Handbook of SPORT MARKETING Research

Handbook of SPORT MARKETING Research

Nancy L. Lough & William A. Sutton
Editors

Fitness Information Technology
A Division of the International Center
for Performance Excellence
262 Coliseum, WVU-CPASS
PO Box 6116
Morgantown, WV 26506-6116

Library of Congress Card Catalog Number: 2011934339

ISBN: 978-1-935412-39-7

Cover Design: Jamie Pein
Typesetter: Jamie Pein
Production Editors: Matt Brann and Ashley Roberts
Proofreader: Rachel Tibbs
Indexer: Rachel Tibbs
Printed by Data Reproductions Corp.
Cover Photo: Courtesy of Orlando Magic

10 9 8 7 6 5 4 3 2 1

Fitness Information Technology
A Division of the International Center for Performance Excellence
262 Coliseum, WVU-CPASS
PO Box 6116
Morgantown, WV 26506-6116
800.477.4348 toll free
304.293.6888 phone
304.293.6658 fax
Email: fitcustomerservice@mail.wvu.edu
Website: www.fitinfotech.com

Contents

SECTION VII. CELEBRITY ATHLETE ENDORSEMENTS

SECTION VIII. ETHICAL ISSUES

Acknowledgments

We would like to thank all the authors who agreed to have their work represented in this handbook. The accumulated wisdom provided by their dedication to understanding and advancing the sport industry has served as the foundation for this young and growing field. We would also like to thank the team at Fitness Information Technology, specifically Matt Brann and Steven Pope. Their expert guidance and support were instrumental in creating this work. Nancy Lough would also like to thank Ted Peetz and Jennifer Pharr for their assistance and unwavering support. Projects like this only come to be through the dedication of many players on the team. Our gratitude is extended to each of these individuals.

In addition, we would like to thank all of the editors whose collective efforts have resulted in making the *Sport Marketing Quarterly* an important medium for the publication of sport marketing research during the past 20 years. These editors have also helped initiate and develop the careers of countless academics beginning their scholarly pursuits or helped already established academics refine and focus their research. Those editors include Dallas Branch, Stephen Hardy, Bill Sutton, Lynn Kahle, Brian Crow, Jacquelyn Cuneen, Matthew Shank, and Nancy Lough.

Original references for the chapters included in this project are as follows:

Chapter 1, The Four Domains of Sport Marketing: A Conceptual Framework. From *Sport Marketing Quarterly*, 2008, 17(2), 90-108.

Chapter 2, The Foreign Invasion of the American Sporting Goods Market. From *Sport Marketing Quarterly*, 1998, 7(3), 19-29.

Chapter 3, A Conceptual Framework for Evaluating Marketing Relationships in Professional Sport Franchises. From *Sport Marketing Quarterly*, 1997, 6(2), 27-32.

Chapter 4, Examining the Importance of Brand Equity in Professional Sport. From *Sport Marketing Quarterly*, 1999, 8(1), 21-29.

Chapter 5, Brand Extensions by U.S. Professional Sport Teams: Motivations and Keys to Success. From *Sport Marketing Quarterly*, 2002, 11(4), 205-214.

Chapter 6, Segmenting Sport Fans Using Brand Associations: A Cluster Analysis. From *Sport Marketing Quarterly*, 2007, 16(1), 15-24.

Chapter 7, Consumer Research and Sport Marketing: Starting the Conversation Between Two Different Academic Discourses. From *Sport Marketing Quarterly*, 1998, 7(2), 24-31.

Chapter 8, Sport Consumer Typologies: A Critical Review. From *Sport Marketing Quarterly*, 2003, 12(4), 206-216.

Chapter 9, Comparing Sport Consumer Motivations Across Multiple Sports. From *Sport Marketing Quarterly*, 2004, 13(1), 17-25.

Chapter 10, Measuring the Motives of Sport Event Attendance: Bridging the Academic-Practitioner Divide to Understanding Behavior. From *Sport Marketing Quarterly*, 2009, 18(3), 126-138.

Chapter 11, Tapping New Markets: Women as Sport Consumers. From *Sport Marketing Quarterly*, 1995, 4(4), 9-12.

Chapter 12, Market Analyses of Race and Sport Consumption. From *Sport Marketing Quarterly*, 2004, 13(1), 7-16.

Chapter 13, Marketing to Lifestyles: Action Sports and Generation Y. From *Sport Marketing Quarterly*, 2004, 13(4), 239-243.

Chapter 14, Using the Psychological Commitment to Team (PCT) Scale to Segment Sport Consumers Based on Loyalty. From *Sport Marketing Quarterly*, 2000, 9(1), 15-25.

Chapter 15, Creating and Fostering Fan Identification in Professional Sports. From *Sport Marketing Quarterly*, 1997, 6(1), 15-22.

Chapter 16, Characterizing Consumer Motivation as Individual Difference Factors: Augmenting the Sport Interest Inventory (SII) to Explain Level of Spectator Sport. From *Sport Marketing Quarterly*, 2002, 11(1), 33-43.

Chapter 17, Motivational Profiles of Sport Fans of Different Sports. From *Sport Marketing Quarterly*, 2008, 17(1), 6-19.

Chapter 18, Sponsorship Evaluation: Moving from Theory to Practice. From *Sport Marketing Quarterly*, 2004, 13(1), 61-64.

Chapter 19, A Comparative Analysis of Sponsorship Objectives for U.S. Women's Sport and Traditional Sport Sponsorship. From *Sport Marketing Quarterly*, 2001, 10(4), 202-211.

Chapter 20, Sport Sponsorship in China: Transition and Evolution. From *Sport Marketing Quarterly*, 2002, 11(1), 20-32.

Chapter 21, Effect of Perceived Sport Event and Sponsor Image Fit on Consumers' Cognition, Affect, and Behavioral Intentions. From *Sport Marketing Quarterly*, 2006, 15(2), 80-90.

Chapter 22, Celebrity Athletic Endorsement: An Overview of the Key Theoretical Issues. From *Sport Marketing Quarterly*, 1998, 7(2), 34-44.

Chapter 23, Athletes as Product Endorsers: The Effect of Gender and Product Relatedness. From *Sport Marketing Quarterly*, 2004, 13(2), 82-93.

Chapter 24, To Catch a Tiger or Let Him Go? The Match-Up Effect and Athlete Endorsers for Sport and Non-Sport Brands. From *Sport Marketing Quarterly*, 2009, 18(1), 25-37.

Chapter 25, Good Morning Vietnam: An Ethical Analysis of Nike Activities in Southeast Asia. From *Sport Marketing Quarterly*, 2000, 9(1), 43-52.

Chapter 26, Marketing Implications of Title IX for Collegiate Athletic Departments. From *Sport Marketing Quarterly*, 1999, 8(3), 9-20.

Chapter 27, More Than Just a Game? Corporate Social Responsibility and Super Bowl XL. From *Sport Marketing Quarterly*, 2006, 15(4), 214-222.

Chapter 28, Communicating Socially Responsible Initiatives: An Analysis of U.S. Professional Teams. From *Sport Marketing Quarterly*, 2010, 19(4), 187-195.

Introduction

"We know what we are, but know not what we may be." — *William Shakespeare*

Our understanding of sport marketing has evolved considerably during the course of the past 20 years. In assembling this collection, we enable readers to see firsthand how the growing complexity and importance of sport marketing has pushed scholars and practitioners to respond in increasingly sophisticated ways.

Drawing from the seminal works published during the past two decades in *Sport Marketing Quarterly*, this collection brings to light foundational theories that have guided some of the most pragmatic studies to date. Through the creation of this handbook, we revisit trends, present instruments designed to assess key constructs, and provide critical analysis of industry practices with regard to issues such as gender, race, and ethical practices. We witness a diversity of topics that highlight where we've been while illuminating where we must go next.

The chapters included serve as a "moment in time" captured, a mirror reflecting the state of the industry through applied scholarly work during the past 20 years. In this singular work, we attempt to broaden the scope of interest and encourage a widening lens through which sport marketing is viewed. Increasingly, there is a need for a more global scope in our research and for one to demonstrate sport as more than merely a commodity to sell. As such, each section of this handbook is designed to provide foundational work reflecting development of key conceptual areas, including sport marketing fundamentals, branding, consumer behavior, market segmentation, fan identity, spectator motives, sponsorship, endorsements, and ethical issues. We are given the opportunity to consider throughout the sections how the fundamental issues of communication and consumer response differ in sport in meaningful ways from other types of marketing.

As a whole, this book presents some of the latest thinking on emerging challenges, while simultaneously reflecting foundational thought. We have endeavored to create a compilation that will benefit a wide variety of readers, from students to scholars, and sport managers to top executives. The overarching goal of this book is to inspire future research, including collaboration and cross-disciplinary work that contributes to our understanding of sport marketing.

"Whatever good things we build end up building us." — *Jim Rohn*

Historical Context

Over the past two decades, the field of sport marketing has taken on a level of recognition not previously witnessed. Cuneen and Hannan (1993) pointed out corporate America spent less than $90 million on the "non-traditional" form of advertising referred to as sponsorship in the early 1980s. Ten years later, estimates suggested special event sponsorships were well over $500 million. In 1987, sport was reportedly the 23rd largest industry in the US, totaling $50.2 billion each year (Hofacre & Burman, 1992). As of 1991, corporate sponsorship was considered the fastest growing component of the $63.1 billion Gross National Sports Product, with North American spending estimated to be $2.94 billion on sporting events alone (Irwin & Asimakopoulos, 1992). By the mid-1990s the economic activity associated with the sport industry was gaining widespread attention. The result of one analysis in 1995 found that the sport industry was worth $152 billion, and this was supported by an additional $259 billion in economic activity (Meek, 1997). Many of us have witnessed firsthand the growing value of the industry, and as a result the broadening interest.

Publications such as the *Wall Street Journal*, *New York Times*, and *Forbes Magazine* began publishing sport industry-related articles with growing frequency. By 2010, International Events Group (IEG) estimated 68% of sponsorship money was invested in sporting events. Fragmenting of the industry has led to new categories. For example, the Fantasy Sport Trade Association estimated $800 million was directly spent on fantasy sport products and services, while another $3.5 billion was spent on media services related to this new industry (Dwyer & Drayer, 2010). Still, the most staggering figure reported to date was the estimate of the sport marketplace, ranging between $425 and $450 billion each year (Plunkett, 2009). This growth in the industry has been mirrored by prolific growth in academic programs preparing future industry professionals. One account suggested 8,000 students graduated with sport-focused degrees in 2009 (King, 2009).

Accordingly, a proliferation in research focused on the sport industry has transpired. Scholarly journals can now be found specializing in sport economics, finance, communications, media, management, and statistics, just to name a few. As a result, the development and growing sophistication of both the field and the scholarly work focused on sport marketing are worthy of reflection. Pitts encouraged colleagues to embrace the concept that "theoretical research and development are essential to the foundation of the body of knowledge for sport marketing, and therefore as academics we have a responsibility to produce an appropriate body of knowledge" (2002, p. 85). As scholars in this rapidly changing field, we have been challenged to "bridge the gap" between academe and industry. Yet, some sport management scholars have argued for a demarcation of theory vs. practice oriented research.

Scholarship chosen for inclusion in this book represents a broad perspective of all segments of the sport industry. We recognize that scholarship is critical to the development of sport marketing knowledge, and theoretical research and development are essential to the foundation of the corresponding body of knowledge. As Pitts suggested, "a body of knowledge that includes all known facts, theories, and principles about a subject is necessary for the continued and sustained growth of an academic field" and "should represent the full picture of the field; it is what students need to know to work in the field" (2002, p. 88). In response to the theory or practice debate, Stotlar argues in Chapter 18 of this handbook, "Those who propose theory without a connection to practice are as misguided as practitioners who disregard relevant theory" (p. 256). Serving as an example to follow, Stotlar's contribution illustrates how sponsorship works in sport to draw a parallel in scholarly work, suggesting "theorists and practitioners form a symbiotic relationship where joint efforts are greater than the sum of the parts" (p. 256). Similarly, the authors represented in this handbook have effectively answered the call to bridge the academic-practitioner divide.

Without question there are many sport businesses that need our research and need to be included in our body of literature. The scholars represented in this work have addressed this need and continue to develop additional ways to make the literature reflect theoretical applications and sport industry developments. In 1999, Hardy and Sutton identified eight key trends driving research, teaching, and practice: 1) entertainment, 2) the game as an experience, 3) technology transforming the experience and enhancing activation for sponsors, 4) growth of websites and e-commerce, 5) branding the experience, 6) place as a game-changer (i.e., PSLs), 7) endorsements, and 8) corporate sponsors or someone to pay for it all (p. 10). They followed this identification of trends with delineating the need for more research in targeted areas such as the pitfalls and limitations of websites, branding to effectively reach consumers, the effect naming rights have on brand equity, the impact of economic value associated with symbolic qualities of celebrity athletes, and accountability for sponsor investments. Over the years, many of these trends and topics have been studied. Still, several of them stand out as broad categories that have evolved into distinct conceptual areas fragmenting into new areas of inquiry. For example, the growth of websites and e-commerce now includes opportunities presented by social media, live streaming media coverage, secondary ticket sales, and fantasy sport leagues. In response, the chapters presented in this handbook each contribute in a meaningful way to the development of the field and to the advancement of our understanding of this dynamic industry.

Themes within Sport Marketing

Foundations of Sport Marketing

This handbook begins appropriately with a section focusing on the theme of sport marketing foundations. Fullerton and Merz find no consensus of the term "sport marketing" had been attained. The dichotomy of "marketing through sport" and "marketing of sport" has been well established with sponsorship-based strategies most often identified. In our first contribution, the authors provide more clarity by creating four distinct domains to classify sport marketing. Readers will be well prepared to engage in the dialogue and debate of defining parameters for the field after considering this contribution.

We are also given a unique opportunity to learn from an historical example that is as relevant today as ever. Fielding and Miller use examples from baseball, tennis, golf, and track and field to recount how companies such as Mizuno (Japanese) and adidas (European) gained significant market share in the American market during the 1960s and 1970s. When adidas became the official track and field outfitter of the 1968 Olympic Games, "they banned other companies from the Olympic village" (p. 36). In essence, adidas became synonymous with one of the most global sports of the day, serving as a foundational example of what would come to be known as sport marketing. To regain market share from foreign competitors, American companies employed various research, design, production, and promotion strategies, the latter of which focused on use of American athlete endorsements and autograph models of equipment. In this example, we see how many practices common today were initiated during this period. A key concept gleaned from this study: "Each element in the formula for success depends upon market analysis" (p. 41).

Rounding out the foundations theme, McDonald and Milne recognize the potential technology holds for sport organizations interested in advancing relationship marketing. By focusing on customer retention, as opposed to acquiring new customers, they explore the concept of lifetime value (LTV). In essence, this theme demonstrates the evolution from marketing being transaction based to relationship based. Development of relationships with suppliers and customers is now considered a crucial step in maintaining a competitive advantage.

Brand Building

Our conceptual understanding of brand equity is expanded in this second theme. Gladden and Milne argue that while winning is vitally important in sport, short-term tactics do not guarantee long-term consistent revenue streams. Citing examples where a winning season did not translate to ticket sales and desirable marketplace outcomes, the authors suggest expanding the focus of strategic marketing to include efforts to increase brand awareness, brand associations, and brand loyalty. The myopic focus on winning has plagued sport for decades. Fortunately, the work supporting this theme demonstrates the strategic value attributed to brand building. As an example, Apostolopoulou analyzes brand extensions in US professional sport teams. Focusing on motivations and working directly with 12 marketing managers, she finds brand extensions were often used to enhance the emotional attachment between consumers and the team. Establishing a stronger presence for the franchise in the market, enhancing relationships with fans, and building fan loyalty, even when the team did not have a winning record, all emerged as key motives.

Our understanding of the brand building theme is further strengthened by analyzing how brand associations differ across various segments of the fan base in the contribution by Ross. While segmentation strategies are known to differ from organization to organization, employing multiple categories such as demographic characteristics with values, lifestyles, and product usage results in more effective strategies. Through this theme, we see how sport fans hold different representations of brands. Thus, accurately defining key market segments is critical to efforts designed to enhance brand equity, sponsorships, positioning strategies, and relationship marketing.

Understanding Sport Consumers

Incorporating relevant work from consumer behavior research and sport sociology, our understanding of sport consumers is extended beyond the traditional sport fan. Kates points out how critical ideas from feminism, Marxism, and post-structuralism could be utilized to broaden sport marketing perspectives with regard to the disenfranchised. As a follow up to Kates' work, Stewart, Nicholson, and Smith acknowledge that while many models of sport consumption identify interesting cognitive and affective differences between consumers, analysis was frequently limited to one or two behavioral traits. The authors propose multidimensional models to reveal subtle nuances that people bring to their sport consumption experiences. To address these issues, the authors suggest "a greater use of multidisciplinary teams using longitudinal studies to collect data that covers both the individual behavior of consumers and the social and economic context in which this behavior takes place" (p. 122).

James and Ross seek to better understand sport consumers by identifying motives that influence an individual's interest in non-revenue collegiate sports. Traditionally, sports such as volleyball, tennis, and swimming have not been represented in sport marketing research. We can deepen our understanding of sport consumers through examination of motives related to each sport, along with motives pertaining to self-definition and personal benefits. Even though this collegiate sport model remains limited to the US, the motives identified are relevant to each sport studied, and as such provide guidance for strategically reaching potential consumers.

More recently, Funk, Filo, Beaton, and Pritchard find sport consumer studies rarely report or explain game attendance behavior. In response, the authors present a hybrid approach blending the demands of both academicians and practitioners for theoretical and applied scales to investigate motives capable of explaining sport event attendance. The authors identify five motivational themes used in previous empirical studies to develop a parsimonious set of motives including: Socialization, Performance, Excitement, Esteem, and Diversion. Validation of the resulting SPEED scale has created new opportunities for understanding sport event attendance, and thereby understanding sport consumers.

Market Segmentation

Studies focused on specific market segments demonstrate a meaningful evolution in sport marketing thought. Beginning with the recognition of women as sport consumers, Branch opens the dialogue for discussion of emerging or new market segments. Data demonstrates that by the mid-1990s women accounted for an increasing share of sport consumption dollars, and women were becoming sport consumers at a rate paralleling men in the coveted 18-24 age bracket. Branch points to incidences of sport "softening" the presentation of the core product, as a direct response to this "new" target market.

Similarly, race is a factor influencing consumption dynamics in professional women's sport, as detailed by Armstrong and Stratta. Specifically, racial classification of the individual consumer, the racial characteristics of the sport team (players and management) as the product to be consumed, and the racial demographics of the environment in which the sport consumption took place influenced consumers' behavior. Clearly, specific marketing strategies must reflect such nuances. Armstrong and Stratta demonstrate a clear need to understand consumer attributes typically overlooked or neglected both in academic work and in the industry.

Influencing the highly coveted youth market, yet another vital segment, can be a difficult task. Bennett and Lachowetz use action sport as the context to examine the unique attributes of young male consumers utilizing Hanan's (1980) definition of lifestyle marketing. The incorporation of the edginess, irreverence, and exhilaration of action sports is found to be the perfect fit for promotion of a non-sport product like Mountain Dew, which utilized its action sports association to become a part of a culture that provides endless ways of communicating or reaching its targeted youth market.

A segmentation theme in sport would be incomplete without addressing the notion of loyalty. Fortuitously, Mahony, Madrigal, and Howard establish a scale for measuring attitudinal loyalty, or the strength of a fan's commitment to a particular team. By demonstrating how the "dispositional nature of attachment is crucial to establishing true loyalty" (p. 193), we are provided a practical tool upon which teams can base market strategies most likely to successfully exploit and consequently build fan loyalty.

Fan Identity and Spectator Motives

Building on the idea of consumer motives, the book's next section explores fan identity and spectator motives. In their conceptual framework, Sutton, McDonald, Milne, and Cimperman identify three distinct levels of fan identity, along with managerial factors and benefits, combined to inform four strategies for increasing fan identification. Given the interest in building upon known motives to enhance levels of identity among a fan base, the framework serves as a pragmatic model for sport organizations intent on developing fan identity.

In an effort to further explain levels of spectator support, Funk, Mahony, and Ridinger augment the Sport Interest Inventory (SII) by studying women's sport. Based largely on the success of the 1999 Women's World Cup held in the US, the Women's United Soccer Association (WUSA) was created shortly thereafter and served as the focal point for evaluation of the SII, which has proven to be a useful tool for examining sport spectators motives. Marketing unique or niche-based sport events will be most successful when these five motivational characteristics are integrated: (a) sport interest, (b) team interest, (c) vicarious achievement, (d) role modeling, and (e) entertainment value. In essence, this groundbreaking study provides a foundational framework for marketing women's sport.

In keeping with the theme, Wann, Grieve, Zapalac, and Pease investigate eight fan motives: escape, economic (i.e., gambling), eustress (i.e., positive arousal), self-esteem, group affiliation, entertainment, family, and aesthetics. Sport types are found to maintain a unique compilation of motives. From each of the studies supporting this theme, profound benefits have been offered to the sport industry. Through review of this scholarly work we see how significant questions have been answered while the research guides us to pose new questions.

Sponsorship

The topic of sponsorship is often considered synonymous with sport marketing. After all, where would sport be without sponsorship? From the 1984 Olympic Games, in which the Los Angeles Olympic Organizing Committee utilized sponsorship to become the first profitable host, to recognition as the fastest growing segment in sport marketing, some have suggested sport could not survive today without sponsorship. As an expert on the topic, Stotlar points out how many corporations fail to assess their sponsorship's effectiveness, and often overlook the fit with broader marketing objectives. He creates an evaluation model for sport sponsorship with the intent to provide a comprehensive overview of how theory relates to and shapes current practice.

Still, the majority of support for this theme comes from studies examining sponsorship objectives. Once again, the significant place women's sport held at the turn of the 21st century created an intriguing context for study. With noted increases of girls and women competing and becoming sport fans, the question potential sponsors were facing was whether sponsorship of women's sport would achieve desired marketing objectives. With prior studies establishing an array of known sponsorship objectives including increased exposure, recognition, product sales, and brand loyalty, Lough and Irwin set out to determine if these objectives were similar or different based on the gender of the sport product sponsored. The authors find that the catalyst for women's sport sponsorship was the 1996 Olympic Games in Atlanta. Evidence for this benchmark is provided by the increasing levels of prize money available for established women's sport properties, as well as in the increasing number of sponsors reporting involvement with women's sport during and after the 1996 Olympic Games. This particular study represents one of the few that have focused specifically on the relationship between sponsors and women's sport properties.

As the sponsorship theme evolved over time, the globalization of sport became more significant. Geng, Burton, and Blakemore find that the sport-centered ideas practiced in China were unfamiliar to Western sport practitioners. As Western corporations initiated sponsorships with Chinese sports events and properties, their capitalistic attitudes (i.e., economic profit motives) were often in conflict with China's distinct socialism (i.e., social profit motives). We learn from this example that American sport marketers need to develop a better understanding of how views on sponsorship have cultural implications. As marketers seek to develop international relationships, the overarching theme of a win-win or symbiotic strategy becomes particularly relevant for the ongoing globalization of the sport market.

As sponsorship progressed from a philanthropic orientation prior to 1984 to the objective-driven orientation we see today, corporate image, brand attitude, and brand recognition became important dimensions, along with the relationship to purchase intentions. Spectators with a high image fit have been found to have a more positive image of the sponsor, demonstrate a more positive brand attitude, and demonstrate an increased likelihood of correctly recognizing a sponsor's brand. Koo and Quarterman reveal how future work will need to demonstrate clear connections between theory and practice to accomplish the objectives aligned with each entity involved in the sponsorship relationship.

Celebrity Athlete Endorsements

The foundational work of Brooks and Harris serves as an appropriate introduction to celebrity athlete endorsement. By defining the term "celebrity endorser" and examining four product endorsement styles, the authors broaden our understanding of this key theme. Four questions they pose remain intriguing today: Under what condition is a celebrity athlete most persuasive? What type of celebrity athlete is most persuasive? How does celebrity endorsement work? Do celebrity athletes sell product?

In a related piece, Boyd and Shank examine the effects of endorser gender, consumer gender, and the type of product advertised on consumer perceptions of endorser trustworthiness, expertise, and attractiveness. Their findings demonstrate that regardless of product type, subjects rate endorsers of the same gender as more trustworthy. Interestingly, again we see research focusing on women leading to a better understanding of this theme. Endorsement effectiveness must take into consideration gender differences and develop appropriate marketing strategies to achieve success.

Recognizing celebrities are ineffective as endorsers for some brands, the match–up hypothesis is utilized by Koernig and Boyd to explain the congruence between the image of a spokesperson, the brand image, and the advertisement. Linking the relationship between the endorser-brand fit and endorser credibility, endorsements worked largely to enhance the image of the celebrity. "From a managerial standpoint, this raises the issue of whether a highly accomplished athlete endorser benefits more than the brand they endorse" (p. 354). Current industry practice of endorsing athletes who have no obvious match with the product category is found to be an inefficient use of company resources. As a result, we know "it is the fit of the athlete with the brand that is driving positive attitudes rather than the fame of the athlete" (pp. 355–356).

Ethical Issues

The final section of this handbook examines an important but often overlooked theme—ethical issues that sport marketers face. Kahle, Boush, and Phelps analyze the environment in which Nike was working when it was accused of unethical behavior in Southeast Asia. Noting the poor infrastructure in developing countries as one reason for low wages and suppressed productivity, the authors provide a broader view of the circumstances companies face when engaging in foreign labor markets. In their analysis, the authors suggest that by investing in the work force, companies such as Nike improve the economy of the developing country. The greatest likelihood for stakeholder conflict arises when accepted principles and business practices in the US are not upheld in other countries. Their ethical examination of the issue included Kant's categorical imperative from foundational philosophy. Public perception of the sport brand (Nike) and the resulting strategic response both serve as guidance to practitioners interested in maintaining ethical business practices.

In the unique realm of US collegiate sport, a different set of ethical issues warrants exploration. Barr, Sutton, and McDermott identify revenue potential and attendance as the top two factors influencing marketing allocations. These factors have led to a self-fulfilling prophecy that runs counter to the federal Title IX law employed as an ethical guideline. Top revenue-producing sports receive the bulk of the funding and marketing expertise due to their attendance and revenue potential, thus long-established male sports thrive due to the substantial investment and as a result further increase their revenue potential. The cycle identified has continued for years despite the federal law designed to hold university athletic personnel accountable for some degree of balance between male and female sports. The lack of investment in women's sport demonstrates non-compliance with a federal law as well as a disregard for ethical practices.

At the professional sport level, corporate social responsibility has recently become a focal point. Babiak and Wolfe note that "... the NFL is becoming progressively more invested in corporate social responsibility (CSR) initiatives in an effort to establish itself as a socially conscious organization ..." (p. 393). The influential theme of CSR indicates organizations have responsibilities beyond profit maximization. Through the authors' analysis of marketing activities aligned with the Super Bowl, we see "doing the 'right thing,' in an environment where corporations are increasingly criticized for unethical activity, may ward off backlash and contribute to the NFL's reputation as an entity that cares, and thus may enhance its image" (p. 403). With the NFL recently enduring a contentious labor dispute, the benefits of CSR appear as poignant as ever.

Organizations must also be cognizant of how the growth of the Internet and social media has provided new ways for them to communicate socially responsible initiatives with their stakeholders. Walker, Kent, and Vincent suggest that messages devoted to ethical, environmental, and other social initiatives have increased in popularity with CSR serving as one way in which organizations seek to manage stakeholder pressures, improve organizational reputation, and increase consumer patronage. While teams currently do not display the same eagerness to appear socially responsible in their e-newsletters, the authors provide guidance with regard to how sport marketers can begin to understand what matters most to their fans and select community partnerships and social initiatives that serve mutual interests, as well as promote social change.

Conclusion

This book is premised on the core idea to "bridge the gap" between past and present, between research and practice. We must first understand fundamental concepts of sport marketing and sport consumer behavior if we are to have an effect on the marketing *of* sport, and marketing *through* sport. Building emotional attachments, creating brand equity, and strengthening opportunities offered through sponsorships and endorsements all contribute to our opportunity to influence consumer behavior and design more effective marketing strategies. Through this presentation of seminal work in the field, we can reflect on how well the breadth and depth of the scholarship has shaped the industry, and where we must go next in pursuit of advancing the field.

Just as *Sport Marketing Quarterly* was originally envisioned to "generate, evaluate and synthesize data from the field and package it so as to be accessible and valuable for use in the classroom, the clubhouse, the field house and the front office" (Hardy & Sutton, 1999, p. 10), this book has a parallel mission: to illuminate seminal works and make them accessible in one volume. Through this accessibility, historical lessons are brought back to light, along with foundational and conceptual pieces that have helped to define the field. In each case, the beneficiaries will undoubtedly be those who endeavor to lead us forward.

References

Babiak, K., & Wolfe, R. (2011). More than just a game? Corporate social responsibility and Super Bowl XL. In N. L. Lough & W. A. Sutton (Eds.), *Handbook of sport marketing research*, (pp. 393–405). Morgantown, WV: Fitness Information Technology.

Cuneen, J., & Hannan, M. J. (1993). Intermediate measures and recognition testing of sponsorship advertising at an LPGA tournament. *Sport Marketing Quarterly, 2*(1), 47–56

Dwyer, B., & Drayer, J. (2010). Fantasy sport consumer segmentation: An investigation into the differing consumption modes of fantasy football participants. *Sport Marketing Quarterly, 19*, 207–216.

Fielding, L., & Miller, L. K. (2011).The foreign invasion of the American sporting goods market. In N. L. Lough & W. A. Sutton (Eds.), *Handbook of sport marketing research*, (pp. 29–44). Morgantown, WV: Fitness Information Technology.

Geng, L., Burton, R., & Blakemore, C. (2011). Sport sponsorship in China: Transition and evolution. In N. L. Lough & W. A. Sutton (Eds.), *Handbook of sport marketing research*, (pp. 273–289). Morgantown, WV: Fitness Information Technology.

Hanan. M. (1980). *Life-styled marketing*. New York: Anacom.

Hardy, S. & Sutton, W. A. (1999). The SMQ and the sport marketplace: Where we've been and where we're going. *Sport Marketing Quarterly, 8*(4), 9–14.

Hofacre, S., & Burman, T. K. (1992). Demographic changes in the U.S. into the twenty-first century: Their impact on sport marketing. *Sport Marketing Quarterly, 1*(1), 31–36.

Irwin, R. L., & Asimakopoulos, M. K. (1992). An approach to the evaluation and selection of sport sponsorship proposals. *Sport Marketing Quarterly, 1*(2), 43–51.

King, B. (2009, August 24). New lessons to learn. *SportsBusiness Journal*, p. 04a.

Koernig, S. K., & Boyd, T. C. (2011). To catch a Tiger or let him go? The match-up effect and athlete endorsers for sport and non-sport brands. In N. L. Lough & W. A. Sutton (Eds.), *Handbook of sport marketing research*, (pp. 341–357). Morgantown, WV: Fitness Information Technology.

Mahony, D. F., Madrigal, R., & Howard, D. (2011). Using the Psychological Commitment to Team (PCT) Scale to segment sport consumers based on loyalty. In N. L. Lough & W. A. Sutton (Eds.), *Handbook of sport marketing research*, (pp. 215–230). Morgantown, WV: Fitness Information Technology.

Meek, A. (1997). An estimate of the size and supported economic activity of the sport industry in the United States. *Sport Marketing Quarterly*, *6*(4), 15–21.

Pitts, B. (2002). Examining sport management scholarship: An historical review of the Sport Marketing Quarterly. *Sport Marketing Quarterly*, *11*, 84–92.

Plunkett, Research, Ltd. (2009). *Introduction to the sports industry.* Plunkett Research. Retrieved from Plunkett Research, Ltd. Database.

Stewart, B., Nicholson, M., & Smith, A. C.(2011). Sport consumer typologies: A critical review. In N. L. Lough & W. A. Sutton (Eds.), *Handbook of sport marketing research*, (pp. 109–124). Morgantown, WV: Fitness Information Technology.

Stotlar, D. K. (2011). Sponsorship evaluation: Moving from theory to practice. In N. L. Lough & W. A. Sutton (Eds.), *Handbook of sport marketing research*, (pp. 253–257). Morgantown, WV: Fitness Information Technology.

SECTION I.

Foundations of Sport Marketing

1

The Four Domains of Sports Marketing: A Conceptual Framework

Sam Fullerton and G. Russell Merz

Introduction to Sports Marketing

The concept of "sports marketing" is ambiguous in its meaning for both practitioners and academicians. Discussions about its application in the popular press and in many textbooks include categories ranging from tickets to spectator sports to sport-related wagers in legal gambling establishments (Shannon, 1999). Some tend to take a narrow view about what the discipline of sports marketing encompasses. To them, the primary task is one of selling tickets and putting fans in the seats at organized sports events (Sports Marketing Surveys, 2002), thereby equating the sports product to tickets for spectator sports. This definition, broadly applied, may include the sale of tickets for minor events such as high school sports and minor league ice hockey, but the prevailing thinking focuses on major sports properties such as an NCAA Division I-A (FBS) college football game, a NASCAR event, the Super Bowl, and the Olympics. Undoubtedly, this perspective reflects the vast marketing expenditures for these major properties.

With the 2008 Summer Olympics fast approaching, Du Wei, the Vice Chairman of the Institute of Beijing Olympic Economy, recently stated in comments directed to Chinese companies that "sports marketing has become one of the most effective of all marketing strategies" (Anonymous, 2006). However, Wei was not narrowly referring to the tasks associated with the selling of tickets to Olympic events. Rather he was using a broader definition by suggesting that marketers of nonsports products can benefit by becoming more involved with the 2008 Olympic Games. But since these firms are not selling sports products, how are their actions characterized as sports marketing? In order to fully appreciate and understand the dynamics and differing perspectives of sports marketing, it is imperative that the task of *marketing through sports* also be accepted as an integral component of the industry. Coca-Cola has been associated with the Olympic Games since 1928; however, this relationship was not focused on demand creation for one of the world's premier sporting events. Clearly, it focused on the sale of Coca-Cola products. Many marketers use a sports platform as the basis for appeals to consumers across a vast array of products, the majority of which have little or nothing to do with sports. The *marketing through sports* component of sports marketing tends to be overlooked by some texts (Pitts & Stotlar, 1996). This is unfortunate because it is in this domain that many marketing practitioners are employed and use their skills to implement sports marketing strategies. A comprehensive review of recently published sports marketing textbooks reveals inconsistencies in the definitions of *sports marketing* (Van Heerden, 2001). This conceptual weakness illustrates the need for including both the *marketing of sports* and *marketing through sports* in a broader sports marketing platform that encompasses the entire realm of sports marketing practice. It is the purpose of this article to propose a broadened framework built upon this conceptual dichotomy.

A "Veritable Plethora"[1] of Definitions

Exactly what does the practice of sports marketing encompass? In other words, how can we define sports marketing? The reality is that there exists a veritable plethora of definitions of sports marketing. In fact, some spokespersons seek to differentiate between "sport" marketing and "sports" marketing. Much like any other business concept, the realm of sport(s) marketing has continued to evolve while encompassing a broader array of business activities. The disparity clearly indicates a need to re-conceptualize the construct. Consider the following definitions.

The genesis of the term "sport marketing" can be attributed to a story in a 1978 issue of *Advertising Age.* In that venerable publication, sport marketing was characterized as "the activities of consumer and industrial product and service marketers who are increasingly using sport as a promotional vehicle" (Gray & McEvoy, 2005). In their recent contribution to a compilation of sports marketing literature, Gray and McEvoy noted that this set of activities is best characterized as "marketing *through* sport; that is using sport as a promotional vehicle or sponsorship platform for companies that market consumer, and to a lesser extent, industrial products" (p. 229). Gray and McEvoy further noted a perceived shortcoming of that definition by calling attention to the absence of any reference to the "marketing *of* sport." The implication is that there is a second major dimension of sports marketing, one entailing "the application of marketing principles and processes to market goods and services directly to sports participants and spectators" (p. 229). The amalgamation of *marketing through sport* and the *marketing of sport* provided the foundation for Gray and McEvoy's broad-based definition: "the anticipation, management, and satisfaction of consumers' wants and needs through the application of marketing principles and practices" (p. 229). Presumably, this definition encompasses both major dimensions. Some organizations market sport products to a targeted set of consumers, while others market an array of nonsports products to market segments that have a "personal investment" in sports entities such as athletes, events, and teams (Merz & Fullerton, 2005).

Similarly, Mullin, Hardy, and Sutton (2000) characterize sports marketing in a way that encompasses either dimension, or thrusts, as they describe them. Their resultant definition is based on the premise that

> "sport marketing consists of all activities designed to meet the needs and wants of sports consumers through exchange processes. Sport marketing has developed two major thrusts: the marketing of sport products and services directly to consumers of sport, and the marketing of other consumer and industrial products or services through the use of sports promotions." (p. 9)

This definition was subsequently embraced in a contribution by Gladden and Sutton (2005) in the text edited by Masteralexis, Barr, and Hums (2005). Yet readers may question the concept of "sports promotions." Exactly what actions comprise this activity? Is it limited to sponsorship or would an advertisement featuring a generic sports theme fit within this thrust of sport marketing? A second question concerns the exclusive province of sport promotion. Can strategic initiatives other than promotion be used to create a sports overlay that would fit within the realm of marketing through sports?

Questions such as these were addressed by Blann and Armstrong (2003) when they articulated the point that the term sport marketing has been used in many contexts, thereby leading to confusion as to exactly what the term really means. Not only do they incorporate both dimensions, but they also expand one of the earlier perspectives by stating that marketing through sports encompasses far more than just advertising and public relations.

Schlossberg's (1996) early book on sports marketing did not specifically define the concept; however, it focused on the efforts of marketers who use sports as a marketing platform for nonsports products. More specifically, Schlossberg states that "sports has become a marketing medium in and of itself with the ability to target, segment, promote, and cast products and services in heroic lights. More and more companies you'd never think of being remotely attached to sports are using sports to enhance and embellish their marketing" (p. 6). In describing the efforts of companies such as Coca-Cola and Visa, Schlossberg's reference seems to be directed toward sponsorship activities.

With their focus on sports products, Pitts and Stotlar (1996) offer a different perspective of the practice of sport marketing. In their text, sport marketing is defined as "the process of designing and implementing activities for the production, pricing, promotion, and distribution of sport product to satisfy the needs or desires of consumers and to achieve the company's objectives" (p. 80). This definition was reiterated in Stotlar's (2001) later book that delineated the process of developing "successful sport marketing plans." Of note is the inclusion of pricing, distribution, and promotion—three traditional elements of the marketing mix. This inclusion represents a meaningful extension of the assertion by Gladden and Sutton (2005) that sport marketing was based solely upon promotional efforts by the marketer.

Similarly, while stating that "sports marketing does not have a single, consistent definition," Moore and Teel (1994) offer a definition that focuses on the marketing of sports products as a basis for the generation of revenue for sports entities while developing marketing plans that will lead to the maximization of revenues accruing to the sports entity. Yet they still incorporate marketing through sports by referring to sports entities such as athletes, teams, and programs in the firm's marketing plan. Sponsorships such as Lenovo's involvement in "the Olympic Partner (TOP)" program for the cycle that included the 2006 Winter Olympics in Torino and the 2008 Summer Games in Beijing would fit within the parameters of their definition of sports marketing. Their early work offers a forward-looking perspective via their assessment that "attention to marketing tools is long overdue" in the marketing of sports products.

This brings us to two of the most recent entries into the sports marketing textbook arena. Shank (2005) defines sports marketing as the "specific application of marketing principles and processes to sports products and to the marketing of nonsports products through association with sports" (p. 3). Finally, Fullerton (2007) provides no specific definition of the term, yet the book is divided into the two aforementioned dimensions: *marketing through sports* and the *marketing of sports.*

Purpose of the Paper

While there continues to be no single, universal definition of the concept of sports marketing, one key consideration is evident. As articulated earlier, the practice of sports marketing is generally recognized as consisting of two fundamental thrusts. However, while recognition of this dichotomy in sports marketing practice is a necessary part of conceptualizing a sports marketing framework, it is insufficient for clearly distinguishing among the multitudes of sports marketing practices that exist today. It is the objective of this article to refine and extend this dichotomy into more detailed constituent components based on actual sports marketing activities in the environment. The authors adopt a grounded theory building approach (Glaser & Strauss, 1967) based upon numerous observations of actual sports marketing activities to develop a preliminary conceptualization of the field of sports marketing[2]. The resulting framework provides a more comprehensive classification of sports marketing practices than has heretofore been advocated, and is suggestive of sports marketing decision-making guidelines. In the remainder of this article two important distinctions that underlie sports marketing practices are identified and discussed. These two distinctions are then combined to form a new sports marketing framework consisting of four categories of sports marketing domains. The article provides support for the framework by discussing and illustrating each domain with examples of actual sports marketing activities.

Identifying Domains within the Sports Marketing Environment

Two important product-related aspects of the sports marketing environment are noteworthy. First is the strategic focus aimed at the marketing of pure sports products. Less evident is the marketing of nonsports products while using a sports platform as the foundation of the firm's marketing efforts. Therefore, two prominent initiatives in sports marketing are identified. They are the *marketing of sports products,* and the *marketing of nonsports products through sports.* Some universities offering sports marketing programs have opted to offer courses using this nomenclature. This is particularly evident when the program is offered through a business or management school. However, even with the acknowledgement of these two broad initiatives, the question of exactly what constitutes a sports product still begs to be answered.

Sports Products versus Nonsports Products

In developing a model that depicts the sports marketing environment, an essential distinction is the difference between sports products and nonsports products. Making this distinction is not as simple as it may sound. The following overview is provided in an effort to clarify the difference.

Sports Products

Sports products have been described in many studies. In fact, an early article that sought to estimate the gross domestic sports product (GDSP) in the United States went so far as to include agent services, sports law services, golf course construction, and pari-mutuel betting receipts (Meek, 1997). While some readers may agree with the breadth of this eclectic array, others will view it as having no real focus. The latter view is shared by the authors of this article. For the purpose of describing the sports marketing environment, three categories of sports products have been identified. They are spectator sports, participation sports, and a third eclectic category that is comprised of sporting goods, apparel, athletic shoes, and sports-related products.

(1) Spectator Sports

From college sports, to minor league sports, to the highest level of professional sports, and for international events such as the Olympics, one key marketing objective is that of selling tickets. Yet, it is not only those who purchase tickets to a game or event who are important; sports marketers also work to increase viewership and listenership on a variety of broadcast media. This includes television options such as free-to-air TV, premium cable and satellite networks, pay-per-view for special events, enhanced access to a sport's broadcasts (such as DIRECTV's NFL Sunday Ticket), and devoted networks such as the Rugby Channel and the Golf Channel that are dedicated to an array of programming germane to a single sport. Other media include traditional radio, satellite radio, audio/video streaming on the Internet, and an emerging emphasis on mobile technology such as the cellular phone and podcasts.

With this in mind, the spectator sports product can be viewed from two perspectives. First is the sale of access to events; that access may legitimately be viewed as the product. Second is the reality that access has no value without the competition on the field of play. Thus, whether audiences are live or media-based, it is the game or event that represents the product in the spectator sports market.

(2) Participation Sports

The category of participation sports rightfully includes an array of activities that might not normally be perceived as sports. While organized soccer leagues, golf, and tennis are recognized as participation sports, other activities that are done on an individual basis are not always acknowledged as sports. The absence of competition that identifies a winner and loser may be the basis for this reluctance. Individuals who jog around the neighborhood or who lift free weights at home or at the health club are not typically characterized as athletes. There is yet another tier of activities that represent participation and competition although only the most liberal definition would permit them to be classified as sports. The most recent addition to this category is poker; even sports networks such as Fox Sports and ESPN have begun to broadcast "Texas hold'em" poker tournaments. Other activities such as darts, fishing, competitive eating, and billiards are also noteworthy from a participation perspective.

In many cases, marketing's role is to increase the number of participants and the frequency of participation in a specific activity. For example, golf courses want to attract new golfers while at the same time inducing current golfers to play even more. The primary benefit to these sports marketers is that increased participation keeps facilities such as golf courses, tennis clubs, swimming pools, and health clubs busy. A secondary benefit is that it creates demand for more sports equipment and apparel. This leads us to the third and final category of sports products.

(3) Sporting Goods, Apparel, Athletic Shoes, and Sports-Related Products

The final category of sports products is somewhat more difficult to define. While sporting goods such as snowboards, apparel such as skiwear, and athletic shoes such as a pair

Table 1.
Products Sold by Sports Marketers

Sports Products
Spectator Sports Products
- The game or event itself
  - Tickets for attendance
  - Viewership and listenership on electronic media

Participation Sports Products
- Organized participation (leagues & tournaments)
- Casual participation
- Access to public and private athletic facilities

Sporting Goods, Apparel, Athletic Shoes, & Sports-Related Products
- Sports equipment (skis, golf clubs, & soccer balls)
- Sports apparel (hunting clothing, swimwear, & team uniforms)
- Athletic shoes
- Sports-related products (souvenirs, lessons, & refreshments)

Nonsports Products
Goods and services not directly related to a sport

of "Air Jordans" are easy to understand, the final component, sports-related products, is very diverse. It includes sports souvenirs, publications, lessons, and a diverse assortment of products that can be purchased at event venues.

Sporting goods include tangible products specific to a participation sport or activity. These products may be sold to casual participants as well as those who take part in organized activities. The 55 million Americans who participate in bowling (Anonymous, 2003c) create a demand for bowling equipment. Golfers throughout the world have fueled a tremendous increase in the sale of clubs, balls, bags, and gloves on a global basis.

Apparel is clothing that falls into one of two categories. First and foremost, it may be purchased to facilitate participation. The annual start of a new season for many sports creates demand for new uniforms. Style changes may induce golfers to abandon last year's clothing in favor of new styles so that they look good on the golf course. The second category is based on the acknowledgement that sports apparel can be fashionable within certain market segments. These buyers may be fans who wear clothing that features the logos of teams that they support. Others may buy the same apparel, not because they support the team, but because the clothing is in vogue among their peers.

The third component of this category is *athletic shoes*. While these were once primarily devoted to the participant market, this has changed significantly since the advent of Nike's Air Jordan shoes. Today, athletic shoes are an integral part of almost everyone's wardrobe. For participants, there are designs that are deemed appropriate for specific activities such as racket sports, basketball, running, walking, and cross training. No longer are athletic shoes combined into the generic category of tennis shoes.

The final component consists of a broad array of *sports-related products*. These include souvenirs that may be purchased at event venues as well as a number of other official retailers. Consumers often purchase sports magazines. These may feature sports in general, but many focus on a single sport or even a specific team. Lessons to improve one's skill at sports like tennis or golf fit best within this category as well. But the broadest set of products in this category is comprised of venue-specific products. While these products are not tied to a sport per se, they are purchased by spectators in attendance. So, while we might be reluctant to classify beer as a sports product, the reality is that it represents an important revenue stream for teams and stadium operators.

Nonsports Products

In contrast to the various sports products, marketers of *nonsports products* have used sports platforms or themes as part of their marketing strategy as well. Examples of nonsports products that have used sports platforms include automobiles, medical services, fast food, consumer electronics, and beverages such as milk, water, and colas. Yet, even this group of products has some grey areas. When beer or fast food is sold at a sports venue, is it a sports product or not?

The above discussion (see Table 1) summarizes the array of products that are sold within some domain of the sports marketing industry. Sports marketers must understand which products are important to their target markets and develop a strategy that meets those needs. Furthermore, the product strategy must be consistent with the other elements of the marketing mix. Only then can the sports marketer take full advantage of the opportunities that exist.

Level of Integration: Traditional versus Sponsorship-Based Strategies

In addressing the marketing of products through sports, the degree of integration with the sport is the second key consideration. Here the choices are broad but can be classified into two categories—traditional and sponsorship-based.

Traditional Integration

The first category represents the use of sport as part of the marketing program and typically involves the basic components of a marketing strategy: a target market and a corresponding marketing mix. As such, these strategies involve no official relationship with a sports entity such as a league, team, or player. Using a *traditional* marketing strategy, the marketer identifies target markets and develops corresponding product, distribution, pricing, and promotion strategies that are designed to appeal to those target markets. A traditional strategy using a sports overlay may simply involve an advertisement that features actors or models playing a sport, it may involve the placement of an ad in a sports publication that reaches the same target market, or it may utilize graphics on the packaging that feature a sports setting. Each component of the marketing strategy can be integrated within the marketer's effort to incorporate a sports theme.

Sponsorship Integration

In contrast to the traditional approach for integrating sport into the marketing of products, *sponsorship* involves an array of activities whereby the marketer attempts to capitalize on an official relationship with an event, a team, a player, or some other sports organization such as the NCAA, the IOC, or FIFA. One article recently referred to sponsorship as having a "fairly loose meaning in sport" (p. 24). In other words, the concept goes beyond the traditional sponsorship arrangement that most readily comes to mind

(Felt, 2003). But it is essential to understand that a sponsorship involves two entities, the sponsor and the sponsee.

The most readily acknowledged sponsorship can be characterized as the **traditional sponsorship.** The traditional sponsorship generally involves the acknowledgement of the sponsor by the sports property and the ability of the sponsor to use the property's trademarks and logos in its efforts to leverage the sponsorship and reinforce the relationship in the minds of members of the sponsor's target market. During the 2006 post-season games in MLB, each sponsor was recognized with a display on the scoreboard and through virtual advertising for those watching on TV. The traditional sponsorship can involve title rights; for example the Accenture Match Play Championship leaves no doubt as to whom the primary sponsor is. In a somewhat more subtle implementation, a marketer might be recognized as the presenting sponsor. Two noteworthy examples are "the Rose Bowl Presented by Citi" and "Chicago Bears Football Presented by US Bank." In addition to these approaches for the implementation of a traditional sponsorship, three special cases of sponsorship are used by today's marketers. These include (1) venue naming rights, (2) endorsements, and (3) licensing. Some readers might question the designation of these three strategies as being sponsorship-based. However, the following review of the literature finds ample support for this premise.

Venue naming rights have often been characterized as *building sponsorships.* The Edmonton Oilers play their home games in the Skyreach Centre. In a recent article, the relationship between the team and the marketer (Skyreach Equipment, Ltd.) was specifically characterized as a "building sponsorship" (Zoltak, 1998, p. 1). A more recent article in *Brandweek* referred to "building sponsors" and the evolution of that type of strategy over the past few years (Green, 2002). Even the venerable publication *Advertising Age* concurs with this characterization. In its review of stadium naming rights, it noted that there are "more than 50 corporations involved in major *sponsorships* of U.S. sports facilities" (Lippe, 2002). Similarly, the International Events Group (IEG) referred to venue naming rights as "title sponsorship deals" (Ukman, 2002). A.C. Nielsen recently added a service called "Sponsorship Scorecard" with the express purpose of developing a better understanding of "the value that sponsors receive from stadium naming rights" (Anonymous, 2004a). The important conclusion that can now be drawn is that venue naming rights do represent a special form of sponsorship. Therefore, when Pepsi-Cola paid to have its name attached to a sports facility in Denver, it was reasonable to presume that the company was implementing a sponsorship-based strategy to sell its nonsports products through sports.

Endorsements have been referred to as "personal (or personality) sponsorships" (Anonymous, 2003a, p. 70). Furthermore, when referring to endorsement opportunities for the NHL's first selection in the 2005 draft, Sidney Crosby, one Canadian publication stated that these personal "sponsorships could prove huge for Crosby's pocketbook" (Anonymous, 2005, p. 14). Another publication referred to Tiger Woods' significant earnings from "sponsor endorsements" (Kedrosky, 2005, p. 17). David Beckham is perhaps the most famous soccer player in the world, and his endorsement power is staggering. *The Economist* magazine specially referred to his deals with Pepsi and adidas as *personal sponsorships* (Anonymous, 2003a). Additional anecdotal support for the premise that endorsement deals fall within the realm of the sponsorship environment can be found on the *SportBusiness International* website. Nike's signing of LPGA golfer Grace Park was touted as a sponsorship deal (Barrand, 2003a), and in a separate posting, *SportBusiness International* referred to Yao Ming's endorsement of Pepsi-Cola as a "sponsorship agreement" (Barrand, 2003b). It should now be evident that the general consensus within the sports marketing industry is that endorsements are indeed a form of sponsorship.

Of the three special cases, **licensing** may be the most debatable as to whether or not it represents a sponsorship-based strategy. Yet, there is ample support for this assertion in the practitioner-oriented literature. Also noteworthy is the fact that many traditional sponsorship deals provide the marketer with the right to use the sport property's logos and trademarks in its own marketing endeavors. One common sponsorship category is that of "official supplier." These sponsors are often granted the right to produce and sell logo apparel and a variety of other licensed products. The NHL recently announced the signing of Reebok as its *official apparel supplier* at the beginning of the 2005-06 season. A recent report out of the UK discussed "sports licensing" within the context of "kit sponsorships" (Barrand, 2005). The report went on to state that licensing provides sponsors with the opportunity to maximize the value of their sponsorship rights. In another example that ties the concept of licensing to that of sponsorship, a recent report indicated that Reebok has an arrangement that allows for the use of the logos of MLB's 30 teams in the marketing of a special line of footwear (Anonymous, 2004b). Until 2008, Sears used a traditional sponsorship with NASCAR with the specific goal of driving the sale of its Craftsman brand of tools. Beyond that relationship, Sears also sold a broad array of NASCAR-licensed merchandise in many of its retail stores (Anonymous, 2003b). EA Sports recently signed a seven-year contract with NASCAR providing the marketer with exclusive rights to use the organization's logos in the video game market (Hein, 2003). The importance of this form of sponsorship was noted by Felt (2003), who observed that "Nike and Adidas now have intellectual property rights whose value far exceeds that of the products through their association with leading sports teams and events." It is also noteworthy that each venue selected to host the Olympic Games is now required to implement a new stringent set of rules that protect this class of sponsors. Clearly, the literature bears witness to the co-mingling of the terms *sponsors* and *licensing.* Given this fact, it seems reasonable to assume that licensing can be classified as a special form of sponsorship. Thus the marketer has a wide array of options available when the decision to implement a sponsorship-based strategy is made.

If the marketing decision maker wishes to integrate a sports theme into the marketing strategy there are two choices. The marketer either opts to use a traditional marketing strategy approach based on the selection of target markets and the development of a corresponding marketing mix for each target, or alternatively the decision maker may integrate sports in a more formal manner by employing one or more of the four sponsorship strategies described on the preceding pages (traditional sponsorships, venue naming rights, endorsements, and licensing agreements).

Basic Principles of Sports Marketing

From the previous discussion, three principles are relevant for the assessment and understanding of today's sports marketing industry. They are

- The nature of the sports marketing focus (marketing of sports or marketing through sports);
- The nature of the product being marketed (sports or nonsports); and

- The level of integration of sports within the marketing strategy (traditional or sponsorship-based).

A summary of the basic components for each area is presented in Table 2. The latter two are used in the development of a detailed framework that extends the previous broad approaches of "marketing through sports" and the "marketing of sports" into a more strategic conceptualization of the four domains of sports marketing.

The Four Domains of Sports Marketing

As illustrated in Figure 1, the four domains that comprise the sports marketing environment are identified as *theme-based* strategies, *product-based* strategies, *alignment-based* strategies, and *sports-based* strategies. An explanation and rationale for each proposed domain, along with illustrations of actual sports marketing strategies, is provided in the following sections.

Theme-Based Strategies

Theme-based strategies can be defined as the use of *traditional marketing strategies* that incorporate a sports theme into the marketing program for *nonsports products*. The marketer might opt to use a sports-related copy platform or advertise products in sports-related media to effectively reach customers. A key aspect of theme-based strategies is that the marketer's efforts are not predicated upon an official relationship with any specific sports property in its effort to create the sports overlay for its marketing efforts. A bank that advertises in a sports magazine or during a TV broadcast of a sports event has incorporated sports at a rudimentary level. As such, this domain represents the lowest level of integration of sports within the sports marketing environment. There is plenty of anecdotal evidence that illustrates how sports marketers have used theme-based approaches in the implementation of target market access, as well as product, promotion, pricing and distribution strategies.

Implementation of a theme-based strategy may be achieved by placing advertisements in vehicles that appeal to one or more of their sports-oriented **target markets**. It is important to note that the advertisements used in this type of strategy will not necessarily have a sports theme. Marketers of

Table 2.
The Basic Principles of Sports Marketing

Nature of Sports Marketing Focus
- Marketing of Sports
- Marketing through Sports

Products
- Sports Products
  - Spectator Sports
  - Participation Sports
  - Sporting Goods, Apparel, Athletic Shoes, and Sport-Related Products
- Non-Sports Products

Level of Integration
- Traditional
  - Target Market Selection
  - Marketing Mix Decisions
- Sponsorship-Based
  - Traditional
  - Venue Naming Rights
  - Endorsements
  - Licensing

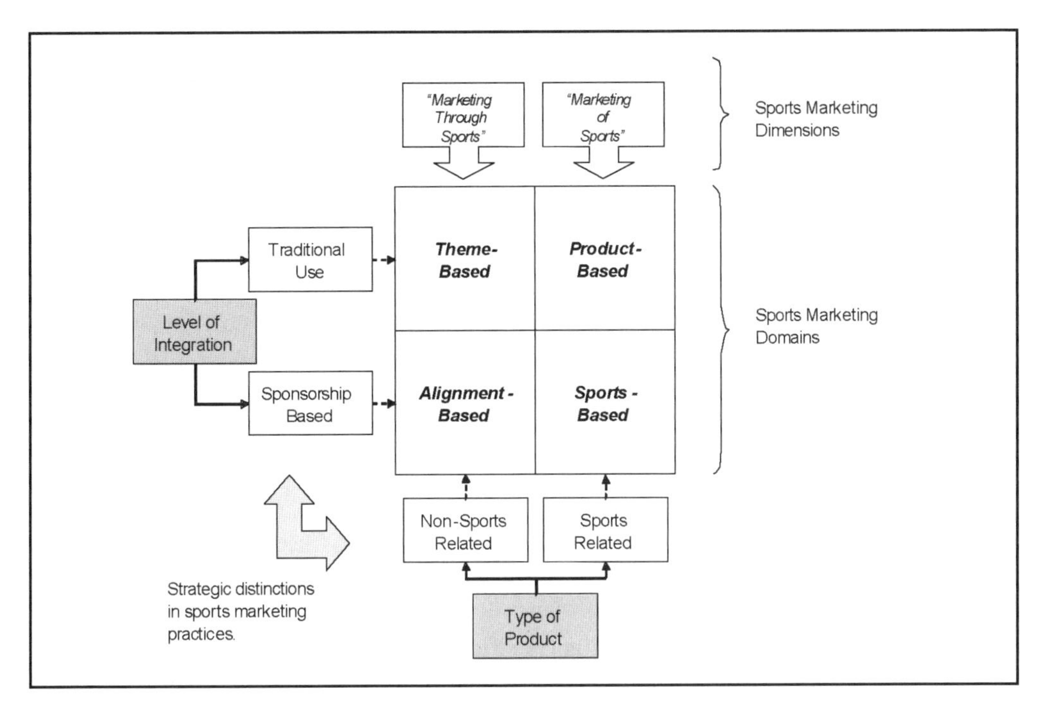

Figure 1.
The Four Domains of Sports Marketing

nonsports products often reach different target markets by objectively selecting their media vehicles.

The use of a theme-based strategy is also evidenced by the incorporation of sports into the other elements of the marketing mix. A well-conceived marketing mix will be tailored so as to coincide with the characteristics of a particular target market. To accomplish this, the marketer must consider the specific initiatives that are used in the task of defining its product, promotion, pricing, and distribution strategies. Thus the task is one of utilizing one or more of these components in such a way so as to create a sports overlay that will appeal to its own target markets.

Product strategies can incorporate sports themes as a way to provide resonance with customers. Sports bars use the promise of televised sports programming as a way to sell food and beverages; fashion labels create clothing that features a sports motif such as polo or golf; and credit card marketers may provide access to member-only sporting events as part of their product offering. Most marketers accept the premise that packaging represents part of the product strategy, so packaging will frequently feature a sports design or motif.

It is common that sports overlays are incorporated into **promotional** efforts for a variety of nonsports products. For example, tie-ins with sports event through the use of hospitality tents at the event; TV advertisements that feature kids being treated to a trip to a favorite fast-food restaurant after winning their game; and commercials suggesting that viewers get more enjoyment from watching televised sports when they watch it on a particular brand of high definition TV all illustrate the use of a theme-based approach.

Technology has also increased the tie-in capabilities of theme-based marketers. Virtual advertising technology can be used to place computer-generated signage at strategic locations during the broadcast of a sports event. During the recent Major League Baseball post-season games, TV viewers were exposed to a sign for a new Gillette razor whereas the fans in the stands simply saw a blank green surface. An advantage of virtual signage is that it can be changed during the broadcast. The Gillette sign that TV viewers

Table 3.
Overview of Theme-Based Strategies (Traditional Strategies for Nonsports Products)

Target Marketing
- Budweiser Using Sports Media to Reach Consumers (Super Bowl; Sports Illustrated)
- Cadillac Using Golf Magazine to Reach Upscale Segment
- Cadillac Appealing to Target Market Based on Ability to Fit Four Sets of Clubs in the Trunk

Product
- Sports Bars Feature Sports TV Programming as Part of their Product Assortment
- Clothing Featuring a Sports Motif (Men's Underwear and Tie Featuring Golf Graphics)
- Kodak Film Packaging Featuring Generic Sports Images
- M&M Packaging Featuring Checkered Flag Graphic and Racing Team Labeling
- Crunch 'n Munch Packaging Featuring a Young Boy Playing Basketball
- Tag Heuer's Invitational Golf Tournament for Buyers of an Expensive Model of Its Watch
- Visa Signature Credit Card Providing Access to Exclusive Properties (Pebble Beach GC)

Promotion
- Detroit Newspaper's Hospitality Facility at Ryder Cup Competition
- McDonald's Advertisement Featuring Kids After Winning a Sports Competition
- Sony Advertisement - You Can Enjoy Sports More on a Sony High Definition TV
- New Zealand Radio Station – 99 FM – "Breakfast with Balls" Theme
- Panasonic Laptop Computers and Football – Toughness and Performance
- Gillette and State Farm Insurance Using Virtual Advertising during MLB Broadcasts
- Kraft's Game Day Cake Recipe during Time Period Preceding the Super Bowl
- Ambush Marketing (Wendy's, American Express, Pepsi-Cola, and Telecom New Zealand)

Pricing
- Bars Offering Discounts to Recreational Sports Participants (softball players)
- Hospitality Industry Offering Discounts to Ticket Holders of Select Sports Events

Distribution
- Hard Rock Café at Rogers Centre in Toronto
- Big Boy Restaurant at Detroit's Comerica Park
- Levy Restaurants at Sports Venues (Wrigley Field, Comerica Park)
- Alcoholic Beverages at Sports Venues (Mike's, Cuervo, & Bass Ale)
- FedEx at Ryder Cup Venue (Oakland Hills)
- Budweiser Distribution in NASCAR Geographic Markets (i.e., Darlington)

first saw became a sign for State Farm Insurance later in the broadcast. It can also be used to display different signage to viewers in different geographic markets.

In each of the aforementioned examples, the intent was not to sell a sports product; rather it was to sell a marketer's nonsports offering. The list of theme-based efforts that feature a sports overlay through promotion is almost endless—no doubt a testament to the popularity and perhaps the effectiveness of this type of strategic initiative.

Strategies involving the **pricing** variable and a sports overlay are a bit more difficult to implement. However, one common strategy is for casual restaurants and bars to offer discounts to patrons who are wearing their uniforms from a participation sport such as softball. Another similar strategy is for hotels, restaurants, and bars to offer reduced prices for patrons holding a ticket to a particular sports event. By coupling this action with effective promotion, the marketers are able to create the sports overlay that can be used to appeal to one or more meaningful target markets.

The final element of the marketing mix is the **distribution (or place)** strategy. The food service industry has been effective and profitable by virtue of its ability to achieve a distribution point at a number of sports venues across the globe. One of the more notable efforts of this type involves the presence of a Hard Rock Café at the Rogers Centre in Toronto, Canada. Similarly, there is a Big Boy Restaurant located inside Detroit's Comerica Park. Not all of these providers are readily recognizable retailers. For example, Levy Restaurants are present at many sports venues across the United States; however, the Levy brand is not emphasized. Marketers of alcoholic beverages have also sought to have their products available at sports venues. In an interesting distribution strategy, FedEx negotiated for the right to have a temporary shipping point located on the Oakland Hills Golf Course during the 2004 Ryder Cup. The strategy provided convenience for the spectators who bought souvenirs as well as incremental revenue for FedEx. Finally, marketers will consider the geographic aspects of their distribution strategy. Budweiser's distribution of 8-packs of beer (in recognition of Dale Earnhardt, Jr. when he was still driving the number 8 car) was initially confined to major NASCAR hotbeds such as Charlotte, Darlington, and Atlanta.

Table 3 summarizes the array of examples delineated in this section on theme-based strategies. It is important to remember that the intent of a theme-based strategy is to use traditional elements of a marketing strategy to create a sports overlay in an effort to sell nonsports products; it is not based upon any type of sponsorship relationship between the marketer and any sports entity. It is also important to note that the five elements of marketing strategy are not mutually exclusive; rather they are integrated in such a way so as to create a synergistic effect. Thus the question is not which element to use; instead, it is how can the firm develop and integrate target marketing, product, promotion, pricing, and distribution strategies so as to capitalize on the opportunities presented by the sports environment while simultaneously avoiding the high fees associated with an actual sponsorship. In answering this question, it is important to note that many firms have adopted strategies that are referred to as ambush marketing. These efforts involve a nonsponsor developing a strategy that creates the false impression that it is an official sponsor of some sports property. Ambushing has become more common as the rights fees for premier properties have continued to escalate. Companies such as Wendy's Hamburgers, American Express, Pepsi-Cola, and Telecom New Zealand have been noted over the years for their effective use of ambush marketing initiatives.[3]

Product-Based Strategies

Efforts to market *sports products* using *traditional marketing strategies* when the marketer has no official relationship with the sports entity being used in its marketing efforts are classified as product-based strategies. These strategies may or may not involve a sports theme beyond the product offering. Consider the marketer of athletic shoes who drops prices and provides incentives for the retailers. It is apparent that these specific strategic decisions are independent from the sports environment; however, since the product is sports-related, the strategy still falls within the realm of sports marketing. Within this product-based domain, it is logical for the marketer to implement strategies that incorporate sports themes. It is also important to understand that such strategies are not achieved solely by virtue of a marketer's promotional efforts.

The NHL changed its rules at the beginning of the 2005-06 season in an effort to make the game more appealing. This effort does not represent a sponsorship-based strategy because it fails to meet the litmus test of having a sponsor and a sponsee involved in an integrated marketing endeavor. A second example is the sporting goods retailer who chooses to give away free caps at a baseball game in an effort to create awareness of its brand. If this strategy is the result of the retailer providing compensation for the right to distribute the caps and not on the basis of an official sponsorship, then it can be classified as a product-based strategy. Clearly, there are varying levels of involvement of sports for strategies within the product-based domain. Since efforts within this domain are implemented using the traditional elements of the marketing mix, it is worth reiterating the point that traditional strategies involve the selection of the target market and the development of a corresponding marketing mix. So the question becomes one of how a marketer of sports products can use its target marketing, product, promotion, pricing, and distribution strategies to influence purchase behavior. How can they get consumers to purchase more of their sports products?

The assessment of the product-based strategies begins with descriptions of how marketers of sports products use traditional strategic initiatives in their efforts to appeal to designated **target markets**. As an example of an effort on the part of one marketer of sports products to reach a key target market, consider an ad that was placed by the PGA for its "Tour Partners" club in *Golf for Women* magazine. It is important to note that while the PGA used another sports entity (in this case, a sports magazine) to reach a key target market (female golfers), that is not a condition of this domain. For instance, had the advertisement been placed in *USA Today* or *BusinessWeek* magazine, the effort would have still qualified as a product-based strategy. The key distinction in this case is the absence of any type of sponsorship relationship between the PGA and the publication. In a somewhat controversial target marketing strategy, the WNBA's Los Angeles Sparks made an overt effort to target the gay and lesbian segment and supported that initiative by staging a pep rally at an area bar that is frequented by gay and lesbian consumers. Less controversial in nature, MLB has targeted the Hispanic segment while the NBA has tried to capitalize on the emergence of Yao Ming by targeting the Chinese-speaking segment of the sports market. Many sports organizations have implemented relationship marketing programs designed to appeal to their most avid fans; one example is the Real Madrid soccer team that featured David Beckham. In the aftermath of the 2006 World Baseball Classic, MLB decided to nurture the interest that had emerged in several European markets. As one component of that strategy, the MLB Road Show, an exhibit that allows "fans" to experience the game of baseball by hitting in batting cages and pitching in an environment that allows the speed of their pitches to be measured, traveled to "new" geographic target markets such as Germany. Target marketing may also involve B2B efforts. For example, in one effort to reach sports business professionals, adidas placed an advertisement in *SportBusiness International* magazine.

It should now be apparent that any alteration in the organization's target marketing strategy is typically supported by other changes in its marketing mix. The product is tweaked; the promotion is altered; the price is modified; or the distribution strategy is changed so as to better work in harmony with the efforts to reach a new target market.

There are numerous examples for **product** decisions. The San Diego Padres provide a Spanish-language broadcast for their aforementioned Hispanic target market. This modification of the team's product provides a better fit for some members of its media-based audience. Marketers of spectator sports often target large business accounts; the product that has become a prominent part of every new sports venue built in the past 15 years is the luxury box. There are few individual fans who would be interested in purchasing this product; in fact, even the few "super-wealthy" fans who can afford a luxury box would prefer to spend their money on the expensive premium seats at the venue. TV viewers will frequently see actor Jack Nicholson in the front row of Lakers games, director Spike Lee in the front row of Knicks games, and singer Kid Rock in the front row of Pistons games.

Some sports have opted to change the rules that govern their game. As mentioned above, after losing a season because of the inability to reach an agreement with the players association, the NHL introduced substantial modifications to its rules beginning with the 2005-06 season. Similarly, in an effort to speed up its football games, the NCAA introduced rules changes that governed the starting and stopping of the clock at the beginning of the 2006 season. Virtually every major sport has changed its core product in some meaningful way over the past 20 years. Marketers of spectator sports must carefully consider any decision to modify the way their game is played or officiated as any changes will inevitably be met with resistance by some segment of the fan base. Yet, such changes are often viewed as an improvement to the product that will enhance its appeal among members of one or more key target markets. Another key product decision for team management concerns the players who are on the field. A team may sign a new star play in order to improve the quality of play and to induce a more positive perception of the team on the part of fans and the media.

Sports equipment is often altered in an effort to create brand preference. Even though they violate the official rules of the game, golf balls that float or travel too far are sought by some golfers. Golf clubs have been modified in an effort to provide players with the opportunity to hit the ball further and straighter; tennis rackets have larger sweet spots; and bowling balls have stronger hooking characteristics. The sale of basketballs has been enhanced by modifying its dimensions. A slightly smaller ball is used by women who play organized basketball (such as the WNBA). This smaller ball is also more likely to be purchased by women who participate informally as a form of recreation and exercise.

There are many **promotions** used to sell sports products. Examples abound from the use of TV ads by New Balance; the use of the Internet by FIFA, the New York Yankees, the Plymouth Whalers, and Nike; direct mail campaigns by the Chicago Bears; and local newspaper ads by the PGA and the NBA's Memphis Grizzlies. Sports teams often use sales promotion as a marketing tool; one of the more popular techniques is the giveaways that are designed to encourage attendance and to nurture relationships. For MLB's Los Angeles Dodgers, one of the more popular giveaways is the infamous bobble-head doll. In another example, for the 2007 tour of the Harlem Globetrotters, anyone purchasing a minimum of six tickets could enter a special code in the Internet ticketing service dialog box and receive a free basketball. Sales promotions like these reflect many people's narrow perspective of sports marketing, one that focuses on the question: how can we put more fans in the seats?

Spectator sports are not the sole province for sports marketers who utilize promotion as a means of implementing a product-based strategy. Marketers of participation sports products and the varied array of sporting goods, apparel, shoes, and other sports-related products also rely extensively on promotion as an important component of their strategies. For example, Bowflex uses TV advertisements, the Internet, and a CD-ROM that is sent to prospects in their efforts to nurture demand. The popular women's fitness center, Curves, has used two-for-one coupons while Bally's Fitness Centers have used 30-day free trial membership periods to get customers through the door. A bowling center in Westland, Michigan, sent coupons to all of the registered league bowlers in its database providing them with the opportunity to bowl a free game during the late summer, a notoriously slow period for bowling centers nationwide. Marketers everywhere acknowledge that trial is often the prelude to adoption, so manufacturers and retailers of golf clubs often stage "Demo Days" at local pro shops; this promotion is designed to get prospects to try new equipment in a risk-free environment. Finally, some marketers will provide premiums for buyers much the way that the marketers of spectator sports use the giveaway strategy. The example in this case is for subscribers of *Golf* magazine to receive a dozen new Titleist golf balls.

In regard to **pricing**, many MLB teams work with local organizations and provide their members with discounts. Examples include a team's decision to sell discounted tickets to members of AAA and AARP. Another is the group sales strategy that provides discounts for employee groups and students at certain schools. Many marketers of spectator sports have begun to use bundling strategies as a mechanism for providing discount pricing. During the 2007 season, MLB's Atlanta Braves offered fans their Grand Slam Ticket Pack that included four game tickets, four hot dogs, four Coca-Colas, four team bucket hats, one game program, and parking at prices starting as low as $59.

One interesting strategy for a participation sport involves the task of making golf affordable. The USGA and its "First Tee" program have sought to reach kids, especially inner-city kids who generally do not have the financial resources required to play a round of golf. The marketing of athletic shoes has long been marked by controversy as the high prices often led to robberies and even murders by kids who simply could not afford to pay $150 for a pair of desirable sneakers (Telander & Ilic, 1990). Some marketers have begun to offer new shoes at greatly reduced prices.[4]

In an interesting example that illustrates potential pitfalls in establishing prices that benefit the organization, the Chicago Cubs were recently sued because of the team's decision to sell highly desirable tickets through its Wrigley Field Premium Tickets service. The result was that prices escalated far beyond the face value printed on the ticket. When the team was absolved of any legal violations, it was stated that this tactic would likely become more prevalent in situations where the demand for tickets exceeds the supply (Rovell,

2003). In fact, some teams and events (as well as other entertainment events such as concerts) have begun to offer the best seats through auctions in an effort to maximize revenue. The Detroit Tigers auctioned off some of the front row seats at the team's on-deck circle during the final days of its run to the 2006 MLB playoffs. Similarly, the organizers of a boxing match between Lennox Lewis and Kirk Johnson sold 300 VIP ringside tickets to the highest bidders.

From these examples, it should be evident that pricing decisions do not always involve discounted prices. While the focus has been on ticket prices for spectator sports, those marketers also have to think about the prices for access by the media-based audiences—those using TV, radio, the Internet, and mobile technology to watch or listen to the event. Pricing decisions can also be a key part of the strategy for marketers of participation sports, sporting goods, apparel, and athletic shoes.

The final area to consider in the product-based quadrant is distribution. How can the marketer implement **distribution** strategies that assist in the marketing of sports products? For marketers of spectator sports, this involves access to the event and efforts to distribute tickets to the fans. For the live audience, consideration must be given to the location of franchises. The NHL engaged in an aggressive expansion program that resulted in the location of new franchises in warm weather locations such as Phoenix and Miami. Leagues must also evaluate opportunities involving the relocation of struggling franchises. One of the most recent moves involved the relocation of MLB's Montreal Expos to Washington, DC. Many marketers of spectator sports have begun to reach out to new international markets; the non-defunct NFL-Europe is one example of this phenomenon. The location of special events often involves a series of difficult decisions. The Super Bowl, the Olympics, and the World Cup of Soccer evaluate the infrastructure of candidate cities as part of the decision-making process.

Tickets for most sporting events are now available through a variety of outlets; no longer is the fan limited to the traditional box office. Teams and events offer tickets through independent agencies such as Ticketmaster and Stubhub.com. Fans can purchase tickets over the Internet; in fact, they can even print their tickets on their own computer.

The media-based audience has become increasingly vital to the well-being of every marketer of spectator sports. We have seen the emergence of numerous TV options including team-dedicated networks (Manchester United Network), general sports networks (ESPN), specific sport networks (the Rugby Channel), sports tiers (NBA League Pass), free-to-air TV (Fox), and pay-per-view (PPV for boxing matches). The growth of satellite radio has also provided another distribution outlet. For example, NASCAR broadcasts many of its races on Sirius Radio. Perhaps the most significant innovation of the past few years has been the ability to use the Internet for audio and video streaming. Major League Baseball was quick to capitalize on this emerging source of revenue with its MLB TV programming. An emerging application is the distribution of sports programming through mobile technology such as cellular phones and Blackberry PDA units.[5]

In the distribution of participation sports facilities, the emphasis is on supply and demand. Brunswick once evaluated each geographic area on the basis of the number of bowling lanes that it could support. Then, based on the number of existing lanes in that area, Brunswick would calculate the surplus or deficit and use that statistic as the basis for determining whether or not a new facility should be built. In the absence of this type of objective assessment, the golf industry has overbuilt; as a result, decisions have had to be made regarding the closure of many courses (Fullerton, 2007).

For the marketing of sporting goods, apparel, and shoes, consider Reebok's distribution strategy; it is quite different from that of most of its key competitors. While most marketers of athletic shoes seek to use channels that emphasize large retailers, Reebok has historically focused on small specialty stores that provide an enhanced level of customer service (Rohm, 1997). The final example to consider is that of Callaway's marketing of golf clubs. It uses the Callaway Golf Tour Fit Van to go to remote locations and reach out to consumers. The van reaches golf enthusiasts who are given easy access to the marketer's products.

From these preceding examples, it is evident that marketers of each category of sports products will seek to implement traditional strategies that will allow them to take advantage of the opportunities that the marketplace presents. These actions may or may not result in a competitive advantage to the marketer. In many cases the actions taken are quickly imitated and thus become *points of parity*. However, an interesting research question to answer might be the extent to which marketing innovations in the sports marketing arena are sustainable and provide competitive advantages. Marketers are acutely aware of the need to identify viable target markets and to develop a series of corresponding marketing mixes that will appeal to each target market. Table 4 provides an array of examples that illustrate the traditional strategic initiatives employed in the implementation of product-based strategies.

Alignment-Based Strategies

Many marketers of *nonsports products* officially align themselves with sports properties via one or more of the four forms of *sponsorship* previously described (traditional sponsorships, venue naming rights, endorsements, and licensing agreements). The nature of this sponsorship-based relationship reflects a higher level of integration of sports within the sports marketing environment. A common strategy involves a sponsor who uses an association with sports to market nonsports products; this combination emphasizes initiatives that are classified as alignment-based strategies. In an effort to sell more fast food, McDonald's advertising and packaging feature its official partnership with the Olympic Games. Volvo uses its sponsorship of a high profile sailing event to strengthen the public's perception of the carmaker as one that exudes prestige while concurrently emphasizing safety and technology. While the strategic initiatives that augment the sponsorship are important, the foundation for the resultant strategy is the fact that the marketer, by virtue of its official sponsorship, is highly integrated within the sports environment. Thus, the task for these marketers of nonsports products is one of implementing strategic initiatives that allow them to capitalize upon their position within this realm of the sports marketing environment. Such initiatives are alternatively characterized as leveraging or activation.

Examples using **traditional sponsorship** abound; however, two of the most noteworthy examples are Coca-Cola's relationships with the World Cup of Soccer and the Olympics. Other noteworthy Olympics sponsors include McDonalds, Lenovo Computers, and John Hancock Life Insurance (see Table 5 for several examples).

In addition to traditional sponsorship, there are three special forms of sponsorship that are available to today's marketers. The professional teams in Denver provide excel-

Table 4.
Overview of Product-Based Strategies (Traditional Strategies for Sports Products)

Target Marketing
- PGA Focus on Women (through Golf for Women Magazine Ad)
- WNBA's Los Angeles Sparks Targeting the Gay & Lesbian Segment
- MLB Targeting the Hispanic Market
- NBA Targeting Chinese-Speaking Fans
- Adidas' Advertisement in SportBusiness International to Reach Sport Business Professionals
- Real Madrid's Relationship Marketing Program Targeting Avid Fans
- MLB Road Show in 13 Cities in Germany

Product
- NHL Changes in Rules to open up the Game and Eliminate Ties
- MLB's San Diego Padres' Spanish Language Radio Broadcast
- Luxury Boxes for Large Corporate Customers
- Expensive Premium Seats for Wealthy Fans
- NCAA Football Rules Changes to Speed up the Game
- Signing Star Player to Improve Product (Chicago Bulls Signing of Ben Wallace)
- Sporting Goods with Performance Characteristics (golf clubs, golf balls, tennis rackets, bowing balls)
- Sporting Goods Tailored to Target Market (Smaller Basketball for Female Players)

Promotion
- Creative Appeals in Advertising (New Balance – "for the love of the game")
- Internet Site for Dissemination of Information (FIFA, New York Yankees, Plymouth Whalers, Nike)
- Direct Mail (Chicago Bears Season Ticket Renewal Solicitation)
- Newspaper Advertising (Teams and Events (Memphis Grizzlies and the PGA Championship))
- Sales Promotion – Giveaways (Los Angeles Dodgers Bobblehead Dolls; Harlem Globetrotters Ball)
- CD-ROM (Bowflex Mails to Prospects Identified through Direct Response Advertising)
- Free Trial (Bally's 30-Day Complimentary Membership; Golf Products "Demo Days")
- Discount Coupons (Curves 2-for-1 Offer)
- Free Participation (Coupon for Free Game for Registered League Bowlers)
- Premiums (Golf Magazine Giving a Dozen Titleist Balls to Subscribers)

Pricing
- Discounts for Member of Recognized Groups (AARP & AAA)
- Group Discounts for Informal Groups (Parties, Students)
- Bundling of Tickets, Food, Beverages, and Other Products (Atlanta Braves Grand Slam Ticket Pack)
- Bundling of Events (Ford Field College Football Package)
- Programs to Make Participation Affordable (USGA's "First Tee" Program)
- New Lines of Athletic Shoes Selling at Lower Prices
- Premium Tickets Sold at Premium Prices (Chicago Cubs Wrigley Field Premium Ticket Service)
- Auction – Price Determined by Bidding (Lennox Lewis Fight; Detroit Tigers On-Deck Seats)

Distribution
- NHL Expansion to Warm Weather Locations (Miami, Phoenix, Atlanta, Tampa Bay)
- MLB Relocation Decision (Move Montreal Expos Team to Washington, DC)
- Location of Special Events (2010 World Cup of Soccer in South Africa)
- Competitions in International Markets (NFL Europe)
- Internet Ticket Procurement (Ticketmaster, Stubhub.com, Print-at-Home)
- Alternative TV Distribution (i.e., NFL Sunday Ticket, ESPN, the Golf Channel, Pay-Per-View)
- Satellite Radio (NASCAR on Sirius Radio)
- Audio and Video Streaming on Internet (i.e., MLB.TV)
- Distribution via Mobile Technology (i.e., Mobile ESPN)
- Construction of Participation Facilities Based on Supply and Demand (Brunswick Bowling Centers)
- Mobile Retail Facility Going to the Customer (Callaway Golf Tour Fit Van)

lent examples of how marketers of nonsports products use **venue naming rights** (or "building sponsorships") as a platform for creating demand. MLB's Rockies play their home games in Coors Field. The NHL's Avalanche and the NBA's Nuggets both play their home games in the Pepsi Center. In this same vein, the NBA's Memphis Grizzlies play in the FedEx Forum while MLB's San Diego Padres play their games in Petco Park. Significant growth has also occurred in the American collegiate market and in minor league professional sports; consider Ohio State's Value City Arena and the Memphis Redbirds in AutoZone Park. Virtually every major venue in the United States now has a naming rights sponsor; as a result, much of the recent growth in this type of sponsorship activity has taken place in international markets. A few examples are Allianz Arena in Munich, Germany; Lexus Centre in Melbourne, Australia; Coca-Cola Stadium in Xi'an, China; T-Mobile Arena in Prague, Czech Republic; and DeBeers Diamond Oval in Kimberly, South Africa.

Venue naming rights inevitably provide benefits far beyond that of simply putting a corporate moniker on the façade of some sports facility. For example, the Pepsi Center serves Pepsi products, and all of the ATMs in Comerica Park belong to Comerica Bank. Thus, venue naming rights can be an integral component of a marketer's strategy in its efforts to influence consumer attitudes and preferences as well as the purchase of its nonsports products by members of the organization's target markets.

A second special form of sponsorship is that of the implementation of an **endorsement** strategy or what has been referred to as a "personality sponsorship" (Gillis, 2005, p. 4). One can seldom watch a TV program or read a magazine without seeing at least one effort to use an athlete's endorsement as a means of cutting through the clutter. These celebrity endorsers are generally easily recognized, in part because they have achieved a high standard of performance. While there are many types of personalities who can perform in the role of a celebrity endorser, within the realm of sports marketing, the focus is on athletes. Indianapolis Colts' quarterback Peyton Manning has become a popular endorser. Among his recent spate of endorsements is one for Sony High Definition TV. It is worth noting that no NFL trademarks or logos are used in these advertisements because another marketer, Samsung, is the official High Definition TV sponsor for the NFL. Some critics may actually refer to Sony's effort as ambush marketing

The final special form of sponsorship involves the use of **licensing** to sell nonsports products. Consider the relationship between Mattel and NASCAR. By using select NASCAR trademarks, Mattel is able to capitalize on the sport's popularity and sell more of its Hot Wheels toy cars. Consumers may also purchase a slow cooker from Rival; the marketer's "Crock Pots" bear the likeness of one of several NASCAR drivers including Jeff Gordon and Dale Jarrett. Major credit card companies have entered into licensing agreements with virtually every major sports league and their teams. The resultant affinity credit cards can represent an attractive offering for fans. Two examples are the Visa "NFL Extra Points" card and the MasterCard that features MLB's St. Louis Cardinals.

It is important to reiterate the fact that each of the examples delineated represents a marketer's effort to sell nonsports products. However, the efforts reflect a higher level of integration of sports within the marketing strategy than is in evidence with theme-based strategies. This is achieved through the use of some form of sponsorship that ties the marketer to some important sports entity. Table 5 provides a compendium of examples of alignment-based strategies.

Table 5.
Overview of Alignment-Based Strategies (Sports Sponsorship-Based Strategies for Nonsports Products)

Traditional Sponsorship
- Olympic Sponsorships (McDonald's, Lenovo, & John Hancock Life Insurance)
- Volvo's Sponsorship of the Ocean Race
- World Cup Sponsorships (Google!, Coca-Cola, McDonald's)
- NASCAR Sponsorships (DeWalt, DuPont, Best Western, Budweiser & Pepsi-Cola)
- Weetabix Women's British Open
- PGA Tournament Title Sponsors (FedEx)
- NFL "Official" Products (Coors Lite, Samsung HDTV)
- Official Energy Bar of the New Zealand All Blacks (Moro)
- Official Energy Source of the PGA Tour (Nature Valley Granola Bars)
- Barclay's Premiership League
- MLB's Chicago White Sox sponsorship by 7-11
- Red Bull Sponsorship of MLS Team (New York Red Bulls)

Venue Naming Rights
- Denver Sports Facilities (Coors Field, Pepsi Center)
- Memphis Sports Facilities (FedEx Forum and AutoZone Park)
- San Diego MLB Facility (Petco Park)
- Detroit MLB Facility (Comerica Park)
- College Venues (Ohio State's Value City Arena)
- Minor League Sports (Memphis Redbirds' AutoZone Park)
- International Venues (Allianz Arena, Lexus Centre, Coca-Cola Stadium)
- Other International Venues (T-Mobile Arena, DeBeers Diamond Oval)

Endorsements
- Sony High Definition TV and Peyton Manning
- "Got Milk?" and Peyton, Eli, & Archie Manning
- Prilosec and Brett Favre
- Tag Heuer Watches and Tiger Woods & Michelle Wie
- Buick and Tiger Woods
- Accenture and Tiger Woods
- Arnold Palmer and Invacare
- Menard's Home Improvement and Dale Earnhardt, Jr.
- Old Spice Fragrances and Tony Stewart

Licensing
- Mattel "Hot Wheels" Cars and NASCAR
- Rival "Crock Pots" and NASCAR
- Monogram Lunch Meats and NASCAR
- Visa and the NFL
- MBNA and MLB's St. Louis Cardinals
- Van Dillen Asiatech and FIFA World Cup
- Hawthorne Village and the NHL
- York Heating and Air Conditioning and NCAA Sports Teams (U of Michigan)
- Danbury Mint (Watches) and NCAA Teams (University of Michigan)
- Glidden Paint and an Array of Sports Entities (i.e., NFL, NCAA, NBA, & USOC)
- Oak Grove Caskets and NCAA Teams (i.e., Ohio State University)

Table 6.
Overview of Sports-Based Strategies (Sports Sponsorship-Based Strategies for Sports Products)

Traditional Sponsorship
- Adidas and FIFA (World Cup of Soccer)
- Adams Golf and the PGA (Tight Lies Tour)
- Adidas and the New Zealand Rugby Football Union (New Zealand All Blacks)
- Adidas and National Soccer Teams (e.g., Germany and Argentina)
- Quiksilver and the X Games
- Real Madrid Soccer Team and a Formula 1 Race Team

Venue Naming Rights
- Reebok Stadium in Bolton, England
- Fila Forum in Milan, Italy
- Pro Player Stadium in Miami, Florida, USA (contract terminated)

Endorsements
- Nike and Michelle Wie, Tiger Woods, and Michael Jordan
- Adidas and David Beckham
- Burton Snowboards and Shaun White
- Storm Bowling Balls and Pete Weber
- Callaway Golf and Arnold Palmer
- PGA Golf and Star Players ("These guys are good")
- NBA and Star Players ("The NBA is FANtastic")
- MLB and International Star Players (World Baseball Classic)

Licensing
- Nike and Major Universities (e.g., North Carolina, Duke, and Ohio State)
- Upper Deck and MLB (collectable trading cards)
- Reebok and NHL (apparel and equipment)
- Gilbert and Super 14 Rugby (balls)
- Wilson and the NFL (balls)

Sports-Based Strategies

The final domain, sports-based strategies, is characterized by *official sponsors of a sports property* who are selling other *sports products*. Because of the role of sports in both the product and integration dimensions, this domain may reflect the greatest reliance on sports-oriented initiatives. It may also represent the least common type of strategy employed by today's sports marketers. Within this domain, the most common strategy features the marketer of sporting goods or sports apparel in a traditional sponsorship of a sports team or a sporting event. Strategies in this domain can be very effective when appealing to customers who are excited by the sports that are used in the implementation of the specific strategic initiatives (Fullerton, 2007). For example, adidas sells sporting goods and it uses advertising that complements its traditional sponsorship of FIFA and the World Cup of Soccer. This consistency produces the synergy that is characteristic of the sports-based domain.

An example that features a **traditional sponsorship** is Adams Golf and the PGA. The maker of the "Tight Lies" brand of clubs sponsors a lower-level regional series of golf tournaments that comprise the Tight Lies Tour. Another example is the traditional sponsorship for adidas and the New Zealand All Blacks (New Zealand Rugby Football Union). While this is similar to the sponsorship of the World Cup of Soccer by adidas, the difference lies in the type of property with which the sponsor is aligned. In the former case, adidas is sponsoring an event; in the latter case, the marketer is sponsoring an organization and its famous team. While each of these examples best fits within the realm of traditional sponsorship, the sponsors' contracts typically provide them with opportunities to sell officially licensed merchandise and to gain the services of key players for endorsements. Thus, there is often an overlap in the types of sponsorships used by any marketer that is operating in the sports-based domain.

The three special forms of sponsorship can also be employed by marketers operating in the sports-based quadrant. For example, Reebok has **venue naming rights** for a soccer stadium in Bolton, England; the Reebok Stadium is the result. While this strategy has seldom been chosen as an appropriate sponsorship endeavor by marketers of sports products, it may become more common as new stadia are built with a focus on revenues from the marketers holding the naming rights for each venue.

Endorsements for sports products that use athletes as spokespersons represent the best examples of the sports-based domain. Nike's personal sponsorship of Michelle Wie is one of the most recent and most noteworthy efforts of this type. Early in Tiger Woods' career, Nike was criticized for its substantial payment for the golfer's endorsements of Nike's new line of golf products. Given the terms of their new contract, it is evident that Nike felt like the world's number one golfer contributed to its sales in a positive way, much the way that Michael Jordan did throughout his illustrious NBA career. Marketers of spectator sports can also implement endorsement-based strategies. Most often, these involve spokespersons who are still active in the sport. The PGA has long run a "these guys are good" campaign that features current golf stars. Similarly, the National Basketball Association has relied on its "the NBA is FANtastic" advertising theme that features current NBA stars such as Dwayne Wade and Yao Ming. Because of their potential impact, endorsements are a commonly employed strategy within the sports-based domain.

Finally, we turn our attention to **licensing.** It is important to reiterate the earlier point that the other forms of sponsorship may convey to the sponsor the right to produce and sell an array of merchandise that features the trademarks, logos, and likenesses of the sponsee. Nike has licensing deals with a number of top tier university athletic programs. Among the most noteworthy are the University of North Carolina, Duke University, and The Ohio State University. Upper Deck uses a licensing agreement with professional sports leagues and players such as those in Major League Baseball as the foundation of its efforts to sell collectable trading cards. It is important to understand that the licensee is using its relationship with a sports property to influence demand for its own sports products.

For each of the aforementioned examples, the synergy emanating from the two sports entities should be evident. As noted earlier, this domain represents the one with the greatest overall immersion into the world of sports; therefore, it can be extremely effective when the target market is comprised of fans of the sports entity with which the marketer has an official relationship. Clearly, the marketing of sports products can be impacted in a positive manner via the incorporation of the sponsorship of a recognizable sports property within an integrated marketing communications strategy. Table 6 provides a summary of the sports-based strategies that were cited in this section.

Conclusions

The purpose of this conceptual paper is to provide a grounded theory-based framework for classifying activities that comprise sports marketing strategies. It begins with the recognition that there are two distinct dimensions within the sports marketing industry: the marketing *of sports* products and marketing *through sports*. Thus, sports marketing is not solely focused on how to get more fans in the seats at a specific sports venue. By taking the type of product sold and the level of sports integration into account, four strategic domains have been identified. The types of products have simply been identified as sports products and nonsports products. The marketers' level of integration concerns its involvement with some sports entity in some form of official sponsorship. As such, the two broad areas for integration have been designated as traditional and sponsorship-based. Using these dimensions, the two-by-two matrix shown in Figure 1 emerges. This matrix provides the foundation for the definition and description of the four domains of the sports marketing industry.

At the most fundamental level, *theme-based* strategies use the traditional components of a marketing strategy—target market and marketing mix decisions—to sell nonsports products. This can be differentiated from the *product-based* strategies that represent the use of traditional marketing mix and target marketing decisions in an effort to sell sports products. Representing a higher level of integration, many marketers have aligned themselves with sports properties via some form of sponsorship. The sponsorship-based strategies are represented by the *alignment-based* and *sports-based* strategies. Alignment-based strategies use sponsorship in the efforts to sell nonsports products; it is the fact that the marketer is aligned with some sports entity that qualifies this type of strategy as one of the sports marketing domains. Conversely, sports-based strategies involve some form of official sponsorship of a sports property in the task of marketing one of the many sports products that crowd the marketplace.

The classification of recent examples within the sports marketing industry provides evidence and further documents the fact that these four domains are mutually exclusive and collectively exhaustive, thus meeting a basic test for the usefulness of this proposed framework. In addition, the broadened set of sports marketing domains articulated herein provides a method for classifying the many strategies that have recently evolved in the practice of sports marketing. This classification system is an initial first step for the development of theory in a field, it allows for the development of testable hypotheses to guide the development and execution of research, and finally it provides guidance to decision-makers in the field.

Directions for Future Research

The classification framework presented herein gives rise to a number of interesting and potentially fruitful research topics related to sports marketing. We mention several here.

A key question is the relative performance of these various sports marketing approaches in the accomplishment of business objectives. The performance characteristics should consider the advantages and disadvantages of each approach. For instance, there is some evidence that sponsorship strategies may stimulate negative societal attitudes toward the practices in particular and sports in general (Merz, Fullerton, & Taylor, 2006).

In addition, the development of descriptive research to document the relative costs associated with each of the four domains and the identification of contingencies for choosing one approach over another would help establish useful decision-making guidelines. For instance, strategy research can identify conditions under which it is more advantageous for a marketer of non-sports related products to use a theme-based versus an alignment-based strategy.

Finally, the practice of sports marketing strategies internationally is another area of fruitful inquiry. As many of the examples used in this paper reveal, while the underlying framework as a theory possesses face validity, clearly how the approaches are executed varies dramatically in a cross-cultural context. Marketers engaged in global activities need guidelines about how best to use sports marketing strategies in the international arena.

Endnotes

[1] Howard Cosell first uttered the expression "veritable plethora" in a sports context during the broadcast of a Monday Night Football game in the 1970s. That phrase seems to be an appropriate description of the current state of sports marketing.

[2] A grounded theory approach has as goals the identification of concepts, categories and propositions. Concepts and categories are the basic units of analysis and the starting point for most grounded theory applications. It is the conceptualization and categorization of observed events (the data) that establishes the bases and means for integrating the emerging theory. In its formation the grouping of concepts into categories is supported by examples (samples of data) observed by the researcher.

[3] For example, Qantas Airway's ambushing of Ansett Australia during the Sydney Olympics, and Nike's ambushing of the official adidas sponsorship of the World Cup of Soccer.

[4] Grabbing many of the headlines in recent days is the pricing strategy used by Steve and Barry's University Sportswear store to sell its new basketball shoe for $14.98. In light of Payless Shoe Source's marketing of its successful $35 Amp running shoe, one sports marketing firm issued a stern warning that, "If I were a branded athletic company right now, I'd be reconsidering my whole approach" (Holmes 2007).

[5] ESPN attempted to provide this type of service, but it was met by general disinterest by American consumers.

References

Anonymous (2006, September 19). *Experts urge Chinese companies to back Beijing Olympics.* Retrieved from http://www.sportbusiness.com/news/ 160453/experts-urge-Chinese-companies-to-back-Beijing-Olympics

Anonymous (2005, August 15). Sidney Crosby: Already an NHL endorsement superstar. *Marketing, 110*(27), 14.

Anonymous (2004a). *Nielsen expands sports arm.* Retrieved from http://www.sportbusiness.com/ news/index

Anonymous (2004b, May). News Briefs. *Sporting Goods Business, 37*(5), 12.

Anonymous (2003a, July 5). Business: Branded like Beckham; Sporting endorsements. *The Economist, 368*(8331), 70.

Anonymous (2003b, July). Sears maximizes tools of the NASCAR trade. *Retail Merchandiser, 43*(7), 44.

Anonymous, (2003c). *SGMA sports participation trends.* Retrieved from http://www.SGMA.com

Barrand, D. (2005, June). Why brands are banking on sport. *Promotions & Incentives*, 13-14.

Barrand, D. (2003a). *Nike signs up first female golfer.* Retrieved from http://www.sportbusiness. com/news/ index?news_item_id=150250

Barrand, D. (2003b). *Yao and Coke resolve image row.* Retrieved from http://www.sportbusiness.com/news/? news_item_id=152825

Blann, F., & Armstrong, K. (2003). Sport marketing. In J. Parks & J. Quarterman (Eds), *Contemporary Sport management* (2nd edition). Champaign, IL: Human Kinetics.

Felt, J. (2003, December/January). How sponsorship can help your brand. *Managing Intellectual Property, 125*, 24.

Fullerton, S. (2007). *Sports marketing.* New York, NY: McGraw-Hill/Irwin.

Gillis, R. (2005). Harnessing the power of personality. *Sponsorship Works,* (2), London, UK: SportBusiness International, 4-6.

Gladden, J., & Sutton, W. (2005). Marketing principles applied to sport management. In L. Masteralexis, C. Barr, & M. Huns (Eds), *Principles and practice of sport management.* Sudbury, MA: Jones and Bartlett Publishers.

Glaser, B., & Strauss, A. (1967). *The discovery of grounded theory.* Chicago: Aldine.

Gray, D., & McEvoy, C. (2005). Sport marketing strategies and tactics. In B. Parkhouse (Ed), *The management of sport: Its foundation and application.* New York, NY: McGraw-Hill Inc.

Green, P. (2002, December 9). Sponsorship with no booths or logos. *Brandweek, 43*(45), 16.

Hein, K. (2003, September 22). EA drives into the action as NASCAR's solo gamer. *Brandweek, 44*(34), 9.

Holmes, S. (2007, January 22). Changing the game on Nike: How budget sneakers are tripping up its basketball business. *Business Week,* 80.

Kedrosky, P. (2005, March 14). Tiger, tiger burning bright. *Canadian Business, 78*(6), 17.

Lippe, D. (2002, October 28). Inside the stadium-rights business. *Advertising Age.* Retrieved from http://www.adage.com/news.cms?newsID=36406

Masteralexis, L., Barr, C., & Hums, M. (Eds). (2005). *Principles and practice of sport management.* Sudbury, MA: Jones and Bartlett Publishers.

Meek, A. (1997). An estimate of the size and supported activity of the sports industry in the United States. *Sport Marketing Quarterly, 6*(4), 15-21.

Merz, G. R., & Fullerton, S. (2005, March 24-26). Developing a personal investment measurement scale for sport spectator behavior. In J. Chapman (Ed.), *Expanding marketing horizons into the 21st Century; Proceedings Association of Marketing Theory and Practice* (pp. 394-399). Jekyll Island, GA.

Merz, G. R., Fullerton, S., & Taylor, D. (2006, March 23-25). An exploratory study of societal attitudes in the United States and New Zealand toward sport sponsorship: Differences, structure and effects. In J. Chapman (Ed.), *Enriching theoretical and practical understanding of marketing; Proceedings Association of Marketing Theory and Practice* (pp. 69-70). Hilton Head, SC.

Moore, E., & Teel, S. (1994). Marketing tools for sports management. In P. Graham (Ed), *Sport business: Operational and theoretical aspects.* Dubuque, IA: Brown & Benchmark.

Mullin, B., Hardy, S., & Sutton, W. (2000). *Sport marketing.* Champaign, IL: Human Kinetics.

Pitts, B., & Stotlar, D. (1996). *Fundamentals of sport marketing.* Morgantown, WV: Fitness Information Technology.

Rovell, D. (2003, November 24). *Judge decides business is legit.* Retrieved from http://www. sports.espn.go.com/mlb/news/index?news_item_id=1670041

Rohm, A. (1997). The creation of consumer brands within Reebok Running. *Sport Marketing Quarterly, 6*(2), 17-25.

Schlossberg, H. (1996). *Sports marketing.* Cambridge, MA: Blackwell Publishers, Inc.

Shank, M. (2005). *Sports marketing: A strategic perspective.* Upper Saddle River, NJ: Pearson Education, Inc.

Shannon, J. R. (1999). Sports marketing: An examination of academic marketing publication. *The Journal of Services Marketing, 13*(6), 517-34.

Sports Marketing Surveys (2002, October 7). *Insights Newsletter,* 1-3.

Stotlar, D. (2001). *Developing successful sport marketing plans.* Morgantown, WV: Fitness Information Technology.

Telander, R., & Ilic, M. (1990, May 14). Senseless: In America's cities, kids are killing kids over sneakers and other sports apparel favored by drug dealers: Who's to blame? *Sports Illustrated, 72*(20), 36-42.

Ukman, L. (2002, February 21). *Naming rights: Not just for stadiums anymore.* Retrieved from http://www.sponsorship.com/learn/namingrights.asp

Van Heerden, C. R. (2001, September 9). Factors affecting decision-making in South African sport sponsorships. *Doctoral Thesis* (etd-11072001-165433). University of Pretoria, South Africa.

Zoltak, J. (1998, October 12). Skyreach Equipment Ltd. purchases naming rights at Edmonton. *Amusement Business, 110*(49), 1.

2

The Foreign Invasion of the American Sporting Goods Market

Lawrence W. Fielding and Lori K. Miller

Introduction

American sporting goods firms have always prided themselves on their ability to compete successfully. They have been particularly effective at recognizing market signals, aiding market development, and promoting sport (Hardy, 1990; Fielding & Miller, 1996). Industry leaders like Spalding Brothers, Wilson, MacGregor, and Rawlings have understood each other and used this knowledge to curb the intensity of rivalry (Fielding & Miller, 1996). Beginning in the early 1920s, industry members acted in concert to improve industry structure by promoting and organizing participation and by refraining from cutthroat competition (Fielding, Miller, & Pitts, 1994). Competitive conduct, based upon years of repetitive experiences and expectations, was predictable. American sporting goods firms competed against other American sporting goods firms. Quality and price decisions relied upon evaluations of neighboring companies and took for granted consumer needs and preferences (Fielding & Miller, 1996; Kotler, Fahey, & Jatusripitak, 1985).

This comfortable scenario changed during the 1960s with the emergence of foreign competitors in American sporting goods markets. Foreign competitors saw some market opportunities sooner and more clearly than did American companies. European and Japanese firms, for example, responded to customer readiness for new high-tech sport products manufactured from new kinds of raw material. Foreign firms also saw the need for higher product quality and lower consumer prices (Kotler et. al., 1985). The success of the foreign invaders brought challenges to American sporting goods firms.

James Dubow, president of J.A. Dubow Sporting Goods Corporation, told Congress in 1964 how the foreign invasion affected his company: The Japanese have put us out of business. . . . All the people that worked for us in baseball gloves are gone. . . . I believe it is strictly a case of drop dead and hope your next life will be better. (Testimony of James Dubow, 1964). For many members of the sporting goods trade, the end of baseball glove production at Dubow Sporting Goods Corporation provided ample proof that the foreign invasion of the American sporting goods market had reached crisis proportions. Dubow was a venerable company. They pioneered the manufacture of baseball gloves during the 1890s. By the turn of the century, Dubow was a leading promoter of the American game on both the national and the local scale. During the 1930s, Dubow sponsored softball and promoted its growth and popularity. During the 1950s, Dubow sponsored Little League, American Legion, and other forms of amateur baseball. When Dubow stopped baseball glove production in 1962, it had been a promoter of baseball for over 70 years. Dubow survived five depressions, the intense competition that followed both the First and the Second World Wars, government luxury and excise taxes, labor disputes, hostile buyouts, and attacks on its market share and distribution chain by mail-order houses, chain stores, and department stores. The company was resilient. The company grew with the game and, in turn, helped the game to grow.

The company did not survive the Japanese invasion into the baseball glove and mitt market. Company president J. A. Dubow cited low-cost Japanese imports as the cause. Top-grade Dubow gloves cost the retailer approximately $20.00. Retailers sold the glove for $34.95 (Sandifer, 1964a). Japanese gloves of equal quality cost the dealer $5.00 and sold at $8.95 (Sandifer, 1964a). The Japanese had even greater advantages with medium-and lower priced gloves. The Dubow medium-priced baseball gloves sold for $13.95. Japanese gloves of the same leather quality sold for $6.88 and had more features. Further, inexpensive Japanese gloves sold for $3.88 and had all the features identified with American models that sold for $12.95 (Sandifer,1964a). Baseball glove manufacturing was labor intensive. Much of Dubow's cost resulted from the labor necessary to manufacture quality gloves. Unable to compete against Japanese prices at retail sporting goods specialty stores, Dubow turned to the large chain stores and mail-order houses. This proved fruitless. Dubow lost its Sears, Roebuck account and its Montgomery Ward account in 1960. Declaring that his company could not match the low wages Japanese companies paid their employees, Dubow stopped production of baseball gloves and mitts in 1962 (Sandifer, 1964a).

The Dubow scenario is important for four reasons. First, it reflects the concerns and the attitudes of many sporting goods manufacturers. These concerns and attitudes will be developed in Part I of this paper. Second, Dubow's remarks were widely quoted and widely used by sporting goods proponents of protective tariffs and opponents of free trade agreements to document the need for protection against imports. The free trade policy of President Kennedy and later of President Johnson affected the sporting goods industry by making the foreign invasion easier. Part II of this paper will discuss attempts by the sporting goods industry to convince the Tariff Commission, the President, and Congress of the need for higher tariffs and quotas on foreign sporting goods in order for American companies to survive. Third, Dubow's conclusions about the cause of Japanese success in American markets are not completely accurate. Part III of this paper will emphasize how Japanese companies manipulated marketing mix to gain a competitive advantage in the American sporting goods market. Fourth, Dubow's decision to quit the manufacture of gloves and mitts reflects one of many responses adopted by sporting goods companies. Part IV of this paper will elaborate how American sporting goods employed strategies that manipulated marketing mix to regain market share. Part V of the paper will develop the implications of the foreign invasion and the American response to it in terms of the contemporary emphasis upon market-mix strategies and the basis for the development of these strategies.

Part I: Attitudes and Concerns

Many segments of the sporting goods industry were concerned about the yearly increases in the number of imports and market share by foreign companies. The invasion of Japanese-made baseball and softball gloves and mitts is one example. In 1957 imports accounted for only 4.2% of the market. By 1966 foreign manufacturers controlled 84% of the glove and mitt market. Between 1957 and 1966, imports of gloves and mitts rose from 149,000 to 3,989,691, an increase of 2,578%. During the same period, domestic production decreased by over 2.6 million ("Collier's Bill, "1966). Smaller companies like Dubow and Denkert Company ceased production. Larger companies like Rawlings, Goldsmith, MacGregor, Spalding Brothers, Wilson, and Stall and Dean curbed American production. In an emotional appeal before the U.S. Tariff Commission, protectionists declared that foreigners controlled the glove market for America's national game and that soon there would be no American companies left (*U.S. Tariff Commission Hearings*, 1960).

The attitude of many sporting goods manufacturers was that they should be protected by higher tariffs, quota systems,[1] or selling-price agreements.[2] Sporting goods manufacturers claimed that they wanted only a level playing field. They argued that the lower wages paid to workers in foreign countries formed an insurmountable competitive advantage. The cost of labor in Japan, for example, was between 10 and 14 cents per hour compared to an average $1.75 in America ("Let's Take a Look at the Record," 1961). According to Tyler B. Davis, president of Bancroft Racket Company, foreign competitors captured 27% of the tennis racket market in 1951, 59% in 1960, and 80% in 1966. Davis attributed this increase in market share to the differential in wages paid to employees. As stated by Davis, "The main cause on the inability of domestic manufacturers to compete with foreign manufacturers is the vast difference in factory wages" (Testimony of T. B. Davis, 1966).

The wage problem was compounded by the fact that Congress placed high tariffs on key raw materials. Thomas Elliott, vice president of Rawlings, complained to the Tariff Commission during the July 1960 hearings that high tariffs on imported leather increased the cost of production for gloves and mitts, baseballs and softballs, as well as other types of sport equipment. In comparison, Elliott noted that Japan and European countries placed no tariff restrictions on raw material imports (Sandifer, 1960a). P. C. Mathewson, operations manager of Pennsylvania Products, a division of the General Tire and Rubber Company, echoed Elliott's concerns for tennis-ball manufacturers. The import duty for wool into the United States, stated Mathewson, was 24 cents per pound. European competitors enjoyed an advantage because this wool entered their countries duty-free (Testimony Davis, 1966). Improved American technology, a cost-cutting strategy that developed and utilized labor-saving machines, was negated by government policies that gave advanced technologies to key foreign competitors. As Representative Frank Scherer (Ohio Republican) pointed out to the Tariff Commission in 1961, one main problem with the American glove and mitt industry was that the Japanese had been given, free of cost, the most modern mass-producing leather equipment in existence. Japanese equipment, a goodwill gift from the U.S. government, was better than the equipment used by most American sporting goods firms (Sandifer, 1961c).

Foreign firms engaged in cutthroat competitive practices such as dumping and trademark and patent infringement. Before the 1960s, dumping referred to a strategy of eliminating inventory by cutting prices to promote consumer buying. Price cutting was an acceptable practice when used in this capacity. The Japanese, the West Germans, and the Australians changed the meaning of and attitude toward dumping. They used dumping as a penetration strategy to obtain market share. Dumping became defined as foreign companies' selling a product below the cost of production or selling below the price charged in their own country.[3] In the 1960s Japanese companies infringed on American trademarks by using the names of American baseball stars on their products. They also labeled their baseballs as the Official American League, or National League, or Little League ball. Some foreign companies became involved in patent infringement. The MacGregor Company, for example, introduced a six-finger baseball glove in 1960. The Japanese had a copy within 3 months that matched MacGregor quality and sold for about one third the price (Spink, 1960). Members of the American Fishing Tackle Manufacturers Association had similar complaints. Japanese firms produced replicas of American high-priced reels and sold them on the American market for 1/4 the price. Tennis racket manufacturers, golf club producers, sporting arms and ammunition manufacturers, and manufacturers of bicycles offered similar complaints (Spink, 1960).

American sporting goods firms also complained about the difficulties of competing in foreign markets. Besides production costs being higher in American, sporting firms faced the additional problem of high protective tariffs sponsored by foreign governments. The European Economic Community (EEC), Japan, Britain, and the Soviet bloc countries maintained high tariffs that made American goods less competitive. American tariff policy opened American markets to foreigners, but foreign countries, because of their high tariff policies, were less open to American sporting goods firms. Sporting goods firms wanted these inequities changed. During the 1960s, many firms looked to the American government to provide solutions that would level the competitive playing field.

Part II: Tariffs and Fair Trade

Many sporting goods manufacturers blamed Congress, presidents Kennedy and Johnson, and the Tariff Commission for adopting and supporting free trade policies (Calleo, 1987; Gilpin, 1987; Gray, 1979; Lundestad, 1990; Zeiler, 1992). Free trade emphasized equal access to world markets for all nations. For sporting goods companies, this meant the elimination of a protective tariff policy that dated from the 1930s (Zeiler, 1992). To accomplish its free trade objectives, the United States government insisted on multilateral trade agreements that included tariff and trade barrier reductions (Zeiler, 1992). The drive for multilateral trade agreements resulted in the General Agreement on Tariffs and Trade (GATT). GATT, created in 1947, gave American leaders a means with which to carry out their free trade policies through meetings and agreements with foreign nations.[4] The first round of the GATT meetings lowered global tariffs and was credited with stimulating a boom in world trade. The next meetings in 1949, 1951, and 1955 reduced tariffs and included specific concessions to West Germany and Japan. GATT rounds in 1956 and 1962 provided more modest cuts, primarily because Congress, bombarded by appeals to halt tariff reductions, sought to freeze tariff reductions until it addressed the problem of growing imports into the United States (Curzon, 1965; Dam, 1970; Zeiler, 1992).

The sporting goods trade was involved, as a minor player, in congressional hearings and in the Tariff Commission Hearings where the debate for lower tariffs took place. Trade members believed that the GATT rounds in 1955 and 1956 resulted in tariff reductions that threatened the survival of American sporting goods companies.[5] Trade leaders Rawlings, Dubow, Wilson, Brunswick, Stall and Dean, Hillerich and Bradsby, Spalding Brothers, Bancroft, MacGregor, Weber Tackle Company, Horrocks-Ibbotson, General Tire and Rubber Company, Arco Skates, and representatives of the Sporting Goods Manufacturers Association and the American Fishing Tackle Manufacturers Association appealed to the Tariff Commission for relief under the escape clause in 1960, 1961, and 1964 (Zeiler, 1992).[6] Except for the glove and mitt industry in 1961, the Tariff Commission rejected all arguments by trade members for relief in the form of higher tariffs. On March 19, 1962, President Kennedy turned down the Tariff Commission recommendation for relief for the glove and mitt industry. Even though the glove and mitt industry was a small segment of the American sporting goods industry, members of the sporting goods industry felt rejected by the Tariff Commission and the President.

Industry members found little solace in the outcome of congressional Hearings. House committee hearings in 1962 and 1966 provided a forum for the concerns of sporting goods manufacturers, but the results were meager (HC, Ways & Means, 1962; HC, Subcommittee on Labor, 1966). Although tariffs on imported sporting goods products were not lowered, they were not raised either. By 1967, everyone in the sporting goods industry was forced to concede that the solution to competitive advantages enjoyed by foreign producers of sporting goods did not lie with the United States Congress or the executive branch of government.

Part III: The Off-Shore Manipulation of Marketing Mix

The GATT agreements opened American markets to foreign sporting goods manufacturers from Japan, the EEC, and the Soviet bloc countries, but the lowering of tariffs does not explain the success of these off-shore invaders. The triumph of the foreign invaders can be best explained in terms of competitive strategies foreign sporting goods manufacturers employed to manipulate specific parts of the traditional marketing mix. In the paragraphs that follow, we discuss how the invaders executed competitive strategies in terms of product, price, distribution, and promotion.

Product Strategies

Product strategies involved three approaches. First, off-shore companies copied American models. The six-finger baseball glove is an example of this strategy. Rawlings introduced the glove in May of 1959. The company used Davega Sporting Goods Company to sales test the glove in New York City. Davega, a highly successful retail sporting goods chain, spent a great deal of money advertising and promoting the glove, which sold for $30.00 retail. According to Charles Jacobson, sporting goods merchandise manager for Davega, by August of 1959 the Japanese (led by Mizuno) had a six-finger glove of the same quality that sold for $10.00. Jacobson reported that he was forced by competitive conditions to add the Mizuno model to the Davega inventory (Sandifer, 1961c). Similar stories about copied models were related by Edwin Parker, president of Spalding Brothers (tennis, football, and baseballs); Carl Benkert, vice president of Hillerich & Bradsby (golf clubs and baseball bats); Tyler Davis, president of Bancroft (tennis and badminton rackets); and Richard Balch, president of Horrocks-Ibbotson (fishing reels and fishing tackle) (Sandifer, 1961a,b,c).[7]

A second strategy adopted by foreign competitors was to improve upon successful American models. Lawrence Brown, president of Cortland Racket Company; Tyler Davis, Bancroft; Edwin Parker, Spalding; Lewis Crager, executive vice-president of MacGregor; and Olen Parks, vice-president of Wilson Sporting Goods, told members of the Tariff Commission about improvements foreign competitors made in tennis rackets. Foreign firms added a seventh ply to the traditional American six-ply tennis racket, making it stronger and more durable. Foreign companies also added throat overlays, over-wrapping, better leather grips, full counter-sinking and improved slotting and grooving. These features substantially improved upon American models (Sandifer, 1961c).

A third strategy came as a result of improved technologies and can be most fully seen in the athletic shoe industry. Bernard Benowitz, president of Saucony Shoe and president of the Athletic Goods Manufacturing Association, noted that the success of foreign athletic shoe manufacturers, like Adidas and Puma, was due in part to an improved vulcanizing process that made Adidas shoes lighter and more durable. This same process permitted mass production of molded soles, making it possible for foreign competitors to develop a greater variety of sizes and styles at less cost.

Price Strategy

Perhaps the most extensive and successful competitive strategy employed by foreign competitors dealt with price and corresponds directly with what James Quinn has termed logical incrementalism (Quinn, 1980). The Japanese were by far the most effective at utilizing this strategy. They began by entering the low-end market in such products as baseball gloves, baseball bats and balls, footballs and basketballs, tennis rackets, bowling balls, golf clubs, and fishing reels and tackle. Japanese companies like Mizuno used penetration pricing to introduce high-quality products into the American sporting goods market. The low-end market was an unguarded area in American sporting goods. Major sporting goods manufacturers like Rawlings, Spalding, MacGregor, Wilson, and H&B produced low-grade products merely to fill out their lines and to keep their employees working (Spink, 1960). According to Claude Carr, president of Rawlings, none of the major sporting goods manufacturers paid much attention to this market niche. Japanese emergence into and takeover of this niche went virtually unnoticed (Spink, 1960).

Once the Japanese had secured approximately 40% of the low-grade market, they moved into the middle-range market and finally into the top-grade market (Spink, 1960). Price was a significant competitive factor in the middle-and upper grade American market. Japanese companies offered identical or superior quality at lower prices (Sandifer, 1960 a,b;1961b,c; Spink, 1960). Retailers like Davega, mentioned earlier, found it impossible to compete without stocking Japanese products (Sandifer, 1961b).

The essence of the Japanese competitive strategy was to slip unnoticed into an unguarded market niche, take it over, and then expand into other market niches. American sporting goods manufacturers were caught off-guard. They did not feel the impact of the foreign invasion until the Japanese firms moved into the middle- and top-grade areas of the market ("Athletic Shoes," 1967). By then, for some American firms, it was too late. Dubow is a good example. Unable to compete with Japanese firms like Mizuno in the top-grade niche, they chose to compete in the low-grade gloves market. Unfortunately for Dubow, Mizuno and other Japanese glove makers already controlled this market niche. Dubow's attempt to recapture the forgotten segment came too late.

Distribution Strategies

Japanese distribution strategies were closely aligned with pricing strategy. American sporting goods firms presented significant barriers to entry for top-grade products. Top-grade products were distributed primarily through sporting goods stores and club pros. In the late 1950s and early 1960s, Japanese firms could not gain access to these distribution channels. This required Japanese firms to establish other distribution channels.

Japanese firms established new distribution channels in three important areas. First, many Japanese firms targeted the discount stores that developed in the later 1950s and early 1960s. The shopping mall movement of the late 1950s spurred the growth of discount stores (Historical Overview, 1992; Markowitz, 1987). Discount stores found low-end sporting goods a significant consumer attraction. Japanese firms discovered and developed this ever-expanding low-end market. Second, Japanese firms targeted mail-order houses, department stores, and chain stores. High-quality and low-priced Japanese sporting goods were sold by Sears, Montgomery Wards, Gimbel Brothers, Hecht, Macy's, J.C. Penny, and Goldblatt's ("Bigger Stores," 1961; Burke, 1961). Third, Japanese firms sold sporting goods through nontraditional retail outlets. Japanese sporting goods could be found at the grocery stores like the A&P, 5&10 stores like Woolworth and Newberry's, as well as hardware stores, drug stores, and variety stores (Burke, 1961). Other foreign competitors followed the Japanese model. By the late 1960s, consumers could buy top-grade sporting goods products ranging from bicycles to fishing tackle to baseball bats, golf clubs and golf balls at discount stores, drug stores, supermarkets, department stores, and mail-order houses (Sandifer, 1961a,b,c). These new distribution channels at first supplemented and then circumvented traditional sporting goods distribution outlets.

Promotion Strategies

Foreign competitors adopted different promotion strategies in different segments of the sporting goods industry. These strategies can be divided into two broad categories: reseller aids and personal selling. In baseball, golf, tennis, and fishing equipment, foreign manufacturers, principally the Japanese, offered reseller aids in the form of larger margins. This was an effective strategy in selling sporting goods to discount houses, department stores, chain stores, and mail-order retailers. These kinds of firms relied upon low margins and high-volume sales. They depended upon price advertising and loss leaders to pull customers into their stores. They emphasized the use of displays and other forms of merchandising to motivate customers to purchase products. Discount houses, for example, advertised name-brand gloves at wholesale prices and used displays of baseballs and baseball bats to sell these items (Sandifer, 1960b). The larger margins offered by Japanese baseball and bat manufacturers meant that discount stores could sell sporting goods products for less than American-made goods and still make a significant profit. Discount stores, department stores, chain stores, and even supermarkets grouped related sporting goods in tangential displays on the theory that such forms of merchandising motivated customers to buy. Claude Carr, president of Rawlings, emphasized the effectiveness of discount stores' merchandising techniques for increasing sporting goods sales. Carr believed that discount stores set the standard for merchandising (Spink,

1960). They arranged, organized, and displayed goods more effectively than did sporting goods retailers (Spink, 1960).

In the athletic shoe and athletic apparel segments of sporting goods, foreign competitors like Adidas and Puma emphasized personal selling and sales promotions. Adidas sales representatives dealt directly with coaches and athletes. They outfitted track teams for free. They gave away shoes and athletic apparel at all the major track meets. Adidas sales representatives talked to college and high school track coaches about ways to improve athletic shoes and hawked Adidas equipment (Autz, 1967; "Competitors Co-operate," 1965). Bernard Benowitz, president of the Sporting Goods Manufacturers Association (SGMA), pointed out that American athletic shoe manufacturers had stopped doing this during the 1950s ("Athletic Shoes," 1967). The Europeans simply filled in the gaps left by American complacence. Many American and world track and field stars wore Adidas. High school and collegian track athletes demanded the same shoes and apparel as the stars wore. By 1967, 80% of all Olympic track and field athletes wore Adidas. When Adidas became the official track and field outfitter at the 1968 Olympics, they banned other companies from the Olympic village ("Olympics Fire Up Seriousness of Imports," 1968). Direct selling and promotional giveaways made Adidas synonymous with track and field success.

Part IV: American Responses to the New Competition

Foreign competitors from Japan, Europe, and Asia were successful because they employed competitive strategies that manipulated the traditional marketing mix to their advantage. Companies like Adidas and Mizuno employed product, price, distribution, and promotion as weapons first to penetrate and then to gain control of American sporting goods markets. Their success introduced what Philip Kotler (Kotler et al., 1985) and others have termed the new competition. According to Kotler (Kotler et al.,1985), the new competition stressed market analysis and market exploitation, employing the elements of marketing mix as a part of competitive strategy. The success of foreign invaders demonstrated the importance of this approach. American sporting goods firms adjusted in order to compete against the foreign firms and to gain a competitive advantage over other American firms.

American sporting goods companies responded to the foreign invasion in the following six different generic ways: (a) movement to offshore production, (b) emphasis upon research and development (R&D), (c) improved promotions, (d) expanded distribution, (e) merger as a means of horizontal expansion, (f) improved industry analysis through cooperative efforts. Each of these responses will be discussed in the paragraphs that follow.

Offshore Production

Several companies moved operations offshore. Companies that moved manufacturing operations offshore did so for three reasons. First, the manufacture of sporting goods is labor intensive. Foreign competitors in Japan, Europe, Korea, Taiwan, and the Soviet bloc countries had lower labor costs. Many American manufacturers believed that the only way to compete with sporting goods producers from these countries was to establish factories in foreign lands where labor was cheaper. Second, Japan, the EEC, and the Soviet bloc countries maintained protective tariffs. By establishing manufacturing plants in these countries, American sporting goods companies avoided the high tariffs levied on imported products. Third, American companies moved offshore to escape escalating legal costs associated with liability suits (Miller & Fielding, 1995).

A. G. Spalding, a division of Questor Corporation of Toledo, led the movement to offshore production. Spalding moved its tennis-ball operation to Ireland in 1961. During the same year, it transferred the manufacture of tennis rackets to Belgium. A year later, it developed manufacturing plants for tennis rackets and tennis balls in Sweden and Britain (Sandifer, 1961c, 1962, 1964b). Spalding baseballs were manufactured in the West Indies as early as 1960. Complete baseball manufacturing operations were transferred to the West Indies in 1970 ("Spalding to Shift Baseball Production," 1970). The company moved its production of baseball and softball mitts and gloves to Korea in 1965 ("Business & Financial News," 1965). Manufacture of golf equipment was transferred overseas in 1970. Early in 1972, Spalding merged with Bridgestone Tire Company, LTD., of Tokyo to produce golf gear ("Spalding, Japanese Team Up," 1972). During this same year Spalding set up manufacturing plants in Spain and Italy to produce ski equipment ("Spalding in Spain and Italy," 1972). By early 1974, Spalding did most of its manufacturing in Canada, Australia, Japan, Korea, and Europe. American plants were limited to the production of basketball and football equipment, active wear, and some baseball, tennis, and golf equipment ("Dick Gersler Succeeds Paul Collins at Spalding," 1974; "Gary Grimes Prexy of Spalding U.S.," 1973).

Other companies followed the Spalding example. In the glove and mitt industry, MacGregor moved production to Puerto Rico early in 1961. Hutchenson Brothers transferred all of its production of mitts and gloves to Japan during 1962. Rawlings joined with Fulkui Sports of Tokyo in 1965 and became a part of the powerful Mitsui Dussan, a general trading company, during the same year. After 1965, Rawlings gloves were made with American leather, produced by a Japanese manufacturing company, and distributed worldwide by a Japanese trading company. Wilson Sporting Goods and Regent Sporting Goods moved glove and mitt operations to Korea in 1965. The Wells Lamont Company set up operations in Ireland in 1970 ("Business and Financial News," 1965; Sandifer, 1964b; "Wells Lamont Co.," 1970). The manufacture of baseballs followed the same exodus. MacGregor was in Puerto Rico by 1961. Stall and Dean moved production to Puerto Rico early in 1962. Rawlings' baseballs were made in Japan by 1965. Wilson had moved all of its baseball operations to Korea by 1972 ("Business and Financial News," 1965, 1972).

Manufacturers of golf, tennis, and fishing equipment also moved overseas during the 1960s and early 1970s. Wilson and Bancroft established plants to manufacture tennis equipment in Belgium (1961) and Japan (1962) respectively (Sandifer, 1961c; "Tragic Condition of Tennis," 1964). Wilson, Rawlings, and MacGregor transferred the manufacture of golf equipment overseas during the mid-1960s ("Pepsi Co. Inc. Buys Wilson," 1970). Japan was the chosen site for fishing-tackle manufacturers. Between 1964 and 1970, Roddy Recreation Products, Garcia, Shakespeare, and Heddon built plants on Japanese soil ("Profit Off 23% for Shakespeare," 1970; Sandifer, 1964b; "Shakespeare Firm in Japan," 1970; "Tokyo Tackle Firm, Heddon Sign Pact," 1970).

R&D Strategies

A second strategy emphasized research and development (R&D). This led to the production of new products using new materials and new technologies. Rawlings, Wilson, Spalding, MacGregor, Lannom, and Hillerich and Bradsby turned to the use of aluminum at least in part as a response to the increase in golf and baseball imports ("Aluminum Shaft—Here's Where It Helps," 1970; "Carr Staying on as Rawlings President," 1964; "Change for the Better at Alcoa," 1969; "Engineered Aluminum Bats," 1970; "Lannom Marketing Aluminum Bat Line," 1970; "Look of a Leader Theme at Rawlings," 1973; "MacGregor Force Told of Dramatic Progress," 1970; "Wilson Produces Aluminum Bat," 1970). R&D efforts led to the development of other materials and new manufacturing processes. Worth introduced the solid-core baseball and the synthetic "Dura-Hyde" baseball in 1972 ("Worth Unveils Solid Core Ball and New Bat, 1972). These new processes cut production costs and improved product durability. Wilson and Rawlings introduced aluminum and fiberglass composition tennis rackets in the late 1960s. During this same period, golf clubs were redesigned using new types of materials for club heads and shafts to improve club performance and durability.[8] Firms emphasized R&D as a means for introducing new products and for improving manufacturing processes to cut production costs.

Promotion Strategies

Third, American sporting goods companies increased promotional efforts in terms of sales promotions, personal selling, and reseller support. Aluminum bats were color coded by length and packaged in plastic wrapping. Packaging for golf clubs and tennis rackets was made more attractive. Many firms reemphasized endorsements by professional athletes. Adirondack produced a 600 series autograph model Willy Mays bat to commemorate and capitalize on May's 600th home run. MacGregor launched the Jack Nicklaus, Golden Bear, line of golf clubs and used Nicklaus-led golf clinics and other on-site promotions to sell golf equipment ("MacGregor Force Told of Dynamic Progress," 1970). Wilson replaced its outdated Jack Kramer and Doris Hart autograph model rackets with Arthur Ashe, Jimmy Conners, and Billy Jean King autograph models. Other athletic goods manufacturers redoubled their sponsorship efforts. Tennis equipment manufacturers gave more money for youth tennis tournaments and for support of USLTA programs ("Competitors Co-operate," 1965). Baseball and softball equipment manufacturers promoted youth league baseball, gave away rule books, and spent considerable money to help enforce standardization of youth league equipment. Many American firms redoubled efforts to display their goods at sporting goods fairs ("Competitors Co-operate," 1965).

American firms emphasized personal selling. Sporting goods manufacturers increased the size of sales forces in order to more effectively cover assigned territories. Efforts to meet with high school and college coaches increased. SGMA officials began attending meetings of track and field, basketball, and football coaches associations. SGMA members attended NCAA meetings and meetings of the National Federation of State High School Athletic Association. Companies like Wilson, MacGregor, and Rawlings instituted training programs for their sales personnel. Face-to-face selling and personal contacts had always been important in the sporting goods business ("Competitors Co-operate,"1965). Sporting goods firms increased efforts in these areas to meet the new competition from foreign firms and the intensified personal selling efforts of other American sporting goods producers.

The intensified competition from foreign and other American companies also led to a reemphasis on reseller support. American sporting goods firms increased regional advertising efforts and provided local firms with advertising copy. Sales representatives helped local retailers with information about displays and provided tips about effective merchandising techniques. Factory representatives spent more time explaining product features to retailers and providing sales information.

Diversification Strategies

Diversification was a fourth strategy. Shakespeare, a fishing equipment manufacturer, moved into the ski equipment industry. Garcia, another producer of fishing equipment, began the manufacture of firearms. Spalding, Rawlings, Wilson and MacGregor each began producing new lines of sport equipment ("Garcia Taking Aim at Firearms Market," 1968; "MacGregor Crew Kicks Off Opportunity," 1972; "Shakespeare Signs Elan Skis Pact," 1971).

Mergers

A fifth strategy was merger. In the fishing industry, for example, Gladdon, Shakespeare, Garcia, and Heddon were each involved in mergers ("Garcia Buying its Supplier," 1973; "Gladdin Acquires U.S. Fiberglass," 1967; "Shakespeare Buys Pfluger," 1966; "Tokyo Tackle Firm, Heddon Sign Pact," 1970). Spalding, Rawlings, Wilson, and MacGregor, called the big four by contemporaries, were involved in mergers into larger companies. Spalding became a division of Questor Corporation. Rawlings was part of Automatic Sprinkler. Pepsi-Cola owned Wilson, and MacGregor became a division of Brunswick. These mergers were not a strategic response to competition from foreign imports. However, in each instance the merger provided additional cash and promoted economies of scale and scope that strengthened the company's competitive advantage against foreign imports ("Automatic Sprinkler Moves to Acquire Rawlings," 1967; "MacGregor Begins Move," 1965; "Pepsi Co. Inc. Buys Wilson," 1970).[9]

Cooperative Efforts

A sixth strategy involved cooperative efforts. This took four forms. First, American companies cooperated through the SGMA and the Athletic Institute to obtain better information about industry conditions. American sporting goods firms had become painfully aware that foreign competitors often had more accurate information on consumer needs and wants and on market segments and their size. Participation statistics used by Americans, for example, were mere estimates based upon updates of inaccurate figures compiled from previous years. American firms realized the necessity of cooperation to compile more accurate sport-consumer information. Second, American firms cooperated in efforts to promote American-made sporting goods products. A key factor in this approach was an agreement among manufacturing firms to label products "made in America." A third approach involved the attempt to enforce product standards as prescribed by athletic association rules. Baseball and softball equipment producers, for example, provided money and expertise to help Little League officials test youth league equipment for compliance with published Little League standards. The emphasis upon enforcement of standards grew out of an attempt by baseball and softball equipment producers to have Little League officials ban the use of foreign-made products in all youth league contests (Autz, 1967). Fourth, sporting goods firms initiated several efforts to establish resale price maintenance (Miller & Fielding, 1995a).

Part V: Implications of the New Competition

By lowering tariffs, the GATT agreements opened American markets to a greater degree than ever before, but the success of foreign competitors was a result of careful manipulation of the marketing mix. The new competition relied upon competitive strategies that were not new. The formula for success had four distinct parts.

First, competitors developed products that met customer needs and wants. In sporting goods, this meant introducing new products that improved performance. In baseball, tennis, and golf, foreign competitors first copied American products and then improved upon them. In track and field, it meant the introduction of new high-tech products. American competitors responded by developing R&D departments and producing their own high-tech equipment. In baseball and softball, R&D led to the aluminum bat and then to the use of other materials like graphite and titanium to make bats that sent the ball further. In tennis, the seven-ply racket was replaced by fiberglass and aluminum and then by other kinds of compositions. Manufacturers turned to larger size rackets to increase the "sweet spot" and forgive less accurate swings. In golf clubs, firms moved from wood to aluminum to graphite to titanium and also introduced larger club heads that increased hitting surface and were more forgiving of mis-hits. Golf balls were designed to meet the specifics of individual play and style. In track and field, the Nike Waffle shoe was only a first example of technology improving performance and comfort. Athletic shoe design became highly specialized. Participants of the 1990s have special shoes for walking, hiking, jogging, running, aerobics, and weight training as well as special shoes for each sport in which they participate. In today's highly competitive athletic shoe industry, R&D is a large part of the price of doing business.

The key point in contemporary product strategies is meeting customer needs and wants. R&D functions to help sporting goods firms meet predetermined customer wants. Hillerich & Bradsby's graphite bat is a good example. According to Bill Williams, H&B vice president in charge of marketing, the graphite bat was developed as a result of market studies that determined customer needs (personal communication, 17 April 1993). The same is true in tennis and golf where rackets, clubs, and even golf balls are designed to meet the needs of individual skill levels and playing styles. Marketing determines customer needs and wants. R&D develops products to fulfill these needs and wants (Urbanski, 1997).

The second part of the success formula involves pricing strategies. Japanese sporting goods firms entered the American market at the low-end segment, offering quality goods at low prices. Success in the low-end niche led to invasion of middle and high-end markets. Penetration pricing strategies worked effectively in these segments as well. American sporting goods firms learned an important lesson from the Japanese invasion. Firms cannot ignore particular segments. Claude Carr, president of Rawlings, put it most succinctly back in 1960: "Low-end merchandise also affects medium-priced merchandise" (qtd. in Spink,1960, p. 96). He might have added that low-end and medium-priced merchandise also affect high-priced merchandise. The key lesson here is that firms need to understand different segments in terms of size, needs and wants, price decisions, and the potential for customer movement from one niche to another. This point has been recently emphasized by Mullin, Hardy, and Sutton (1993) when they argue that marketers need to concentrate on developing strategies to move medium-level participants into higher levels of participation. Avid participants not only play more, but they are also willing to pay more for their equipment.

A third part of the success formula involves the choice of distribution channels. Foreign competitors were successful in low-end markets because they chose the right distribution channels. They correctly determined that price-conscious shoppers would choose discount stores and that time-conscious shoppers would visit department stores, chain stores, and supermarkets that offered a wide variety of merchandise in one place. They also knew, as did American sporting goods manufacturers, that high-tech/high-priced sporting goods required personal selling. These products were channeled through club pros, specialty sporting goods stores, and wholesalers who met directly with coaches and athletic equipment buyers. A key element of foreign success was understanding consumer shopping habits as the basis for choosing the right distribution channel. When foreign competitors distributed sporting goods through shopping malls and discount stores, they tapped into changing consumer habits. Today the problem is more complicated. Shopping centers have increased nearly 48% in the past 10 years, and the time consumers spend shopping has decreased by nearly 25% (Holstein & Hannon, 1997). Like other shoppers, sporting goods shoppers are more selective about where they buy, and most know where to go to purchase what they want (Holstein & Hannon, 1997). This requires sporting goods firms to be more selective in matching channel choice with consumer purchasing habits.

All of this places additional emphasis on the fourth part of the success formula, promotion. Foreign competitors relied upon personal selling, sales promotions, and reseller support to move their products. American firms retaliated in these same areas, but also reemphasized endorsements by professional athletes. Adirondack's 600 series autograph model Willy Mays bat is a good example. This process continues unabated today as Nike's Air Jordan shoes amply demonstrate. However, the process has been expanded to include promotional ideas introduced by the Japanese. Today, unheralded athletes endorse equipment, attracting and motivating consumers who have difficulty relating their potential exploits to the likes of Michael Jordan or Jackie Joiner Kersey (Fielding & Miller, 1996).

One key element runs through all of the above. Each element in the formula for success depends upon market analysis. Our discussion has concentrated upon the invasion of foreign sporting goods manufacturers into American markets and how this invasion influenced the development of competitive strategies that relied upon the manipulation of marketing mix to achieve a competitive advantage. The retaliation of American companies to regain market share relied upon the same strategy. Effective manipulation of the marketing mix depends upon market analysis. Sporting goods manufacturers, wholesalers, and retailers must understand and intelligently apply this principle in order to compete successfully in today's highly competitive sporting goods market.

Endnotes

[1] Quota systems sought to limit the number of specific products that could be imported. Usually this was determined by an estimated percentage of the market. The most discussed example was the Japanese agreement to limit the number of baseball and softball gloves it exported to America. American companies claimed that the quota system never worked. Japan increased the quota as it saw fit. It always shipped more than its agreed–to limits. Japan used several methods to bypass the quota system. It shipped to Canadian companies that then sold to American companies. It sold products to American companies through an intermediary like Okinawa.

[2] The generic name for selling-price agreements was American Selling Price (ASP). ASP meant that imports would have to be sold at the same price that comparable American products sold for. The concept was popular during the 1960s and 1970s.
[3] Dumping was made illegal under the Antidumping Act of 1974.
[4] Zeiler (1992). Zeiler explains that the GATT paralleled a larger effort under the International Trade Organization (ITO) to institutionalize comprehensive rules and principles on a wide range of issues that affected trade.
[5] This perception was not completely accurate. The 1949 GATT agreement actually made the largest cut, decreasing tariffs that directly affected the sporting goods trade from 30% to 15%. With the exception of the bicycle industry, which felt the impact of tariff cuts by the middle 1950s, most sporting goods manufacturers did not feel the impact until the early 1960s. The significance of the 1951 GATT and the 1955 GATT was that West Germany (1951) and Japan (1955) joined the GATT.
[6] Zeiler (1992). Congress adopted the "escape clause" as a formal mechanism in trade negotiations in 1947. The escape clause permitted the withdrawal of tariff concessions from a trade agreement when imports threatened the survival of an industry. The Tariff Commission had the responsibility to investigate complaints and to advise the President about a proper course of action. The withdrawal of concessions and the raising of tariffs, that is, the breaking of multilateral agreements, was presidential prerogative.
[7] Sandifer was reporting on the testimony of sporting goods manufacturers and retailers at the U.S. Tariff Commission Hearings that were taking place in Washington, D.C., from February through September of 1961.
[8] Citations are too numerous to list. See, for examples, the "New Products" sections of the *Sporting Goods Dealer (SGD)* for the years 1970–1976. New Products sections were standard sections averaging 12 to 15 pages each month.
[9] Our intent here is not to cover all of the mergers. This is just the tip of the iceberg. In 1967 alone, there were 35 mergers within the sporting goods industry. Mergers were so numerous during the period that the editors of the *SGD* developed a special section to keep industry members up to date. See, for example, "Here's Your 1967 Scorecard," November 1967, p. 84.

References

Aluminum shafts—here's where it helps. (1970). *Sporting Goods Dealer, 142*(6), 68.

Athletic Shoes: European or American. (1967). *Sporting Goods Dealer, 136*(4), 290–293.

Automatic Sprinkler moves to acquire Rawlings. (1967). *Sporting Goods Dealer, 136*(1), 206–207.

Autz, H. (1967). Athletic imports still disturbing. *Sporting Goods Dealer, 137*(2), 139–142.

Bigger stores import direct. (1961). *Sporting Goods Dealer, 125*(3), 237.

Burke, R. (1961). Report import threat spreading. *Sporting Goods Dealer, 124*(2), 91–92.

Business and financial news. (1965). *Sporting Goods Dealer, 131*(4), 258.

Business and financial news. (1972). *Sporting Goods Dealer, 145*(5), 173.

Calleo, D.P. (1987). *American hegemony.* New York: The Twentieth Century Fund.

Carr staying on as Rawlings president flanked by veteran executive team. (1964). *Sporting Goods Dealer, 130*(3), 137.

Carton awards to Wilson, 3M, Foster Grant. (1973). *Sporting Goods Dealer, 147*(3), 84.

Change for the better at Alcoa. (1969). *Sporting Goods Dealer, 140*(3), 13.

Collier's bill to curb baseball glove imports presented to House. (1966). *Sporting Goods Dealer, 134*(6), 242–243.

Competitors co-operate: Athletic goods manufacturers pull together for good of entire industry; Check spread of many imports. (1965). *Sporting Goods Dealer, 132*(2), 56–60, 100.

Curzon, G. (1965). *Multilateral commercial diplomacy: The General Agreement on Tariffs and Trade and its impact on national commercial policies and techniques.* New York: Praeger.

Dam, K.W. (1970). *The GATT: Law and international economic organization.* Chicago: University of Chicago Press.

Davis,T.B. *Impact of imports and exports on American labor: Hearings Before the General Subcommittee on Labor, Committee on Education and Labor, House of Representatives,* 89th Congress, 2d Sess. 387(1966), (testimony of T.B. Davis).

Dick Gersler succeeds Paul Collins at Spalding. (1972). *Sporting Goods Dealer, 148*(4), 372.

Dubow, J. (1964). *Hearings before the General Subcommittee on Labor of the Committee on Education and Labor:* House of Representatives, 89th Congress.

Engineered aluminum bats. (1970). *Sporting Goods Dealer, 142*(3), 54.

Fielding, L.W., Miller, L.K., & Pitts, B.G. (1994). "Anxious decades: The sporting goods industry during the 1920s and 1930s," *Proceedings: North American Society for Sport History.* Hamilton, Ontario Canada.

Fielding, L.W. & Miller, L.K. (1996). Historical eras in sport marketing. In B.G. Pitts & D.K. Stotlar, *Fundamentals of sport marketing.* Morgantown, WV: Fitness Information Technology, Inc.

Garcia buying its supplier of Mitchell Tackle. (1973). *Sporting Goods Dealer, 149*(2), 156.

Garcia taking aim at firearms market. (1968). *Sporting Goods Dealer, 138*(4), 315–316.

Gary Grimes prexy of Spalding U.S. (1973). *Sporting Goods Dealer, 146*(5), 73.

Gilpin, R. (1987). *The political economy of international relations.* Princeton: Princeton University Press.

Gladdin acquires U.S. Fiberglass, other changes. (1967). *Sporting Goods Dealer, 136*(4), 444.

Gray, H.P. (1979). *International trade, investment, and payments.* Boston: Houghton Mifflin.

Hardy, S. (1986). "Adopted by all the leading clubs: Sporting goods and the shaping of leisure, 1800–1900," In R. Busch (Ed.), *For fun and profit: The transformation of leisure into consumption.* Pp. 31–61. Philadelphia: Temple University Press.

Historical Overview: 1962–92, (1992). *Discount Store News, 31*(4), 40–44.

Holstein, W.J., & Hannon, K. (1997), They drop till you shop. *U.S. News & World Report, 123*(3), 51–52.

Kotler, P., Fahey,L., & Jatusripitak, S. (1985). *The new competition.* Englewood Cliffs,NJ: Prentice-Hall, Inc.

Lannom marketing aluminum bat line. (1970). *Sporting Goods Dealer, 142*(3), 142.

Let's take a look at the record. (1961). *Sporting Goods Dealer, 124*(6), 132–133, 267.

Look of a leader theme at Rawlings seminar. (1973). *Sporting Goods Dealer, 147*(3), 372–373.

Lundestad, G. (1990). *The American "empire".* Oslo: Norwegian University Press.

MacGregor begins move to new home. (1965). *Sporting Goods Dealer, 132*(4), 396.

MacGregor crew kicks off opportunity. (1972). *Sporting Goods Dealer, 147*(6), 234–235.

MacGregor force told of dramatic progress. (1970). *Sporting Goods Dealer, 143*(6), 240–241.

Markowitz, A. (1987). Retailing leadership: A quarter-century history of the discount industry. *Discount Store News, 26*(19), 36–40.

Miller, L. K. & Fielding, L. W. (1995a). Resale price maintenance: A historical view of its impact on the sporting goods industry. *Journal of Legal Aspects of Sport, 5*(1), 1–27.

Miller, L. K. & Fielding, L. W. (1995b). Product liability reform from the perspective of the sporting goods manufacturer. *Journal of Legal Aspects of Sport. 5*(2), 1–33.

Mullen, B. J., Hardy, S. & Sutton, W. A. (1993). *Sport Marketing.* Champaign, IL: Human Kinetics.

Olympics fire up seriousness of import inroads. (1968). *Sporting Goods Dealer, 138*(2), 122.

Pepsi Co. Inc. buys Wilson 80 million deal. (1970). *Sporting Goods Dealer, 142*(6), 230.

Profit of 23% for Shakespeare. (1970). *Sporting Goods Dealer, 143*(2), 213.

Quinn, J. B. (1980). Strategies for change: Logical incrementalism. Homewood, IL: Irwin.

Sandifer, T.N. (1960a). Rising tide of Japanese sporting goods imports described. *Sporting Goods Dealer, 122*(5), 164–165, 173, 265.

Sandifer, T.N. (1960b). Fishing tackle industry faces total destruction. *Sporting Goods Dealer, 123*(6), 195, 279.

Sandifer, T.N. (1961a). Latest from Washington. *Sporting Goods Dealer, 124*(2), 137.

Sandifer, T.N. (1961b). Plea for higher glove tariffs granted. *Sporting Goods Dealer, 124*(2), 77.

Sandifer, T.N. (1961c). Situation alarming, baseball industry declares at hearings on foreign invasion. *Sporting Goods Dealer, 124*(6), 127–131, 140.

Sandifer, T.N. (1962). Baseball plea back to president. *Sporting Goods Dealer, 126*(4), 180–181.

Sandifer, T.N. (1964a). Plight in baseball gloves worsens. *Sporting Goods Dealer, 130*(6), 143–144, 149.

Sandifer, T.N. (1964b). Reel and tennis producers ask help. *Sporting Goods Dealer, 131*(1), 141–142.

Sandifer, T.N. (1968). New Washington campaign may upset investments overseas. *Sporting Goods Dealer, 138*(5), 248.

Shakespeare buys Pfluger. (1966). *Sporting Goods Dealer, 125*(4), 182.

Shakespeare firm in Japan. (1970). *Sporting goods Dealer, 143*(5), 212.

Shakespeare signs Elan skis pact. (1971). *Sporting Goods Dealer, 144*(5), 226.

Spalding in Spain and Italy to manufacture ski equipment. (1972). *Sporting Goods Dealer, 143*(4), 68–69.

Spalding, Japanese team up to market gold gear in Japan. (1972). *Sporting Goods Dealer, 142*(1), 258.

Spalding to shift baseball production. (1970). *Sporting Goods Dealer, 143*(1), 258.

Spink, T.J.G. (1960). Carr has rounded all the curves. *Sporting Goods Dealer, 122*(1), 96–100, 138.

Tokyo tackle firm, Hedden sign pact. (1970). *Sporting Goods Dealer, 143*(3), 143.

Tragic condition of tennis discussed by manufacturers. (1964). *Sporting Goods Dealer, 131*(1), 141–142.

Urbanski, A. (1997). Chasing DeMarini. *Sporting Goods Dealer, 196*(2), 25–27.

U.S. Tariff Commission Hearings, July 28, 1960.

Wells Lamont Co. builds in Ireland. (1970). *Sporting Goods Dealer, 142*(3), 176.

Williams, B. (1993). Interview. April 17.

Wilson blitzes U.S. with 21 sales meetings. (1971). *Sporting Goods Dealer, 144*(4), 416, 435.

Wilson innovations hailed in Illinois, California, and Pennsylvania. (1970). *Sporting Goods Dealer, 142*(4), 448–450.

Wilson produces aluminum bat. (1970). *Sporting Goods Dealer, 143*(3), 136.

Worth unveils solid core ball and new bat. (1972). *Sporting Goods Dealer, 146*(1), 113.

Zeiler, T.W. (1992). *American trade and power in the 1960s.* New York: Columbia University Press.

3

A Conceptual Framework for Evaluating Marketing Relationships in Professional Sport Franchises

Mark A. McDonald and George R. Milne

Introduction

With the number of competing sport and entertainment options, and the subsequent shift of emphasis from acquiring customers to retaining customers, sport marketers are beginning to embrace relationship marketing. This article contributes to the growing knowledge about relationship marketing by offering segmentation approach that will help sport organizations serve their customers better.

Relationship marketing has been defined as

> ...to establish, maintain, and enhance and commercialize customer relationships (often but not necessarily long term relationships) so that the objectives of the parties are met. This is done by a mutual exchange and fulfillment of promises. (Gronroos, 190, p. 5)
>
> ...an integrated effort to identify, maintain, and build a network with individual consumers and to continuously strengthen the network for the mutual benefit of both parties, through interactive, individualized and value added contracts over a long period of time. (Shani & Chalasani, 1992, p. 44)

These definitions stress that relationship marketing is the individual customer seller interaction that takes place over time. The definitions emphasize expectations and benefits of the relationships. Also, the definitions suggest that retention is a valuable goal for the marketers.

Outside of sport, service marketers have been quick to embrace relationship marketing because it directly affects service quality. The term *relationship marketing* was introduced into the service-marketing literature by Berry (1983), who defined relationship marketing as "attracting, maintaining and—in multiservice industries—enhancing customer relationships" (p. 25).

The adoption of relationship marketing is being fueled by the availability of information technology. Databases allow marketers to store information on consumers, assess their value to the organizations, and create individualized marketing efforts. In sport, we are seeing the beginning of database creation for tracking season-ticket holders, mapping participation patterns, and fundraising operations.

In sport, as well as in marketing in general, efforts toward measuring customer relationship value are scarce in the literature. One measure of the value of a customer to a marketing organization is lifetime value. A customer's lifetime value (LTV) is "the present value of expected benefits (e.g. gross margin) less the burdens (e.g. direct costs of servicing and communicating) from customers" (Dwyer, 1989).

$$\Sigma \frac{\text{Revenues - costs}}{(1+r)n}$$

This formula indicates that customers have different value levels to an organization depending on the amount of revenue they contribute, the costs to serve them, and the estimated length a customer is projected to be with an organization. Efficient marketing requires an organization to put more of its marketing budget toward satisfying the most valuable customers.

Despite its appealing conceptual promise, LTV has been utilized primarily by database-marketing companies. Although the model focuses on identifying difference in current and projected customer financial value, it does not offer managerial insights for improving retention levels and strengthening relationships with customers. There are other factors that can moderate the strength of a customer's position with an organization. More personal—loyalty and affliction-based—relationship measures also affect a customer's potential to stick with an organization over the long haul. As relationship marketing moves forward, there is a need to develop better measures of customer relationships and to utilize this information to improve individual customer-seller relationships.

In this article, we conceptualize a measure of the intangible bonds between customers and professional sport franchises. We call this relationship measure Relative Relationship Strength (RRS). Additionally, we show how RRS, in conjunction with customer LTV, can be used as a segmentation tool to provide managers with a new approach to understand and improve relationships with current customers. The remainder of this paper is divided into three sections. The next section details the development of the RRS measure. The following section describes managerial implications of using RRS and LTV as segmentation tools. The last section of the paper describes concrete managerial actions required to implement relationship-marketing strategies.

Developing a Relative Relationship Strength (RRS) Measure

In the professional sport context, measuring a customer's RRS is complex and requires consideration of a number of factors unique to their industry in addition to the standard financial information This section conceptualizes a relative relationship strength measure applicable to professional sport franchises incorporating the behavioral and psychological commitment of sport consumers.

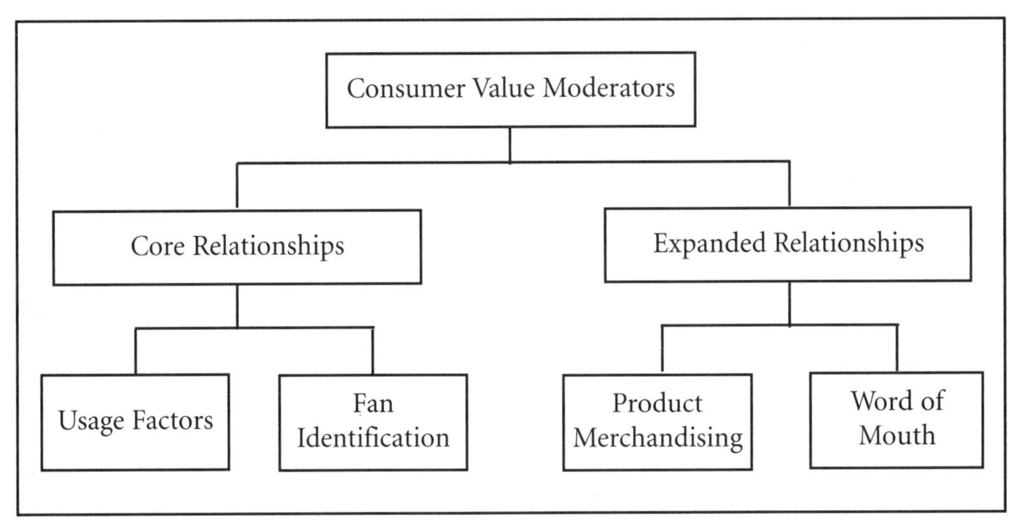

Figure 1.
Factors Modifying Lifetime Value (LTV)

Figure 1 depicts factors that impact the relationship between customers and a professional sport franchise. These moderators are separated into core and expanded relationship factors. Core relationship factors. Core relationship moderators relate to the relationship between the customer and the core product. The core relationship comprises both the usage index and fan identification index.

Usage refers to the length and intensity of the relationship, as well as the frequency and nature of the contact between customers and a franchise. Frequency of utilization is not limited to attendance, but is inclusive of television viewership. If a season-ticket holder chooses not to attend a home or away game, but instead views the game on television, this type of utilization still has value to the franchise. Television viewership leads to improved ratings, which translate to increased advertising rates, ultimately resulting in higher broadcast rights fees for the franchise.

In addition to the usage index, the core relationship also comprises the fan identification index. Fan identification refers to the level of personal commitment and emotional involvement customers have with a franchise (Sutton, McDonald, Milne, & Cimperman, 1997). Sport differs from other sources of entertainment through evoking high levels of emotional attachment and identification that other forms of entertainment are lacking. When a customer identifies closely with an organization, a sense of connectedness ensues, and he or she begins to define him- or herself in terms of the organization (Mael & Ashforth, 1992).

This identification leads to increased member loyalty to the organization (Adler & Adler, 1987), decreased turnover (O'Reilly & Chatman, 1986), high brand loyalty and positive word of mouth (Aaker, 1994; Peter & Olsen, 1993). This increased loyalty results in improved retention rates. Given that it can cost an organization six times more to attract new consumers than it does to retain current customers (Rosenberg & Czepiel, 1984), improved retention rates can have a marked impact on the bottom line.

Research indicates that identification is equally important for sport organizations as it relates to fan behavior. The degree to which fans identify with a sports team has significant consequences to that team's fiscal success. Wann and Branscombe (1992), for example, found that higher levels of fan involvement and investment in a team translated to greater attendance and price insensitivity. Additionally, highly identified fans are less likely to disassociate themselves from a team during unsuccessful periods (Wann & Branscombe, 1990).

As presented in Figure 1, the second of the factors composing RRS is the strength of the expanded relationship. The expanded relationship relates to aspects that transcend usage and identification with the core product. Specifically, it refers to the additional revenue generation derived from licensing and merchandising, as well as the financial impact of developing future customers. As such, the expanded relationship index comprises the merchandising index and the word-of-mouth index.

The merchandising index consists of the general proclivity to purchase merchandise through the mail and the specific desire to purchase franchise merchandise through catalogs. In addition to the direct impact merchandise sales have on the revenue of a franchise, individuals wearing the logoed merchandise further advertise the team. This type of exposure enhances interest in the franchise and indirectly increases the level of support.

Word of mouth refers to the propensity of current customers to encourage others to become franchise customers. Positive word of mouth results in the cost-efficient development of a future customer base. Given the high cost associated with attracting new customers, positive word of mouth is an extremely cost-efficient way to ensure the continual development of a future customer base.

Conceptually, as the strength of the core and expanded relationships between the customer and franchise increases, so does the overall relationship with the customer. Thus, both core relationship measures (the average of usage factors and fan identification) and expanded relationship measures (the average of merchandising index and word of mouth) should have a positive impact on RRS. Because both core and expanded relationship measures have a multiplicative positive impact on the overall RRS of a customer, index scores should be bounded between 1.0 and the maximum relationship value normed by the sample average.

In addition to the core and expanded relationship indices, measuring the strength of the relationship should account for an opportunity cost implicit in choosing to invest time and money in this relationship, as opposed to other options. This factor that influences RRS is represented as the opportunity-cost adjustment index.

This index reflects the implicit opportunity cost of being a season account holder of a professional sport franchise. These customers have chosen to invest their time and money in this relationship. Implicitly, the have chosen this option over other alternative uses of these resources. The opportunity cost index impacts the RRS of customers based on their level of satisfaction with the choice they made. When customers are satisfied (have lower opportunity costs), the RRS is positively influenced. In contrast, RRS declines when customers are dissatisfied (have higher opportunity costs). The opportunity-cost adjustment index can increase or decrease the relative relationship strength. As with the core and expanded relationship indices, this index should be normed by the sample average and centered at 1.0.

The calculation of RRS reflects the impact of all the above described factors. Specifically, the strength of the customer relationship is a function of usage, fan identification, merchandising, word of mouth, and the opportunity-cost adjustment index. Formally,

RRS = number of years x [core relationship index + expanded relationship index] x (opportunity cost adjustment index)

In this equation, number of years refers to the anticipated number of years remaining in the relationship. This is calculated by subtracting the current age of the season-ticket holder from an upper bound constrained by the age of the oldest season-ticket holder in the database.

The next section of this paper reviews the managerial implications of utilizing RRS, in combination with LTV, to segment professional sport customers.

Managerial Implications

Many a successful franchise, like the Boston Celtics, has had valuable long-term fans leave when their winning days were over. The franchise is left not really understanding which customers to spend its marketing effort and money on in order to rebuild fan base.

In order to evaluate a customer's worth to an organization, it is necessary to measure both financial value and personal relationship strength. Arraying customers on these two principal dimensions should provide an organization with ample information with which to effectively manage its fan base. Table 1 presents a framework for segmenting customers based on their LTV and RRS. Customers in a database can be classified according to these variables and arrayed on a two-dimensional space. Customers, based on their LTV and RRS scores, are placed in one of four cells: Cell 1 (high RRS/high LTV); Cell 2 (high RRS/low LTV); Cell 3 (low RRS/high LTV); Cell 4 (low RRS/low LTV).

Armed with this information sport managers can develop and implement strategies to effectively manage their fan base. A franchise's most valuable customers are located in Cell 1. These customers have a high financial and emotional investment in the team.

An effective, and easily implemented strategy, is to recognize and reward these customers for their continued loyalty. Special events in their honor and increased opportunities for contact with players and coaches should be sufficient to continue the quality of these relationships. This recognition for loyalty serves the additional purpose of providing an incentive for other customers to improve their relationships with the franchise to reap similar rewards.

In contrast to customers located in Cell 1, customers in Cell 4 are not vested emotionally or financially in the team. As such, their relationship with the sport organization is likely to fluctuate with team performance. These fans hop on the bandwagon when times are good and jump ship when team fortunes decline. Team performance, however, is largely

Table 1.
Conceptual Framework

Relative Relationship Strength (RRS)		Financial Value (LTV) High	Low
	High	1	3
	Low	2	4

out of the control of sport marketers. For this reason, few financial resources should be expended on customers in this segment.

Customers located in Cell 2 have high financial investment coupled with low relationship strength. For most franchises, this cell will comprise the following two distinct customer groups:

Corporate users. High financial investment could reflect the purchase of a large number and/or high-priced (e.g. luxury seating) season tickets. Many of the customers in Cell 2 are likely to be corporate clients. This accounts for the low level of emotional investment. It is unlikely that these customers will be successfully moved to Cell 1. Fortunately, it does not matter. Because these customers are purchasing tickets for corporate reasons, including client hospitality, their demand for tickets is essentially inelastic. These customers will be relatively insensitive to changes in ticket process and team performance.

These customers, however, will be very sensitive to changing levels of service quality. Corporate users are utilizing the product to better serve the needs of their current and future customers. Consequently, the level of service provided to them and their clients is crucial to continuing the relationship. Marketing dollars expended on customers in Cell 2 should be allocated in the area of enhanced service quality. This service quality should be delivered in terms of improved business communications and individualized attention during games.

Dissatisfied users. Low relationship strength could reflect high opportunity costs. Customers in this cell might be dissatisfied with the value they are receiving given the time and financial resources they have expended to continue the relationship. This segmenting could be large for franchises that are benefiting from sold-out buildings and a corresponding season-ticket holder waiting list. Annual price increases and lack of individualized attention might be increasing customer opportunity costs. These fans might be continuing the relationship because of superior seat location or team performance.

Customers in this segment offer a prime opportunity for sport marketers to apply the techniques of relationship marketing. These customers need to be rewarded for their continued patronage. Individualized marketing efforts and value-added programs are perfectly suited to this segment of customers. Good examples of programs designed to increase customer loyalty are the San Diego Padres' Compadre Club and the Pirates Advantage Card promotions. These programs are outlined in Brenner's article titled "Pursuing Relationships in Professional Sport" also included in this special issue on relationship marketing.

Customers classified into Cell 3 have high emotional but low financial ties with the franchise. Thus, strategic marketing initiatives have the potential to move these customers toward Cell 1. Managers must ensure that proper mechanisms are in place for these customers to move up in the escalator to higher levels of financial and emotional commitment. For example, a variety of ticket plans need to be available to move single-game attendees to more frequent usage. Additionally, all efforts must be made to ensure that these marginal fans have the opportunity to follow the team in the media (television, radio, newspaper, and Internet) and purchase merchandise and memorabilia at the playing facility, as well as offsite at easily accessible locations.

A bonus system providing additional emotional rewards for increased financial rewards should be established. Point system should be based on number of games attended, number of tickets purchased, and concession-and-merchandise-purchasing habits. Rewards should serve to further enhance emotional ties with the team. Most notable would be an opportunity to travel with the team, an opportunity to sit in owner's luxury box for a game, and access to players and/or coaches once a year prior to a game.

The last section of this paper provides a brief overview of specific steps sport marketers need to take to implement relationship-marketing programs in their organizations.

Managerial Actions

Relationship marketing requires sport marketers to be proactive. The benefits from building strong and lasting relationships with customers only accrue to those who take the proper steps to really know their customers and understand their needs and wants. This can be accomplished effectively through building and managing a database storing information on current and potential customers. The following is a list of required action steps to participate in the world of relationship marketing:

1. *Build a customer database.* All personnel who can benefit from relationship-marketing efforts should be involved in designing the database, determining types of reports to be produced, and scheduling communication programs. This includes the marketing director, ticket manager, community relations director, sponsorship sales and licensing/merchandising personnel.

   The customer database should include basic information such as names, addresses, telephone numbers, number and type of tickets, and seat locations. Additionally, specific personal data such as birth dates for all household members, alma mater, preferred radio station, purchasing history, response to previous mailings, preferred activities, preferred opponent, and prior communications should be part of the database.
2. *Collect customer-level data.* There are a variety of methods for collecting the information comprising database. One method is to include a survey in scheduled mailings to existing customers (i.e., ticket renewals). A second method is to distribute surveys at events and provide space for responders to provide name and address to be added to the mailing list.

   A third way to collect the relevant data is through ID cards. Ticket holders can be admitted to games by passing their barcoded ID cards through a machine. Similar machines can track merchandise and concession purchases to track consumer purchasing habits. In order to ensure involvement from customers, it is important to continually convey the benefits of participation (i.e., improved service, targeted programs).
3. *Differentiate your customers.* Customers should be segmented based on measurements of lifetime value and relationship strength. Means and style of communication with customers should differ depending on how they responded to past efforts.
4. *Develop innovative programs.* The applications of the database to enhance and measure relationships with customers are nearly unlimited. The most valuable customers could be given free entrance to a preferred membership club. These customers, for example, might qualify for opportunities to travel with the team, participate in special events, or gain access to specialty merchandise. Customers

can be provided with coupons for their favorite restaurant on their special days (birthday, anniversary).

Customers can be segmented based on purchasing habits, demographics, or psychographics. This information can be utilized to develop game program advertising and sponsorship proposals. If the franchise also owns the facility and/or another sport team, information in the database regarding preferred activities and radio stations can be used to generate a qualified list of prospective purchasers to receive direct mail.

As marketing evolves from being transaction based to relationship based, sport organizations that take the proper steps to develop and manage supplier and customer relationships will have an advantage over the competition.

References

Aaker, D. (1994). Building a brand: The Saturn story. *California Management Review, 36*(2), 114.

Adler, P., & Adler, P.A. (1987). Role conflict and identity salience: College athletics and the academic role. *Social Science Journal, 24*, 443-455.

Berry, L. (1983). Relationship marketing. In *Emerging Perspectives on Service Marketing* (pp. 25-28). L.L. Berry, G.L. Shostack, & G. Upah (Eds.), Chicago, IL: American Marketing Association.

Dwyer, F.R. (1989, Autumn). Customer lifetime valuation to support marketing decision making. *Journal of Direct Marketing, 3*, 8-15.

Gronroos, C. (1990). *Service management and marketing. Managing the moments of truth in service competition.* New York: Lexington Books.

Mael, F., & Ashforth, B.E. (1992). Alumni and their alma mater: A partial test of the reformulated model of organizational identification. *Journal of Organizational Behavior, 13*, 103-123.

O'Reilly III, C., & Chatman, J. (1986). Organizational commitment and psychological attachment: The effects of compliance, identification, and internalization of prosocial behavior. *Journal of Applied Psychology, 71*(3), 492-499.

Peter, J.P., & Olson, J.C. (1993). *Consumer behavior and marketing strategy.* Homewood, IL: Richard D. Irwin, Inc.

Rosenberg, L.J., & Czepiel, J.A. (1984, Spring). A marketing approach to customer retention. *Journal of Consumer Marketing, 1* (Spring), 45-51.

Shani, D., & Chalsani, S. (1992). Exploiting niches using relationship marketing. *The Journal of Consumer Marketing, 9*(3), 33-43.

Sutton, W.A., McDonald, M.A., Milne, G.R., & Cimperman, J. (1997). Creating and fostering fan identification in professional sports. *Sport Marketing Quarterly, 6*(1), 15-22.

Wann, D.L., & Branscombe, N.R. (1990). Diehard fans and fair weather fans: Effects of identification on BIRGing and CORFing tendencies. *Journal of Sport and Social Issues, 14*, 103-117.

Wann, D.L., & Branscombe, N.R. (1992). Role of identification with a group, arousal, categorization processes, and self-esteem in sports spectator aggression. *Human Relations, 45*, 1013-1034.

SECTION II.

Building Brands

4

Examining the Importance of Brand Equity in Professional Sport

James M. Gladden and George R. Milne

Introduction

Strategic brand management is an important focus of both marketing academics and practitioners. A brand is a name or symbol attached to a product that allows for differentiation from similar product offerings (Keller, 1998). Management of brands is important because consumers base purchase decisions on their awareness, perception, and attachment to brands. Recently, the study of brands has focused on brand equity, or the "marketing effects uniquely attributable to the brand" (Keller, 1998, p. 42). Specifically, brand equity represents positive or negative associations with a particular brand name (or logo/mark) that adds to (or subtracts from) the value provided by the product (Aaker, 1991).

Brand equity is also a vitally important tool for sport managers. Examples of sport-related business' employing brand management strategies to grow revenues are increasingly evident. Disney-owned ESPN has recently become very aggressive with brand extensions aimed at solidifying its place as the definitive source for all sports information. Through the introduction of "ESPN – The Store," a concept entertainment store featuring ESPN-licensed merchandise ("ESPN Store Moves," 1997), and the creation of "ESPN Grill," a sports-themed restaurant, ESPN is attempting to improve its brand equity ("New ESPN Grills," 1997).

Such a strategic focus is not limited to corporately owned sport business entities. Executives of professional sport teams are turning to long-term strategic brand management as the overriding philosophy for their marketing efforts. The San Antonio Spurs (of the NBA) utilize integrated marketing to manage the Spurs brand (R. Bookbinder, personal communication, May 29, 1997). Similarly, Terdema Ussery, the president of the Dallas Mavericks (of the NBA), has suggested his priority was to make the Mavericks one of the top brands in sports (Alm, 1997).

A long-term focus on brand management strategies is warranted given the volatility of success in team sport. Recent estimates suggest that one in five professional sport franchises

(Major League Baseball, National Basketball Association, National Football League, and National Hockey League) lost money in 1995 (Atre et al., 1996). In the past, substandard revenue generation has usually been blamed on a lack of on-field success. In response, sport managers have largely resorted to short-term tactics such as firing a head coach or signing a free agent to a multimillion-dollar contract. Although winning is vitally important, implementing short-term tactics does not necessarily guarantee long-term and consistent revenue streams. Further, sport managers have realized that winning is only part of the consumer's experience. Therefore, as sport managers adopt brand management strategies, the study of brand equity is particularly relevant.

Although the strategic use of brand equity is beginning to be implemented by sport managers, there has been little sport-specific research available to guide these efforts. Gladden, Milne, and Sutton (1998) proposed a conceptual framework for evaluating brand equity in the Division I college athletic setting. This added to the earlier efforts of Boone, Kochunny & Wilkins (1995) in Major League Baseball. Given the importance of professional sport to the economy, research on brand equity in this area is also needed. Such research could build upon previous sport research that focused on examining relationships between predictors of positive marketplace outcomes. There is a wealth of literature examining the impact of success on the achievement of marketplace consequences (Branvold, Pan, & Gabert, 1997; Cialdini et al., 1976; Hansen & Gauthier, 1989; Jones, 1984; Schofield, 1983; Sigelman & Bookheimer, 1983; Whitney, 1988). Research efforts have also examined the impact of individual variables, such as a star player, promotional events, competitive forces, and the head coach, on the attainment of positive outcomes (Branvold et al., 1997; Hansen & Gauthier, 1989; Marcum & Greenstein, 1985; Scully, 1989).

The purpose of this paper is to (a) expand the brand equity conceptual framework (Gladden et al., 1998) to include the entire team sport setting and (b) examine the importance of brand equity compared with the importance of winning in the realization of a marketplace outcome in the professional sport setting.

Conceptualizing Brand Equity in Team Sport

The conceptual framework for evaluating brand equity in the Division I college athletic setting built upon Aaker's (1991) model of brand. Aaker conceptualized brand equity as consisting of four major components that can be managed:

1. Perceived quality — consumer judgments of a product's overall excellence relative to its intended purpose
2. Brand awareness — the familiarity of the consumer with a particular brand
3. Brand associations — any mental connections (often experiential) a consumer makes with a particular brand
4. Brand loyalty — the ability to attract and retain customers.

The conceptual framework developed by Gladden et al. (1998) suggests antecedent conditions (team related, organization related, and market related) lead to the creation of brand equity (perceived quality, brand awareness, brand associations, and brand loyalty). Based on a team's brand equity, six forms of marketplace consequences result: national media exposure, merchandise sales, individual donations, corporate support, atmosphere, and ticket sales. The product of the antecedents, brand equity, and consequences then creates a marketplace perception. The importance of developing brand equity over time is captured by feedback loops, which suggests that the marketplace perception impacts the antecedents and, by consequence, brand equity.

Whereas the Gladden et al. (1998) framework is useful for managers of Division I college athletics, there are some components that lead to the creation of brand equity in other team sports that were not originally included. With modifications, the conceptual framework for assessing brand equity in Division I college athletics can be expanded to provide for an understanding in the broader context of team sport (see Figure 1). Such changes allow for application of the framework to professional sport, both in North America and abroad. With the changes, two additional antecedents need to be recognized: the design of a team's logo and the stadium/arena in which the team plays are included as antecedents of brand equity. In addition, the consequence donations is expanded to "additional revenues" in order to better capture the abundance of miscellaneous marketing outcomes that result from brand equity. The following section describes the new components of the framework.

Logo Design

In recent years, professional sports teams have proven that brand equity can be created based on the logo and name of the team. By 1991, the San Jose Sharks of the National Hockey League (NHL) built up brand equity using logoed merchandise sales prior to the team's playing its first game. Through extensive research, San Jose developed a nickname (the Sharks) and a fashionable logo that created equity prior to ever playing a game (Hardy, 1996). The use of a logo to introduce a team has become a common tactic in both major and minor professional sport. In addition, teams with low brand equity are now turning to logo redesigns and color changes as a means of changing their image. For example, the Tampa Bay Buccaneers of the National Football League (NFL) recently attempted to change their identity through new colors (red, black, and gray) and a new logo (featuring a skull and crossbones).

Stadium/Arena

The building in which a sport team plays may significantly impact the development of brand equity. This may occur for two reasons. First, the relationship between the stadium and the organization varies across the sport industry. Some team owners own their stadiums/arenas and benefit greatly from complete control over the stadium's ancillary activities and revenue sources. However, often teams do not own their stadium/arena and are forced to negotiate lease arrangements. In some cases, these lease agreements allow for little control by the team (e.g., the Pittsburgh Pirates with Three Rivers Stadium). Overall, those teams that have more control over the stadium are likely to generate more revenues from the stadium-related extensions such as concessions, parking, and luxury suites (Atre et al., 1996). Such enhanced control also allows for increased marketing activity and consequently increased brand equity. University athletic departments, who are increasingly building or renovating university-controlled stadiums, have also recognized the importance of the stadium as a means of developing brand equity.

Second, the stadium tradition and design may play an important part in the development of brand equity. Certain stadiums possess significant histories (Fenway Park, Lambeau Field, Cameron Indoor Arena), whereas others are more generic (Veterans Stadium, the Metrodome, the Carrier Dome). In addition, many new stadiums are being designed with nostalgic themes in mind (Jacobs Field, Oriole Park at Camden Yards), thus emphasizing the aesthetic qualities of the stadium or arena. A sport consumer's brand associations may be enhanced when the stadium itself plays a part in the attending or viewing experience. Extending this reasoning, the area in which the stadium or arena exists can also enhance the associations with the team sport product (e.g., Wrigley Field's existing in the "Wrigleyville" section of Chicago).

Additional Revenues

Rather than focusing solely on donations to a university, this consequence is expanded to include all other marketing activities (aside from corporate support, ticket sales, and merchandise sales) that may benefit or suffer depending on the creation of brand equity. If a team possesses high brand equity, its ability to create revenue-generating marketing extensions will increase. Such extensions would include, but not be limited to, donations to the university, increased applications/enrollment at the university, and team-owned or licensed restaurants, practice facilities, and merchandise stores. For example, the Orlando Magic has capitalized on high brand equity by constructing a state-of-the-art practice facility in which the team now charges admission to watch practice. Similarly, the recently opened Buckeye Hall of Fame Café capitalizes on the brand equity of The Ohio State University (Horovitz, 1997).

Implications of Brand Equity Framework

Marketing literature suggests brand equity is not created instantaneously. Aaker (1991) contends that building the brand requires a long-term vision, thus implying brand equity is developed over time. Although specific antecedents to brand equity may not occur in a given year, the existence of brand equity from past development may suffice to produce positive marketplace outcomes. The conceptual framework for brand equity in the team sport setting reflects this view.

Given the framework, the next logical step is to assess the importance of brand equity in the realization of marketplace outcomes. If sport managers can predict which consequences result from brand equity (even in the absence of specific antecedents), they will be better able to manage their team's brand and realize positive marketplace consequences. Historically, winning has been consistently linked to increased team revenues and increased attendance (Whitney, 1988). Such knowledge largely justifies a short-term marketing approach that is geared around the success of the team. Therefore, in an effort to establish the utility of brand equity for sport managers, this study examines the importance of brand equity as compared to winning in the realization of a selected marketplace outcome (merchandise sales) over time.

Methodology

Data Collection

Secondary data were gathered from a variety of recognized secondary sources that provide comprehensive information on the professional sport industry. Table 1 depicts the various secondary sources used to gather data for this study. The data set included information on all teams competing in Major League Baseball (MLB), the National Basketball Association (NBA), and the National Hockey League (NHL) for the time period 1992 to

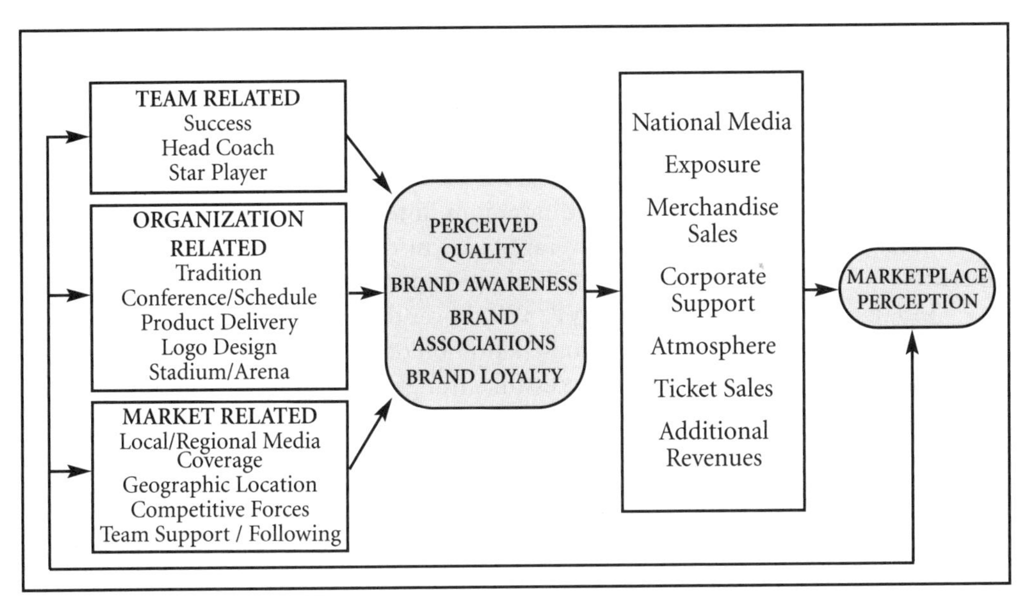

Figure 1.
Conceptual Framework of Brand Equity in the Team Sport Setting

1995. Based on the availability of comprehensive data, the 4-year time period was selected in an effort to monitor the development and changes in brand equity over time. For the 4-year period, 112 observations were collected from MLB data, 108 observations from NBA data, and 104 observations from NHL data.

Measures

This study examined the impact of success and brand equity on merchandise sales. Therefore, operational definitions were needed for these predictor variables.

Brand equity. Although the marketing literature abounds with discussion and operational definitions of brand equity, one consistent measure has not emerged (Uncles, 1996). In fact, brand equity has been measured from three different perspectives: based on consumer perceptions, based on consumer behavior, and based on financial indicators (Cobb-Walgren, Ruble, & Danthu, 1995). Lacking an accepted measure for brand equity, researchers commonly define brand equity in the context of a particular product category or type. Given the differences between sport and mainstream consumer products, such an adaptation seems appropriate for brand equity in team sport.

Because the examination of brand equity in the team sport setting was a new research endeavor, several operational definitions for brand equity were derived. Boone et al. (1995) suggested that the "franchise values" annually published by *Financial World* provide an indicator of brand equity. It can also be suggested that a team that is able to sell out its stadium or arena on a regular basis possesses brand equity. However, if a team can generate revenues and crowds without the assistance of a success, then the brand equity of that team would be even higher. Therefore, the first definition of brand equity (BE1) encompasses franchise value (FV), percentage of stadium/arena seats sold (%SAS), and history of success (WP25YRS):

$$(1) \qquad BE1 = \frac{\text{FV x \%SAS}}{\text{WP25YRS}}$$

Winning percentage over 25 years was utilized to reflect the importance of time in developing brand equity and to smooth out anomalies in the data.

Brand equity has also been measured using the price premium commanded by the product (Simon & Sullivan, 1992). Aaker (1996) contends that price premium may be the best single measure of brand equity because it captures the loyalty aspect of brand equity. In order to establish a true price premium in team sport, data on average ticket prices (AVETIX) were collected. The average ticket price was standardized across North America using cost-of-living indices. Based on previous rationale, the ability to sell tickets (%SAS) and winning percentage (WP25YRS) over the past 25 years were incorporated into the measure. Therefore, the second definition of brand equity (BE2) posited that those teams that have not been as successful throughout history yet still charge high prices and sell tickets have the most brand equity:

$$(2) \qquad BE2 = \frac{\text{AVETIX x \%SAS}}{\text{WP25YRS}}$$

Success. Success was defined based on a team's ability to win the games it participated in during a given year. Therefore, success was measured in terms of winning percentage:

$$(3) \qquad SUCCESS = \frac{\text{Games Won}}{\text{Games Played}}$$

Table 1.
Secondary Sources for Variables Studied

Variable	Sources
SUCCESS	The National Basketball Association, League Office The National Hockey League Official Guide and Record Book The Official NBA Basketball Encyclopedia (2nd ed.) The Sporting News Baseball Guide
BE1	The Complete Four Sport Stadium Guide Financial World Places Rated Almanac The Sporting News Baseball Guide The Sports Business Daily
BE2	The Complete Four Sport Stadium Guide Financial World Places Rated Almanac The Sporting News Baseball Guide The Sports Business Daily Team Marketing Report
MERCH	Team Licensing Business

Table 2.
Logistic Regression Results for Merchandise Sales as a Function of Brand Equity and Success

Analysis	NHL Stand. Beta	NHL z	NBA Stand. Beta	NBA z	MLB Stand. Beta	MLB z
BE1	0.755	4.08[a]	0.334	2.51[b]	0.380	2.96[a]
Success	0.447	2.58[a]	0.489	3.45[a]	0.103	0.81
Pseudo R^2	0.27		0.17		0.10	
χ^2(with 2 DF)	32.18		24.85		13.45	
Probability	0.00		0.00		0.00	
BE 2	0.313	2.35[b]	0.161	1.07	0.376	2.90[a]
Success	0.426	2.84[a]	0.494	2.88[a]	0.091	0.70
Pseudo R^2	0.11		0.15		0.10	
χ^2(with 2 DF)	12.90		91.32		13.08	
Probability	0.00		0.00		0.00	

Merchandise sales. Merchandise sales were defined as the sales of apparel and other items that contain the team name or logo. Aaker (1991) suggests the ability to license one's marks provides an excellent example of the strength of a brand name. Sport consumers purchase team-logoed merchandise in an effort to be affiliated with a given team (Sutton, McDonald, Milne, & Cimperman, 1997). Such affiliation, or "fan identification," may be largely the result of the brand loyalty and brand associations possessed by sport consumers. Because a team's logoed merchandise is sold outside of the home market, merchandise sales would provide a national indicator of brand equity. Unfortunately, the professional sport leagues do not release the team-by-team sales figures. However, rankings by team are published every year by *Team Licensing Business.* Therefore, in lieu of having actual sales figures, dummy variables were assigned based on whether or not a team was ranked in the top 10 teams for logoed merchandise sales in a given year.

Procedure

Logistic regression analysis was employed to examine the relationship between the independent variables brand equity and winning percentage and the dependent variable merchandise sales in MLB, the NBA, and the NHL. The relationship was examined in each of the 4 years for each of the three leagues. Logistic regression analysis was conducted to examine the model:

MERCHt = f (BEQUITYt, SUCCESSt).

Examination of correlation matrices and variance inflation factors did not suggest that the independent variables were highly correlated. Thus multicollinearity was not present.

Results

The results of logistic equations that examine the impact of brand equity and success on merchandise sales are shown in Table 2. Six regressions were run for three leagues (NHL, NBA, and MLB) using two definitions of brand equity. All regressions reported statistically significant χ_2 values.

Brand equity was found to significantly impact merchandise sales across all three professional sport samples when brand equity was defined in terms of franchise value (BE1). Statistically significant relationships between brand equity and merchandise sales were found in the NHL sample ($\beta = 0.755$, z=4.08, $p<.01$), NBA sample ($\beta = 0.334$, z=2.51, $p<.05$), and the MLB sample ($\beta = 0.380$, z=2.96, $p<.01$). However, the impact of success on merchandise sales for these same regressions was mixed. Statistically significant relationships between success and merchandise sales were found for the NHL ($\beta = 0.447$, z=2.58, $p<.01$) and NBA ($\beta = 0.489$, z=3.45, $p<.01$). However, this relationship was not significant for the MLB ($\beta = 0.103$, z=0.81).

A second set of three regressions using the second definition of brand equity 2 (in terms of price), revealed a slightly different pattern. For this definition, the relationship between brand equity and merchandise sales was only statistically significant for the NHL ($\beta = 0.313$, z=2.35, $p<.05$) and MLB ($\beta = 0.376$, z=2.96, $p<.01$). Like the first definition, the relationship between success and merchandise was statistically significant only for the NHL ($\beta = 0.426$, z=2.84, $p<.01$) and NBA ($\beta = 0.494$, z=2.88, $p<.01$).

Discussion and Implications

This section focuses on (a) comparing the importance of brand equity and winning (b) evaluating the utility of the two brand equity measures employed in this study. A summary of the key findings and implications of the study are provided in Table 3.

Comparisons of the Importance of Brand Equity and Winning

Interesting differences occurred in the relationship between brand equity and winning percentage and merchandise sales across the three professional sport leagues. In general, brand equity was more important to the sales of merchandise in the NHL and in MLB whereas winning percentage was more important in the NBA. Such findings have significant implications for sport managers.

There were positive relationships between both brand equity and winning percentage with the sales of team-logoed merchandise in the NHL. In order to assess the relative impact of brand equity and winning percentage, the standardized betas were compared. The standardized betas provide a common unit of comparison with respect to which independent variable accounts for the most variance in the dependent variable. Such a comparison revealed higher betas for brand equity for the first definition of brand equity ($\beta_{\text{brand equity}} = 0.755$, $\beta_{\text{winning \%}} = 0.447$). Meanwhile the beta was higher for winning percentage with respect to the second definition of brand equity ($\beta_{\text{brand equity}} = 0.313$, $\beta_{\text{winning \%}} = 0.426$).

The difference in standardized betas suggests that teams that have developed brand equity over time sell more team-logoed merchandise than do teams that experience short-term success or reap the benefits of recent entry into the league. Expansion teams such as the Mighty Ducks of Anaheim and San Jose Sharks experience high merchandise sales after unveiling their logos. However, this finding suggests the realization of such an outcome is only short-term. An analysis of the data set reveals that established teams with long histories in the league, such as the Detroit Red Wings, Chicago Blackhawks, and Montreal Canadiens, are annually the leaders in merchandise sales for the NHL.

Brand equity was more important to the attainment of merchandise sales in MLB. Across both definitions, only brand equity exhibited a positive relationship with merchandise sales. Again, the long-term development of brand equity was more important than short-term success. This is not surprising given the rich and lengthy history of Major League Baseball. The heritage and popularity of baseball stretches back more than 100 years. No other sport league in North America has been around for nearly this long. As a result, MLB teams have had longest history of forging relationships and associations with sport consumers. Teams such as the Chicago Cubs, Los Angeles Dodgers, and New York Yankees were leaders in merchandise sales in the years studied despite not always having winning records.

These findings suggest NHL and MLB sport managers should focus their efforts toward building their team brand in addition to putting a winning team on the ice or field. Therefore, efforts should be made to increase the brand associations and brand loyalty for each team in these leagues. Particularly in the days of eight-figure annual salaries, it becomes even more important to focus on building the bond with the sport consumer. Given such high salaries, it is easier than ever for fans to feel disassociated with a professional sports team. The Chicago Cubs have not won a championship since 1905. However, the neighborhood surrounding fosters associations with the Cubs above and beyond the team's performance on the field. This, in turn, fosters loyalty and identification with the team, ultimately resulting in more merchandise sales.

These findings also have implications for managerial action specifically with respect to team-logoed merchandise. Teams with established and consistent levels of brand equity should definitely consider owning and operating merchandise stores. Because each of the leagues equally shares the royalties from the cumulative sales of logoed merchandise with all league members, teams that sell more merchandise do not receive a disproportionate payout. Therefore, to capitalize on high consumer demand and identification with the team, the sport team should open a merchandise store in which they will reap all of the profits. Such stores are now commonplace in most professional sport arenas. However, teams should also consider separate locations in high-traffic shopping areas. Along these lines, teams should explore creating their own catalogs and opening cyberstores at each of their individual Web site locations. Increased sales of logoed merchandise also serves to build brand awareness as the people purchasing the logoed merchandise then serve as walking billboards.

Winning percentage was a more important predictor of merchandise sales in the NBA. Although brand equity was positively related to merchandise sales in the equation with BE1, winning percentage was positively related to merchandise sales in both definitions of brand equity. In addition, winning percentage (β= 0.489) was more important than brand equity (β= 0.334) for the first definition of brand equity. This suggests that team-operated merchandise stores may be more reliant on success for sales, and are thus riskier ventures. Further, it also suggests apparel licensees of the NBA must be prepared to capitalize mostly on a short-term basis associated with winning seasons.

Table 3.
Summary of Key Findings and Marketing Implications

Key Finding	Marketing Implication
Both brand equity and success are positively related to merchandise sales.	Incorporate long-term brand management approach based on conceptual framework for brand equity in the team sport setting.
Brand equity is more important to realizing merchandise sales in the NHL and MLB.	Consider the creation of team-owned merchandise stores. Explore the possibility of auxiliary uniforms.
Success is more important in the NBA.	Team-owned merchandise stores are more of a risky venture. Licensees and league must be prepared to capitalize on success when it occurs.
Success is an important predictor of merchandise sales in all 3 leagues.	Logo redesigns should be introduced when a team is improving and in conjunction with other manipulations of brand equity antecedents.
Both brand equity measures yield significant results.	Given the limitations of each measure, sport managers should continue to use both measures in all benchmarking efforts.

Overall, winning was a significant predictor of merchandise sales in two of the three professional sport leagues examined. Based on these results, teams should consider implementing logo redesigns when their team is winning rather than when their team is losing (as is so often the case in today's marketplace). Logo redesigns should be employed to change or enhance the image of a team. If a losing team redesigns its logo and changes its colors, the new brand associations developed by the consumer will still be attached to a losing team. Therefore, sport managers should wait until their team begins to improve (or has a better chance of improving) before they attempt to make image modifications through their logo. In addition, the sport manager should manipulate other antecedents to brand equity concurrent with attempts to maximize marketplace outcomes. For example, when a team experiences moderate success and introduces a new logo, it may also want to sign a highly acclaimed free agent to further fuel the development of brand equity. Clearly, this suggests that the adaptation of a strategic brand management focus requires commitment from the top of the organization such that the marketing, business, and player personnel divisions of the team work together.

Evaluation of the Brand Equity Measures

A further contribution of this study is the creation of two brand equity measures for use in the team sport setting. The main difference between the two measures was that the first definition relied on team franchise values and the second definition relied on price premiums. In general, the findings were consistent across all three measures. Given such results, it is difficult to determine the relevance of relying more on one definition than another in future research efforts. Further, each definition has inherent strengths and weaknesses. Franchise values should represent an expert approximation of the true marketplace value of a team. However, this measure is based on the analysis of team financial figures, and the creation of consistent figures across all teams in a league requires significant estimation. This could result in significant measurement error. Meanwhile, the analysis of brand equity in terms of price premiums illustrates the ability of brand loyalty to override cost considerations. However, given the many different types of seats, calculation of average ticket prices is very difficult. In addition, examining the price elasticity of ticket prices ignores the brand equity that is created at a national level. Thus, future research efforts should incorporate both definitions of brand equity.

Limitations

There are several limitations associated with this study that are important to recognize when interpreting the findings. First, there have been two basic approaches to the evaluation and measurement of brand equity: financial-based evaluations and consumer-based evaluations (Ambler & Styles, 1996). In providing an econometric evaluation of selected hypothesized links in the brand equity framework, this dissertation relies on the former. As such, this study does not solicit direct consumer feedback in examining brand equity. Blackston (1992) suggests the consumer ultimately controls the creation of brand equity. Keller (1998) details how brand associations are created through links in the consumer's memory.

Therefore, in order to enhance the understanding of how brand associations and brand loyalty are developed in the team sport setting, attempts to measure brand equity from the consumer's perspective must be undertaken. Future research efforts to evaluate the conceptual framework should target sport consumers and experts. Using a national sample of sport consumers, one study could investigate people's perceptions of the various professional sport teams given the four components of brand equity as defined by Aaker (1991). An alternative study could ask similar questions to experts from the sport industry, such as sports writers who had traveled to various cities, stadiums, and arenas. Experts would likely have a more expanded base of comparison when evaluating professional sport teams on the different elements of brand equity. Results from such a study could be combined with this study's financial-based definition of brand equity to form an index of brand equity that would incorporate both financial and customer-based evaluations.

Second, the predictor variables, although statistically significant, explained between 10 and 27% of the variance in merchandise sales. Although these results are quite acceptable for cross-sectional research, other predictors may contribute to the realization of merchandise sales. Therefore, sport managers should proceed with caution when considering the implementation of the actions recommended herein. Additional research incorporating operationalizations for many of the brand equity antecedents is needed to further assist sport managers in making strategic marketing decisions.

Conclusion and Future Directions

This study has established that, in addition to winning, a focus on strategic brand management is also warranted in professional sport. Sport is unique in the way that it impacts its customers and fan base (Gorman & Calhoun, 1994). The core product, performance in competition, is inconsistent and very difficult for the sport manager to control. In addition, there are cases where winning occurs but positive marketplace outcomes do not result. For example, the Atlanta Hawks won 57 of their 84 regular season NBA games during the 1993–94 season but failed to sell 25% of their tickets for their home playoff games (Lister, 1997). By expanding the focus of strategic marketing to include efforts to increase brand awareness, brand associations, and brand loyalty, the sport manager can improve the frequency and degree to which positive marketplace consequences are realized.

Future research efforts should focus on expanding the evaluation of the conceptual framework for brand equity in team sport. Additional data could be gathered to allow for the examination of the antecedent's role in the creation of brand equity and realization of marketplace outcomes. In addition, if the conceptual framework is to apply to the team sport setting, then similar studies need to be conducted in other team sport industries. Although this study examined three professional team sports, secondary data could be gathered that would allow for evaluation of the framework as applied to the National Football League, Major League Soccer, and the Division I college athletic setting.

The impact of the antecedents and consequences could be different across sport settings examined. For example, at the Division I college sport setting, the head coach may have a larger impact on the creation of brand equity. It could also be hypothesized that logo design would be important to minor league professional sport teams, where the struggle for brand awareness is hindered by the proliferation of minor leagues.

Finally, it would be instructive to begin evaluating the development of brand equity by professional athletes competing in individual, rather than team, sports. Professional tennis players, golfers, and even extreme athletes develop brand equity associated with their names and images. For example, Jack Nicklaus parlayed the equity associated with his nickname into Golden Bear Enterprises, a multimillion-dollar golf marketing company. A conceptual framework that would explain the development of professional athletes could assist the agencies representing athletes in more effectively targeting their marketing efforts.

References

Aaker, D.A. (1991). *Managing brand equity.* New York: The Free Press.

Aaker, D.A. (1996). *Building strong brands.* New York: The Free Press.

Alm, R. (1997, August 4). Mavericks would like to get into brand-name game. *Dallas Morning News,* p. 2B.

Ambler, T., & Styles, C. (1996). Brand development versus new product development: Towards a process model of extension decisions. *Marketing Intelligence & Planning, 14* (7), 10–19.

Atre, T., Auns, K., Badenhausen, K., McAuliffe, K., Nikolov, C. & Ozanian, M.K. (1996, May 20). The high stakes game of team ownership. *Financial World,* pp. 52–70.

Blackston, M. (1992). Observations: Building brand equity by managing the brand's relationships. *Journal of Advertising Research, 32* (3), 79–83.

Boone, L.E., Kochunny, C.M., & Wilkins, D. (1995). Applying the brand equity concept to Major League Baseball. *Sport Marketing Quarterly, 4* (3), 33–42.

Branvold, S.E., Pan, D.W. & Gabert, T.E. (1997). Effects of winning percentage and market size on attendance in minor league baseball. *Sport Marketing Quarterly, 6* (4), 35–42.

Cialdini, R.B., Borden, R.J., Thorne, R.J., Walker,M.R., Freeman, S., & Sloan, L.R. (1976). Basking in reflected glory: Three football field studies. *Journal of Personality and Social Psychology, 34,* 366–375.

Cobb-Walgren, C.J., Ruble, C.A., & Donthu, N. (1995). Brand equity, brand preference, and purchase intent. *Journal of Advertising Research, 24* (3), 25–40.

ESPN Store moves into crowded "retail-tainment" arena. (1997, September 17). *Sports Business Daily*, p. 9.

Gladden, J.M., Milne, G.R., & Sutton, W.A. (1998). A conceptual framework for assessing brand equity in Division I college athletics. *Journal of Sport Management, 12,* (1), 1–19.

Gorman, J., & Calhoun, K. (1994). *The name of the game: The business of sports.* New York: John Wiley & Sons, Inc.

Hansen, H., & Gauthier, R. (1989). Factors affecting attendance at professional sport events. *Journal of Sport Management, 3*, 33–43.

Hardy, S. (1996). SMQ profile/interview with Matt Levine. *Sport Marketing Quarterly, 5* (3), 5–12.

Horovitz, B. (1997, October 9). New Buckeye Café gives old college try. *USA Today*, p. 1B.

Jones, J.C.H. (1984). Winners, losers and hosers: Demand and survival in the National Hockey League. *Atlantic Economic Journal, 12* (3), 54–63.

Keller, K.L. (1998). *Strategic brand management: Building, measuring, and managing brand equity.* Upper Saddle River, NJ: Prentice Hall.

Lister, V. (1997, February 14). Hawks seek more hometown hoopla: Winning hasn't put fans in the seats. *USA Today*, p. 6C.

Marcum, J.P., & Greenstein, T.N. (1985). Factors affecting attendance of major league baseball: II. A within-season analysis. *Sociology of Sport Journal, 2*, 314–322.

New ESPN Grills to serve a mean berman bouillabaisse? (1997, October 15). *Sports Business Daily*, p. 10.

Schofield, J.A. (1983). Performance and attendance at professional team sports. *Journal of Sport Behavior, 6* (4), 197–206.

Scully, G.W. (1989). *The business of major league baseball.* Chicago: The University of Chicago Press.

Sigelman, L. & Bookheimer, S. (1983). Is it whether you win or lose? Monetary contributions to big-time college athletic programs. *Social Science Quarterly, 64* (2), 347–358.

Simon, C.J., & Sullivan, M.W. (1992, June). A financial approach to estimating firm-level brand equity and measuring the impact of marketing events. Working Paper, *Marketing Science Institute*, pp. 1–43.

Sutton, W.A., McDonald, M.A., Milne, G.R., & Cimperman, J. (1997). Creating and fostering fan identification in professional sports. *Sport Marketing Quarterly, 6*, (1).

Uncles, M.D. (1996). Reflections on brand management: An introduction to the special issue. *Marketing Intelligence & Planning, 14*, (7), 4–9.

Whitney, J.D. (1988). Winning games versus winning championships: The economics of fan interest and team performance. *Economic Inquiry, 26*, (10), 703–724.

5

Brand Extensions by U.S. Professional Sport Teams:

Motivations and Keys to Success

Artemisia Apostolopoulou

Introduction

The economic constraints of managing a sport organization (e.g., player salaries, fluctuating attendance and increased competition) have heightened the need to generate additional revenue streams. One tactic for increasing revenue, while still effectively managing risk and cost, is to leverage existing brand names to create new products (Kardes & Allen, 1991). The offering of additional products and services beyond the organization's core product (the actual event/game) is known as a *brand extension.* Brand extensions may help an organization strengthen its brand image, broaden its customer base, and, perhaps most importantly, contribute to its long-term viability (Keller, 1998).

Sport organizations regularly introduce new products, attempting to capitalize on the popularity of the organization's brand name. For example, the European football (soccer) club Real Madrid recently unveiled their own television network (Stuart, 2000). The Chicago Bulls, Orlando Magic, and Washington Redskins have practice facilities that generate revenue through spectator visits. And the Cleveland Browns capitalized on their long history to produce successful radio and television shows one year prior to the team's re-entry into the National Football League (Brockinton, 1998).

While many sport organizations have utilized extension strategies to create products (e.g., team-operated merchandise stores, youth clinics and team-branded credit cards), the width/depth and efficiency of these strategies has yet to be evaluated. Limited research specifically examining brand extensions in the sport setting has been published. In one such study, Chadwick and Clowes (1998) examined how Premier League soccer clubs utilize brand appeal to enter non-traditional sport markets (e.g., club-branded male toiletries). No formal research uncovering the determinants of a successful brand extension in sport has been undertaken. Given the increased reliance on brand extensions as a marketing strategy, it is important for sport marketers to better understand what constitutes a successful brand extension. The purpose of this study was to explore the nature of brand extensions and the keys to successful brand extensions in professional team sport. The paper is presented in four sections. First, an overview of brand extension literature is presented, with a focus on sport applications. Second, based on the overview, the paper suggests some keys to successful brand extensions in professional team sport. Third, the results of a descriptive study exploring brand extensions in the sport setting are presented. Finally, the paper provides suggested directions for future research efforts.

An Overview of Brand Extensions

Traditionally, the driving reasons behind extending a brand have been the development of additional revenue streams, the opportunities for an organization to grow in different directions, and to build brand equity (Aaker, 1990; Reddy, Holak, & Bhat, 1994). Using an existing brand name can reduce the risks associated with introducing a new product, thereby increasing chances for success (Aaker, 1990). Risk is diminished, because a known brand name provides consumers with the initial assurance that product quality is similar to other products associated with the brand name (Romeo, 1991).

Moreover, an extension product can have a positive impact on the parent brand. Tauber (1988) suggests that the promotional support for an extension can positively impact the parent brand, helping, for example, to increase sales for the parent brand. Keller and Aaker (1992) demonstrated that successful extensions might improve consumer evaluations of the parent brand. This could be important in the sport setting, because it suggests that professional teams that do not possess strong brands (or any brands) could enhance their image through the implementation of successful extension strategies. For example, the San Jose Sharks introduced their logo and apparel well in advance of their first game, and used the merchandise as a way to build brand equity (Hardy, 1996).

Nevertheless, sport managers should be aware of the underlying risks for brand extensions. While introducing extensions that are closely related to the family brand increases the probability of consumer acceptance, managers should realize that the use of the brand name alone does not guarantee success for the extension, especially if the introduction occurs in a market that has already established competitors (Aaker, 1990). For instance, the ESPN SportsZone restaurants cannot succeed unless real value is added through the use of the ESPN name, and a competitive advantage is thus gained over the numerous large theme restaurants in today's marketplace. ESPN's restaurants must go beyond those elements that will make it a quality restaurant (excellent food and service) by also offering features related exclusively to its brand (sports programming throughout the restaurant).

Probably the biggest risk associated with introducing a brand extension is the potential damaging effect that the extension product may have on the perceived quality and goodwill of the organization if the extension proves to be unsuccessful. Extensive research has been conducted on the effects of brand extensions on brand name dilution (Gürhan-Canli & Maheswaran, 1998; Loken & John, 1993; Romeo, 1991). Aaker and Keller (1990) argue that an unsuccessful extension can generate negative brand associations that have long-term detrimental effects on the parent brand. For example, if people have a bad experience with an extension offered by a sport franchise, such as a sport camp, they might begin to adopt a negative attitude toward the franchise. Similarly, Loken and John (1993) argue that brand extensions can take away from (i.e., dilute) the parent brand, if the extension is perceived to be inconsistent with or working against the parent brand. Also, the undisciplined use of the brand name through a great number of extensions may, under certain circumstances, decrease the effectiveness of a brand (Aaker, 1990), or even conflict with the position of the parent brand (Ries & Trout, 1993). Fans may have a hard time accepting that their team's name and logo is on a number of products that seem unrelated to sport and they could potentially express frustration toward the franchise. However, as Dacin and Smith (1994) argue, a brand could be affiliated with a number of products without being diluted, as long as there is high quality across all those products. This means that if a team offers a number of extensions that are all of high quality, there is less chance that this will have a negative impact on fan perception.

Keys to Successful Brand Extensions

Significant efforts have been undertaken in the marketing literature to understand and evaluate brand extensions. As a basis for developing an evaluation model applicable to the sport setting, an extensive literature review resulted in the identification of three commonly accepted factors that are critical to the success of a brand extension:

- The relative strength of the parent brand (i.e., the brand name that is the basis for extension)
- The perceived fit between the parent brand and the extension product (i.e., similarity and consistency between the parent brand and the extension product)
- The promotional support and positioning surrounding the introduction of a brand extension.

Strength of the Parent Brand

Research findings support the idea that stronger brands facilitate the introduction of extensions more than weaker brands (Aaker, 1990; Keller & Aaker, 1992; Rangaswamy, Burke, & Oliva, 1993). Reddy et al. (1994) discovered that line extensions of relatively strong brands have a greater chance of success than those of weak brands. This implies that if the L.A. Lakers and the L.A. Clippers were introducing youth clinics in the greater Los Angeles area, the Lakers' product extension would enjoy higher success as a result of their brand's more notable strength. The impact of the strength of the parent brand may be even more acute in sport, given the fact that the sport product is an experience good (attributes must be assessed through usage) (Smith & Park, 1992).

Wernerfelt (1988) suggests that consumers use the performance of one product (parent brand) to infer the quality of other products using the same name (brand extensions). For example, the Buckeye Hall of Fame Café is a Columbus, Ohio dining and entertainment facility featuring a museum/shrine to the history of Ohio State University athletics, mostly football. In order for consumers to accurately assess the quality of this particular facility they would actually have to visit the Buckeye Café. However, the strength (image) of the Ohio State University brand can possibly lead consumers to make positive inferences about the café's quality before having a personal experience. Similarly, English Premier League clubs routinely capitalize on the value of brand names (such as "Manchester United") and the central role that the sport of 'football' plays in people's lives to extend their brand to different product categories with minimal risk (Chadwick & Clowes, 1998).

Perceived Fit

According to Tauber (1988), fit is defined by customer acceptance of a new product as a logical extension of the brand. The importance of perceived fit between the parent brand and the extension has been supported by a number of theoretical and empirical research studies (e.g., Aaker & Keller, 1990; Boush & Loken, 1991). Most of these studies cited past literature suggesting that consumer affect or attitude related to a brand transfers more so to other products of that brand if there is fit between the two product categories (Fiske & Pavelchak, 1986). This implies that if a sport franchise with a loyal following introduces an extension product that is perceived by fans as a logical extension of the brand, then the extension will be embraced by the team's supporters.

Earlier studies that examined the notion of perceived fit have defined it in terms of product feature similarity and product category fit between the parent brand and the extension product (e.g., Boush & Loken, 1991). However, there have been studies expanding the notion of fit to include other dimensions, such as fit between the image of the brand and its extensions (brand image fit) (Bhat & Reddy, 1997), or brand concept consistency (Park, Milberg, & Lawson, 1991). These findings are very significant for sport, since it is not always plausible to achieve feature similarity and organizations extend their brands to include products from very different categories, which are considered "stretches" (e.g., theme restaurants). Moreover, Bridges, Keller, and Sood (2000) examined perceived fit as a function of explanatory links that connect the parent brand and the extension, and studied the use of communication strategies in successfully creating those links. In their sport-related study on brand extensions, Chadwick and Clowes (1998) argue that when an organization introduces a brand extension, there should be a level of congruence in the values consumers associate with both products.

Regardless of the way that perceived fit is defined, it is clear that sport managers may need to be concerned with how to achieve this consistency between extension products and their organizations. Dacin and Smith (1994) suggest that it is very important to maintain quality across all the products under a brand name. This suggests that sport franchises could gradually offer a variety of sport-related and non sport-related products and services (e.g., beverages, health and fitness clubs, etc.), as long as they ensure high quality in all these extension products. Broniarczyk and Alba (1994) further argue that the specific attributes of the brand and the extent to which those attributes are relevant to the extension is more important than category similarity. They also indicate that the benefits the extension product provides to the consumer can become the selling point for the extension. Based on their argument, one could assume that if a sport club were to open a restaurant, for instance, people might be willing to support the new business as long as they thought it satisfied their need to affiliate with a particular sport club brand.

While perceived fit is important, research has demonstrated that this factor can be mediated by the consumer's belief in the organization's ability to extend into a new category. In their study, Smith and Andrews (1995) found that perceived fit is less important if the consumer believes that the parent brand has the capabilities to introduce the extension product. In other words, sport entities that are strong brands and enjoy high credibility among their fans could extend above and beyond their original product category, and feel more comfortable in exploring new product markets, as long as they can convince fans/customers that they are capable of handling the requirements of such an endeavor.

Promotional Support and Positioning of Brand Extension

Promotional support and advertising have proven essential to the success of brand extensions, particularly when first introduced to the market (Reddy et al., 1994). The importance of the promotional support of a brand extension was stressed early in the 1970s, when companies started to introduce product extensions as alternative growth opportunities (Morein, 1975). More recently, Broniarczyk and Alba (1994) argued that even a well conceived extension might require significant levels of promotional support to become competitive. Thus, it can be suggested that a marketing campaign to support a brand extension should focus on making consumers aware of the extension product, but also on highlighting the connection (fit) between the two products. It is commonly observed how sport clubs utilize their team name, logo and colors on their extension products (e.g., apparel) as a means to emphasize the tie of these products to the parent organization. However, it is absolutely essential that the promotional campaign also highlights the extension's unique characteristics, and stresses the salient features of the new product (Aaker & Keller, 1990).

Therefore, it is important – especially when entering a different industry and competing against established firms in the marketplace – that the extension of the sport organization is presented as equally competitive and effective as all other existing products. For example, should a team introduce an Internet portal, the focus of the advertising campaign should be dual: first, to promote the fact that this service is offered by the team and is part of the team's product line, and, second, to emphasize that this service is of comparable quality with others in the market. So, although the purchase of the team's Internet services package enhances customers' identification and affiliation with the team (Sutton, McDonald, Milne, & Cimperman, 1997), the fans need not compromise on the quality of the product or services they are receiving in order to gain this attachment.

Methodology

In order to examine the keys to successful brand extensions in the team sport setting, interviews with marketing personnel from U.S. professional teams were conducted. The purpose of the descriptive research was to explore the strategic considerations and tactics utilized by team marketing executives when introducing extension products. Ultimately, the information collected aimed to study the success and failure of brand extensions, and to examine whether strength of the parent brand, perceived fit, and promotional support were critical factors to the success of brand extensions in team sport. Twelve professional clubs from three of the four major sport leagues in the U.S. were contacted. Seven of the interviews were with National Basketball Association (NBA) teams, three with National Football League (NFL) clubs, and two with Major League Baseball (MLB) clubs. Although the 12 teams represented 10 different U.S. states, this was a convenience sample and was not selected using any particular criteria (e.g., geography, size of the organization, win-loss record, etc.). None of the team representatives contacted declined participation.

To ensure that the information was consistent, the interviews were only conducted with marketing decision makers that would have responsibility for brand extensions – Senior Vice Presidents, Vice Presidents of Marketing, and Marketing Directors. The interviews took place during October—December 1999. Two of the interviews were conducted in person, with the remaining interviews conducted over the phone. To ensure consistency in the format of the interviews, a standardized interview guide was used for all 12 contacts.

Table 1.
Types of Extension Strategies Employed by U.S. Professional Sport Teams

Extension Types	Examples
Sport-related extensions	Extension teams and leagues (e.g., NBA – WNBA) Sport camps and clinics Youth leagues Tournaments Street teams Merchandise stores
Entertainment-related extensions	Team mascots Cheerleaders Bands
Media-related extensions	TV and radio shows Broadcasting stations Pay-per-view programs
Information-related extensions	Team publications Web sites
Low perceived fit extensions	Art galleries Health and fitness clubs Credit cards and banking accounts Water and beverages Stores (not team merchandise) Software packages Advertising services

The interview guide included questions in six different areas, five pertaining to the extension strategies and one to the size of the organization. More specifically, questions were directed to the type of extension products the organization currently offers (including control and distribution of the extensions) and the organization's goals for introducing the extensions; the association of the extensions with the parent brand; the support provided to the extension; the evaluation process; and future intentions of the organization in terms of engaging in brand extension strategies.

Results

The findings of this research revealed five main categories of extension products offered by professional teams: sport-related, entertainment-related, media-related, information-related, and miscellaneous products with low perceived fit with the parent brand ("stretch extensions"). These extensions are presented in Table 1. Although some of the extensions – such as the extension leagues – were closely related to the core product and could even qualify as *line extensions* (i.e., extensions in the same product category as the one served by the brand), a large number were not considered traditional extensions of the organization, and in many cases had low perceived fit with the core product (e.g., beverages, credit cards, software packages, etc.). Such "low-fit" extensions were introduced either under the name of the organization (e.g., the official team credit card), or as something separate, under a different name. Further, these extensions were owned and operated solely by the organization, or were under the joint control of the club and a club's corporate sponsor or another agency.

Objectives of Extensions

As expected, one of the main objectives for the introduction of brand extensions was the generation of additional revenue for the sport franchises. This revenue came in the form of cash collected from the exploitation of the extension products (e.g., merchandise sales) or was generated indirectly by creating new business opportunities for the franchise (e.g., selling advertisements or making new sponsorship deals). However, a number of interviewees provided examples of extensions that, although they did not generate any significant revenue for the organization, accomplished another important goal: the enhancement of fans' emotional connectedness with the team. In other words, even extension products that did not benefit the organization financially were introduced as a means to establish a stronger presence in the market, to enhance its relationship with the fans, and to build fan loyalty – even when the team did not have a winning record. The most frequently cited examples of such extension products were publications, junior programs, and clinics. As one of the interviewees said, "We would not hesitate to introduce an extension product that would just break even, as long as it accomplished other goals, such as to build our fan base and help us communicate with the people during the off-season." On the same note, the Marketing Director of a professional basketball franchise noted that, "This particular extension (i.e., magazine) may be a break-even proposition, but it is an important tool to inform and excite the fans."

Such a perspective is somewhat unique to sport. Ultimately, teams are not only seeking to inform and excite fans, but they are also trying to foster a stronger relationship through fan identification. Previous studies (Sutton et al., 1997) have suggested that fan identification represents an emotional connection between the fan and the team that can be enhanced via interactions between the organization and the fan. Branscombe and Wann (1991) also argued that strong identification with a sports team promotes feelings of belongingness and self-esteem. Similarly, Gladden and Funk (2001) discuss the symbolic benefits (fan identification and peer group acceptance) and experiential benefits (escape, nostalgia, and pride in place) that a fan may derive from a team. These points provide the foundation for teams introducing extension products even when they are not "money-makers," as long as they enhance the emotional bond between fans and the team and give fans the opportunity, by supporting the extension, to show their loyalty to the franchise.

Keys to Successful Extensions

In order to assess the keys to successful brand extensions in U.S. professional sport, team managers' responses with respect to both successful and unsuccessful extensions were analyzed. Six factors that assist the success of product extensions were identified:

- The strength of the parent brand
- The perceived fit between the club and the extension
- The promotional support offered by the sport organization to the extension

- The quality of the extension product
- The distribution strategy
- The management of the extension.

A summary of findings as well as their managerial relevance are presented in Table 2.

Strength of the parent brand. The findings are consistent with prior research findings (Keller & Aaker, 1992; Reddy et al., 1994; Sappington & Wernerfelt, 1985; Smith & Park, 1992) that illustrated the importance of a strong parent brand for the success of an extension. Most of the team executives interviewed seemed to agree that the strength of the parent brand affects their extensions. According to the Marketing Director of a NBA team, "The name brings credibility; the reputation of the brand can be used to grow the

Table 2.
Summary of Key Findings and Management Implications

Keys to Successful Brand Extensions	Managerial Implications
1. Strength of the parent brand	Whenever applicable, teams should consider launching new extensions in conjunction with winning seasons.
2. Perceived fit between the club and the extension	Establish a meaningful association between the club and the extension. Enter a new market after extensive research has been conducted, and only if the organization has knowledge and expertise in the new industry.
3. Promotional support offered by the sport	Sign promotional partners that are a good fit with the extension organization to the extension product and that will spend money promoting the product.
4. Quality of the extension product	Offer extensions that are of high quality and can effectively satisfy consumers needs.
5. Distribution strategy	Extension products should be located close to the facility or even, if plausible, have permanent displays in the facility.
6. Management of the extension	If outsourcing, the organization should have control over the vendor that is managing the extension. Challenging contract deals can control for the lack of vested interest of the operating agency.

business." The success of the team may be a proxy for the strength of the parent brand. Although previous brand extension research has included the strength of parent brand variable and operationalized it typically as consumers' assessment of the quality of the parent brand (Aaker & Keller, 1990), there have been only limited cases where the strength of the core brand has been measured with objective criteria (such as market share, in Reddy et al., 1994). It became clear from the responses that the success of the team on the field seemed to be one of the most significant reasons for the success of extension products. Respondents agreed that a winning team was a key point to success and also the best promotional tool for the extension products. A representative of a NBA club clearly stated, "There is a direct correlation between the team's success on the court and the success of our extensions." Yet, respondents acknowledged that success cannot be controlled by sport marketers. As one interviewee from a NFL team said, "We cannot control the outcome of the game. Therefore, we have to become more aggressive with the fans and make them have not only an emotional but also a financial stake in the team." This finding, nonetheless, suggests that, whenever applicable, teams should consider launching new extensions in conjunction with winning seasons. In addition, attending to the five other factors leading to success (discussed hereafter) could be a way for management to account for the lack of control over the performance of the team.

Perceived fit between the club and the extension. The findings of this study provide some support for the importance of perceived fit between the extension and the parent brand. Professional teams, realizing the value of the parent brand and its role to the success of the extension, commonly try to establish a meaningful association (i.e., fit) between their brand and the new product by using the team name and marks on the extension product. A respondent from a professional baseball team seemed to believe that, "With the team's logo and the word 'official' people are more likely to buy." This is the reason why many merchandise stores, although not owned and operated by the team, still use "official" to imply the authenticity of products and attract customers by associating the stores with the team.

The importance of the perceived fit notion was also demonstrated through examples of unsuccessful extensions. Either by management decision or poor promotion, some products were not introduced under the team's umbrella (with the team's name and logo), so the fans failed to make the connection of the extension with the franchise. As a result, the extensions were viewed as independent products or services, and gained no advantage from the strength and equity of the parent brand, or even from the fans' affinity with the team. An example of such a case was given by the Marketing Director of a professional baseball team that decided to open a sport-themed art gallery initially without using the team's name. It was planned that the gallery would be presented, not as an extension of the team, but rather as a separate, new brand of its own. As the representative of that team said later, "The fans failed to see the gallery as an extension of our organization, and did not show the support we expected." That outcome, perhaps driven also by the nature of the extension, led to management's decision to reintroduce the gallery, this time using the team's name on the extension.

When defining "perceived fit" earlier in their study, Smith and Andrews (1995) presented a view of fit being mediated by consumer confidence that the organization can successfully provide the extension product. Such certainty and credibility allow for the brand to extend to very different product categories. Consistent with past research (e.g., Aaker & Keller, 1990) the findings of this study, albeit from the perspective of sport managers, suggested that the knowledge and expertise of the franchise in the new product category or industry are important to the success of the extension. Some brand extensions were unsuccessful because the product or service to be introduced utilized very different business models, on which the sport organization had no expertise and could not compete for consumers on equal terms. As the Vice President of Marketing of a professional basketball team stated, "How can we go into someone else's business and compete with professionals? With what resources do we compete? It would be as if someone would come into our industry, and try to compete against our established franchises!" This inexperience could lead to a perceived lack of professionalism, thereby impacting consumer confidence in the ability of the organization to provide the product. The same interviewee went on to mention that once-popular side businesses have been abandoned, because franchises are starting to realize that it may not be in their best interest to take on that risk.

Although previous research has shown that strong brands stretch farther than average or weak brands, no sport organization, regardless of how strong of a brand, should attempt to enter a new market without prior extensive research and the resources, knowledge, and experience that enable the organization to compete equally with established businesses. The Vice President of Marketing of a NBA team said that, "The effort to enter a new business requires special handling and should definitely be treated differently." Any sport organization attempting to introduce an extension in an industry other than the sport industry should not only have a high quality product and the ability to offer adequate promotional and financial support to the extension, but should additionally have sufficient human resources and experience in that specific industry. These results suggest that the more different (atypical) the extension is from the core product, and the less knowledge and expertise the organization has on that specific industry, the higher the perceived risk for the organization.

Promotional support. Consistent with past studies (e.g., Reddy et al., 1994), this research showed that the level of promotional support and the advertising means used by professional sport clubs to position their new products were keys to successful sport brand extensions. As one NBA marketer stated, "99.9% of the success of any extension depends on the advertising support." Sport organizations should not introduce any brand extensions unless they are willing and able to offer ample promotional support. As one respondent said, "Why extend and not tell people about it?" Similarly, the Senior Vice President of Marketing of a NFL team stated, "No matter how strong the brand is, there is always a need to support and advertise an extension." Traditional advertising (i.e., TV and radio advertisements and shows, print advertisements, direct mail, newsletters, web site advertisements, in-stadium and in-arena announcements, signage and banners, outdoor billboards, player appearances, special events, word of mouth, cross-promotions), either through the team's existing media resources or through corporate partners' efforts, was common practice among the sport organizations examined. Even though stronger brands (i.e., teams experiencing more success, possessing more tradition, etc.) may be falsely under the impression that their products don't require much advertising, sport managers should not rely on the illusion that the extensions will promote themselves.

Poor promotional support was also cited as a reason for failed extensions, thus reinforcing the results of Reddy et al.'s (1994) research. The Senior Vice President of a professional baseball team suggested that part of this promotional support comes in the form of participation from team players. In their case, management was unable to get players to commit early enough, and when they did, it was already too late to successfully promote that extension. As the respondent said, "We just didn't promote it enough ….. and we started promoting it too late." Another impediment to extension success was the selection of the wrong promotional partners. For example, as one interviewee said, their choice of a grocery store as a kids' club sponsor did not prove successful in attracting interested parents or children. Other respondents echoed this sentiment:

"In some occasions, sponsors might acquire a sponsorship deal just to say that they work with the team. However, they often do not utilize the rights that that deal gives them, and they don't activate their partnerships in a way that will benefit both the organization and the sponsors. As a result, they do not help with the promotion of our extensions."

Given the importance of adequate and effective promotional support to a new product, it is apparent from the findings that both a good fit with promotional partners and the active participation of sponsors are critical to extension success.

Quality of the extension product. Another point that appeared to be very critical at the outset was the quality of the extension product. Previous studies stressed the importance of a quality extension product (Dacin & Smith, 1994), as well as the lack of guarantee from use of the brand name alone (Aaker, 1990), suggesting that even strong brands need to provide high quality extensions that effectively satisfy consumer needs. The Marketing Director of a NBA team said: "The name brings credibility, however the product (the extension itself) is most important; it is the key to the success of the extension. You cannot fool the public by offering a bad extension product under the organization's name. And there is also the risk with a bad product of damaging your core product (parent brand)."

These findings imply that no sport manager should depend on the brand name to do all the work, no matter how strong the parent brand may be. The team must be able to guarantee a quality product, one that will satisfy fan needs in the same way traditional products do. For example, a franchise introducing a health and fitness club should be able to guarantee quality services, comparable to other health and fitness clubs. Everything else being equal, it will be the recognition and reputation of the franchise, as well as the identification and affiliation of fans with the team, that will give an advantage to that extension over other health clubs. Also, the positioning of the extension should convince consumers that the team's health club is comparable with other brands, and that by choosing it they not only support their team, but fully satisfy their training needs.

Distribution strategy. The physical location of the extension appears to play an important role in the success of brand extensions. With respect to the aforementioned art gallery, it was located outside the team's stadium. Coupled with not using the team's name, this made it difficult for fans to associate the gallery with the franchise. Their perceptions may have been different had the gallery been located closer to the parent brand, meaning inside the stadium (as usually happens with merchandise stores). Another example was presented by the representative of a professional baseball team, who said that one of the reasons their retail stores were not as successful was the fact that they were not located close to the stadium. It appears that extension products are more successful when they are close to the facility or even have permanent displays in the facility (where feasible), because that facilitates the association of the extension to the team. This finding is consistent with Broniarczyk and Alba's (1994) suggestion that in-store factors, such as physical proximity, could impact consumer perceptions of brand extensions.

Management of the extension. Some unsuccessful extensions were caused by the lack of control over the vendor managing the extension. The Marketing Director of a baseball team, referring to their merchandise stores, recounted his team's experiences:

"Three years ago our two retail stores were not successful, because they were not controlled by the team. An outside company was responsible for managing them. However, it seems that our extensions were just not as important to the people that were running the stores as they were to us. That is why we decided to take them back under our control, and since then they have been more successful."

This failure could be attributed to the lack of direct control from the organization, the inefficiency of the agency, or a combination of both factors. While outsourcing the management of operational areas is a common practice, the example above clearly indicates that the lack of vested interest and commitment from the outside operating agency had a negative impact on the success of the extensions. In order to alleviate these problems, organizations can attempt more challenging contract deals linking the compensation of the agency with the financial success of the extension, or even the collaboration of the team with the managing agency.

Limitations and Directions for Future Research

Given the increasing implementation of extension strategies in the sport industry, this study generates many questions that need timely answers. The primary goal of this research was to investigate the nature of the extension products currently offered by U.S. professional sport franchises and recognize key factors for successful brand extensions. The findings did provide support for the three key variables identified early in the study; however new factors became apparent, some of which seem to be unique to the sport setting (e.g., winning). Further research should be conducted to develop a theoretical framework that could be used as a guide by sport organizations introducing extension products. The original three key points, as well as the other factors identified through the interviews, require further examination. Also, how variables such as fan identification and loyalty affect consumer extension evaluations needs to be studied. Since this study explored management's point of view, it is important that future research address the consumers' perspective. In particular, assessing consumer perceptions of fit is vital to understanding the importance of fit to the success of team brand extensions (as well as how fit is achieved).

Data for this research was collected from U.S. major league franchises. More extensive empirical research is required in a larger sample of U.S. professional sport clubs, as well as other sectors of the sport industry (e.g., colleges and sporting goods companies). Furthermore, the globalization of sport and the strength of traditional sport brands overseas – such as Manchester United and Ajax – suggest research of extensions introduced internationally. Finally, a number of previous studies have examined the issue of parent brand enhancement or dilution due to extensive expansion or the introduction of the wrong extensions. An investigation topic for the future could be how far sport brands can "stretch" in terms of introducing extensions from dissimilar product categories, and whether sport franchises run the risk of harming their image if they introduce an extension product that does not prove successful.

Conclusion

The increasing costs of maintaining a successful sport entity will continue to support reliance on brand extension strategies. In the future, we are likely to witness more sport facilities resembling amusement centers, more services of everyday utility linked to ticket packages, and more teams reaching across the country and overseas with a variety of non-traditional sport products. The accurate identification of key variables will assist the design and implementation of successful extension strategies and tactics, and will minimize the risks of the new introductions by the sport industry. This research provides a starting point. Using theory and depth interviews, it identifies some potential critical success factors for brand extensions in the sport setting. Future empirical research should seek to build on this effort, so as to better inform sport marketers regarding brand extension decisions.

References

Aaker, D. A. (1990). Brand extensions: The good, the bad, and the ugly. *Sloan Management Review,* 31, 47–56.

Aaker, D. A., & Keller, K. L. (1990). Consumer evaluations of brand extensions. *Journal of Marketing,* 54, 27–41.

Bhat, S., & Reddy, S. K. (1997). Investigating the dimensions of the fit between a brand and its extensions. *American Marketing Association,* 8, 186–194.

Boush, D. M., & Loken, B. (1991). A process-tracing study of brand extension evaluation. *Journal of Marketing Research, XXVIII,* 16–28.

Branscombe, N. R., & Wann, D. L. (1991). The positive social and self concept consequences of sports team identification. *Journal of Sport and Social Issues, 15,* 115–127.

Bridges, S., Keller, K. L., & Sood, S. (2000). Communication strategies for brand extensions: Enhancing perceived fit by establishing explanatory links. *Journal of Advertising, XXIX,* 1–11.

Brockinton, L. (1998, September 7–13). Browns' television and radio shows prosper, despite the lack of a team. *Sports Business Journal,* p. 46.

Broniarczyk, S. M., & Alba, J. W. (1994). The importance of the brand in brand extension. *Journal of Marketing Research, XXXI,* 214–228.

Chadwick, S., & Clowes, J. (1998). The use of extension strategies by clubs in the English Football Premier League. *Managing Leisure, 3,* 194–203.

Dacin, P. A., & Smith, D. C. (1994). The effect of brand portfolio characteristics on consumer evaluations of brand extensions. *Journal of Marketing Research, XXXI,* 229–242.

Fiske, S. T., & Pavelchak, M. A. (1986). Category-based versus piecemeal-based affective responses: Developments in schema-triggered affect. In R. M. Sorrentino and E. T. Higgins (Eds.), *The Handbook of Motivation and Social Cognition: Foundations of Social Behavior* (pp. 167–203). New York: Guilford Press.

Gladden, J. M., & Funk, D. C. (2001). Understanding brand loyalty in professional sport: Examining the link between brand associations and brand loyalty. *international Journal of Sports Marketing and Sponsorship, 3,* 67–94.

Gürhan-Canli, Z., & Maheswaran, D. (1998). The effects of extensions on brand name dilution and enhancement. *Journal of Marketing Research, XXXV,* 464–473.

Hardy, S. (1996). SMQ profile/interview with Matt Levine. *Sport Marketing Quarterly, 5,* 5–12.

Kardes, F. R., & Allen, C. T. (1991). Perceived variability and inferences about brand extensions. *Advances in Consumer Research, 18,* 392–398.

Keller, K. L. (1998). *Strategic brand management: Building, measuring, and managing brand equity.* Upper Saddle River, NJ: Prentice Hall.

Keller, K. L., & Aaker, D. A. (1992). The effects of sequential introduction of brand extensions. *Journal of Marketing Research, XXIX,* 35–50.

Loken, B., & John, D.R. (1993). Diluting brand beliefs: When do brand extensions have a negative impact? *Journal of Marketing, 57,* 71–84.

Morein, J. A. (1975). Shift from brand to product line marketing. *Harvard Business Review, 53 (September–October),* 56–64.

Park, C.W., Milberg, S., & Lawson, R. (1991). Evaluation of brand extensions: The role of product feature similarity and brand concept consistency. *Journal of Consumer Research, 18,* 185–193.

Rangaswamy, A., Burke, R. R., & Oliva, T. A. (1993). Brand equity and the extendibility of brand names. *International Journal of Research in Marketing, 10,* 61–75.

Reddy, S. K., Holak, S. L., & Bhat, S. (1994). To extend or not to extend: Success determinants of line extensions. *Journal of Marketing Research, XXXI,* 243–262.

Ries, A., & Trout, J. (1993). *Positioning: The battle for your mind.* New York: Warner Books.

Romeo, J. B. (1991). The effect of negative information on the evaluations of brand extensions and the family brand. Advances in Consumer Research, 18, 399–406.

Sappington, D. E. M., & Wernerfelt, B. (1985). To brand or not to brand? A theoretical and empirical question. *Journal of Business, 58,* 279–293.

Smith, D. C., & Andrews, J. (1995). Rethinking the effect of perceived fit on customers' evaluations of new products. *Journal of the Academy of Marketing Science, 23,* 4–14.

Smith, D. C., & Park, C.W. (1992). The effects of brand extensions on market share and advertising efficiency. *Journal of Marketing Research, XXIX,* 296–313.

Stuart, J. (2000, February 28-–March 5). Real TV. *Sports Business Journal,* p. 45.

Sutton, W. A., McDonald, M. A., Milne, G. R., & Cimperman, J. (1997). Creating and fostering fan identification in professional sports. *Sport Marketing Quarterly, 6,* 15–22.

Tauber, E. M. (1988, August/September). Brand leverage: Strategy for growth in a cost-control world. *Journal of Advertising Research,* 26–30.

Wernerfelt, B. (1988). Umbrella branding as a signal of new product quality: An example of signalling by posting a bond. *RAND Journal of Economics, 19,* 458–466.

6

Segmenting Sport Fans Using Brand Associations:
A Cluster Analysis

Stephen D. Ross

Introduction

Sport organizations now faced with a saturated marketplace and increased competition for consumer dollars are compelled to alter the way they access their sport products' patrons. While this competition has not deterred sport organizations from offering a broad range of products and services for varying consumer groups, it has, however, pushed the identification of smaller divisions of consumers within existing customer bases to the wayside. That is to say, sport managers often stop working to identify distinctive subdivisions of consumers, and give more attention to increasing the strength of relationships with the existing customer base or uncovering followers which they can target as new loyal fans. The practice of pinpointing groups within the current fan base is necessary for success, because a sport organization cannot gain a strong foothold within the marketplace if these individuals are not identified and managed appropriately. As a way of optimally meeting the needs of all fans and establishing a strong position in the sport marketplace, an organization should not only identify the distinct groups of members, but also develop marketing strategies that are tailored to these different groups. This process of identifying well-defined clusters of consumers is known as segmentation, and a wide variety of strategies have been used to achieve organizational goals.

Segmentation Strategies

During the past few decades of market segmentation research, several bases have been used (Wedel & Kamakura, 1998). These include, but are not limited to, demographic and socioeconomic characteristics, personality, values and lifestyle characteristics (psychographics), product usage patterns, attitudes towards products, benefits sought, and attitudes toward marketing strategies (Beane & Ennis, 1987; Dickson & Ginter, 1987; Tynan & Drayton, 1987; Wind, 1978). However, conceptual understanding between the various segmentation bases is not always clear. One specific example is the often interchangeable conceptual and measurement distinctions found between psychographics, values, and attitudes (Kahle & Chiagouris, 1996). Regardless of the terminology and the differences in conceptual underpinnings, segmentation approaches are wide ranging in both subject matter and methodological strategy.

While segmentation strategies differ from organization to organization, segmentation using attitudinal measures as bases was the most popular segmentation development in the 1990s (Honkanen, Olsen, & Myrland, 2004). When using this approach, consumers who possess comparable preferences, beliefs, or attitudes within a specific group are clustered together. Attitudes are defined as psychological tendencies that are expressed by evaluating a particular entity or objects with some degree of favor or disfavor (Eagly & Chaiken, 1993). Generally, attitudes are often defined as a general term of global evaluation (Fazio, 1995). The expression "object" in the formal definition is used in an especially broad meaning, including individuals, tangible entities, situations, and acts. For the purposes of this research, the object is defined as the sport team.

Segmentation via Brand Associations

One segmentation basis focusing on attitudes that can aid sport managers is the image of the sport organization from a spectator's point of view. These thoughts connected to a sport object are known as brand associations (Gladden & Funk, 2002). Such information regarding the perceptions of a sport organization is important for making marketing decisions. With the increasing competition among sport organizations for the discretionary dollar of consumers, competition for new and existing customers is forcing organizations to rethink methods for targeting their fan base. In the area of sport marketing, this importance is heightened given that sport teams provide an experiential service that leaves nothing but memories for the spectator (Gladden, Irwin, & Sutton, 2001).

It has been well documented that spectator sport is a service product and therefore the core product (i.e., the game or event) is an intangible, subjective, and unpredictable occurrence. In view of the fact that sport services hold specific characteristics that pose challenges to brand management, recollections of the brand will have a significant impact on the attitudes and behaviors of consumers (Berry, 2002). From a consumer's perspective, the thoughts that come to mind when a service is encountered are often the same information used to make consumption decisions (Aaker, 1996). Specifically, because of the unique characteristics of sport services, segmenting based upon an experiential mindset, where the brand associations held by spectators are paramount, is needed for understanding the various needs and desires of spectators. Customers are quite often actively involved in helping to create the service product (Lovelock, 1996), and consequently, customer perceptions of service encounters are important elements of customer satisfaction, perceptions of quality, and long-term loyalty (Brown, Fisk, & Bitner, 1994).

The strong reliance on service provision and managing customer perceptions in the sport marketing sphere necessitates a different perspective with regards to segmenting spectators. That is, the brand associations of spectators take on an increased importance in the creation of brand equity and long term team loyalty. As such, research seeking to increase our understanding of brand equity in sport must include and acknowledge the possibility that brand associations may differ across various segments of a fan base. In fact, Gladden et al. (2002) suggest that in terms of building brand equity, the challenge for major professional sport teams in the next decade will be to learn as much as possible about their customers. One way in which managers may begin to learn about their customers is to identify like-minded individuals through the use of cluster analysis.

Cluster Analysis

Cluster analysis has become a common tool for marketing research in both academia and in the professional sector. The method has been widely used in a number of different areas, including travel and tourism (Arimond & Elfessi, 2001; Mazanec, 1984), marketing management (Schaffer & Green, 1998), international banking (Safdari, Ohanian, & Scannell, 2005), and sport participation (Harwood, Cumming, & Fletcher, 2004; Ogles & Masters, 2003). Despite this popularity in the mainstream marketing literature, the method is often ignored as a viable technique in sport consumer research. The catch-all term "cluster analysis" covers a great variety of methods and algorithms for identifying groups of similar objects. This heuristic procedure allocates objects or persons to groups (clusters) on the basis of their similarity, whereby the cluster should be internally homogenous, and externally as easy to distinguish from other clusters as possible (Mueller & Kaufmann, 2001). Unlike other statistical methods for classification, it makes no prior assumptions about differences in the population.

The primary use of cluster analysis has been for marketing segmentation. However, it has shown to be extremely useful in a number of different contexts. The technique has been used to seek a better understanding of buyer behaviors by identifying homogenous subsets of buyers (Kim & Kim, 1998). Cluster analysis has also been employed in the development of potential new product opportunities (Hair, Anderson, Tatham, & Black, 1998). By clustering brands and products, groups of likely product options can be determined within the marketplace. Finally, cluster analysis has been used as a general data reduction technique to develop aggregates of data that are general and more easily managed than individual observations (Harwood et al., 2004).

The primary purpose of this research is to use cluster analysis to identify segments of spectators based upon the brand associations held for a professional sport team. By identifying the specific associations that consumers hold, sport organizations can emphasize important associations and de-emphasize less important associations attached to the brand. However, before teams can benefit from the brand associations customers have for their teams, they must begin by identifying the images of the brand within the existing customer base. Segmentation based on brand associations in general can help a sport organization identify groups of customers, and then target and position their product in a satisfactory manner. A secondary purpose is to identify the similarities and differences among these segments based upon demographic variables. Using demographic variables to describe and distinguish the market segments can result in greater effectiveness in managing marketing campaigns.

Method

Sample

The study was conducted with a sample of sport consumers from a Midwestern National Basketball Association (NBA) team. A mail survey was sent to 1,600 full season ticket holders during the 2004-2005 NBA season. Six hundred sixty-five surveys were returned for a 41.5% effective response rate. However, 662 of the surveys were deemed useable for the data analysis after screening, cleaning, and omitting outliers.

Survey Instrument

The survey form, four pages in length, included demographic information and brand association measures utilized in the TBAS (Ross, James, & Vargas, 2006). Two different versions of the instrument were used to prevent order and fatigue biases. The demographic information collected included age, ethnicity, gender, marital status, educational level, and household income.

The TBAS measures 11 team brand associations for professional sport teams. The associations measured included: (1) the non-player personnel associated with a particular professional sport team (Non-player Personnel); (2) the quality, performance, and/or success of a team (Team Success); (3) the history of a particular sport team (Team History); (4) the stadium and community in which the team calls "home" (Stadium Community); (5) specific characteristics that a team displays upon the field of play (Team-play Characteristics); (6) the identifying marks associated with a specific sport team (Brand Mark); (8) eating and consuming beverages at the stadium (Concessions), (9) associating with others such as friends and other fans of team (Social Interaction), (10) the competition among teams that are known to be historically significant competitors (Rivalry); and (11) an individual's enduring affiliation to a particular professional sport team (Commitment). These 11 associations served as the basis for comparing consumer segments. All brand association items in the instrument were measured on seven-point Likert-type scales with response categories anchored by *Disagree (1)* and *Agree (7).*

Data Analysis

Given the objective of finding distinct segments of sport consumers based on brand associations, cluster analysis was the chosen method in this study. The two-stage cluster analysis utilizing hierarchical and non-hierarchical methods was used following the suggestions put forth by Punj and Stewart (1983). The first step in this clustering process was to determine the number of clusters contained within the sample, if any, using hierarchical methods. Specifically, Ward's method was used to identify the number of clusters within the sample of respondents. The optimal number of clusters is determined by analyzing the clustering coefficients (i.e., the within-cluster sum of squares) in the agglomeration schedule produced through the analysis. Small coefficients indicate that somewhat homogenous clusters are being merged, while the joining of two very different clusters results in a large coefficient (Hair et al., 1998). The optimal number of clusters is determined by finding the largest difference among clustering coefficients.

The second step involves using a non-hierarchical K-means analysis on the solution discovered in the hierarchical clustering procedure to define cluster membership. In contrast to the hierarchical method, K-means clustering does not involve the treelike construction process. Instead, K-means assigns individuals into clusters once the number of clusters to be formed is specified. The K-means procedure in SPSS 13.0 was used to assign individual respondents into clusters. In addition to the cluster analyses, a one-way analysis of variance was performed to show which brand association dimensions contribute to the cluster formation. Finally, a canonical discriminant analysis was used to determine whether clusters could be distinguished from one another based upon the demographic characteristics collected from the respondents.

Table 1.
Demographic Profile of All Respondents

	Frequency	Percentage
Marital status		
Married	506	77.8
Single	106	16.3
Divorced/widowed	38	5.9
	650	100.0
Education level		
Attended high school	4	0.6
High school graduate	34	5.1
Attended college	90	13.7
College graduate	327	49.6
Post-graduate degree	204	31.0
	659	100.0
Household income		
Less than $35,000	11	1.8
$35,001 - $50,000	32	5.1
$50,001 - $75,000	70	11.2
$75,001 - $100,000	86	13.8
$100,001 - $125,000	88	14.1
$125,001 - $150,000	57	9.1
$150,001 - $175,000	50	8.0
$175,001 - $200,000	33	8.0
Over $200,000	196	31.5
	623	100.0
Race		
Black/African American	14	2.1
Native American	2	0.3
Hispanic	3	0.6
White/Caucasian	632	96.0
Asian or Pacific Islander	6	1.0
	657	100.0
Gender		
Female	117	17.8
Male	541	82.2
	658	100.0
Age		
18 - 29 years	44	6.7
30 - 39 years	127	19.4
40 - 49 years	196	29.9
50 - 59 years	200	30.5
60 - 69 years	72	11.0
70 years or older	16	2.5
	655	100.0
	Mean age: 47.3	

Results

Description of Respondents

In terms of the overall sample, nearly two-thirds (60.4%) of the respondents were between 40 and 59 years of age, while 19.4% of the respondents were between the ages of 30 and 39 (see Table 1). The majority of the respondents (96.0%) were White/Caucasian; 2.1% were African-American, and 0.5% were Hispanic. The gender distribution of respondents was 17.8% female and 82.2% male. The majority of the respondents were married (76.8%), and well educated, with 31.0% having a post-college graduate degree. Finally, one-third (31.5%) of the respondents had a household income of $200,000 or higher.

Brand Association Clusters

Ward's method was used to identify the number of clusters within the sample of respondents. The results of the agglomeration schedule revealed that going from two to one cluster produces the largest increase in the clustering coefficients. Because of this, the two-cluster solution was selected as the appropriate number of clusters. The K-means procedure was then used by specifying the desired number of clusters to two, resulting in the respondents being assigned into the two clusters. Cluster One (n=316) made up 48% of the sample and Cluster Two (n=346) made up 52% of the sample. The results of the ANOVA indicated that all eleven brand association dimensions contributed to the cluster formation (Table 2). When comparing the

Table 2.
NOVA Table

	Cluster One	Cluster Two	F	*p* value
Commitment	5.63 (.755)	4.59 (.936)	248.33	<.001
Concessions	4.50 (1.18)	3.17 (1.20)	204.83	<.001
Team History	5.10 (.823)	3.82 (.901)	356.27	<.001
Brand Mark	6.06 (.766)	5.12 (.986)	182.07	<.001
Organizational Attributes	5.60 (.712)	4.28 (.863)	455.63	<.001
Rivalry	5.30 (.845)	4.21 (.961)	237.00	<.001
Personnel	5.16 (.779)	3.75 (.953)	429.34	<.001
Stadium Community	4.97 (.933)	3.57 (1.10)	307.54	<.001
Social Interaction	4.81 (1.16)	3.64 (1.15)	168.51	<.001
Success	5.17 (.786)	3.59 (.935)	546.76	<.001
Team Play	4.99 (.857)	3.29 (.986)	555.109	<.001

mean factor scores across the two clusters it is evident that the individuals comprising Cluster One have more frequent and positive thoughts that come to mind when thinking about their favorite team. For Cluster One, all factor means were greater than the 4.0 mid-point. On the contrary, for Cluster Two all but four factor means were below the 4.0 mid-point.

Discriminant Analysis

Following the classification of respondents, the next step was to describe the characteristics of each cluster based on data not included in the cluster procedure (Hair et al., 1998). The descriptive statistics for each of these variables across clusters are shown in

Table 3.
Comparison of Cluster Demographic Profiles

	Cluster One		Cluster Two	
	Frequency	Percentage	Frequency	Percentage
Marital status				
Married	237	75.9	267	80.6
Single	56	17.9	49	14.8
Divorced/widowed	19	6.2	15	4.6
	312	100.0	331	100.0
Education level				
Attended high school	2	28.3	2	0.7
High school graduate	20	6.4	14	4.1
Attended college	56	46.8	33	9.6
College graduate	147	0.7	178	52.0
Post-graduate degree	89	17.8	115	33.6
	314	100.0	659	100.0
Household income				
Less than $35,000	6	2.0	4	1.2
$35,001 - $50,000	24	8.1	8	2.5
$50,001 - $75,000	43	14.5	26	8.0
$75,001 - $100,000	46	15.5	40	12.3
$100,001 - $125,000	47	15.9	41	12.7
$125,001 - $150,000	36	12.2	21	6.5
$150,001 - $175,000	23	7.8	27	8.3
$175,001 - $200,000	11	3.7	22	6.8
Over $200,000	60	20.3	135	41.7
	296	100.0	324	100.0
Race				
Black/African American	10	3.2	4	1.2
Native American	1	0.3	1	0.3
Hispanic	1	0.3	2	0.6
White/Caucasian	301	95.6	328	96.5
Asian or Pacific Islander	2	0.6	5	1.4
	315	100.0	340	100.0
Gender				
Female	76	24.2	40	11.7
Male	238	75.8	301	88.3
	314	100.0	341	100.0
Age				
18 - 29 years	26	8.3	18	5.3
30 - 39 years	67	21.3	60	17.8
40 - 49 years	93	29.5	102	30.3
50 - 59 years	82	26.0	116	34.4
60 - 69 years	37	11.7	35	10.4
70 years or older	10	3.2	6	1.8
	315	100.0	337	100.0
	Mean: 46.6		Mean: 47.7	

Table 4.
Discriminant Analysis

	Wilks' Lambda	F	df_1	df_2	p value
Gender	0.97	17.10	1	606	<.001
Ethnicity	0.99	13.89	1	606	n.s.
Marital Status	1.00	0.09	1	606	n.s
Educational Level	0.99	5.73	1	606	<.05
Household Income	0.94	40.56	1	606	<.001
Age	0.99	0.88	1	606	n.s

Table 3. Given that past research has shown that brand evaluations and perceptions differ based on demographic characteristics (Chao & Rajendran, 1993; Darley & Smith, 1995; Lindstrom, 2004), it was important to investigate any potential differentiation among the clusters identified. Therefore, a discriminant analysis was used to determine whether the two clusters could be distinguished in terms of demographic characteristics collected through the mail survey. The results of the analysis (Wilk's Lambda = .916, d.f. = 6, p<.001) revealed that the two clusters do indeed have characteristics that differentiate themselves (Table 4). Specifically, they significantly differ on gender, educational level, and household income.

Discussion

While the statistical method employed (two-part cluster analysis) in this study has been used for some time in other fields and was previously validated in those studies (Arimond & Elfessi, 2001; Harwood et al., 2004; Mazanec, 1984; Ogles & Masters, 2003; Safdari et al., 2005; Schaffer & Green, 1998), it has never been used in the study of sport brand associations. This sport consumer study confirms that by using this statistical approach, it is possible to use a traditional large-scale consumer survey to identify viable segments in the sport spectator market based on brand perceptions.

This type of analysis enables several major factors of strategic importance. First, it allows managers to identify segments of consumers that may be vulnerable to competitors' marketing strategies; that is, consumers having a negative perception may be influenced to switch to a competing brand. Second, this type of analysis allows managers to identify market gaps that are not currently satisfied by market offerings. For example, findings may indicate that consumers may feel unsatisfied with a current service and would like additional offerings. Finally, and most importantly, this analysis allows managers to discover ways in which the consumer thinks about the market. Specifically, a general understanding of consumer perceptions is critical to the success of an organization. In many cases, the findings will reinforce what managers already know. However, in some instances it may provide fresh insight into the clusters of consumers who hold particular brand association sets.

Brand Association Clusters

The primary purpose of this research was to use cluster analysis to identify segments of spectators based upon the brand associations held for a professional sport team. The results of the cluster analysis revealed that the total sample could be clustered into two distinct groups. The two clusters were significantly different in terms of the frequency and nature of which the brand association dimensions were elicited from memory. Specifically, Cluster One agreed with all 11 brand association dimensions more often than did Cluster Two. These results lend support to the notion that sport spectators can be classified into smaller market subsets based upon the perception of a sport brand. Furthermore, these results show that the cluster analysis technique is a viable solution to the identification of smaller subsets of consumers within the larger existing sport consumer base.

Demographics

A secondary purpose of the current study was to identify the possibilities of similarities and differences among these segments based upon demographic variables. Specifically, the membership of each cluster group was profiled and discriminant analysis was used to examine potential differences in age, ethnicity, gender, marital status, educational level, and household income. The results of the analysis revealed that the two clusters do indeed have demographic characteristics that differentiate it from other. In particular, Cluster One and Cluster Two members differed in regards to gender, educational level, and household income.

Although females and males could be found in each cluster group, there was a bias towards a larger proportion of the total female sample to be included in Cluster One. In fact, two-thirds (64%) of all females in the full sample were members of this cluster. Research related to information-processing may provide some explanation for this finding. Specifically, previous research has indicated that substantial gender differences do exist when processing information. For example, females appear to have superior ability in correctly recalling task sequences (Nicholson & Kimura, 1996) and in object recognition from studying visual stimuli (Harshman, Hampson, & Berenbaum, 1983). In a similar vein, other research suggests that females prefer a sequential, elaborative strategy, whereas males prefer an impulsive, global strategy to cognitive processing (Klinteberg, Levander, & Schalling, 1987; Pogun, 2001).

The two cluster groups that emerged in the study also could be distinguished by their educational level. A highly educated profile emerged as the most common pattern among the members of Cluster Two. Conversely, members of Cluster One were more likely to have attended college, but did not attain a degree. Perhaps those individuals with greater educational attainment have learned specific processing techniques, and therefore have greater propensities for detailed processing, allowing them to access brand associations more frequently. Finally, the results found that Cluster One and Cluster Two could be differentiated based upon household income. Specifically, the members of Cluster Two indicated having a much greater household income than did the members of Cluster One. One potential explanation for this finding is that members of Cluster Two were attending the sport event for the purposes for status, rather than interest in the game itself, and as such, the experiences sought from the game were more social in nature. The clusters were not significantly different in terms of martial status and age. While segments of consumer having different demographic profiles is nothing new, the current study showed that by investigating demographic profiles among segments based on other variables, such as brand image, it is worthwhile for further understanding of consumers.

Managerial Implications

All sport fans are not the same. Quite to the contrary, fans often differ in demographic characteristics, values, lifestyles, and product usage. One additional characteristic in which fans differ is in their perceptions about a sport brand. Specifically, sport fans will frequently hold different representations of a brand. One way in which to better understand these differences to properly meet the needs and wants of the consumer is through segmentation identification. Once the larger market for a sport product or service is divided into more manageable groups of consumers, a full investigation into the perceptual differences can take place. This research is a first attempt at using cluster analysis techniques to investigate the perceptions of brand associations among professional sport consumers.

Given that sport consumers are often actively involved in creating the service product (cheering, interacting socially, etc.) (Lovelock, 1996), each consumer experience is quite varied. In view of the fact that perceptions of sport brands repeatedly fluctuate between consumer segments, and understanding that managing the brand perceptions is tremendously important, it becomes crucial for managers to investigate and examine the brand associations across distinct subgroups of their customer base. This is particularity critical for managers when determining the effectiveness of marketing and positioning strategies.

By examining brand associations through the use of such segmentation strategies as cluster analysis, managers can have greater control over the equity of their sport brand. The image of a product or service is thought of as being a critical component of brand equity, and managing this equity is critical to the long-term success of a brand in that it has the ability to enhance brand loyalty among customers. Marketing theory has established that an organization's net value is largely created by the customer loyalty it commands (Aaker, 1996), typically with 80 percent of sales coming from 20 percent of the customers (Mullin, Hardy, & Sutton, 2000). If a consumer has negative perceptions of a service, then the likelihood of that consumer spending his or her dollars on that particular service is reduced. On the contrary, sport service providers with "good" reputations have the potential for high levels of customer loyalty (Aaker, 1996), and therefore strengthen the value of the brand. These issues have strong implications for the evaluation of positioning strategies.

Positioning involves communicating what the organization wants the consumer to think about the service. It is a critical element in marketing because it has long been known that the effect of positioning strategies affect how consumers perceive brands by establishing a particular set of brand associations linked to the service in the consumers mind (Kapferer, 1997; Keller, 1993). Therefore, in order to evaluate positioning activities, it is important to examine multiple segments of consumers based upon brand associations such as the current study proposes.

A demographic difference in cluster membership is another important piece of information that managers can use to more effectively reach and serve consumers. If sport managers are able to determine the demographic composition of a specific cluster of consumers, more specific and effective marketing strategies could be employed. For example, if managers discover that a specific group of consumers access certain brand associations frequently, and those cluster members are predominantly female, more specific promotional strategies could be developed to target those female sport consumers. Conversely, if future market research finds that cluster membership cannot be determined through gender, broad-based promotional strategies disregarding a gender-specific campaign could be employed as a cost savings measure. While demographic segmentation strategies are only one small portion of an overall marketing strategy, a customer's gender and the relationship of this demographic characteristic to the network of brand associations is important for sport administrators to consider.

Locating segments of consumer with similar perceptions of a sport brand can be a powerful tool for sponsorship development as well. Sport managers who develop sponsorship packages can use this information in order to better solicit sponsorship partners. For instance, a segment of consumers with like perceptions may be distinguished by average household income (as was found in the current study). This information could be used to target potential sponsors with high-priced or exclusive products or services. For example, sponsorship relationships with companies selling high-priced automobiles could be established to access the segments with higher levels of household income. In a similar vein, potential sponsor partners could be identified for those psychographics matching the members of less affluent segments, such as that of Cluster One. Given that the members of this segment were found to be less affluent, perhaps discount retailers (such as Wal-Mart) could be targeted as potential sponsorship partners to reach this specific segment of consumers. In practice, sponsorship is much akin to alignment marketing where an attempt is made to build a relationship in the consumer's mind between a brand name and an organization or event. Therefore, the image in the consumer's mind is extraordinarily important in assessing a sponsorship fit. Likewise, potential sponsors may be able to assess the image of a property in order to make accurate decisions before paying large sums of money to be a sponsor.

A final implication arising from the current study involves the value of segmenting ticket holders for the purposes of relationship marketing. Specifically, relationship marketing strategies may aid managers in the quest for increased retention and renewal rates among season ticket holders, and could be employed to promote advancement in loyalty rates. Zeithaml and Bitner (2000) suggest that there are four points related to relationship marketing. Financial bonding is the first point of relationship marketing and focuses on offering monetary encouragement such as discount ticket prices. However, for season ticket holders the financial investment has already been realized. Furthermore, it should be noted that season ticket holders have been found to be less motivated by financial issues such as price promotions offered through ticket discounts. That is to say, research has suggested that season ticket holders respond more positively to exclusive benefits (Funk & James, 2001) not available to general fans. Therefore, the remaining points in relationship marketing take on a greater importance for these individuals.

Social bonding, the second point, provides a considerable opportunity to impact the loyalty of season ticket holders. By recognizing season ticket holders and making them feel valuable to the organization, relationships between the two entities can be enhanced. One suggestion for marketers would be to organize "meet and greet" programs for season ticket holders and team personnel to interact in a sociable atmosphere.

Opportunities such as this would help facilitate an increase in an individual's self-appreciation and assist in the creation of greater loyalty towards the team.

The third point, customization, may also aid in the retention and renewal rate among season ticket holders. When specific programs and events are molded to individuals, customization occurs. The concept here is to discover what individuals specifically seek through their affiliation with a sport organization. Once thorough understandings of these needs are achieved, the organization can make an effort to provide services that meet those needs. The final point, structural bonding, provides another robust method to develop a connection to the organization. Structural bonding involves providing services that are designed for a specific client or customer (e.g., fan loyalty programs, venue kiosks), often based on technology (Funk & James, 2001). Fan loyalty programs would encourage a stronger relationship between season ticket holders and the organization, perhaps leading to greater proportions of retention.

Future Research

One potential question pertaining to future research would be to determine the underlying reasons as to why one cluster differs from another in terms of association elicitation. Additionally, future research using cluster-analysis methods regarding brand association groups seems warranted. A series of investigations is needed to determine whether similar brand perception clusters can be identified in other samples of sport consumers. Certainly the current study focuses on a specific sample of consumers, and care should be taken as to the generalizability across sport as a whole. Specifically, the sample used in the current study (one NBA season ticket holder base) is certainly not generalizable to other teams within the league. In addition, the results are not generalizable to the perceptions among fans for other professional sport teams given that all sports, leagues, and markets have idiosyncrasies that prevent such comparison. It is suggested here that in order to develop a full understanding of these principles in the sport marketplace, future research should replicate the current study among intercollegiate sport consumers, other sports at the professional level, and consumers across a variety of sports. In a similar vein, it is suggested that cluster-analysis methods be used to examine the existence of other clustered groups based on different variables. The possibility of consumers being segmented into smaller market subsets according to such variables as motivations for attendance, sponsorship recognition, and psychological commitment to a team is a fruitful line of research that needs to be pursued.

References

Aaker, D. (1996). *Building strong brands.* New York: The Free Press.

Arimond, G., & Elfessi A. (2001). A clustering method for categorical data in tourism market segmentation research. *Journal of Travel Research, 39*(4), 391-397.

Beane, T., & Ennis, D. (1987). Market segmentation: A review. *European Journal of Marketing, 21*(5), 20–42.

Berry, L. (2002). Cultivating service brand equity. *Journal of the Academy of Marketing Science, 28*, 128-137.

Brown, S., Fisk, R., & Bitner, M. (1994). The development and emergence of services marketing thought. *International Journal of Service Industry Management, 5*(1), 28-48.

Chao, P., & Rajendran, K. (1993). Consumer profiles and perceptions: Country-of-origin effects. *International Marketing Review, 10*(2), 22-39.

Darley, W., & Smith, R. (1995). Gender differences in information processing strategies: An empirical test of the Selectivity Model in advertising response. *Journal of Advertising. 24*, 41-56.

Dickson, P., & Ginter, J. (1987). Market segmentation, product differentiation, and marketing strategy. *Journal of Marketing, 51*, 1–10.

Eagly, A., & Chaiken, S. (1993). *The psychology of attitudes.* Harcourt Brace Jovanovich: Fort Worth, TX.

Fazio, R. (1995). Attitudes as object-evaluation associations: Determinants, consequences, and correlates of attitude accessibility. In R. E. Petty & J. A. Krosnick (Eds.), *Attitude strength: Antecedents and consequences,* (pp. 247-282). Mahwah, NJ: Lawrence Erlbaum Associates, Inc.

Gladden, J., & Funk, D. (2002). Developing an understanding of brand associations in team sport: Empirical evidence from consumers of professional sport. *Journal of Sport Management, 16,* 54-81.

Gladden, J., Irwin, R., & Sutton, W. (2001). Managing North American major professional sport teams in the new millennium: A focus on building brand equity. *Journal of Sport Management, 15,* 297-317.

Hair, J., Anderson, R., Tatham, R., & Black, W. (1998). *Multivariate data analysis: With readings* (5th ed.). New Jersey: Prentice-Hall.

Harshman, R., Hampson, E., & Berenbaum, S. (1983). Individual differences in cognitive abilities and brain organization. *Neuropsychologica, 36,* 37-43.

Harwood, C., Cumming, J., & Fletcher, D. (2004). Motivational profiles and psychological skills use within elite youth sport. *Journal of Applied Sport Psychology, 16,* 318-332.

Honkanen, P., Olsen, S., & Myrland, O. (2004). Preference-based segmentation: A study of meal preferences among Norwegian teenagers. *Journal of Consumer Behavior, 3*(3), 235-250.

Kahle, L., & Chiagouris, C. (1996). *Values, lifestyles and psychographics.* Erlbaum: Hillsdale, NJ.

Kapferer, J. (1997). *Strategic brand management* (2nd Edition). London: Kogan Page Publishing.

Keller, K. (1993). Conceptualizing, measuring, and managing customer-based brand equity. *Journal of Marketing, 57,* 1-22.

Kim, C., & Kim, S. (1998). Segmentation of sport center members in Seoul based on attitudes toward service quality. *Journal of Sport Management, 12,* 273-287.

Klinteberg, B., Levander, S., & Schalling, D. (1987). Cognitive sex differences: Speed and problem-solving strategies on computerized neuropsychological tasks. *Perceptual and Motor Skills, 65,* 683-697.

Lindstrom, M. (2004). Branding is no longer child's play. *Journal of Consumer Marketing. 21*(3), 175-182.

Lovelock, C. (1996). *Services marketing.* (3rd Edition). Upper Saddle River, NJ: Prentice Hall.

Mazanec, J. (1984). How to detect travel market segments: A clustering approach. *Journal of Travel Research, 23*(1), 17-21.

Mueller, H., & Kaufmann, E. (2001). Wellness tourism: Market analysis of a special health tourism segment and implications for the hotel industry. *Journal of Vacation Marketing, 7*(1), 5-17.

Mullin, B., Hardy, S., & Sutton, W. (2000). *Sport marketing* (2nd edition). Champaign, IL: Human Kinetics.

Nicholson, K., & Kimura, D. (1996). Sex differences for speech and manual skill. *Perceptual and Motor Skills, 82,* 3-13.

Ogles, B., & Masters, K. (2003). A typology of marathon runners based on cluster analysis of motivations. *Journal of Sport Behavior, 26*(1), 69-85.

Pogun, S. (2001). Sex differences in brain and behavior: Emphasis on nicotine, nitric oxide and place learning. Personality and individual difference. *International Journal of Psychophysiology, 42,* 195-208.

Punj, G., & Stewart, D. (1983). Cluster analysis in marketing research: Review and suggestions for application. *Journal of Marketing Research, 20,* 134-148.

Ross, S. (2006). A conceptual framework for understanding spectator-based brand equity. *Journal of Sport Management, 20,* 22-38.

Ross, S., James, J., & Vargas, P. (2006). The development of a scale to measure team brand associations professional sport. *Journal of Sport Management, 20,* 260-279.

Safdari, C., Ohanian, R., & Scannell, N. (2005). A statistical approach to peer-groupings: The case of banks in Armenia. *Journal of American Academy of Business, 6*(2), 24-31.

Schaffer, C., & Green, P. (1998). Cluster-based market segmentation: Some further comparisons of alternative approaches. *Journal of the Market Research Society, 40*(2), 155–163.

Tynan, A., & Drayton, J. (1987). Market segmentation. *Journal of Marketing Management, 2*(3), 301–335.

Wedel, M., & Kamakura, W. (1998). *Market segmentation: Conceptual and methodological foundations.* Kluwer Academic Publishers: London, UK.

Wind, Y. (1978). Issues and advances in segmentation research. *Journal of Marketing Research, 15,* 317–337.

SECTION III.

Understanding Sport Consumers

7

Consumer Research and Sport Marketing: Starting the Conversation Between Two Different Academic Discourses

Steven M. Kates

Is Sport a Form of Consumption?

For many individuals, much of their everyday behavior involves the consumption of sporting (or leisure) goods and services. For the most part these products share some common properties. First, they are generally high-involvement goods and services that are self-relevant and potentially risky in a social or financial sense (Holbrook & Hirschman, 1982). Second, many of these goods and services may be utilized within groups (such as teams or cliques of friends), or among large crowds of people engaged in a form of arousing, pleasurable, and hedonic consumption activity (Holbrook & Hirschman, 1982), such as spectatorship. The following questions emerge: What renders a sport 'special' or unique as a form of consumer behavior? Are there any examples of sport that are definitively not consumer behavior?

In the most simplistic sense, sport can be classified as a type of consumption because it normally involves the purchase (or rental), use, and/or disposition of a good (such as a Frisbee, basketball, climbing rope, or bathing suit) or a service (such as swimming lessons, coaching hours, or rink time). People's choices of what sporting events to attend or what brands of baseball gloves to purchase can be explored by employing traditional models of cognitive information processing developed within the consumer research discipline (Bettman, 1979; Olson, 1980). The movement in consumer research to study aspects of symbolic and experiential modes of consumption (Holbrook 1987; Holbrook & Hirschman, 1982) is fortunate in that it may inspire researchers to broaden their foci to the uses and meanings of sport. In the experiential view, researchers are urged to focus upon how a consumer derives fun and enjoyment from a product so that it results in feelings of pleasure (Holbrook & Hirschman, 1982). Sport, as a potentially unique form of consumption, allows consumers to experience the remarkable phenomenon of extraordinary experience (Arnould & Price, 1993). That is, those engaging in activities like river rafting, skydiving, bungee jumping, and skiing may become so engaged by the wonder and magic of the novelty of perception that they may experience flow. This is a sense of total, transcendental involvement while partaking in an activity (Celsi et al, 1993; Czikszentmihalyi, 1990), peak performance, communion with nature, communitas with other participants (Turner, 1969), and a sense of self-renewal. Many other forms of consumption, by contrast, are constituted by a repetitive, low-involvement, mundane, everyday activity, such as shopping for groceries, paying the electric bill, or filling the car with gas. Although these latter activities may very well be symbolic and meaningful to consumers, sporting activities are somewhat unique in that they are often highly communicative, social, and symbolic—attributes they share with many high-involvement consumer rituals such as gift-giving (Belk, 1979; Belk & Coon, 1993; Sherry, 1983), self-care practices (Thompson & Hirschman, 1995) or even cosmetic surgery (Schouten, 1991).

Other aspects of sport that set it apart from consumption are its institutionalized and formalized manifestations and its competitiveness. In its most institutionalized framework, sport is commonly constructed as a form of work or production. For example, one might argue the professional football player is not really "playing" at a game, but is fulfilling the specific and formalized roles of a job description or legal contract. From a broader sociological perspective, modern sport in its corporate or professional capacity has often been conceptualized as an institutionalized set of practices that exemplify and celebrate competitiveness, a hegemonic form of masculinity (Connell, 1995), the acquisition of skill and expertise, and an adversarial form of accomplishment (Gruneau, 1988). Thus, sport may be productively delineated and conceptualized as a separate societal "field" (Bourdieu, 1984) or institution with its own sets of meanings, practices, patterns, and rules of conduct that seem to perpetuate and reproduce themselves over time (Gruneau, 1988).

It is tempting to assert that sport and consumption are mutually exclusive societal fields because of sport's supposedly unique tendency to socialize children into a whole range of complementary and contradictory norms and values. Such values include hard work, competitiveness, reward through merit, team effectiveness, fair play, co-operation, helpfulness, aggression, patriotism, "family values," respect for hierarchy, and individualism. From the standpoint of consumer behavior, what is interesting about these beliefs is that they are so pervasive (Grove & Dodder, 1982; Spreitzer & Snyder, 1975) despite the fact that research suggests the benefits obtained depend entirely on the nature of the sport program's implementation (McCormack & Chalip, 1988). In other words, benefits are not intrinsic to sport, they depend on program design. Green (1997) has shown that the breadth of sport's market penetration is enhanced by inclusion of programs that are specifically redesigned to foster particular benefits. Thus, although popular beliefs about sport may enhance its appeal, those beliefs are neither universally nor uncritically held. Programs can be designed and implemented to attract those into sport who are otherwise skeptical about its purported benefits.

Consumption is a field that possesses socialization capabilities. The consumer research literature is replete with evidence that strongly suggests that consumers—adults and children—learn the values and norms of their respective cultures as they are socialized into consumption and through consumption (see especially Belk, 1979; Belk, Bahn & Mayer, 1982). Although evidence of the precise mapping between macro values and actual consumption choices is scant, people are socialized through a wide variety of consumption into values, such as materialism (e.g., Richins & Dawson, 1992), norms of self-control, denial, and adherence to prescribed idealized images of beauty (e.g., Richins, 1991; Schouten, 1991; Thompson & Hirschman, 1995), assumption of risk (Celsi et al.,

1993), and community and care for others (Belk & Coon, 1993). As a cultural institution symbolic consumption is thought to influence individual socialization. An emerging branch of a more poststructuralist orientation of consumer research is devoted to the study of power and consequence of consumption (Holt, 1997; Thompson & Haytko, 1997; Thompson & Hirschman, 1995). One productive area of research potentially involves the study of the specific meanings of socialization within various sport contexts. The work in sport subcultures is one variant of this direction (Beal, 1995; Donnelly, 1993; Donnelly & Young, 1988; Green & Chalip, in press; Klein, 1986, 1987; Theberge, 1995; Varpalotai, 1987). Thus, we might consider sport and consumption as overlapping institutions of meanings, practices, norms, values, and rituals. The boundaries between these fields are quite problematic in that they are permeable and negotiated by individuals, groups, and institutions over time. Professional hockey, for example, is commonly considered a formal, institutionalized form of sporting activity. Yet, it may also be viewed as a form of consumption because team players provide a symbolic and involving performance for spectating audiences. Some of the team activities are consumption rituals, such as suiting up or paying penalties, that are embedded within the game itself (McCracken, 1986). Is it sport, or is it consumption? Perhaps the most productive answer is that certain activities incorporate meanings, traditions, norms, values, and practices from both realms, and it is useful to view formal, institutionalized sporting activities (or events) and informal sport activities ("play") as potential sites for symbolic consumption. In this respect they are subject to theoretical inquiry from academics in consumer research and sport marketing.

This insight has some interesting implications for the marketing of sport, particularly in the context of event organizing. Increasingly, sporting activities are embedded within a highly commercialized context, such as the Gay Games, the Summer and Winter Olympics, and smaller tournaments and events (Thoma & Chalip, 1996). It should be noted that the holistic experience of these events, although centering on sporting activities, also incorporates other "fun" activities including organized dances, pub crawls, social mixers, and parties. The challenge for marketers is to develop an innovative overall product mix of activities whose shared cultural meanings complement and enrich each other to achieve a product "fit." The common relationship between alcohol consumption and sports has been noted elsewhere (Donnelly & Young, 1988), but excess levels of partying may not be acceptable to all segments of sport-event consumers. More interesting experiences that acknowledge and reinforce the social bonds among participants may include the incorporation of lectures on the relevant activity by noted sport figures and company-sponsored tours of the surrounding areas (e.g., a hike through a subtropical rainforest in Australia or a sightseeing tour of historic sights in London or Paris). What is important is that marketers recognize the "linking value" (Cova, 1997) of these events: that their most important source of utility is found not necessarily in the relationship between the person and the product, but in their capacity to enrich the experience and to facilitate the creation and maintenance of social relations among consumers.

Shared Meanings and Identity: (Sport) Subcultures of Consumption

One of the most interesting branches of both the sport marketing and the consumer research disciplines—from both theoretical and managerial perspectives—is the study of subcultures whose social organization revolves around various brands or activities

(Donnelly & Young, 1988; Irwin, 1973; Klein, 1986, 1987; Schouten & McAlexander, 1995; Stratton, 1985), providing sophisticated insights on the contextualized, in situ meanings of various forms of socialization. In their comprehensive ethnography of the new urban bikers, Schouten & McAlexander articulate four distinctive themes associated with these forms of subculture: hierarchical structures based upon levels of commitment and perceived authenticity, a distinctive ethos composed of shared norms and values, self-transformation to the biker identity, and the symbiotic relationship between marketing institutions and the subculture itself. Most importantly this particular study in consumer research provides an in-depth theoretical treatment of a form of consumer socialization into the new biker norms and values. When we take into consideration other literature on sport subcultures as well, some general observations can be made about this process. First, although the experiential manifestations of each subculture are probably distinct and unique to the local context, most subcultures exhibit the notably contradictory features of conformity to core values and calculated "deviance" from those constraints. Consumer practices—such as wearing Harley-Davidson jackets and riding Harley bikes—are key symbolic actions in demonstrating individual adherence to group expectations. Yet, given that these subcultures are hierarchically structured and tolerate some departure from norms, senior members are allowed to be more expressive and individualistic in their public consumer behaviors, (e.g., by decorating their bikes in manners that would be deemed unacceptable for neophyte members).

This study, along with others within the symbolic interactionist stream, provides an interesting insight into the workings of socialization into a subculture of sport. So-called conformity to norms and values of an institution is a negotiated phenomenon. That is, the possibility for action and the learning and adoption of meanings are "opened up" whereas others are foreclosed. Moreover, this process of socialization via negotiation changes over time. The neophyte biker, surfie, or football player, for example, is relatively constrained in his or her social behaviors (due to pressures for conformity—the social "sacrifice" necessary for inclusion) and even meaning construction, relying upon stereotypical notions of what it means to be, say, a biker, climber, or rugby player (Donnelly & Young, 1988; Irwin, 1973; Schouten & McAlexander, 1995). Nevertheless, over time, as one progresses through the social hierarchy of the subculture, greater freedom is accorded to the senior member to express himself or herself in a more idiosyncratic, individualistic manner.

An alternative theoretical perspective of sport enculturation is provided by a major ethnographic study of skydiving and high-risk leisure pursuits (Celsi et al., 1993). The unique aspect of this work is its particularly intriguing account of how skydivers acculturate to a high-risk, dangerous sport over time. The process of self-identity construction is key to understanding the motivations of normally safety-conscious people (who, for example, use seat belts regularly). In this study, socialization assumes a qualitatively unique set of meanings or local knowledge (Geertz, 1983): Skydivers achieve a sense of efficacy within the context of a previously frightening, challenging task. They conquer their fears and gradually learn to perceive risk in a relative, neutral manner.

From a theoretical perspective, this account of skydiving is embedded within a sophisticated model of high-risk leisure consumption, fundamentally based upon the dramaturgical framework of human interaction. In contrast to Schouten & McAlexander's (1995) study of the urban bikers, Celsi et al. (1993) provide a theory that incorporates a societal backdrop to consumers' shared motivations for partaking regularly of the sport. In particular, the mass media, social specialization, and technology are cited as critical macroenvironmental socializing influences of the dramatic worldview; the news, historical accounts, commercials, stories, soap operas, and particularly social relations serve to enculturate people into a "catalogue of possible behaviors," outcomes, expectations, and possibilities: "[Social specialization] couples with the behavioral alternatives presented in the mass media, and the instrumentality provided by the technology, creates a context conducive to dramatic high-risk leisure behavior" (Celsi et al., 1993, p. 4).

Many productive theoretical insights questions for future research and managerial insights can be generated when this model is translated to other sporting activities. For example, do mass media messages and products (e.g., television commercials, print ads, movies) reinforce traditional notions of hegemonic masculinity and, in turn, encourage teenage males to engage in potentially dangerous sports, such as football and hockey? Do these same mass media products promote a particularly masculine ("no pain, no gain;" "take it like a man!") orientation to risk and serious injury? Assuming that young teenagers feel alienated at school or part-time jobs, does sport provide them with an outlet for meaning creation, exercising their potential skills and creativity, and acquiring pleasurable, meaningful lived experience? What forms of technological products provide the requisite props for risk taking in sport? The dramatic worldview model lends itself to further analyses that explore the relationships between macrosocietal influences and consumers' lived experience. Moreover, further studies may employ both theory and substantive findings from both consumer research and sport sociology, crossing and integrating these two separate academic discourses.

Studies of sport subculture may also inspire researchers to provocative methodological insights as they "go native" or become what they research. It should be noted that in both studies cited above, the authors invested years as they entered the biker and skydiving communities respectively and learned the "lingo," norms, and values associated with the phenomenon in question. Thus, they themselves were socialized into sporting subcultures and gained the local knowledge. Their insights are hermeneutic; that is, they are understood by the researchers within the context of the subcultures in question. Their insights are also generated in the context of background experience, knowledge, meanings, and biases they bring to the research process. Thus, a healthy measure of self-reflexivity must be maintained (see Gould, 1991) and described so that others can understand "where the researcher was coming from" as they read accounts of the research.

For managers, the key challenge is to establish, develop, and maintain a continuing symbiotic relationship with sport and leisure subcultures, as exemplified by the Harley-Davidson brand (Gottdiener, 1985; Klein, 1986, 1987; Schouten & McAlexander, 1995). Ethnographic forms of market research may be employed to explore the deep meanings (often found in sport subcultures) connected to existing consumers' use of and experience with the brands in question. These meanings may then be incorporated into product designs and advertising the brand. The Harley-Davidson company, as an example, has incorporated various symbols of the outlaw biker subculture into its chopper-style motorcycles. Marketers are advised to redefine and change subculture meanings—in other words, to "sanitize" them so that they are acceptable to members of the larger population. This is not a rare phenomenon in marketing or fashion merchandising. In theoretical terms, it represents the co-optation of subcultural meanings into the larger fashion system (Hebdige, 1979) so that the resulting products are acceptable to larger segments of mainstream consumers. High-fashion designers in the early 1980s adopted certain punk rock styles and marketed them with the slogan "To Shock is Chic." Mainstream consumers are then enabled to form a kind of identification with marginalized or exotic groupings, sharing vicariously in their culture.

The Post Structuralist Turn: Sport as a Site of Struggle

Both sport and consumer research literatures have begun to incorporate perspectives from critical theory, feminist cultural studies, or poststructuralism (e.g., Hargreaves, 1988; Holt, 1997; Messner & Sabo, 1990; Thompson & Haytko, 1997). It should be noted that "socialization" is not generally in the accepted lexicon of poststructuralism. Rather, critical or conflict theories might view sport or consumer behavior as hegemonic processes or as sites of dominance, subordination, and resistance. Moreover (at the risk of some oversimplification; the critical perspectives cited here are quite diverse and contradictory in many instances), studies drawing upon these more critical perspectives may assume the contentious position that sport is an institution for reproducing dominant societal discourses associated with sexism, racism, homophobia, and overall conformity to repressive norms. In other words, sport is an arena of contested meanings and manifested power (Hargreaves, 1988; Pronger, 1990; Varpolotai, 1987), particularly relating to issues of gender (e.g., Fischer & Gainer, 1994; Varpolatai, 1987), race, or sexuality (e.g., Pronger, 1990). The Gramscian view of hegemony is particularly relevant to the study of power relation in sport consumption (Gramsci, 1971; Gruneau, 1988). According to this reformulation of Marxist thought, people instantiate norms and values within the contexts of mundane, everyday activities. Domination is characterized not simply by violence or the threat of violence (although this can be a meaningful component of any hegemonic process), but by the explicit or implicit consent of the subordinated group or individual. Hegemony is further complicated by the resistance that complements it. Oppressed groups or individuals may contest and negotiate different and perhaps more liberating meanings to the practices of everyday life, obtaining some consciousness of the social dynamics of their subordination.

Sport sociology and consumer research disciplines have both addressed the question of hegemonic structures operating within their respective fields. It should be noted, however, that sport sociology appears to be significantly more advanced in incorporating Marxist, feminist, or poststructuralist perspectives. Sport as a pervasive, political, and reputedly conservative institution may lend itself more to these kinds of social critique, whereas many other forms of consumer behavior appear at first glance to be value or power neutral (Beal, 1995; Hargreaves, 1988; Holt, 1997; Theberge, 1995; Thompson & Haytko, 1997; Thompson & Hirschman, 1995; Varpolatai, 1987). There are two theoretical issues that deserve future comment and research. First, on the individual level of analysis, play, exercise, and related leisure pursuits and consumer self-care practices establish a problematic relationship between the person and his or her body (see Thompson & Hirschman, 1995). In other words, the parts of the body, or the whole body itself, are problematized in relation to pervasive and idealized images of what the body should be. This relationship may be reinforced and instantiated through dietary practice, exercise, and sporting activities. Thus, consumers may find themselves trapped within discursive formations emphasizing strict regimen and the disciplining of the body—that is, monitoring, criticizing, and self-regulating it (Foucault, 1979). Many sporting activities then may be viewed as forms of insidious social control that promote a panoptic self-understanding of the socialized body. Further, consumers may negotiate among a number of sports-related discourses (e.g., "sport as character building "or "sport as a manner of conformity" or "activity as producing tangibly experienced health benefits" or "sport as masculine territory") to negotiate personal identity, social identity, and gender identity (see Thompson & Haytko, 1997). The analysis and interpretation of such negotiation processes that form dialogic relationships between self and cultural discourse may emerge as a productive field of endeavor, as such activities may yield insights into the dynamics of entering and participating in a sport subculture.

Although power dynamics within sporting activities or sport subcultures can be studied at the individual, psychological level, there is also an opportunity for scholars to study sport or leisure subcultures from a more collective standpoint, inquiring how practices are situated within (often unequal) social relations and how the consumers of these leisure pursuits are hailed (or interpellated) into various subject positions. For example, Beal (1995), in her study of a skateboarding subculture, notes that this form of unstructured play constitutes a form of active, conscious resistance to the sport status quo of organized competition, structure, and rules. One may interpret the skateboarders as having a strong, unproblematic form of self-identity based upon the use of the same product category. Yet, from an alternative, more antivoluntaristic position (now being expounded in the consumer research discipline; see Holt, 1997), one could assert that these young men and women are part of a social category, structured by a symbolic boundary, beyond the scope of their individual agency and generally inaccessible to self-reflexive understanding. Further analysis yields another more sophisticated insight: Indeed this form of activity may be emically experienced or even etically interpreted as a form of resistance to (or emancipation from) an existing dominant discourse involving sport. From a theoretical perspective, participation in a form of sporting resistance (as expressed within a subculture or by a shared form of identity) is not in a position of exteriority to power dynamics. It is, to a large extent, an indirectly defined and elaborated phenomenon. This is not to assert that participants join subcultures against their free will. Membership in subcultures and the negotiated social construction of the symbolic boundaries that define them operate (paradoxically) through free will or choice or in spite of it. Symbolic boundaries of a subculture are defined more by their members' treatment by the dominant culture than by their sense of self-identification with the subculture itself (Crosset & Beal, 1997).

It is difficult to determine managerial insights derived from critical or poststructuralist perspectives because these perspectives are often inimical to and critical of business interests. Yet this does not necessarily preclude the event organizer, manufacturer, or sporting goods retailer from following socially enlightened policies when marketing products. Organizations may gain insight and market share from the notion that they can refrain from specific activities that are problematic from the consumers' point of view. They might even engage in a prosocial marketing campaign. For example, Nike and other sporting goods marketers have recently been criticized by African-American intellectuals for their aggressive marketing tactics in the African-American communities. These marketing campaigns may validate the ambitions of youth to become basketball stars. Because only a small number of these young men will ever play in the NBA, many may find themselves without alternative skills. To compound the problem, Nike funds a basketball camp, recruits the best players from inner-city schools, and donates Nike equipment to adolescents. Critics see this as exploitation that perpetuates a cycle of poverty and hopelessness. Of course, one would hope that this is not Nike's intention and that Nike's motives are philanthropic. Nike can avoid criticism and benefit African-American communities by linking sport to education in ways that promote upward mobility (cf., Hawkins, 1987).

Gender issues involving equality are also significant. There is still a strong cultural discourse that excludes women from being participants or fans on a par with men (Fischer & Gainer, 1994). As a pervasive, public, and influential form of cultural practice, sport marketing tactics have the potential to denigrate women, even when women are the target market. For example, gender stereotypes or sexy imagery can perpetuate sexist attitudes. In popular film and television, to cite another form of cultural practice, there has been quite a positive phenomenon in the recent emergence of competent, physically capable, athletic, and intelligent women, such as Ripley in the *Alien* series of films and Buffy in *Buffy the Vampire Slayer.* Sport marketers have an opportunity to portray women athletes in ways to foster their empowerment. They can employ female athletes to endorse products, provide media coverage for the games within women's leagues, and organize special events.

Conclusions

This paper has endeavored to link literatures from consumer research, sport sociology, and sport marketing. The goal is to stimulate idea cross-fertilization among these communities of discourse. When ideas from these fields are connected, new substantive insights may result.

Some scholarly work within consumer research has focused upon the study of subcultures or subcultures of consumption, yielding theoretical frameworks and substantive findings regarding the enculturation of people into a new set of norms and values while interacting with others. Moreover, the study of sport subcultures has linked socialization into sport to the expression of identity through sport consumption. The common aspects of these two research streams are greater than any differences. By linking these discourses, new marketing tactics can be formulated. Yet, the theoretical insights and managerial prescriptions may be of value in that they can be transferred to new sporting events and subcultures of consumption.

Critical views from feminism, Marxism, and poststructuralism are also useful. They provide a unique perspective on sport consumption as sites of hegemony and resistance, elaborating upon how the body is problematized and regulated. They also identify how symbolic boundaries are negotiated between groups of people through self-care practices and sporting activities. Perhaps one of the most needed contributions is an exploration of how marketing tactics, sporting activities, and commercial organizations contribute to consumers' discontent and alienation and the many ways of connecting and enriching their lives. By bringing the discourses of consumer behavior, sport sociology, and sport marketing together, new research agendas and new marketing insights will result.

References

Arnould, A. J., & Price, L. L. (1993, June). River magic: Extraordinary experience and the extended service encounter. *Journal of Consumer Research, 20,* 24–45.

Beal, B. (1995). Disqualifying the official: An exploration of social resistance through the subculture of skateboarding. *Sociology of Sport Journal, 12,* 252–267.

Belk, R. W. (1979). Gift-giving behavior. In J. N. Sheth (Ed.), *Research in Marketing,* (Vol. 2, pp. 95–126). Greenwich, CT: JAI.

Belk, R. W., Bahn, K. D., & Mayer, R. N. (1982, June). Developmental recognition of consumption symbolism. *Journal of Consumer Research, 9,* 306–312.

Belk, R. W., & Coon, G. S. (1993, December). Gift-giving as agapic love: An alternative to the exchange paradigm based on dating experiences. *Journal of Consumer Research, 20,* 393–417.

Bettman, J. (1979). *An information processing theory of consumer choice.* Reading, MA: Addison-Wellesley.

Bourdieu, P. (1984). *Distinction.* Cambridge, MA: Harvard University Press.

Celsi, R. L., Rose, R. L., & Leigh, T. W. (1993, June). An exploration of high-risk leisure consumption through skydiving. *Journal of Consumer Research, 20,* 1–25.

Connell, R. W. (1995). *Masculinities.* London: Polity Press.

Cova, B. (1997). Community and consumption: Toward a definition of the "linking value" of product or services. *European Journal of Marketing, 31*(3–4), 297–316.

Crosset, T., & Beal, B. (1997). The use of "Subculture" and "Subworld" in ethnographic works on sport: A discussion of definitional distinctions. *Sociology of Sport Journal, 14,* 73–85.

Czikszentmihalyi, M. (1990). *Flow: The psychology of optimal experience.* New York: Harper & Row.

Donnelly, P. (1993). Subcultures in sport: Resilience and transformation. In A. G. Ingham & J. W. Loy (Eds.), *Sport in social development: Traditions, transitions, and transformations,* (pp. 119–145). Champaign, IL: Human Kinetics.

Donnelly, P., & Young, K. (1988). The construction and confirmation of identity in sport subcultures. *Sociology of Sport Journal, 5,* 223–240.

Fischer, E., & Gainer, B. (1994). Masculinity and the consumption of organized sports. In J. A. Costa (Ed.), *Gender issues and consumer behavior,* (pp. 84–103). Thousand Oaks, CA: Sage Publications.

Foucault, M. (1979). *Discipline and punish.* New York: Pantheon.

Geertz, C. (1983). *Local knowledge.* New York: Basic Books.

Gottdiener, M. (1985). Hegemony and mass culture: A semiotic approach. *American Journal of Sociology, 90*(5), 979–1001.

Gramsci, A. (1971). *Selections from prison notebooks of Antonio Gramsci.* New York: International Publishers.

Green, B. C. (1997). Action research in youth soccer: Assessing the acceptability of an alternative program. *Journal of Sport Management, 11,* 29–44.

Green, B. C., & Chalip, L. (in press). Sport tourism as the celebration of subculture: Parading identity at a women's football tournament. *Annals of Tourism Research.*

Grove, S. J., & Dodder, R. A. (1982). Constructing measures to assess perceptions of sport functions: An exploratory investigation. *International Journal of Sport Psychology, 13,* 96–106.

Gruneau, R. S. (1988). Modernization or hegemony: Two views on sport and social development. I. In J. Harvey & H. Cantel (Eds.*), Not just a game: Essays in Canadian sport sociology.* (pp. 9–32). Ottawa: University of Ottawa Press.

Hargreaves, J. (1988). *Sport, power, and culture: A social and historical analysis of popular sports in Britain.* London: Polity Press.

Hawkins, L. (1987). Media and sports in the urban high school. *Gannett Center Journal, 1*(2), 83–87.

Hebdige, D. (1979). *Subculture: The meaning of style.* New York: Routledge.

Holbrook, M. B. (1987, June). What is consumer research? *Journal of Consumer Research, 14,* 128–132.

Holbrook, M. B., & Hirschman, C. H. (1982, September). The experiential aspects of consumption: Consumer fantasies, feelings, and fun. *Journal of Consumer Research, 9,* 132–140.

Holt, D. B. (1997, March). Post-structuralist lifestyle analysis: Conceptualizing the social patterning of consumption in postmodernity. *Journal of Consumer Research, 23,* 326–350.

Irwin, J. (1973). Surfing: The natural history of an urban scene. *Urban Life and Culture, 2,* 131–160.

Klein, A. (1986). Pumping irony: Crisis and contradiction in bodybuilding. *Sociology of Sport Journal, 3,* 112–133.

Klein, A. (1987). Fear and self-loathing in Southern California: Narcissism and fascism in bodybuilding subculture. *The Journal of Psychoanalytical Anthropology, 10*(2), 117–137.

McCormack, J. B., & Chalip, L. (1988). Sport as socialization: A critique of methodological premises. *Social Science Journal, 25*(1), 83–92.

McCracken, G. (1989, June). Culture and consumption: A theoretical account of the structure and movement of the cultural meaning of consumer goods. *Journal of Consumer Research, 13,* 71–84.

Messner, M. A., & Sabo, D. F. (1990). Football ritual and the social reproduction of masculinity. In M. A. Messner & F. Sabo (Eds.), *Sport, men, and the gender order: Critical feminist perspectives* (pp. 115–126). Champaign, IL: Human Kinetics.

Olson, J. C. (1980). Encoding processes: Levels of processing and existing knowledge structures. In J. Olson (Ed.), *Advances in consumer research,* (pp. 154–160). Ann Arbor, MI: Association for Consumer Research.

Pronger, B. (1990). *The area of masculinity: Sports, homosexuality and the meaning of sex.* Toronto: Summerhill.

Richins, M. L. (1991, June). Social comparison and the idealized images of advertising. *Journal of Consumer Research,, 18,* 71–83.

Richins, M. L., & Dawson, S. (1992, December). A Consumer values orientation for materialism and its measurement: Scale development and validation. *Journal of Consumer Research, 19*, 303–316.

Schouten, J. W. (1991, March). Selves in transition: Symbolic consumption in personal rites of passage and identity reconstruction. *Journal of Consumer Research, 17*, 412–425.

Schouten, J. W., & McAlexander, J. H. (1995, June). Subcultures of consumption: An ethnography of the new bikers. *Journal of Consumer Research, 22*, 43–61.

Sherry, J. F. (1983, September). Gift-giving in anthropological perspective. *Journal of Consumer Research, 10*, 147–168.

Spreitzer, E., & Snyder, E. E. (1975). The psychosocial functions of sport as perceived by the general population. *International Review for the Sociology of Sport, 10*, 87–95.

Stratton, J. (1985, July). Youth subcultures and their cultural contexts. *Australian and New Zealand Journal of Sociology, 221*, 194–218.

Theberge, N. (1995). Gender, sport and the construction of community: A case study from women's ice hockey. *Sociology of Sport Journal, 12*, 389–402.

Thoma, J. E., & Chalip, L. (1996). *Sport governance in the global community.* Morgantown, WV: FIT.

Thompson, C. J., & Haytko, D. L. (1997, June). Speaking of fashion: Consumers' uses of fashion discourses and the appropriation of countervailing cultural meanings. *Journal of Consumer Research, 23*, 15–42.

Thompson, C. J., & Hirschman, E.C. (1995, September). Understanding the socialized body: A poststructuralist analysis of consumers' self-conceptions, body images, and self-care practices. *Journal of Consumer Research, 22*, 139–153.

Turner, V. W. (1969). *The ritual process.* Chicago: Aldine.

Varpolotai, A. (1987). The hidden curriculum in leisure: An analysis of a girl's sport subculture. *Women's Studies International Forum, 10*(4), 411–422.

8

Sport Consumer Typologies: A Critical Review

Bob Stewart, Matthew Nicholson, and Aaron C. T. Smith

Introduction: Differentiating Sport Consumers

Sport consumers display a bewildering array of values, attitudes, and behaviors (Meir, 2000; Shank, 2002; Westerbeek & Smith, 2003). Not all consumers are equally passionate and fanatical, nor use their team to confirm their personal identity (Redden & Steiner, 2000). Neither are they all totally loyal, engrossed in club history, or resistant to change that threatens team values and practices. Some attend games on a regular basis, while others attend only on special occasions. Some consumers spend most of their time engaging in sport chatter and trawling the Internet, while others display their fandom by watching pay television sport channels. They experience sport in different ways, and use team affiliations to meet a diverse range of needs (Wann, Melnick, Russell, & Pease, 2001). This complexity challenges the view that sport consumption can be reduced to a narrow set of homogeneous traits.

This complexity also underpins the desire to construct models of sport consumption that make sense of this disparate behavior, and provides the foundation for models of market segmentation that links behavior to different demographic, social, and cultural groupings. Effective segmentation can reveal distinctive preferences and needs, identify sources of loyalty and commitment, and highlight differences in spending patterns of sport consumers (Pitts & Stotlar, 1996; Shilbury, Quick, & Westerbeek, 1998). In short, sport consumer typologies allow sport marketers to refine marketing activities, redesign sport products, monitor price sensitivities, reconfigure playing arenas, adjust promotional campaigns, and generally customize the sport experience to fit the peculiar needs of each customer segment.

The purpose of this paper is to critically examine the approaches taken to classify sport consumers, discuss the strengths and limitations of the approaches, and recommend areas of future research for both theoreticians and practitioners. This will be achieved by discussing sport consumption from three perspectives. The first perspective focuses on dualistic models, which essentially involve contrasting one form of sport consumer behavior with its opposite. The second perspective covers tiered models where sport consumers are grouped and then ranked according to the strength of their emotional or financial commitment to the sport or team. The third perspective focuses on multidimensional approaches that combine underlying motives for consuming sport products, factors that give sport meaning, indicators of loyalty, levels of emotional attachment, and frequency of game attendance, to produce an array of sport consumer types.

Dualistic Approaches

Some of the earliest typologies arose out of the changes that took place in European soccer in the 1970s and 1980s. Clarke (1978) developed a simple typology to show how some individuals had been marginalized by the commercial transformation of English soccer. He contrasted **genuine** fans, who used their local teams to construct a sense of community, with **others**, who viewed soccer as a pleasant afternoon's entertainment. Boyle and Haynes (2000) drew similar conclusions about the profile of English soccer fans by distinguishing between **traditional** fans, who were true supporters with a strong sense of the game's history and culture, and **modern** fans, who were attracted to the game because it offered an entertaining, if ephemeral experience. Nash (2000) used the same assumptions to distinguish between **core** fans, who grew up with the game and built enduring emotional attachments to teams, and **corporate** fans who used the game to consolidate their social and professional networks.

Ferrand and Pages (1996) and Quick (2000) also used dualistic approaches in their examination of French soccer followers and Australian sport consumers respectively. They distinguished between **irrational** fans, who had strong tribal and emotional connections with a club or team, and **rational** fans, who were more inclined to use their club and team connection to secure a social or commercial benefit. Rational fans asked questions like What pleasure or return will I get on my investment in a sport team?

These typologies, which are summarized in Table 1, confirm that in an increasingly commercialized sport-world, individuals often take an instrumental approach to sport consumption. However, the typologies are also constrained by an ideological assertion that genuine sport followers have been marginalized by modern consumers, and need to reclaim their pivotal place as authentic sport consumers. From a sport marketing perspective, dismissing a segment because it is not authentic is a recipe for failure, since it limits the potential for attracting new market segments. At the same time, the rational/irrational distinction provides a starting point for understanding the different ways individuals affiliate with their favorite sports and teams.

Table 1.
Dualistic Fan Typologies

Type 1 Fans	Type 2 Fans
Old	New
Genuine	Corporate
Traditional	Modern
Expressive	Submissive
Irrational	Rational
Symbolic	Civic
Die–hard	Less-loyal

Lewis (2001) has also presented a dualistic approach, but instead of differentiating between genuine and modern fans, focused on the different ways individuals identified with their clubs and teams. He examined a sample of North American professional sport consumers and found that some aligned themselves primarily with the city the team represented, while others aligned themselves with the team itself. The individuals who identified themselves with the city, which in this case was Houston, were labelled **civic** fans. Those who identified with the team, which in this case was the Oilers, were labelled **symbolic** fans.

The complex dynamics of identifying with sports teams were also revealed in a study by Hughson (1999), who examined ethnic-Australian soccer supporters. He distinguished between **expressive** supporters, who were driven by the search for adventure, excitement, and thrills, and **submissive** supporters, who, while strongly committed to their teams, did not share the transgressive and neo-tribal qualities of expressive supporters. Expressive supporters identified most closely with their ethnic and cultural traditions, and used the team as a conduit for displaying this other identity.

Bristow and Sebastian (2001) used the concept of brand loyalty to undertake a dualistic analysis of fans of the Chicago Cubs baseball club. They noted that models of consumer brand loyalty usually assumed that high brand loyalty was linked to strong brand identification, a long historical connection with the brand, and performance expectations that were continually met. The first two elements were used to distinguish **die-hard** or extremely loyal fans from **less loyal** fans. They found that die-hard fans were more brand loyal, had a stronger connection to the club as children, spent more time talking about the club, went to see more games, and spent more money on paraphernalia. Interestingly both die-hard and less loyal fans liked the club to the same extent.

The studies of Lewis (2001), Hughson (1999), and Bristow and Sebastian (2001) mark a significant shift in the use of dualistic models to inform sport consumption analysis. Unlike the English models, neither Lewis nor Hughson privileged one sport-consumption type over the other. They clearly articulated the different ways consumers identify with their favorite teams, and provide a solid foundation for more complex analyses of team identity and attachment. Bristow and Sebastian also broaden our knowledge of sport consumer behavior by highlighting the different meaning consumers attach to the sport experiences and the tenuous relationship between liking a team, being loyal to a team, and regularly attending games.

However, despite these conceptual advances, dualistic models of sport consumption tend to conflate a range of practices into a behavioral straitjacket. By aiming for a neat simplicity, they inhibit our understanding of sport consumer beliefs and attitudes, and restrict attempts to discover new patterns of sport consumer behavior. As such, dualistic typologies should be seen as a starting point for the design of more multifaceted models of sport consumption.

Tiered Typologies

During the early 1990s, a number of North American studies broadened the analysis of sport consumers by measuring the level and intensity of team attachments. In doing so, they found that sport consumers could be not only be differentiated, but also ranked on the basis of their beliefs and behavior.

Wann and Branscombe (1993) differentiated North American sport consumers on the basis of the intensity of their relationship with a club or team, and measured this intensity by constructing a sport spectator identification scale (SSIS). They concluded that individuals who read a lot of sport material, talked to others about sport a lot, frequently attended games, had a strong general interest in sport, and had a good general sport knowledge, also had strong attachments to teams and players. These **high identification** supporters linked their favorite team to their sense of self and publicly displayed their team loyalty. On the other hand, supporters with weaker attachments read and talked about sport less, attended fewer games, watched less sport on television, and had less knowledge about sport. They were the **low identification** supporters. The Wann and Branscombe model consequently laid the foundation for a sport fan continuum that provided for multiple levels of attachment, loyalty, and identification.

Mullin, Hardy, and Sutton (1993) used a similar set of assumptions about North American sport followers to produce their model of sport consumption. They claimed that sport consumers could be located along a frequency escalator, with **highly committed** consumers who attend games regularly at the top of the escalator, those with **low commitment** or low attenders at the bottom of the escalator, and **moderately committed** consumers somewhere near the middle. They suggested that the goal of sport marketers was to move consumers up the escalator and consequently increase their consumption of sport products.

Kahle, Kambra, and Rose (1996) focused their analysis on North American consumers, and used the experiences of college football spectators to construct a three-level typology. The first type was labeled **internalized and highly involved.** These individuals sought close attachment and identification, and constructed strong tribal relationships with their team. At a lower level of intensity were **self expressives** who sought excitement and the big experience, but were less inclined to incorporate the team in their sense of self. Finally, there were **camaraderie** sport consumers who had only a slight commitment to the team, but enjoyed the social interaction with other team supporters.

Sutton, McDonald, Milne, and Cimperman (1997) also developed a three-tier model of sport consumption from North American sources. On the top tier were **vested fans,** who had a strong sense of ownership, high levels of emotional investment in their team, and a greater tendency to define themselves through their team or club. On the middle tier were **focused fans,** whose commitment and investment of emotional energy was contingent upon the success of the team. On the bottom tier were **social fans** who, while low on team identification, were attracted to the entertainment value of the game.

Clowes and Tapp (1999) also developed a three-part typology from English football data and used the same tiered approach to distinguish between **fanatics, committed casuals,** and **care-free casuals.** Like Kahle et al. (1996) they suggested a clear hierarchy of loyalty and commitment, with fanatics at the top and care-free casuals at the bottom.

When Wann and Branscombe (1993), Mullin et al. (1993) Kahle et al. (1996) Sutton et al. (1997), and Clowes and Tapp (1999) are compared, three common sport consumer types emerge. At the top of the tier are the vested and highly committed consumers, in the middle are the expressive and focused consumers, while at the bottom are the social and camaraderie consumers who display the lowest levels of commitment. The tiered models are summarized in Table 2 below.

The tiered models have added substantially to our knowledge of sport consumption, demonstrating that sport consumers have different relationships with their favorite teams and that they approach their sport consumption in different ways. That is, consumption is expressed through not only tribal connections to teams, but also through social interaction and being entertained. On the other hand, tiered models of sport consumption cannot readily accommodate differences within each step or tier. Neither do they say much about what causes sport consumers to move from one tier to the next. They also assume a positive link between loyalty, identity, and consumption without

Table 2.
Common Elements in Tiered Fan Typologies

Tier	Primary focus of fan	Secondary focus of fan	Type
1 to team	Emotional connection experience	Excitement and special vested	Internalised, focused,
2	Excitement and entertainment, the big experience	Emotional connection to team	Self expressive, committed casual
3	Social interaction and entertainment	Team identification	Camaraderie, care-free casual, social

providing strong empirical support. Finally, they give us only a partial understanding of the underlying beliefs and motives that drive an individual's loyalty, attachment, and sport consumption behavior.

Multidimensional Typologies

Some of the limitations of tiered models of sport consumption have been addressed with the development of typologies that run across two or more dimensions. Holt (1995) constructed one of the earliest multidimensional models of sport consumption using consumers of the Chicago Cubs Baseball Club as primary data. The first dimension centered on the subjective **experiences** of consumers and how they connected to the team using both rational and emotional behaviors. The second dimension centered on the ways consumers went about **integrating** the club and its personality into their sense of self. The third dimension centered on the ways consumers used the sport experience to classify their **relationships** to the club, and project that relationship to the wider community. The final dimension focused on the **play** element in consumption and how consumers played out their sport experience alongside fellow consumers. Holt concluded that sport consumption not only involved a forum for expressing emotional attachments to a team, but was also used to engage in strategic analysis, confirm individual identity, signify one's social position, converse with other sport consumers in a common setting, and indulge in playful exchanges.

McDonald and Milne (1997) used relationship marketing theory to construct a two-dimensional model of sport consumer behavior. They categorized sport consumers on the basis of their value to the team or club (their lifetime value or LTV) and their level of commitment to the club or team (their relative relationship strength or RRS). Consumers were subsequently characterized by one of four types. The first type was the most attractive to the club, being highest on both value (LTV) and relative relationship (RRS). The second type was high on value but low on relative relationship. The third type was low on value but high on relative relationship. The final type was low on both value and relative relationship, and the least attractive to the club or team.

McDonald and Milne suggested that type 1 consumption represented the ideal relationship since it combined a high commitment with the highest levels of financial support. Like Mullin et al. (1993), they concluded that sport marketers should focus their attention on designing strategies to move customers up the sport consumption escalator to higher levels of commitment and financial support.

Using Australian sport leagues data, Smith and Stewart (1999) produced a typology that focused on the attitudes and behaviors of sport consumers. By examining motives for attending games and frequency of match attendance, Smith and Stewart identified five different sport consumer types. The first were the **passionate partisans** who attended games regularly, were loyal to their team, and identified closely with its players, traditions and collective image. The second were the **champ followers** who were less fanatical, and committed only when their team performed well. The third category was the **reclusive partisans,** whose commitment to the team was strong, but attended infrequently. In contrast to these parochial consumers, who valued team affiliation above all else, Smith and Stewart identified two additional types who were more interested in the quality of the game. The first type were **theatergoers** who primarily sought entertainment and were attracted to comfortable venues, star players, and the expectation of a close contest. The second type was **aficionados,** who, like theatregoers, were attracted to exciting games but were also attracted to games that provided skill and tactical complexity, even if they were likely to be one-sided.

Mahony, Madrigal, and Howard (2000) adopted a similar conceptual approach to Smith and Stewart in examining North American sport consumers. They created a psychological commitment to team (PCT) scale to measure commitment levels and reveal the strength of an individual's relationship with a team. Attendance was measured by asking individuals how often they went to home games. These two indicators were used to construct a two-dimensional measure of loyalty. The first dimension was an attitudinal component (my team is important to me, and I am highly committed), while the second dimension was a behavioral component (I go to my team's home games and attend regularly).

Four types of team loyalty resulted from the Mahony et al. (2000) research. The highest level of loyalty was labeled **true loyalty** and involved both strong commitment and strong attendance. The next level was labeled **spurious loyalty,** which involved weak commitment, but strong attendance at home games. The next level of loyalty was labeled **latent loyalty** and included a strong commitment to the team, but a low level of attendance at home games. The most fragile type was labeled **low loyalty** and included both weak commitment, and weak home game attendance.

Hunt, Bristol, and Bashaw (1999) also used commitment as a way of distinguishing between sport consumers, but added a time and space dimension to their analysis. Using themes that centered on identification, attachment and the processing of sport-related information, they identified five types of sport consumers. The first type were **temporary fans** whose identification with players and teams was time constrained. Temporary fans were committed so long as the team was winning, star players were performing, and events had media reinforcement. They wanted value from their sport experience and lost interest when the pay-off from their fandom fell. The second type were **local fans** whose identification was linked to a geographic area. Local fans supported their local team because it represented their town or city, rather than using the team to confirm their own sense of self. The third type were **devoted fans** whose identification was linked to a sense of self. They were more strongly committed than temporary and local fans, more loyal to the team, and therefore less likely to jettison the team when it performed poorly. The fourth type were **fanatical fans** whose team identification was expressed in very public ways. They not only attended games more frequently, but also painted their body in team colors and continually collected memorabilia. The fifth type were **dysfunctional fans** whose identification with team was so strong that it dominated their lives. They obsessively connected with the team, believed that winning mattered more than anything else, and often engaged in anti-social behavior when their team performed poorly.

Funk and James (2001) developed a more complex model of sport consumer behavior that they titled the Psychological Continuum Model (PCM). Instead of using tiers and escalators, they adopted an incremental stage metaphor to frame their analysis. According to Funk and James, sport consumers move through four stages or floors of sport and team identification. The first stage or floor was labeled **awareness.** At this ground floor level, individuals were aware of the existence of different sports and teams, but had little commitment or interest in them. The next level, or first floor, was labeled **attraction.** In these instances, consumers used sport as an escape from the routines of daily life and were attracted to a team because it provided amusement and excitement.

Table 3.
Multidimensional Approaches to Sport Consumption

Cluster type	Differentiating behaviors
Underlying motivations	Escape (to a less stressful 'sports-world') Eustress (excitement, and entertaining event) Social interaction
Emotional attachment	Obsessive attachment and strong commitment Moderate attachment and conditional commitment Slight attachment and fragile commitment
Economic attachment	High value: strong financial commitment Moderate value: intermediate financial commitment Low value: weak financial commitment
Identity	Team used to confirm self-concept Team used to confirm civic and community pride Team used to confirm social or cultural identity
Loyalty	Loyalty through game attendance Loyalty through displaying team colors Loyalty through chatter and conversation
Connective focus	Team is primary connection Sport or league is primary connection Player is primary connection
Overt experiences	Rational: strategic analysis Symbolic: gestures, ceremonies and rituals Social: play and social integration
Attendance at games	Frequent Moderate Low

However, they did not strongly identify with the team. The next level, or second floor of commitment was labeled **attachment.** Individuals with a strong attachment developed a more stable connection with the sport or team and invested more time and emotional energy into team activities. The top or third floor contained fans with the most passionate level of commitment, which was labeled **allegiance.** In these instances consumers gave a high priority to loyalty, and incorporated the team image into their own sense of self. They spent more time reading about the team, engaging in sport chatter with other fans, and attending games.

Gladden and Funk (2002) used the concepts of brand equity and brand association to create a three-dimensional approach to team identification. By examining the attitudes and behaviors of a sample of North American sport consumers they found that association with teams were formed in three specific ways. First, consumers connected to teams via **product features** that included the coach, team management, the team logo, team colors, star players, and facilities and services. Second, they connected to teams via **product benefits** that were either experiential (an escape from daily routines and pressures, a means of connecting to the past, and as a way of developing pride in place and community solidarity) or symbolic (self-enhancement, role position, group membership and ego-identification). Finally, they connected to teams via **attitudes**, which included the importance of the team to the individual and knowledge of the team. In total, Gladden and Funk identified sixteen brand association factors that they used to construct a Team Association Model (TAM) which provided the foundation for establishing profiles of sport consumers.

The above multidimensional models show that sport consumption involves a broad range of motivations and beliefs. At the same time they can be consolidated into a number of behavioral clusters that highlight the different ways in which consumers express their sporting interests. These clusters include primary motivators, emotional commitment, economic and financial commitment, levels of identification, loyalty, connective focus, overt experiences, and frequency of game attendance. These eight dimensions of sport consumption are summarized in Table 3 below.

These models not only confirm that sport consumption has cognitive, effective and behavioral components, but also challenge the view that loyalty and commitment are directly translated into active consumption. Mahony et al. (2000) noted that some individuals displayed latent loyalty that involved high commitment but low attendance. Similarly Smith and Stewart's (1999) passive partisan displayed strong team affiliation, but relatively low levels of attendance. So too did McDonald and Milne's (1997) type 3 sport consumer, who rated high on team attachment, but low on financial value. These contradictions were not revealed in the tiered models of sport consumption.

The multidimensional models also provide a richer description of the factors that underpin sport consumption. Holt (1995) in particular revealed a multiplicity of social and psychological factors that shape the behavior of sport consumers. Moreover, Holt convincingly demonstrated that sport consumers engage in entangled displays of fandom that combine identity formation with social interaction, and strategic analysis with play and ritual.

Finally Hunt et al. (1999), Funk and James (2001), and Gladden and Funk (2002) demonstrate that sport consumption involves more complex patterns of team identification than the tiered models suggest. Hunt et al., and Funk and James showed that committed sport consumers can be differentiated, while Gladden and Funk identified sixteen variables that defined the sport consumption experience.

Toward a Better Understanding of Sport Consumption

The first thing to be said about the above studies is that they provide a rich and varied analysis of sport consumption. At the same time, there is a significant overlap, and the empirical support for some of the models is slim. In general though, they confirm that sport consumption is multifaceted, and involves far more than simply turning up to a game, tuning in, and going home. In the following section we aim to draw together the main themes and issues arising from our earlier discussion and analysis, and critically assess the strengths and weaknesses of sport consumption research undertaken so far.

Defining Sport Consumption

The studies reviewed in this paper show that it impossible to describe the archetypal sport consumer, because there are a multitude of interdependent values, attitudes, and behaviors to consider (Holt, 1995). While some of the early dualistic models of sport consumption confined fandom to displays of passionate attachments to teams, and habitual game attendance (Clarke, 1978; Mason, 1999), Wann and Branscombe (1993) correctly noted that a sport fan is someone who says they are a sport fan. In other words, sport consumption is a self-defining phenomenon. As Jones (1997) noted, being a sport fan "comprises more than attending and observing a sporting event" (p. 1). Taking a broad view of sport consumption can only be a good thing from a researcher's perspective.

Identifying Differences

The above studies also show that sport consumers can be segmented from many perspectives. Moreover, they have their origins in not only what sport consumers do (their behavior) but also what they feel and say (their motivations and beliefs). This distinction underpins the studies of Funk and James (2001), Holt (1995), Gladden and Funk (2002), Hunt et al. (1999), Mahony et al. (2000), and Smith and Stewart (1999). Some sport consumers are passionate and obsessive, while others more casual about their team relationship (Kahle et al., 1996). Some primarily identify with a team, while others connect more with the game and the league (Smith & Stewart, 1999; Hill & Green, 2000). Some committed consumers regularly attend games, while others with a high level of commitment do not (Mahony et al., 2000). Some sport consumers express their fandom through chatter, reading newspapers, and television viewing, while others dress up in team colors as a way of displaying their team affiliation (Hunt et al., 1999; Gladden & Funk 2002). Some slavishly surf the Internet, while some spend lavishly on memorabilia and collectables. Many sport consumers use their team allegiance to socialize with other true believers (Holt, 1995). Others consume sport in order to escape the routine of daily life (Gladden & Funk, 2002).

Benefits of Demarcation

While models of sport consumption tend to fragment sport consumer behaviors and can dilute their strategic value for sport marketers, they also capture important distinctions. Lewis' (2001) contrast of civic and symbolic fans is a good example, as is the distinction Hunt et al. (2000) make between fanatical and dysfunctional fans. So too is Hughson's distinction between sport consumers that individually identify with the team and those who use the team to express a broader cultural identity.

As a result, researchers should be encouraged to examine sport consumption behavior in accordance with an individual's self-perception, since it produces more personalized and divergent responses. While recording every microscopic difference creates a mass of disparate data waiting to be classified, these subjective experiences can also reveal distinctive sport consumer traits that previously went unrecognized.

Rational-Irrational Distinctions

Many of the typologies discussed above, particularly, Ferrand and Pages (1996), Holt (1995), Hunt et al. (1999), and Quick (2000) show a rational-irrational division between sport consumers. Some sport consumers want tangible outcomes like an entertaining experience, comfortable seating at the venue, and access to merchandise and memorabilia (Wakefield & Sloan, 1995; Wakefield, Blodgett, & Sloan, 1996). In contrast, other consumers connect to their team in emotional ways, and poor team performance and substandard facilities are no impediment to their commitment and sense of identification (Funk & James, 2001; Hunt et al., 1999). This distinction between the highly rational fan and the highly emotional fan is an interesting one, and has been closely examined by Holt (1995) who found that most participants in his study were simultaneously rational and irrational. They not only displayed their passionate team allegiance, but also spent time analyzing team selection, tactics, and performance. The rational-irrational distinction has been under-researched, and would be a productive area for more detailed empirical study.

Understanding the Emotional Connection

Studies of sport consumption also show that the emotional connection that individuals have with a sport, team, or player becomes more complex the deeper we look. They can be temporary and slight, or permanent and obsessive, and are most clearly articulated in the studies of Funk and James (2001), Hunt et al. (1999), and Kahle et al. (1996). These connections not only vary in their intensity, but also in their form. For example, some consumers incorporate their favorite team into their sense of self and create a personal identity around the team (Holt, 1995). Others use the sport or team as a means of identifying with a town or city (Hunt et al., 1999; Lewis, 2001), while others may use the team to strengthen a racial, class, gender, or ethnic identity (Hughson, 1999; Jones, 2000). In other words, the identification process is more complex than some sport marketers would have us believe, since sport consumers can link a team to their sense of self in fundamentally different ways.

The above studies also demonstrate that loyalty is a pivotal part of the sport consumer experience. As Mahony et al. (2000) and Bristow and Sebastian (2001) show, most consumers see loyalty as a defining feature of their relationship with a sport team or player. Elevator models of the Funk and James (2001) type and multidimensional approaches that capture the escalation of fandom conceptualize this relationship the best.

However, the link between loyalty, identity, and consumption can be problematic. While sport consumers who have a highly emotional attachment to a team will be loyal, the studies of Bristow and Sebastian (2001) and Clowes and Tapp (1999) found that individuals with a more casual connection to a team may also possess a great store of loyalty. Moreover, loyalty does not necessarily translate into frequent match attendance. While Wann and Branscombe (1993) and Funk and James (2001) suggested that sport consumers who attended most frequently were also loyal, the studies of Clowes and Tapp (1999) and Mahony et al. (2000) indicated that many committed and loyal team fans did not attend regularly. At the same time, there were also a group of less committed and loyal consumers who attended more frequently. These findings suggest that sport consumers express their loyalty in various ways. Regular attendance is one way, while reading newspapers, chatter, purchasing club merchandise, and watching games on television are other ways. This fractured connection between loyalty and attendance is compounded by the growing tendency for some consumers to value match-day entertainment over the parochial support of their team (Smith & Stewart, 1999). Models that distinguish between emotionally connected high-attendees and emotionally connected low-attendees are therefore essential to accommodate this crucial, but often ignored, aspect of sport consumer behavior. Empirical studies that can illuminate the different patterns of behavior within groups of emotionally connected and loyal sport consumers will provide valuable insights for sport marketers.

Fan Hierarchies and Weightings

Many of the above studies also contain an implied hierarchy of sport consumers. For the most part, passionate supporters are given the most weight because of their high level of emotional investment and game attendance. They have been variously described as tribal, irrational, expressive, internalized, vested, fanatics, allegiance, and passionate partisans. Their privileged position is encapsulated by the use of the term genuine (Clarke, 1978; Nash, 2000). At the other end of the continuum are the less committed supporters who have been variously described as rational, submissive, expressive, social, carefree-casuals, attraction, and theatregoers. There is some merit in the hierarchy approach since it correctly implies that some sport consumers contribute more equity than others (Pitts & Stotlar, 1996). It also highlights the crucial importance of committed consumers to the ongoing financial health of sporting competitions and organizations (McDonald & Milne, 1997).

On the other hand, a heavy-handed application of hierarchical models of sport consumption to sport marketing can marginalize consumers who are not as passionate or committed, or indeed are seen to be too passionate and anti-social (Hunt et al., 1999). Hierarchical models of sport consumption consequently require critical re-assessment by sport marketers, since they are underpinned by heavily value-laden assumptions (Nash, 2000).

Hierarchical models also imply that it is not necessary to hard-sell to committed consumers, and that we should be cautious about investing resources in so-called casual consumers. This ambivalence about transitional consumers is short sighted since it assumes they are low yield. However, this notion denies the possibility that an incremental shift in their behavior will produce a significant benefit. Indeed, McDonald and Milne (1997) contend that effective sport marketing is all about getting customers to "move up the escalator to higher levels of financial and emotional commitment" (p. 31). These lower bands of casual consumer types are empirically tantalizing, but conceptually underdeveloped. Further analysis and development is needed to tease out more data on their underlying beliefs about attachment, loyalty, identity, and sport consumption.

Avoiding Duplication

Our review of the sport consumption research literature shows there has been a sustained progression in its breadth and sophistication. Rudimentary analysis that contrasted real and authentic consumers with their opposite has given way to multifaceted models grounded in solid theories of consumer behavior. These theories have been used to construct detailed typologies that differentiate sport consumers around a number of factors including emotional attachment to teams, loyalty, and identity, which are then linked to specific patterns of consumption like game attendance, television viewing, and the purchase of team merchandise. However, as the number of sport consumption typologies expands, it becomes increasingly clear that many types and segments can be conflated into a small number of common core dimensions. Many of the studies examined in this paper were very often saying the same thing with a different nomenclature. The tiered models of Wann and Branscombe (1993), Mullin et al. (1993), Kahle et al. (1996), Sutton et al. (1997), and Clowes and Tapp (1999) are good examples. As Funk and James (2001) politely noted, "any effort to re-write the literature (on sport consumption) becomes an exercise in untangling semantic differences" (p. 120). Typologies that may, on the surface, look quite different are frequently saying the same thing. In short, the desire for an expanded demarcation of sport consumer types may have to be tempered by critical analysis that weighs the benefit of constructing a new sport consumer segment against the cost of converting it into an operational marketing strategy. The need to formalize every unique consumer experience should be balanced against the expediency of a more generalized segmentation model.

Implications for Future Sport Consumption Research

Our analysis of sport consumption studies suggests that there is no single best conceptual model, since they all have strengths and limitations. At the same time, the strongest models of sport consumption have a number of distinguishing features. First, they are grounded in solid theories of consumer behavior, with the studies of Funk and James (2001), Gladden and Funk (2002) and Holt (1995) being exemplars in this respect. Second, they clearly articulate each sport consumer type or segment, and link their behavior to underlying beliefs and motives. The models of Bristow and Sebastian (2001), Funk and James (2001), Hunt et al. (1999), Mahony et al. (2000) and Lewis (2001) meet this criteria. Third, they explain the implication of each sport consumer type and segment for subsequent marketing strategies. This task was impressively completed by Kahle et al. (1996), Mahony et al. (2000), McDonald and Milne (1997), and Sutton et al. (1997). Finally, they are supported by a broad base of empirical support. The survey by Funk (2002) was particularly relevant in this respect, since it was based upon the previously constructed Psychological Continuum Model (PCM) (Funk & James, 2001). Funk confirmed the theoretical foundations of PCM by identifying casual, moderate, and loyal market segments using six sport consumer associations (like team identification and nostalgia) and eighteen survey questions at an accuracy level of more than 70%. Funk's empirical study validates the claim that while sport consumer typologies can be theoretically sound by encompassing a full spectrum of beliefs, meanings, and behaviors, their ultimate value comes from capturing real consumer experiences.

Nevertheless, there are also a number of areas where research into sport consumption requires further development. There is a crucial need for additional empirical studies that can be used to test the conceptual models discussed above. For example, Holt (1995), Hunt et al. (1999), Lewis (2001), and Smith and Stewart (1999) have designed some tantalizing models of sport consumption, but need more detailed empirical surveys to test the credibility of their sport consumer types. Specifically, the aficionado segment in the Smith and Stewart model and the dysfunctional fan described by Hunt et al. are fascinating types, but are currently underdeveloped. They need to be tested to establish their significance and market value. In this respect, there are strong grounds for undertaking more qualitative research that uses in-depth interviews to tease out some of the more subterranean beliefs and motivations that underpin the above models of sport consumption (Jones, 1997).

More work also needs to be undertaken on methodologies that can assist practitioners in designing strategies for many of the market segments identified in the studies examined in this paper. For example, the assumption that different sport consumer types respond indifferently to standard marketing communications, and therefore require customized messages to elicit greater team attachment, is often not supported by hard evidence. As with all aspects of sport marketing, sport consumer typologies need to be tempered in the forge of market practice.

The relationship between a consumer and a sport team is complicated by the fact that individuals bring their own personalities and values to their sport experience. Moreover, they are subject to a broad range of external factors that mediate their relationship with their favorite sport, team and players (Funk & James, 2001; Kates, 1998). These mediating factors include gender, family structure and values, household income, friendship groups, the social milieu in which sport consumers run their daily lives, the class or subculture to which they belong, their sensitivity to price, and the cost of sport activities (Fort, 2003; Hunt et al., 1999; Wann et al., 2001). Contextual factors have usually been ignored by sport consumer researchers. This constitutes a serious weakness, and the quality of sport consumption research would be enhanced by more multidisciplinary studies that locate sport consumption in a cultural and economic context. (Fort, 2003; Kates, 1998; Shank, 2002).

Neither do many of the above studies have much to say about the ways in which sport consumption originates and evolves. Yet, this is fundamental to the development of a supporter base for any sporting competition. As Bristow and Sebastian (2001) suggest, understanding the behavior of the very young sport consumers may be the key to unlocking the door to fan loyalty (p. 271). The issue of how young people in particular construct their patterns of sport team attachment constitutes an important challenge for subsequent research.

Finally, apart from Funk and James (2001), the studies reviewed in this paper reveal little about the mobility of consumers along the frequency escalator, or from one type to another. Future models of sport consumption could enhance their explanatory powers by saying more about those factors that may cause an individual to change their sport consumption behavior. Funk and James (2001) have laid the foundation, and more studies that focus on changing patterns of sport consumption would be very instructive. The most useful models of sport consumption should be capable of specifying the gatekeepers and drivers of movement between levels and forms of fandom and the consequent change in consumption. To this end, there are significant pay-offs from undertaking longitudinal studies that trace the behavior of sport consumers over time. Whereas life-cycle metaphors and processes have been successfully applied to sport products (Mullin et al., 2000), no equivalent studies have been undertaken on sport consumers.

Implications for Sport Marketers

The above analysis makes a strong case for employing some form of segmentation model in developing marketing strategies for attracting sport consumers to sport products. A segmented model not only forces sport marketers to differentiate the market, but also encourages them to develop a more detailed understanding of the motives and values that underpin specific aspects of consumer behavior.

To this end, a number of practical issues need to be addressed. First, the studies discussed above suggest that sport consumption has both an irrational and rational component. The irrational component signals the need to provide experiences that enable sport consumers to identify with teams, and escape into a world of passion, exuberant ritual, and idle chat. At the same time, the rational component signals the need to provide experiences that involve strategic analysis, commercial exchanges, and value adding.

Second, sport marketers should not only promote the benefits of identifying with the team and its players, but also the benefits of witnessing a spirited contest and high quality game. A number of typologies identified customer segments that involved high value supporters being attracted to the game as a whole rather than to a particular team. These game-quality, high value segments, which comprise both corporates and individuals, are likely to become increasingly lucrative sources of income for sport organizations and a strategic focal point for sport marketers.

Third, sport marketers need to select models of sport consumption that fit their tactical intentions. While in some cases the acquisition of new sport consumers will be a priority, in other cases the primary aim will be to maximize post-purchase relationships. As a result, marketers should be aware of the power different sport consumption models have in targeting and revealing consumer readiness. Moreover, some models excel at identifying and classifying motivations for consumption decisions, but are less useful in specifying the preconditions to gain consumer attention, interest, and desire. In short, some models will provide a strong theoretical base, while others will have a more concrete application to market place strategies.

Conclusion

In summary, the desire to understand the consumption patterns of sport consumers has been a long-standing goal for sport marketers. This goal has often been framed by typologies that aim to reveal the motivations and behaviors upon which to base segmentation models of sport consumption. Sport consumer typologies allow sport marketers to customize their marketing communications to sport consumers, but differentiating the motivational complexities of individuals can be problematic. While many models of sport consumption identify interesting cognitive and affective differences between consumers, their analysis is frequently limited to one or two behavioral traits. Some of the multidimensional models are more effective in segmenting consumers and frequently reveal subtle nuances that people bring to their sport consumption experiences. However, they also have their limitations, since they rarely discuss how individuals move between different segments or change their beliefs and behaviors. Nor do they explain precisely how relationships between consumers and teams are formed in the first place. Sport consumer research will be enhanced by a greater use of multidisciplinary teams using longitudinal studies to collect data that covers both the individual behavior of consumers and the social and economic context in which this behavior takes place. They will provide a rich description of consumer values and beliefs, and changes in their sport-related behavior (Jones, 1997). This will not only add to the body of knowledge on sport consumption, but also assist sport marketers to more effectively meet the needs of what is an increasingly complex and idiosyncratic market.

References

Boyle, R., & Haynes, R. (2000). *Sport, the media, and popular culture.* Harlow: Pearson Education.

Bristow, D., & Sebastian, R. (2001). Holy cow! Wait 'til next year! A closer look at the brand loyalty of Chicago Cubs baseball fans. *Journal of Consumer Marketing, 18*(3), 256-275.

Clarke, J. (1978). Football and working class fans. In R. Ingham, S. Hall, J. Clarke, P. Mann, and J. Donovan (Eds.). *Football hooliganism: The wider context.* London: Inter-action Imprint.

Clowes, J., & Tapp, A. (1999). Market segmentation in football clubs: An empirical investigation. *Proceedings of European Association for Sport Management Conference, 1998.* Thessaloniki, EASM, 66-72.

Ezzy, D. (2002). *Qualitative analysis: Practice and innovation,* Sydney, Australia: Allen and Unwin.

Ferrand, A., & Pages, M. (1996). Football supporter involvement: Explaining football match loyalty. *European Journal for Sport Management, 3*(1), 7-20.

Fort, R. D. (2003) *Sports economics,* Upper Saddle River, NJ: Prentice Hall.

Funk, D. (2002). Consumer-based marketing: The use of micro-segmentation strategies for understanding sport consumption. *International Journal of Sports Marketing and Sponsorship,* September/October, 231-256.

Funk, D., & James, J. (2001). The psychological continuum model: A conceptual framework for understanding an individual's psychological commitment to sport. *Sport Management Review, 4*(2), 119-150.

Gladden, J., & Funk, D. (2002). Developing an understanding of brand association in team sport: Empirical evidence from consumers of pro sport. *Journal of Sport Management, 16,* 54-81.

Hill, B., & Green, C. (2000). Repeat attendance as a function of involvement, loyalty, and the sportscape across the football codes. *Sport Management Review, 2*(3), 145-162.

Holt, D. (1995). How consumers consume: A typology of consumption practices. *Journal of Consumer Research, 22* (June), 1-16.

Hughson, J. (1999). A tale of two tribes: expressive fandom in Australia's A-league. *Culture, Sport, Society,* 11-30.

Hunt, K., Bristol, T., & Bashaw, R. (1999). A conceptual approach to classifying sport fans. *Journal of Services Marketing, 13*(6), 439-452.

Jones, I. (2000). A model of serious leisure identification: the case of football fandom, *Leisure Studies, 19,* 283-298.

Jones, I. (1997). Mixing qualitative and quantitative methods in sport fan research. *The Qualitative Report, 3*(4), 1-6. Retreived from http://www.nova.edu//sss/QR.

Kahle, L., Kambra, K., & Rose, M. (1996). A functional model of fan attendance motivation for college football. *Sport Marketing Quarterly, 5*(3), 51-60.

Kates, S. (1998). Consumer research marketing: Starting the conversation between the different academic discourses. *Sport Marketing Quarterly, 7*(2), 24-31.

Lewis, M. (2001). Franchise relocation and fan allegiance. *Journal of Sport and Social Issues, 25*(1), 6-19.

Mahony, D. F., Madrigal, R., and Howard, D. R. (2000). Using the psychological commitment to team (PCT) scale to segment sport consumers based on loyalty. *Sport Marketing Quarterly, 9*(1), 15-25.

Mason, D. (1999). What is the sport product and who buys it? The marketing of professional sport leagues. *European Journal of Marketing, 33*(3/4), 402-418

McDonald, M., and Milne, G. (1997). Conceptual framework for evaluating marketing relationships in professional sport franchises, *Sport Marketing Quarterly, 6*(2), 27-34.

Meir, R. (2000). Fan reaction to the match day experience: A case study in English professional rugby league, *Sport Marketing Quarterly, 9*(1), 34-42.

Mullin, B., Hardy, S., & Sutton, W. (1993). *Sport marketing,* (1st ed.), Champaign, IL: Human Kinetics.

Mullin, B., Hardy, S., & Sutton, W. (2000). *Sport Marketing,* (2nd Ed.), Champaign, IL: Human Kinetics.

Nash, R. (2000). Contestation in modern English football. *International Review for the Sociology of Sport, 35*(4), 439-452.

Pitts, B., & Stotlar, D. (1996). *Fundamentals of sport marketing.* Morgantown, WV: Fitness Information Technology.

Quick, S. (2000). Contemporary sport consumers: Some implications of linking fan typology with key spectator variables. *Sport Marketing Quarterly, 9*(3), 149-156.

Redden, J., & Steiner, C. (2000). Fanatical consumers: Toward a framework for research, *Journal of Consumer Marketing, 17*(4), 322-337.

Shank, M. (2002). *Sports marketing: A strategic perspective.* New Jersey: Prentice Hall.

Shilbury, D., Quick, S., & Westerbeek, H. (1998). *Strategic sport marketing.* Sydney, Australia: Allen and Unwin.

Smith, A., & Stewart, B. (1999). *Sports management: A guide to professional practice.* Sydney, Australia: Allen and Unwin.

Sutton, W. A., McDonald, M. A., Milne, G. R., & Cimperman, A.J. (1997). Creating and fostering fan identification in professional sport. *Sport Marketing Quarterly, 6*(1), 15-29.

Wakefield, K., Blodgett, J., & Sloan, H. (1996). Measurement and management of the sportscape. *Journal of Sport Management, 10,* 15-31.

Wakefield, K., & Sloan, H. (1995). The effect of team loyalty and selected stadium factors on spectator attendance. *Journal of Sport Management, 9,* 103-117.

Wann, D., & Branscombe, N. (1993). Sport fans: Measuring degree of identification with the team. *Journal of Sport Psychology, 24,* 1-17.

Wann, D., Melnick, M., Russell, G., & Pease, D. (2001). *Sport fans: The psychology and social impact of spectators.* New York: Routledge.

Wann, D., Royalty, J., & Roberts, A. (2000). The self presentation of sport fans. *Journal of Sport Behavior, 23*(2), 198-206.

Westerbeek, H., & Smith, A. (2003). *Sport business in the global marketplace.* New York: Palgrave Macmillan.

9

Comparing Sport Consumer Motivations Across Multiple Sports

Jeffrey D. James and Stephen D. Ross

Introduction

The provision of intercollegiate athletic programs involves a myriad of complex financial challenges. An increasing number of athletic administrators must manage their programs in environments characterized by declining revenue sources and increasing operating costs. A report on the revenues and expenses of NCAA athletic programs from Fulks (2000) indicates that most athletic programs depend on institutional support to avoid operating at a deficit. Given the fact that the figures reported by Fulks (2000) do not include debt service and capital expenses, it is reasonable to conclude that the majority of athletic programs struggle to balance revenues and expenses. In the near future, athletic programs at best can expect to receive current levels of institutional support while expenses continue to rise; a more realistic expectation is that they will receive lower levels of financial support. Faced with declining institutional support, athletic administrators must decide whether to reduce their budgets and potentially eliminate sports or try to generate additional income to offset expenses.

The financial pressure on athletic programs is coming from a number of rising costs. The increasing costs of scholarships, equipment, Title IX compliance, and salaries for coaches and personnel, all contribute to the current financial situation that many athletic administrators are facing (Masteralexis, Barr, & Hums, 1998). In light of declining revenues and increased costs, while at the same time motivated to satisfy increased demands, athletic administrators are seeking ways to maintain current programs (Branvold, 1992). Within most athletic programs, men's football and basketball are the only revenue-generating enterprises (Howard & Crompton, 2003). The ability of one or both of these sports to produce substantial income is often crucial to maintaining all other nonrevenue producing sports.

One approach to meeting the financial challenges of the future is to generate income from what have historically been low or nonrevenue sports (e.g., baseball, softball, and wrestling). Potential sources of increased revenue include income from sponsorship deals, merchandise sales, concessions, and gate receipts. Given the fact that nonrevenue sports are not high profile, it is not likely that sponsors will be lining up to spend substantial dollars to form associations. There may be opportunities for package deals by bundling various sports together, but institutional restrictions on sponsorship deals and existing deals with sponsors of revenue sports will likely limit the opportunities.

Merchandise sales in collegiate sport are another potential source of revenue for athletic programs. Very few programs currently realize the full benefit of this revenue source. Previous research indicates that one out of every four athletic programs receives no annual licensing revenue, and another 25% receive 50% or less of the revenue generated through merchandise sales (Howard & Crompton, 2003). These figures indicate that while merchandise sales are a potential revenue enhancer, programs at best can only expect a small percentage of the returns. Similarly, food service plays a smaller role in collegiate sport compared to the professional level. Fulks (2002) noted that concessions represented only 2% of total revenues for Division-IA programs. Food service is a minor revenue source in collegiate sports for two primary reasons: smaller disposable income of fans and lack of beer sales (Howard & Crompton, 2003). Most colleges do not allow beer sales, which results in concession volumes that are at least 35% below the sales volume at the professional level.

At the collegiate level, a potential and many-times-overlooked source for increased revenues across multiple sport programs is ticket sales. Athletic programs currently rely on gate receipts from the revenue sports, primarily football, to help fund nonrevenue programs (Howard & Crompton, 2003). For example, on average football and men's basketball account for 93% of Division-IA men's program revenues and 58% of Division II with football men's program revenues (Fulks, 2002). Although ticket sales at nonrevenue sporting events are not expected to generate sufficient income to fully fund respective programs, it is reasonable to expect that increased income from ticket sales would help offset some of the expenses. This is a particularly appealing option given that ticket pricing and promotion of ticket sales represent areas over which an athletic department has direct control. In order to develop strategies for increasing ticket sales for various low or nonrevenue sports, it is necessary to better understand why individuals have an interest in these sports and what factors may motivate them to attend live events.

Sport Consumer Motives

Early research on sport spectator consumption centered principally on the topic of sport demand. Research has examined the effect of economic factors, promotions, and residual preference factors (e.g., scheduling of games, new arenas, accessibility) on attendance at sporting events and has studied the relationship between sociodemographic variables and watching sports (Baade & Tiehen, 1990; Greenstein & Marcum, 1981; Hansen & Gauthier, 1989; Schofield, 1983; Zhang, Pease, Hui, & Michaud, 1995; Zhang, Smith, Pease & Jambor, 1997).

The sport demand variables help sport marketers appreciate how pricing issues (setting ticket prices that are affordable based on a community's average household income), promotions (giveaways and events that stimulate single game attendance), and residual preference factors (game time, weather, accessibility) affect attendance. At the same time, these variables are often beyond the control of sport marketers (e.g., game times set by television broadcast schedules; weather) or do not relate to the core product, the event on the field or court (e.g., promotional giveaways, concerts, fireworks shows).

More recent research has examined the intrapersonal motives of sport consumers (Kahle, Kambara, & Rose, 1996; Milne & McDonald, 1999; Trail & James, 2001; Wann, 1995) to help explain sport consumption. A wide array of motives has been proposed to explain sport consumption including aesthetics, catharsis, drama, entertainment, escape, social interaction, and vicarious achievement (Sloan, 1989; Trail, Anderson, & Fink, 2000). Researchers have focused on testing and refining scales that assess the intrapersonal motives of sport consumers (Trail & James, 2001; Wann, 1995). An emerging body of work has most recently begun reporting the importance of various intrapersonal motives relative to sport consumption. Research has examined motives across different professional sports (Funk, Mahony, & Ridinger, 2002; James & Ross, 2002), professional sports in other countries (Mahony, Nakazawa, Funk, James, & Gladden, 2002), and college football and basketball (James & Ridinger, 2002; Kwon & Trail, 2001). With the exception of the work by James and Ridinger, work to date has yet to examine the motives of consumers relative to nonrevenue collegiate sports.

James and Ridinger (2002) examined the motives of consumers attending men's and women's college basketball games. The results indicated that those attending men's and women's games were influenced by the action in the games and the opportunity to escape from one's daily routine. Differences between male and female consumers regardless of sport were also reported; compared to women, men experienced a greater sense of vicarious achievement, enjoyed the aesthetic value of basketball, and had a greater knowledge of the game. The findings suggest that the motives for following and attending nonrevenue sports are similar to the motives for following and attending revenue sporting events.

The purpose of the current study was two-fold. First, to extend our understanding of sport consumers by identifying the motives that help explain an individual's interest in nonrevenue collegiate sports. Second, to ascertain whether similar motives influence consumption across multiple nonrevenue sports. For intercollegiate athletic administrators seeking to generate additional ticket sales from nonrevenue sports, it is essential to assess the importance of different motives to ascertain which may exert the greatest influence on consumption of specific sports.

Method

Sample

Three sport programs offered at a large Midwestern university (men's baseball, women's softball, and men's wrestling) were included in the current study. These sports were chosen because they took place concurrently, were characterized as nonrevenue sports by the athletic department, and each attracted at least 250 spectators per game or match. Information was collected from people attending wrestling matches, baseball games, and softball games. Questionnaires were distributed at three wrestling matches, three baseball games, and three softball games. Volunteers were recruited and trained to assist with the data collection. Following a prepared script, the volunteers approached individuals sitting in randomly selected seats prior to the beginning of a game or match, explained the project, and asked if they would be willing to participate. A total of 1,125 questionnaires were distributed at the nine events, 125 per match or game. Two hundred ninety-two useable questionnaires were collected from those attending the wrestling matches (78% return rate). Three hundred fifty-four useable questionnaires were collected from those attending baseball games (94% return rate), and 301 useable questionnaires were collected from those attending softball games (80% return rate).

Procedure

Participants were asked to complete a four-page questionnaire assessing their reasons for following the respective teams and attending games. Individual items were distributed throughout the survey to reduce order and other biases. Those responding were also asked to provide demographic information (age, gender, level of education completed, ethnicity, household income, and marital status) so that a profile of people attending the three sports could be developed.

Sport Consumer Motives

The sport consumer motives in the current study included eight constructs drawn from previous research (James & Ross, 2002; Trail & James, 2001) and two developed by the authors. Six of the nine factors from the Motivation Scale for Sport Consumption (MSSC) (Trail & James, 2001) were utilized (Achievement, Drama, Escape, Family, Skill, and Social). Officials at the university asked that the Physical Attraction items not be used so this factor was omitted. The Knowledge factor was omitted because a review of the individual items led the authors to conclude that the items examine whether a person currently has knowledge about players or a team's win/loss record and various statistics, but they do not measure a desire for knowledge influencing the individual's sport consumption. After reviewing the wording of the items for Aesthetics and Physical Skill, and noting the high correlation for the two constructs reported by Trail and James (2001), the decision was made to include only the items measuring physical skill (Skill). It seemed reasonable to expect that the aesthetic enjoyment of some sports may come from watching the athletes demonstrate their physical skills.

Team Affiliation, or the desire to feel a connection to or an affiliation with the team, and Entertainment, the enjoyment of a sport as a source of entertainment, initially tested by James and Ross (2002) were also included in the study. To more accurately measure the motivations, the wording of some items was altered to include the specific sport being examined. For example, the first Escape item, "Games represent an escape for me from my day-to-day activities," was altered to read, "For me, softball games are an escape from my day-to-day activities." Similarly, the first Family item, "I like going to games with my family," was changed to, "Being with my family is why I enjoy softball games." Wording changes were also made to some items based on the recommendations of Trail and James in an effort to improve the respective factors.

The authors developed two additional constructs, Team Effort and Empathy. Unlike professional athletes, college athletes do not receive direct monetary compensation for their participation. Athletes in nonrevenue sports in particular are thought to participate because of a love for the game. The authors hypothesized that some sport consumers may attend games and matches based on their enjoyment of watching athletes give their best efforts in a sport they enjoy. The current study provided an opportunity to test this idea.

Empathy, the extent to which an individual shares in the disappointment of a lost or poorly played game was also measured. Research suggests that individuals desiring to enhance their self-esteem through an association with a team feel proud when the team plays well and engage in a BIRGing (basking in reflected glory) process (Cialdini, Borden, Thorne, Walker, Freeman, & Sloan, 1976; Sloan, 1989). As noted in previous research, individuals with a strong connection to a team do not dissociate themselves when the team plays poorly (Wann, 1993; Wann & Branscombe, 1990); these individuals maintain their association suggesting that they experience some level of frustration. The authors hypothesized that a more complete measure of self-esteem enhancement should include items assessing whether an individual shares in the disappointment of a lost or poorly played game. Three items were developed by the authors to measure whether an individual experienced empathy as well as vicarious achievement relative to a team's performance. The ten factors, each represented by three items, were evaluated by the respondents using seven-point Likert scales anchored by Strongly Disagree (1) and Strongly Agree (7) (see Table 1 for a list of the motives and individual items).

Results

Sample Characteristics

The complete frequency and percentage of responses for the demographic measures are available by contacting the authors. The majority of respondents recruited from the baseball games were male (59%), 43% were between 20 and 34 years old, single (55%), Caucasian (95%), and most were well educated (i.e., 45% had completed at least an undergraduate degree). Those recruited from the softball games were evenly split by gender (49% female and 51% male), 33% were between 20 and 34 years old, married (49%), Caucasian (91%), and well educated (i.e., 53% had completed at least an undergraduate degree). Those recruited from the wrestling matches were predominantly male (75%), 26% were between 20 and 34 years old, married (59%), Caucasian (93%), and well educated (i.e., 49% had completed at least an undergraduate degree).

Sample Characteristic Comparisons

Cross tabulations between sports revealed several differences regarding the demographic makeup of the audience. Spectators at baseball games were significantly more likely to fall within the 20-34 age range than those attending wrestling or softball ($\chi^2=40.218$, $df=8$, $p<.001$). Similarly, baseball spectators were found to be more likely to only have completed a high school degree at the time of data collection than spectators at the other two sports ($\chi^2=83.554$, $df=8$, $p<.001$). Spectators at baseball games were also significantly more likely to be employed part-time or be unemployed ($\chi^2=41.078$, $df=10$, $p<.001$), earn an income of $25,000 or less ($\chi^2=31.971$, $df=6$, $p<.001$), not have children ($\chi^2=15.974$, $df=2$, $p<.001$), and not be married ($\chi^2=28.345$, $df=8$, $p<.001$). These findings suggest that the association of the respondents to the university could explain these differences. That is, a higher percentage of those attending baseball games could be students who attend the university, explaining the younger age, present educational level, present employment status, household income, and current marital status. Additionally, spectators at baseball and wrestling events were found to be more likely to be male than those attending softball games ($\chi^2=36.660$, $df=2$, $p<.001$). Finally, no differences were found among the ethnic makeup of spectators at the three nonrevenue sports examined ($\chi^2=7.338$, d$f=10$, $p=.693$).

Table 1.
Confirmatory Factor Analysis for the Sport Consumer Motivations: Item Loadings (β), Confidence Intervals (CI), Standard Errors (SE), t-values (t), Construct Reliability (CR) and Average Variance Explained (AVE)

Factor and Items[abc]	β	CI	SE	t	CR	AVE
Empathy					.86	.67
Right after a(n) *team name* loss I feel sad.	.821	.780-.861	.025	33.47		
I feel upset as I leave the stadium/arena after a(n) *team name* loss.	.807	.767-.847	.024	33.48		
When the *team name* lose a big game, I feel like I have lost.	.831	.790-.872	.025	33.54		
Social Interaction					.85	.65
I enjoy *team name* games/matches because they provide an opportunity to be with my friends.	.822	.779-.866	.026	31.22		
Wanting to spend time with my friends is one reason I go to *sport* games.	.793	.751-.853	.026	30.96		
Having a chance to see friends is one thing I enjoy about *sport* games.	.812	.769-.855	.026	31.14		
Family					.85	.65
Being with my family is why I enjoy *sport* games.	.716	.677-.755	.024	30.44		
The opportunity to spend time with my family is something I like about attending games.	.784	.742-.825	.025	31.22		
I enjoy *team name* games because they are a good family activity.	.908	.861-.954	.028	32.02		
Team Effort					.84	.64
I support the *team name* because the team gives 100% every game.	.797	.759-.836	.024	33.91		
One reason I am a(n) *team name* fan is because the team plays hard all the time.	.828	.788-.868	.024	34.08		
The effort by the players to always do their best is a primary reason why I follow *sport.*	.779	.741-.817	.023	33.80		
Team Affiliation					.82	.60
I want to feel like I am a(n) *team name.*	.702	.666-.737	.022	32.33		
It is important for me to feel connected to the *team name.*	.814	.774-.855	.025	33.09		
I come to *sport* games so that I will feel like part of the team.	.796	.756-.836	.024	33.00		
Achievement					.80	.58
When the *team name* win I feel like I have won.	.762	.724-.800	.023	32.93		
I feel a personal sense of achievement when the team does well.	.742	.705-.779	.023	32.82		
I feel proud when the team plays really well.	.779	.741-.818	.024	33.03		

Table 1, continued
Confirmatory Factor Analysis for the Sport Consumer Motivations: Item Loadings (β), Confidence Intervals (CI), Standard Errors (SE), t-values (t), Construct Reliability (CR) and Average Variance Explained (AVE)

Factor and Items[abc]	β	CI	SE	t	CR	AVE
Entertainment					.79	.55
The main reason I like *team name* games is because *sport* is good entertainment.	.743	.705-.782	.024	31.62		
I like going to *team name* games because watching *sport* is fun.	.728	.690-.766	.023	31.50		
Team name games are a fun way to spend my time.	.764	.724-.803	.024	31.75		
Skill					.78	.54
One reason I like *team name* games is being able to see well-executed play.	.663	.628-.698	.021	31.13		
Getting to see the superior skills of college athletes is why I enjoy *team name* games.	.734	.696-.772	.023	31.72		
I like *team name* games because I value seeing some of the top college *sport* players.	.810	.768-.851	.025	32.11		
Drama					.77	.53
I enjoy watching *sport* because of the dramatic turn of events that a game can take.	.810	.767-.852	.026	31.37		
An important reason why I go to games is the excitement of two teams "battling" to the end.	.763	.723-.804	.024	31.15		
I like the suspense of a game where the lead changes back and forth.	.589	.556-.622	.020	29.45		
Escape					.74	.49
For me, *sport* games are an escape from my day-to-day activities.	.729	.690-.768	.024	30.57		
I enjoy *team name* games because they are a great change from what I regularly do.	.690	.652-.727	.023	30.30		
I like going to games because when I'm there I forget about all my troubles and cares.	.688	.651-.726	.023	30.29		

Note. [a] Measured on a scale using 1 = Strongly Agree and 7 = Strongly Disagree
[b] Insert name of team for *team name*

Table 2.
A Comparison of Sport Consumption Motives by Sport: Means (Standard Deviations), F-statistics, and p-value.

Motive[a]	Total Sample	Baseball	Softball	Wrestling	F Statistic	p value
	Sport					
Entertainment	5.80 (1.08)	5.71 (1.11)	5.82 (1.04)	5.90 (1.06)	2.535	n.s.
Skill	5.53 (1.13)	5.17 (1.14)	5.61 (1.04)	5.87 (1.05)	34.812	<.01
Drama	5.34 (1.13)	5.05 (1.12)	5.29 (1.09)	5.82 (1.05)	48.689	<.01
Team Effort	5.26 (1.23)	4.88 (1.27)	5.41 (1.15)	5.57 (1.16)	29.384	<.01
Achievement	4.95 (1.31)	4.72 (1.37)	5.08 (1.27)	5.12 (1.26)	9.506	<.01
Social Interaction	4.88 (1.28)	4.85 (1.24)	4.84 (1.28)	4.96 (1.32)	.881	n.s.
Family	4.80 (1.41)	4.64 (1.44)	4.80 (1.41)	4.98 (1.36)	4.573	<.05
Team Affiliation	4.58 (1.44)	4.42 (1.47)	4.65 (1.40)	4.70 (1.44)	3.493	<.05
Empathy	4.37 (1.52)	4.19 (1.55)	4.43 (1.52)	4.52 (1.45)	4.257	<.05

Note. [a] 1 = Strongly Disagree; 7 = Strongly Agree

[b] A multivariate GLM was utilized to assess whether there were differences across sport relative to the sport consumption motives (L=.826, F = (20, 1870), 9.405, $p<.001$). The univariate F-statistics reported in the table were produced by the MANOVA.

Sport Consumer Motives

Before testing whether there were differences in the motives of consumers across the three sports, a confirmatory factor analysis (CFA) was computed using the RAMONA Covariance Structure Modeling technique (available in the SYSTAT 9.0 (1999) statistical package) to verify the internal consistency and the construct validity of the sport consumption motives. The CFA was necessary because two new constructs were included, and the wording of several items was changed for this study. The results reported in Table 1 indicate that nine of the ten factors showed good internal consistency and construct reliability.

The construct reliabilities for the ten motives ranged from .77 to .86, which exceed the minimum level (.70) recommended by Nunnally and Bernstein (1994). Regarding individual item loadings, Skill, Team Affiliation, and Drama each had one item that did not load at the recommended .707 level (Fornell & Larcker, 1981). Two of the Escape items did not load at the recommended level. The measures of average variance extracted (AVE) for nine of the motives indicated that the amount of variance explained by the constructs was greater than the variance explained by measurement error, including the three constructs that had one item loading below .707. The measure of AVE for Escape indicated that the amount of variance explained by the construct (AVE=0.49) was less than the variance explained by measurement error. The Escape factor was deemed unreliable and consequently was not included in the subsequent data analysis.

Overall Difference Tests

A multivariate GLM was used to assess whether there were significant differences across the three sports with respect to the sport consumer motives. Results indicated that there were significant differences across the three sports (L=.826, $F(20, 1870)=9.405$, $p<.01$) on seven of the nine motives (see Table 2). Entertainment and Social Interaction were the only motives on which there were no significant differences.

For Skill and Drama, there were significant differences across all three sports. Those attending wrestling matches expressed the strongest agreement with the ideas that they enjoyed the athletes' physical skills ($M=5.87$) and the drama of matches ($M=5.82$); consumers of women's softball had the next highest ratings for the two factors ($M=5.61$ and $M=5.29$ respectively). Those attending baseball games had the lowest ratings for Skill ($M=5.17$) and Drama ($M=5.05$).

Consumers of wrestling matches and women's softball games had similar ratings for Team Effort ($M=5.57$ and $M=5.41$ respectively) and Achievement ($M=5.12$ and $M=5.08$ respectively). The ratings of Team Effort and Achievement for those attending baseball games were neutral ($M=4.88$ and $M=4.72$ respectively). The only significant differences for Family, Team Affiliation, and Empathy were between those attending baseball games and those attending wrestling matches. Although the ratings were statistically different, the mean scores on the three motives indicate that across the three sports Family, Team Affiliation, and Empathy were not primary motives driving peoples' interest in the sports.

Discussion and Implications

Sport managers within intercollegiate athletics are faced with the challenge of generating more revenues to offset rising program costs. One option to consider is generating additional revenues from ticket sales for nonrevenue sports. The two-fold purpose of the current study was (1) to identify some of the motives that influence an individual's interest in nonrevenue collegiate sports, and (2) to ascertain whether similar motives influence consumption across multiple nonrevenue sports. Understanding some of the intrapersonal motives that drive consumers' interest in nonrevenue sports will provide sport marketers with information that can be used to develop promotional campaigns to target specific consumer motivations helping to increase attendance, and ultimately offset costs to the programs.

Overall, the results suggest that interest in the three nonrevenue sporting events was based on factors associated with sport in general. Consumers of men's baseball, women's softball, and men's wrestling all rated the sport-related motives (i.e., entertainment, skill, drama, and team effort) higher than the motives pertaining to self-definition (i.e., achievement, empathy, and team affiliation) and motives related to personal benefits (i.e., social interaction and family). These results support the authors' supposition that some sport consumers attend college sporting events based on their enjoyment of watching athletes give their best efforts in a sport they enjoy playing. The higher ratings for the sport-related motives are an important finding for marketers of intercollegiate athletics because they suggest that consumers were most interested in components that are easily promoted.

One implication of the results is that the promotional campaigns of nonrevenue sports may be conducted in a blanket fashion in order to cut or eliminate costs. Considering that there was no significant difference across the sports regarding entertainment value, marketers can decide whether to promote individual sports, or to develop promotions that emphasize the entertainment value of multiple nonrevenue sports. Sport marketers at the intercollegiate level may be able to efficiently cross-promote nonrevenue sports through the use of a single campaign focusing upon the entertainment aspect of various sports, which could include highlighting the skill of the athletes, the drama of events, and/or watching athletes give their best efforts. Other suggestions for cross-promotion include in-game announcements of upcoming events of other in-season events, as well as inserting flyers in sports programs highlighting the entertainment aspects of other in-season nonrevenue sport programs. Going further, athletic programs may develop special offerings like a multisport pass that can be used for attending multiple nonrevenue sporting events.

Looking at the differences between specific sports, the wrestling spectators rated all of the motives higher than the baseball and softball spectators. Similarly, those attending softball games rated all but one of the motives (Social Interaction) higher than the baseball spectators. These findings are noteworthy because they provide information to athletic administrators regarding potential promotional themes for specific nonrevenue sports. For example, because wrestling spectators rated the Drama higher than the baseball spectators, promotional materials for the wrestling matches could focus upon the suspense and uncertainty of outcome associated with wrestling matches.

The lack of strong agreement with eight of the nine motives among those attending baseball games suggests that people attended games just for the entertainment value or, more likely, due to other motives not measured. Considering the differences in the demographic characteristics between the consumers of baseball, softball, and wrestling, other possibilities that bear further investigation are that students may attend nonrevenue sports because of the (generally) low cost to attend or because they want to enjoy a spring afternoon. Promotional campaigns could focus on the entertainment value in terms of fun at low or no cost, or as a chance to enjoy a beautiful spring day in an effort to foster increased student attendance at baseball games.

A second contribution of the study is extending our knowledge of sport consumer motivations. Previous research has found that people attend sporting events because they are interested in a specific sport or team (Funk et al., 2002), they enjoy the entertainment of sports (James & Ross, 2002), the drama and action of sports (James & Ridinger, 2002; Kwon & Trail, 2001), and the athletes' physical skills (James & Ross, 2002). Considering the results of previous research and the findings from the current study, two points are important for marketers to consider. First, there are aspects of sport that appeal to consumers that cut across sport and the different levels of sport. The entertainment of sport that is likely drawn from the drama, physical skills, and action associated with sport are motives that may serve as topics for promotional campaigns regardless of the sport or the level of a sport (e.g., college or professional). At the same time, there are specific motives associated with different sports and different levels of a sport that may also be developed in promotional campaigns. For example, marketers of college athletics may concentrate on broad campaigns to attract consumers based on the entertainment of sport, using pictures or clips of multiple sports that emphasize the ideas of drama and action. If the resources are available to focus on specific sports, marketers may choose to highlight motives that have a distinct appeal for specific sports. For example, promotional campaigns for wrestling could focus on the drama involved in matches and the effort put forth by the athletes. In other levels of sport, such as minor league baseball, marketers may focus on the entertainment of games and the opportunity to socialize with friends (James & Ross, 2002). The results suggest that marketers need a better appreciation of sport consumer motivations that cut across sport and those that are unique to specific sports.

As with any study, several limitations should be noted. The current study examined fans of only three sports: men's baseball, women's softball, and men's wrestling. Additional research should examine other nonrevenue sports to determine whether there are other similarities and differences (e.g., volleyball, swimming, tennis, track and field). The current study only measured ten motives thought to influence the consumption of sport. As noted, there was strong agreement only for one of the motives among baseball consumers. Future research should consider what other motives may be unique to different sports. Additional work is also needed to refine and improve the items used to measure sport consumer motives. Finally, the current study only examined intrapersonal motives; future research should examine the influence of demand variables and intrapersonal motives on sport consumption. For example, the low cost to attend nonrevenue sports may be a key motivator for college students. Work should continue in this area in order to provide marketers with a better understanding of the multiple factors that influence sport consumption.

References

Baade, R. A., & Tiehen, L. J. (1990). An analysis of Major League Baseball attendance, 1969 –1987. *Journal of Sport and Social Issues, 14*, 14-32.

Branvold, S. (1992). The utilization of fence signage in college baseball. *Sport Marketing Quarterly, 1*(2), 29-32.

Cialdini, R. B., Borden, R. J., Thorne, A., Walker, M. R., Freeman, S., & Sloan, L. R. (1976). Basking in reflected glory: Three (football) field studies. *Journal of Personality and Social Psychology, 34*, 366-375.

Fornell, C., & Larcker, D. (1981). Evaluating structural equation models with unobservable variables and measurement error. *Journal of Marketing Research. 28*(1), 39-50.

Fulks, D. (2002). *Revenues and expenses of Division I and II intercollegiate athletic programs: Financial trends and relationships-2001.* National Collegiate Athletic Association. Indianapolis, IN.

Fulks, D. (2000). *Revenues and expenses of Division I and II intercollegiate athletic programs: Financial trends and relationships-1999.* National Collegiate Athletic Association. Indianapolis, IN.

Funk, D., Mahony, D., & Ridinger, L. (2002). Characterizing consumer motivation as individual difference factors: augmenting the Sport Interest Inventory (SII) to explain level of spectator support. *Sport Marketing Quarterly. 11*(1), 33-43.

Greenstein, T. N., & Marcum. J. P. (1981). Factors affecting attendance of major league baseball: Team performance. *Review of Sport & Leisure, 6*(2), 21-34.

Hansen, H., & Gauthier, R. (1989). Factors affecting attendance at professional sport events. *Journal of Sport Management, 3*, 15-32.

Howard, D., & Crompton, J. (2003). *Financing Sport* (2nd ed.). Fitness Information Technology, Inc., Morgantown, WV.

James, J., & Ridinger, L. (2002). Female and Male Sport Fans: A Comparison of Sport Consumption Motives. *Journal of Sport Behavior, 25*(3), 1-19.

James, J., & Ross, S. (2002). The motives of sport consumers: A comparison of Major and Minor League baseball. *International Journal of Sport Management, 3*(3), 180-198.

Kahle, L. R., Kambara, K. M., & Rose, G. M. (1996). A functional model of fan attendance motivations for college football. *Sport Marketing Quarterly, 5*(4), 51-60.

Kwon, H., & Trail, G. (2001). Sport fan motivation: A comparison of American students and international students. *Sport Marketing Quarterly, 10*(3), 147-155.

Mahony, D. F., Nakazawa, M., Funk, D. C., James, J. D., & Gladden, J. M. (2002). Motivational factors impacting the behavior of J. League spectators. *Sport Management Review, 5*(1), 1-24.

Masteralexis, L., Barr, C., & Hums, M. (1998). *Principles and Practice of Sport Management.* Gaithersburg, MD: Aspen Publishers, Inc.

Milne, G. R., & McDonald, M. A. (1999). Motivations of the sport consumer. In *Sports marketing: Managing the exchange process* (pp. 21-38). Sudbury, MA: Jones and Bartlett Publishers.

Nunnally, J., & Bernstein, I. (1994). *Psychometirc theory* (3rd ed.). New York, NY: McGraw-Hill.

Schofield, J. A. (1983). Performance and attendance at professional team sports. *Journal of Sport Behavior, 6*, 196-206.

Sloan, L. R. (1989). The motives of sports fans. In J. H. Goldstein (Ed.), *Sports, games, and play: Social and psychological viewpoints* (2nd ed.) (pp. 175-240). Hillsdale, NJ: Lawrence Erlbaum Associates.

Trail, G. T., Anderson, D. F., & Fink, J. (2000). A theoretical model of sport spectator consumption behavior. *International Journal of Sport Management, 3*, 154-180.

Trail, G., & James, J. (2001). An analysis of the sport fan motivation scale. *Journal of Sport Behavior, 24*, 108-127.

Wann, D.L. (1993). Aggression among highly identified spectators as a function of their need to maintain positive social identity. *Journal of Sport and Social Issues. 17*(2), 134-143.

Wann, D. L. (1995). Preliminary validation of the Sport Fan Motivation Scale. *Journal of Sport and Social Issues, 19*, 377-396.

Wann, D.L., & Branscombe N.R. (1990). Die-hard and fair-weather fans: Effects of identification on BIRGing and CORFing tendencies. *Journal of Sport and Social Issues. 14*(2), 103-117.

Zhang, J. J., Pease, D. G., Hui, S. C., & Michaud, T. J. (1995). Variables affecting the spectator decision to attend NBA games. *Sport Marketing Quarterly, 4*(4), 29-39.

Zhang, J. J., Smith, D. W., Pease, D. G., & Jambor, E. A. (1997). Negative influence of market competitors on the attendance of professional sport games: The case of a minor league hockey team. *Sport Marketing Quarterly, 6*(3), 34-40.

10

Measuring the Motives of Sport Event Attendance:

Bridging the Academic-Practitioner Divide to Understanding Behavior

Daniel C. Funk, Kevin Filo, Anthony A. Beaton, and Mark Pritchard

Measuring Core Facets of Motivation for Sport Event Attendance

Sport event attendance represents a significant aspect of leisure and recreation in many countries. Few hedonic consumptive experiences create greater interest and investment than watching competitive sports (Baade, 2003; Pons, Mourali, & Nyeck, 2006). In 2005-06, 10.5 million Australians over the age of 15 participated in organized sport and physical recreation (Australian Bureau of Statistics, 2007a). Furthermore, 7.1 million Australians over the age of 15 attended at least one sport event (Australian Bureau of Statistics, 2007b). These numbers reflect the large audience in place for sport organizations; however, the demand for spectator sport can fluctuate and fragment due to market forces (Andreff & Szymanski, 2006), while competition among mass entertainment sport in Australia has increased.

A number of challenges exist for sport franchises to confront the fluctuation of spectator interest to build and sustain volume. General population surveys reveal overall attendance at sport events has remained virtually unchanged from 1995 despite the introduction of the Hyundai A-League in 2005 and expansion of teams in the National Rugby League and Australian Football League. Gender and age considerations demonstrate men (56%) are more likely to attend a sport event than women (41%), but both groups steadily declined after age 24. This decline is problematic given Australians are living longer than ever—life expectancy for women is 83 years of age, while men are expected to live to 78 (Australian Bureau of Statistics, 2007c). In addition, the cost of replacing one spectator can be six times more expensive than retaining an existing spectator (Rosenberg & Czepiel, 1983).

An aging population with a declining attendance rate, along with increased competition among sport and entertainment products, has made it important for sport managers to better understand what motivates individuals to attend events. Academic research has provided some guidance in this area by developing an array of multi-attribute scales to measure motives for attending professional and collegiate competitive sport events (Funk, Mahony & Ridinger, 2002; Madrigal, 2006; Trail & James, 2001; Wann, 1995). On the surface, attending a sport event would appear a simple behavior, but academic tools used to explain such behavior are complex and use a number of measures so as to be comprehensive enough to capture a wide variety of individual motives. In addition, the specific sport event (e.g., football, women's basketball, motorsport) also involves contextual differences (Wann, Grieve, Zapalac, & Pease, 2008) that must be considered. This has led to a proliferation of survey tools with multiple constructs making survey content decisions difficult for academics and industry professionals. However, the ability of these scales to explain past game attendance is often not reported and the few studies that do report this information reveal explanatory ability of 20% or less.

The purpose of this research is to provide a parsimonious measurement tool capable of providing guidance to academics and practitioners for explaining sport event attendance behavior. A 10-item multi-attribute scale that assesses five facets of motivation: Socialization, Performance, Excitement, Esteem, and Diversion (SPEED) is offered and tested. Details of this research are divided into five sections. First, a review of prior work on sport consumer motivation is given. Second, scale requirements by academe and industry are discussed. Third, the conceptualization of the SPEED scale is provided. Fourth, the research methods employed are described. Finally, the results are reported, leading to conclusions regarding managerial implications, limitations, and directions for future research.

Literature Review

Sport Consumer Motivation

Motivation represents an activated internal state that arouses, directs, and leads to behavior (Iso-Ahola, 1982; Mowen & Minor, 1998). A general definition suggests motivation reflects a process with five sequential stages: a) need recognition; b) tension reduction; c) drive state; d) want; and e) goal-directed behavior (Schiffman & Kanuk, 2001). The want stage within this process receives considerable attention from academics and marketers because it represents the pathway toward a specific form of behavior to satisfy a need or acquire benefits. There are numerous pathways a person may take to receive desirable outcomes based on a unique set of experiences, socio-cultural upbringing, and personality. Hence, motivation reflects an internal desire to take a pathway because it provides opportunities to satisfy needs and receive benefits through acquisition (MacInnis, Moorman, & Jaworski, 1991).

Motives for sport event attendance are dynamic, multifaceted, and have been examined through a number of different frameworks. These approaches include Maslow's (1954) hierarchy of needs, Iso-Ahola's (1982) escape-seeking model, the premise of push-pull factors (Crompton, 1979), psychological needs (Sloan, 1989), and stages of increasing involvement (Funk & James, 2001). The variety of paradigms underscores the challenges that exist in effectively assessing sport consumer motivation. Research suggests that motives for leisure activity are dynamic and should be viewed as changing throughout a consumer's lifetime (Beaton & Funk, 2008; Iso-Ahola, 1980). Such fluctuations can also be found in spectator sport (Funk & James, 2006; Ross, 2007). In addition, comparative studies reveal motives may vary by country, sport, and emotional attachment (Koo &

Hardin, 2008; Wann et al., 2008; Won & Kitamura, 2007). These ongoing challenges, along with increasing importance for understanding the motivations driving sport consumers among sport managers, contributed to the development of a vast array of instruments for investigating consumer motivation to attend sport events.

Existing Motivation Scales

Sport event research has utilized a number of discrete facets of motivation or motives among spectators and fans (Funk, Ridinger, & Moorman, 2004; Madrigal, 2006; Pease & Zhang, 2001; Trail & James, 2001; Wann, 1995). In general, these motives can be categorized as utilitarian or hedonic (Hirshman & Holbrook, 1982). Utilitarian motives are functional and represent objective desires or tangible attributes of a sport product or service including venue services, admission costs, marquee players and coaches, promotions, scheduling of games, new arenas, accessibility, and the relationship between socio-demographic variables and watching sports (Gladden & Funk, 2002; Ross, 2007; Wakefield & Sloan, 1995). In contrast, hedonic motives are experiential in nature involving subjective emotional responses to the product such as excitement, fantasy, eustress, vicarious achievement, escape, aesthetics, group affiliation, and social interaction (Funk et al., 2004; Madrigal, 2006; Trail & James, 2001; Wann, 1995). The dominance of scales to measure hedonic motives compared to utilitarian motives stems from the subjective nature of the sport experience and the unique aspects of various sport experiences (Kahle, Kambara, & Rose, 1996; Madrigal, 2006).

The growing body of knowledge in sport consumer behavior has provided a number of beneficial scales to measure intrinsic motives for attending sport events. This line of inquiry represents a micro approach to understanding spectator motivation by dividing the construct into smaller representative dimensions (i.e., motivational content types or motives) to assess the intimate workings of motivation. Kiesler, Collins, and Miller (1969) suggest one way social science can understand constructs like motivation is via "the delineation of gross variables into more atomistic ones" (p. 279), which divides motivation into smaller representative factors. This has led to the proliferation of scales ranging from 7 to 18 constructs to measure motivation. In general, each construct is measured with three items requiring 21 to 48 questions to be placed on a survey.

A critique of published research using existing motivation scales reveals most studies rarely report or explain game attendance behavior. Only four published articles were found that report this information and the variance explained in game attendance ranged from 15% and 20%. Hoye and Lilis (2008) used the *Motivation Scale for Sport Consumption* (MSSC) to explain 20% of the variance in attending away games among 93 members of an Australian football club. Ridinger and Funk (2006) used the *Sport Interest Inventory* (SII) to explain 14% and 18% in home game attendance among 951 spectators at men's and women's NCAA basketball games. Neale and Funk (2006) used the SII to explain 19% of the variance in home game attendance among 651 club supporters in Australia. Mahony and colleagues (2002) used elements of the SII and MSSC to explain 15% of the variance in games attended among 1201 spectators at J League matches. Beyond these studies, the vast majority of published research uses existing constructs and scales to explain variance in attitudes (e.g., team commitment, behavioral intention) or a composite attitude-behavior measure (e.g., loyalty variable of commitment and attendance behavior) or describe differences between segments (Funk et al., 2002;

Theodorakis, & Alexandris, 2008; Trail & James, 2001). Hence, the multi-attribute scales appear to be more relevant for explaining attitude-related information among consumer groups than game attendance behavior.

An alternative approach used in related disciplines of leisure and marketing has adopted a macro perspective to measure complex constructs such as motivation (Gerbing & Anderson, 1988; Iwasaki & Havitz, 2004). The macro approach focuses on developing a nomological understanding of a construct to help examine its interrelationships with other key variables. Motivation to engage in a leisure activity can either be measured with four dimensions of escape, competency, mastery, and socialization (Beard & Ragheb, 1983) or a single strength of motivation dimension (Carroll & Alexandris, 1997). Early work on the involvement construct examined the internal structure and definition (Dimanche, Havitz, & Howard, 1991), while later efforts examined links with other key constructs (Iwasaki & Havitz, 2004). The involvement construct as an enduring state of motivation has been measured as unidimensional (Mittal, 1995; Zaichkowsky, 1985) or three dimensions of pleasure, sign, and centrality (Kyle & Mowen, 2005). The macro approach has been used in sport to explain larger constructs such as identification and satisfaction, allowing a more parsimonious examination of the constructs' relationship to antecedents and outcomes (Kahle, Kambara, & Rose, 1996; Laverie & Arnett, 2000). In addition, some researchers suggest the feasibility of a single-item measure for a psychological construct (Drolet & Morrison, 2001; Kwon & Trail, 2005), but this can become problematic for model testing.

Hybrid Approach

This research adopts a hybrid approach incorporating both macro and micro means to measure and explain sport attendance behavior. The hybrid approach blends the demands of both academics and practitioners for theoretical and applied scales to investigate motives capable of explaining sport event attendance. Academics have labeled practice-oriented research as unintellectual and desire a clear delineation between theory and practice-oriented research (Razzaque, 1998). Although academics focus on theorizing and producing new knowledge, practitioners typically desire pragmatic solutions with a bottom line focus (Razzaque, 1998). Henderson, Presley, and Bialeschki (2004) suggest such demarcations are unnecessary and call for bridging the academic-practitioner divide. Flynn and Pearcy (2001) argue that the "the ideal characteristics of a scale are not the same if a researcher is measuring a construct for diagnostic or managerial reasons vs. measuring the same construct for theoretical explanation"(p. 415). The authors suggest that if "the aim of the research is to test theory by examining constructs in relation to other phenomena then 'no longer is an inventory of items necessary'" (p. 418). Although academic demands have led to the proliferation of multi-attribute scales, explanations of game attendance remain limited. In addition, practitioners demand shorter scales to increase efficiency because shorter scales place fewer burdens on respondents (DeVellis, 2003).

The hybrid approach meets both academic and practitioner demands. A concise list of core constructs to measure motives could provide an efficient means to explain game attendance and examine motivation's relationship with other theoretical constructs in complex models (Flynn & Pearcy, 2001; Iwasaki & Havitz, 2004). In addition, the number of items used to measure each construct could be reduced to two, allowing for complex model testing (Hair, Black, Babin, Anderson, & Tatham, 2006). Such an approach would also allow for tests of convergent, discriminant, and nomological validity to provide a stable and known factor structure so theorists may rely on its consistent performance in complex models (Flynn & Pearcy, 2001; Spector, 1992). In doing so, it is important to recognize that to provide a stronger research-practice relationship, the key words and language of constructs used and tested by researchers needs to correspond to that of practitioners (Henderson et al., 2004). The hybrid approach represents a refinement of existing work in order to guide future research on sport consumer behavior and places significance on both theoretical and practical relevance. The next section provides a discussion from which a parsimonious set of motives capable of explaining game attendance is developed.

SPEED Facets of Motivation

The present research conceptualizes spectator motivation as representing five motivational content facets: Socialization, Performance, Excitement, Esteem, and Diversion (SPEED). These themes represent a parsimonious set of motives for why individuals seek out and attend sport events that have been used in previous research. The themes also represent a convergence of constructs from previous instruments. The five themes reflect core motivational facets that drive individuals to seek out sport experiences to satisfy needs and receive benefits. The acronym SPEED is useful for industry to refer to core motivational themes. A detailed description of each SPEED facet of motivation is provided in the Appendix and the facets are briefly reviewed next.

Socialization relates to the interpersonal aspect of sport. Specifically, socialization represents a desire for sociability and the extent to which a person perceives attending a sport event as an opportunity to interact with family, friends, and other spectators. Individuals are motivated to seek a sport event experience due to opportunities for the enhancement of human relationships through external interaction with other spectators, participants, friends, and family. This definition overlaps with group affiliation, family bonding, friends bonding, social interaction, and camaraderie (Funk et al., 2004; Madrigal, 2006; Trial & James, 2001; Wann, 1995). Performance relates to the extent to which an individual believes that sport events provide excellence, beauty, and creativity of athletic performance. Individuals are motivated to seek a sport event experience due to opportunities to enjoy the grace, skill, and artistry of athletic movement. Performance encompasses motives of aesthetics, aggression, physical skill, flow, and performance evaluation (Funk et al., 2004; Madrigal, 2006; Trial & James, 2001; Wann, 1995).

Excitement represents the extent to which a sport event is perceived as providing stimulation provided by the consumption experience. Excitement represents a desire for intellectual stimulation. Individuals are motivated to seek a sport event experience due to opportunities for mental action and exploration from the atmospheric conditions created by the uncertainty of participation and competition, and the spectacle of associated activities. Excitement includes motives of entertainment, eustress, economic, drama, entertainment, player and sport interest, wholesome environment, and physical and celebrity attraction (Funk et al., 2004; Madrigal, 2006; Trial & James, 2001; Wann, 1995). Esteem reflects the extent to which an individual perceives attending a sport event as providing an opportunity for vicarious achievement. Individuals are motivated to seek a sport event experience due to opportunities for achievement and challenge that produce a sense of mastery and a heightened sense of personal and collective self-esteem. Esteem relates closely to motives of self-esteem, group affiliation achievement, community support, and vicarious achievement (Funk et al., 2004; Madrigal, 2006; Trial & James, 2001; Wann, 1995). Finally, diversion reflects the extent to which a person perceives attending a sport event provides an opportunity to escape the hassles and normal routine of everyday life. Diversion represents a desire for mental well-being. Individuals are motivated to seek a sport event experience due to opportunities to escape and remove themselves from daily work and life routines that create stress. Diversion highlights previous motives of escape and fantasy (Funk et al., 2004; Madrigal, 2006; Trial & James, 2001; Wann, 1995).

The five SPEED facets reviewed provide a parsimonious conceptualization of the multi-faceted nature of sport consumer motivation. The current research follows a hybrid approach to conceptualize core facets of motivation in order to develop a valid number of practically useful motivational constructs as a means toward better understanding their relationship with consumption activities (Flynn & Pearcy, 2001). Such conceptualization is not without controversy as the potential for theoretical overlap among the five facets is likely, as well as the potential loss of specific information in reducing the number of constructs and items to measure each construct.

The SPEED conceptualization represents an initial step in bridging the gap between academics' and practitioners' demands in hopes of creating further research discussion (DeVellis, 2003). Such conceptualization also conforms to the idea of "sensemaking" proposed by Weick (1993) such that reality is an ongoing accomplishment that emerges from efforts to create order and make retrospective sense of what occurs "... [and] make things rationally accountable to themselves and others" (p. 635). Hence, five facets are considered to measure motivation rather than attempting to directly reconcile existing scales and literature. As the initial step, empirical evidence is needed to substantiate these core motivational facets. Of particular relevance would be the ability of a 10-item SPEED scale to explain game attendance.

In summary, explaining and predicting sport event attendance remains important to sport marketers and academics. Academic research has provided a variety of measurement tools with various motivational constructs to examine sport attendance, but such tools often are perceived as burdensome and complex by practitioners and the prediction of attendance behavior is limited. To meet the research demands of both practitioner and academic, a theoretical and applied measurement tool is required to foster a stronger research-practice relationship. The examination of constructs from a number of scales led to the identification of five motivational themes used in previous empirical studies from which a parsimonious set of motives was developed: Socialization, Performance, Excitement, Esteem, and Diversion. These SPEED facets represent a hybrid approach to measuring a parsimonious set of motives to explain game attendance behavior. The method employed to test the reliability and validity of these measures is described next.

Method

The objective of the data collection was to assess the psychometric properties of the SPEED scale and test its ability to explain game attendance. A survey was developed to measure the five facets based on the existing literature and commonalities shared among the instruments reviewed. The SPEED scale was distributed to spectators at a professional football game and to individuals in the general population.

Participants

The survey group consisted of 410 spectators attending an Australian Rules Football (AFL) game and 2,421 individuals intercepted at various locations within the geographic location of three sport teams in southern Queensland. The sample characteristics were 65% male, 44% in the age range 25-44 years, 38% had a high school degree followed by 37% with a university degree, 48% were of Oceania/Australia ethnicity followed by 27% European and 9% Asian, 52% were living with a partner, 37% had children, and 56% earned between $2500-6000 AUD per month. The breakdown per sport team surveyed were (Australian Rules Football; AFL = 49%), (Australian Football League; A-League = 27%), and (National Rugby League; NRL = 24%).

Materials

A paper and pencil questionnaire was used to collect responses. The 10-item SPEED questionnaire was adopted and adapted from previous work in measuring spectator sport motives (i.e., Funk et al., 2004; Madrigal, 2006; Trail & James, 2001; Wann, 1995). Each facet was assessed using two items randomly placed within the questionnaire on Likert scale items using seven-point scales anchored with [1] strongly disagree to [7] strongly agree. Outcome measures of game attendance behavior and team commitment were included to examine the explanatory ability of the SPEED facets. Behavior was assessed with a single self-report measure of past behavior "number of games attended last season." A three-item commitment scale (Neale & Funk, 2006) was used to measure the level of psychological commitment to the team (i.e., I am a committed fan of the team, I am a loyal supporter of the team; Win, lose or draw I'm a loyal fan of the team) on Likert scale items using seven-point scales anchored with [1] strongly disagree to [7] strongly agree. A battery of questions was used to assess demographics of gender, income, ethnicity, education, and age.

Procedure

The 10 items representing the five SPEED facets were included in a single-page questionnaire administered to spectators attending an Australian Rules Football match in Brisbane, Australia. Questionnaires were distributed by 10 student researchers stationed at five randomly selected gates at the venue. Every fifth spectator was intercepted upon entrance and asked to complete the questionnaire and return the instrument to the researcher upon completion. The number of refusals was low. A total of 410 usable questionnaires were collected.

The SPEED scale was also administered at various locations within geographic proximity of three sport teams (Australian Rules Football, A-League Soccer, and National Rugby League) in southern Queensland. Questionnaires were distributed by 20 trained researchers at shopping malls, local sport competitions, train stations, cinemas, car washes, and sport centers. Individuals were intercepted and asked a qualifying question: "Are you aware of Team X?" If the response was affirmative, the individual was asked to complete the questionnaire and return it immediately to the researcher. Again, the number of refusals was low. A total of 2,421 usable questionnaires were collected for the analysis. The surveys were entered into the Statistical Package for the Social Sciences (SPSS) 14.0 for analysis.

Table 1.
Correlations, Means, Standard Deviations and Reliability Measures for the SPEED Facets of Sport Event Motivation, Game Attendance and Team Commitment (N = 2,831)

	SOC	PER	EST	EXC	DIV	BEH	COM	M	SD	α
SOC	1							4.08	1.73	.86
PER	.43*	1						3.79	1.73	.83
EST	.47*	.56*	1					3.70	1.95	.85
EXC	.53*	.68*	.67*	1				4.57	1.77	.77
DIV	.62*	.52*	.52*	.61*	1			3.89	1.66	.83
BEH	.32*	.41*	.51*	.49*	.37*	1		3.53	2.01	
COM	.45*	.57*	.84*	.71*	.52*	.60*	1	4.11	2.08	.95

Table 2.
Measurement Results for Confirmatory Factor Analysis of SPEED Facets (N = 2,831)

	β	T values
Socialization (SOC)	VE = .60	
The chance to socialize with others	.74	33.07
The opportunity to interact with other people	.80	34.72
Performance (PER)	VE = .78	
The gracefulness associated with the game	.89	38.79
The natural elegance of the game	.87	34.76
Excitement (EXC)	VE = .77	
I enjoy the excitement associated with the games	.88	30.85
I find the games very exciting	.88	29.35
Esteem (EST)	VE = .75	
I feel like I have won when the team wins	.92	45.24
I get a sense of accomplishment when the team wins	.80	41.15
Diversion (DIV)	VE = .75	
I can get away from the tension in my life	.85	35.65
It provides me with a break from my daily routine	.88	32.35

Note:
β = Standardized Regression Coefficients

Results

The means and standard deviations for each of the five SPEED facets are reported in Table 1. The mean scores ranged from 3.70 to 4.57, with Excitement revealing the highest mean score and Esteem the lowest mean score. The Cronbach alphas were calculated since multi-item scales were used and indicate the items used to measure the constructs were reliable and all above the $\mu = .70$ benchmark (Nunnally & Bernstein, 1994). Correlations are presented in Table 1 and reveal significant correlations between the five constructs ranging from 0.43 to 0.68.

Measurement Details

A confirmatory factor analysis (CFA) using AMOS 7.0 (Arbuckle, 1994) indicated an acceptable fit for the psychometric properties of the SPEED facets: $\chi^2 = 280.12/df = 25$. A covariance matrix taken from these respondents was used as the input data. The measurement model examined the relationships between the five SPEED facets and 10 manifest items. The five latent SPEED facets were left to freely correlate. The parameter estimates and the accompanying *t*-test of significance for the relationships between each scale item and its respective SPEED facet were significant ($p < .01$). The standardized regression coefficients (β) reported in Table 2 for each construct exceeded the required .707 minimum, the squared multiple correlation coefficient for each item exceeded .50, and the average variance extracted by the three items for each construct was above the .50 benchmark (Bagozi & Yi, 1988). A test of discriminant validity revealed the average variance extracted by each of the items representing a construct exceeded the square of correlation between each construct (Fornell & Larcker, 1981). See Table 2 for Average Variance Extracted (VE).

Five fit indexes were used to evaluate how well the measurement model fit the data collected: Root Mean Squared Error of Approximation (RMSEA), Normed Fit Index (NFI), Goodness of Fit Index (GFI), Comparative Fit Index (CFI), and Standardized Route Mean Squared (SRMR) (Bagozzi & Yi, 1988; Bollen, 1989; Hair et al., 2006; Hu & Bentler, 1999; Tabachnick & Fidell, 1996). Fit statistics were: RMSEA = .06; SRMR = .02; GFI = .98; NFI = .99; and CFI = .99.

A comparison of SPEED facets by game attendance is presented in Table 3. Reported number of games attended was used to create two groups: No Prior Game Attendance (N = 1,224) and Previous Game Attendance (N = 1,607). The two groups were used to compare responses to SPEED facets to assess the role of prior attendance on responses. Multivariate Analysis of Variance (MANOVA) revealed respondents in the previous game attendance group were more likely to agree attending games provided SPEED benefits of SOC $F(1, 2892) = 38.37$, PER $F(1, 2892) = 539.97$, EXC $F(1, 2892) = 1123.11$, EST $F(1, 2892) = 961.86$, and DIV $F(1, 2892) = 551.60$). A one sample *t*-test using a test value of 4.0 revealed that the No Prior Game Attendance group rated the SPEED facets significantly below the 4.0 mid point, indicating they did not agree that attending games provide SPEED benefits. In contrast, the Prior Game Attendance group rated the SPEED facets significantly higher than the 4.0 midpoint, indicating they were more likely to agree that games provided SPEED benefits.

The means, standard deviations, and correlations for past game attendance and team commitment are reported in Table 1. Multiple linear regression was employed to examine the predictive ability of the five SPEED factors for game attendance and team commit-

Table 3.
MANOVA Comparison of Past Attendance Group on SPEED Facets Ratings (N = 2,831)

	No Prior Game Attendance N = 1,224	Prior Game Attendance N = 1,607
SPEED Facet	**Mean ***	**Mean +**
Socialization	3.39 (1.77)	4.62 (1.50)
Performance	3.00 (1.67)	4.42 (1.52)
Esteem	2.57 (1.77)	4.66 (1.62)
Excitement	3.49 (1.77)	5.41 (1.25)
Diversion	3.12 (1.50)	4.45 (1.76)

* Mean scores significantly lower than 4.0 midpoint $p < .01$
\+ Mean scores significantly higher than 4.0 midpoint $p < .01$

ment. The regression model presented in Table 4 indicates that 30% (R^2 = .30) of the variance in past attendance was explained by three of the SPEED facets, PER, EST, and EXC $F(5, 2{,}825) = 244.56$ $p < .01$. Multiple linear regression was next employed to examine the predictive ability of the five SPEED factors for team commitment. The regression model is presented in Table 4 and indicates that 75% (R^2 = .75) of the variance in team commitment was explained by facets of SOC, EST, EXC, and DIV $F(5, 2{,}825) = 1705.39$ $p < .01$.

Discussion

The current research provides a 10-item multi-attribute measurement tool capable of measuring parsimonious facets of motivation for sport event attendance. The SPEED motivational facets of Socialization, Performance, Excitement, Esteem, and Diversion represent five unique but related reasons why individuals seek out spectator sport experiences because the consumption experience provides opportunities to acquire needs and benefits (MacInnis et al., 1991). The psychometric properties of the SPEED motives and their ability to explain past attendance behavior and team commitment were tested using data collected during an Australian Rules Football (AFL) match and surveys distributed to the general population at various locations within geographic proximity of three sport leagues. The following section provides a discussion of the research findings.

SPEED Conceptualization

The SPEED motives represent a hybrid approach to conceptualize sport event attendance motivation. The hybrid approach provides a parsimonious set of motives to meet theoretical and practical demands (DeVellis, 2003; Flynn & Pearcy, 2001). SPEED motives are not intended to provide new theoretical development nor scale development advancement, but are listed based upon the principles of "sense making" to build a stronger research-practice relationship (Weick, 1993). Definitions for each motive were provided in the Appendix to clarify definitional meaning for the constructs. Hence, SPEED creates a stronger research-practice relationship as the work of researchers can easily be translated and used by practitioners (Henderson et al., 2004). SPEED motives can now be used to focus on interrelationships with other key variables (Gerbing & Anderson, 1988). This work reverses the micro trend in sport consumer research that has led to the proliferation of scales and items to measure a list of factors comprehensive enough to capture a wide variety of individual characteristics (Koo & Hardin, 2008; Wann et al., 2008; Won & Kitamura, 2007). The SPEED scale reduces the number of factors to explain motivation, allowing a more parsimonious examination of the constructs' relationship to antecedents and outcomes (Laverie & Arnett, 2000). This conceptualization represents an initial step in bridging the gap between academics and practitioners.

SPEED Measurement

The measurement of each SPEED motive was also based on a hybrid approach. Item measures were adapted from previous scales to explain sport consumer behavior (Funk et al., 2004; Madrigal, 2006; Trail & James, 2001; Wann, 1995). Each SPEED motive was measured with two items per construct compared to the common practice of using three items and the feasibility of using a single item to measure each construct. Confirmatory factor analysis results support the reliability of 10 items as a means to measure a parsimonious set of five motives. Each SPEED motive represents a relatively narrow, one-dimensional facet of motivation. As such, arguments could be made for the use of single-item measures in the name of parsimony (e.g., Drolet & Morrison, 2001; Kwon & Trail, 2005). To do so, however, would require the unrealistic assumption that each facet can be measured without error and proves difficult to use in model testing (Hair et al., 2006). Therefore, each facet was measured with two items to allow reliability to be assessed and reported. Overall, the results provide evidence of reliability for the SPEED measures. However, reliability is sample dependant (Streiner, 2003), and although a necessary condition of validity, it does not ensure validity (Hair et al., 2006). A discussion of the explanatory validity of the SPEED measures follows.

Table 4.
Regression of Past Attendance and Team Commitment on SPEED Facets (N = 2831)

	Game Attendance	Team Commitment
SPEED Facet	**Beta**	**Beta**
Socialization	.01	-.03
Performance	.07 *	.03 *
Esteem	.30 *	.66 *
Excitement	.21 *	.25 *
Diversion	.04	.03 *
F	244.56	1705.39
Adjusted R^2	.30	.75

* $p < .05$

SPEED Explanatory Validity

The results provide evidence of explanatory validity for the SPEED measures. The MANOVA results in Table 3 indicate the five SPEED motives are able to differentiate individuals based on previous consumption experience. The experience gained from direct consumption of the live sport product was evident as individuals who had attended at least one game perceived receiving benefits of socialization, performance, excitement, esteem, and diversion from attendance more than individuals who had not attended a prior game. This level of knowledge reflects the realization that a specific sport consumption activity provides opportunities to satisfy needs and acquire benefits (Funk & James, 2006; MacInnis et al., 1991). In addition, responses for the prior attendance group were significantly above the 4.0 midpoint, indicating their agreement that attending a sport contest provides the five SPEED benefits. Hence, the scale is particularly useful for individuals who have prior direct experience with attending games to understand what benefits the spectator sport experience provides.

The SPEED facets demonstrate evidence for predictive validity as three facets possess the ability to explain an individual's past behavior and current team commitment level (Heiman, 1999). In regard to past attendance, multiple linear regression reported in Table 4 indicate the more games an individual attended the more likely he/she agreed attending games provided the opportunity for excitement, to enjoy live performances, and increase esteem. The three facets explained 30% of the variance in past game attendance. The explanatory ability of these three SPEED motives represents an increase in predictive validity from the 20% or less reported in previous research (Hoye & Lilis, 2008; Neale & Funk, 2006; Ridinger & Funk, 2006). The remaining two measures of diversion and socialization were not significant predictors explaining prior attendance behavior. This finding is surprising given past research but these two motives may reflect benefits that individuals can obtain through non-sport related entertainment consumption activities.

The ability of the SPEED facets to explain current levels of team commitment was robust. Individuals who reported higher levels of team commitment were more likely to agree that attending games provided the opportunity for excitement, to enjoy live performances, increase esteem, and escape daily routines. These four motives explained 75% of the variance in team commitment. The socialization facet was not significant. These findings indicate that higher levels of team commitment are associated with consumption activities that provide four unique but related benefits.

In summary, the SPEED scale provides a parsimonious measurement tool of motives to explain past sport event attendance. Each motive within the scale represents a construct examined within existing motivation scales. The SPEED motives demonstrate reliability and were able to explain 30% of past game attendance and 75% of team commitment. Collectively, the SPEED scale is a reliable and valid measurement tool that is relatively concise, facilitating implementation by practitioners, while effectively representing sport event attendance motives uncovered through existing academic research.

Implications

The findings of this research introduce a variety of theoretical and practical implications. First, the results provide empirical evidence that the SPEED scale represents a concise 10-item instrument with sound psychometric properties to measure and explain why people attend spectator sport contests. The SPEED scale integrates previous scales applied to sport consumer motivation research and provides a reliable and valid tool that researchers can apply and further test in additional sport contexts.

Second, this research further highlights the importance of delineating among different types of motives useful for explaining behavior versus attitudes (Koo & Hardin, 2008; Pritchard & Funk, 2006). Research applying the SPEED scale can continue to classify consumers to further investigate motivational differences that may exist (Ross, 2007). Finally, the findings demonstrate the relative importance of esteem, excitement, and performance facets for both behavior and team commitment (e.g., Neale & Funk, 2006; Ridinger & Funk, 2006). This finding highlights benefits provided by the gameday sport experience (Zuckerman, 1983).

From a practical perspective, the application of the SPEED facets presents managers with a relatively brief tool for the assessment of consumer motivation. Administration of the SPEED scale in both a gameday environment and natural setting through intercepts demonstrates the convenience of being able to solicit feedback without extended interruption. This procedure illustrates how a core set of motives based on theoretical and practical relevance can be easily examined to provide a stronger research-practice relationship (Henderson et al., 2004). The results can aid sport marketing professionals in survey development decisions related to selecting the most appropriate motives and items (DeVellis, 2003) that can later shape marketing communication.

Specific findings of the current research indicate marketing communication should highlight the benefits of excitement, performance, and esteem associated with attending professional sport contests. Excitement reflects the desire for intellectual stimulation of which thrills related to the contest and associated activities are attractive. In marketing excitement, Durgee (1988) advocates a focus on storytelling with an emphasis on setting, characters, opposition, symbols, mood, and plot associated with the product. As a means to facilitate this, the author suggests interacting with consumers about the stimulation inherent to their experiences, focusing on the minor details that reflect how individuals experience the product (Baker, Grewal, & Parasuraman, 1994). Performance represents the desire to watch an artistic movement that provides the excellence, beauty, and creativity of athletic performance. Marketing content should emphasize pictorial and verbal forms of performance that communicate these aesthetic characteristics (Madrigal, 2006). For consumers with direct first-hand experience attending a previous game, this task revolves around reinforcing the positive outcomes that can be achieved through attendance. However, for individuals who are aware but have not previously attended a game, efforts should be more informational to increase the knowledge and realization that these benefits can be obtained through attendance.

Finally, the relative importance of esteem reaffirms the importance of leveraging the potential sense of accomplishment received from a sport team (Kahle et al., 1996). Trail, Anderson, and Fink (2005) indicate that as a consumer builds and maintains self-esteem through a sport team, they are more likely to attend future games and purchase merchandise. The authors suggest facilitating these behaviors through means such as post-game events involving players, coaches, and fans is critical; as well as the creation of specific sections within stadia for the most loyal fans. Furthermore, to capitalize on the emotions and accomplishment evoked by a sport team, managers can launch season ticket and membership sales campaigns immediately following the completion of the season (Trail et al., 2005). Even after unsuccessful seasons, these campaigns can still work to leverage this construct as negative influences on esteem among highly involved fans may be temporary (Bizman & Yinon, 2002).

Limitations

Three limitations to this research should be recognized. First, respondents were required to self-report their consumption behaviors. Inconsistencies may exist between what was reported and an individual's actual game attendance and other related behaviors. Second, the sport teams have experienced varying degrees of success and the history of each franchise is quite diverse. Third, the sport teams examined were professional and the SPEED scale should be implemented using non-professional sport teams as the object.

Future Directions

Using this research as a starting point, future work can be done to replicate the findings of the current study and to continue developing the SPEED motives. First, the hybrid approach adopted by this research provides the ability to use SPEED facets to create consumer profiles through segmentation research similar to enduring involvement research that commonly utilizes facets to develop unique involvement profiles (Havitz & Dimanche, 1997). A SPEED profile allows researchers and practitioners to examine specific aspects of motivation that provide unique information about a consumer. For instance, an individual may regularly attend cricket matches because s/he enjoys meeting with friends to take in the game and appreciates the excitement and uncertainty surrounding the outcome of each match, while paying little attention to, and having limited knowledge of, the skills and techniques exhibited by the players. This individual's SPEED profile towards cricket may reflect high levels of excitement, along with low levels of performance.

Second, qualitative data can be collected to further examine the relative importance of each motive and perhaps broaden the items underlying each construct. Focus groups can be organized with aware non-consumers, light, medium, and heavy users to explore the differences found among these groups. In addition, one-on-one interviews can be conducted prior to matches to further study the game attendance experience and the factors that drive attendance. An important area is to further explore why socialization and diversion were not rated as important as other SPEED facets especially among non-sport game attendees. Third, the current study looked at three different types of professional sport. Future research can apply the SPEED motives to a wider variety of sports, including both men's and women's, as well as different levels (e.g., amateur, semi-professional, youth). Furthermore, the SPEED motives could be examined across different geographical regions as the current study focuses solely on Australian sport.

Next, the current study concentrated on game attendance as sport consumption behavior; however, the SPEED motives may be relevant and important for individuals who choose to follow and watch sport via media (e.g., television, Internet) (Pritchard & Funk, 2006). Additional work examining these consumers can assist sport marketers in maintaining or improving television ratings and customizing Internet marketing communication. Finally, the instrument can be further employed within the sport event context. The SPEED motives can be assessed for the different types of events (mega, hallmark, major, and local) to assist event managers in tailoring their event marketing communication. Finally, a link between the SPEED motives and the event location as a tourist destination could be explored.

Conclusion

This research introduces and tests a 10-item instrument to measure sport consumer motivation and explain past game attendance behavior. Results reveal that the SPEED facets of Socialization, Performance, Excitement, Esteem, and Diversion (SPEED) demonstrate adequate reliability and validity. Results provide both academics and sport marketing professionals guidance in survey development decisions related to selecting the most appropriate motives and items needed to understand sport consumers. This research can lead to further application and examination of the SPEED motives across a variety of sport contexts.

References

Andreff, W., & Szymanski, S. (2006). *Handbook on the economics of sport.* Cheltenham, UK: Edward Elgar Publishing Limited.

Arbuckle, J. L. (1994). AMOS: Analysis of moment structures. *Psychometrika, 59,* 135-137.

Australian Bureau of Statistics (2007a). *Australian social trends.* Retrieved from http://www.abs.gov.au/AUSSTATS/abs@.nsf/Latestproducts/0F4B69DDFF667646CA25732C00207F44?opendocument

Australian Bureau of Statistics (2007b). *Sports attendance, Australia.* Retrieved from http://www.abs.gov.au/ausstats/abs@.nsf/productsbyCatalogue/1F8FAC9C2C7B1623CA2568A900139417?OpenDocument

Australian Bureau of Statistics (2007c). *Measures of Australia's progress: Summary indicators, 2007 (Edition 2).* Retrieved from http://www.abs.gov.au/AUSSTATS/abs@.nsf/Latestproducts/1383.0.55.001Main%20Features42007%20(Edition%202)?opendocument&tabname=Summary&prodno=1383.0.55.001&issue=2007%20(Edition%202)&num=&view=

Baade, R. A. (2003). Evaluating subsidies for professional sports in the United States and Europe. *Oxford Review of Economic Policy, 19,* 585-602.

Baker, J., Grewal. D., & Parasuraman, A. (1994). The influence of store environment on quality inferences and store image. *Journal of the Academy of Marketing Science, 22,* 328-339.

Bagozzi, R. P., & Yi, Y. (1988). On the evaluation of structural equation models. *Journal of the Academy of Marketing Science, 16,* 74-94.

Beard, J. G., & Ragheb, M. G. (1983). Measuring leisure motivation. *Journal of Leisure Research, 15,* 219-228.

Beaton, A. A., & Funk, D. C. (2008). An evaluation of theoretical frameworks for studying physically active leisure. *Leisure Sciences, 30,* 53-70.

Bollen, K. A. (1989). *Structural equations with latent variables.* New York: Jon Wiley and Sons.

Bizman, A., & Yinon, Y. (2002). Engaging in distancing tactics among sport fans: Effects on self-esteem and emotional responses. *The Journal of Social Psychology, 142,* 381-392.

Carroll, B., & Alexandris, K. (1997). Perception of constraints and strength of motivation: Their relationship to recreational sport participation in Greece. *Journal of Leisure Research, 29,* 279-299.

Crompton, J. L. (1979). Motivations for pleasure vacation. *Annals of Tourism Research, 6,* 408-424.

DeVellis, R. (2003). *Scale development -Theory and applications* (2nd ed.). Thousand Oaks, CA: Sage Publications

Dimanche, F., Havitz, M. E., & Howard, D. R. (1991). Testing the involvement profile (IP) scale in the context of selected recreational and touristic activities. *Journal of Leisure Research, 23,* 51-66.

Drolet, A. L., & Morrison, A. G. (2001). Do we really need multiple-item measures in service research? *Journal of Service Research, 3,* 196-204.

Durgee, J. F. (1988). Understanding brand personality. *The Journal of Consumer Marketing, 5,* 21-25.

Flynn, L., & Pearcy, D. (2001). Four subtle sins in scale development: Some suggestions for strengthening the current paradigm. *International Journal of Market Research, 43*(4), 409-433.

Fornell, C., & Larcker, D. F. (1981). Evaluating structural equation models with unobservable variables and measurement error. *Journal of Marketing Research, 18,* 39-50.

Funk, D. C., & James, J. (2001). The psychological continuum model: A conceptual framework for understanding an individual's psychological connection to sport. *Sport Management Review, 2,* 119-150.

Funk, D. C., & James, J. (2006). Consumer loyalty: The meaning of attachment in the development of sport team allegiance. *Journal of Sport Management, 20,* 189-217.

Funk, D. C., Mahony, D. F., & Ridinger, L. (2002). Characterizing consumer motivation as individual difference factors: Augmenting the Sport Interest Inventory (SII) to explain level of spectator support. *Sport Marketing Quarterly, 11,* 33-43.

Funk, D. C., Ridinger, L., & Moorman, A. J. (2004). Exploring origins of involvement: Understanding the relationship between consumer motives and involvement with professional sport teams. *Leisure Sciences, 26,* 35-61.

Gerbing, D. W., & Anderson, J. C. (1988). An updated paradigm for scale development incorporating unidimensionality and its assessment. *Journal of Marketing Research, 25,* 186-192.

Gladden, J. M., & Funk, D. C. (2002). Developing an understanding of brand associations in team sport: Empirical evidence from consumer of professional sport. *Journal of Sport Management, 16,* 54-81.

Hair, J. F., Black, W. C., Babin, B. J., Anderson, R. E., & Tatham, R. L. (2006). *Multivariate analysis* (6th Edition). Upper Saddle River, NJ: Pearson.

Havitz, M. E., & Dimanche, F. (1997). Leisure involvement revisited: Drive properties and paradoxes. *Journal of Leisure Research, 31,* 122-149.

Heiman, G. W. (1999). *Research methods in psychology* (2nd ed.). Boston, MA: Houghton Mifflin.

Henderson, K. A., Presley, J., & Bialeschki, M. D. (2004). Theory in recreation and leisure research: Reflections from the editors. *Leisure Sciences, 26,* 411-425.

Hirshman, E., & Holbrook, M. B. (1982). Hedonic consumption: Emerging concepts, methods and propositions. *Journal of Marketing, 46,* 92-101.

Hoye, R., & Lillis, K. (2008). Travel motivations of Australian Football League fans: An exploratory study. *Managing Leisure, 13*(1), 13-22

Hu, L., & Bentler, P. M. (1999). Cutoff criteria for fit indexes in covariance structure analysis: Conventional criteria versus new alternatives. *Structural Equation Modeling, 6,* 1-56.

Iso-Ahola, S. E. (1980). *The social psychology of leisure and recreation.* Dubuque, IA; Wm. C. Brown.

Iso-Ahola, S. E. (1982). Toward a social psychological theory of tourism motivation: A rejoinder. *Annals of Tourism Research, 9,* 256-262.

Iwasaki, Y., & Havitz, M. E. (2004). Examining relationships between leisure involvement, psychological commitment, and loyalty to a recreation agency. *Journal of Leisure Research, 36,* 45-72.

Kahle, L. R., Kambara, K. M., & Rose, G. (1996). A functional model of fan attendance motivations for college football. *Sport Marketing Quarterly, 5,* 51-60.

Kiesler, C., Collins, B. E., & Miller, N. (1969). *Attitude change: A critical analysis of theoretical approaches:* New York: Wiley.

Koo, G-Y., & Hardin, R. (2008). Difference in interrelationship between spectator motives and behavioral intentions based on emotional attachment. *Sport Marketing Quarterly, 17,* 30-43.

Kwon, H., & Trail, G. (2005). The feasibility of single-item measures in sport loyalty research. *Sport Management Review, 8,* 69-89.

Kyle, G. T., & Mowen, A. J. (2005). An examination of the leisure involvement—Agency commitment relationship. *Journal of Leisure Research, 37,* 342-363.

Laverie, D. A., & Arnett, D. B. (2000). Factors affecting fan attendance: The influence of identity salience and satisfaction. *Journal of Leisure Research, 32,* 225-246.

MacInnis, D. J., Moorman, C., & Jaworski, B. J. (1991). Enhancing and measuring consumers' motivation, opportunity, and ability to process brand information from ads. *Journal of Marketing, 55,* 32-53.

Madrigal, R. (2006). Measuring the multidimensional nature of sporting event consumption. *Journal of Leisure Research, 38,* 267-292.

Mahony, D. F., Nakazawa, M., Funk, D. C., James, J., & Gladden, J. M. (2002). Motivational factors impacting the behavior of J. League spectators: Implications for league marketing efforts. *Sport Management Review, 5,* 1-24.

Maslow, A. (1954). *Motivation and personality.* New York. Harper and Row.

Mittal, B. (1995). A comparative analysis of four scales of consumer involvement. *Psychology and Marketing, 12,* 663-682.

Mowen, J. C., & Minor, M. (1998). *Consumer behavior* (5th ed.). Upper Saddle River, NJ: Prentice Hall.

Neale, L., & Funk, D. C. (2006). Investigating motivation, attitudinal loyalty and attendance behaviour with fans of Australian Football. *International Journal of Sports Marketing and Sponsorship, 7,* 307-317.

Nunnally, J. C., & Bernstein, I. H. (1994). *Psychometric theory* (3rd ed.). New York, NY: McGraw-Hill.

Pease, D. G., & Zhang, J. J. (2001). Socio-motivational factors affecting spectator attendance at professional basketball games. *International Journal of Sport Management, 2,* 31-59.

Pons, F., Mourali, M., & Nyeck, S. (2006). Consumer orientation toward sporting events. *Journal of Service Research, 8,* 276-287.

Pritchard, M. P., & Funk, D. C. (2006), Symbiosis and substitution in spectator sport. *Journal of Sport Management, 20,* 297-320.

Razzaque, M. A. (1998). Scientific method, marketing theory development and academic vs practitioner orientation: A review. *Journal of Marketing Theory and Practice, 6,* 1-15.

Ridinger, L., & Funk, D. C. (2006). Looking at gender differences through the lens of sport spectators. *Sport Marketing Quarterly, 3,* 123-134.

Rosenberg, L., & Czepiel, J. (1983). A marketing approach for consumer retention. *Journal of Consumer Marketing, 1,* 45-51.

Ross, S. D. (2007). Segmenting sport fans using brand associations: A cluster analysis. *Sport Marketing Quarterly, 16,* 15-24.

Schiffman, L. G., & Kanuk, L. L. (2001). *Consumer behavior* (7th ed.). Upper Saddle River, NJ: Prentice Hall.

Sloan, L. R. (1989). The motives of sports fans. In J. D. Goldstein, *Sports, games and play: Social and psychology viewpoints* (2nd ed., pp. 175-240). Hillsdale, NJ: Erlbaum Associates.

Spector, P. E. (1992). *Summated rating scale construction: an introduction.* Newbury Park, CA: Sage Publications.

Streiner, D. L. (2003). Starting at the beginning: An introduction to coefficient alpha and internal consistency. *Journal of Personality Assessment, 80,* 99-103.

Tabachnick, B. G., & Fidell, L. S. (1996). *Using multivariate statistics* (3rd ed.). New York: Harper Collins.

Theodorakis, N. D., & Alexandris, K. (2008). Can service quality predict spectators' behavioural intentions in professional soccer? *Managing Leisure, 13*(3-4), 162-178.
Trail, G. T., Anderson, D. F., & Fink, J. S. (2005). Consumer satisfaction and identity theory: A model of sport spectator conative loyalty. *Sport Marketing Quarterly, 14*, 98-111.
Trail, G. T., & James, J. D. (2001). The motivation scale for sport consumption: Assessment of the scale's psychometric properties. *Journal of Sport Behavior, 24*, 108-127.
Wakefield, K. L., & Sloan, H. J. (1995). The effects of team loyalty and selected stadium factors on spectator attendance. *Journal of Sport Management, 9*, 153-172.
Wann, D. L. (1995). Preliminary validation of the sport fan motivation scale. *Journal of Sport and Social Issues, 19*, 377-396.
Wann, D. L., Grieve, F. G., Zapalac, R. K., & Pease, D. G. (2008). Motivational profiles of sport fans of different sports. *Sport Marketing Quarterly, 17*, 6-19.
Weick, K. E. (1993). The collapse of sensemaking in organizations: The Mann Gulch disaster. *Administrative Science Quarterly, 38*, 628-652.
Won, J., & Kitamura, K. (2007). Comparative analysis of sport consumers' motivations between South Korea and Japan. *Sport Marketing Quarterly, 16*, 93-105.
Zaichkowsky, J. L. (1985). Measuring the involvement construct. *Journal of Consumer Research, 12*, 341-352.
Zuckerman M. (1983). Sensation seeking and sports. *Personality and Individual Differences, 4*, 285-293.

Appendix

Construct Definitions Measure for SPEED Facets of Sport Event Motivation

Socialization

The extent to which a person perceives attending a sport event is viewed as an opportunity to interact with family, friends, and other spectators

- Socialization represents a desire for sociability. Individuals are motivated to seek a sport event experience due to opportunities for the enhancement of human relationships through external interaction with other spectators, participants, friends, and family.

Performance

The extent to which an individual believes that sport events provide excellence, beauty, and creativity of athletic performance

- Performance represents a desire for aesthetic and physical pleasure. Individuals are motivated to seek a sport experience due to opportunities to enjoy the grace, skill, and artistry of athletic movement and physiological movement.

Excitement

The extent to which a sport event is perceived as providing excitement and drama with an element of uncertainty as to the outcome of the game

- Excitement represents a desire for intellectual stimulation. Individuals are motivated to seek a sport event experience due to opportunities for mental action and exploration from the atmospheric conditions created by the uncertainty of participation and competition and the spectacle of associated activities.

Esteem

The extent to which an individual perceives a heightened sense of personal and collective esteem based on vicarious achievement when his/her favorite team wins

- Esteem represents a desire for competency. Individuals are motivated to seek a sport event experience due to opportunities for achievement and challenge that produce a sense of mastery and a heightened sense of personal and collective self-esteem.

Diversion

The extent to which a person perceives attending a sport event provides an opportunity to escape or "get away" from the hassles and normal routine of everyday life

- Diversion represents a desire for mental well-being. Individuals are motivated to seek a sport event experience due to opportunities to escape and remove themselves from daily work and life routines that create stress.

SECTION IV.

Market Segmentation

11

Tapping New Markets:
Women as Sport Consumers

Dallas D. Branch

Introduction

Women as sport consumers have been maligned in the sport marketplace over the years. Traditional and stereotypical thinking has placed women as an afterthought in the minds of most sport marketers, promoters, and corporate advertisers when it comes to identifying women as a potential target market. This revelation should not be surprising, as these professions are controlled by men who have decided "*that women weren't interested in sport and if they were, that they could get away with producing a pretty but inferior quality product that of course did not sell. As a result, the industry found itself marketed almost exclusively to men*" (Lopiano, 1993, p. 1). In short, women have been given the short end of the stick when it comes to being viewed as a viable and emerging target market segment.

The stereotypical manner in which women are still portrayed by most of the sport industry is summed up by Donna Lopiano (1993), Executive Director of the Women's Sports Foundation, when she states, "*It is fine (for women) to be active and fit. It is even okay to play sports as long as you maintain your femininity. Women still wear makeup when they play sport even though they sweat and makeup don't make sense. Women are still decorative objects in our society. They still define themselves by the clothes they wear*" (p. 1).

Sport marketers concluded that sport was something that could not be appropriately targeted to women. After all, women weren't serious athletes, they didn't understand the game(s), and they attended or viewed sporting events as appendages to men—either husbands or male friends. Sport marketers may have felt justified in their neglect of women as a consumer group, as marketers into the media trap that "concluded that women weren't interested in the sport pages, even when the sports pages catered to men and covered few if any events involving or of interest to women" (Lopiano, 1993, p. 1).

Designer Genes

In the 23 years since the passage of Title IX, the role of women in sport as participants and spectators has begun to change dramatically. Generations of women are becoming more active and fit, pursuing sport as well as other fitness activities at an ever-increasing rate. With this increase in participation and spectating, women are consuming more sports and sport-related products than ever before, as they now account for an increasing share of the sport consumption dollar in many segments of the sport industry. Women have become a market force that can no longer be ignored and must be reckoned with.

As a consumer group, women now possess the marketing potential to make a significant impact upon the bottom line of consumer and spectator sport organizations that are willing to consider these obvious trends in the sport marketplace. As a result, some companies are beginning to change their attitudes about women as a viable consumer group and target market. This change in attitude comes none too soon. With 60% of Division I-A intercollegiate athletic programs and 30%+ of the professional sport franchises losing money by some estimates, as well as stagnant markets for many sport (spectator and consumer) products designed for men, it is timely that sport marketers, promoters, and advertisers would be searching for new markets (Fulks, 1994; Ozanian, 1994).

Today, a few sporting goods manufacturers are offering quality products developed and designed specifically for women ("Center court," 1995; Ruffenach, 1995). The response to Nike, L.A. Gear, Danskin, and Reebok, in their attempts to appeal to women athletes through a dedicated line of apparel and athletic footwear, has been that "when a company does come out with a serious product and treats [a woman] like a serious athlete, she responds with appreciation and loyalty" (Grim, 1994; Hollreiser, 1995; Lopiano, 1993, p. 1). Nike's sales to women jumped 25% in 1990, the first full year of their EMPATHY campaign, and grew an additional 25% in 1991 and 28% in 1992 ("They just did it," 1993). Adidas, looking to improve its marketing to women, has just announced the launching in January (1996) of a new women's fitness line called WORKOUT ("Women's market," 1995). The company projects that the worldwide advertising campaign entitled "Adidas: A woman's brand since 1932" could help boost total sales by 30-35% ("Woman's market," 1995). Active Apparel Group (AAG) is likewise targeting women sport consumers by "taking established brand names from the men's market and aggressively marketing them to women" ("Women's market," 1995, p. 2). These examples highlight the fact that targeting women sport consumers is not only smart, but also profitable, due largely to the fact that many male-dominated sport markets are now saturated and stagnant. Lisa Voorhees, owner of The Sporting Women in Denver, says that "men's apparel sales are flat" and that "manufacturers realize that if they want to experience growth, it has to come from women" ("Women's markets," 1995, p. 2).

Designing sport products to meet the unique and discerning needs of women consumers should be a no-brainer for sport marketers. Who would argue that women have traditionally been the better shoppers of the two sexes? As Donna Lapiano (1993) asserts, "At the risk of using sexist humor, let's face it, women are genetically superior to men with regard to the shopping gene. Women participate in most purchasing decisions for men and families as well as their own" (p. 1).

In a 1993 study and three-part report jointly sponsored by the National Golf Foundation (NGF) and the Ladies Professional Golf Association (LPGA) entitled

Women in Golf, the American woman of today was generally characterized as having "no equal in her relentless search for quality, good selection, fair prices, and dependable customer service" ("Women in golf," 1994b, p. 13). In particular, the 5.2 million "occasional" and "core" women golfers were profiled as being young (69% were <49 years of age), affluent (60% with HHI > $40K), well-educated (72% with at least "Some College"), and highly influential "in decisions concerning the household" ("Women in golf" 1994c, p. 17). The report concluded that, *"although women make up a smaller portion of the golf industry than do men, it is clear that they are an economic force that helps drive the golf industry... Recognizing these facts and addressing concerns unique to women golfers should aid in ensuring a solid future not only for women in golf, but for the game itself"* (p. 20).

Jeff Urban, Sports Marketing Manager for USA Today, and Deborah Larkin, former Executive Director of the Women's Sports Foundation, presented the results of a compelling study entitled Active Women: Who Are They? at the Women's Sports Foundations Annual Conference in June 1993. This study, which utilized several different methodologies for data collection including the 1992 Simmons study of media and markets, personal interviews, and self-administered questionnaires, identified 21 million "active" women, defined as those women who exercised regularly (2+ times per week). The demographics of these active women included a profile of their age (69% <45 years old), marital status (60% married), household income (50%+ > $45K), employment (71% work at least part-time and 28% top-middle management), education (50%+ attended or graduated college), and homeowner status (70% are homeowners). As far as trends in product consumption are concerned, these active women are 78% more likely to own or use a MasterCard, 62% more likely to buy slacks or pants, 50% more likely to buy a jogging or athletic suit, 59% more likely to travel (domestic) by plane, 91% more likely to use fresh pasta, 41% more likely to own a car bought new, and 32% more likely to own a 35mm camera (Urban & Larkin, 1993). In short, the 21 million active women identified in this study are a powerful group of potential sport consumers who can significantly impact the bottom line of sport organizations that are ready, willing, and able to tap into this virtually untapped market segment.

Sport Spectatorship: Women Are Watching

Whereas the potential impact of women consumers on the sport retail and product industry is all too apparent, the sport spectator marketplace is not immune to these trends, as sport organizations that are responsible for producing live events likewise have the opportunity to "grow" their businesses by tapping into the growing women's sport spectator marketplace.

Len Deluca, vice president of programming for CBS, recently assessed the network's overwhelming media success of the 1994 Winter Olympics in Lilehammer, Norway, in which the ladies' technical skating program was viewed by an estimated 127 million Americans, a 48.5 share, making it the fourth most-watched television event in U.S. television history (Grabarek, 1995). As figure skating is the most popular spectator sport among U.S. women and their daughters (and second overall in TV viewership behind the NFL, but ahead of baseball, basketball, and hockey), it is a little wonder that "Where this kind of audience—read younger women—goes, advertisers marketers and broadcast executives follow." Deluca concludes that "there are now as many young female heroines as there are young male heroes. And this translates into more girls and women watching sports. This is great news for the networks" (Grabarek, 1995, p. 99).

Females of all ages are becoming fans of spectator sports. National Sports Study II, the largest sports and lifestyle study ever conducted in this country, presented its findings in 1993 at the Women's Sports Foundation Annual Conference. Under the direction of Nye Lavalle, chairman of the Sports Marketing Group located in Dallas, this study described how "a generational and gender revolution is quietly sweeping American sports" ("National Sports," 1993, p. 9).

Women are becoming an increasingly significant market segment for spectator sports organizations at the same time that men's interest in spectator sports is stagnating or waning. In particular, Lavalle's study found that, *"among women 18 and older, the total popularity of the NBA (has) soared 70% since 1989, the NFL 45%, and baseball 40%... among men 18 and older, the popularity of the NBA rose 10%, the NFL barely 1%, and baseball 7%" (p. 9).* With more recent problems that have beset Major League Baseball (strike and lock-out), a Harris poll found that baseball had lost about 33% of its fans (mostly men) since last year ("Fan Loss," 1995). In addition, attendance (mostly men) at major league parks this season is down about 25% over last year ("All-Star Plight," 1995). Lavelle's study highlights further a surge in sports interest by women as closing the traditional disparity in spectator sports..."In baseball, for example, fan appeal varies only about 5 percentage points between men and women in all age groups under 65" ("National Sports," 1993, p. 9). The implications are that women today are becoming fans of men's and women's spectator sports at a rate greater than or equal to men in many age categories, especially among young women 18-24 years old. The most significant outcome in this study is Lavelle's revelation that "what it all means is the sports demography landscape of America is shifting, and the majority of the industry isn't paying attention, including some advertisers, networks, newspapers, leagues, and teams" (p. 9).

NASCAR, the fastest growing spectator sport in America today, may be ahead of its time and behind the times (at the same time), as "mixed messages" in promoting this spectator sport to women maintain a "redneck" element in the sport while "the ambience at the track is still white male" (Silver, 1995, p. 23). Even so, the approximately 40% of race fans who are women "cope with the panting sexuality that permeates the crowd" while they are being skillfully influenced with the most effective and targeted corporate advertising campaign in sport featuring Tide, Miracle Whip, Underalls (pantyhose), Folger's (coffee), 7-Eleven, Red Baron (pizza), McDonald's, Kellogg's, Lifebuoy, Butter Flavor Crisco, and Wrangler cars that are displaying on their hoods the very consumer household products these women will go home and buy (Bauer, 1987). With this kind of demographic "fit," it is a little wonder that corporate sponsors are racing to win one of the 100+ available car sponsorship deals.

Conclusions

Several trends identified in this paper combine to increase the potential of successfully marketing sport to women in the future. First, women are consuming sport and sport-related products at an ever-increasing rate. Second, consumption of sport and sport-related products by men has plateaued or, in some cases, has fallen. Thus, men are less likely to be "moved" to consume more, as their sluggish consumption patterns indicate that they may be at or neat their "salutation point," the point at which further advertising, promotion, and marketing efforts will not influence them to purchase more of a given product category. Women have demonstrated, on the other hand, that they can be influenced and "moved," in some cases dramatically, to consume more of the sport product if the approach and product are designed for and with the female consumer in mind. The key for sport organizations and sport-related businesses is in the design of strategies that appeal to a woman's sensitivities toward quality, price value(s), feelings, and emotional well-being. If sport organizations can find the right marketing "mix" of products and services to meet the discriminating needs of women in this regard, they are well on their way to improving their future success and ultimate survival. It makes little sense and earns fewer cents to ignore in some cases 50% of one's viewing audience or of the consumers of one's products. To the contrary, sport organizations that position themselves to take full advantage of this opportunity to market successfully to a growing segment of consumers—women—who have begun to exercise their consumer spending power in the sport marketplace will find themselves with a greater share of the sport market and its profits.

Donna Lopiano concluded her remarks at the 1993 Sport Summit by saying that "it is a good time to invest in the women's sports market" (p. 1). For sport organizations, the media, corporate sponsors, and marketers of sport, now may be the best time ever simply to invest in women.

References

All-Star plight: Can anybody fix this game? (1995, July 9). *The Dominion Post*, p. 8C.

Bauer, B. (1987, June 29). A new way to reach America's good ol' girls. *U.S. New and World Report*, 41.

Center court: Ironic isn't it? (1995, July 26). *Sports Business Daily*, 213, 1.

Fan Loss (1995, July 3). *USA Today*, p. C-1.

Fulks, D. (1994, August). *Revenues and Expenses of Intercollegiate Athletic Programs.* National Collegiate Athletic Association.

Grabarek, B. (1995, February 14). Ladies, don't touch that dial. *Financial World, 164*(4), 99-102.

Grim, M. (1994, February 7). Strategy: Women role models are Bok. *Brandweek, 35*, 4.

Hollreiser, E. (1995, January 39). L.A. Gear recasts for women, kids. *Brandweek*, 36,13.

Lopiano, D. (1993, January 26). *Marketing trends in women's sports and fitness.* Paper presented at the 1993 Sports Summit, New York, NY.

National Sports Study II Summary (1993). Dallas, TX: The Sports Marketing Group.

Ozanian, M. (1994, May 10). The $11 billion pastime. *Financial World, 163*(10), 50-59.

Ruffenach, G. (1995, February 3). Designing for women: Bats bikes, even golf balls. *Wall Street Journal*, p. B12.

Silver, M. (1995, July 24). A daay at the races. *Sports Illustrated, 83*(4), 18-24.

They just did it: Nike's bold campaign to women strikes a chord (1993, March). *Lear's, 6*, 92-111.

Urban, J., & Larkin, D. (1993, June 20). *Active Women: Who are they?* Paper Presented at the 1993 Women's Sports Foundation Annual Conference, New York.

Women in golf: 1988-1993 (1994, November). National Golf Foundation: Jupiter, FL.

Women in golf: Attitudes, behaviors, and expectations (1994, November). National Golf Foundation and the Ladies Professional Golf Association: Jupiter, FL.

Women in golf: Purchasing patterns and spending data (1994, November). National Golf Foundation and the Ladies Professional Golf Association: Jupiter, FL.

Women's market a target strategy for both adidas and AAG (1995, July 26). *Sports Business Daily*, p. 2.

12

Market Analyses of Race and Sport Consumption

Ketra L. Armstrong and Terese M. Stratta

Introduction

A number of sociodemographic variables have been found to influence the consumption of sport. Among them are age (Pan, Gabert, McGaugh, & Branvold, 1997), gender (Pan et al., 1997; Sutton & Watlington, 1994), income (Baade & Tiehen, 1990), and occupation (Zhang, Pease, Hui, & Michaud, 1995). Another sociodemographic variable that has been posited to influence sport consumption is race/ethnicity. Zhang et al. (1995) revealed that race may influence the decision-making process in which sport spectators engage as they ponder the decision to attend professional sport events. In that study, differences were found in spectators' responses to a decision-making inventory concerning sport attendance based on the spectators' race/ethnicity. Zhang et al. (1995) also revealed that game promotions in particular equally influenced African Americans' (used interchangeably with Blacks in this study) and Hispanics' decisions to attend games of the National Basketball Association (NBA). However, game promotions influenced the attendance decisions of African Americans and Hispanics more than those of Asians and Caucasians. Additionally, Zhang et al. (1995) also revealed that African Americans' decisions to attend NBA games were influenced by schedule convenience more often than for any other ethnic group. According to Schurr, Wittig, Ruble, and Ellen (1988), race was statistically significant in explaining the difference between college basketball game attendees and non-attendees. Schurr et al. (1988) also found an interaction between race and gender, suggesting that Black males, Black females, and White males were equally likely to attend the respective basketball games, with such likelihood being significantly lower for White females. Goldsmith (2003) offered further evidence of the influence of race-related factors on Blacks' participation in sport.

The racial composition of the environments in which sport events take place may also influence sport consumption. According to Noll (1974), the presence of ethnic groups in a population had a negative effect on sport attendance such that as the number of ethnic groups increased, overall attendance at respective sport events decreased. Schofield

(1983) also revealed that the composition of ethnic groups in an environment had a negative effect on game attendance. In contrast, Baade and Tiehen (1990) offered findings to refute those presented by Noll (1974) and Schofield (1983) by revealing that as the percentage of a city's total population represented by Blacks increased, so would attendance at sport events (when everything else is equal).

Another likely influence on sport consumption is the race/ethnicity of the players on the participating sport teams. According to Zhang et al. (1995), the general influence of the home team had a similar effect on attendance decisions by each ethnic group (e.g., Caucasians, Asians, African Americans, and Hispanics). However, Sapolsky (1980) offered findings to the contrary. To specifically examine the influence of the race of the athletes competing on spectators' enjoyment of the contests, Sapolsky (1980) conducted an experimental study in which Black and White male spectators viewed a video presentation of an edited basketball game featuring an all-Black and an all-White team. The results revealed that the Black spectators enjoyed scores by the Black athletes significantly more than did the White spectators. There were no significant differences between the Black and White spectators' enjoyment of scores made by White players. Additionally, Black spectators' enjoyment of the game was not predicated on the suspense of the contest as it was for Whites, as Blacks were significantly more pleased with the game when the Black team won.

Purpose of the Study

While many sociogeographic factors undoubtedly influence sport consumption, the primary foci of this exploratory investigation were race-based factors: (a) the racial/ethnic classification of the sport consumers, (b) the environments' residential racial/ethnic composition, and (c) the racial/ethnic composition of the respective home teams. The collection of research previously reported on the expressed and/or implied influence of race/ethnicity on sport consumption has yielded varied and often conflicting results, warranting further investigation of this topic. This study continued the exploration of race and sport consumption by examining whether Black and White consumers of professional women's basketball teams from two different (environmental) markets in the United States differed significantly regarding (a) communication tools they relied on for game or team information, (b) their game/event purchase patterns, (c) their active participation in basketball, (c) factors motivating their game-attendance decisions, and (d) predictors of their game attendance frequency.

Market Analysis of Selected Sites

General Market Characteristics

The sites selected for this study differed in their geographical location: One was located in the southern region of the United States and the other was located in the midwestern region. Nevertheless, they were strikingly similar regarding their predominant sociodemographic market characteristics: (a) both had a gender composition of 51% female and 49% male; (b) both were perceived as young markets with a median age of 33; (c) both had a number of colleges and universities in close proximity yielding a student population of at least 90,000; (d) over 70% of residents in both markets completed high school, and at least 16% held college degrees; (e) both had unemployment rates that were approximately 4%; and (f) both cities were listed in *Fortune Magazine's* top 10 rankings for their economic and business opportunities (Greater Columbus Chamber of Commerce Research Department, 1995; Metro Atlanta Chamber of Commerce, 1996).

One notable difference between the two environments was the population size. The midwestern market was ranked as the 16th largest city in the United States and the 29th largest *metropolitan statistical area* (MSA; Greater Columbus Chamber of Commerce Research Department, 1995). In comparison, the southern market had a smaller city population (ranked 37th) but a larger MSA (ranked 11th; United States Bureau of the Census, 1994, 1997). Another difference in the two environments was that the southern market had a higher household *effective buying income* than did the midwestern market, reporting incomes of $46,099 and $39,283, respectively (Metro Atlanta Chamber of Commerce, 1996). Thus, the overall sociodemographic characteristics of the two environments were more similar than dissimilar, notwithstanding the population size and (to a lesser extent) income differences.

Racial Composition of Markets' Residents

The most striking difference between the two environments under investigation, and the one most central to this study, was the racial composition of the individuals residing therein. The midwestern market had an MSA with an ethnic/racial composition of 86% White, 12% Black, 0.7% Hispanic, and 1.5% Asian (the midwestern city proper had a racial/ethnic composition of 74% White, 23% Black, 2% Asian, and 1% Hispanic). The southern market had an MSA with a racial/ethnic composition of 71% White, 26% Black, 3% Hispanic, and 3% Asian (the southern city proper had a racial/ethnic composition of 67% Black, 30% White, 2% Hispanic, and 1% Asian). While both markets were predominately White, the southern market had an MSA Black population that was more than twice that of the midwestern market, and the southern city's Black population was approximately three times that of the midwestern city's Black population.

Racial Demographics of Home Team

Based on the findings of Sapolsky (1980) and the disposition that spectators may have for athletes who are racially similar, it was important to note the racial composition of the home teams (professional women's basketball) for the respective environments. The home team for the midwestern market included five Blacks, four Whites, and one athlete classified as interracial. The team's 'star' players were of both races. In addition, the team had an all-White coaching staff and one Black in a management position. The home team for the southern market included eight Blacks, two Whites, and one athlete classified as international. The team's celebrated star player was Black, the head coach was Black, and Black personnel held most of the front office positions.

Methodology

Data Collection Procedures

Data were collected in two separate consumer studies at professional women's basketball games held in the southern and midwestern markets using similar data collection methods. In both studies, data were collected by randomly distributing questionnaires to spectators as they entered the respective sport arenas. For the midwestern market, data were collected on two separate occasions at the end of the season (at a weeknight game and at a weekend game). Attendance at each game was 2,165 and 5,429 respectively, for an average attendance of 3,797. The average home attendance for the team for the season was 2,682. A total of 736 questionnaires were gathered; however, only the questionnaires from respondents who classified themselves as Black or White were used in the analysis. This procedure yielded a usable sample size of 710 (606 Whites and 104 Blacks), which was deemed generally representative of the racial composition of the attendance population (approximately 84% and 14%, respectively).

Data in the southern market were collected on seven separate occasions throughout the season, during games held on both weeknights (n = 3) and weekends (n = 4). Attendance at each game: 2,325; 3,489; 2,187; 2,482; 2,251; 3,683; and 1,224, for an average attendance of 2,520. The average home attendance for the season was 2,780. A total of 1,361 questionnaires were collected during the seven games; however, only the questionnaires from respondents classifying themselves as Black or White were used for the analyses. This procedure yielded usable sample size of 1,284 (716 Blacks and 568 Whites), which was deemed generally representative of the racial composition of the attendance population (approximately 53% and 42%, respectively).

Data Analysis

Descriptive statistics were calculated for each of the sociodemographic and sport consumption profile variables. An analysis of variance (ANOVA) was performed to examine the differences between the spectators' game attendance frequency. A multivariate analysis of variance (MANOVA) was performed to examine responses to the summated game attendance motivation variable and the different factors posited to influence game attendance decisions. A multiple regression analysis was performed to examine the degree to which active basketball participation and the summated attendance motive predicted game attendance frequency.

Results

Summary Demographic Profile

The demographic profiles of the Black and White spectators were similar in that for both samples from the midwest and southern markets (a) females comprised the majority (70% and 72%, respectively); (b) Blacks were generally younger, with greater percentages in the age range 25-34 (for the midwest market) and 25-39 (for the southern market); (c) more Blacks were single in both samples (69% and 58%, respectively); (d) Whites reported higher incomes for both samples (with 25% and 35% reporting incomes that exceeded $75,000 in the respective markets); (e) Whites had higher levels of education, with a greater percentage in both samples holding graduate or professional degrees; and (f) the majority of Blacks and Whites in both samples had professional occupations.

Pre-Game Activities

A similar percentage of White and Black spectators from the midwest market were at home prior to the basketball games (47% and 42%, respectively). However, over twice as many White than Black spectators were at a restaurant or a bar prior to the games (27% and 11%, respectively). Conversely, over twice as many Black spectators compared to White spectators (21% and 9%, respectively) were at work prior to the games.

The pre-game behaviors of spectators in the southern market were similar to those revealed for the midwestern market. Similar percentages of Black and White spectators were at home prior to the games (57% and 51%, respectively) and approximately three times more White than Black spectators (17% and 6%, respectively) were at a restaurant prior to the games. Unlike the midwestern market, similar percentages of Black (22%) and White (19%) spectators were at work prior to the games.

Communication Tools

The communication tools regarding game or team information that were examined in this study were determined by the researchers in consultation with the teams' marketers. The communication tools examined included: word of mouth advertising (from friends or associates), team schedules, radio, television, newspaper, and the internet. For the midwestern market, the tools that the spectators utilized to obtain information about the team's games were ascertained. The results revealed similarities between the Black and White spectators. The majority of both groups relied on team schedules for game information (i.e., 63% of Whites and 60% of Blacks). Regarding other communication methods: word-of-mouth advertising informed 33% of the White spectators and 28% of the Black spectators; radio informed 11% of the Black spectators and 9% of the White spectators; the newspaper informed 20% of the White spectators and 14% of the Black spectators; television informed 11% of Blacks and 6% of Whites; and the internet was negligible as a source of awareness of the team's games for both races of spectators (utilized by 3% of the Black spectators and 2% of the White spectators).

For the southern market, the communication tools the spectators relied on for general information about the team was ascertained. The results revealed that both Black (32%) and White (38%) spectators from the southern market most often relied on word-of-mouth advertising for information regarding the team. Both Black and White spectators also relied on the newspaper as the second most popular source of information (18% and 27%, respectively). While radio informed substantially more Black (14%) than White (2%) spectators, television appeared to inform both Black and White spectators similarly (8% and 5%, respectively). Pocket schedules were utilized by 7% of Blacks and 4% of Whites.

Sport Purchase Patterns

Ticket Purchases. For the midwestern market 43% of the White spectators purchased tickets prior to game day, compared to 26% of Blacks. Similar percentages of Blacks and Whites purchased their tickets just before the game (41% and 37%, respectively). Differences were also found in the time of ticket purchases for Black and White spectators in the southern market. Most notably, almost twice as many White spectators as Black spectators purchased tickets 15 days or more in advance of the games (35% versus 18%). On the other hand, more Black spectators (25%) than White spectators (16%) purchased tickets within 24 hours of the games.

Game and Team Merchandise Purchases. In terms of sport purchases made during the game, there were similarities between Black and White spectators from the midwestern market, as both races were equally likely to purchase game programs, concession items, and team merchandise. Thirty percent of Whites and 29% of Blacks purchased game programs; 68% of Whites and 66% of Blacks purchased concession items; and 22% of Blacks and 20% of Whites purchased team merchandise.

Specific purchases were not ascertained for consumers in the southern market. Instead, spectators from the southern market were asked the frequency with which they purchased products that they saw or heard advertised at the team's games. Forty percent of the Black spectators and 49% of the White spectators indicated that they frequently (i.e., sometimes or often) purchased products associated with the team.

Game Attendance Frequency

Seventy-six percent of the Black spectators in the midwestern market had attended from 1-5 games; more specifically, 53% had attended only one or two games. Comparably, approximately 70% of the White spectators were also considered light users, with 57% of them having attended only one or two games. The ANOVA revealed no statistically significant differences in the basketball game attendance frequency among the Black and White spectators in the midwestern market [$F(1, 706) = 1.65$, $p = .20$, M for Blacks = 4.6, M for Whites = 5.5]. Thus, race did not appear to significantly influence the frequency of basketball attendance.

Spectators in the southern market were also categorized as predominantly light users. Forty-six percent of Black spectators and 59% of White spectators attended only one of the professional women's franchise basketball games. Twenty percent of both Black and White spectators attended two games, while only nine percent of Black and three percent of White spectators attended three games. Unlike the midwestern market, the ANOVA revealed that the game attendance frequency in the southern market significantly differed based on the race of the spectator, with Blacks attending at a higher frequency, $F(1, 1184) = 16.16$, $p < .001$; M for Blacks = 1.92, and the M for Whites = 1.55.

Active Basketball Participation

For the midwestern market, approximately 59% of the Black spectators compared to 42% of the White spectators were active participants in basketball. For the southern market, both past and current basketball participation patterns were ascertained. The rates of basketball participation for both Black and White spectators in the southern market were similar: (a) 47% of Black spectators and 50% of White spectators previously participated in competitive basketball, and (b) 14% of Black spectators and 13% of White spectators were current participators in organized basketball leagues.

Motivations for Game Attendance Decision

Midwestern Market. For the Midwestern market, items that were identified as motives for the spectator's attendance decision included: (a) being fans of the game of basketball, (b) the opportunity to see positive role models (i.e., professional women athletes), (c) to see the team's players, (d) to support the league, (e) the quality of the play, (f) for entertainment, (g) to share the experience with family, and (h) to see the opposing team. Participants were asked to respond to the manner in which each factor influenced their decision to attend the team's games using a Likert scale of 1 (not influential at all) to 7 (very influential). The MANOVA revealed that two of the factors were significantly more important to the attendance decisions of the Black rather than White spectators: (a) the opportunity to support the league, $F(1, 612) = 6.72$, $p = .01$; M for Blacks = 6.51, M for Whites = 6.13 and (b) the opportunity to see the opposing team, $F(1, 612) = 18.86$, $p < .001$; M for Blacks = 4.25, M for Whites = 3.14. See Table 1.

Table 1.
MANOVA Results of Black and White Spectators' Responses to Factors Influencing Attendance Decision in the Midwestern Market *(7 = Very Influential; 1 = Not Influential at All)*

Attendance Factors	Black Spectators Mean (Std. Dev)	White Spectators Mean (Std. Dev.)	F-value
1. Fan of the game of basketball.	6.03 (1.34)	5.74 (1.71)	2.32
2. To see positive role models.	5.89 (1.54)	5.62 (1.74)	1.82
3. To see the team's players.	6.35 (1.03)	6.09 (1.28)	3.35
4. To support the league.*	6.51 (1.04)	6.13 (1.35)	6.72
5. The quality of the play.	6.26 (1.04)	6.09 (1.24)	1.42
6. Entertainment.	6.32 (.960)	6.23 (1.12)	.404
7. Share experience with family.	5.11 (2.18)	4.68 (2.33)	2.66
8. To see the opposing team. **	4.25 (2.21)	3.13 (2.12)	21.30
Composite Attendance Motive Variable**	5.84 (.936)	5.47 (1.04)	10.19

* Denotes factor that is significant at the .01 level.
** Denotes factors that are significant at the .001 level.

Table 2.
MANOVA Results of Black and White Spectators' Responses to Factors Influencing Attendance Decisions in the Southern Market *(5=Most Important; 1=Least Important)*

Attendance Factors	Black Spectators Mean (Std. Dev)	White Spectators Mean (Std. Dev.)	F-value
1. Basketball Action	4.70 (.75)	4.70 (.69)	.001
2. Entertainment*	2.66 (1.52)	1.95 (1.28)	80.52
3. Social Atmosphere*	3.33 (1.39)	2.99 (1.42)	17.80
4. Adult Giveaways*	2.52 (1.59)	2.00 (1.42)	38.79
5. Children Giveaways*	2.46 (1.71)	1.65 (1.44)	81.78
6. Special Promotions*	2.80 (1.62)	2.11 (1.46)	60.93
7. Food*	2.34 (1.69)	1.73 (1.44)	49.87
8. Ticket Price*	3.59 (1.57)	3.05 (1.52)	36.66
Composite Attendance Motive Variable*	3.05 (1.03)	2.52 (.920)	90.06

* Denotes factors that are significant at the .001 level.

The attendance decision motives had a reliability coefficient of .78. Based on the internal consistency of the responses, a composite attendance motivation variable was computed to examine the differences between the overall responses of Black and White spectators. Also revealed in the MANOVA was that the summated attendance motive variable was more important in the attendance decisions of the Black rather than White spectators, $F(1, 612) = 10.19$, $p = .001$; M for Black spectators = 5.84, M for White spectators = 5.47.

Southern Market. Factors that were posited as motives for the attendance decision at the professional women's basketball games in the Southern market included the following variables: (a) basketball action, (b) pre-game entertainment/activities, (c) social atmosphere, (d) promotional/giveaway items for adults, (e) promotional/giveaway items for children, (f) other special promotions, (g) quality of food, and (h) ticket price. Using a Likert scale of 1 (least important) to 5 (most important), participants were asked to respond to each item in terms of its importance in determining their decision to attend the game. The MANOVA revealed that seven of the eight motives were more influential in the attendance decision of the Black rather than White spectators. The only factor the spectators did not respond significantly different to was basketball action, F (1, 1226) =.001, p=.98 (means for both groups = 4.70). See Table 2.

The attendance decision motives had a reliability coefficient of .85. Based on the internal consistency of the responses to the items, a composite attendance motivation variable was computed to examine the differences between the overall responses of Black and White spectators. The MANOVA revealed that the summated attendance motivation variable was more important to the attendance decision of the Black rather than White spectators, $F(1, 1226) = 86.95, p < .001$; $M = 3.05$ for the Black spectators and $M = 2.52$ for the White spectators.

Predictors of Game Attendance Frequency

To examine the manner in which active basketball involvement- and attendance-decision motivations (previously discussed) actually predicted attendance frequency at the professional women's basketball games, multiple regression analyses were performed for Black and White spectators. For the midwestern market, the results revealed that the model of predictors was significant for the White spectators, explaining approximately 21% of the variance in attendance [$F(2, 510)$, =67.44, R^2=.209, p<.001 with both variables being significant at the univariate level: (a) active participation in basketball, Beta = .286, t =7.23, p<.001, and (b) the summated attendance-decision motivation, Beta = .390, t =9.84, p<.001]. In contrast, the model for the predictors was not significant regarding the attendance frequency for the Black spectators [$F(2, 86)$ = .981, R^2 =.02, p=.38].

The predictor variables for the southern market included past basketball participation, current basketball participation, and the summated attendance-decision motivation variable. For the southern market, the multiple regression analysis revealed findings that were opposite the ones found for the midwestern market. The model of predictors were not significant for the attendance frequency of the White spectators [$F(3, 526) = 2.20$, R^2 = .012, p=.09]. However, the model of predictors was significant for the Black spectators [$F(3, 652) = 3.12$, p=.03, although it explained only a negligible amount of the variance in attendance (R^2=.014)]. The results indicated that while current basketball participation was not significant at the univariate level (B=.043, p=.28), past basketball participation was significant (B=.091, t=2.29, p=.02), as was the composite attendance-decision motivation variable (B =.076, t = 1.94, p=.05).

Discussion

The profile of the participants in this study revealed demographic differences among the subsamples of Black and White spectators; however, the demographic differences between Blacks and Whites were similar in both markets (e.g., more Blacks were younger and single, more Whites were educated and affluent, yet both Blacks and Whites were employed in professional occupations). Based on these findings, in both markets, demographic segmentation strategies based on age, income, and marital status may not capture the Black and White spectators similarly. The communications tools used for team/game information were more similar than dissimilar for the Black and White spectators in the midwestern and southern markets, with the exception of Black spectators in the southern market relying more on radio for team information. This latter finding reiterated the effectiveness of radio in promoting sport to Black consumers as discussed by Johnson (1995).

The finding regarding pre-game activities highlighted the potential attractiveness of pre-game social activities to the White spectators, because White spectators were more likely to make their sport experience an extension of a social outing at a bar or restaurant than were the Black spectators. Black and White spectators in both markets exhibited similar behaviors regarding their game purchases or willingness to purchase team merchandise. A noteworthy difference regarding team purchases was that a greater percentage of the White spectators in both markets were more likely to engage in advanced ticket purchases. Therefore, marketing activities related to last-minute promotions and impulse buying may be more effective for the Black than the White spectators as the Whites tended to engage in planned or advanced purchases.

Burnett, Menon, and Smart (1993) discussed the need for sport marketers to examine the manner in which sport spectators may differ from sport participants in order to further segment the market for sport consumers. Shank (1999) also contended that in some instances the sport spectator and sport participant markets overlap. The findings of this study suggested that basketball participant and spectator markets among Black and White consumers existed and overlapped to varying degrees in the respective markets; however, differences in the basketball spectator and participant markets between the Black and White consumers were also revealed (such that active basketball participation was a particularly positive predictor for Whites' attendance in the midwestern market and past basketball participation was predictive of attendance for Blacks in the southern market). These findings indicated that promotional activities that seek to involve spectators in active basketball participation may vary in their appeal to Black and White spectators in different regions of the country.

Concerning the spectators' attractions to the respective games, in both markets the Black and White spectators' attendance was primarily influenced by game- and basketball-related attributes. These findings supported those of Ferreira and Armstrong (2003) regarding the importance of product attributes to sport-attendance decisions. Zhang et al. (1995) revealed promotions were more influential on game attendance for Blacks than for Whites. This study supported the findings of Zhang et al. (1995) in that Black spectators in both the southern and midwestern markets responded significantly higher to the summated attendance-motivation variable. Moreover, for the southern market adult giveaways, children giveaways, and other special promotions were more important to the attendance decision of Black than White spectators, and the summated attendance motivations were significant predictors of Blacks' game-attendance frequency, offering further support for the influence of promotional activities on ethnic minorities' sport consumption decisions.

According to Zhang et al. (1995) the influence of the home team was similar for ethnic groups; however, this study revealed that for the midwestern market (where the home team reflected a racial balance between Black and White players) the opportunity to see the *opposing team* (rather than the home team) was more important to the attendance decisions of Black spectators than of White spectators. For the southern market, the influence of the players on the home team (predominately Black) on the spectator's attendance decision was not directly ascertained. Nonetheless, a comparison of the findings for the two markets offered insight into a likely latent influence of race of home team on attendance.

For example, Gouke (1987) suggested that two distinct markets exist: one for general (mainstream) consumers and one primarily for Black consumers. Blacks and Whites may purchase a product that is designed for the general market at similar rates; however, a product primarily designed for the Black consumer market is most often purchased by Black consumers only. Relating Gouke's (1987) contentions to this study, since the team in the midwestern market had a racially balanced composition, it may have been perceived as a product for the "general" market and therefore, consumed by Blacks and Whites similarly. The ANOVA findings supported this premise in that game-attendance frequency in the midwestern market did not differ statistically based on the spectators' race. Consequently, the racial composition of the attendees at the professional women's basketball games for the team in the midwest generally reflected and represented the racial composition of the MSA (approximately 14% and 12%, respectively). These findings supported Baade and Tiehen's (1990) contention that the representation of Black and White sport attendees would generally correspond to their representation in a population.

Conversely, also based on Gouke's (1987) premise, the team (and management) in the southern market was predominately Black, and therefore may have been perceived as a product with a specific appeal to the "Black" consumer market, and thus more likely to be consumed more often by Black consumers. The ANOVA findings supported this premise in that game attendance frequency for the southern market differed significantly based on the spectators' race, such that Black spectators attended the games of the predominately Black home team at a frequency that was significantly higher than that of the White spectators. Consequently, the representation of Blacks generally in attendance at this team's games was more than twice the percentage of Blacks living in this metropolitan area (53% and 26%, respectively). Black spectators were overrepresented at the games, while White spectators were underrepresented. These results collectively imply modest support for: (a) Schurr et al. (1988), regarding race being statistically significant in explaining differences between basketball attendees and nonattendees; (b) Sapolsky (1980), regarding the disposition Black spectators may have to watch Black athletes perform; and (c) the premise offered by Gouke (1987), regarding the race of a consumer-product features - and rate of product consumption phenomenon, such that certain product features are likely to influence the consumption rates of certain consumers.

Implications for Sport Marketers

The findings of this study illustrated similarities and differences in the consumption-related profiles of two regional samples of Black and White spectators. There are a number of practical implications of the results of this study. The racial differences revealed implied that race effects may influence (a) sport consumer/target market segmentation, (b) advertising and marketing communications strategies, (b) the sale and distribution of sport event tickets, (c) effectiveness of pre-game promotions, and (d) the success of community-relations activities involving basketball participation. This study also demonstrated that the impact of race on sport consumption may be geographically influenced, such that the impact of race on sport marketing strategies (and subsequently sport consumer behavior) might be more pronounced in some regional locations than in others.

The results of this study also have theoretical implications regarding the nuances of sport consumer behavior. For example, although attendance at the professional women's basketball games in the midwestern market was relative to the racial demographics of the environment's population, the substantial Black attendance at the games in the southern market was anomalous and offered an illustration of an exceptional consumption pattern referred to by Mason (1981) as *conspicuous consumption*. Conspicuous consumption has traditionally been viewed as an economic, status-directed activity (i.e., a consumption pattern that affirms a desired economic status for the consumer); however, it may be influenced by a myriad of personal and social factors as well (Mason, 1981). In the context of this study, it may be surmised that an illustration of socially conspicuous consumption was displayed by the Black spectators in the southern market in that social factors such as racially/ethnically related consumer, environmental, and/or product utility characteristics may have collectively influenced their sport consumption patterns.

Limitations and Future Considerations

The nature of this investigation did not allow the researchers to infer causality; therefore, inferences could only be made from the descriptive data gathered (as inferred from and supported by previous, related research). As such, this study offered valuable insight into the similarities and differences of the sport consumptions of Black and White professional women's basketball attendees from different geographical markets. Nevertheless, the results of this study are not generalizable to (a) Black and White sport consumers in general, (b) Black and White sport consumers in the respective markets, or (c) Black and White basketball consumers in particular. One limitation of this study was comparing similar data ascertained using different instruments (albeit relevant to the respective consumer studies in each market) for each team under investigation. Future research on market analyses should seek to standardize the instruments used at the outset.

Race does not exist in isolation, as it undoubtedly interacts with a myriad of sociodemographic and psychographic variables to influence behavior. Additionally, race is not a homogeneous or finite construct, and therefore is a difficult 'variable' to measure. The amount of uncontrolled and unexamined variance in this study prevented the researchers from attributing the differences found between the Black and White spectators exclusively to their race. Future research should examine how demographic (particularly age, gender, income, marital status and education), social, and psychological factors may interact with facets of race to influence sport attendance.

Sport does not exist in isolation from the sociocultural environment in which it operates. Based on the manner in which attitudes often influence behavior (Fazzio, 1990), it is likely that the prevailing attitudes and beliefs of consumers in an environment may also influence the sport behaviors therein. As such, another limitation of this investigation was that racial attitudes were not ascertained. Due to the manifestations of race in the findings for the southern market, which has a history of overt racial demonstrations (Viorst, 1981), future research should examine the degree to which racial attitudes and perceptions (at the macro and micro levels) contribute to differences in Blacks' and Whites' sport consumption behaviors.

Conclusion

Undoubtedly, environments help to shape human behavior. As Danielson (1997) contends, "markets create probabilities, rather than determine outcomes" (p. 46). Therefore, one of the greatest challenges sport marketers may face, in light of an increasingly racially and ethnically diverse population of sport consumers (Hofacre & Burman, 1992), is ascertaining the manner in which sociocultural and environmental market factors influence sport consumption. Social scientists such as Hacker (1992) have long concluded that racial dynamics pervade various factions of human life including social institutions that guarantee or contest it such as economics, politics, education, religion, etc. Mullin, Hardy, and Sutton (2000) asserted that "race is the enduring American conundrum, especially in the sport marketplace" (p. 62) and ". . . there is little evidence that the patterns of Black sport involvement have any basis in 'race'" (p. 61). However, Harrison, Lee, and Belcher (1999) revealed that race serves as a self-schema that influences sport involvement, and Goldsmith (2003) revealed that while Whites' participation in sport was influenced more by structural and socioeconomic variables, Blacks' sport participation was influenced more by race relations.

Notably, of the two markets under comparison, the one in which a significant influence of race was revealed (i.e., the southern market) was the one that had the most pronounced minority racial characteristics. With other sociodemographic and market characteristics being fairly equal and more similar than dissimilar, the results of this study implied that differences in Blacks' and Whites' active and vicarious sport consumption may indeed be based in latent and manifest elements of race [e.g., the racial classification of the individual consumer, the racial characteristics of the sport team (players and management) as the product to be consumed, and the racial demographics of the environment in which the sport consumption takes place]. Thus, the findings of this study implied support of Hacker's (1992) contention, reiterated the premise of Goldsmith's (2003) findings, and thus refuted the previous assertion of Mullin et al. (2000).

Although the focus of this study was on the sport of basketball, the findings supported previous studies on race and baseball attendance (Noll, 1974; Staples, 1987). Given baseball's storied racist past (Staples, 1987), a negative relationship between race and attendance was not surprising. Just as baseball has had a traditional social role in American culture, basketball has had a historical presence in the Black community and has long been thought to be a sport with particular appeal to the Black culture (Sachs & Abraham, 1979). Therefore, it was not too surprising that racial differences were also manifested in this study involving basketball consumption. Previous research on the influence of race on sport consumption has focused on men's sports. This study revealed that racial dynamics might also influence the consumption of professional women's sports.

References

Baade, R. A., & Tiehen, L. J. (1990). An analysis of major league baseball attendance, 1969-1987. *Journal of Sport and Social Issues, 14*(1), 14-32.

Burnett, J., Menon, A., & Smart, D. T. (1993). Sports marketing: A new ball game with new rules. *Journal of Advertising Research* (September/October), 21-35.

Danielson, M. N. (1997). *Home team: Professional sports and the American metropolis.* Princeton, NJ: Princeton University.

Fazio, R.H. (1990). Multiple processes by which attitudes guide behavior: The mode model as an integrated framework. In M.P. Zanna (Ed), *Advances in Experimental Social Psychology* (Vol. 23, pp. 75-109). New York: Academic Press.

Ferreira, M., & Armstrong, K.L. (2003). *An examination of attributes influencing students' decisions to attend college sport events.* Manuscript submitted for publication.

Goldsmith, P.A. (2003). Race relations and racial patterns in school sports participation. *Sociology of Sport Journal, 20*(2), 147-171.

Gouke, C. G. (1987). *Blacks and the American economy.* Needham Heights, MA: Ginn Press.

Greater Columbus Chamber of Commerce Research Department. (1995). *Columbus profile* [Brochure]. Columbus, OH: Author.

Hacker, A. (1992). *Two nations: Black and White, separate, hostile, unequal.* New York: Ballantine Books.

Harrison, L., Lee, A. L., & Belcher, D. (1999). Race and gender differences in sport participation as a function of self-schema. *Journal of Sport and Social Issues, 23*(3), 287-307.

Hofacre, S., & Burman, T. K. (1992). Demographic changes in the U.S. into the twenty-first century: Their impact on sport marketing. *Sport Marketing Quarterly, 1*(1), 31-36.

Johnson, P. (1995). Black radio's role in sports promotion: Sports, scholarships, and sponsorships. *Journal of Sport and Social Issues, 19*(4), 397-414.

Mason, R. S. (1981). *Conspicuous consumption: A study of exceptional consumer behavior.* New York: St. Martin Press.

Metro Atlanta Chamber of Commerce. (1996). *Atlanta MSA labor force and employment* [Brochure]. Atlanta, GA: Author.

Mullin, B. J., Hardy, S., & Sutton, W. (2000) *Sport marketing* (2nd Ed.). Champaign, IL: Human Kinetics.

Noll, R. G. (1974). Attendance and price setting. *Government and the sports business.* Washington, DC: The Brookings Institute.

Pan, D. W., Gabert, T. E., McGaugh, E. C., & Branvold, S. E. (1997). Factors and differential demographic effects on purchases of season tickets for intercollegiate basketball games. *Journal of Sport Behavior, 20*(4), 447-463.

Sachs, M. L., & Abraham, A. (1979). Playground basketball: A qualitative field examination. *Journal of Sport Behavior, 2*(1), 27-36.

Sapolsky, B. S. (1980). The effect of spectator disposition and suspense on the enjoyment of sport contests. *International Journal of Sport Psychology, 11,* 1-10.

Schofield, J. A. (1983). Performance and attendance at professional team sports. *Journal of Sport Behavior, 6*(4), 196-206.

Schurr, K. T., Wittig, A. F., Ruble, V. E., & Ellen, A. S. (1988). Demographic and personality characteristics associated with persistent, occasional, and non-attendance of university male basketball games by college students. *Journal of Sport Behavior, 9*(1), 3-17.

Shank, M. D. (1999). *Sports marketing: A strategic perspective.* Upper Saddle River, NJ: Prentice Hall.

Staples, B. (1987, May 17). Where are the Black fans? *The New York Times Magazine,* 27-31.

Sutton, W. A., & Watlington, R. (1994). Communicating with women in the 1990s: The role of sport marketing. Sport Marketing Quarterly, 3(2), 9-14.

United States Bureau of the Census. (1994). Land area, population 1992. *County and city data book* [Online]. Retrieved from http://www.census.gov/statab/ccdb/ccdb301.txt.

United States Bureau of the Census. (1997). Metropolitan area rankings. State and metropolitan area data book (5th ed.) [Online]. Retrieved from http://www.census.gov/Press-Release/metro01.prn.

Viorst, M.(1981). *Fire in the streets: America in the 1960's.* New York: Simon & Schuster.

Zhang, J. J., Pease, D. G., Hui, S. C., & Michaud, T. J. (1995). Variables affecting the spectator decision to attend NBA games. *Sport Marketing Quarterly, 4*(4), 29-39.

13

Marketing to Lifestyles: Action Sports and Generation Y

Gregg Bennett and Tony Lachowetz

Introduction

The youth market is a highly coveted consumer segment that is difficult to both reach and influence. The current youth market has been called the Echo Boom Generation, but it is most commonly known as Generation Y. This generation of Americans consists of individuals born between 1982 and 2003 (Howe & Strauss, 2000). Generation Y makes up almost 25% of the United States population, while Generation Y's predecessor, Generation X, makes up only 16% of the population. Individuals born between 1946 and 1964 comprise the Baby Boom Generation, which currently makes up a larger percentage (28.2%) of the United States population (Gardyn & Fetto, 2000); however, this advantage will decrease as Baby Boomers continue to age. As the number of Baby Boomers decreases, the spending power and influence of Generation Y will subsequently increase. The sheer size of Generation Y, coupled with the reported spending habits of young people, makes this segment a desirable target of corporations and sport marketing professionals.

The action sports genre is a growing segment of the sport industry that has, in many cases, connected with the elusive Generation Y market (Bennett, Henson, & Zhang, 2002; Bennett, Henson, & Zhang, 2003; Bennett & Henson, 2003). Action sports are an eclectic collection of risky, individualistic, and alternative sports such as skateboarding, BMX biking, surfing, street luge, wakeboarding, and motocross. The growth of action sports has been demonstrated by increased media coverage and the addition of several major tours and events; concurrently, there have been increased athlete endorsements, corporate sponsorships, branding, and lay-athlete participation rates among members of Generation Y (Bennett et al., 2002; Kelly & Warnick, 1999).

Much of the aforementioned growth is partially due to the sport consumption habits of Generation Y. For example, McCarthy (2001) suggests that action sports boast over 58 million consumers between the ages of 10 and 24 who wield $250 billion in buyer power. Members of Generation Y consume action sports more than any preceding generation, leading some to label action sports as "Gen-Y sport" (Gordon, 2000; Petrecca, 1999).

Accordingly, aggressive lifestyle marketing campaigns implemented by marketing specialists and practitioners have effectively targeted the Generation Y market through action sports using ad campaigns and platforms and activations at action sports events.

The marketing and promotion of action sports does not simply focus on the individual, collective sporting events, or athletes. This genre of sport has merged with music, apparel, and movie industries to form a large sporting culture (Fitzgerald, 2000). The action sport culture includes numerous apparel lines, video games, movies and documentaries, events, and concert tours. The influence of action sports is pervasive in Generation Y culture. A cursory look at commercials targeting Generation Y (i.e., Saturday mornings) demonstrates the influence of the genre. Companies and advertisers are more likely to use teens riding skateboards to promote products than traditional athletes like baseball or football players. Moreover, one of the highest grossing films of 2002 was XXX, an action film supposedly representing the modern day secret agent or James Bond. In this movie, actor Vin Diesel participates in action sports throughout the film. Perhaps nowhere are the effects of action sports more ubiquitous than in the video gaming business, which has grown into an extremely lucrative industry. Tony Hawk's Underground and Pro Skater 4 have sold quite well among young consumers. As Liberman (2004) informs, Hawk's videogame franchise is only outsold by John Madden's professional football video game.

Another important indicator of the powerful influence of the action sports segment on Generation Y includes the explosion of grassroots and large-scale events, most of which have managed to obtain substantial corporate sponsorship. Currently, the five major action sports events include the Gravity Games, Gorge Games, Great Outdoor Games, Winter X Games and Summer X Games. Recently, Clear Channel-NBC announced it would sponsor the Mountain Dew Action Sports Tour, an event that will commence in May of 2005 (Lefton, 2004). The Dew Action Sports Tour will serve as a professional action sports regular season with stops in five cities. At the end of the Dew Action Sports Tour, individual leaders in event categories will be awarded prize money and the "Dew Cup" (Lefton, 2004).

These events represent an attempt by broadcasters, marketing firms, and advertisers to commercialize action sports into a package that will reach Generation Y in the form of a large-scale event. The first large-scale event was created by ESPN in 1995, an event initially called the Extreme Games and currently known as the X Games (Pedersen & Kelly, 2001). Originally, ESPN intended to create a marketing platform that would enable broadcast companies and sponsors to reach the elusive, and hard to influence, youth market. This creation of large-scale events and tours represents a critical step towards successfully influencing Generation Y consumers. Bill Carter, the president and partner of Fuse Integrated Sports Marketing, reinforces this message:

> The media and advertising community are those responsible for developing, in part, the landscape that allows for any sport to become a successful platform for a brand. They have a simple formula: they respond to the interests of the demographics by way of developing advertising and media that sells to those groups. When they finally figured out, about five years later than it was actually happening, that action sports were a key pillar within youth culture, media and advertising responded accordingly. Since the involvement of TV networks and the advertising community, action sports have snowballed into something bigger and bigger, now with over 30 million participants. (personal communication, June 20, 2003)

Action sports are also popular on a grassroots level because many companies connect with action sports tours, such as Tony Hawk's Boom-Boom Huck Jam, in an effort to reach Generation Y. Broadcasted by NBC, the Vans Warped Tour is an annual festival that tours throughout the United States and combines fashion, music, and action sports. Mountain Dew's Free Flow Tour is another example of a grassroots effort that will likely expand the genre. Furthermore, action sports camps where beginning athletes can improve and refine their skateboarding and/or snowboarding skills have developed throughout the United States. In fact, a few of these camps have begun to attract older, more skeptical adult members of Generation X (Bennett et al., 2003).

Lifestyle Marketing (LM) and Action Sports

According to Hanan (1980), lifestyle marketing (LM) is "a strategy for seizing the concept of a market according to its most meaningful, recurrent patterns of attitudes and activities, and then tailoring products and their promotional strategies to fit these patterns" (pp. 2-3). LM targets the consumer segment by addressing the patterns common within the group (Swenson, 1990). As stated by Michman (1991), the goal of LM is to connect with the consumer through their lifestyle choices by assessing "how individuals spend their time, what they consider important about their surroundings, their opinions on various issues, and their interests" (p. 19). Some of these lifestyle choices include product usage and purchasing habits, media usage, preferred recreational activities, heroes and role models, ethnic and religious associations, and product awareness (Hanan, 1980; Michman, 1991; Swenson, 1990). Demographic and psychographic characteristics are also important considerations when implementing LM strategies.

Mullin, Hardy, and Sutton (2000) suggest that the integration of a company's message with the lifestyle pursuits of a targeted market adds immediate credibility to the corporation or sponsor. Because leisure pursuits are such an effective avenue for presenting sales messages to consumers, association with a sporting event has become an important LM strategy. Events that are viewed favorably by a particular target market allow investors and sponsors to be viewed favorably as well (McDaniel, 2002; Mullin et al., 2000). In fact, the popularity of action sports events has led to commercial successes for sponsors, media, and athletes.

The lifestyle habits of Generation Y consumers have been well documented (Bennett et al., 2002; Bradish, Lathrop, & Sedgwick, 2001; Lim & Turco, 1999). Many youth in this demographic population are avid Internet surfers, are technologically savvy, and enjoy various forms of media, including television, magazines, and video games. In fact, media consumes a large portion of Generation Y members' time, often between 33 and 38 hours a week (Henry J. Kaiser Foundation, 1999).

In addition to simply viewing action sports, it appears that members of Generation Y assume the lifestyle and actively participate in the sports. Skateboarding (20.1%), in-line skating (163.1%), snowboarding (238.8%), and roller hockey (51.9%) each realized significant and, in some cases, remarkable percentage growth rate increases from 1991 to 2001 among young people (National Sporting Goods Association, 2002). These growth rates were apparent across all age groups, but much of this change is due to the increases realized within the youth segment: Snowboarding rose from 1.8 million to 3.6 million participants during the 1990s; skin and scuba diving participation increased 75% from 1979 to 1996; rock climbing realized an increase of 3.3 million participants, from just under 5 million participants in 1993 to 8.3 million in 1997; and the number of people riding mountain bikes soared, from less than 4 million in the early 1990s to more than 8 million in 1998 (Bennett et al., 2003; Kelly & Warnick, 1999). Some individuals are spending large sums of money for extreme sports vacations at exotic locales, and serious extreme sports athletes compete in eco challenges throughout the world (Esquire, 2000).

Another characteristic fueling the action sports phenomenon is the grassroots campaign being driven by individual lay-athletes. Much of the increase in the participation rates of action sports can be tied directly to the individual nature of the sports, which appears to be an attractive feature for Generation Y. As a result, the more traditional team sport of baseball saw a participation rate decrease of 33% from 1990 to 2002, while sports such as skateboarding and snowboarding are among the few to experience large increases in participation patterns (Bennett, Dees, & Tsuji, 2004; Sporting Goods Manufacturers Association, 2004). Children are opting for skateboards instead of baseball bats and gloves, and an increase in "skate moms" signals a correlation with the "soccer mom" phenomenon of the 1990s (Bennett et al., 2004; McCarthy, 2001).

As reported by Coakley (2001), action sports provide members of Generation Y with an enticing alternative to the "increasingly exclusive, structured, performance-oriented, and elitist" organized youth sport programs prevalent in America (p. 118). According to Coakley, when children play by themselves, they are typically interested in action, personal involvement, a close score, and opportunities to reaffirm friendships. The importance of activity, excitement, and movement to members of Generation Y is easily correlated to the recent growth of the action sport genre as it focuses on intense, action-packed, risky, individualistic sporting endeavors.

Action Sports Target Lifestyles

Action sports events attempt to connect with Generation Y by capturing the lifestyle and culture surrounding these sports through live music and interactive elements. Event marketing allows broadcast companies like ESPN, NBC, and the Outdoor Life Network to aggressively seek corporate partners and sponsors whose products and image parallel the lifestyles exhibited by spectators and TV viewers of the different events. According to the general manager of the Dew Action Sports Tour, Wade Martin, companies are

> interested in action and lifestyle sports for a number of reasons. First, the growth and popularity of these sports, from a viewership and participation perspective, are overwhelming. Second, this category is an attractive and elusive demographic for advertisers. Third, companies believe they can be a leader in the area of action and lifestyle sports with respect to providing opportunities for corporate partners and sponsors through their brand. (personal communication, June 15, 2003)

The fact that this genre has recently flourished allows companies to re-focus their marketing efforts in an attempt to manipulate the consumption habits of Generation Y. Companies have the potential to sell more apparel and equipment to Generation Y if action sports and events thrive and prosper. Since action sports have the innate attractiveness and magnetism to reach this target market, a clear objective of the different events is to remain competitive and appealing. Carter explains:

> Action sports speak to youth culture, as they represent elements that this demographic sees as important, including creativity, individuality, friendship/camaraderie (even within a competitive setting), and a style that can only be developed when not

> constrained by teams and rules found in traditional sports like football, baseball, and basketball. Our clients don't necessarily utilize action sports for the "sport" of it, but rather to connect to a culture that teens identify with and claim as their own. Action sports are cool and why wouldn't a brand want to be where cool is? (personal communication, June 20, 2003)

Action sports events also cater to the lifestyles of Generation Y consumers through interactive elements and live music. According to Eliza Russell, event coordinator of the Gravity Games,

> The event includes various elements that capture the essence of the action sports culture, including an interactive village, live concerts from every genre, and professional demonstrations, in addition to amazing athletic competitions. Event attendees can ride a BMX bike on a dirt course or try skateboarding and inline skating on a street course, both built by the same guys who created our professional courses. People who come to the Gravity Games have the chance to be more than simply a spectator. They really become part of the action. (personal communication, January 15, 2003)

The fascination that Generation Y consumers have with action and lifestyle sports has generated increased interest among sport marketing agencies, major TV networks, and corporate entities. The marketplace is becoming much more competitive for companies involved with action sports; consequently, strategies shift the focus from development and awareness to continual growth and enhancement of brand image in order for the events to remain viable with Generation Y. This appears especially true since this generation is responsible for the increase in action sports popularity and retail spending. Capitalizing on this increase in popularity and Generation Y spending, through the enhancement of their brand image and partnerships with major TV networks, action sports events can continue to provide marketing opportunities for their clients who seek to influence this highly sought after, but very elusive, target segment. According to Carter,

> Implementing and reinforcing this strategic initiative is critical if we are to provide added value for our corporate sponsors and remain a leader in the action sports arena. Our clients include brands that target teens and young adults, typically between the ages of 13-25. Sponsors include Pepsi's Mountain Dew brand, Gillette's Right Guard Xtreme Sport brand, Ford Motor Company, Motorola, Quiksilver, Burton Snowboards, and others. While their products differ (e.g., beverages, deodorant, automobiles, cell phones, surf-inspired casual clothing, and snowboards), what they have in common is a difficult-to-influence target. Note that I said difficult to influence, not difficult to reach, as they are very easy to reach—TV, radio, events, and magazines all reach them. What is difficult is to cut through the clutter of the millions of messages they are bombarded with and get them to identify with your brand. (personal communication, June 20, 2003)

According to Bennett et al. (2002), corporate sponsors continue to view action sports and action sports events as effective mediums for their message. One brand, Pepsi's Mountain Dew, seems to have managed to get their message to Generation Y (Bennett et al., 2002). In fact, Pepsi has repositioned the Mountain Dew brand to be seemingly ubiquitous in the action sports world. Mountain Dew seems inextricably linked to action sports for an entire generation of consumers (Bennett et al., 2002). Thus, it seems appropriate that Mountain Dew would become the presenting sponsor of the Dew Action Sports Tour (Lefton, 2004). Heidi Sandreuter, a marketing manager with Pepsi-Cola

Sports Marketing, contends that the brand sponsors action sports because of the positive consequences that have been documented. Sandreuter further explains the importance of leveraging Mountain Dew with Generation Y by attempting to connect and associate with the lifestyles of its members:

> The edginess, irreverence and exhilaration of Action Sports was/is the perfect fit for Mountain Dew. These shared equities resonate powerfully with the teen male target, so by aligning with such edgy activities that teens enjoy or admire, Mountain Dew increases its brand affinity among a critical demographic. Mountain Dew also benefits from the fact that the Action Sports association is not just about tapping into a sport ... it's about becoming part of a culture that provides endless ways of communicating to consumers ... through music, fashion, sports etc. Instead of just showing snowboarders and skateboarders in its advertising, Mountain Dew wanted to stand out as a true supporter of Action Sports. As a result, Dew became a sponsor of the ESPN XGames and the Vans Triple Crown as well as of numerous Action Sport athletes. And to further legitimize its presence in this space, the brand started its own grassroots skate park tour, the Mountain Dew Free Flow Tour, that recognizes and supports amateur skaters across the country. (personal communication, April 25, 2003)

Conclusion

Action sports events may increase in popularity over the next few years. Since action sports were founded by individuals seeking to be involved in participant-controlled sports, the genre may continue to have some mass appeal for the members of Generation Y (Coakley, 2001). Therefore, many companies and marketers will seek to benefit from the transfer of brand associations resulting from the firms aligning themselves with the events and athletes that appeal to the youth segment.

Certainly, there are valuable lessons that can be learned from the substantial growth of the action sports industry. Since there has been such a dramatic rise in the popularity and strength of the genre, practitioners should analyze the efforts made by those responsible for expanding the industry. For example, marketing campaigns and sporting event activations that connect with youth market lifestyles have an evident influence on the popularity of the sports and athletes. Obtaining sponsors that appeal to targeted markets or have the capability of transferring images is another objective that has been utilized by action sports marketers and managers. Finally, marketers should consider being authentic or creating a "cool" image when attempting to influence the youth market, especially one so large and filled with cynicism toward corporate sponsorship. Choosing sponsors that can deliver on authenticity rather than simply provide a revenue stream may allow greater return on investment in the future for those targeting Generation Y.

The Dew Action Sports Tour and the action sports industry in general will provide a fertile ground of investigation for scholars and potential growth opportunities for the industry. It will certainly be interesting to investigate the effects of a professional tour on the action sports industry. Additional research efforts may focus on sponsorship and the advertising effectiveness of tours, events, athlete endorsements, and other marketing communication efforts. Since the events are more like festivals, with interactive elements, festival villages, and music, an examination on how these additional features affect consumer behavior would provide valuable research. Comparing the growth of action sports, including participation patterns and equipment sales trends, to more traditional and established segments of the sport industry through trend analyses seems especially important. Since events and tours are vitally important to the industry, exploration of consumer satisfaction with these events could add to the literature and aid practitioners. Finally, important social issues warrant analysis when considering action sports as a research stream. For instance, the health-related benefits associated with sports like skateboarding and BMX biking should be studied since the genre appeals to and depends on the youth market. Additional social issues should be assessed, including how the genre affects the family, organized youth sport, traditional coaching, and other social institutions.

The action sports industry could serve as a model for marketers, promoters, practitioners, and corporations attempting to connect with members of Generation Y. Associating their brands with large-scale, multi-purpose events, such as the X Games, Gravity Games, or the Dew Action Sports Tour may be a viable strategy for firms attempting to reach this elusive market. These events are replete with athletes, music, and interactive components that appeal to the lifestyle behaviors of Generation Y.

References

Bennett, G., Dees, W., & Tsuji, Y. (June 3, 2004). *Exploring the action sports phenomenon: Trendy fad or established segment?* Paper presented at the annual conference of the North American Society for Sport Management, Atlanta, GA.

Bennett, G., Henson, R., & Zhang, J. (2003). Generation Y perceptions of the action sports industry segment. *Journal of Sport Management, 17*(2), 95-115.

Bennett, G., & Henson, R. (2003). Status of the action sports segment among college students. *International Sports Journal, 7*(1), 124-138.

Bennett, G., Henson, R., & Zhang, J. (2002). Action sport sponsorship recognition. *Sport Marketing Quarterly, 11*(3), 185-196.

Bradish, C., Lathrop, A., & Sedgwick, W. (2001). Girl power: Examining the female pre-teen and teen as a distinct segment of the sport marketplace. *Sport Marketing Quarterly, 10* (1), 19-24.

Coakley, J. (2001). *Sociology of sport: Issues and controversies* (7th ed.). New York: McGraw-Hill.

Fitzgerald, K. (2000, May 15). Bash is a smash: Beach volleyball, extreme sports join forces in Mervyn's event. *Advertising Age, 71*, 60.

Gardyn, R., & Fetto, J. (2000, June). Demographics: It's all the rage. *American Demographics, 22*(6), 72.

Gordon, D. (2000, January 1). Up, up, and away, dude! Extreme sports: What in the world is freestyle motorcross? *Newsweek*, pp. 78-80.

Hanan, M. (1980). *Life-styled marketing.* New York: Anacom.

Henry J. Kaiser Foundation. (1999). *Kids & media @ The new millennium.* Retrieved from http://www.kff.org/entmedia/1535- index.cfm

Howe, N., & Strauss, W. (2000). *Millenials rising: The next great generation.* New York: Random House.

Kelly, J., & Warnick, R. (1999). *Recreation trends and markets: The 21st century.* Champaign, IL: Sagamore.

Lefton, T. (2004, July 12-16). Mountain Dew will title Clear Channel-NBC Tour. *SportBusiness Journal, 7*(11), p. 1, 39.

Liberman, N. (2004, July 12-16). New heights or a crash landing? *SportBusiness Journal, 7*(11), p. 25-26.

Lim, C., & Turco, D. (1999). The next generation of sport: Y. *Cyberjournal of Sport Marketing, 3*(4).Retrieved from http://pandora.nla.gov.au/nph-arch/1999/Z1999-Nov-1/http://www.cjsm.com/vol3/ lim34.htm

McCarthy, M. (2001, August 14). ESPN's promotion of X Games goes to extremes. *USA Today*, C.

McDaniel, S. (2002). An exploration of audience demographics, personal values, and lifestyle: Influences on viewing network coverage of the 1996 Olympic Games. *Journal of Sport Management, 16*(2), 117-131.

Michman, R. (1991). *Lifestyle marketing segmentation.* New York: Praeger.

Mullin, B., Hardy, S., & Sutton, W. (2000). *Sport marketing.* Champaign, IL: Human Kinetics.

Pedersen, P., & Kelly, M. (2001). *ESPN X Games: Commercialized extreme sports for the masses.* Retrieved from http://sptmgt.tamu.edu/espnx.htm

Petrecca, L. (1999, October 11). Defying gravity: NBC, Petersen connect with cynical teens via sports fest. *Advertising Age, 70*(42), 36, 38, 40.

Sporting Goods Manufacturers Association (2004).*State of the industry 2004.* Retrieved from http://www.sgma.com/reports/2004/report1073334018-29562.html

Swenson, C. (1990). *Selling to a segmented market: The lifestyle approach.* Westport, CT: Quorum.

14

Using the Psychological Commitment to Team (PCT) Scale to Segment Sport Consumers Based on Loyalty

Daniel F. Mahony, Robert Madrigal, and Dennis Howard

"Marriages come and go. So do jobs, hometowns, friendships. But a guy's attachment to a sports team? There's a bond that holds the heart."

The preceding statement on fans' obsession with sports teams appeared recently as the lead sentence in a feature article in *USA Today*, the United States' largest daily newspaper (Eisler, 1997). The quote captures the fanaticism or intense partisanship that Guttmann (1986) uses to define fans as "emotionally committed consumers of sporting events" (p. 6). The attention given to sport by hard-core fans and other spectators is well documented. Americans buy almost 200 million tickets to attend professional and collegiate sporting events each year (U.S. Bureau of Census, 1993), spending about $5 billion annually for admission (Bureau of Economic Analysis, 1996). In 1996, the retail sales of products bearing the trademark or logo of teams in the four major professional sports leagues in the United States and Canada totaled $8.8 billion, an increase of 126% over the $3.9 billion spent in 1990 (National Sporting Goods Association, 1996). Although fans' time and monetary investments in sports seem to have grown exponentially in recent years, it is important to recognize that not all those who watch or attend sporting events are fans committed to the teams they view. Zillman and Paulus (1993) characterized *spectators* as individuals who watch a game but then forget about the experience once it is over, whereas Sloan (1989) said a *fan* is one who watches as an enthusiastic devotee.

The Concept of Fan Loyalty

Although the notion of loyalty to team extends back to antiquity (Lee, 1983), very little is known about the social-psychological factors that produce strong emotional attachment to sports teams or organizations. Previous research outside the sport-fan literature has shown that individuals who are emotionally involved devotees to a particular product or service are far more likely to repurchase that product or service and to evaluate the brand or experience more positively (e.g., Havitz & Howard, 1995). Smith, Patterson, Williams, and Hogg (1981) found the same relationship extended to sport fans. Although not addressing the concept of loyalty directly, their study of avid sport fans found that "deeply committed fans" displayed a much greater propensity to watch and attend sporting events featuring their favorite teams. More recently, Wakefield and Sloan (1995) concluded that "team loyalty," defined as enduring allegiance to a particular team, was the most important factor in determining spectators' desire to attend live sporting events.

Although there are many behaviors that may be an expression of fan loyalty (e.g., television viewing, radio listening, team merchandise purchases), prior research has relied heavily on attendance data to measure fan loyalty to sports teams. Total attendance (e.g., Baade & Tiehan, 1990), increases in ticket sales (e.g., Howard & Crompton, 1995), and the extent of repeat attendance (e.g., Mullin, Hardy, & Sutton, 1993) have been used as behavioral indicators of consumers' loyalty to a sports team or organization. Mullin and his associates demonstrated the potency of repeat patronage, confirming the application of the "80-20 principle" (Evans & Berman, 1994) to sports teams. In their analysis of season attendance at Pittsburgh Pirates games, Mullin et al. found that 80% of the increase in ticket sales from one season to another was produced by 20% of the existing attendees' buying more tickets. Although repeat attendance may be the most evident manifestation of a person's attachment to a team, this strictly behavioral indicator ignores the underlying psychological processes explaining why some people attend more games over time.

In fact, research has shown attendance alone is a poor measure of loyalty. Murrell and Dietz (1992) found individuals' support for a particular team may be strong regardless of actual attendance. Backman and Crompton (1991a) identified several factors explaining why strictly behavioral or "observable" measures like attendance are inadequate indicators of loyalty. They contend that "behavioral measures do not discriminate between purchasing based on habit or lack of convenient opportunities" (p. 206). For example, an NFL fan in Nashville, Tennessee, may attend Tennessee Titans games because there are no other professional football options in the area, and he or she may not necessarily be a committed fan of the Titans. Therefore, "true" loyalty exists only when the consumer regularly purchases the product or service and also displays a strong, positive attitude toward a specific brand (Day, 1969).

Loyalty as a Two-Dimensional Construct

The multidimensional nature of loyalty has long been of interest to brand loyalty researchers. In order to provide a focus for this research, Olson and Jacoby (1971) developed a six-point definition of brand loyalty, which is now widely cited. Their definition, later restated slightly by Jacoby and Kyner (1973), states that brand loyalty is "(1) a biased (i.e., nonrandom), (2) behavioral response (i.e., purchase) (3) expressed over time (4) by some decision making unit (5) with respect to one or more alternative brands (6) as a function of psychological (decision making, evaluate) processes" (p. 2). Although Jacoby and Kyner (1973) focused on testing all six of the elements, most of the loyalty research has focused primarily on two main dimensions, behavioral and attitudinal (e.g., Backman & Crompton, 1991a, 1991b; Jacoby & Chestnut, 1978). Although Day (1969) was the first to propose a two-dimensional conceptualization of loyalty integrating both behavioral and attitudinal components, later research provided empirical evidence that consumer loyalty was in fact composed of these two separate but related elements (e.g., Backman & Crompton, 1991a, 1991b; Olson & Jacoby, 1971).

		Strong	Weak
Behavioral Consistency (Attendance Frequency)	High	High (True) Loyalty	Spurious Loyalty
	Low	Latent Loyalty	Low (Non) Loyalty

Figure 1.
Loyalty Model

For example, Backman and Crompton (1991a) used attitudinal and behavioral scores to segment respondents in their study of golf and tennis participants. A 13-item semantic differential scale was used to measure "participants' general feelings toward the activities" (p. 208). The researchers referred to this dimension as attitudinal loyalty. The proportion of participation devoted to golf or tennis during the previous 12-month period was used as the measure of behavior. They then used a two-dimensional matrix to distinguish four discrete levels of loyalty (Figure 1). The resulting four-quadrant matrix served to classify participants into specific groups by weak or strong attitudes and high or low behavioral consistency.

Following Day's (1969) earlier characterization, those demonstrating strong psychological attachment (i.e., high attitudinal loyalty) as well as active participation (i.e., high behavioral loyalty) were placed in the upper left quadrant, labeled "High (True) Loyalty." Consumers placed in the upper right quadrant, labeled "Spurious Loyalty," were those who exhibited high behavioral loyalty, but low attitudinal loyalty. Because of the low level of attitudinal loyalty, dropout rates among these spuriously loyal consumers tends to be high. In contrast, respondents who were strongly attached to their activity (i.e., high attitudinal loyalty), but exhibited a low frequency of participation (i.e., low behavioral loyalty) were placed in the lower left quadrant, labeled "Latent Loyalty." Latently loyal consumers often express a strong desire to participate, but may lack the means (e.g., time, money, equipment) to engage in the activity on a regular, ongoing basis. Finally, those in the lower right quadrant, or "Low Loyalty" segment, were respondents who exhibited low levels of both behavioral and attitudinal loyalty.

Backman and Crompton (1991b) advanced the understanding of loyalty in a sport and leisure context in two important ways. First, their two-dimensional approach reaffirmed and extended Day's (1969) claim that any measure of a person's commitment to a brand or, in the case of Backman and Crompton's work, a sport "activity" must take into account the individual's disposition toward that activity (i.e., attitude) as well as the frequency of his or her participation (i.e., behavior). Second, their identification of four discrete levels of loyalty provided important insights into the complexity of the construct. They demonstrated that the traditional all-or-none portrayal of loyalty as a simple dichotomy between loyal and nonloyal consumers was far too narrow. For example, the ability to measure consumers' strength of attachment to a particular sport product or service in order to separate the highly loyal from the spuriously loyal is crucial to distinguishing genuine loyalty from habitual purchase behavior.

Commitment as Attitudinal Loyalty

Although Backman and Crompton (1991a) demonstrated the importance of linking attitudes with behaviors in measuring loyalty, the approach they used in operationalizing the attitude component, which they termed "psychological attachment," was very limited. Pritchard, Havitz, and Howard (1999) were the first to provide both a theoretically grounded and psychometrically sound basis for measuring the attitude bias component of loyalty. These researchers developed a scale for measuring loyalty toward specific travel-service providers, such as airlines and hotels. They used the construct of commitment as the foundation for explaining the psychological processes underlying and leading to consumer loyalty. A number of researchers have argued that psychological commitment best describes the attitude component of loyalty. Day (1969) contended true loyalty exists only when there is "commitment to a brand or product." Jacoby and Chestnut (1978) further elaborated the construct's connection to loyalty, stating that "as a result of this evaluative process, the individual develops a degree of commitment to the brand in question; he is 'loyal.' The concept of commitment provides an essential basis for distinguishing between brand loyalty and other forms of repeat purchasing behavior" (p. 84).

According to Crosby and Taylor (1984), people who are high in psychological commitment "resist changing their preference in response to conflicting information or experience" (p. 414). Drawing heavily from the work of Crosby and Taylor, Pritchard et al. (1999) operationalized psychological commitment as the tendency to resist changing one's preference based on the desire to maintain cognitive consistency. The desire for consistency between an individual's beliefs and feelings toward an object produces a stable behavioral intention toward that object (Rosenberg, 1965). Support for Crosby and Taylor's interpretation of commitment based on resistance to change is found in Kiesler's (1971) earlier work on commitment. Kiesler and associates established in several experiments that the "effect of commitment is to make an act less changeable" (Kiesler & Mathog, 1971; Kiesler & Sakamura, 1966, p. 349). Moreover, recent research suggests "that loyal consumers—those who have a strong commitment to a service or brand—show strong resistance to counter persuasion attempts" (Schiffman & Kanuk, 1997, p. 223).

Proceeding, then, on the belief that psychological commitment was a strong barometer of preference stability, Pritchard et al. (1999) developed a scale that measured the attitude component of loyalty on the basis of how committed people were toward a specific travel service. Following a rigorous scale construction procedure (Churchill, 1979; Dawis, 1987), the researchers developed a 13-item scale that demonstrated strong psychometric qualities. Using samples across three travel-service subsets (destination golf resorts, airlines, hotels), Pritchard and his associates produced an instrument displaying consistently high reliability as well as discriminant and convergent validity.

Creating a Commitment to Team Scale

The purpose of this study is to extend Pritchard et al.'s (1999) work to establish a scale for assessing the strength of an individual's commitment to sport teams. It is expected that fans who demonstrate loyalty toward a sports team possess an attitude bias that is both resistant to change and persistent over time. In addition, it is expected that strong and weak attitudes, or levels of personal commitment, toward a team would be effective guides to behavior (Fazio, 1995; Petty, Haugtvedt, & Smith, 1995). Those individuals scoring high on the personal commitment scale would accurately represent those fans truly devoted to a particular team. Conversely, those scoring low would be classified, at best, as spuriously loyal, with a substantial number having little or no emotional attachment to the team. Determining the strength of an individual's attitude or commitment, therefore, would allow for meaningful differentiation between "fair-weather" and "deeply committed" fans (Smith et al., 1981).

Scale Development

The Psychological Commitment to Team (PCT) scale (see Table 1) was developed using multiple steps and four phases of data collection. Instrument development relied heavily on the work of Pritchard et al. (1999) and the suggestions of Churchill (1979) on scale development (e.g., generating items, purifying the measure, assessing reliability and validity). Specifically, the following steps were taken in the current study: (a) items were generated; (b) items were pretested; (c) scale was tested with three separate samples in three different team sport settings (i.e., professional football, college football, professional basketball) to establish internal consistency and reliability; and (d) scale was tested with two samples (one from the University of Oklahoma and one from The Ohio State University) to determine if it had construct and predictive validity.

Generating Items

Based on the findings of Crosby and Taylor (1983) and the results of recent attitude strength studies (Haugtvedt & Petty, 1992; Haugtvedt & Wegener, 1994), resistance to change was believed to be a critical factor underlying commitment. Therefore, items were generated that emphasized the importance of resistance to change. In particular, the authors attempted to measure whether fans would remain committed to the team when something occurred that might change their commitment (i.e., poor team performance, loss of good players, change in the coach).

A couple of items from the original Pritchard et al. (1999) PCI scale were determined to be easily adaptable to a sports context and were included in the item pool. As suggested by Churchill (1979), additional items based on a review of the literature on sport fans were then generated by the authors. Churchill's suggestion that items be worded both positively and negatively was also followed. The Psychological Commitment to Team (PCT) scale used a 7-point Likert scale ranging from *strongly disagree* to *strongly agree.* Positively worded items were scored from 1 for strongly disagree to 7 for strongly agree, whereas negatively worded items were scored from 7 for strongly disagree to 1 for strongly agree. Therefore, a higher score always represented greater psychological commitment to the team. The 15 total items generated were then sent to a panel of judges to determine the appropriateness of each item with respect to clarity and face validity. The panel, which included experts in research related to sport consumer behavior, provided unanimous support for the inclusion of all 15 items.

Pretesting Items

A convenience sample (*N*=100) was then used to examine the scale for internal consistency. Using an initial sample to purify the measure is also a suggestion made by Churchill (1979). All surveys collected were usable. The respondents were incoming freshmen at The Ohio State University who were recruited from the 1994 summer orientation program. Each was asked to answer the questions with regard to his or her favorite National Football League (NFL) team. Professional football was selected because of its popularity in the United States and because of the general awareness of NFL teams. A *USA Today/Gallup Poll* found that professional football ranked first in popularity among the four major professional sports in the United States (as cited in Mihoces, 1995). Examination of the item-to-total correlations found one item ("It is normal for a person to change their allegiance to a local team after relocating") had a low negative correlation with the total (*r*=.08). Because the item had such a low correlation and did not ask about the fan's personal relationship with his or her favorite team, the item was eliminated from the scale, resulting in the 14-item PCT scale that was further tested with the three remaining samples.

Establishing Internal Consistency and Reliability

A second convenience sample (*N*=151) was recruited from undergraduate classes at the University of Oklahoma. The original sample size was 153, but 2 respondents were eliminated because they indicated they had no favorite team. The final sample (*N*=151) included 89 men (58.9%) and 62 women (41.1%) with a mean age of 23.45 (approximately 23 years 6 months old). Respondents were again asked to answer the questions with regard to their favorite NFL team. As per Churchill's (1979) recommendation, Cronbach's (1951) coefficient alpha was used initially to examine the measure's internal consistency to help establish reliability. Cronbach's coefficient alpha estimate for the 14-item PCT scale was .88. This estimate was greater than the .70 minimum that has been suggested by Nunnally and Bernstein (1994). Examination of the item-to-total correlations (see Table 1) found that only item number 2 had an item-to-total correlation of less than .30 (r = .25). This item was not eliminated from the scale for several reasons: (a) eliminating this item would not have changed the coefficient alpha estimate; (b) the item-to-total correlation was very close to the .30 mark being used in this study; (c) the item had an item-to-total correlation well above .30 during the pretesting of the scale (r = .54); and (d) the item was believed to be important in measuring psychological commitment to team (PCT) because of the results of prior research and the studies related to the domain of this construct (Crosby & Taylor, 1983).

A third convenience sample (*N*=157) was recruited from a number of graduate and undergraduate classes at the University of Louisville. The sample included 113 men and 44 women with a mean age of 23.01 years. This time respondents were asked to answer the questions with respect to their favorite National Basketball Association team. Cronbach's coefficient alpha was used once again to examine the scale's internal consistency. Cronbach's alpha estimate for the 14-item scale was again .88, establishing the reliability of the scale items. The item-to-total correlations (see Table 1) were .30 or better for all items. In

Table 1.
Item-to-Total Correlations and Alpha Coefficients If That Item Were Deleted for the PCT Scale

Item	Item-to-Total Correlations			Alpha If Deleted		
	Sample 2 (*N*=151)	Sample 3 (*N*=157)	Sample 4 (*N*=76)	Sample 2	Sample 3	Sample 4
1. I might rethink my allegiance to my favorite team if this team consistently performs poorly.	.595	.481	.739	.87	.88	.94
2. I would watch a game featuring my favorite National Football League (NFL) team regardless of which team they are playing.	.255	.353	.679	.88	.88	.94
3. I would rethink my allegiance to my favorite team if management traded away its best players.	.371	.473	.773	.88	.88	.94
4. Being a fan of my favorite NFL team is important to me.	.635	.550	.760	.87	.87	.94
5. Nothing could change my allegiance to my favorite NFL team.	.673	.684	.723	.87	.87	.94
6. I am a committed fan of my favorite NFL team.	.733	.713	.808	.86	.86	.94
7. It would not affect my loyalty to my favorite NFL team if management hired a head coach that I disliked very much.	.513	.497	.653	.88	.88	.94
8. I could easily be persuaded to change my favorite NFL team preference.	.690	.564	.791	.87	.87	.94
9. I have been a fan of my favorite team since I began watching professional football.	.360	.516	.569	.88	.88	.94
10. I could never switch my loyalty from my favorite NFL team even if my close friends were fans of another team.	.690	.728	.814	.87	.86	.94
11. It would be unlikely for me to change my allegiance from my current favorite NFL team to another.	.765	.754	.781	.87	.86	.94
12. It would be difficult to change my beliefs about my favorite NFL team.	.813	.760	.714	.86	.86	.94
13. You can tell a lot about a person by their willingness to stick with a team that is not performing well.	.354	.300	.465	.88	.88	.94
14. My commitment to my favorite NFL team would decrease if they were performing poorly and there appeared little chance their performance would change.	.426	.346	.739	.88	.88	.94

particular, the item-to-total correlation for item 2 was .353. Therefore, the authors believe the decision to keep this item was appropriate.

The fourth convenience sample (*N*=76) was collected from students at The Ohio State University. Selfidentified Ohio State fans were asked to fill out the scale with regard to the OSU football team. The only item that had to be adjusted somewhat was item number 3. The item, which was worded "I would rethink my allegiance to my favorite team if management traded away its best players" when examining professional sport teams, was changed to "I would rethink my allegiance to the Ohio State football team if their best players left the team (i.e., transfer, graduate, etc.)." All questionnaires were completed, and they were all usable. Cronbach's coefficient alpha was used once again to examine the scale's internal consistency to help further establish reliability. Cronbach's alpha estimate for the 14-item scale was .94, again exceeding the minimum threshold of .70 suggested by Nunnally and Bernstein (1994). The item-to-total correlations, shown in Table 1, were better than .45 for all items.

Establishing Construct and Predictive Validity

The authors used a number of methods to establish construct and predictive validity. First, the authors examined the PCT scale with a known group. One common method for determining the validity of a scale is to distribute the scale to a group that should score high on the scale (Churchill, 1979). If the group does in fact indicate a high score, this would be further evidence to support the scale's construct validity. When examining the fourth convenience sample, fans who indicated they had a very strong interest in Ohio State football (*N*=43; a score of 6 or 7 on a one-item measure with 1=Minimal Interest to 7=Strong Interest), the PCT score was very high (*M*=88.09, *S.D.*=8.76). This is much higher than the average score on the PCT scale with the professional football sample (*M*=70.12) and the professional basketball sample (*M*=62.60). In addition, a one-way ANOVA (with interest in OSU football as the independent variable and score on the PCT as the dependent variable) showed that fans who indicated a strong interest in OSU football (6 or 7) scored significantly higher on the PCT scale than did fans who had less interest in OSU football (*N*=33; less than 6 on a scale of 1 to 7), $F(1, 74) = 104.33$, $p < .001$. Therefore, the examination of the known group provided support for the construct validity of the PCT scale.

Second, another method for determining if an attitude scale is valid is to examine if scores derived from the scale can predict related behaviors. In fact, a recent metaanalysis by Kraus (1995) found that attitudes have been very useful in predicting future behavior in a variety of settings. Because a strong relationship is expected between attitudinal loyalty and behavioral loyalty, a series of analyses were used to determine if the Psychological Commitment to Team (PCT) scale was significantly related to various measures of behavioral loyalty. Using the second convenience sample, the current study examined the relationship between score on the PCT scale and (a) the duration of one's commitment to a team, (b) the frequency with which, according to their own report, the respondents generally watched their favorite team on television, and (c) the percentage of games featuring their favorite team that the respondents actually watched during the NFL regular season.

The correlations between the Psychological Commitment to Team (PCT) scale and all three behavioral loyalty measures were examined to determine whether the scale demonstrated effective predictive validity. High correlations with these behavioral loyalty measures would indicate that the measure is appropriate for assessing attitudinal loyalty. First, there was a significant positive correlation between the PCT scale and the number of years as a fan of the favorite team, $r = .426, p < .001$. Second, there was a significant positive correlation between the PCT scale and how often the respondents generally watched their favorite team, $r = .584, p < .001$. Third, there was a significant positive correlation between the PCT scale and the percentage of the favorite-team games respondents actually watched during the NFL season, $r = .563, p < .001$.

The Psychological Commitment to Team scale again demonstrated good predictive validity when used to analyze Ohio State football fans in the fourth convenience sample. The relationship between score on the PCT scale and three behavioral measures of fan loyalty was examined. First, a regression analysis was used to determine whether the respondents' scores on the PCT scale could be used to predict the number of Ohio State football games attended during the last season. The results indicated that psychological commitment to the Ohio State football team did make a significant contribution to the prediction of the number of games attended, ($R^2 = .273, p < .001$). Second, a chi-square analysis examined whether scores on the PCT scale (a median split was used on PCT score) could predict whether students had purchased Ohio State football tickets during the prior season. The results of the chi-square analysis indicated there was a significant relationship between psychological commitment to the OSU football team and the purchase of season tickets, χ^2 $(df=1) = 8.85, p < .003$. Analysis of the frequencies indicated that those who scored higher on the PCT scale were more likely to buy season tickets. Third, another chi-square analysis examined whether "score" on the PCT scale (a median split was again used on PCT score) could predict whether the student "makes every effort to watch or listen" to Ohio State football games he or she does not attend. The results of the chi-square analysis indicated there was a significant relationship between psychological commitment to the OSU football team and making an effort to watch or listen to the team, χ^2 $(df=1) = 14.77, p < .001$. Analysis of the frequencies indicated those who scored higher on the PCT scale were more likely to make every effort to watch or listen to the team.

Overall, the PCT scale demonstrated strong predictive validity, and the analysis provided evidence of its construct validity. Therefore, the scale appears to be useful with both college and professional teams.

Conclusion and Implications

The Psychological Commitment to Team (PCT) scale provides researchers with a reliable and valid tool for measuring attitude loyalty, or the strength of fans' commitment to a particular sports team. Previous research has shown that capturing the dispositional nature of attachment is crucial to establishing true loyalty (Day, 1969; Dick & Basu, 1994). Research by Howard and Thompson (1984) has shown that customers' level of loyalty to a particular brand or service mediates their responsiveness to accompanying information and their intentions to repurchase that good or service. The stronger the attitude typically the greater the likelihood of congruent behavior. Not surprisingly, then, the more positively disposed individuals are toward a particular object, the more likely they are to attend to advertising messages relevant to that object, share positive affirmations (e.g., word of mouth) about the object, and ultimately, purchase the product.

The initial tests conducted in this study demonstrated the score derived from the PCT scale by itself can be very useful in predicting attendance at sporting events and television viewing behavior. The scale's capabilities for predicting loyal behavior in the future, however, are more fully realized when the PCT score is combined with a measure of past behavior. As Backman and Crompton (1991a, b) and Pritchard et al. (1999) demonstrated, combining attitude loyalty with behavior (e.g., frequency of repeat purchase) provides a basis for differentiating customers into meaningful loyalty segments. The easy-to-administer PCT scale provides sport marketers with a tool for assessing the extent to which their existing fan base falls into deeply committed or fair-weather fan categories. Knowing what percentage of a team's existing fan base falls into high, spurious, latent, or low loyalty categories provides the basis for developing a marketing program that optimizes the potential for strengthening fans' attachment to the team.

Knowing what percentage of a team's existing fan base falls into high, spurious, latent, or low loyalty categories provides a starting point for developing customized programs that account for varying levels of attachment held by fans. The varying attitude-behavior combinations represented in each cell in Figure 1 suggest that different approaches to changing or maintaining current levels of loyalty are required for each segment (see Table 2). The following sections discuss specific marketing strategies and tactics for optimizing the strength of fans' attachment to a team for each of the four loyalty segments.

High-Loyalty Segment

Description

In the upper left quadrant of Figure 1 are the truly loyal fans (i.e., high loyalty). Fans in this segment score high on the PCT scale (i.e., high attitudinal loyalty) and exhibit strong behavioral loyalty (e.g., attending games, watching games on television). For these fans, the relationship with the team has probably become a significant part of their lives, and they are unlikely to change their behavior or level of commitment. However, the loyalty level of this group may decrease slowly over time if this segment is ignored by marketers or may decrease more quickly if something very drastic happens.

Strategy

A reinforcement strategy is the best means for marketing to the highly loyal fans (Pritchard et al., 1999; Sheth, 1987). This strategy should focus on reinforcing existing cognitions, allaying the potential for dissonance to occur (Pritchard et al., 1999; Sheth, 1987). Because they are so valuable to the team, marketers want to avoid a situation in which highly loyal fans would decrease their behavior or reconsider their allegiance to their favorite team. Moreover, marketers want to focus on increasing the behavior of these loyal fans (e.g., number of games attended, amount of merchandise purchased) and increasing the strength of their commitment. Therefore, the reinforcement strategy involves a two-pronged approach. First, behavioral loyalty can be reinforced extrinsically through economic incentives (e.g., discounts, value-added services). Second, psychological reinforcement based on intrinsic rewards can be provided by personalized encouragement (e.g., newsletters, VIP treatment). The objective is to progressively increase the yield from these best consumers by developing a long-term, interactive, value-added relationship.

For example, the San Diego Padres have developed a successful program for rewarding their most loyal customers ("With Frequency," 1996). Recently, this Major League Baseball team developed a loyalty program designed to reward frequent attendance, as

Table 2.
Suggestions for Marketing to the Four Loyalty Segments

Segment	Suggestions
High Loyalty	Marketers should use a reinforcement strategy that includes reinforcing behavioral loyalty through economic incentives and attitudinal loyalty through personalized encouragement. This strategy is designed to increase the yield from this segment and to avoid any chances of losing the segment.
Spurious Loyalty	Marketers should focus on increasing the fans' psychological commitment through the use of a rationalization strategy. This can be done by promoting the positive attributes of the product or service, getting the fans to articulate why they support the team, and/or coupling attendance with support of a relevant social cause.
Latent Loyalty	Marketers should focus on increasing the positive behaviors of the latently loyal fan by using a market inducement strategy. This can be done by removing significant barriers to behavior and by offering economic incentives to engage in certain behaviors.
Low Loyalty	Although some might suggest marketers use a confrontation strategy, which requires a direct attack on the fan's existing attitudes, others believe this may only lead to strengthening the fan's low level of commitment. Many strategists instead recommend focusing on using either a rationalization strategy to increase commitment or an inducement strategy to increase behavior as a first step to high loyalty.

well as to encourage fans to attend as many games as possible. The Padres reward fans by allowing those who attend games to register for membership in the Compadres Club. Based on frequency of game attendance, club members earn points ("hits") toward increasingly attractive prizes, including exclusive autograph sessions and inclusion in pregame chalk talks. Registration for club membership also allows the Padres to identify their most loyal customers, to send customized newsletters, and to solicit consumer satisfaction feedback from these most desirable fans.

Spurious-Loyalty Segment

Description

Spuriously loyal fans, those in the upper right quadrant of Figure 1, are fans who exhibit high levels of behavioral loyalty, but score low on the PCT scale. These fans may appear to most observers to be loyal fans of the team because they behave in the same manner as the truly loyal fans (e.g., frequently attending games, frequently watching games on television). However, they are not committed fans of the favorite team and could drop out at any point with little dissonance. There may be a number of reasons for this high level of behavior accompanied by low commitment, such as (a) they attend games primarily because friends or family want to attend; (b) they attend games of the home team, but are fans of a team in another location; (c) games are a relatively cheap source of entertainment; (d) they are given the tickets for free (by an employer or another business); or (e) they go to the game for other reasons (e.g., business interactions, socializing, drinking, gambling).

Strategy

With spuriously loyal fans, the strategy would be to increase the psychological commitment to the team they are already supporting behaviorally. Again, increased attitudinal loyalty among this segment is extremely important because these are generally the fans who will stop supporting the team when something goes wrong (e.g., team performance decreases; a popular player is traded). Sheth (1987) recommends a market rationalization strategy as a way to strengthen consumers' commitment toward a product they are already buying. The intent is to create rationalized reasons to justify their behavior.

One approach is to focus on promoting the attributes of the product or service (Sheth, 1987) in an attempt to provide the spuriously loyal fan with rational reasons why he or she should support the team (e.g., first-class tradition, fan-friendly team). Second, it would also be helpful to get the fans "to articulate, at least on a rationalized basis, why they buy or use the product/service" (Sheth, 1987, p. 27). Prior research suggests that as consumers try to justify their purchase, they tend to become more committed to the product or service they purchased (Schiffman & Kanuk, 1997).

Third, coupling attendance with support for a relevant social cause may be an important rationalized reason for some spuriously loyal fans. An emerging strategy, called alignment marketing, attempts to improve a brand or company's fortunes by linking it to some highly valued celebrity or cause (IEG, 1995). Alignment marketing is based on the belief that if an organization is able to build a link in the consumer's mind between the product name and a cause that is of great importance to that consumer (e.g., feeding and sheltering the homeless, civic pride), then there is a strong probability that the consumer's perception of that particular brand or product will improve. This strategy may also provide the basis for fans to rationalize and, therefore, strengthen their emotional commitment to a team. A team, for example, that demonstrates its commitment to helping battered women by pledging a portion of each ticket sold to fund or construct a new shelter provides the spuriously loyal fan one more important reason to care about the organization and to attend games. In a college sport setting, it may be possible to focus on the team's high graduation rate, suggesting this is a program that values education first, or focus on the number of local players on the team, playing on the belief of some that it is important to support local "kids."

Latent-Loyalty Segment

Description

In contrast to spuriously loyal fans, latently loyal fans (lower left quadrant of Figure 1) are those who scored high on the PCT scale, but exhibit low levels of behavioral loyalty. Although these fans are unlikely to change their team allegiance, they do not exhibit many of the behaviors that would benefit the team (e.g., attending games). There may be a number of reasons for their low level of behavior including the high cost of some games, the time it takes to attend a game, and the accessibility of games. Many people in this segment may constitute what Mullin et al. (1993) refer to as "media consumers," those whose commitment is high but whose behaviors related to their favorite team are limited to more passive, indirect involvement through watching or listening to games and reading about the team in the newspaper. Moreover, fans who live outside their favorite team's region may have difficulty obtaining even media access to games and would, therefore, exhibit even less loyalty-related behavior.

Strategy

According to Sheth (1987), the market inducement strategy is most useful in reaching latently loyal consumers. To induce these fans to move toward more active, direct participation and into the "high-loyalty" group, where their behavior matches their attitude, Sheth recommends two approaches. First, the facilitation of inducement involves eliminating any obstacles that prevent consumers from purchasing the product or service they like. "It involves removal of time, place and possession barriers in target segments" (Sheth, 1987, p. 26). Second, economic incentives are another way to induce people to engage in behavior toward which they have a positive predisposition. Incentives could include a range of sales and promotional programs, such as coupons, ticket-price discounts, and the offering of lottery prizes.

The Milwaukee Brewers initiated a ticket-package campaign intended to reach fans who had not historically purchased season ticket packages (Eisengerg, 1993). Rather than just offering traditional full- (81 games) or halfseason (40 games) ticket options, the Major League Baseball club created a series of miniticket packages (13 games) tailored to the specific interests and abilities of their fan base (Eisengerg, 1993). In effect, fans were offered the opportunity to attend Brewer games on the dates (e.g., weekdays, Saturdays, and/or Sundays only) they most preferred and at the time they most preferred (afternoon or evenings) and to watch the combination of teams they most preferred, all at a substantial discount. The new program was enormously successful, increasing new or first-time season ticket sales by 41% (Eisengerg, 1993). Meanwhile, teams may also want to focus on increasing the media coverage of their games in order to reach fans who are not geographically close to their favorite team. For example, many college sport teams are focusing on increasing the radio reach of their games (e.g., picking stations with a wider reach, offering games over the internet) and on increasing access to televised games (e.g., pay-per-view) in order to reach their fans and alumni who do not live in their geographic region.

Low-Loyalty Segment

Description

Finally, low-loyalty fans (lower right quadrant of Figure 1) are those who scored low on the PCT scale and exhibited low levels of behavioral loyalty. These fans are not committed to the team and rarely support the team by attending games or by watching on television. It is likely that when these fans do attend games, it is merely for some reason unrelated to the team itself (e.g., to watch a particular player, to watch the opposing team, to socialize). They could drop out, and this would have no psychological impact on them and would result in almost no change in their daily lives.

Strategy

Low-loyalty consumers are the most challenging segment. These infrequent or nonattending patrons hold, at best, an ambivalent attitude toward the sports team. Converting this segment's behavior and predisposition is likely to be very expensive, and even then, the probability of success is low. Sheth (1987) recommended a confrontation strategy for reaching this disenfranchised market. This approach requires a direct attack on existing attitudes of the consumer. However, achieving the desired change may be very difficult. As Kiesler (1971) points out, this approach often results in a "boomerang effect" in which counterpersuasive communication strengthens the recipient's resistance to change. Moreover, the confrontation process is not a cost-efficient approach in terms of actually turning consumer attitudes and behavior.

A second approach would be to allow the movement of fans toward genuine loyalty to be undertaken gradually, concentrating on either behavioral or attitudinal change first (i.e., movement to spuriously or latently loyal). Marketers could focus on increasing the behavior first. This could be done by offering packages to various groups (e.g., families, businesses) that may result in the low-loyalty fans attending more games, by selling the game to the low-loyalty fans as part of an entire entertainment package, or by focusing on attributes other than the team (e.g., opposing team, star player). In addition, the rationalization strategy could be used to first focus on building a level of commitment to the team. However, both of these approaches are unlikely to produce highly successful results with this segment and may not be the best use of resources. Consequently, many strategists recommend focusing on the more attractive, less resistant spuriously loyal and latently loyal fans (Hawkins, Best, & Coney, 1995; Rothschild, 1987).

Summary

In general, the PCT scale can be very helpful to sport marketing practitioners who wish to use psychographic information to better target their fans and to better assess the current feelings about the team among fans and/or local residents. The scale is relatively short (it could even be used as part of a phone survey), easy to administer, and easy to adjust to different team sports at different competition levels. Use of the scale will allow marketers to better assess loyalty toward their team and to be better prepared for their future. The scale can also be useful in assessing the impact of past and current marketing and customer service efforts. Sport marketers who wish to move beyond the "build it and they will come" philosophy of sport marketing should find this scale useful in moving their marketing efforts forward.

References

Baade, R. A., & Tiehan, L. J. (1990). An analysis of major league baseball attendance: 1969–1987. *Journal of Sport and Social Issues, 14,* 14–32.

Backman, S. J., & Crompton, J. L. (1991a). The usefulness of selected variables for predicting activity loyalty. *Leisure Sciences, 13,* 205–220.

Backman, S. J., & Crompton, J. L. (1991b). Using a loyalty matrix to differentiate between high, spurious, latent and low loyalty participants in tow leisure services. *Journal of Park and Recreation Administration, 9,* 117.

Bureau of Economic Analysis (1996, January/February). *Survey of current business, 6.* Washington, DC: U.S. Department of Commerce.

Churchill, G. A., Jr. (1979). A paradigm for developing better measures of marketing constructs. *Journal of Marketing Research, 16,* 64–73.

Cronbach, L. J. (1951). Coefficient alpha and the internal structure of tests. *Psychometrika, 16,* 297–334.

Crosby, L. A., & Taylor, J. R. (1983). Psychological commitment and its effect on postdecision evaluation and preference stability among voters. *Journal of Consumer Research, 9,* 413–431.

Dawis, R. V. (1987). Scale construction. *Journal of Counseling Psychology, 34,* 481–489.

Day, G. S. (1969). A two dimensional concept of brand loyalty. *Journal of Advertising Research, 9,* 29–35.

Dick, A. S., & Basu, K. (1994). Customer loyalty: Toward an integrated conceptual framework. *Journal of the Academy of Marketing Science, 22,* 99–113.

Eisengerg, J. (1993, October). Small-market success: How the Milwaukee Brewers sold 43% more season tickets. *Team Marketing Report,* pp. 9–11.

Eisler, P. (1997, March 27). Guys go awry over losing. *USA Today,* p. 1D.

Evans, J. R., & Berman, B. (1994). *Marketing* (6th ed.). New York: Macmillan.

Fazio, R. H. (1995). Attitudes as object-evaluation associations: Determinants, consequences, and correlates of attitude accessibility. In R. E. Petty & J. A. Krosnick (Eds.), *Attitude strength: Antecedents and consequences* (pp. 247–282). Mahwah, NJ: Lawrence Erlbaum Associates.

Guttmann, A. (1986). *Sports spectators.* New York: Columbia University.

Haugtvedt, C. P., & Petty, R. E. (1992). Personality and persuasion: Need for cognition moderates the persistence and resistance of attitude changes. *Journal of Personality and Social Psychology, 63,* 308–319.

Haugtvedt, C. P., & Wegener, D. T. (1994). Message order effects in persuasion: An attitude strength perspective. *Journal of Consumer Research, 21,* 205–218.

Havitz, M., & Howard, D. R. (1995). How enduring is enduring involvement? A seasonal examination of three sports activities. *Journal of Consumer Psychology, 4,* 255–276.

Hawkins, D. I., Best, R. J., & Coney, K. A. (1995). *Consumer behavior: Building marketing strategy* (7th ed.). New York: McGraw-Hill.

Howard, D. R., & Crompton, J. L. (1995). *Financing sport.* Morgantown, WV: Fitness Information Technology, Inc.

Howard, D. R., & Thompson, P. (1984). The critical importance of the distribution variable in marketing strategy. *Visions in Leisure and Business, 3*(2), 34–40.

International Events Group (1995). *IEG's complete guide to sponsorship.* Chicago, IL.

Jacoby, J., & Chestnut, R. W. (1978). *Brand loyalty: Measurement and management.* New York: Wiley.

Jacoby, J., & Kyner, D. B. (1973). Brand loyalty V. repeat purchase behavior. *Journal of Marketing Research, 10,* 19.

Kiesler, C. A. (1971). *The psychology of commitment.* New York: Academic Press, Inc.

Kiesler, C. A., & Mathog, J. (1971). Resistance to influence as a function of number of prior consonant acts: A test. In C. A. Kiesler (Ed.), *The psychology of commitment.* New York: Academic Press, Inc.

Kiesler, C. A., & Sakamura, J. (1966). A test of a model for commitment. *Journal of Personality and Social Psychology, 3,* 349–353.

Kraus, S. J. (1995). Attitudes and the prediction of behavior: A metaanalysis of the empirical literature. *Personality and Social Psychology Bulletin, 21,* 58–75.

Lee, H. M. (1983). The sport fan and team loyalty in ancient Rome. *ARETE: The Journal of Sport Literature, 1,* 139–145.

Mihoces, G. (1995, May 23). Fans fight poststrike hangover. *USA Today,* pp. C1–C2.

Mullin, B. J., Hardy, S., & Sutton, W. A. (1993). *Sport marketing.* Champaign, IL: Human Kinetics Publishers.

Murrell, A. J., & Dietz, B. (1992). Fan support of sports teams: The effect of a common group identity. *Journal of Sport and Exercise Psychology, 14,* 28–39.

National Sporting Goods Association. (1996). *The sporting goods market in 1995.* Mt. Prospect, IL: National Sporting Goods Association.

Nunnally, J. C., & Bernstein, I. H. (1994). *Psychometric theory* (3rd ed.). New York: McGraw-Hill.

Olson, J. C., & Jacoby, J. (1971). A construct validation study of brand loyalty. *Proceedings of the American Psychological Association, 6,* 657–658.

Petty, R. E., Haugtvedt, C. P., & Smith, S. M. (1995). Elaboration as a determinant of attitude strength: Creating attitudes that are persistent, resistant, and predictive of behavior. In R. E. Petty & J. A. Krosnick (Eds.), *Attitude strength: Antecedents and consequences* (pp. 93–130). Mahwah, NJ: Lawrence Erlbaum Associates.

Pritchard, M. P., Havtiz, M. E., & Howard, D. R. (1999). Analyzing the commitment-loyalty link in service contexts. *Journal of the Academy of Marketing Science, 27,* 333–348.

Rosenberg, M. J. (1965). When dissonance fails: On eliminating evaluation apprehension from attitude measurement. *Journal of Personality and Social Psychology, 1,* 28–43.

Rothschild, M. L. (1987). *Marketing communications: From fundamentals to strategies.* Lexington, MA: D. C. Heath & Company.

Schiffman, L. G., & Kanuk, L. L. (1997). *Consumer behavior* (6th ed.). Upper Saddle Run, NJ: Prentice-Hall.

Sheth, J. N. (1987). A normative theory of marketing practice. In G. Frazier & N. Sheth (Eds.), *Contemporary views of marketing practice* (pp. 19–31). Lexington, MA: Lexington Press.

Sloan, L. R. (1989). The motives of sports fans. In J. H. Goldstein (Ed.), *Sports, games, and play: Sociological and psychological viewpoints* (2nd ed.; pp. 175–240). Hillsdale, NJ: Lawrence Erlbaum Associates.

Smith, G. J., Patterson, B., Williams, T., & Hogg, J. (1981, September). A profile of the deeply committed male sports fan. *Arena Review, 5,* 26–44.

U.S. Bureau of Census. (1993). *Statistical abstract of the United States: 1993* (113th ed.). Washington, DC: U.S. Department of Commerce.

Wakefield, K. L., & Sloan, H. J. (1995). The effects of team loyalty and selected stadium factors on spectator attendance. *Journal of Sport Management, 9,* 153–172.

With frequency promotion and database marketing, Padres expect fans to have many happy returns. (1996, March). *Team Marketing Report,* pp. 3, 8.

Zillman, D., & Paulus, P. B. (1993). Spectators: Reaction to sporting events and effect on athletic performance. In R. N. Singer, M. Murphey, & L. K. Tenant (Eds.), *Handbook of research on sport psychology* (pp. 600–619). New York: Macmillan.

SECTION V.

Fan Identity and Spectator Motives

15

Creating and Fostering Fan Identification in Professional Sports

William A. Sutton, Mark A. McDonald,
George R. Milne, and John Cimperman

Introduction

Fan identification is defined as the personal commitment and emotional involvement customers have with a sport organization. When a customer identifies closely with an organization, a sense of connectedness ensues and he or she begins to define him- or herself in terms of the organization (Mael & Ashforth, 1992). Sport differs from other sources of entertainment through evoking high levels of emotional attachment and identification.

The marketing and communication functions of a sports team cannot directly influence on-field success. Therefore, fan identification is an important concept because it may minimize the effects of team performance on long-term fiscal success and position in the sport entertainment hierarchy of its community. The Boston Red Sox, for example, have not won the World Series since 1906. Failure to win the championship, however, has not stopped fans from vigorously supporting the Red Sox by attending games on NESN, a regional sports television channel offering coverage of the Red Sox throughout New England.

Although people in the U.S. society are becoming disconnected from a sense of community as a result of changing lifestyles, societal interests and technological innovations (Putnam, 1995), interestingly this does not hold true for spectator sports. Spectator sports, in contrast, are deeply rooted in Rooney's (1974) concept of "Pride in Place" — meaning a key expression of community identification and expression. Sport promotes communication, involves people jointly, provides common symbols, a collective identity and a reason for solidarity (Lever, 1983). Noting the effect that sports has upon a community, Hall of Fame basketball star Kareem Abdul-Jabbar states, "Our (L.A. Lakers) collective success has forged some kind of unity in this huge and fragmented metropolis, and it cuts across class cultural lines" (Fox, 1994, p. 89).

In recent years, franchise movement, or the threat of such movement, has galvanized fan identification into not only a social force but also a political and judicial force. The recent move of the NFL's Cleveland franchise to Baltimore (where they will operate as the Ravens) demonstrates the depth of fan identification. At the time of the move, the

Browns had ranked among the top five teams in the NFL in terms of attendance for 12 of the previous 20 years.

When Art Modell, the owner of the Cleveland Browns, announced he was moving the team to Baltimore, it mobilized the community into a cohesive entity with a mission to retain their beloved franchise. Advertisers responded by pulling their advertising from Cleveland Stadium. The city received a preliminary injunction against the relocation, and at least nine independent law suits were filed by Browns' season ticket holders and fan groups against Modell and the Browns (Rushin, 1995).

Fans describe the Browns as part of the history of their families and refer to Modell as a murderer for killing their memories and future. Fan identification with the Browns was so established that the Browns Backers included over 63,000 members located in 200 chapters throughout the United States, the United Kingdom, and Japan. Despite the history, tradition, and support of the city of Cleveland, Art Modell was given permission to move his franchise to Baltimore for the 1997 season. However, in a negotiated settlement, the City of Cleveland retained the colors and nickname "Browns" and are to be awarded an NFL expansion team when the city constructs a new facility (Rushin, 1995).

During the same year, the Oilers, after 35 years in Houston, announced they were planning to move to Nashville, Tennessee. Support days were planned, protests scheduled, and lawsuits contemplated in response to the potential relocation. In contrast to the Cleveland Browns' situation, fan interest and support were lacking, indicative of small amounts of fan identification with the franchise. As a result, the Oilers will be moving to Nashville after the completion of their existing lease within the next 3 years. Although fan identification is clearly a powerful social and market force, there are no guarantees that it will develop for every team.

The purpose of this paper is to present a normative model to create and foster fan identification. Specifically, our objectives are to a) discuss the characteristics that lead to, and create, the identification between a sports team and its fan base and b) outline steps a sport organization can take to nurture and develop fan identification. We begin by presenting a conceptual framework for fan identification.

Conceptual Framework For Fan Identification

What factors increase levels of fan identification? What are the benefits of having highly identified fans? Social identification researchers believe that the level of identification with an organization depends on such factors as satisfaction with the organization, frequency of contact, and the visibility of affiliation (Bhattacharya, Rao & Glynn, 1995).

Bhattacharya's (1995) model relates member identification to three broad factors (a) organizational and product characteristics, (b) affiliation characteristics, and (c) activity characteristics.

Organizational and product characteristics relate to members' perceptions of the focal organization and its offerings, specifically, the perceived prestige of the focal organization and satisfaction with the membership benefits. Affiliation characteristics refer to the characteristics of a person's membership, such as length of membership, visibility of membership, and number of other similar organizations he or she patronizes. Activity characteristics refer to behavior patterns such as level of contact with the organization and donation of money to the focal organization (Bhattacharya, et al., 1995).

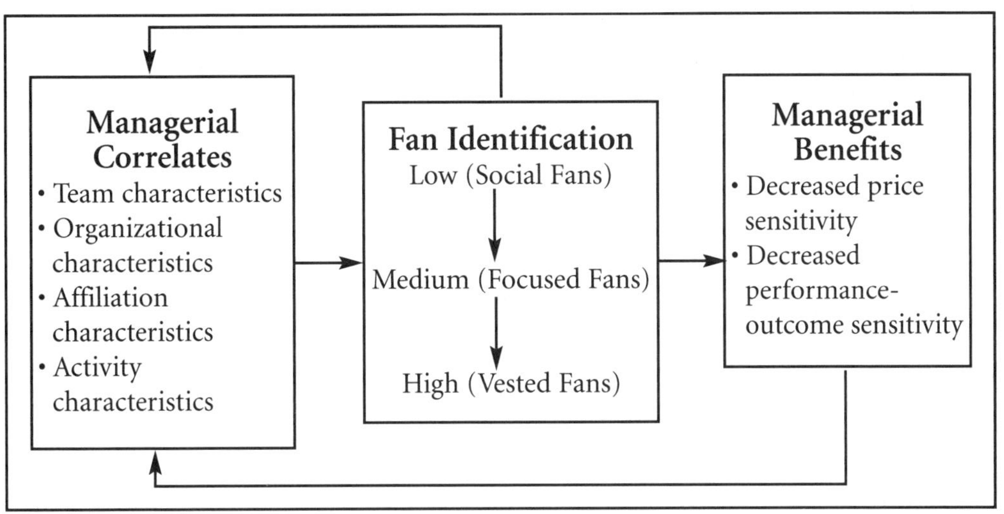

Figure 1.
Conceptual Framework for Fan Identification

Several aspects of this model are adaptable for sport organizations. Our conceptual model proposes that managerial factors influence the level of fan identification, which then results in managerial benefits. The model depicts this process as a closed system where managerial factors are influenced by feedback loops from fan identification and managerial benefits. The feedback loops produce ever higher levels of fan identification.

As shown in Figure 1, the level of fan identification with a sport organization (team) is directly impacted by four managerial factors: (a) team characteristics, (b) organizational characteristics, (c) affiliation characteristics, and (d) activity characteristics. Each of these factors contributes to the attraction and, ultimately, the identification a fan has for a sports team.

Fan identification can be divided into three discernible levels: (a) low identification (social fans), (b) medium identification (focused fans), and (c) high identification (vested fans). Fan identification leads to two notable managerial benefits: (a) decreased price sensitivity and (b) decreased performance-outcome sensitivity.

Levels of Fan Identification

Fanatics, by Webster's definition, are exaggeratedly zealous for a belief or a cause. In the case of sports fans, this belief or cause is that of the team they support and the subject of their faith and beliefs. Not all fans have the same level of fervor, devotion, and commitment to their favorite team. We suggest that there are three discernible levels of fan identification, with certain key characteristics associated with each level.

Level 1: Low Identification

(Social Fans). This refers to a relatively passive long-term relationship with the sport — low on emotion, low on financial commitment, low on involvement, but a definite relationship exists. Fans characterized as low in identification may be attracted purely by the entertainment value of the product. Fans who are attracted to sports exclusively for the entertainment value do not, initially, have an emotional attachment to a team or a particular sporting event, but rather are attracted to the sport for its pleasure and stress-relieving qualities or the opportunities for social interaction within the community.

Fans with this level of identification are followers of sport entertainment and not necessarily the team. For these fans, the outcome of the sporting event is less important than the overall quality of the entertainment opportunity provided. For this group of fans, a tailgating party, post game concert, picnic at the ballpark, or enjoyment of social interaction with fellow attendees might be the most important aspect of the evening's sport entertainment experience. It should also be noted that this initial attraction to a sport for its entertainment value or opportunities for social interaction can lead to a great liking and, ultimately, greater degree of identification with the team. It may also be the introductory phase of a relationship that could grow and intensify to a much stronger relationship and level of involvement —- meeting players, attending a team function such as a team preview of draft party, purchasing a ticket plan, and so forth.

Level 2: Medium Identification

(Focused Fans). This refers to an association with a sport or team that is based upon some attributes or elements found to be attractive. In many cases, this level of identification may be based upon fad, social factors, team performance, or player personality. Fans attracted to the achievement-seeking aspect of sport project many of the qualities of the strongly identified fan Although the high-achievement-seeking fan will make significant personal and financial investments for the team, the behavior is directly correlated to team performance and therefore may only be short term. These fans may also be attracted to the event, that being the big game. Examples of this attraction include the purchase of baseball season tickets to guarantee the right to All Star Game tickets or the purchase of football season tickets for Purdue University to ensure a ticket for the Notre Dame game. It is at this time when the greatest short-term, emotional attachment to a team is displayed. A common behavior of the achievement-seeking fan would be the wearing of team apparel, again to build the positive association between the fan and the team. These types of involvement with the team may lead to a greater relationship and identification or may follow the fate of fads and die out after the involvement has run its course —- poor team performance, identified player traded, and so forth.

Level 3: High Identification

(Vested Fans). This refers to the strongest, most loyal and longest term-relationship a fan/participant can have with a sport or team. This relationship speaks of a heavy investment and commitment either financially or in terms of time or both. A strongly identified fan (participant) can feel an "emotional ownership" in the sport (product), refer to the entity as "WE," recruit other fans (participants). Most importantly, according to Pooley (1978), fans who strongly identify with a team (activity) often devote significant portions of their day to following the team (activity).

The fan with a strong identification is a team follower. Although such fans will be attracted to sports, their loyalty to their team, just like their loyalty to their community, is unwavering and long-term. Fans who view the team as an extension of their community have strong emotional attachment to the team. Although the success of the team reflects personally upon individual fans, it also reflects upon the collective identity of the community. A lawsuit was filed in Cleveland, Ohio, resulting in a negotiated settlement for the city to retain ownership of the names and trademarks associated with the Cleveland Browns and Browns (Rushin, 1995).

Wann and Branscombe (1993) found that individuals highly identified with a sports team were more involved with the team. This involvement translated into a greater number of years as a fan, greater attendance at both home games and away games, and high expectations for future attendance-related behaviors. Additionally, fan identification was related to investment. Highly identified fans were willing to invest greater amounts of money and time in their attempts to follow their team. James Michener (1976) interviewed Russel Swanson, a Nebraska football fan, who noted:

> Fans in other states think that football fever strikes the nation from late summer to midwinter, but in Nebraska we follow it longer. We expect news coverage from August practice, through the fall season, including bowl practice in December and the bowl game in January. The balance of January and February are ugh. We look at the line-ups in March, follow spring practice in April and attend the spring Red-White squad game in May. Somehow we manage through June, but pro football with some former Big Red players starts in July, which carries us back to August practice. (Quoted in Michener, 1976, p. 276)

Managerial Factors

Fan identification with sport organizations (teams) is impacted by four factors under the direct influence of managers. By manipulating these factors, managers can incrementally increase levels of fan identification with their teams.

1. *Team characteristics.*

   Successful teams and seasons attract fans who desire the positive association to be reflected upon them. In many cases, this results in jumping on the bandwagon and embracing teams such as the Atlanta Braves, San Francisco 49ers, Chicago Bulls, and Dallas Cowboys, who have been very successful and popular. Also worth noting is that fans of a team, described as *affiliated others*, can attract the achievement-seeking fan. If, for example, the team is perceived to attract a socially desirable fan base, other fans will look to associate themselves with the team to gain stature in the eyes of their peers and to enhance their feelings of personal worth.

   The existence and success of team support groups such as the Baltimore Orioles Designated Hitters, who function as unpaid sales personnel to help promote the team, are excellent examples of personal image-enhancement and prestige-building associations. As noted, this attraction may be short-term and heavily dependent, for many people, upon team performance. Fans may avoid associations with a team when team performance falters as a means of protecting their (the fan's) own image.

   Similar findings can be found when examining the purchases of professional team sports apparel. Consistently, the merchandise sales of championship teams outrank that of the competition. For example, merchandise sales for the National Basketball Association's Houston Rockets increased 397% after their 1994 NBA Championship season. Thus, people associate themselves in terms of interest, appearance, speech, and behavior with winning sports teams to enhance their prestige in others' eyes and very probably to increase their own self-esteem.

2. *Organizational characteristics.*
Organizational characteristics differ from team characteristics in that they encompass the "off-field" image of ownership, decision making, and tradition of the franchise. For example, recent criticism of the Browns' move to Baltimore was directed at the organization and not the team. Organizational characteristics, which can contribute to fan identification, also include the reputation of the franchise and the league/conference in which the team competes, the prestige and reputation associated with a franchise's league, and affiliated division within that structure. For example, the New York Yankees are one of the most prestigious teams in professional baseball. Their presence in the Eastern Division of the American League may increase fan interest and identification with the other teams in the league and the division. Teams do not exist and thrive in isolation. Teams that play in competitive divisions with well-developed rivalries typically have fans who identify with who they are, as well as define the team based upon their competition.
An organization's reputation depends on a history of on-field success, constant commitment to excellence from team ownership, and a record of dealing with the surrounding community with integrity. Commitment to excellence is reflected by the continuous striving to bring in top coaches/managers and a willingness to invest financial resources to acquire available impact free agents. Strong community relations and forthright and honest negotiations with community representatives regarding stadium leases and capital improvements (new or enhanced facilities) reflect high levels of organizational integrity.

3. *Affiliation characteristics.*
Community affiliation is the most significant correlate of fan identification. This component is potentially the most instrumental in building fan identification and, consequently, has the strongest long-term effects. The community affiliation component was derived from the friendship and bonding research and is defined as kinship, bond, or connection the fan has to a team. Community affiliation is derived from common symbols, shared goals, history, and a fan's need to belong. The expression of common symbols, history, shared goals, and the fan's need to belong links the team to the community and provides an identity for the team that is inseparable from that of the community. As an embodiment of the community, a fan's affinity for his or her community is associated and extended to the team.
This association, or "BIRG" (Basking in Reflective Glory) phenomenon, was found to manifest itself in a number of ways by Cialdini et al. in their 1976 study of college students. In this study, students used the pronoun "WE" to describe a team victory while using the pronoun "THEY" to describe a team defeat. It was also discovered that the wearing of school-related apparel increased after team victories.
The community-affiliation component is comprised of an individual's need to belong. As the friendship research suggests, individuals seek a sense of belonging and an opportunity for communication and interaction. A sports team provides the individual an attachment to a larger community with similar interests and goals, functioning much like a fraternal organization. Proprietary research conducted through focus groups for the Orlando Magic reveals that ticketholders

form relationships in their searing section to exchange tickets during the season and often have social activities after the season with their new friends who are also season ticketholders (Audience Analysts, 1993).

4. *Activity characteristics.*
   While attendance at the actual event can lead to increased involvement, so can the exposure received via electronic and print media coverage and programming. The combination of opportunities through the purchase of tickets and/or the access through the media ensures opportunity for stimulation and exposure at various levels of economic investment and time commitment, as well as geographic considerations for fans living outside the immediate area. As technology, particularly media-related developments, has evolved, so has the opportunity for the fans to become more and more identified with respect to the object (team or player) of their identification. National and regional 24-hour sport television networks, World Wide Web home pages, radio call-in shows, pay-per-view television, print media devoted exclusively to particular teams, and fan clubs have all provided the sport fan access to whatever degree of identification he or she wishes to achieve. For example, a cable television subscriber in western Massachusetts has access to three 24-hour-a-day sport channels (ESPN, Sport Channel America, and the New England Sports Network [NESN]), plus sports coverage through WTBS (Atlanta) as well as limited sports offerings available through USA Network, and the regular networks (ABC, CBS, NBC, & Fox). In addition, the cable subscriber also has access to many pay-per-view sporting events throughout the year.

   The convenience and affordability of satellite programming now offer the fan the opportunity to follow a favorite team regardless of the location of that team in relationship to the residence of the fan. The National Football League has in fact created a package with RCA's Direct TV satellite package to promote this opportunity to its fans throughout the United States. Similar programs are also offered by the National Basketball Association, National Hockey League, Major League Baseball, and the NCAA.

Managerial Benefits

The four factors described in the preceding paragraphs lead to the establishment of fan identity and are essential in preserving and expanding the levels and types of expressions associated with that fan identity. From a managerial perspective, fan identity produces two beneficial outcomes, decreased price sensitivity and decreased performance-outcome sensitivity.

1. *Decreased price sensitivity.* The relative price inelasticity among sports fans is demonstrated annually for each sport franchise or organization. In spite of ever increasing ticket process, sports teams continue to attract fans in record numbers. Entering their respective 1994-95 seasons, the average ticket prices for the major sports in the United States were as follows:
   National Basketball Association..........$27.12
   National Football League..........$31.05
   National Hockey League..........$33.66
   Major League Baseball..........$10.25
   (*Team Marketing Report, 1994).*

This price insensitivity has also manifested itself in several other forms of commitment. First of all, as the level of identification increases and the fan becomes a ticket holder, the fan must pay for these tickets as much as 6 months in advance prior to the first game of the next season. This willingness to pay in advance has not been lost upon the more astute sport marketers such as Max Muhleman of Charlotte-based Muhleman and Associates, who created the concept of personal seat licensing (PSL) for the Charlotte Panthers of the National Football League. Modeled in part after the priority seating systems that are prevalent in college sports, PSLs are advance payments by the fan merely for the right to purchase a ticket. This "right" can be permanent or, as in the case of the NFL's Oakland Raiders, can be for a fixed term (20 years).

2. *Decreased performance-outcome sensitivity.* As the degree of fan identification and involvement increases, the less likely the fan's behaviors will be impacted by team performance —- it has been over 70 years since the Red Sox won the World Series, yet attendance (percentage of capacity) consistently ranks among the highest in the league. This is due in part to "vesting" —- which in this context refers to improving seat location on an annual basis to the point that it would be foolish to lose the prime location that the fan has "earned" as a result of renewing his/her tickets. Other sport teams are in the process of developing benefit packages based upon accumulating points —- similar to frequent flyer/buyer programs —- for their fans. This type of program essentially rewards a fan for increased involvement and investment in the team.

Strategies for Increasing Fan Identification

Although a number of the environmental influences on the team or a sport, such as history, rules, team composition and team performance, are beyond the scope of teams' marketing and communication strategies (Mullin, Hardy, & Sutton, 1993), this examination focuses upon strategies for increasing fan identification that are within the control of sport managers and marketers.

1. *Increase team/player accessibility to the public.* Crosset (1995), in his study detailing the relationships between players and fans on the PLGA tour, explains the concept of reciprocity. This reciprocity is, in marketing terminology, an exchange process between the athlete who gives of this talent to the fans who in exchange "give" their adulation and support to the golfer. This mutual exchange is a critical ingredient in establishing and maintaining fan interest. The gift that fans want more than any other is accessibility, and in the 1990s this is the gift that players and the team are most reluctant to give. Thus when accessibility is offered, it is highly valued and appreciated.

   Accessibility of the team and its players will lead to greater attraction for the team among fans. Advertising and exposure relating to player appearances, autograph sessions, and youth clinics are all methods of increasing the team's exposure in the community. It has become common practice in the NBA for each team to host its own "Draft Party" in conjunction with the annual NBA Draft in June. These events often feature current and past players as well as team personnel who interact with the fans in attendance throughout the evening. These types of events create a sense of community essential in building fan identification.

2. *Increase community involvement activities.* The community relations efforts of professional sports teams and their players play a significant role in building fan identification. As supported by friendship and attraction theories, community involvement demonstrates the team's shared goals, in this case, improvement of the quality of life in general for the community. Underscoring the activities that the team is endorsing is the fact that they usually take place on the "turf" of the community and not necessarily in the facilities owned by the team. This gives the activities more credibility and makes the gesture on behalf of the team/players more meaningful. Community relations programs are often grassroots oriented and may include any or all of the following: charity work, social cause projects, involvement with literacy or reading programs at elementary schools, drug education programs, and programs designed to develop leadership abilities in youth. Many of these programs are handled by various departments within the organizational structure of the team, whereas other teams, most notably the Orlando Magic, have established a nonprofit charitable foundation to coordinate their efforts and programs.

   Philanthropic efforts reinforce the team's position in the community and reflect positively on the team as well as its fans. As the achievement theories demonstrate, a positive effort by the team will reflect positively on the fans and, consequently, draw more fans to the team through the positive association. It is important to note that in addition to implementing the community relations efforts, the team must increase awareness of these efforts to receive maximum benefit. Proactive media campaigns should be developed and implemented to communicate the goodwill efforts of the team to constituency in order to impact their levels of fanship. Teams often promote these activities during telecasts of their games by showing film of the actual programs and activities.

   Teams must also capitalize on community acceptance and the abilities and interests of their individual players as well. Shaquille O'Neal, while a member of the Orlando Magic, sponsored an annual Shaqsgiving celebration in November, whereas the community involvement and image of the Boston Red Sox's Mo Vaughn was a critical consideration in his recent contract extension.
3. *Reinforce the team's history and tradition.* When possible, and wherever applicable, the reinforcement of a team's history on the playing field/court and in the community can also be a method of building fan identification. The evocation of childhood memories and associations can increase entertainment value by eliciting positive memories, emotions, associations, and loyalties.

   Additionally, the reinforcement of the team's history will serve to increase the connection between the team, the community, and the fans. This same reinforcement will also enhance the sense of belonging for the fans. A team's history will communicate the fact that a fan group spans not only seasons, but generations. Finally, the sense of belonging is increased by providing vehicles for communication through the expression of opinions and emotional responses.

   Common vehicles to accomplish this reinforcement of history and tradition include: Turn Back the Clock games where both competing teams wear replica uniforms of past teams to commemorate their success and history; Old Timers games and events which provide the heroes of the past with an opportunity to meet their past fans and allow the current fans to meet the legends and traditional heroes of the game; creation of Hall of Fame and retirement of uniform numbers; construction of new facilities that are actually a celebration of the past such as baseball parks like Camden Yards in Baltimore and Jacobs Field in Cleveland; and contests to select the all-time team, etc., which again creates awareness of the ties between the city and the team while also generating publicity promoting this relationship. Finally, geared to the more active fans are fantasy camps, which provide fans an opportunity to play and compete with their heroes of the past in the game that they love. For Pittsburgh Pirate fans, the Pirates offer an annual fantasy camp at the Pirates' spring training site in Bradenton, Florida. Here the campers socialize and are coached by former Pirate greats such as such as Bill Mazeroski and Elroy Face. The week then culminates in a fantasy game in which the "campers" actually play a game against the former Pirate stars. Product extensions involve uniforms and personalized baseball cards.

4. *Create opportunities for group affiliation and participation.* Fans look to sport as a means of belonging. Teams should strive to promote this sense of belonging and affiliation. Teams need to communicate the fact that fans are "part of the team." That this is "their team" and that "WE" compete together as a unit. Establishing fan clubs and newsletters and organizing trips to away games, etc., are all effective methods of promoting affiliation and participation.

   Additionally, marketing communications should reinforce and display positive group behaviors of attending an event and following a team, as well as positive attributes of the fan group. Again, fans want to be associated with positive others. If the followers of a team are perceived in a positive way, more fans will be attracted to the fan group and, in turn, the team.

Labor disputes in the National Hockey League and Major League Baseball have impacted many fans at various levels of fandom. Franchise and player movement, and salaries that the fans cannot relate to but must still help finance are detrimental to the growth of fan identification. The concepts set forth in this paper can be part of a long-term relationship-building process with the fans that will ultimately be determined by the accord between labor and management and the acceptance by fans that sport is a business involving many more activities and considerations than those that take place between the lines of a playing field or court.

References

Audience Analysts (1993). *Orlando Magic season ticketholder report.* Unpublished consulting report. Amherst, MA.

Bhattacharya, C.B., Rao, H., & Glynn, M.A. (1995). Understanding the bond identification: An investigation of its correlates among art museum members. *Journal of Marketing, 59,* 46-57.

Cialdini, R.B., Borden, R.J., Thorne, R.J., Walker, M.R., Freeman, S., & Sloan, L.R. (1976). Basking in reflected glory: Three football field studies. *Journal of Personality and Social Psychology, 34,* 366-375.

Crosset, T.W. (1995). *Outsiders in the clubhouse.* Albany, NY: State University Press.

Fox, S. (1994). *Big leagues.* New York: Morrow.

Lever, J. (1983). *Soccer madness.* Chicago, IL: University of Chicago Press.

Mael, R., & Ashforth, B.E., (1992). Alumni and their alma mater: A partial test of the reformulated model of organizational identification. *Journal of Organizational Behavior, 13,* 102-123.

Michener, J.A. (1976). *Sports in America.* New York: Random House.

Mullin, B., Hardy, S., & Sutton, W.A. (1993). *Sport Marketing.* Champaign, IL: Human Kinetics.

"NHL fans pay top dollar: Average ticket costs surpass NFL, NBA and MLB," (October). *Team Marketing Report, 7*(1), 1. Chicago, IL: TMR Publishing.

Pooley, J.C. (1978). *The sports fan: A psychology of misbehavior.* Calgary, Alberta: CAPHER Sociology of Sports Monograph Series.

Putnam, R.D. (1995). Bowling alone: America's declining social capital. *Journal of Democracy, 6*(1), 65-78.

Rooney Jr., J.F. (1974). *The geography of American sport.* Reading, MA: Addison Wesley Publishers.

Rushin, S. (1995, Dec. 4). The heart of a city: Cleveland won round 1 in what will be an agonizing battle to hold on to its beloved Browns. *Sports Illustrated, 83*(23), 58-70.

Wann, D.L., & Branscombe, N.R. (1993). Sports fans: Measuring degree of identification with their team. *International Journal of Sport Psychology, 24*, 1-17.

16

Characterizing Consumer Motivation as Individual Difference Factors: Augmenting the Sport Interest Inventory (SII) to Explain Level of Spectator Support

Daniel C. Funk, Daniel F. Mahony, and Lynn Ridinger

Introduction

Participation in women's sports has been increasing consistently since the passage of Title IX of the Educational Amendments in 1972 (e.g., Acosta & Carpenter, 1994; Coakley, 1998; Mahony & Pastore, 1998; Sabo & Snyder, 1993). However, a more recent change has been the increasing spectator interest in women's sports (e.g., Lough, 1996). Attendance at women's sporting events and media coverage of women's sports have been increasing steadily (e.g., Coakley, 1998; Lough, 1996). This increase in interest has given rise to several questions of interest to sport consumer researchers: What motivates people to watch women's sports? Are these motivations the same as or different from the motivations for watching men's sports? Do these motivations differ among various types of spectators (e.g., men vs. women; old vs. young)? Will the interest in women's sports continue to grow?

For sport managers, the advent of the Women's United Soccer Association (WUSA) and numerous commercial soccer enterprises has made it imperative to examine these questions. A better understanding of the factors contributing to spectator motivation is crucial for the continued financial viability and growth of the women's professional sports leagues that have emerged recently in the United States.

Women's World Cup

Spectator interest in women's professional sports hit a high point in the United States during the 1999 Women's World Cup (WWC). The attendance and media attention exceeded the optimistic projections of those associated with the event (Mitchell, 1999). In fact, the attention paid the team was so extensive that they ultimately were named the "Sportswomen of the Year" by *Sports Illustrated*, marking the first recognition ever for a women's sports team (Bamberger, 1999). While many in the media hypothesized about reasons for the strong interest in the team (e.g., Bernstein, 1999) and whether that interest might be used to help jump-start a new professional women's soccer league in the United States (e.g., Mullen, 1999), only Funk, Mahony, Nakazawa, and Hirakawa (2001) actually attempted to assess scientifically the various motivations of Women's World Cup spectators.

Motivations of Spectators

General Literature

The study of motivation in consumer research seems to involve two fundamental challenges. The first is to understand the interrelationships between motives and specific behavior, and the second is to develop a list of consumer motives comprehensive enough to capture the wide variety of motivating forces that stimulate and shape behavior (Foxall & Goldsmith, 1994). *Motivation* refers to an activated state within a person—consisting of drive, urges, wishes, and desires—that leads to goal-directed behavior (Mowen & Minor, 1998). Within the social-psychological viewpoint of sport behavior, motivation has been examined from two different perspectives: (a) as an outcome variable measured in the form of choice, effect, and/or persistent behavior and (b) as an individual difference factor that initiates a sequence of events leading to behavior (Weiss & Chaumeton, 1992). The latter perspective focuses on how individuals who vary in levels of motivational characteristics differ on criterion measures of concern (e.g., interest, attitudes, behavior); it is especially relevant for understanding differences in spectator and fan support of managed professional sport teams.

The central purpose of the present research was to identify different motivational factors and to examine their usefulness in explaining various levels of support in a specific sport. However, there appears to be little consensus in the literature as to which factors or combination of factors best explains and predicts the motives and behavior of sport spectators and sport fans. A variety of theories have been set forth in an attempt to explain the appeal of spectator sports (Duncan, 1983; Sloan, 1989; Smith, 1988; Trail, Anderson, & Fink, 2000; Wann, 1995), but empirical evidence is scant. Moreover, most of the sport spectator literature has focused on just two of these areas—individual motives and identification (Trail et al., 2000). Not only that, but the majority of the literature has examined men's sports or sports in general, rather than women's sports. While claims have been made that the crowds at women's sporting events differ from those at men's sporting events (Lopiano, 1997), there is an absence in the literature of empirical studies attempting to find factors that may be unique to consumers of women's sports. The following section provides a brief discussion of the spectator behavior literature as it applies to women's sports in particular and to team sports in general.

Women's Sports

Several studies have sampled spectators of women's sports to assess various factors including fan satisfaction (Madrigal, 1995), involvement (Kerstetter & Kovich, 1997), commitment (Weiller & Higgs, 1997), and marketing strategy (Antonelli, 1994). However, most of this research applied models or theories that were developed based on men's sports or on sports in general. Few efforts have been made to determine whether there are any factors that may be unique in contributing to consumptive behavior as it applies to women's sports. These studies have focused exclusively on issues pertaining to the spectators at women's sporting events.

Weiller and Higgs (1997) identified achievement seeking and entertainment as motivations for committed fans of the American Girls Professional Baseball League (AGPBL) of the 1940s. Armstrong (1999) examined factors that influenced attendance at professional women's basketball games in the now-defunct American Basketball League (ABL). She investigated some of the traditional motives and objects of identification found in the literature, along with a few exploratory factors. These new factors included the opportunity to support professional women's basketball and the opportunity to see positive role models. Armstrong's results revealed that entertainment, support of the women's league, the quality of play, and the players themselves substantially influenced overall attendance. Surprisingly, the opportunity to see role models had only a marginal influential on attendance at professional women's basketball games. In contrast, Funk, Ridinger, and Moorman (2000) reported that support for competitive opportunities for women in sport, players serving as role models, the traditional style of play, the wholesome environment, and the entertainment value of games were rated as being important attendance motives among season-ticket holders and single-game attendees of a Women's National Basketball Association (WNBA) franchise.

Interestingly enough, while the more traditional sport spectator motives have been based on hedonic principles, the new factors that have emerged in preliminary investigations of women's sports are based more on a utilitarian perspective (Armstrong, 1999). Rather than being motivated simply by factors associated with individual pleasure, women's sports fans also may be motivated by the utility or function served by those sports (i.e., providing positive role models for youth and representing an avenue for equal rights that transcends the world of sports).

The general literature addressing sport consumption by spectators continues to evolve. Researchers have investigated a variety of motives and other factors linked to fan behavior; however, few of these studies have focused on or even included women's sports. Funk et al. (2001) used a number of prior studies on spectator motivation (e.g., Kahle, Kambara, & Rose, 1996; Madrigal & Howard, 1999; Sloan, 1989; Sloan, Bates, Davis, & Schwieger, 1987; Wann, 1995) to develop a 30-item Sport Interest Inventory (SII). The SII was used to assess 10 potential motives of spectators attending the 1999 Women's World Cup (WWC), including drama, vicarious achievement, aesthetics, interest in team, interest in player, interest in soccer, national pride, excitement, social opportunities, and support for women's opportunities. The psychometric properties of the SII were tested, drawing upon 1,303 spectators at five different venues across the United States during opening-round matches of the 1999 WWC. Confirmatory factor analysis supported the instrument's reliability, and regression analysis indicated that six of the motives predicted 34% of the total variance in interest in the tournament (i.e., interest in team, excitement, interest in soccer, vicarious achievement, drama, and support for women's opportunities). A significant negative relationship between interest in the 1999 WWC and both drama and vicarious achievement was observed.

Open-ended questions also were used to determine whether additional motives existed for women's professional soccer spectators (Funk et al., 2001). A qualitative analysis of these open-ended questions indicated four additional factors that emerged to explain spectator motivation in this setting. A number of the spectators made comments suggesting the importance of these factors: (a) The players served as important role models for young children; (b) the entertainment provided at the World Cup was a good value for the money; (c) the event provided a valuable opportunity for family members to bond with one another; and (d) the matches presented a wholesome environment.

The current study attempted to confirm and extend the Sport Interest Inventory by examining the level of continued interest in the U.S. Women's team subsequent to the 1999 Women's World Cup. The U.S. Women's team toured the United States and played a number of games as part of the 1999 U.S. Nike Cup. The final game was played in Louisville, Kentucky, in October of 1999. Spectator motive items were generated for 14 possible factors, which included the 10 original factors examined by the SII plus the additional four factors that emerged from the qualitative analysis done in that study. Hence, the factors examined in the current study were (a) drama, (b) vicarious achievement, (c) aesthetics, (d) interest in team, (e) interest in player, (f) interest in soccer, (g) national pride, (h) excitement, (i) social opportunities, (j) support for women's opportunities, (k) players as role models, (l) entertainment value, (m) bonding with family, and (n) wholesome environment.

Methodology

Procedures

The data for the current study were collected using the following procedures. Spectators attending the 1999 U.S. Nike Cup on October 10, 1999, in Louisville, Kentucky, were surveyed. The SII questionnaire contained 15 behavioral and demographic items in addition to the 42 items measuring 14 individual difference factors (three items per factor). The SII was distributed to males and females aged 12 and older. The surveyors randomly selected sections in the stands at the venue and approached spectators at their seats before the first match and between matches. Efforts were made to include a broad representation of the people sitting in each section, and no more than two persons per party were given the survey. Participation was voluntary, so those who chose not to participate were replaced; however, a surveyor's request was rarely rejected. It took respondents approximately 15 minutes to complete the questionnaire. A sample of 580 spectators received the SII. Of these, 520 surveys were returned, for a response rate of 90%. Of the collected surveys, 504 were usable, for a final response rate of 86%.

Analysis

Descriptive statistics were utilized to develop a general profile of spectator characteristics. A confirmatory factor analysis was conducted using Joreskog and Sorbom's LISREL 8.3 (1999) to purify the scale and to estimate how well the 42 scale items represented 14 latent motivational factors. Per Kline's (1998) recommendation, five fit indices were used to evaluate the model's fit (2/*df*, RMSEA, NNFI, CFI, SMRM). Alpha coefficients were computed to examine the interreliability of the derived factors and were reported along with factor means and standard deviations. Multiple linear regression analysis was employed to examine the relationship between the 14 factors and spectator support level. An individual's spectator support level was derived from five Likert-type scales with end points ranging from 1 to 4 and 1 to 7. Respondents were asked to rate (a) their level of interest in women's soccer, (b) their degree of interest in the 1999 Women's World Cup,

Table 1.
Means, Standard Deviations, and Cronbach Alphas for Spectator Motives and Spectator Level of Support for Soccer

Spectator motives	*M*	*SD*	α
Role model (ROLE)	4.58	.71	.88
Excitement (EXC)	4.34	.70	.81
Drama (DRAMA)	4.29	.74	.74
Wholesome environment (WHOENV)	4.28	.72	.83
Aesthetics (AESTH)	4.21	.76	.76
Entertainment value (ENTV)	4.17	.84	.88
Interest in soccer (SOCCER)	4.16	.95	.87
Interest in team (TEAM)	4.08	.77	.78
Support women's opportunity in sport (SWOS)	3.98	.87	.82
Bonding with family (BON)	3.79	.98	.87
National pride (PRIDE)	3.81	.83	.70
Vicarious achievement (VIC)	3.77	.93	.84
Socialization (SOCIAL)	3.33	.83	.64
Interest in player (PLAYER)	2.78	.92	.82

(c) the number of years they had been fans of soccer, (d) their knowledge of the rules of soccer, and (e) how often they watched soccer on television.

Results

Behavioral Profile

Well over half (61%) of the spectators in the sample were female, and the mean age of all spectators was 31. The mean age of the females (29.0) was significantly lower than that of the males (34.0), indicating the presence of a younger female audience. The modal response (MODE = 15) indicated that a vast number of attendees were young, Caucasian females who lived in Louisville, Kentucky, and attended in groups of approximately six persons. While these individuals indicated a high interest in the 1999 FIFA Women's World Cup, they generally had no history of attending men's or women's soccer games in person. They considered soccer to be their favorite sport, and had played in organized soccer for 7 years.

In addition, spectators indicated they possessed a high level of soccer knowledge and a strong understanding of the rules. Of the sample, 45% indicated gender was not an important factor in their preference for watching soccer. Taken together, these results indicate that the event drew a young group of Caucasian spectators who had been soccer fans for many years. The spectators attended in groups, often with family members and friends.

Scale Analysis

Internal consistency measures were computed for each of the 14 factors from the overall purified sample ($N = 432$) and ranged from $\alpha = .64$ to $\alpha = .91$. Only the SOCIAL $\alpha = .64$)

Table 2.
Correlation Matrix of Involvement Antecedents From Standardized Phi Matrix (N = 300)

	swos	social	soccer	exc	drama	team	vic	player	pride	role	entv	whoenv	bon	aesth	supp
swos	1														
social	.44	1													
soccer	.59	.35	1												
exc	.77	.35	.78	1											
drama	.54	.20	.46	.63	1										
team	.87	.33	.85	.96	.59	1									
vic	.52	.40	.41	.60	.32	.62	1								
player	.10	.29	.08	.05	-.07	.05	.32	1							
pride	.68	.34	.33	.60	.35	.64	.80	.18	1						
role	.70	.24	.45	.73	.64	.73	.38	-.04	.58	1					
entv	.60	.27	.48	.70	.47	.64	.38	.03	.49	.70	1				
whoenv	.71	.37	.48	.76	.56	.76	.45	.01	.61	.87	.85	1			
bon	.41	.28	.18	.38	.26	.41	.26	-.04	.44	.45	.41	.66	1		
aesth	.70	.39	.75	.80	.59	.78	.51	.06	.51	.65	.66	.79	.45	1	
supp	.21	.07	.32	.41	.12	.50	.41	.31	.39	.24	.23	.35	.55	.41	1

Note.
swos = Support Women's Opportunity in Sport
vic = Vicarious Achievement
bon = Family Bonding
social = Socialization
player = Interest in a Specific Player
aesth = Aesthetics
soccer = Interest in Sport of Soccer
pride = National Pride
supp = Soccer Support Level
exc = Excitement
role = Role Model
drama = Drama
entv = Entertainment Value
team = Interest in the Team
whoenv = Wholesome Environment

dimension was below the .70 benchmark (Nunnally & Bernstein, 1994). The means, standard deviations, and Cronbach alphas for the sample are reported in Table 1. The means for each construct ranged from 2.78 for PLAYER to 4.58 for ROLE. Standard deviations ranged from .70 to .98. It is interesting to note that the four factors added to the SII examined by Funk et al. (2001)—ROLE, WHOENV, ENTV, and BON—were rated as the first, fourth, fifth, and ninth most important factors, respectively. These results appear to support the addition of these four factors to the SII. A correlation matrix was computed and is reported in Table 2. Examination of the correlation matrix (see Table 2) revealed moderate discriminant validity among the 14 factors. All correlation coefficients except three were well below the $r < .85$ ceiling (Kline, 1998).

Confirmatory Factor Analysis

The results of the confirmatory factor analysis revealed that the Sport Interest Inventory was psychometrically sound and confirmed the existence of 14 unique factors related to women's professional soccer. The results of the confirmatory factor analysis are presented in Table 3, and the regression model is presented in Table 4. See the Appendix A for detailed discussion. While the 14 dimensions explained 67% of the variance, National Pride and Socialization each had a single item that should be reworded to increase the predictive validity. Overall, these results validate the SII's predictive ability in measuring

Table 3.
Results of Confirmatory Factor Analysis: Factor Loadings for Individual Items, Path Coefficients, t-Values, and Average Variance Explained by Latent Factors

Item	Factor loadings	Lambda X	*t*-values	Avg. var. explained
Interest in soccer (SOCCER)				77%
First and foremost, I consider myself a fan of soccer.	.68	.86	20.53	
I love to follow the game of soccer.	.80	.87	23.53	
I am a huge fan of soccer in general.	.84	.95	24.32	
Vicarious achievement (VIC)				67%
When my favorite team wins, I feel my status as a fan increases.	.43	.70	14.68	
I feel a sense of accomplishment when my team wins.	.74	.88	21.32	
When my team wins, I feel a personal sense of achievement.	.80	.96	22.61	
Excitement (EXC)				60%
I find the U.S. Cup matches very exciting.	.51	.60	16.53	
I enjoy the excitement surrounding a U.S. Cup match.	.60	.63	18.42	
I enjoy the high level of excitement during the U.S. Cup competition.	.69	.70	20.57	
Interest in team (TEAM)				54%
I consider myself to be a big fan of my favorite U.S. Cup team.	.54	.73	17.28	
Compared to how I feel about other sports teams, the Women's U.S. Cup team is very important to me.	.51	.69	16.67	
I am a loyal fan of my favorite U.S. Cup team no matter if they are winning or losing.	.56	.66	17.77	
Supporting women's opportunity in sport (SWOS)				62%
I attend the U.S. Cup games because I believe it is important to support women's sport.	.52	.74	16.54	
I see myself as a major supporter of women's sports.	.59	.81	18.17	
Attending the U.S. Cup demonstrates my support for women's sport in general.	.75	.81	21.58	
Aesthetics (AESTH)				57%
There is a certain natural beauty to the game of soccer.	.68	.75	20.57	
I enjoy the gracefulness associated with the sport of soccer.	.75	.77	20.37	
Successful plays and strategies performed by the players are an important component of the soccer game being enjoyable.	.32	.54	12.09	

Table 3, continued
Results of Confirmatory Factor Analysis: Factor Loadings for Individual Items, Path Coefficients, t-Values, and Average Variance Explained by Latent Factors

Item	Factor loadings	Lambda X	*t*-values	Avg. var. explained
Social opportunities (SOCIAL)				45%
I like to talk with other people sitting near me at the U.S. Cup soccer games.	.17	.44	8.03	
The U.S. Cup soccer games give me a great opportunity to socialize with other people.	.77	.86	17.17	
I attend the U.S. Cup because of the opportunities to socialize.	.42	.72	12.82	
National pride (PRIDE)				45%
I attend the U.S. Cup to support my country's team.	.32	.62	11.83	
When my country's team wins, I feel proud to be a citizen.	.63	.77	17.86	
Patriotism is a big reason I attend the U.S. Cup.	.41	.70	13.71	
Drama (DRAMA)				52%
I prefer watching a close game rather than a one-sided game, even when my favorite U.S. Cup team is playing.	.50	.71	15.17	
I like watching matches where the outcome is uncertain.	.35	.52	12.39	
A close match between two teams is more enjoyable than a blowout.	.72	.73	18.39	
Interest in player (PLAYER)				60%
I tend to follow individual players more than the team.	.58	.77	16.92	
I am more a fan of individual players than I am of the team.	.69	.88	18.74	
The main reason I attend the U.S. Cup is to cheer for my favorite player.	.53	.79	16.05	
Role model (ROLE)				71%
U.S. Cup players provide inspiration for girls and boys.	.68	.68	20.53	
I think U.S. Cup players are good role models for young girls and boys.	.80	.65	23.53	
The U.S. Cup players provide inspiration for children.	.84	.69	24.32	
Entertainment value (ENTV)				73%
The U.S. Cup is affordable entertainment.	.73	.79	21.63	
The U.S. Cup is great entertainment for the price.	.84	.78	23.97	
I attended the U.S. Cup because it is an entertaining event for a reasonable price.	.61	.76	18.82	

Table 3, continued
Results of Confirmatory Factor Analysis: Factor Loadings for Individual Items, Path Coefficients, t-Values, and Average Variance Explained by Latent Factors

Item	Factor loadings	Lambda X	*t*-values	Avg. var. explained
Wholesome environment (WHOENV)				62%
I like attending the U.S. Cup because it is good, clean fun.	.63	.65	19.43	
There is a friendly, family atmosphere at the U.S. Cup.	.64	.66	19.51	
I value the wholesome environment evident at the U.S. Cup.	.60	.69	18.62	
Family bonding (BON)				69%
I enjoy sharing the experience of attending the U.S. Cup with family members.	.68	.83	19.89	
Attending the U.S. Cup gives me a chance to bond with my family.	.76	1.00	21.52	
An important reason why I attend the U.S. Cup is to spend time with my family.	.62	.93	18.71	

Note. Factor loadings represent the squared multiple correlation coefficients for manifest indicators. For example, the latent variable Family Bonding accounts for 68% of the variance in scale item "I enjoy sharing the experience of attending the U.S. Cup with family members." Lamba X's are the standardized measurement paths for each parameter from the Lambda Matrix. The average variance extracted is the average amount of variance that the latent factor explains in all three of the scale items used to measure the construct.

unique motives using a survey questionnaire. Once the SII was confirmed, multiple linear regression was employed to examine the relative importance of the 14 factors to level of spectator support in women's soccer.

Regression Analysis

Since the goal of the present study was to explain the spectator support level among those attending the 1999 U.S. Cup, simultaneous regression was employed to examine the 14 motives (Stevens, 1998). The mean response for spectator support level was 3.83 (SD = .79), and the interreliability measure was α = .78. The correlation matrix for the independent and dependent variables is presented in Table 2. The regression model is presented in Table 3 and indicates that 54% (R^2 = .54) of the variance in spectator support level was explained by SOCCER, TEAM, VIC, ROLE, and ENTV ($F = 40.33$, $df = 503$ $p < .01$). Examination of the Beta coefficients revealed that SOCCER (b = .47) was the most influential with regard to spectator support level, followed closely by TEAM (b = .41) and, to a lesser degree, VIC (b = .09), ROLE (b = .13), and ENTV (b = .09). Assumptions of multiple regression were examined and indicated the residuals did not deviate from a normal distribution, were constant in variance, and were not correlated with the independent variable. The R-square value (R^2 = .54), adjusted (R^2 = .52), and the small standard error (SD = .70) indicated the model was robust (Stevens, 1998). Moreover, the 54% of the variance in support level predicted in the current study represents a considerable improvement over the 34% of interest in the Women's World Cup predicted by Funk et al. (2001).

Discussion

The current study clearly builds and expands on the contributions made by the Funk et al. (2001) study. Therefore, the results of this study have implications for both sport marketers and sport marketing researchers. While the current study focused on U.S. Cup spectators, the results of this study can still be used to better understand sport spectators in a number of settings, particularly those involving women's sports. This study makes important contributions in that it (a) expands the understanding of sport spectator motivation beyond the traditional motives; (b) provides a more complete scale for examining the motives of spectators at women's sporting events; and (c) provides suggestions for marketing a variety of sport events, particularly the games of the new WUSA.

Augmenting Traditional Motives to Better Understand Sport Spectators

The Sport Interest Inventory extends the available knowledge of potential motives useful in determining the type and level of support for women's professional soccer in particular and for team sport in general. In addition to examining traditional spectator motives (e.g., drama, vicarious achievement), the study utilized other motives, including (a) players serving as role models, (b) entertainment value, (c) bonding with family, (d) supporting women's opportunity in sport, and (e) the presence of a wholesome environment at games. All of these factors were confirmed through the use of factor analysis. It is interesting to note that players as role models ($M = 4.58$) was identified by the spectators as being the most important factor. The mean importance of entertainment value ($M = 4.17$) and wholesome environment ($M = 4.28$) was higher than that of such factors as interest in soccer ($M = 4.16$) and interest in the team ($M = 4.08$), while that of family bonding ($M = 3.79$) was higher than that of such factors as vicarious achievement ($M = 3.77$).

Although many of these differences are small, the results do suggest that, at least in this particular sport setting, there are some new factors that are at least as important as some of the traditional ones. Moreover, these new factors can be used to examine sport spectators in variety of settings. In fact, it might be particularly interesting to examine the importance of these factors at male sporting events, where prices are much higher and the role-model status of players has frequently been questioned. In addition, the results suggest that further research is needed to continue the search for important spectator motives and that such research may be quite fruitful.

Examining Motives of Spectators at Women's Sporting Events

The current study extends the work of Funk et al. (2001) by providing a more complete scale for understanding spectator motivations. The SII received further support for its construct validity, and its psychometric properties were again confirmed as reliable. Moreover, the 14 motives represented 67% of the variance in the scale items of the SII, an improvement over the 60% predicted in Funk et al. Furthermore, the results of the regression analysis indicated that interest in the sport of soccer, interest in team, vicarious achievement, players serving as role models, and entertainment value explained 54% of the variance in spectator support level. Again, this represents an improvement over the SII presented by Funk et al.

Table 4.
Regression of Spectator Support Level on Fourteen Motives (N = 504)

Variable	*b*	*SE*	β
SOCCER	.47	.04	.57 *
TEAM	.41	.06	.40 *
VIC	-.09	.04	-.11 *
ROLE	-.13	.06	-.12 *
ENTV	.09	.04	.10 *
WHOENV	-.11	.07	-.10
PRIDE	-.05	.04	-.06
BON	.03	.03	.04
EXC	-.05	.06	-.05
DRAMA	-.03	.04	-.04
AESTH	.04	.05	-.04
SWOS	.03	.04	.04
PLAYER	-.01	.03	-.02
SOCIAL	-.01	.03	-.02

Note. Full Model: R^2 = .54; Adjusted R^2 = .52; F = 40.33, p < .01 df = 503. AESTH = aesthetics, BON = family bonding, DRAMA = drama, EXC = excitement, ENTV = entertainment value, PLAY = interest in players, PRIDE = national pride, ROLE = role modeling, SOCCER = interest in soccer, SOCIAL = social opportunities, SWOS = support for women's opportunities, TEAM = interest in team, VIC = vicarious achievement, WHOENV = wholesome environment.*p < 05.

The SII can be a valuable tool for both future researchers and practitioners. The scale is relatively short, requiring only 15 minutes to complete, and can be adapted for use in a variety of settings. In particular, the factors and items utilized in the SII could very easily be adapted to other women's sport events and soccer events. The confirmation of the instrument's psychometric properties, completed in two separate studies, should increase researchers' and practitioners' comfort with using these items. While more research is still needed relative to the factors motivating sport spectators, the SII provides future researchers with a number of potential factors to examine in various spectator sports and provides those researchers with statistically supported items to measure those factors.

The SII is a meaningful tool for sport organizations, enabling them to better understand the motivations of spectators who attend their events. This has a number of potential applications. First, the SII can be used in developing content for advertising campaigns. Understanding why fans are interested in a sporting event makes it much easier to determine what kind of advertisement content to include in promotional materials for that event. For example, a sport marketer can use the SII to measure the relative importance of the various objects of attachment (e.g., team, sport, player) and can then focus his or her advertising efforts on the most critical object of attachment. Second, the SII can be used in determining how to present the event in the sport facility. The presentation of the event involves a variety of aspects, including the music that is played and the half-time entertainment. Third, a motivational profile of spectators can be used in the sale of sponsorships. Corporate sponsors increasingly are concerned with reaching their "consumers." It is the sport organization's responsibility to demonstrate that the sport event's consumers match the sponsor's consumers; creating motivational profiles is one way to do so. For example, the entertainment value attendees attribute to the event might align with businesses that emphasize product value in promotional marketing campaigns.

Providing Suggestions for Marketing Sport Events

Finally, the authors believe the current study provides a number of suggestions for the marketing of women's sports. In particular, the results of the study would be particularly helpful to those organizing the new professional women's soccer league in the United States, the WUSA. A number of suggestions emerge upon examining the means for the 14 motivational factors. First of all, it is important to continue to convince the public that female soccer players are good role models. This has implications both for the way that teams market these players and for the way that the players market themselves. League officials must stress to the athletes the importance of maintaining a positive public image and must convey to them the impact this image has on the success of the league.

Second, league marketers must focus on providing entertainment for the fans both relative to the game itself and during breaks in the game. The spectators at the U.S. Nike Cup indicated entertainment was the second most important motivational factor to them, which suggests that simply presenting the game itself, without ancillary entertainment, would be insufficient for the fledgling league. However, fans also indicated the importance of drama and of their interest in soccer. Therefore, providing high-quality, exciting soccer games would be essential.

Third, the spectators indicated that the wholesome environment at the game was important to them. This has implications for a variety of decisions made by marketers and promoters, including the type of entertainment provided at the game and the music played in the stadium. For example, XFL-style cheerleaders clearly would not be a welcome addition in the eyes of many WUSA fans.

Fourth, the league must maintain reasonable prices. Many of the spectators at the Nike Cup indicated that the entertainment value influenced their decision to attend the game. As the cost of attendance for team sports continues to escalate (Howard, 1999), women's soccer provides a less expensive alternative. This cost factor may also have been associated with the notion that the event provided an opportunity for parents and children to bond in a wholesome environment, something rarely found at traditional sporting events that are constrained by cost elements and may be seen as less wholesome.

Fifth, league officials must focus on creating fan attachments to the teams in the WUSA. Efforts to foster team identification (Sutton, McDonald, Milne, & Cimperman, 1997) and to strengthen attachment could be utilized to increase a team's consumer base. However, this generally is much more of a challenge for new leagues, which cannot rely on the long-term relationships between teams and their fans that more established leagues enjoy. The U.S. women's soccer team had strong support, in part because of national pride, but the new league will have to create new interest in new teams to be successful. Sutton et al. (1997) suggest increasing team/player accessibility to the public and increasing community-involvement activities as means of creating identification. Another feasible way to increase attachment to and identification with a team is to develop supporter clubs. Such clubs already are common in male soccer leagues around the world (Nakazawa, Mahony, Funk, & Hirakawa, 1999), as well as in multisport organizations (Hall & Mahony, 1997). In many cases, the teams provide a number of incentives for joining the clubs, such as discounts on tickets and merchandise, increased access to tickets, and special events for club members. As a result of such efforts, behavioral patterns relative to purchasing team-related merchandise or game tickets should mirror the increase in team attachment.

Sixth, the league should make an effort to market the WUSA to groups and individuals who support an increase in opportunities for women. The spectators at the Cup reported that support for women's opportunities was important to them. Armstrong (1999) also found support for a similar factor in her examination of the ABL, another women's sport league. It is possible that the league might attract fans who have less interest in soccer than do traditional fans, but who feel it is important that women be given an equal chance. Local women's organizations, for example, would be good targets for marketers.

Seventh, the league should not focus too much effort on marketing individual players in order to spur interest in the league. While the players are important as role models, interest in specific players was rated the lowest of the 14 factors ($M = 2.78$) and this factor was not a significant predictor of spectator support level. Funk et al. (2001) reported similar findings in that players were rated the lowest of 10 factors during the 1999 FIFA Women's World Cup ($M = 2.55$) and were not a significant predictor of interest in the event. Despite considerable anecdotal evidence to the contrary, provided through the media, these results suggest that individual players do not in fact appear to be major factors in stimulating interest in women's soccer.

Finally, the regression results suggest that using different marketing strategies for different segments may be particularly effective. A high level of spectator support was associated with a strong interest in soccer, a strong interest in the team, and the desire for good entertainment value. Therefore, a marketing strategy aimed at core soccer fans should focus on these factors. For example, a marketing campaign targeted toward those participating in soccer leagues or those subscribing to soccer-related publications should stress the high quality of soccer being played in the WUSA. The campaign also should focus on the entertainment value of league games, and teams would be well advised to offer reasonably priced entertainment packages to increase attendance during the early years. It might also be effective to approach adult and youth leagues with group-package deals. In fact, encouraging these fans to join team supporter clubs could be useful in increasing the value of the games (e.g., by offering discounts to club members) and could help to increase attachment to the team, something core fans indicated was important to them.

In contrast, there was a significant negative relationship between spectator support level and vicarious achievement and the importance of players as role models. There also was a moderately significant negative relationship between spectator support level and the wholesome environment at the games. It is important to note that these factors were not negatively related to attendance, because all of the respondents were attendees at the game. The negative relationship suggests that those fans with a more moderate interest in professional women's soccer—the fringe fans—indicated these factors were more important to them. For example, fans with a low level of interest in soccer may have had a stronger desire for vicarious achievement, something they could experience even if their overall interest was low. Therefore, different marketing strategies should be used when attempting to attract these fringe fans; a campaign that focuses simply on the high quality of soccer will fail. For example, advertisements directed toward these fans should emphasize that players are role models who can have a positive impact on the lives of young children and that the games provide a wholesome environment, appropriate for children of all ages. Such advertisements could be especially effective if they were directed toward the parents of recreational players, who are less involved in the sport of soccer but have observed their children's admiration of a sport figure (e.g., Biskup & Pfister, 1999).

Limitations of the Study

There are a few limitations of the current study that suggest the need for further research. First, not all individual difference factors were identified. Although 14 factors from previous literature were utilized, 46% of the variance in spectator support level remained unexplained. More qualitative analysis is needed to identify additional motivational characteristics in order to augment understanding of spectator differences. Second, the current study did not utilize an attendance element in the dependent measure. With the advent of the new WUSA, future data collection using the SII could incorporate an attendance-frequency measure to augment the five existing items used to derive an overall level-of-support variable. Third, the sample included only those who attended the event—a typical scenario in the study of sport spectators. Eventually, comparisons of attendees and non-attendees will be important in this line of research.

Conclusion

The present study focused on women's professional soccer and demonstrated that consumer motivation can be partitioned into individual difference factors to better understand interest in a specific sport product. The psychometric properties of the Sport Interest Inventory (SII) were confirmed as viable for measuring individual differences in consumer motivation. The results indicate that while 14 distinct motivational characteristics could be identified among spectators, only five were useful in explaining how individuals differed in spectator support level. The five individual difference factors were sport, team, entertainment value, vicarious achievement, and role modeling; combined, they explained 54% of the variance in support for women's professional soccer. Taken together, the results suggest further investigation is needed to fully understand the characteristics of spectator motivations. Simply relying on past studies of sport spectators in other settings to predict motives in future events may be ineffective when developing marketing approaches. In particular, the significant negative relationship between interest in the Women's World Cup and both role modeling and vicarious achievement suggests far more research is needed to more fully understand the motives of sport spectators. It would be advisable to survey consumers in a specific situation before using motives to develop marketing strategies. In general, the current study provides a greater understanding of women's sports consumers, as well as some preliminary suggestions for those seeking to market similar events.

References

Acosta, R. V., & Carpenter, L. J. (1994). The status of women in intercollegiate athletics. In S. Birrell & C. L. Cole (Eds.), *Women, sport, & culture* (pp. 111–118). Champaign, IL: Human Kinetics.

Antonelli, D. (1994). Marketing intercollegiate women's basketball. *Sport Marketing Quarterly, 3*(2), 29–33.

Armstrong, K. L. (1999). A quest for a market: A profile of the consumers of a professional women's basketball team and the marketing implications. *Women in Sport and Physical Activity Journal, 8*(2), 103–126.

Bagozzi, R. P., & Yi, T. (1988). On the evaluation of structural equation models. *Journal of the Academy of Marketing Science, 16*(1), 74–94.

Bamberger, M. (1999, December 20). Dream come true. *Sports Illustrated, 91*, pp. 46–60.

Bentler, P. M. (1990). Comparative fit indexes in structural models. *Psychological Bulletin, 107*, 238–246.

Bernstein, A. (1999, July 19–25). World Cup kicks off talk of pro league: Marketers learn lessons from smashing success. *Street & Smith's SportsBusiness Journal*, pp. 1, 48.

Biskup, C., & Pfister, G. (1999). I would like to be like her/him: Are athletes role-models for boys and girls? *European Physical Education Review, 5*, 199–218.

Browne, M. W., & Cudeck, R. (1993). Alternative ways of assessing model fit. In K.A. Bollen & J.S. Long (Eds.), *Testing structural equation models*. Newbury Park: Sage Publications.

Coakley, J. J. (1998). *Sport in society: Issues and controversies* (6th ed.). Boston, MA: McGraw-Hill.

Duncan, M. C. (1983). The symbolic dimensions of spectator sport. *Quest, 35*, 29–36.

Foxall, G. R., & Goldsmith, R. E. (1994). *Consumer psychology for marketing*. London: Routledge.

Funk, D. C., Mahony, D. F., Nakazawa, M., & Hirakawa, S. (2001). Development of the Sport Interest Inventory (SII): Implications for measuring unique consumer motives at sporting events. *International Journal of Sports Marketing and Sponsorship, 3*, 291–316.

Funk, D. C., Ridinger, L., & Moorman, A. J. (2000, June 1–3). *An empirical examination of spectator motives in women's professional basketball*. Paper presented at the North American Society for Sport Management, Colorado Springs, CO.

Hair, J. F., Anderson, R. E., Tatham, R. L., & Black, W. C. (1998). *Multivariate data analysis* (4th ed.). Englewood Cliffs, NJ: Prentice-Hall.

Hall, J. S., & Mahony, D. F. (1997). Factors affecting methods used by annual giving programs: A qualitative study of NCAA Division I athletic departments. *Sport Marketing Quarterly, 6*(3), 21–30.

Howard, D. R. (1999). The changing fanscape of big-league sports: Implications for sport managers. *Journal of Sport Management, 13*, 78–91.

Joreskog, K. G., & Sorbom, D. (1999). *LISREL VIII*. Chicago: SPSS.

Kahle, L. R., Kambara, K. M., & Rose, G. (1996). A functional model of fan attendance motivations for college football. *Sport Marketing Quarterly, 5*(4), 51–60.

Kerstetter, D. L., & Kovich, G. M. (1997). The involvement profiles of Division I women's basketball spectators. *Journal of Sport Management, 11*(3), 234–249.

Kline, R. B. (1998). *Principles and practice of structural equation modeling*. New York: Guilford Press.

Lopiano, D. (1997). *Tomorrow in women's sports: Now is just the tip of the iceberg*. Paper presented at the Women's Sports Foundation Summit, Bloomingdale, IL.

Lough, N. L. (1996). Factors affecting corporate sponsorship of women's sports. *Sport Marketing Quarterly, 5*(2), 11–20.

Madrigal, R. (1995). Cognitive and affective determinants of fan satisfaction with sporting event attendance. *Journal of Leisure Research, 27*(3), 205–227.

Madrigal, R., & Howard, D. R. (1999). *Measuring the multidimensional nature of spectators' attraction to sport events*. Manuscript submitted for publication.

Mahony, D. F., & Pastore, D. (1998). Distributive justice: An examination of participation opportunities, revenues, and expenses at NCAA institutions—1973–1993. *Journal of Sport and Social Issues, 22*, 127–148.

Mitchell, E. (1999, July 19–25). Ticket run smashes all expectations. *Street & Smith's SportsBusiness Journal*, p. 48.

Mowen, J. C., & Minor, M. (1998). *Consumer behavior* (5th ed.). Englewood Cliffs, NJ: Prentice-Hall.

Mullen, L. (1999, July 19–25). World Cup kicks off talk of pro league: Despite losses, MLS owners eye investment. *Street & Smith's SportsBusiness Journal*, p. 1, 47.

Nakazawa, M., Mahony, D. F., Funk, D. C., & Hirakawa, S. (1999). Segmenting J. League spectators based on length of time as a fan. *Sport Marketing Quarterly, 8*(4), 55–65.

Nunnally, J. C., & Bernstein, I. H. (1994). *Psychometric theory* (3rd ed.). New York: McGraw-Hill.

Sabo, D., & Snyder, M. (1993). *The Miller Lite report on sport and fitness in the lives of working women*. Milwaukee, WI: Women's Sport Foundation.

Sloan, L. R. (1989). The motives of sports fans. In J. H. Goldstein (Ed.), *Sports, games and play: Social and psychology viewpoints* (2nd ed., pp. 175–240). Hillsdale, NJ: Erlbaum Associates.

Sloan, L. R., Bates, S., Davis, W., & Schwieger, P. K. (1987). *Are sports' appeal and sports' consequences derived from the same fan motives? Support for the achievement seeking needs*. Paper presented at the meeting of the Midwestern Psychological Association.

Smith, G. J. (1988). The noble sports fan. *Journal of Sport and Social Issues, 12*(1), 54–65.

Stevens, J. (1998). *Applied multivariate statistics for the social sciences* (3rd ed.). Hillsdale, NJ: Lawrence Erlbaum Associates.

Sutton, W. A., McDonald, M. A., Milne, G. R., & Cimperman, J. (1997). Creating and fostering fan identification in professional sports. *Sport Marketing Quarterly, 6*(1), 15–22.

Tabachnick, B. G., & Fidell, L. S. (1996). *Using multivariate statistics* (3rd ed.). New York: Harper Collins.

Trail, G. T., Anderson, D. F., & Fink, J. (2000). A theoretical model of sport spectator consumption behavior. *International Journal of Sport Management, 3,* 154–180.

Wann, D. L. (1995). Preliminary validation of the sport fan motivation scale. *Journal of Sport & Social Issues, 20,* 377–396.

Weiller, K. H., & Higgs, C. T. (1997). Fandom in the 40's: The integrating functions of All American Girls Professional Baseball League. *Journal of Sport Behavior, 20*(2), 211–231.

Weiss, M. R., & Chaumeton, N. (1992). Motivational orientations in sport. In T. S. Horn (Ed.), *Advances in sport psychology* (pp. 61–99). Human Kinetics Publishers: Champaign IL.

17

Motivational Profiles of Sport Fans of Different Sports

Daniel L. Wann, Frederick G. Grieve,
Ryan K. Zapalac, and Dale G. Pease

Introduction

Over the past 20 years, sport scientists (e.g., sport psychologists, sport sociologists, and sport marketing professionals) have shown an increased interest in the psychological factors that motivate individuals to consume sport. Although the list of potential motives is naturally quite extensive, eight motives appear to be particularly common among fans (see Wann, Melnick, Russell, & Pease, 2001, for an in-depth discussion of various motivational typologies): escape, economic, eustress, self-esteem, group affiliation, entertainment, family, and aesthetics.

The escape motive involves the use of sport fandom and spectating as a diversion from the rest of one's life (Sloan, 1989; Smith, 1988). That is, individuals who are dissatisfied by their home life, work, college experience, and so forth may be able to temporarily forget their troubles while consuming sport. Consequently, the use of sport as an escape may be particularly prevalent during personally difficult and/or stressful times (e.g., during times of war; see Wann, 1997).

The economic motive is found among individuals who are attracted to the potential economic gains to be accrued through sport wagering (Eastman & Land, 1997; Gantz & Wenner, 1995; Guttmann, 1986). Some researchers (e.g., Wann, 1995) have failed to find a relationship between level of economic motivation and self-proclaimed fandom. This suggests that these individuals may not be "fans" in the normal sense of the word (e.g., rooting for a favored team, identifying with players, etc.).

A third motive is eustress (i.e., euphoric stress), which involves a desire to gain excitement and stimulation through sport (Gantz, 1981; Sloan, 1989). Fans with high levels of eustress motivation become involved with the pastime because they enjoy the excitement and arousal they experience watching sport. A fourth motive, group affiliation, concerns the social nature of sport spectating. In general, fans report a clear preference for consuming sport as a part of a group (Aveni, 1977; Mann, 1969). For some fans, the opportunity to spend time with friends is a driving motivational force behind their decisions to consume sport (Melnick, 1993; Pan, Gabert, McGaugh, & Branvold, 1997).

Another important fan motive is entertainment. Many individuals become involved in sport fandom simply because it is perceived as an enjoyable pastime (Gantz, 1981; Gantz & Wenner, 1995; Sloan, 1989). In these instances, sport fans are motivated in much the same way as fans of other recreational pursuits, such as going to the theater, watching television, or reading books. A number of researchers have examined the characteristics of sporting events that are perceived as entertaining. This literature indicates that watching one's favorite teams succeed (Su-Lin, Tuggle, Mitrook, Coussement, & Zillmann, 1997), watching a rival lose (Bryant, 1989; Sapolsky, 1980), and watching violent sports (Bryant, Comisky, & Zillmann, 1981) are viewed by many fans as entertaining.

The family motive is similar to the group affiliation motive. However, rather than involving a desire to be with others, the family motive involves the consumption of sport because it provides an opportunity to spend time with family members (Evaggelinou & Grekinis, 1998; Guttmann, 1986; Weiller & Higgs, 1997). As one would expect, this motive is particularly common among sport fans that have children and/or are married (Wann, Lane, Duncan, & Goodson, 1998). Wann, Schrader, and Wilson (1999) suggested that sport fans with high levels of family motivation may prefer to consume nonaggressive sports rather than aggressive sports because they did not want to expose their children to the violent actions found in aggressive sports. However, subsequent work failed to find a relationship between level of family motivation and preferences for aggressive or nonaggressive sports (Wann & Ensor, 2001; Wann et al., 1998).

A final factor underlying fan consumption of sport is the aesthetic motive (Guttmann, 1986; Hemphill, 1995; Rinehart, 1996; Wertz, 1985). This motive involves an individual's desire to participate in sport as a fan because he or she enjoys the artistic beauty and grace of sport movements. Artistic sports such as figure skating and gymnastics can be attractive to fans because of their inherent beauty and the artistic expressions of the athletes. However, it is important to note that the aesthetic motive is not limited to fans of "stylistic" sports (Sargent, Zillmann, & Weaver, 1998); rather, those interested in other sports may also express a high level of aesthetic motivation (e.g., golf fans often discuss the beauty of a well-executed golf swing).

Research examining the aforementioned eight sport fan motives has indicated several interesting patterns that differentiate the various motives. For instance, investigators have examined gender differences in sport fan motivation (Dietz-Uhler, Harrick, End, & Jacquemotte, 2000; James & Ridinger, 2002; MacLardie, 2002; Wann, 1995; Wann, Schrader, et al., 1999). This research consistently replicated several gender differences in fan motivation, including higher scores for male fans on eustress, economic, self-esteem, and aesthetic motivation, and higher scores for female fans on family motivation. Similarly, other researchers have noted that members of different ethic and racial groups report different fan motivational patterns (e.g., Armstrong, 2002; Bilyeu & Wann, 2002; Wann, Bilyeu, Breenan, Osborn, & Gambouras, 1999) as do fans seated in different areas of the sports arena (Wigley, Sagas, & Ashley, 2002).

Understanding different spectator motivations can be of significant benefit to the sport marketer looking to boost team revenues and gate receipts. Of particular interest are both the marketing manager understanding the specific motivations that drive a spectator or fan to consume a sport (Bernthal & Graham, 2003) and the subsequent development of marketing communications based on these motivations (McDonald, Milne, & Hong, 2002). These effective marketing communication plans can often help build groups of "die-hard" fans, thus expanding the customer base for a team (Pease & Zhang, 2001). Spectator and fan motivation can also be used as an effective psychographic segmentation method that can result in more effective marketing campaigns. A comprehensive marketing model that includes motivation and other important spectator and fan variables, such as identification or loyalty, can be very useful in marketing a team or sport (Trail, Fink, & Anderson, 2003; Trail & James, 2001).

Motivational Differences for Fans of Different Sports

The literature described above indicates that there are numerous motives that underlie fans' decisions to consume sport, and that patterns of these motives differ across spectator groups (e.g., males and females). Another important area of research concerns potential differences in motivational patterns for fans of different sports. To date, a handful of studies have examined the possibilities that fans of different sports report distinctly divergent motivational patterns. Perhaps the first study to investigate this possibility was conducted by Wenner and Gantz (1989). As part of a larger telephone interview project, these authors examined potential motives for indirect sport consumption via television. Participants were segmented based on the sport they most frequently watched on television. They were then asked a series of questions assessing, among other things, their motives for watching their favored sport. The results indicated that professional basketball fans were particularly likely to report motives related to eustress (i.e., consuming to "get psyched up"). Differences among the target sports were not found for motives related to escape (e.g., "to relax/unwind").

A second study, conducted by Wann, Schrader, and Wilson (1999), asked participants to list the sport they most enjoyed watching and then complete a measure assessing their motivational pattern as a fan. The participants were classified as having a preference for an aggressive sport (e.g., boxing) or a nonaggressive sport (e.g., baseball), and as having a preference for an individual sport (e.g., figure skating) or a team sport (e.g., volleyball). The results revealed at least one significant difference for each motive. Relative to team sports, participants with a preference for an individual sport reported lower levels of eustress, self-esteem, escape, entertainment, group affiliation, and family motivation, and higher levels of aesthetic motivation (no differences were found for economic motivation). Relative to nonaggressive sports, participants with a preference for an aggressive sport reported lower levels of aesthetic motivation and higher levels of eustress, self-esteem, economic, and group affiliation motivation (no differences were found for escape, entertainment, and family motivation).

A third assessment of sport type differences in fan motivation was conducted by McDonald, Milne, and Hong (2002). These researchers mailed 5,000 surveys to a sample of sport enthusiasts; over 1,600 useable surveys were returned. Subjects were asked to list their favorite sport and then to answer the motivational items specifically for that sport. Unlike the Wann, Schrader, and Wilson (1999) research, this methodology allows for direct comparison of motivational patterns across different sports. Nine target sports were examined: auto racing, college baseball, professional baseball, college basketball, professional basketball, college football, professional football, golf, and ice hockey. A number of motives were assessed, including several that were directly or peripherally related to the eight common motives described previously. The results revealed a large number of motivational differences across sport. Of specific interest were the particularly high levels of group affiliation motivation for fans of auto racing, the particularly high levels of aesthetic motivation for fans of golf, and the low aesthetic motivation for fans of football. No target sport differences were found for escape motivation (referred to by these authors as "stress release"). McDonald et al., (2002) also noted that understanding these motivations is "fundamental to the marketing concept" (p. 110) and this improved understanding can assist sport marketers with the development of effective psychographic evaluation methods.

A final study was recently completed by James and Ross (2004). These authors examined the motivational patterns of fans consuming three non-revenue college sports: baseball, softball, and wrestling. Their results failed to detect sport differences in entertainment or group affiliation (referred to as social interaction). Wrestling had particularly high scores on eustress (termed drama by James & Ross), self-esteem (called the achievement motive), and family motivation. Baseball had lower scores for these motives, while motivational levels for softball were between wrestling and baseball. As noted by the authors, an enhanced understanding of these motives can help with revenue generation, which is a very important concern common to most intercollegiate athletic programs. However, it should be noted that additional revenue generation for a sport team at any level is a concern, as consumers are being presented with an increasing number of entertainment options. Thus, the lessons learned from this study, as well as other studies examining sport fan motivation, can be very useful to the sport manager/marketer.

The Current Investigation

The current investigation was designed to expand the aforementioned work on the differential motivational patterns for different target sports (e.g., James & Ross, 2004; McDonald et al., 2002; Wann, Schrader, and Wilson, 1999; Wenner & Gantz, 1989). Specifically, the current work expanded on previous efforts in several important ways. First, and perhaps foremost, previous efforts (referred to here as target sport analyses) employed specific sports such as basketball and football as the unit of analysis. Although such an approach is certainly worthwhile and yields vital information, we attempted to move beyond such a level of analysis by additionally focusing on various types of sports (referred to in the current work as sport type analyses). Only one previous effort, Wann, Schrader, and Wilson (1999), employed such an approach and was limited to comparisons of individual versus team and aggressive versus nonaggressive sports. The current investigation extended this line of investigation by also comparing the motivational patterns underlying the consumption of stylistic and nonstylistic sports. Second, at the target sport level, the current study examined motivational patterns for consuming sports not previously examined in past research. Previous efforts focused on popular sports such as baseball and basketball. In addition to examining these sports, we were also interested in establishing motivational patterns for previously unexamined sports. Third, the current work extended past efforts by investigating motives that were neglected in some of the earlier investigations and by using a well-tested protocol to assess motivation. For instance, McDonald et al. (2002) and Wenner and Gantz (1989) did not examine economic or family motivation, and neither study used a previously established and psychometrically sound measure of fan motivation. Fourth, in some of the past work it is unclear as to whether or not the participants were truly fans of a specific sport. For instance, in the Wann, Schrader, and Wilson (1999) research, although the fans were asked to list the sport they most enjoyed following, there was no guarantee that they were actually involved as a fan of the sport listed. That is, someone could say they most enjoyed watching football while not truly being a fan of the sport. And finally, some of the previously cited works (Wann, Schrader, & Wilson, 1999) had methodological shortcomings, such as small sample sizes and confusion over whether the subjects were completing a general measure of fandom or a motivational pattern specific to the consumption of a target sport.

Because of the exploratory nature of this research, the development of direct hypotheses was often not plausible. That is, given the lack of applicable theory and/or research, it was not appropriate to develop an expectation for each motivational pattern for each sport. Rather, the current work simply attempted to answer the research question, "How and to what degree do motivational patterns differ with respect to the consumption of different sports as well as among different types of sports?" The discussion section presents a comparison of the current data with previous data (James & Ross, 2004; McDonald et al., 2002; Wann, Schrader, & Wilson, 1999; Wenner & Gantz, 1989).

Method

Participants

The original sample consisted of 1,372 college students attending universities located in the Mid-south and South. However, 96 of the participants returned incomplete questionnaire packets. In addition, subsequent analyses (see descriptions below) indicated that 390 of the participants were not fans (at least in a moderate sense) of any of the 13 target sports. Consequently, these respondents were also dropped from the sample. The result was a final sample consisting of 886 sport fans (285 male, 263 female, 338 not reporting) with a mean age of 21.41 years ($SD = 3.42$).

Procedure

All respondents (i.e., the 1,372 participants in the original sample) were tested in small groups ranging from 5 to 50 in university classrooms. Upon providing their consent to participate, the subjects were asked to complete a questionnaire packet containing four sections. This first section simply contained demographic items designed to assess age and gender.[1] The next section of the questionnaire asked subjects to report their level of interest in 13 different sports. For example, the first item read, "I follow professional baseball (for example, watch it on TV, read about it in newspapers, etc.)." Participants were to report their level of following by circling one of three response options: never, sometimes, or often. In addition to professional baseball, the participants reported their level of interest in college football, professional football, figure skating, gymnastics, professional hockey, boxing, auto racing, tennis, professional basketball, college basketball, professional wrestling, and golf.

Upon completion of this section of the packet, subjects returned the questionnaire to the researcher, who then examined participants' responses to the interest items. Specifically, the researcher was looking for the most instances of the response "often", and for which sport. Based on this finding, and if there was only one such sport, the participant was asked to target this sport for the remainder of the items in the questionnaire.

If there were more than one such sport, the researcher randomly chose one of the target sports. If participants had no sports they followed "often," they were asked to target a sport they followed "sometimes," with the method of choosing the particular sport similar to that for sport viewed "often." If subjects did not follow any sport at least "sometimes," they were simply asked to return the questionnaire and they were excused from the study. The aforementioned procedure was designed to result in a sample consisting of fans who are at least moderately interested in the target sport (i.e., it made little sense to assess the fan motives of persons who were not actually fans of a given sport).

The next section of the questionnaire contained one page printed front and back. Subjects were instructed to write the name of their target sport at the top of each side of the page and to focus on this sport when answering the items. On the front side, subjects completed the Sport Fandom Questionnaire (SFQ), a reliable and valid five-item instrument (Likert scale format) assessing level of sport fandom (Wann, 2002), of the target sport. Response options to the questionnaire range from 1 (*low fandom*) to 8 (*high fandom*).

The final section of the questionnaire packet, located on the back side of the final page, contained the 23-item Sport Fan Motivation Scale (SFMS; Wann, 1995; Wann, Schrader, & Wilson, 1999). This valid and reliable instrument assesses motivation for eight different fan motives described earlier in the introduction: escape, economic, eustress, self-esteem, group affiliation, entertainment, family, and aesthetics. Each subscale contained three items, with the exception of the family subscale, which contained two. Response options to the motivation questionnaire ranged from 1 (*low motivation*) to 8 (*high motivation*). Thus, higher numbers indicate greater levels of motivation for following the target sport. Items on each subscale were summed and this total was divided by the number of items in the subscale (i.e., 2 or 3), resulting in all subscales being standardized to the range of the original items (i.e., 1 to 8).

After the participants had completed both sides of the final page, the questionnaire packet was stapled and returned to the researcher. The participants were then debriefed, provided information on obtaining a final report of the project, and excused from the testing session. Each session lasted approximately 15 minutes.

Results

Preliminary Analyses

Prior to examining the impact of target sport on motivational patterns, several preliminary analyses and calculations were required. First, the five items comprising the SFQ were summed to create a single index of level of fandom for the participant's target sport. Next, Cronbach's analyses were used to examine the reliability of the SFQ and the eight subscales of the SFMS. These analyses supported the reliability of each scale or subscale (alphas ranged from .69 to .91). Finally, SFQ scores were used to eliminate participants who were not at least moderately interested in their target team. Specifically, subjects with an SFQ score of less than 16 (scale ranges from 5 to 40, i.e., participants must have a mean item score of at least 3 on the 1-8 Likert scale) were deleted from the sample, resulting in the final sample of 886 participants. (This procedure was employed to ensure that the participants were truly fans of their target team, at least at a moderate level.)

Table 1.
Means and Standard Deviations for the Motivation Subscales by Target Sport.

Target Sport	ESC	ECO	EUS	S-E	G A	ENT	FAM	AES	n
Professional Baseball	3.37_{a}	1.45_{a}	5.50_{cd}	4.51_{c}	4.77_{b}	6.60_{bc}	3.57_{ab}	3.87_{abcd}	106
	(2.08)	(0.98)	(1.49)	(1.43)	(1.64)	(1.18)	(2.07)	(2.04)	—
College Football	3.23_{a}	1.72_{a}	5.56_{cd}	4.27_{c}	5.16_{b}	6.56_{bc}	3.71_{b}	2.95_{a}	84
	(1.83)	(1.25)	(1.65)	(1.48)	(1.71)	(1.18)	(1.94)	(1.72)	—
Professional Football	3.64_{a}	1.55_{a}	5.63_{d}	4.15_{bc}	5.13_{b}	6.76_{bc}	3.36_{ab}	3.33_{abc}	87
	(2.02)	(1.01)	(1.55)	(1.48)	(1.69)	(1.06)	(2.11)	(1.71)	—
Figure Skating	3.53_{a}	1.18_{a}	4.38_{a}	3.11_{a}	3.04_{a}	6.17_{ab}	2.68_{ab}	6.97_{f}	34
	(2.07)	(0.49)	(1.87)	(1.55)	(1.46)	(1.38)	(1.80)	(1.22)	—
Gymnastics	3.09_{a}	1.18_{a}	4.68_{abc}	3.33_{ab}	3.36_{a}	6.22_{abc}	2.47_{a}	6.50_{f}	51
	(1.64)	(0.46)	(1.64)	(1.430	(1.44)	(1.16)	(1.55)	(1.30)	—
Professional Hockey	3.73_{a}	1.28_{a}	5.73_{d}	3.79_{abc}	4.59_{b}	6.89_{c}	3.13_{ab}	3.26_{ab}	40
	(2.09)	(0.60)	(1.71)	(1.41)	(1.34)	(1.18)	(2.37)	(1.98)	—
Boxing	3.27_{a}	2.28_{b}	6.02_{d}	3.75_{abc}	4.46_{b}	6.61_{bc}	2.83_{ab}	4.90_{e}	43
	(2.10)	(1.50)	(1.56)	(1.59)	(1.47)	(1.14)	(2.05)	(1.96)	—
Auto Racing	3.79_{a}	1.61_{a}	5.37_{bcd}	4.04_{bc}	4.86_{b}	6.62_{bc}	3.74_{b}	3.06_{a}	52
	(1.84)	(1.06)	(1.69)	(1.32)	(1.45)	(1.10)	(2.21)	(1.83)	—
Tennis	3.58_{a}	1.28_{a}	5.11_{abcd}	3.90_{abc}	3.62_{a}	6.08_{ab}	2.48_{a}	4.83_{e}	67
	(2.01)	(0.64)	(1.80)	(1.78)	(1.62)	(1.38)	(1.81)	(1.67)	—
Professional Basketball	3.27_{a}	1.65_{a}	5.58_{cd}	4.29_{c}	4.96_{b}	6.48_{bc}	3.42_{ab}	4.10_{bcde}	79
	(1.86)	(1.20)	(1.39)	(1.33)	(1.50)	(1.08)	(2.03)	(1.74)	—
College Basketball	3.35_{a}	1.52_{a}	5.59_{cd}	4.27_{c}	5.23_{b}	6.58_{bc}	3.88_{b}	3.37_{abc}	138
	(1.93)	(1.14)	(1.59)	(1.44)	(1.61)	(1.13)	(2.08)	(1.82)	—
Professional Wrestling	4.84_{b}	1.27_{a}	5.19_{abcd}	3.74_{abc}	5.06_{b}	6.67_{bc}	3.11_{ab}	4.21_{cde}	36
	(1.80)	(0.64)	(1.82)	(1.56)	(1.81)	(1.19)	(2.12)	(2.24)	—
Golf	3.72_{a}	1.69_{a}	4.55_{ab}	3.63_{abc}	3.60_{a}	5.69_{a}	3.08_{ab}	4.70_{de}	69
	(2.23)	(1.29)	(1.89)	(1.69)	(1.52)	(1.55)	(2.02)	(1.71)	—
All Sports Combined	3.50	1.53	5.36	4.03	4.60	6.47	3.31	4.07	886
	(1.99)	(1.06)	(1.68)	(1.53)	(1.72)	(1.23)	(2.07)	(2.07)	—

Notes: Standard deviations appear in parentheses below each mean. SFMS subscale scores range from 1 (*low motivation*) to 8 (*high motivation*). ESC = escape subscale, ECO = economic subscale, EUS = eustress subscale, S-E = self-esteem subscale, G A = group affiliation subscale, ENT = entertainment subscale, FAM = family subscale, AES = aesthetic subscale, *n* = number of subjects for whom that was the target sport. For each motivation scale (i.e., column), means sharing a common subscript are not significantly different (Student-Newman-Keuls tests).

Motivational Patterns

Comparisons across target sport. The first set of examinations involved a Multivariate Analysis of Variance (MANOVA) in which the target sport served as the grouping variable and motivation subscale scores were employed as the multiple dependent measures. Means and standard deviations for the SFMS subscales by target sport appear in Table 1. The MANOVA yielded a highly significant multivariate effect, Wilks' Lambda (8, 866) = 3292.99, $p < .001$.

Because of the significant multivariate effect, a series of eight separate univariate tests were conducted, one test for each of the eight motivation subscales (target sport again served as the grouping variable). The results of these analyses are found in Table 1 (see subscripts to means in Table 1). The univariate analysis on the escape subscale resulted in a significant between-subjects effect, $F(12, 873) = 2.21, p < .02$. Post hoc analyses (all such analyses were Student-Newman-Keuls) indicated that escape motivation subscale scores were higher for professional wrestling than the 12 other sports, none of which were significantly different. The univariate analysis on the economic subscale also resulted in a significant between-subjects effect, $F(12, 873) = 3.90, p < .001$. Post hoc analyses indicated that economic motivation subscale scores were higher for boxing than the 12 other sports, none of which were significantly different. The univariate analysis on the eustress subscale also resulted in a significant between-subjects effect, $F(12, 873) = 4.75, p < .001$. Post hoc analyses indicated that eustress subscale scores were lower for figure skating and higher for professional football, hockey, and boxing. However, this is an oversimplification as a rather complex pattern of effects was found (see Table 1). The univariate analysis on the self-esteem subscale also resulted in a significant between-subjects effect, $F(12, 873) = 4.42, p < .001$. Post hoc analyses revealed several different effects, including the finding of lower self-esteem subscale scores for figure skating and higher scores for college football, college basketball, professional basketball, and professional baseball.

The univariate analysis on the group affiliation subscale also indicated a significant between-subjects effect, $F(12, 873) = 14.14, p < .001$. Post hoc analyses indicated that group affiliation motivation subscale scores were lower for figure skating, gymnastics, golf, and tennis, and higher for the other subscales. No other comparisons were significant. The univariate analysis on the entertainment subscale also resulted in a significant between-subjects effect, $F(12, 873) = 4.65, p < .001$. Post hoc analyses revealed many different effects, including the finding of lower entertainment subscale scores for golf and higher scores for professional hockey. The univariate analysis on the family subscale also revealed a significant between-subjects effect, $F(12, 873) = 3.81, p < .001$. Post hoc analyses revealed lower family subscale scores for gymnastics and tennis than for college football, auto racing, and college basketball. No other comparisons were significant. And finally, the univariate analysis on the aesthetic subscale also revealed in a significant between-subjects effect, $F(12, 873) = 25.66, p < .001$. Post hoc analyses revealed a highly complex pattern of effects, which included particularly high aesthetic subscales scores for gymnastics and figure skating.

Comparisons of individual and team sports. The next set of analyses involved comparisons of motivational patterns for team sports versus individual sports. Of the 13 target sports, seven were classified as individual sports: figure skating, gymnastics, boxing, auto racing, tennis, professional wrestling, and golf.[2] The remaining six target sports were categorized as team sports: professional baseball, college football, professional football, pro-

Table 2.
Means and Standard Deviations for the Motivation Subscales by Sport Type.

Sport Type Comparison	ESC	ECO	EUS	S-E	G A	ENT	FAM	AES	n
Individual versus Team									
Individual	3.65	1.51	5.03	3.67	3.96	6.24	2.91	4.94	352
	(2.02)	(1.02)	(1.81)	(1.59)	(1.67)	(1.34)	(1.97)	(2.06)	—
Team	3.40	1.54	5.58	4.27	5.02	6.62	3.58	3.50	534
	(1.96)	(1.09)	(1.55)	(1.44)	(1.62)	(1.13)	(2.09)	(1.86)	—
Aggressive versus Nonaggressive									
Aggressive	3.63	1.64	5.63	4.02	4.96	6.68	3.32	3.55	290
	(2.01)	(1.13)	(1.64)	(1.51)	(1.65)	(1.14)	(2.11)	(1.96)	—
Nonaggressive	3.44	1.48	5.23	4.03	4.43	6.36	3.31	4.32	596
	(1.96)	(1.09)	(1.55)	(1.44)	(1.62)	(1.13)	(2.09)	(1.86)	—
Stylistic versus Nonstylistic									
Stylistic	3.26	1.18	4.56	3.24	3.23	6.20	2.55	6.69	85
	(1.83)	(0.47)	(1.73)	(1.47)	(1.45)	(1.24)	(1.65)	(1.28)	—
Nonstylistic	3.53	1.57	5.45	4.11	4.75	6.49	3.40	3.79	801
	(2.00)	(1.10)	(1.65)	(1.51)	(1.68)	(1.23)	(2.09)	(1.94)	—

Notes: Standard deviations appear in parentheses below each mean. SFMS subscale scores range from 1 (*low motivation*) to 8 (*high motivation).* ESC = escape subscale, ECO = economic subscale, EUS = eustress subscale, S-E = self-esteem subscale, G A = group affiliation subscale, ENT = entertainment subscale, FAM = family subscale, AES = aesthetic subscale, *n* = number of subjects in that sport type.

fessional hockey, professional basketball, and college basketball. The MANOVA for this analysis employed sport type (i.e., individual or team) as the grouping variable and motivation subscale scores served as the multiple dependent measures. Means and standard deviations for the SFMS subscales by target sport type are presented in Table 2. The MANOVA yielded a highly significant multivariate effect, Wilks' Lambda (8, 877) = 3645.19, $p < .001$. Post hoc analysis of variance (ANOVA) tests were then computed for each motivation subscale. Two of these comparisons failed to find a significance difference in level of motivation between individual and team sports: escape motivation, $F(1, 844) = 3.44$, $p > .05$, and economic motivation, $F(1, 844) = 0.27$, $p > .60$. The remaining six comparisons found significant differences. In one comparison focusing on aesthetic motivation, individual sport scores were higher than those for team sports, $F(1, 844) = 116.19$, $p < .001$. In the five remaining comparisons, scores were greater for team sports than for individual sports: eustress, $F(1, 844) = 24.01$, $p < .001$; self-esteem, $F(1, 844) =$

32.92, $p < .001$; group affiliation, $F(1, 844) = 90.36$, $p < .001$; entertainment, $F(1, 844) = 20.92$, $p < .001$; and family, $F(1, 844) = 23.11$, $p < .001$.

Comparisons of aggressive and nonaggressive sports. The next set of analyses involved comparisons of motivational patterns for aggressive sports versus nonaggressive sports. Of the 13 target sports, five were classified as aggressive: college football, professional football, hockey, boxing, and professional wrestling. The remaining eight sports were categorized as nonaggressive: professional baseball, figure skating, gymnastics, auto racing, tennis, professional basketball, college basketball, and golf. The MANOVA for this analysis employed sport type (i.e., aggressive or nonaggressive) as the grouping variable and motivation subscale scores served as the multiple dependent measures. Means and standard deviations for the SFMS subscales by target sport type are found in Table 2. As in other instances, the MANOVA yielded a highly significant multivariate effect, Wilks' Lambda (8, 877) = 3406.16, $p < .001$. Post hoc analysis of variance (ANOVA) tests were then computed for each motivation subscale. Three of these comparisons failed to find a significant difference in level of motivation between aggressive and nonaggressive sports: escape motivation, $F(1, 844) = 1.77$, $p > .15$; self-esteem motivation, $F(1, 844) = 0.01$, $p > .85$; and family motivation, $F(1, 844) = 0.00$, $p > .95$. The remaining five comparisons were statistically significant ($p < .05$). In one comparison, aesthetic motivation, nonaggressive sport scores were higher than those for aggressive sports, $F(1, 844) = 27.58$, $p < .001$. In the four remaining comparisons, scores were greater for aggressive sports than for nonaggressive sports: economic, $F(1, 844) = 4.41$, $p < .05$; eustress, $F(1, 844) = 10.75$, $p < .001$; group affiliation, $F(1, 844) = 19.07$, $p < .001$; and entertainment, $F(1, 844) = 13.86$, $p < .001$.

Comparisons of stylistic and nonstylistic sports. The final set of analyses involved comparisons of motivational patterns for stylistic sports versus nonstylistic sports. Two of the 13 target sports were classified as stylistic: figure skating and gymnastics. The remaining 11 sports were labeled nonstylistic: professional baseball, college football, professional football, professional hockey, boxing, auto racing, tennis, professional basketball, college basketball, professional wrestling, and golf. The MANOVA for this analysis employed sport type (i.e., stylistic or nonstylistic) as the grouping variable and motivation subscale scores served as the multiple dependent measures. Means and standard deviations for the SFMS subscales by target sport type are presented in Table 2. The MANOVA yielded a highly significant multivariate effect, Wilks' Lambda (8, 877) = 1323.99, $p < .001$. Post hoc analysis of variance (ANOVA) tests were then computed for each motivation subscale. Only one comparison, escape motivation, failed to reach statistical significance, $F(1, 844) = 1.35$, $p > .20$. The remaining seven comparisons were significantly different. In one comparison, aesthetic motivation, stylistic sport scores were higher than those for nonstylistic sports, $F(1, 844) = 182.06$, $p < .001$. In the six remaining comparisons, scores were greater for nonstylistic sports than for stylistic sports: economic, $F(1, 844) = 10.24$, $p < .001$; eustress, $F(1, 844) = 21.80$, $p < .001$; self-esteem, $F(1, 844) = 25.68$, $p < .001$; group affiliation, $F(1, 844) = 63.84$, $p < .001$; entertainment, $F(1, 844) = 4.38$, $p < .05$; and family, $F(1, 844) = 12.91$, $p < .001$.

Discussion

The current investigation was intended to replicate and extend previous research on the motivational patterns of sport fans by examining potential differences in patterns for different sport types and different target sports. As revealed in Table 1, there were many significant motivational differences among the sports. Further, Table 2 reveals that the consumption of different sport types (e.g., aggressive versus nonaggressive) was characterized by different motivational patterns. In the paragraphs to follow, we will focus our discussion on the sport type differences and highlight the specific sport comparisons when applicable. However, prior to discussing the results, the age of the current sample warrants mention. Clearly, with a mean of 21.41 years and a standard deviation of 3.42 years, the sample was quite homogeneous with respect to age. This was simply a consequence of the convenience sample (i.e., college students) used in this research. It will be important for future researchers to replicate the work conducted here with a sample that is more heterogeneous with respect to age. However, the homogeneous nature of the current sample does not invalidate the results. This is particularly true in light of the fact that previous research using heterogeneous samples (Wann, 1995; Wann, Schrader, & Wilson, 1999) has failed to find significant relationships between age and sport fan motives.

Individual versus Team Sports

The analysis of individual sports versus team sports revealed a number of motivational differences as all motives except escape and economic differed by sport type. Individual sports were more likely to be a function of aesthetic motivation than were team sports. An investigation of Table 1 reveals that this finding was primarily a function of the exceptionally high levels of aesthetic motivation as a driver for figure skating and gymnastics. However, one could likely argue that it is the stylistic nature of these sports that lead to high levels of aesthetic motivation (see below), rather than their categorization as an individual sport. That is, if one were to specifically assess motives for consuming doubles figure skating, one would likely get high levels of aesthetic motivation. There might also be a connection with the method that the sport uses to evaluate performance (i.e., gymnastics and figure skating both use subjective scoring methods that rely on judges to evaluate performance rather than "points" or "goals," which are more objective in nature).

Eustress, self-esteem, group affiliation, entertainment, and family motivations were all more prevalent as factors for consuming team sports, findings that replicate work by Wann, Schrader, and Wilson (1999) and, to a limited degree, Wenner and Gantz (1989), who found low levels of eustress motivation for tennis. As for eustress, it is interesting to note that for most of the individual sports examined here (i.e., figure skating, gymnastics, tennis, and golf), spectators are discouraged from conversing and moving around during play (for instance, officials at professional golf tournaments hold signs reading "QUIET" while the players execute shots). Thus, it shouldn't be surprising to find that fans of these sports are less likely to be motivated by a desire to get excited by the action. Quite to the contrary, the norms surrounding many of these sports discourage such reactions. Such an argument also may partially explain why fans of team sports were more likely to endorse group affiliation and family needs as motives underlying their consumption habits. Again, participants reported low levels of these two motives for figure skating, gymnastics, tennis, and golf—sports with lower levels of contact among fans. If one attends a sporting event to spend time with others and/or his or her family, the fan is likely to choose a sport where such interactions are the norm. Interpersonal communications are less common at the individual sports listed above, likely resulting in group affiliation and family being less powerful drivers in the consumption of these sports.

With respect to the individual/team sport differences in self-esteem, this motive was found to be particularly prominent among fans of four sports: professional baseball, college football, professional basketball, and college basketball. Figure skating and gymnastics were less likely to be consumed due to a desire to enhance one's self-image. Such a finding makes logical sense, given that sport fans often attach to and follow baseball, basketball, and football teams for many years, resulting in particularly high levels of identification with those teams. Conversely, supporting an elite figure skater or gymnast may be less likely to lead to high levels of identification because these individuals only compete for a few years, rather than for decades, as is the case with sport teams.

A close inspection of Table 1 reveals that the individual/team sport difference for entertainment motivation was primarily driven by the levels of entertainment motivation for golf. Why golf fans would report a lower level of entertainment motivation is not clear at this point, given that fans of other individual sports (e.g., professional wrestling and tennis) reported such high levels of this motive. One possibility is that the slower pace of this sport, relative to the other sports, led to the lower entertainment motivation scores. Further, it warrants mention that although entertainment motivation was lower for golf than the other target sports, this motive was still the most powerfully endorsed motive for golf, with a mean Likert-score of 5.69, which is a full point (on the 1-8 scale) higher than any other motive for the consumption of golf. Thus, concluding that golf fans are not motivated by the entertainment value of their sport would be premature.

Aggressive versus Nonaggressive Sports

Comparisons of aggressive and nonaggressive sports revealed significant sport type differences for five of the eight motives: aesthetic, economic, eustress, group affiliation, and entertainment. Differences were not found for escape, self-esteem, or family motivation. Aesthetic motivation was found to be more prominent among fans of nonaggressive sports. This finding precisely replicates work by Wann, Schrader, and Wilson (1999) and also mirrors research by McDonald et al. (2002), who found particularly high levels of aesthetic motivation for the consumption of golf. Based on this pattern of effects, Wann and his associates hypothesized that fans with a high level of aesthetic motivation probably prefer nonaggressive sports because the actions found in aggressive sports may "inhibit the graceful execution of sport movements" (p. 122). Such an argument is consistent with the data presented above. Wann and Wilson (1999) examined this possibility in a pair of studies. In Study 1, participants completed questionnaires assessing their level of aesthetic motivation and their enjoyment of watching several aggressive sports. Wann and Wilson expected a negative correlation between level of aesthetic motivation and enjoyment of violent sports, yet, contrary to expectations, the correlational analyses failed to reveal such a relationship. A second study had subjects complete an inventory assessing their level of aesthetic motivation and then watch a series of violent football plays, rating their enjoyment of each. Once again, there was no significant relationship between aesthetic motivation and enjoyment of violent plays. Wann and Wilson concluded that the suggestions offered by Wann, Schrader, and Wilson (1999) concerning the relationship between aesthetic motivation and enjoyment of aggressive sports were premature because their research indicated that fans who are motivated by the beauty and grace of sport movements are equally likely to enjoy violent and nonviolent sports.

Thus, we are left with a contradiction between the Wann, Schrader, and Wilson (1999) work and the current study on one hand and the research by Wann and Wilson (1999) on the other. Apparently, the key to understanding this paradox is to contrast reasons for consumption with preference for sport. It appears that individuals are less likely to consume aggressive sports for aesthetic reasons (i.e., the current work and research by Wann, Schrader, & Wilson, 1999). However, this does not suggest that these individuals do not like aggressive sports or aggressive sport actions (e.g., Wann & Wilson, 1999). Rather, it means that when they do consume aggressive sports, they are motivated by reasons other than aesthetics (e.g., fans follow hockey for reasons other than aesthetics but these same persons may still enjoy this sport).

The remaining motives, economic, eustress, group affiliation, and entertainment, were all more prominent in the consumption of aggressive sports. With respect to economic motivation, an examination of Table 1 reveals that the significant effect for sport type (i.e., aggressive versus nonaggressive) was driven by the sport of boxing. In fact, in respect to economic motivation for following boxing, only one significant finding was noted, relative to the other sports: Fans were more likely to consume boxing out of a desire to wager on the event. This finding seems reasonable given the reputation of boxing as a gambling sport. Conversely, college and professional football did not involve significantly high levels of economic motivation, which was surprising, as these sports are also targets of sport wagering.

However, eustress was also more likely to be endorsed as a motive underlying the consumption of aggressive sports, a finding that replicates earlier work (Wann, Schrader, & Wilson, 1999; Wenner & Gantz, 1989). This suggests that the violent nature of these activities is arousing and exciting to many fans, and can serve as an attractive component of these sports. People are less likely to consume nonaggressive sports out of a desire to gain excitement and stimulation (however, note that the mean eustress score for the nonaggressive sports was still above the midpoint on the scale, indicating that this is a motive for some fans of these sports). The added excitement of the aggressive content may partially account for the sport type differences in entertainment motivation. Several researchers have noted that violent sport content is often viewed as entertaining, particularly for male fans, fans with violent tendencies, and especially when the announcers highlight its aggressive nature (Bryant, Brown, Comisky, & Zillmann, 1982; Bryant, Comisky, & Zillmann, 1981; Kaelin, 1968). Thus, by combining these effects, it may be that the highest excitement and arousal of aggressive sports impacts the entertainment value of these activities.

Finally, group affiliation scores were also higher for aggressive sports than nonaggressive sports. Such a finding could reflect the types of activities that are commonly associated with these sports. For example, tailgating is a valued and frequent activity associated with football at both at the collegiate and professional levels, where sport fans gather hours before the start of the contest to eat and socialize with friends. In a similar vein, it is not uncommon for people to host parties in their homes to watch important boxing matches, Monday Night Football, and World Wrestling Entertainment events. Or, perhaps the high group affiliation scores for aggressive sports is due to a complex interaction of factors such as social class, ethnic and cultural beliefs, political agendas, and so forth. For instance, for sports such as football and hockey, which often pit community against community, and sports such as boxing and professional wrestling, in which race and ethnicity are often associated with the competition, there are multiple social (i.e., community) and personal identity issues involved. The aggressive sports have a common link of extreme physical contact, which may result in collective action, referred to as *emotional contagion* by Coakley (2004). Under such conditions, group norms may be established and even cherished, leading these fans of these sports to view the group-nature of the event as an important motivational factor.

Stylistic versus Nonstylistic Sports

Comparisons of stylistic and nonstylistic sports revealed significant sport type differences for all motives, with the exception of escape. As one might expect, scores for aesthetic motivation were much higher for the stylistic sports, relative to the nonstylistic sports. In fact, aesthetic motivation scores for the stylistic sports were higher than any other motive for those sports, the mean score aesthetic motivation score for stylistic sports was the highest mean score for *any motive for any sport type*, and the difference in aesthetic motivation for stylistic and nonstylistic sports (*M* difference score = 2.90) was the largest sport type difference for any motive across any sport type comparison (in fact, the second largest sport type difference, group affiliation motivation for stylistic versus nonstylistic sports, was barely half as great; *M* difference = 1.52). With the strength of this effect, it should not come as a surprise that this finding replicates past work (Wann, Schrader, & Wilson, 1999). Thus, it appears that the beauty and grace inherent in stylistic sports is the key motivational factor underlying consumption.

In the six remaining comparisons, motivation subscale scores were greater for nonstylistic sports than for stylistic sports. The difference in group affiliation was rather large (as noted above, the second largest sport type difference detected), a finding that likely reflects the aforementioned fact that spectators are discouraged from conversing during individual sports such as those mentioned above. Likewise, persons were less likely to consume these sports in order to spend time with their family because person-to-person interactions at these events are less feasible. Further, the finding that consumption of stylistic sports is less likely to be a function of eustress motivation may also be a function of the norms for fan behavior surrounding these events. That is, if fans are discouraged from conversing during play, yelling at the players, etc., it shouldn't be surprising that followers of these sports are less inclined to do so in an attempt to gain stimulation. Comparisons of crowds at stylistic sport events and those at nonstylistic events will generally reveal higher levels of arousal among those persons attending the nonstylistic events. Consequently, fans of stylistic sports participate in the pastime for reasons other than to increase arousal and gain excitement.

The significant sport type difference involving entertainment motivation may lead one to conclude that fans of stylistic sports are less inclined to consume their sport because of its entertainment value. However, two factors suggest that this conclusion is generally unfounded. First, while it is true that significant differences in entertainment motivation between stylistic and nonstylistic sports were found, the mean difference was quite small (*M* difference = 0.29). Second, scores for entertainment motivation for stylistic sports were quite high. An examination of Table 2 reveals that aesthetic motivation and entertainment motivation are clearly the most powerful forces for the consumption of stylistic sports.

The significant stylistic/nonstylistic sport difference for economic motivation is a function of the higher levels of this motive for boxing. As noted previously, all other sports were similar in their level of economic motivation. Similarly, the difference in self-esteem motivation (i.e., higher scores for the consumption of nonstylistic sports) was discussed previously in the individual versus team sport section (e.g., fans may tend to identify more strongly with teams participating in team sports, see discussion above).

Additional Findings

A few additional sport differences warrant mention. First, as noted in the previous paragraphs, there were no sport type differences for escape motivation in any of the three comparisons (i.e., individual versus team, aggressive versus nonaggressive, or stylistic versus nonstylistic). However, concluding that the consumption of various sports is not differentially impacted by desires for a diversion is premature. Specifically, an examination of Table 1 revealed that escape motivation was involved in a significant relationship, as the consumption of professional wrestling was more likely to be motivated by escape needs than all other sports. That consumption of professional wrestling is highly motivated by needs for a diversion is quite interesting. Professional wrestling is a highly ritualized form of entertainment in which there are obvious scripts, storylines, protagonists, and antagonists. In fact, in recent years professional wrestling has openly admitted that the outcomes are predetermined (these organizations now tend to refer to themselves as "sports entertainment"). Because of the ongoing storylines, some of which play out like violent soap operas (e.g., wrestlers not only battle over championships, but also over relationships, power, and prestige), it seems logical that the consumption of this activity would be attractive to those individuals in need of an escape. That is, the consumption of professional wrestling appears to be quite similar (with the exception of the level of violence) to other entertainment endeavors such as the theater or the opera (indeed, entertainment motivation was quite high for this sport, see below). Like these other entertainment options, if one does not like the ending (i.e., outcome), he or she can simply rationalize by noting that it was predetermined, a coping strategy that is not available to fans of other sports.

Second, the motivational patterns reported for football and basketball warrant additional discussion. For these two sports, fans of both the professional and college level completed questionnaire packets, allowing for a comparison by competition level. Interestingly, there were no statistically significant differences between college football and professional football or between college basketball and professional basketball on any of the eight motives assessed. Although some competition level differences in motivation have been noted elsewhere (Bernthal & Graham, 2003), the current data suggests that, for the most part, the key factor in predicting differential patterns of fan motivation lies in the target (e.g., baseball versus golf) or type (e.g., stylistic versus nonstylistic) of sport, rather than in the level of competition.

Third, it is interesting to note the grand mean values for the eight motives listed in Table 1 (i.e., across target sport). Entertainment was the most prominent motive, while economic motivation was the lowest rating subscale. Scores for eustress motivation were also quite high, while responses to the family scale were rather low. These findings replicate several previous examinations of sport fan motivation using the SFMS (Wann, 1995; Wann, Schrader, & Wilson, 1999), suggesting that this pattern of effects is quite robust.

Implications for Sport Marketers and Suggestions for Future Research

An enhanced understanding of spectator and fan motivation can be of considerable benefit to the sport marketer (James & Ross, 2004; Trail, Fink, & Anderson, 2003; Trail & James,

2001). Empirical studies of sport spectator and fan motivation should attempt to understand whether the motives to consume a particular sport are different when compared with motivational patterns for consuming other sports (Trail & James, 2001). Thus, the results gleaned from the current study could be of great benefit to the marketing professional that is attempting to develop new strategies to reach sport consumers. Marketers must attempt to understand sport consumer motives that are sport-specific in order to effectively reach their constituents. The development of promotional campaigns and marketing strategies around these sport-specific motives can aid in the marketing of a particular sport, thus driving attendance and consumption. This is an especially critical factor when looking at sports that may have to utilize "blanket" marketing techniques (James & Ross, 2004).

As a result, the utility of the current investigation becomes very clear, as it examines sport spectator and fan motivational patterns across a wide array of sports, which are grouped in categories that are applicable to similar sports or sporting activities not included in the study. Trail et al. (2003) note that these sport-specific motives can then be employed by the sport marketer as a method of segmentation. Thus, the results of the current investigation will allow sport marketers to tailor their promotional methods and marketing strategies to motivations that are prevalent in a particular sport included in the study (i.e., boxing or figure skating), or to those motivations common to a group of sports (i.e., aggressive or nonaggressive sports).

An example of the marketing emphasis placed upon a specific spectator motivation to consume a sport can be found in many of the advertising campaigns conducted by Major League Baseball (MLB). MLB often utilizes many promotional and marketing methods that focus on children and the opportunity for family interaction (Petrecca et al., 2000), which is indicative of family motivation (Wann, 1995). As with other team sports included in this study, baseball has one of the higher family motivation scores (see Table 1). If marketing campaigns focus on spectator motivation for a particular sport, or category of sport, then the results of the current study can assist with the development of other effective marketing campaigns.

For example, responses from the current sample that suggest team sports elicit higher group affiliation scores could assist sport marketers in the development of a campaign communicating to consumers that they will get the spectator experience they desire. By using this study as a guide, sport marketers can look at promoting activities and/or events that facilitate enhanced opportunities to interact and bond with other fans, such as the previously mentioned "tailgating" activities, team rallies, or other interaction opportunities. This is merely one example of ways in which the findings from the current study can have practical application.

Interestingly, the current study also corroborates many of the sport-specific results from McDonald, Milne, and Hong's (2002) study examining a wide range of spectator and fan motivational profiles for different sports. The findings from the current study may provide further evidence that the motivational profiles for a particular sport may be somewhat stable across studies, which could be very useful to the sport marketer looking for consistent consumer motivational trends. However, additional confirmation is needed to verify whether these profiles are in fact stable or if they vary across research studies. Future confirmatory studies investigating the same sports utilized in the current study could be useful in this respect.

Although the data presented here furthers our understanding of the motivational patterns found among fans of various sports, there is still much we do not know about sport fan motivation. For instance, subsequent work should focus on the impact of consumption site on fan motivation. In the current investigation (and previous work as well, e.g., Wann, 1995), fans were asked to report the motives for their consumption in general, regardless of the locale of the consumption. However, we know from past research that the avenue of consumption can impact fan preferences. Wann, Friedman, McHale, and Jaffe (2003) found that fans are far more likely to consume sport alone when listening to the radio than in other environments (e.g., watching sport on television). Consequently, one may find that the motives fans report are also impacted by consumption site. Fans may report greater levels of eustress motivation for the direct consumption of sport (i.e., attending an event in person) than for indirect consumption (e.g., watching a game on television) because of the excitement associated with the crowd.

Future studies should also attempt to replicate the study in different locations, both within the United States and abroad. The motives that drive a spectator or fan of a particular sport to follow or consume that sport may be very different among countries, cultures, and contexts (Kwon & Trail, 2001). Further empirical analyses can assist in understanding whether motivational patterns for a particular sport are universal in nature or whether there may be other factors that help define the motivational profile for a spectator or fan of a particular sport. This could augment international marketing efforts by a sport team. In addition, future studies may want to examine the relationship between spectator and fan identification and motivation for a variety of sports. While this relationship has been examined in other studies (e.g., Trail et al., 2003; Wann, 1995), few, if any, have examined the sheer number of sports included in the current investigation. As a result, motivational patterns of similar sports can be examined, as well as their relationship to identification. It may be possible to identify common motives that feed into an individual's identification with a particular sport or type of sport.

Footnotes

[1]The demographic items were inadvertently left off some of the questionnaires, hence the rather large number of subjects failing to report gender.

[2]For some of these sports, participants do, on occasion, participate as a "team." For instance, tennis players may play in a doubles match or on a larger team (e.g., high school or college). Similarly, auto racing participants have a pit crew, which could be considered a team. However, in general, athletes participating in the previous list of sports do so as an individual. That is, in most cases their performance is a function of their individual level of effort and ability. Hence, these sports were classified as individual sports.

References

Armstrong, K. L. (2002). An examination of the social psychology of blacks' consumption of sport. *Journal of Sport Management, 16,* 267-288.

Aveni, A. F. (1977). The not-so-lonely crowd: Friendship groups in collective behavior. *Sociometry, 40,* 96-99.

Bernthal, M. J., & Graham, P. J. (2003). The effect of sport setting on fan attendance motivation: The case of minor league versus collegiate baseball. *Journal of Sport Behavior, 26,* 223-239.

Bilyeu, J. K., & Wann, D. L. (2002). An investigation of racial differences in sport fan motivation. *International Sports Journal, 6*(2), 93-106.

Bryant, J. (1989). Viewers' enjoyment of televised sports violence. In. L. A. Wenner (Ed.), *Media, sports, and society* (pp. 270-289). Newbury Park, CA: Sage.

Bryant, J., Brown, D., Comisky, P. W., & Zillmann, D. (1982). Sports and spectators: Commentary and appreciation. *Journal of Communication, 32,* 109-119.

Bryant, J., Comisky, P. W., & Zillmann, D. (1981). The appeal of rough-and-tumble play in televised professional football. *Communication Quarterly, 29,* 256-262.

Coakley, J. (2004). *Sports in society: Issues and controversies* (8th ed.). Boston: McGraw Hill.

Dietz-Uhler, B., Harrick, E. A., End, C., & Jacquemotte, L. (2000). Sex differences in sport fan behavior and reasons for being a sport fan. *Journal of Sport Behavior, 23,* 219-231.

Eastman, S. T., & Land, A. M. (1997). The best of both worlds: Sports fans find good seats at the bar. *Journal of Sport & Social Issues, 21,* 156-178.

Evaggelinou, C., & Grekinis, D. (1998). A survey of spectators at the International Stoke Mandeville Wheelchair Games. *Adapted Physical Education Quarterly, 15,* 25-35.

Gantz, W. (1981). An exploration of viewing motives and behaviors associated with television sports. *Journal of Broadcasting, 25,* 263-275.

Gantz, W., & Wenner, L. A. (1995). Fanship and the television sports viewing experience. *Sociology of Sport Journal, 12,* 56-74.

Guttmann, A. (1986). *Sports spectators.* New York: Columbia University Press.

Hemphill, D. A. (1995). Revisioning sport spectatorism. *Journal of the Philosophy of Sport, 22,* 48-60.

James, J. D., & Ridinger, L. L. (2002). Female and male sport fans: A comparison of sport consumption motives. *Journal of Sport Behavior, 25,* 260-278.

James, J. D., & Ross, S. D. (2004). Comparing sport consumer motivations across multiple sports. *Sport Marketing Quarterly, 13*(1), 17-25.

Kaelin, E. F. (1968). The well-played game: Notes toward an aesthetics of sport. *Quest, 10,* 16-28.

Kwon, H., & Trail, G. T. (2001). Sport fan motivation: A comparison of American students and international students. *Sport Marketing Quarterly, 10*(2), 147-155.

MacLardie, J. (2002). *Sport fan motivation.* Unpublished thesis. Aberdeen University.

Mann, L. (1969). Queue culture: The waiting line as a social system. *American Journal of Sociology, 75,* 340-354.

McDonald, M. A., Milne, G. R., & Hong, J. (2002). Motivational factors for evaluating sport spectator and participant markets. *Sport Marketing Quarterly, 11,* 100-113.

Melnick, M. J. (1993). Searching for sociability in the stands: A theory of sports spectating. *Journal of Sport Management, 7,* 44-60.

Pan, D. W., Gabert, T. E., McGaugh, E. C., & Branvold, S. E. (1997). Factors and differential demographic effects on purchases of season tickets for intercollegiate basketball games. *Journal of Sport Behavior, 20,* 447-464.

Pease, D. G., & Zhang, J. J. (2001). Socio-motivational factors affecting spectator attendance at professional basketball games. *International Journal of Sport Management, 2*(1), 31-59.

Petrecca, L., Cuneo, A. Z., Haliday, J., & Nack, J. (2000). MLB pins future on Generation Y. *Advertising Age, 71*(14), 1-3.

Rinehart, R. (1996). Dropping hierarchies: Toward the study of a contemporary sporting avant-garde. *Sociology of Sport Journal, 13,* 159-175.

Sapolsky, B. S. (1980). The effect of spectator disposition and suspense on the enjoyment of sport contests. *International Journal of Sport Psychology, 11,* 1-10.

Sargent, S. L., Zillmann, D., & Weaver, J. B. III. (1998). The gender gap in the enjoyment of televised sports. *Journal of Sport & Social Issues, 22,* 46-64.

Sloan, L. R. (1989). The motives of sports fans. In J. D. Goldstein (Ed.), *Sports, games, and play: Social and psychosocial viewpoints* (2nd ed.) (pp. 175-240). Hillsdale, NJ: Lawrence Erlbaum Associates.

Smith, G. J. (1988). The noble sports fan. *Journal of Sport & Social Issues, 12,* 54-65.

Su-Lin, G., Tuggle, C. A., Mitrook, M. A., Coussement, S. H., & Zillmann, D. (1997). The thrill of a close game: Who enjoys it and who doesn't? *Journal of Sport & Social Issues, 21,* 53-64.

Trail, G. T., Fink, J. S., & Anderson, D. F. (2003). Sport spectator consumption behavior. *Sport Marketing Quarterly, 12*(1), 8-17.

Trail, G. T., & James, J. D. (2001). The motivation scale for sport consumption: A comparison of psychometric properties with other sport motivation scales. *Journal of Sport Behavior, 24*(1), 108-127.

Wann, D. L. (1995). Preliminary validation of the Sport Fan Motivation Scale. *Journal of Sport & Social Issues, 19,* 377-396.

Wann, D. L. (1997). *Instructor's manual to accompany Sport Psychology.* Upper Saddle River, NJ: Prentice Hall.

Wann, D. L. (2002). Preliminary validation of a measure for assessing identification as a sport fan: The Sport Fandom Questionnaire. *International Journal of Sport Management, 3,* 103-115.

Wann, D. L., Bilyeu, J. K., Breenan, K., Osborn, H., & Gambouras, A. F. (1999). An exploratory investigation of the relationship between sport fan motivation and race. *Perceptual and Motor Skills, 88,* 1081-1084.

Wann, D. L., & Ensor, C. L. (2001). Family motivation and a more accurate classification of preferences for aggressive sports. *Perceptual and Motor Skills, 92,* 603-605.

Wann, D. L., Friedman, K., McHale, M., & Jaffe, A. (2003). The Norelco Sport Fanatics Survey: Understanding the behaviors of avid sport fans. *Psychological Reports, 92,* 930-936.

Wann, D. L., Lane, T. M., Duncan, L. E., & Goodson, S. L. (1998). Family status, preference for sport aggressiveness, and sport fan motivation. *Perceptual and Motor Skills, 86,* 1419-1422.

Wann, D. L., Melnick, M. J., Russell, G. W., & Pease, D. G. (2001). *Sport fans: The psychology and social impact of spectators.* New York: Routledge Press.

Wann, D. L., Schrader, M. P., & Wilson, A. M. (1999). Sport fan motivation: Questionnaire validation, comparisons by sport, and relationship to athletic motivation. *Journal of Sport Behavior, 22,* 114-139.

Wann, D. L., & Wilson, A. M. (1999). The relationship between aesthetic motivation andpreferences for aggressive and nonaggressive sports. *Perceptual and Motor Skills, 89,* 931-934.

Weiller, K. H., & Higgs, C. T. (1997). Fandom in the 40's: The integrating functions of All American Girls Professional Baseball League. *Journal of Sport Behavior, 20,* 211-231.

Wenner, L. A., & Gantz, W. (1989). The audience experience with sports on television. In L. A. Wenner (Ed.), *Media, sports, and society* (pp. 241-268). Newbury Park, CA: Sage.

Wertz, S. K. (1985). Artistic creativity in sport. In D. L. Vanderwerken & S. K. Wertz (Eds.), *Sport inside out* (pp. 510-519). Fort Worth, TX: Texas Christian University Press.

Wigley, B. J., Sagas, M., & Ashley, F. B. (2002). A study of collegiate baseball: Examining sport fan motivation and marketing implications. *International Journal of Sport Management, 3,* 90-102.

SECTION VI.

Sponsorship

18

Sponsorship Evaluation:
Moving from Theory to Practice

David K. Stotlar

Introduction

According to the most recent data, projected spending on sponsorship in 2003 in the U.S. will total $10.52 billion, up 3.7% over 2002. Several companies were reported to have spent over $100 million, including Pepsi, Anheuser-Busch, General Motors, Coca-Cola, Miller Brewing, Nike, and Daimler-Chrysler. Sport retained its position as the leading category for sponsorship spending with 69% of expenditures, followed by entertainment (8%), festivals and fairs (8%), cause-related marketing (9%), and arts (6%). Sponsorship has been increasing around the globe as well. Estimated 2003 spending in Europe should top $7.4 billion, the Pacific Rim will account for $4.7 billion, and Central/South America will contribute $2.2 billion to the worldwide total of $26.2 billion (IEG, 2002). With this expanding outlay of capital, one would expect to see the existence of comprehensive and validated means for measuring the effectiveness of sponsorship activities. However, little empirical evidence has emerged in this area. The purpose of this article is to review the theoretical background, assess current practices, and propose a model encompassing sponsorship selection, activation, and evaluation.

Theoretical Background

In the ever-changing environment in which businesses operate, continuous modification of market strategy is essential. Berret and Slack (1999) have confirmed sport sponsorship as a viable component contributing to market strategies. Thus, an examination of sponsorship as a strategic marketing tool seems reasonable.

With the economic recession of late 2001 and 2002, corporations began to more aggressively assess the values and benefits gained through sport sponsorship. Stadium naming rights fees, an area that had seen tremendous growth during the previous 10 years, experienced a 16% decrease in value (Bernstein, 2001a). In addition, the downward movement in many corporate stocks through 2003, projected earnings shortfalls, and decreased company profitability caused some shareholders to question sport sponsorship as an appropriate expenditure of funds. Furthermore, the blackout experienced in many parts of the northeastern United States in August 2003 brought criticism of government officials who had committed taxpayer funding for sports arenas, yet had neglected utility infrastructure such as backup generators for the local water supply (Wiener, 2003). Similarly, in 2001 much of the western United States encountered serious energy shortages, yet energy companies (Edison International, Arizona Public Service, Enron, Portland General Electric, and X-Cell Energy, to name a few) were spending significant sums of money on sport sponsorship.

Much of this corporate reassessment has focused on the measurement of sponsorship effectiveness. Sponsorship activities principally rely on exchange theory (McCarville & Copeland, 1994): an appropriate transfer of value between parties through the sponsorship. In this regard, several questions are being asked. What objectives are being met through the sponsorship? Could these objectives be accomplished through other marketing actions? What is the relative measure of effectiveness of sport sponsorship?

Research in the field has suggested that a variety of corporate objectives are pursued through sport sponsorship including hospitality, trade relations, enhanced corporate image, increased marketshare, client acquisition, product awareness, and on-site sales (Copeland, Frisby, & McCarville, 1996; Irwin & Sutton, 1994; Kuzma, Shanklin, & McCally, 1993; Pope & Voges, 2000; Stotlar, 2001; Thwaites & Aguilar-Manjarrez, 1997).

Through the accomplishment of corporate objectives, sport sponsorship has proven to be effective in shaping competitive advantages in the market (Amis, Pant, & Slack, 1997). However, some corporations have failed to assess sponsorship's effectiveness in meeting these objectives. Appropriate measures have not been taken on the property side either. "It is still not a universal practice among events to provide sponsors with even the most basic post-event report" (IEG, 1999, p. 65). Those events that do supply data that attempts to address sponsorship effectiveness often pay little attention to the sponsor's objectives, but rather detail only attendance figures and media impressions.

The conceptual model that follows is based on the assumption that the most appropriate measure of effectiveness emanates not from what the sponsorship generated, but from whether the specific marketing objectives of the corporation were met. It is hoped that the use of this model will enable corporate sponsors to more accurately assess the effectiveness of sponsorship activities.

The movement from philanthropy to return on investment (ROI) has been well documented in the literature (Copeland, Frisby, & McCarville, 1996; Irwin & Sutton, 1994; Kuzma, Shanklin, & McCally, 1993; Pope & Voges, 2000; Stotlar, 2001; Thwaites & Aguilar-Manjarrez, 1997) and recently Sweet (2002) noted that "Many sport sponsors say they are taking a closer look at their return on investment, especially in light of the slow economy and a sport landscape that offers a wider variety of opportunities" (p. 27). In this environment, a Coke executive noted that "the return on investment continues to shrink" (Perez, 2003, p. 129).

Sponsorship Evaluation Model: Input

The work of Kuzma, Shanklin, and McCally (1993) laid a framework based on a construct for sport organizations engaged in packaging and selling sponsorship with an underlying premise focused on sponsor objectives. The same philosophy can be seen on the sponsor side as well. The manager of sports and events marketing at Federal Express said, "It becomes basic Marketing 101. You have to know your objectives and what you want at every stage and continually question if the property can give you what you want" (Altenburg, 2003, p. 7). Collectively these elements constitute the **Input** section of the model.

The most widely cited definitions for sponsorship (Ukman, 1995; Meenaghan, 1999) confirm that a primary purpose for the sponsor is to utilize the *exploitable commercial potential* of a sport property. Each sport property also has a unique set of exploitable sponsorship components to offer prospective sponsors. This brings to focus one of the basic theoretical changes in marketing with the last 25 years: the move from a product orientation ("sell what you make") to a market orientation ("make what will sell") (Stotlar, 2001). Clearly this orientation must function in the area of sponsorship as well.

Sponsorship Evaluation Model: Filter

Research with the top 50 sponsors in the US indicated that, too often, sport properties were trying to sell their inventory rather than looking to meet sponsor needs (Stotlar, 1999). Thus, the **Filter** section of the model consists of the inventory (*exploitable commercial potential*) that the sport property has to offer through which the sponsor objectives may be realized. Certainly, the sponsor can consider alternative marketing opportunities other than sport sponsorship. These are accounted for in the lower aspect of the Filter component.

Sponsorship Evaluation Model: Activated Components

The flow of objectives through the filter will yield the **Activated Components**, a sample of which is presented in the model. It should be noted that the actual components that are activated in any sponsorship would be ultimately determined by the corporate inputs and the property's filter of viable inventory. Given the unique nature of each sponsor, customized proposals and tailored sponsor benefits must be constructed.

Sponsorship Evaluation Model: Evaluation Protocol

Previous research by Irwin and Sutton (1994) presented and empirically tested criteria utilized by corporations to select appropriate sponsorship opportunities. However, they did not address evaluation. According to the principles set forth in exchange theory, in order to justify continued spending on sport sponsorships, corporations must ascertain if their benefits support their expenditures. An evaluation protocol for sponsors based on this scheme has yet to evolve. This vacuum invites the question "What is the appropriate protocol for measuring the effectiveness of sport sponsorship?" Key performance indicators must be established and an evaluation protocol developed for each performance indicator. Because of the variability of objectives and the complexity of measure, most corporations have not engaged in measuring sponsorship effectiveness. Some have accepted data and reports from sponsored properties that attempted to measure what the sponsorship accomplished, with little regard to the sponsor's objectives. For instance the International Olympic Committee (IOC) conducts research at the Games and provides these data to its corporate sponsors. During the 2002 Winter Olympic Games, the IOC found that "92% of Salt Lake 2002 spectators surveyed agreed that sponsorship support contributes greatly to the staging of a successful Olympic Games" (International

Olympic Committee, p. 57). Furthermore they reported that "95% of Salt Lake 2002 spectator survey respondents who had visited an Olympic sponsor's activity stated that this opportunity positively enhanced their Olympic experience" (p. 62). While these data may be impressive to some, the obvious skew to the questions almost guarantees a positive outcome regarding the IOC, but the findings often have little relevance to the sponsor. As a result, many corporations hire independent research firms or direct their own research.

As noted in the model, these could include recognition and recall measures, qualitative interviews, employee morale measures within the sponsor company, consumer-based focus groups, or sales data collected pre- and post-event.

There have been sporadic measures as illustrated by the following:

1. During the 2002 Olympics, Samsung's research team conducted recognition and recall measures in 10 different markets around the world (Jin, 2002).
2. Through qualitative interviews after the Olympics, VISA consumers were asked about their use of the VISA card. Sixty five percent of all consumers interviewed (18 and over with annual income of over $20,000) were aware of VISA sponsorship of the Olympics.
3. NASCAR has been famous for consumer-based focus groups. Data has been widely reported that indicate that consumers are positively influenced in their purchasing by a sponsor's participation in NASCAR sponsorship (Hagstrom, 1998). Similarly, Pitts (1998) found that the participants of the Gay Games were incredibly loyal to the sponsors.
4. Coca-Cola uses sales data as important measures related to corporate objectives (Perez, 2003). Research on sales during the 2002 Olympic Games found that first quarter sales increased in the US, Japan, Mexico, and Germany more than 5% (International Olympic Committee, 2002).

While these present just a few examples, it is clear that a systematic protocol must be developed from and tied to each activated component. While limited evaluation measures have been reported in the literature, they are all too often not utilized in practice. Therefore, specific and authentic measures related to each objective must be undertaken. Key performance indicators must be assessed through either quantitative or qualitative measures, forming the Residual Measure Data section of the model.

Sponsorship Evaluation Model: Feedback Loop

Finally, the Feedback Loop is provided to reassess the corporate objectives. Thus, corporations can stop asking, "What did the sponsorship do?" and begin answering the more important question "Did the sponsorship accomplish our objectives?"

Conclusion

Hopefully, this model can be utilized to bridge the gap between theory and practice in sport sponsorship. The intent was to present a comprehensive overview of how theory relates to and shapes current practice. Those who propose theory without a connection to practice are as misguided as practitioners who disregard relevant theory. As with sponsorship, theorists and practitioners form a symbiotic relationship where joint efforts are greater than the sum of the parts.

References

Altenburg, N. (2003, January). Negotiations part one: Executives outline approach to say no to a prospective sponsor. *Team Marketing Report, 15*, 4, 7.

Amis, J. Pant, N. & Slack, T. (1997). Achieving a sustainable competitive advantage: A resourced-based view of sport sponsorship. *Journal of Sport Management, 11*(1), 80-96.

Bernstein, A. (2001, August 13-19). The sky is no longer the limit in venue naming rights. *Sport Business Journal*, 1,10.

Berrett, T. & Slack, T. (1999). An analysis of the influence of the competitive and institutional pressures on corporate sponsorship decisions. *Journal of Sport Management, 13* (2), 114-138.

Copeland, R., Frisby, W., McCarville, R. (1996). Understanding the sport sponsorship from a corporate perspective. *Journal of Sport Management, 10*(1), 32-48.

Hagstrom, R. G. (1998). The NASCAR Way. New York: Wiley.

IEG (2002, December 23). 2003 spending to raise as sponsors ask for, receive more for their money. *IEG Sponsorship Report, 21*(24), 1,4-5.

International Olympic Committee (2002). Salt Lake 2002 Marketing Report. Lausanne: International Olympic Committee.

Irwin, R. L. and Sutton, W. A. (1994). Sport sponsorship objectives: An analysis of their relative importance for major corporate sponsors. *European Journal of Sport Management, 1*(2), 93-101.

Jin, W. (2002). Personal interview conducted February 10, 2002. Salt Lake City, UT.

Kuzma, J. R., Shanklin, W. L., McCally, J. F. (1993). Number one principle for sporting events seeking corporate sponsors: Meet benefactor's objectives. *Sport Marketing Quarterly, 2*(3), 27-32.

Ludwig, S. & Karabetsos, JD (1999). Objectives and evaluation processes utilized by sponsors of the 1996 Olympic Games. *Sport Marketing Quarterly, 8*(1), 11-18.

Meenaghan, T. (1999). Commercial sponsorship- the development of understanding. *International Journal of Sports marketing and Sponsorship, 1*(1), 19-31.

McCarville, R, & Copeland, B. (1994). Understanding sport sponsorship through exchange theory. *Journal of Sport Management, 8*(2), 102-114.

Perez, B. (2003). SMQ Profile/Interview: Beatrice Perez. *Sport Marketing Quarterly*, 12 (3), 129-130.

Pitts, B.G. (1998). An analysis of sponsorship recall during gay games IV. *Sport Marketing Quarterly, 7*(4), 11-17.

Pope, N.K. & Voges, K. E. (2000). The impact of sport sponsorship activities, corporate image, and prior use on consumer purchase intention. *Sport Marketing Quarterly, 9*(2), 96-101.

Stotlar, D. K. (1999). Sponsorship in North America: A survey of sport executives. *Journal of Sport Marketing and Sponsorship, 1*(1), 87-99.

Stotlar, D. K. (2001). *Developing successful sport sponsorship plans.* Morgantown WV: Fitness Information Technologies.

Sweet, J. (2002, April 29). ROI drawing closer attention from sponsors. *Sport Business Journal, 27.*

Thwaites, D. and Aguilar-Manjarrez, R. (1997). Sport sponsorship development among leading Canadian companies. Montpellier, France: Forth European Congress on Sport Management.

Turco, D. M. (1996). The effects of courtside advertising on product recognition and attitude change. *Sport Marketing Quarterly, 5*(4), 11-15.

Ukman, L. (1995). *IEG's Complete Guide to Sponsorship.* Chicago: International Events Group.

Wiener, E. (2003, Sept. 3). Metro Views: Cities prefer sports parks to power. *Philadelphia Metro*, D2.

19

A Comparative Analysis of Sponsorship Objectives for U.S. Women's Sport and Traditional Sport Sponsorship

Nancy L. Lough and Richard L. Irwin

Introduction

Increasingly, corporations are relying on the merits of sport sponsorship to market their companies' products and services (Howard & Crompton, 1995). In fact, North American companies increased sponsorship spending in 1998 by 15%, to $5.4 billion (Sponsorship Report, 1998). The emerging role of women in North American sport undoubtedly has been a significant catalyst for this growth trend in sport sponsorship. The number of female sport participants, as well as the number of female spectators, has escalated at a phenomenal pace, warranting attention from corporate America. Perhaps one of the most convincing issues influencing corporate sponsors to consider involvement with women's sport has been the increased recognition of women's strength in the U.S. marketplace and their expanded decision-making power (Lough, 1996). In 1993, Mechem estimated that by the year 2000, 61% of American women would be active in the work force. As increasing numbers of women have discretionary income to spend, and as the number of American women in decision-making roles has increased, corporate sponsors have become more and more interested in this previously neglected market segment. The competitive nature of today's marketplace makes the sponsorship of women's sport a viable avenue for tapping into this desirable market segment. With escalating rights fees and marketplace clutter, corporate rationale for sport sponsorship selection has been altered significantly. Irwin and Sutton (1994) found that results-oriented marketing motives appear to have replaced the philanthropic/image-building philosophy of the past. While such marketplace developments would appear to present opportunities for the funding of U.S. women's sport sponsorship proposals, no empirical evidence has been generated to support this. Two primary questions remain unanswered in the sport sponsorship environment: (a) will sponsorship of American women's sport resemble "traditional" sport sponsorship, with selection decisions based on specific criteria, and (b) will emergence within the contemporary sport sponsorship realm necessitate an objective-driven market orientation? The specific objectives for this study included:

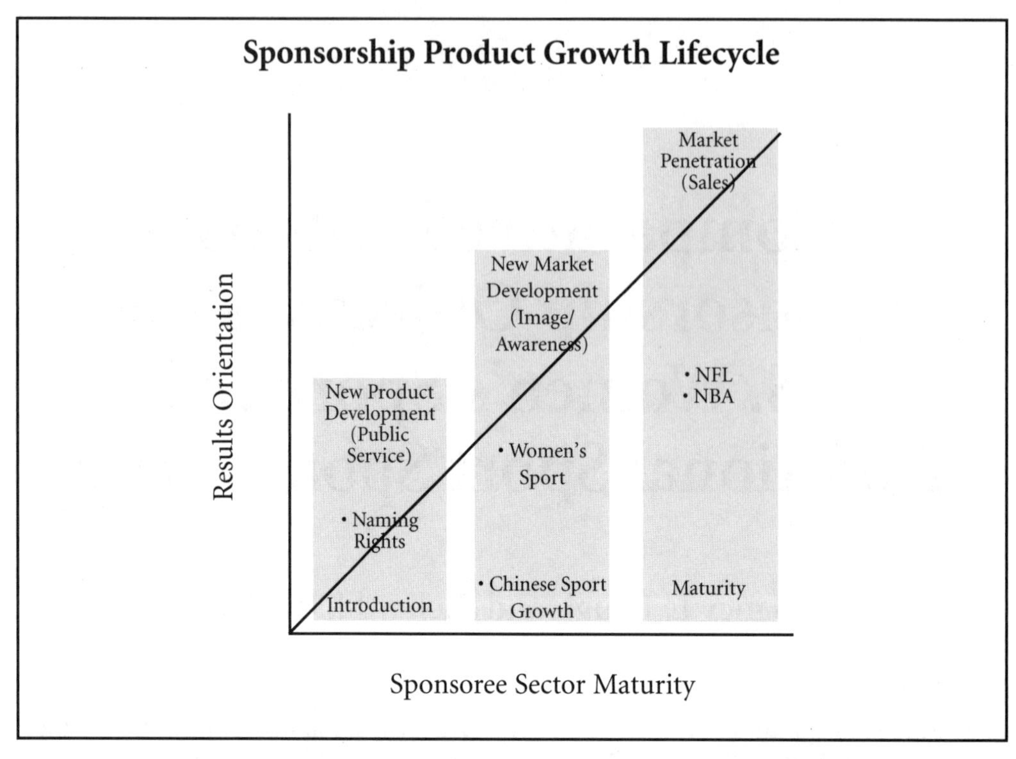

(a) determination of the dominant factors utilized (e.g., motives, objectives, proposal components) by current sponsors of U.S. women's sport in sponsorship selection decisions involving, first, sponsorship proposals from women's sport entities and, second, sponsorship proposals from mainstream sport entities; (b) assessment of the relative importance of each set of factors; and (c) comparative analysis of the two sets of factors. This study utilized survey research methodology incorporating a modification of the Sport Sponsorship Proposal Evaluation Model (Irwin, Assimakopoulos, & Sutton, 1994; Lough, 1996). The results indicate that sponsors of U.S. women's sport desire measurable outcomes, such as increased market share and sales. The comparative analysis found that limited differences exist between general sport sponsorship objectives and women's sport sponsorship objectives. These findings suggest that in order to appeal most to corporate sponsors, those seeking such sponsors for women's sport properties should concentrate on providing business-building opportunities.

Corporate spending on sport sponsorship has increased dramatically within the past decade, reaching almost $19 billion worldwide. Within this same period of time, corporate spending for American women's sport sponsorship has surged more than 100%, from approximately $285 million in 1992 to $600 million in 1998 (IEG Sponsorship Report, 1998). A number of factors appear to have triggered the sudden rise in corporate spending.

First, women's sport has realized remarkable growth. For instance, 55 million women regularly participate in sport in the United States. Further, reports indicate that 55% of all volleyball players, 43% of all runners, and 41% of all soccer players are women (U.S. Industry & Trade Outlook, 1999). At present, over 31 million girls play team sports, and 39% of high school girls play varsity sports. This marks a significant increase, as previous accounts reported that in 1970 one in 27 girls played varsity sports, as compared to one in three in 1996 (National Federation of State High School Associations, 1997). The number of women participating in intercollegiate sport also has continued to increase, with over 110,000 American women active in 1997 (Women's Sports & Fitness, 1998). It is anticipated that increased participation will lead to increased consumer interest. As such, female competitors are more likely to become consumers of women's sport. Further support for this notion was found in 1996, when 85% of U.S. women surveyed reported that they were sports fans. This figure was up from 79% as reported in 1994 (Lopiano, 1999). As *Forbes* magazine noted in 1997, "The market research is clear: women are the next great business opportunity" (p. 130).

In 1997, the IEG Sponsorship Report indicated that $600 million was spent on the sponsorship of women's sport in the United States. This was a significant gain for this newly recognized sport product category, compared to the $285 million spent on such sponsorship in 1992 (IEG Sponsorship Report, 1998). One explanation for a portion of the gain is the creation of new women's sport properties, such as the Women's National Basketball Association (WNBA) and the Women's Professional Softball League (WPSL). Additionally, as companies investing in sport through sponsorship are intent on seeing a return on their investments (Irwin & Morris, 1996), it would appear that such a dramatic increase in sponsorship spending is a direct result of the apparent value derived from association with the women's sport product.

The relationship between the sport product and the sport sponsor is multifaceted. For example, the lifespan of the sport product establishes a level of risk for potential sponsors. Whereas major U.S. professional sports, such as the National Football League (NFL), Major League Baseball (MLB), or the National Basketball Association (NBA), are considered to be mature, familiar commodities to both consumers and sponsors, the fledgling Women's National Basketball Association (WNBA) has a considerably less mature, more unfamiliar status. In more established professional women's sports, such as the Women's Tennis Association (WTA) and the Ladies Professional Golf Association (LPGA), the women's product still may be considered less mature simply because of the exposure, media coverage, and sponsorship spending that have been provided for its more established, male-sport counterparts, such as the Association of Tennis Professionals (ATP) and the Professional Golf Association (PGA). Increasing levels of sponsorship are vital to the growth of any sport property; this is especially true when considering newly recognized sport properties like women's sport properties.

A repeated pairing of the sponsor and the event should facilitate perceived association of the sponsor and event. Through the use of associative learning theory within the context of sport sponsorship, Till and Shimp (1998) found that, in fact, sponsors and the sponsored event do become linked over time. In American women's sport, one of the strongest associations that remained long after the sponsorship relationship ended was the association of Virginia Slims cigarettes with women's tennis, or the WTA. Without the Virginia Slim sponsorship, the WTA may not have been able to achieve the level of recognition and autonomy it was able to achieve as a separate women's sport organization.

The link between the WTA and Virginia Slims in the 1970s was an exemplary use of sport sponsorship. The newly established WTA put forth an image of "women doing it for themselves"—going against the mainstream culture, which wanted to control women's tennis. Virginia Slims was marketing its cigarette brand for women and found the association with the WTA to be powerful; however, the mixed message implicit in a tobacco-product company sponsoring a professional sport tour that considered its athletes to be role models for health and fitness created controversy with the WTA membership. Additionally, the court ruling in *U.S. Federal Trade Commission v. Pinkerton Tobacco Company* (1991) ended virtually all tobacco-related sport sponsorships (Stotlar, 1993).

Another important facet of the sport sponsorship relationship is the size of the potential market, meaning the likelihood that a significant consumer base exists that will associate the sponsor's message with the sport event or organization and, conversely, will associate the sport property with the sponsor's image or products. Sponsorship has been found to affect consumer attitudes through the sponsor's message, the type of products/brands, and the event or organization with whom the sponsor is associated (Cornwell & Maignan, 1998). Thus, for those seeking corporate sponsorship for a sport product, an initial step is to provide sufficient data relative to the size and strength of the consumer base or target market that will be reached through that sponsorship relationship.

The IMG/WTA relationship is a recent example of how the U.S. women's sport market is expanding and how related sponsorship spending is growing. When IMG (International Management Group) sought a new title sponsor for the WTA tour, the goal was to secure $8 million, the largest sponsorship ever in women's sports. With television ratings that have surpassed the comparable men's tour ratings, and with recognizable young stars such as Venus and Serena Williams appealing to a more diverse audience, the WTA was able to sign Sara Lee's Sanex to a 5-year deal (Kaplan, 1999). However, a key aspect of the deal that truly marks a new era in women's sport sponsorship is the contractual obligation Sanex has wherein it agrees to spend at least another $40 million on promotion and advertising to raise awareness of their sponsorship and the WTA tour. This unprecedented obligation will require efforts toward leveraging the sponsorship relationships that have been evident, even expected, in more general sport sponsorship deals, yet have been lacking thus far in women's sport sponsorship.

Spectator exposure to the sponsor's name and logo has been attributed to product awareness and, according to Turco (1994), "may lead to product consumption" (p. 34). Development of awareness, enhancement of image, increased exposure, brand recognition, product sales, and brand loyalty have been found to be primary sponsorship objectives for companies involved with sport (Irwin & Sutton, 1994). Thus, a developing sport product must provide evidence that associating with it will establish a competitive advantage that meets the established objectives of the sponsor(s).

Arguably, the days of philanthropic sponsorship have passed—even in the newly evolving world of women's sport. Today, the primary objective for sponsors involved in sport is a positive return on their investment (Irwin & Morris, 1996). With the increase in U.S. girls and women competing in sport and becoming spectators or fans, the question most sponsors still have is whether an investment in women's sport through sponsorship will in fact translate to the attainment of sponsorship objectives such as increased exposure, recognition, product sales, and brand loyalty.

Value of U.S. Women's Sport Market

Traditionally, sponsorship of sport was thought to be the best way to reach male consumers. With $7.6 billion estimated for sponsorship spending in 1999 (IEG Sponsorship Report, 1998), it seems evident that this tactic has been effective. Consequently, women were not considered as targets of sport sponsorship for the following reasons: (a) women were not considered to be knowledgeable about sport, (b) women were not considered to be serious sports fans, and, most importantly, (c) women were not thought to possess significant discretionary income. Estimates show, however, that female-worker income in the U.S. equals $1 trillion annually (*Forbes,* 1997). Just as women gradually have learned to be athletes and sports fans, they also have climbed the employment ladder to substantially more respectable levels. As a group, women have substantial purchasing power, controlling about 60% of U.S. wealth. Women also are responsible for more than 80% of all purchases (U.S. Industry & Trade Outlook, 1999). Therefore, they would appear to be of vast interest to marketers and sport sponsors.

Support for the notion that women have a substantial economic impact on the sport market also resides in the latest finding that in 33% of dual-income families, the woman earns the higher income (Sporting Goods Dealer, 1995). As evidence that women are spending discretionary income on sport-related purchases, consider that $6 billion was spent on women's athletic footwear in the U.S. in 1995. This figure overlapped comparable men's expenditures of $5.6 billion (Wallenchinsky, 1996). Additionally, women buy out of proportion to their levels of participation. For example, in the U.S., only 20% of all golfers are women, yet women buy 50% of all golf products, with the exception of golf clubs (Lopiano, 1999). With buying power increasing, more women in decision-making roles for the household, and more women experienced in sport on some level, the sport industry is beginning to recognize the economic impact from this segment.

Another aspect of women's sport that would appear to be attractive to sponsors is the fact that this market is also undersaturated, as opposed to the alternative options found in the top-tier U.S. sports (Lough, 1996). For sponsors, saturation translates into money spent on a lost message. Involvement with an undersaturated market could translate into an immediate impact by the sport sponsor on the chosen market, due to greater exposure, recognition, and product/image awareness. For women's sport, this is true due to less advertising "clutter" or "noise" surrounding the sport property. Television exposure is the vehicle most often preferred by corporate sponsors and sport marketers. Once again, the numbers representing U.S. women who watch sport are impressive, and the numbers representing those who watch women's sport are equally so. Women aged 18–34 years increased their viewership of the Olympic Games during the period between 1992 and 1996. The latest estimate indicates that 55–65% of Atlanta's 1996 Olympic audience was female. In 1999, the Women's World Cup was the most-watched soccer tournament or event in the history of network television, with an estimated 40 million U.S. viewers. The turnout of 90,185 at the Rose Bowl also was the largest ever for a women's sporting event (Wahl, 1999). Furthermore, women have been reported to comprise 45% of the NFL and MLB television audience, and the NBA estimates that at least 40% of its television audience is made up of women (Grossi, 1993; Mullin, Hardy, & Sutton, 2000). These figures have not been ignored by the top-tier sports; in fact, every major professional league has a marketing strategy targeting women. Front-runners in the U.S. sport marketing industry, such as NFL Properties, have even developed merchandise lines specifically for women.

The aforementioned figures seem to suggest that U.S. women's sport offers sponsors an opportunity to affiliate with new brands to reach the untapped audience of women's sport. Ironically, the majority of sponsorship dollars are spent in an attempt to appeal to men, who typically are not responsible for product purchases in the United States.

Product sales are carried out predominantly by female consumers. Thus, corporate sponsors who target seeking a return on their investments through product sales should focus their efforts toward gaining recognition and exposure among American women consumers. Utilizing affiliations with women's sport appears to be an effective approach toward reaching women consumers.

Increasingly, sponsors and sport marketers are looking to female athletes to appeal to consumers, especially female consumers. In general, female athletes are perceived as being appreciative, hardworking, and less of an image risk than are many of the high-profile male athletes. An athlete's poor behavior and the resulting negative publicity can damage the image of any company with whom that athlete is associated. Therefore, the opportunity for women athletes to establish positive images in the consciousness of American sport consumers exists more now than ever before.

Identifying Growth Patterns of Women's Sport Sponsorship

In 1995, the total number of women's sports sponsors as indicated by the *Sports Marketplace 1994* was 138. By 1997, after only 3 years, that number had increased by over 10%. With new women's sport properties such as the Women's United Soccer Association (WUSA), launched in April 2001, it is reasonable to speculate that the number of sponsors directly involved with women's sport will continue to increase as opportunities increase (Associated Press, 2000). Also, greater media exposure for women's sport properties has been warranted following the interest generated by the 1996 Olympic Games and the 1999 Women's World Cup (soccer). Combined, these factors suggest that the growth of women's sport sponsorship will continue; however, the number of sponsors for women's sport products has grown increasingly difficult to determine, as corporate sponsors have combined marketing efforts to include women's sport in their overall marketing mixes.

In 1996, Lough reported that 83% of companies responding indicated that the percentage of their budget allocated for advertising and promotions attributed to women's sport was 25% or less. Only 17% indicated that 50% or less of their budget was tagged for women's sport, and no companies reported commitments above 50%. In a similar study conducted in 1999, 39% of the companies reported spending less than 50% of their sponsorship budget on women's sport sponsorship, while 17% of the companies reported spending more than half of their sponsorship budget on women's sport (44% declined to respond based on company policy) (Lough & Irwin, 1999). The change in percentages during the period between the studies confirms an increased corporate commitment to women's sport.

Significant increases in tour prize money available for women's professional tennis and for the LPGA also point to growth in sponsorship spending. Typically, tournament or tour sponsors are responsible for prize money. In professional women's tennis, nearly $40 million was available in 1997 on the WTA tour—over twice the amount available only 10 years prior. In professional women's golf, tour prize money escalated to over $30 million by 1997, which was over double the amount available in 1987 (Women's Sports Foundation, 1999). Just as the 1984 Olympic Games have been recognized as the catalyst for sport sponsorship in general, it appears that the 1996 Olympic Games in Atlanta were the benchmark for women's sport sponsorship. Evidence of this can be found in the increasing amounts of prize money available in established women's sport properties, as well as in the greater number of sponsors reporting involvement with women's sport after the 1996 Olympic Games. New women's sport properties such as the WNBA, which started in 1997, evolved as a direct result of fan interest supported by the television ratings for the 1996 Olympic Games.

The purpose of this study was to determine (a) whether sponsorship of U.S. women's sport will resemble "traditional" sport sponsorship, with selection decisions based on specific criteria, and (b) whether existing within the contemporary sport sponsorship realm will necessitate an objective-driven market orientation. As stated previously, companies investing in sport through sponsorship are intent on seeing a return on their investments. By providing evidence that association with a U.S. women's sport product will establish a competitive advantage and will therefore meet the established objectives of the sponsor(s), it is expected that women's sport will exemplify a similar pattern to that recently established by the "traditional" sport properties sponsorship.

Methodology

A derivative of the questionnaire used by Irwin, Assimakopoulos, and Sutton (1994) was developed employing a 7-point Likert scale to ascertain the importance of each sport sponsorship objective identified in the literature. To be included in the sample, a corporation must have been identified as an active sponsor of (a) one or more sport properties whose contestants are/were comprised exclusively of female athletes (e.g., WNBA) and (b) one or more other sport properties whose contestants are/were not comprised exclusively of female athletes. Survey instruments were forwarded to 74 randomly selected individuals identified within *Sports Marketplace* (1997) as being the key sport sponsorship decision makers at the companies fitting the aforementioned sample profile. All data were reported using descriptive statistics. Furthermore, all sport sponsorship objectives under investigation were categorized according to the sponsorship-objective dimensions established by Lough, Irwin, and Short (2000). Each subsequent dimension was subjected to paired (general sponsorship v. women's sport sponsorship) sample *t* tests (Wilcoxon Signed-Ranks Test). According to Fink (1995), a paired design is most appropriate when attempting to detect the difference between means obtained from the sample group. Due to the exploratory nature of this research, the significance level was set at $p < .10$. Repeated mailings followed by personal contact yielded usable responses from 16 corporate sport sponsorship decision makers, for a response rate of 21%. The Cronbach alpha, used to assess the internal consistency of the instrument, was found to be .94, indicating a high degree of response uniformity among respondents.

Results

Table 1 presents the descriptive statistics for the relative importance of all sport sponsorship objectives under investigation. Responses were found to vary somewhat with respect to the sponsorship type. For instance, when reviewing proposals not specifically related to women's sport, corporate sport sponsorship decision makers appear to be most interested in opportunities that ultimately will yield sales and will influence brand market share. However, when entertaining proposals specifically associated with women's sport, this same group of marketing executives appears to be more concerned with capitalizing on the image associated with the sponsorship and with increasing the awareness of the sport property's target audience. In fact, 78% of the respondents

Table 1.
Importance of Corporate Sport Sponsorship Objective by Sport Sponsorship Type

Mean ratings (1 – 7) Objective	General	Women's
Increase sales/market share	5.94	5.72
Increase target market awareness	5.88	5.89
Enhance general company image	5.81	5.94
Increase public awareness of company	5.56	5.53
Demonstrate community involvement	4.75	4.88
Build trade relations	4.50	4.29
Build trade goodwill	4.31	4.24
Demonstrate social responsibility	4.19	4.57
Block/preempt the competition	4.19	4.00
Enhance employee relations	3.76	3.78
Demonstrate corporate philanthropy	3.13	3.71

assigned a high rating (6 or 7) to "increasing target market awareness" when applied to a sponsorship of women's sport. As an example, the Likert scale utilized ranged from 1 (extremely unimportant) to 7 (extremely important). On the other hand, "increasing sales/market share" was rated as extremely important by 71% of the respondents when applied to general sponsorship arrangements not specifically tailored to women's sport.

For data reduction and analytical purposes, the results were collapsed into the four dimensions of corporate sport sponsorship objectives established by Irwin and Sutton (1994), with existing differences analyzed by way of paired sample *t* tests. The results of this process, as well as the 2-tail level of significance for each, are revealed in Table 2. While the general ranking or position of each dimension was consistent across sponsorship type and was similar to Irwin and Sutton's earlier (1994) findings, the relative differences found between and within dimensions are noteworthy. For instance, further analysis revealed that the sponsorship objectives assigned to the dimension tabbed "public service" were of least importance to all respondents when considering either type of sport sponsorship under investigation. However, a statistically significant difference was found to exist with respect to this specific set of objectives when respondents were considering a general sport sponsorship as compared to a sponsorship involving female athletes. Hence, this set of items may be considered of more importance to marketing decision makers when contemplating sponsorship opportunities specifically targeting women's sport.

An intrasponsorship-type analysis (Table 2) revealed a statistically significant difference to exist for the importance of items classified as "position enhancement" and the dimensions of "trade networking" and "public service," whether respondents were considering a general or a women's sport sponsorship ($p < .10$). This finding highlights the importance marketers place on finding sponsorships that enable them to attain this set of result-oriented outcomes. Similarly, the ratings provided for items comprising the dimension of "public service" were found to differ significantly from the dimensions of "position

Table 2.
Importance of Corporate Sport Sponsorship Objective Dimensions by Sport Sponsorship Type

	Mean ratings		Standard deviation		
Dimension	**General**	**Women's**	**General**	**Women's**	***p* value**
Position enhancement	5.45	5.26	1.02	1.32	.40
Status enhancement	5.02	5.16	1.42	1.44	.89
Trade networking	4.40	4.13	2.15	2.08	.26
Public service	3.81	4.04	1.78	1.77	.08

Table 3.
Frequency Distribution of Ratings Assigned to Sport Sponsorship Objective Dimensions

	Extremely unimportant						Extremely important
Dimension	**1**	**2**	**3**	**4**	**5**	**6**	**7**
Position enhancement							
General	0.0	0.0	6.3	12.6	37.6	30.1	12.5
Women's	0.0	5.9	5.9	5.9	35.7	28.7	17.6
Status enhancement							
General	0.0	6.3	6.3	6.3	43.4	12.6	25.1
Women's	0.0	11.8	0.0	0.0	29.4	41.2	17.7
Trade networking							
General	18.8	6.3	0.0	18.8	18.8	18.8	18.8
Women's	17.6	5.9	0.0	35.3	11.8	5.9	23.5
Public service							
General	6.3	18.8	25.1	12.6	18.8	6.3	12.5
Women's	5.9	17.7	11.8	17.7	35.4	0.0	11.8

enhancement" and "status enhancement" for both sponsorship types under investigation ($p < .10$), thereby illustrating the limited emphasis directed toward the attempt to use sport sponsorship as a vehicle for fulfilling these potential marketing outputs.

Additionally, as revealed in Table 3, a majority (59%) of the averaged responses for items included in the "status enhancement" dimension were rated at a high level of importance (6 or 7) when respondents were asked to apply the motives under investigation to sponsorship programs specifically involving women's sport. No other dimension (i.e., classification of sponsorship objectives) under investigation received a similar proportion of high ratings. To put this into perspective, fewer than half of all respondents rated items contained within "position enhancement"—the overall most important set (dimension) of sponsorship objectives—as being extremely important for either general or women's sport sponsorship (see Table 3).

Discussion

The findings from this investigation mirror the results of investigations conducted within the past few years (Irwin & Sutton, 1994; Stotlar, 1999). This supports the notion that sponsorship, as a promotional vehicle, is viewed by the corporate community primarily as a means of strategically enhancing the company's market position. It would be somewhat redundant to elaborate on the need for sponsor seekers to engineer customized sponsorship packages that incorporate tactical elements (e.g., product sampling, corporate hospitality, point-of-purchase displays) that address objectives contributing to this prioritized outcome. More importantly, the results suggest that distinguishing demographic-type characteristics of the actual sponsorship product, such as sex and age, may in fact influence the prioritization of benefits as well as the outcomes sought by the sport property's corporate benefactors.

Sex-Based Differences. The data generated from this study shed light on the possibility that *sponsorship type* does influence the anticipated outcome(s) and in turn influences the strategic application of the sponsorship arrangement. For instance, while sponsorship objectives comprising the "public service" dimension were found to be of least importance to decision makers, these issues were of significantly greater importance to corporate decision makers with respect to consideration of women's sport sponsorship opportunities. However, of greatest importance may be the fact that sponsorship decision makers appear to be most interested in *enhancing the company image* through the women's sport sponsorship agreement. Such image enhancement can be achieved in a variety of ways. A sponsor endeavoring to distinguish itself on a local, regional, national, or multinational basis would likely seek a sport opportunity that would convey that image (e.g., high school sports, collegiate athletic programs, major professional sport leagues, and Olympics, respectively). In each case the sponsor is able to project a geographical image via the sport sponsorship's geographical magnitude. However, all sport teams, leagues, governing bodies, facilities, events, and even athletes project unique images of value to the corporate sponsor. It may in fact be argued that the image portrayed through the sponsorship of women's sport is one of social responsibility, thus linking these independent objectives and their respective dimensions together and thereby maximizing a sponsorship's appeal to the corporate community.

From a tactical perspective, it would appear that general sport sponsorships (involving male-only or combined-gender sports) more than likely would link sales promotion and corporate hospitality, whereas sponsors of women's sport would be more inclined to develop supplemental advertising conveying a specific message to be projected to a specific audience.

Age-Based Differences. The data generated in this investigation also may provide evidence that the age or maturity of the sponsorship arrangement influences the sponsor's anticipated marketing results. The findings associated with women's sport sponsorship (i.e., importance of image-related items) mirror those generated in early studies conducted in the field of sponsorship (Kuzma, Shanklin, & McCalley, 1993). It can be argued that this previous research was conducted at a period in time when, as a product available for consumption by corporate America, the relatively youthful field of sport sponsorship (1984 is typically acknowledged as the birth of American sport sponsorship as it is known today) was transitioning through a series of life stages or was maturing in a

Table 4.
Sponsorship Growth in North America Since 1985

Year	Number of corporate sponsors	Amount spent
1998	5,200	$6.80 billion
1997	5,000	$5.90 billion
1996	4,900	$5.40 billion
1995	4,800	$4.70 billion
1994	4,600	$4.25 billion
1993	4,500	$3.70 billion
1992	4,300	$3.20 billion
1991	4,200	$2.80 billion
1990	4,000	$2.50 billion
1989	3,850	$2.10 billion
1988	3,700	$1.75 billion
1987	3,400	$1.35 billion
1986	2,100	$1.00 billion
1985	1,600	$850 million

fashion similar to that of other products. The current research appears to indicate that as a sponsorship matures, the sponsor's motives become less image oriented and more results oriented.

A Proposed Sponsorship-Product Life Cycle. Using a typical product life cycle found in any marketing textbook (see Figure 1), the relative position of each "product" under investigation was plotted. According to Czinkota, Kotabe, and Mercer (1997), during the growth stage, as customers become aware of the product and its benefits, usage escalates—whereas during the maturity stage, sales may continue to grow, albeit more slowly. This textbook definition clearly distinguishes U.S. women's sport sponsorship from general sport sponsorship as sales (overall expenditures as well as corporate budgetary allocations) are still in a state of rapid growth. In fact, it would appear that the recent emergence of women's sport sponsorship accounts for a valuable proportion of the overall sponsorship "sales" increases realized over the past few years (see Table 4).

As revealed in Table 4, the expansive growth in sponsorship spending— approximately 20% per year—has slowed considerably within the past few years. Also, the market expansion experienced for traditional sport properties during the late 1980s and early 1990s has permeated the boundaries of the U.S., perhaps indicating a maturation of the general U.S. sport sponsorship product market. Subsequent research conducted during this "maturation" stage has revealed that results-driven objectives have emerged as being most important to corporate marketing decision makers. Moreover, within the sponsorship product category, a "new" line has been introduced specifically targeting women's sport. It is hypothesized that this has triggered a retrospective view of anticipated outcomes focusing on image and awareness building and on a public-service orientation. The sponsorship product's newness may play a role in influencing the inclinations of corporate decision makers to delay expectations of quantifiable outcomes until the product has had sufficient time to sustain market affiliation.

Sponsorship of an "immature" product also may result from the social networks described by Berrett and Slack (1999). In such a case the corporation's decision to sponsor often is guided by personal relations or interests rather than by business-building rationale. It can be hypothesized that the motives of decision makers willing to aid the launch of a new sponsorship product (e.g., women's sport) are likely to be both results driven and service/image driven. Further research is needed to examine the service/image dimension of women's sport sponsorship as it relates to "cause-related" marketing.

Summary

The results indicate that sponsors of U.S. women's sport desire measurable outcomes such as increased market share and sales, along with enhanced image and market awareness. Overall, the comparative analysis found only limited differences between general sport sponsorship objectives and women's sport sponsorship objectives. For example, corporations supporting female sports tend to pursue sponsorship opportunities in an effort to achieve enhanced image and awareness within a targeted market, whereas those sponsoring other events tend to place more importance on capturing sales and market share. However, the participating athlete's sex may not be the only demographic characteristic influencing the prospective sponsor's motives. The results from this analysis shed light on the influence of a sponsorship's age. It would appear that the more mature sport sponsorships, generally involving male or co-ed sporting events, yield higher quantifiable results orientation, whereas less mature sponsorship opportunities typically render a combination of quantifiable expectations and qualitative expectations. While industry-wide figures were used in the analysis to demonstrate this point, future research must focus on defining a mature sponsorship product. As with any product, specific sponsorship factors, such as chronological age and cost, must be assessed. As securing corporate sponsorship for sport grows increasingly competitive, acknowledging differences based on gender and age of sport properties may be one strategy for enhancing existing relationships or improving the acquisition of new partnerships. These findings suggest that those seeking sponsors for women's sport properties should concentrate on providing business-building and image-enhancing opportunities in order to appeal most to corporate sponsors.

References

Associated Press. (2000, April 11). Women's soccer league launched with eight cities. Retrieved from http://my.aol.com/ sports/story

Berrett, T., & Slack, T. (1999). An analysis of the influence of competitive and institutional pressures on corporate sponsorship decisions. *Journal of Sport Management, 13*(2), 114–138.

Cornwell, T. B., & Maignan, I. (1998). An international review of sponsorship research. *Journal of Advertising, 27,* 1–21.

Crimmins, J., & Horn, M. (1996). Sponsorship: From management ego trip to marketing success. *Journal of Advertising Research, 36,* 11–21.

Czinkota, M. R., Kotabe, M., & Mercer, D. (1997). *Marketing management: Text & cases.* Oxford: Blackwell Publishers.

Fink, A. (1997). *How to analyze survey data.* Thousand Oaks, CA: Sage Publications.

Forbes. (1997). Retrieved from http://www.forbes.com/ forbes/ 97/0602

Grossi, T. (1993, November 26). Courting women. *Cleveland Plain Dealer,* pp. 1F, 4F.

Howard, D., & Crompton, J. (1995). *Financing sport.* Morgantown, WV: Fitness Information Technology, Inc..

IEG (1998). 1998 sponsorship spending. *IEG Sponsorship Report, 16*(24), pp. 1, 4–5.

International Events Group. (1999). Sponsorship report: Sponsorship spending in North America. p. 7.

Irwin, R. L., Assimakoupolis, M. K., & Sutton, W. A. (1994). A model for screening sport sponsorship proposals. *Journal of Promotions Management, 2*(3/4), 53–69.

Irwin, R. L., & Morris, D. (1996). The data-driven approach to sponsorship acquisition. *Sport Marketing Quarterly, 5,* 7–10.

Irwin, R. L., & Sutton, W. (1994). Sport sponsorship objectives: An analysis of their relative importance for major corporate sponsors. *European Journal for Sport Management, 1*(2), 93–101.

Kaplan, D. (1999, November 22–28). Persistence pays for WTA Tour. *Street & Smith's SportsBusiness Journal*, p. 8.

Kuzma, J., Shanklin, W., & McCally, J. (1993). Number one principle for sporting events seeking corporate sponsors: Meet benefactor's objectives. *Sport Marketing Quarterly, 2*(3), 27–32.

Lee, J. (1997, June). Fair game: Title IX 25th Anniversary. Women's Sports & Fitness, 37–40.

Lipsey, R. A. (Ed.). (1994, July). *Sports marketplace 1994* (pp. 381–418). Princeton, NJ: Sportsguide, Inc.

Lopiano, D. (1999). *The future of women's sports.* Paper presented at the American Alliance for Health, Physical Education, Recreation & Dance, Boston, MA.

Lough, N. L. (1996). Factors affecting corporate sponsorship of women's sport. *Sport Marketing Quarterly, 5*(2), 11–29.

Lough, N. L., & Irwin, R. L. (1999, June 1). *Objectives sought in sport sponsorship: Women v. general.* Paper presented at the North American Society for Sport Management, Vancouver, BC.

Lough, N. L., Irwin, R. L., & Short, G. (2000). North American sport sponsorship. *International Journal of Sport Management, 1*(4), 283–295.

Mullin, B., Hardy, S., & Sutton, W. (2000). *Sport marketing.* Champaign, IL: Human Kinetics.

Myers, K. J. (Ed.). (1997, Fall). *Sports marketplace* (pp. 498–592). Phoenix, AZ: Franklin Quest Sports Division.

National Federation of State High School Associations. (1997). Public relations survey. Retrieved from http://www.nfhs.org/PR-survey.htm

Peters, T. (1997, June 2). Opportunity knocks. *Forbes,* 130, 132.

Sporting Goods Dealer. (1995). Retrieved from http://www.sportlink.com/press_room/1999_releases/sica99-003.html

Stotlar, D. K. (1993). *Successful sport marketing.* Dubuque, IA: Wm. C. Brown.

Stotlar, D. K. (1999). Sponsorship in North America: A survey of sport executives. *International Journal of Sport Marketing & Sponsorship, 1*(1), 87–100.

Till, B. D., & Shimp, T. A. (1998). Endorsers in advertising: The case of negative celebrity information. *Journal of Advertising, 27,* 67–82.

Turco, D. M. (1994). Event sponsorship: Effects on consumer brand loyalty and consumption. *Sport Marketing Quarterly, 3,* 35–37.

U.S. Industry & Trade Outlook (1999). Leisure products industry survey. U.S. Department of Commerce/International Trade Administration and the McGraw-Hill Companies, Inc. NY, NY.

Wahl, G. (1999). Out of this world. *Sports Illustrated, 91*(3), 38–43.

Wallenchinsky, D. (1996, June 23). Vaults, leaps and dashes. *New York Times on the Web.* Retrieved from http://www.nytimes. qpass.com/qpass-archives.

Zavian, E. (1999, July 12–18). Tournament that once went unnoticed now has cities begging to host. *Street & Smith's SportsBusiness Journal,* p. 18.

20

Sport Sponsorship in China: Transition and Evolution

Lizhong Geng, Rick Burton, and Connie Blakemore Cook

Introduction

On July 13, 2001, International Olympic Committee (IOC) officials from Beijing, China, received word their city would host the 2008 Summer Olympic Games. In addition, in October, China qualified for its first-ever World Cup finals (2002), setting off celebrations throughout the country (Johnson, 2001). Since sport sponsorship is a basic element of sport marketing, sponsorship will be instrumental in China's immediate future as it relates to creating and maintaining athletic events, tournaments, teams, and sports leagues (Andrus, 1996; Boone & Kurtz, 1999; Lizhong, 1996; Mullin, Hardy, & Sutton, 1993). In 2001, IEG projected that North American corporations would spend a combined $6.51 billion on sport sponsorships, with more than 65 companies spending at least $15 million to finance their alignments. The overall North American sponsorship total of $9.5 billion represented a 9.6% increase over the $8.7 billion spent in 2000. In 2001, worldwide spending on sponsorship programs climbed to $24 billion, with Europe spending $7.4 billion and Pacific-Rim countries coming in third with $4.3 billion (IEG Reports, 2001). Given the strength of the Chinese economy, which has been reported as featuring the "fastest economic growth in the world" during the 1980s and 1990s (Wiseman, 2001) and has seen a gross domestic product (real GDP) growth rate of more than 7% every year for the last 6 years (U.S.-China Business Council, 2001), it is not surprising that sponsorship in the Pacific Rim was projected to grow by 12% in 2001 (IEG Reports, 2001). Of the sponsorship amounts noted for North America, sport sponsorship was expected to represent 69% of the total, or $6.51 billion—an increase of 10% over 2000. This may explain why Echikson, Webb, and Fonte (2001) suggested that corporate sponsorship of the Beijing 2008 Olympics is a "no-brainer" (p. 48). A review of the literature suggests that sport sponsorship can (a) offer multidimensional exposure for products; (b) associate a company or a brand name with a specific event; and (c) provide companies with high-visibility activities, particularly those of a national or an international scope, that reward important suppliers and customers (Agnew, 1982; Saxton,

1993; Schlossberg, 1996; Swanson & Spears, 1995; Wilson, 1988). However, sponsorship also carries with it elements of negotiation, delivery of services or products, and written or verbal guarantees. Burton (2001) has suggested that Western-style sponsorship can be defined as "creating mutual exploitation," in that both parties hope to optimize their positions in a created relationship. While Western capitalism in China might seek to focus on profits, the "remnants of the old Marxist system" (Wiseman, 2001, 2B) suggest, perhaps, that sponsorship in China must generate social gain.

Since the 1980 Marlboro Tennis Tournament, the first sponsorship event introduced in China, corporate spending on sport sponsorship programs has increased dramatically (Wu, 1999). The price for a league-title sponsor has risen to more than US$3 million per year. The sponsorship cost for a soccer club runs as high as $1.5 million. Corporate rights surpassed $1 million to produce ceremony uniforms for the Chinese delegation to wear at the 1996 Olympic Games in Atlanta. In 1998, the Chinese government's sport organization budget was $450 million. Additionally, the government raised approximately $200 million from sport sponsorships, or about one half of the government budget allocation (Li, 1999). In exchange for those funds, Chinese sport organizations provided sponsors with promotional and product-sales opportunities for building brand awareness and brand equity, as well as for generating goodwill in communities.

Sport sponsorship programs in China should develop rapidly once sport organizations and commercial businesses more fully recognize the positive features of sponsorship. Today, however, existing sponsors are either terminating their agreements with sport organizations or withdrawing at least some of their financial commitments. In fact, Chinese sport organizations currently are having difficulty finding new sponsors.

A review of the Chinese-language literature (some of which was not used for citation purposes), along with the authors' personal experiences as professional practitioners in China, revealed the possibility of a decline in sponsorship agreements and suggested several possible causes. The most significant reasons suggested included overcommercialization, endorsement scandals, cost-ineffectiveness, misuse of sports, inappropriate communications, lack of public support, lack of state-run media support, marketing clutter, unpredictability, and successful ambush marketing. Furthermore, it is likely these problems were heightened by the major mindset differences evident between country-loyal, sport organization personnel (observing the principles of China's socialism) and Western-style businesses (focusing on profitability). Because Chinese sport previously featured a government-budget orientation (i.e., all elite sport was government funded), it will take time to transform the driving force into a more cooperative model integrating sport into marketing. Assuming Chinese sport will benefit from transitioning to a cooperative sport-marketing model (i.e., one in which the government and the private sector collaborate and find mutual benefit) there is a need to determine successful sponsorship strategies for a workable relationship between sport organizations and corporations in China's relatively complex marketing climate; and while a few Chinese scholars have explored the subject of sport sponsorship in general, a review of the Chinese and Anglo literature suggests that this specific research theme has not been fully examined. The purpose of this study, therefore, was to conduct a gap analysis between sport organizations and commercial corporations for sport sponsorship applications in order to develop successful sponsorship strategies—strategies that will serve the development of sport marketing in China.

Methods

The methods used in this study consisted of three types of marketing research: exploratory, secondary, and primary (Andrus, 2000). The *exploratory* research involved consulting with experienced specialists in sport marketing, both from the United States and from China, to define research problems and possible courses of action. From these consultations, the basic research element in this study was identified as being sponsorship. The *secondary* research involved a thorough review of historical and current documents in the areas of sport marketing, relationship marketing, and the development of Chinese sport. This review contributed to the final decision to design a survey. The *primary* research involved the design of a questionnaire, which was administered to sport officials in China as well as to business executives connected with China's sport marketing enterprises.

The designed questionnaire was pilot tested for language and format purposes within the Chinese community in central Utah, using 40 university graduates working in various business corporations in the area. The pilot study made it possible to finalize the survey questionnaire. Respondents were asked to read and answer a survey document. Sentences were condensed for ease of understanding and were adapted to fit Chinese cultural norms (i.e., traditional patterns of thought). Further, a coefficient alpha test was run to ensure internal-consistency reliability of response. The alpha scores were between 0.77 and 0.63.

The formal questionnaire was developed with three types of questions. The first set of questions addressed sponsorship attitudes, intentions, and perspectives regarding marketing functions, influence factors, favorite events, and misused sports values. The second set addressed sponsorship purposes, interests, opportunities, operational processes, and responsibilities regarding budget, control rights, marketing research, and media connections. The third group of questions requested demographic data regarding age, work experience, gender, and occupation. With the first two groups of inquiries, the same basic question was asked from multiple perspectives in order to promote response validity and reliability.

The pilot-study data helped finalize the survey questionnaire. The data collection was conducted in the People's Republic of China (PRC). Drawing from a representative sample of all major Chinese sport organizations and a large number of commercial corporations known to have purchased sport sponsorships, 180 subjects were surveyed from four groups: two groups in sport organization, and two groups in commercial business. Business group 1 consisted of 50 Chinese executives representing domestic firms. Business group 2 consisted of 40 executives representing international firms. Sport group 1 consisted of 50 Chinese officials involved with local-level and provincial sport organizations. Sport group 2 consisted of 40 Chinese officials involved with national sport organizations. These respondents represented most of the important business and government officials dealing with sport endeavors in China.

Two classes from the Beijing University of Physical Education, of approximately 45 students each, were trained separately to distribute questionnaires and to collect data. Trainees were instructed to deliver the questionnaire in person to officials and executives in sport organizations and corporations and to wait outside the room until the questionnaire was completed. Trainees also were instructed to retrieve the questionnaire in a sealed, coded envelope that prevented them from reading the responses (thus ensuring respondent anonymity). Once the questionnaire was collected, the trainees returned it to their class instructors. Collected data were checked and students were quizzed to ensure that standard-distribution procedures were enforced with respect to data collection. Subsequently, the data were tested for differences across the four described respondent groups. The data were further analyzed through analysis of variance (ANOVA), contrast analysis using post hoc multiple-group comparison, and categorical-data analysis using Chi-square tests (George & William, 1989).

Results

With a total sample size of 180, the average age of respondents was 39.9 years. Respondents had an average of 19.5 years of working experience. A greater percentage of males (79.2%) than females (20.8%) was surveyed. This significant percentage difference between males and females is consistent with the percentage of males and females working in administrative positions, as well as with what typically is seen in gender distribution of sport officials and business executives in China. Approximately 51.8% of the interviews were with sport officials and business executives working in senior positions (the rough equivalent of Western vice presidents or senior directors). The remaining 48.2% of the respondents were directors and executive managers.

Attitudes Toward Sport Sponsorship

Respondents' general attitudes toward sport sponsorship are reviewed in Table 1. Sport organization executives view sport sponsorship more favorably than do the corporations themselves. The attitudes of the sport organization executives toward future involvement in sport sponsorship were seen as being more positive than those of the corporate exec-

Table 1.
Attitudes Toward Sport Sponsorship (Means in Groups)

Internal coefficient alpha = 0.6749						
Variable (Likert Scale of 1 to 5)	*Business groups* 1	2	*Sport groups* 1	2	*F-value*	*p-value*
How do you view sport sponsorship? (1 = strongly in favor)	2.0	2.0	1.4	1.4	16.52	0.000b
What has been your experience with sport sponsorship? (1 = very happy)	2.5	2.3	2.5	2.6	1.146	0.332
Will you become more involved with sport sponsorship? (1 = strongly in favor)	2.6	2.5	1.9	1.9	10.60	0.000b

Note. Business group 1 is domestic corporations; group 2 is international corporations. Sport group 1 is local-level sport committees; group 2 is national sport associations.
b indicates group differences between sport groups and corporations.

utives. The relatively optimistic approach (of sport executives) might reflect the unbalanced situation of supply and demand with regard to sport sponsorship in China. Due to the relatively recent appearance of commercial marketing clutter (in cities such as Shanghai, Beijing, and Guangzhou), sport properties have appeared anxious to provide sponsorship opportunities to leverage high demand for sport sponsorship opportunities.

As China becomes more commercialized (or open to the operating practices of the West), there has been a "gold-rush" effect with sponsors (McDonald's, Coke, Nike, Fuji Film, etc.) coming into the market and properties wanting to immediately offer alignment opportunities (thus anxious). In some cases, sport property organizations are flooding the market with sponsor proposals. In the U.S., sponsors go to the properties (in most cases). In China, in the big cities where there is advertising/commercial clutter, the properties are finding they have to go to sponsor (so that they are seen as a viable option)

Purpose and Marketing Opportunities of Sport Sponsorship

The results in Table 2 indicate the purpose and the marketing opportunities (i.e., sales and advertising) of sport sponsorship as viewed by respondents representing sport organizations and corporations. The categorical data indicate that a significant percentage of the respondents (53% and 45%) in the sport organizations were more likely to expect sponsorship for philanthropic purposes. As shown in Table 2, more than half of the respondents (60% and 50%) from corporations were more likely to view sponsorship as having a marketing-promotion purpose. Both of these purposes are valid; however, such differences in mindset can result in conflict when two parties are attempting to work together. Chi-square analysis indicated that this philosophical difference between groups was almost significant, with a p value of .06.

Table 2.
Purpose and Marketing Opportunities of Sport Sponsorship (Percentage in Groups)

Variable	*Business groups*		*Sport groups*		*Chi-square*	*p-value*
	1	2	1	2		
What Is the Purpose of Sport Sponsorship?					3.532	0.060
Philanthropic purpose only	2	8	4	10		
More philanthropic purpose	30	29	53	45		
More marketing purpose	60	50	37	43		
Marketing purpose only	8	13	6	3		
What Is the Marketing Opportunity of Sport Sponsorship?					0.071	0.789
Advertising opportunity only	24	38	20	38		
More advertising opportunity	56	35	55	48		
More sales opportunity	14	24	20	13		
Sales opportunity only	6	3	4	3		

Note. Business group 1 is domestic corporations; group 2 is international corporations. Sport group 1 is local-level sport committees; group 2 is national sport associations.

Table 3.
Marketing Roles of Sport Sponsorship (Means in Groups)

Internal coefficient alpha = 0.7679

Variable	*Business groups* 1	2	*Sport groups* 1	2	*F-value*	*p-value*
(Likert Scale of 1 to 5. 1 = strongly agree)						
Improve relations w/consumers	2.3	2.2	2.0	2.1	1.993	0.117
Earn goodwill in community	2.1	2.2	2.0	2.2	0.373	0.772
Help test product	2.6	2.3	2.2	2.4	3.229	0.024[b]
Advantage over competitor	3.0	2.5	2.6	2.7	3.247	0.023[a]
Develop company image	2.3	2.2	1.7	1.8	10.145	0.000[b]
Create sales opportunity	2.5	2.3	2.1	2.2	4. 580	0.004[b]
Generate free publicity	2.6	2.4	2.1	2.5	2.827	0.040[b]
Support CEO charity	2.8	2.9	2.4	2.5	2.696	0.048[b]
Build partnership w/customers	2.7	2.5	2.2	2.4	3.914	0.010[b]

Note. Business group 1 is domestic corporations; group 2 is international corporations. Sport group 1 is local-level sport committees; group 2 is national sport associations.
[a] indicates differences within either sport or corporate groups.
[b] indicates group differences between sport groups and corporations.

Table 4.
Factors Influencing Sport Sponsorship Decisions (Means in Groups)

Internal coefficient alpha = 0.6307

Variable	*Business groups* 1	2	*Sport groups* 1	2	*F-value*	*p-value*
(Likert Scale of 1 to 5. 1 = strongly influence)						
Popularity/image of sports	1.9	2.1	1.5	1.5	6.710	0.000[b]
Cost of sponsoring	2.3	2.2	2.4	2.4	0.308	0.820
Coverage of sporting event	2.2	2.2	1.9	2.0	1.912	0.129
Promotional methods	2.3	2.2	2.2	2.0	1.064	0.366
Strength of relationship	2.3	2.6	1.9	2.1	8.125	0.000[ab]
Formal partnerships	2.1	2.7	1.9	2.1	8.713	0.000[ab]
Benefit of sponsoring	2.1	2.3	2.0	2.3	1.549	0.204

Note. Business group 1 is domestic corporations; group 2 is international corporations. Sport group 1 is local-level sport committees; group 2 is national sport associations.
[a] indicates differences within either sport or corporate groups.
[b] indicates group differences between sport groups and corporations.

Marketing Roles of Sport Sponsorship

Perceptions regarding the marketing role of sport sponsorship (i.e., developing company image, creating sales opportunities, and/or building partnerships with customers) are described in Table 3. Local and provincial sport organizations are particularly positive about the marketing benefits of sport sponsorship. Sport organizations view such sponsorship as a charitable, philanthropic effort on the part of cooperating CEOs. Sport organization executives feel that sponsorship is particularly useful in testing products, providing an advantage over competitors, developing company image, creating sales opportunities, generating free publicity, supporting CEO charity, and building customer relationships. Corporate respondents appear to agree with these marketing roles of sport sponsorship; however, they are hesitant to focus themselves on just one of the marketing functions.

Factors Influencing Sport Sponsorship Decisions

Table 4 enumerates several attitudes regarding the factors that influence sport sponsorship decisions. Factors of significance between sport groups and business groups include the popularity and image of sports, the strength of the relationships between the two groups, and the formal partnership negotiations. Sport organizations are especially positive regarding the image of sports. It seems they are proud of their *Olympic achievements* and believe that their Olympic efforts can have a strong impact on sport sponsorship decisions. Although they are less positive than sport groups (1.9 and 2.1 in business groups; more than 1.5 in sports groups), business corporations are still positive about the image of sports. However, their emphasis is different. With their focus on the *popularity/influence of the sporting event,* corporations are more likely to consider using sport sponsorship as a means of receiving economic benefits. Domestic corporations are more likely than are international corporations to consider the strength factor of the relationships between sport and business. International corporations are more likely than are

Table 5.
Approach Strategies for Sport Sponsorship (Means in Groups)

Internal coefficient alpha = 0.6376

Variable (Likert Scale of 1 to 5. 1 = strongly agree)	*Business groups* 1	2	*Sport groups* 1	2	*F-value*	*p-value*
Design customized event	2.3	2.4	2.3	2.3	0.291	0.832
Set mutual benefit goal/s	2.0	2.2	1.7	1.7	6.280	0.000[b]
Generate public interest	2.1	2.0	1.8	2.0	2.117	0.100
Provide financial information	1.9	1.9	1.8	2.1	2.956	0.034[ab]
Present investing opportunity	1.9	2.1	2.1	2.2	1.929	0.127
Ensure pleasant relationships	2.1	1.9	1.7	1.9	2.788	0.042[ab]

Note. Business group 1 is domestic corporations; group 2 is international corporations. Sport group 1 is local-level sport committees; group 2 is national sport associations.

[a] indicates differences within either sport or corporate groups.

[b] indicates group differences between sport groups and corporations.

Table 6.
Favorite Events for Sport Sponsorship (Percentage in Groups)

Event	Rating	*Business groups* 1	*Business groups* 2	*Sport groups* 1	*Sport groups* 2	*Chi-square*	*p-value*
Soccer	Most favorite	79	41	81	92	31.85	0.000
	Somewhat	15	41	17	8		
	Not favorite	6	19	2	0		
Basketball	Most favorite	67	46	80	74	19.24	0.004
	Somewhat	29	35	16	26		
	Not favorite	4	19	4	0		
Table Tennis	Most favorite	57	41	63	60	12.65	0.049
	Somewhat	41	40	31	38		
	Not favorite	2	19	6	3		

Note. Business group 1 is domestic corporations; group 2 is international corporations. Sport group 1 is local-level sport committees; group 2 is national sport associations.

domestic corporations to have an aversion to formal partnership arrangements, because they desire the flexibility to make changes in marketing strategies.

Approach Strategies for Sport Sponsorship

Table 5 presents approach strategies for sport sponsorships between sport organizations and business corporations. As such, the survey asked whether designing customized events; setting mutual, beneficial goals; generating public interest; providing financial information; presenting investment opportunities; and ensuring hospitality relationships were appropriate approach strategies for sport sponsorships. Three significant findings emerged: (a) Sport organizations believe more than do business corporations in setting mutual goals beneficial to both parties (1.7 in sport groups; 2.0 and 2.2 in business groups); (b) sport organizations are more concerned than are business corporations about ensuring sponsors' satisfaction with an event, a factor that results in long-term, positive relations with sponsors (1.7 and 1.9 in sport groups; 2.1 and 1.9 in business groups); and (c) corporate groups are particularly interested in developing feasible financial plans that meet financial goals and are of economic benefit (1.9 in business groups; 1.8 and 2.1 in sport groups). Thus, the message from business groups to sport organizations is clear: Business interest is a top priority in sport sponsorship approaches. While this stance is similar to sponsorship expectations in other countries, the authors believe this is the first time the claim has been validated in China.

Favorite Events for Sport Sponsorship

Table 6 verifies the favorite events for sport sponsorship in China. Of the 17 events listed, soccer, basketball, and table tennis emerged as the most favorable for sponsorship. Climbing, water events, and skiing were the least favored. Soccer was the event most favored by domestic corporations and national sport associations. Not surprisingly, local and provincial sport organizations indicated almost identical levels of support for soccer and basketball (mirroring the near-global support for both sports). International corpo-

Table 7.
Responsibilities of Sport Sponsorship (Percentage in Groups)

Responsibility	*Business groups*		*Sport groups*		*Chi-square*	*p-value*
	1	2	1	2		
Who Should Provide Major Funding for the Event?					7.318	0.007
Sports only provide	16	29	2	0		
Sports provide more	28	30	19	13		
Corporation provide more	44	38	63	55		
Corporation only provide	12	14	17	32		
Who Should Have Control Over the Event?				3.117	0.077	
Sports control only	12	11	15	25		
Sports more control	66	58	71	67		
Corporation more control	16	19	13	8		
Corporation control only	6	11	2	0		
Who Should Pay Expenses for Marketing Research?					2.613	0.106
Sports pay only	8	14	33	23		
Sports pay more	40	40	39	40		
Corporation pay more	32	29	20	30		
Corporation pay only	20	17	8	8		
Who Should Coordinate Media Coverage?				0.105	0.746	
Sports only coordinate	6	11	6	5		
Sports more coordinate	26	22	31	23		
Corporation more coordinate	20	19	14	15		
Corporation only coordinate	48	47	49	58		

Note. Business group 1 is domestic corporations; group 2 is international corporations. Sport group 1 is local-level sport committees; group 2 is national sport associations.

rations preferred basketball, followed closely by soccer. Table tennis was the third most-preferred sport by all groups. Other events preferred for sport sponsorship, although not significantly, were volleyball, tennis, swimming, and badminton.

Responsibilities as Viewed by Both Groups

Table 7 illustrates similarities and differences between sport organizations and corporations regarding the sponsorship responsibilities of funding, control, marketing research, and media connections (i.e., public relations). Sport organizations believe that corporations should provide major funding for events. Some domestic corporations agree; however, international corporations believe that sport organizations should provide more capital for actual event implementation. Regarding the second responsibility, all groups agree that sport organizations should have more control over sporting events than should corporations. While it is not statistically significant between groups, 40% of the respondents in the four groups concur that sport organizations should take responsibility for marketing research. Regarding media interaction, most groups lean heavily

Table 8.
Future Plans for Sport Sponsorship Programs (Percentage in Groups)

Variable	*Business groups* 1	2	*Sport groups* 1	2
Do You Plan to Have One or More Sponsorships in the Future?				
Yes	33	32	77	82
No	67	68	23	18
About How Much Money Has Been Budgeted to Donate/Raise?				
<$100,000	27	28	16	8
$100,001–$200,000	14	6	14	13
$200,001–$400,000	19	28	18	10
$400,001–$600,000	34	28	39	68
>$600,000	5	9	12	3

Note. Business group 1 is domestic corporations; group 2 is international corporations. Sport group 1 is local-level sport committees; group 2 is national sport associations.

toward making corporations responsible for the media connections. There is no consensus concerning who should coordinate media coverage.

Future Plans for Sport Sponsorship Programs

Results in Table 8 indicate the future plans of both sport organizations and corporations regarding sport sponsorship programs. Of the sport organization respondents, approximately 80% expressed their willingness to be involved in sport sponsorship in the future. Of those same respondents, 54% expected at least $400,000 to $600,000 in financial contributions from corporations. In contrast, approximately 68% of the corporate respondents indicated a reluctance to be involved in sport sponsorship in the future. This suggests a possible problem for sport sponsorship in China (i.e., a difficult seller's market), if fewer than one third of the corporations (32%) intend to fund future sponsorship opportunities. The information in Table 8 shows that the sport organizations' demand for sport sponsorship is much higher than the corporations' supply desires. The outcome remains a matter of which parties will be fortunate (and skilled) enough to obtain possible sponsorships and how they will secure them.

Highlights of the Research

1. Both sport organizations and corporations view sport sponsorship as a positive medium for achieving marketing/promotion objectives. Sport organizations are more willing than are commercial corporations to establish personal relationships (i.e., with corporate executives), and they are more likely to build long-term partnerships (i.e., with corporations). With the belief that sport sponsorship benefits both sport and commercial parties, a question remains as to how to formulate successful sport sponsorship strategies that will bring the positive emotions and enthusiasm of sport groups into the partnership.
2. The relatively negative attitude of corporations (based on charitable expectations and cost-ineffective experiences) offers two messages to sport organiza-

Sport-Centered Perspective	*Marketing-Centered Perspective*
With country in mind	With individual in mind
Group development	Individual development
Mission is glory	Mission is service
Core value is competition	Core value is cooperation
Vision focus is a success outcome	Vision focus is a win-win outcome
Platform from physical education	Platform from sports and fitness
Priority in organizational structure	Priority in strategic planning
Organizational satisfaction	Consumer satisfaction
Commitment equates to heritage	Commitment equates to quality of life
Expectation of fund raising	Expectation of marketing shares
Sponsorship approach	Partnership approach
Objective orientation	Process orientation
Concept analysis	Statistical analysis
Investment concern	Profit concern
Focus on economic comfort	Focus on cost-effectiveness
Motivation linked to reputation	Motivation linked to product sales
Avoid risk taking	Incorporate risk taking
Benefit for the cause	Benefit for all involved
Driven by rules and regulations	Driven by joy, fun, and entertainment
Participation encouraged	Consumption encouraged
Involvement is disciplined	Involvement is emotional
Leadership style: I am No. 1	Leadership style: everyone is equal
Favor structured task	Favor creativity
Traditional activities	Opportunity activities
Express motives	Express appreciations
Builds social image	Builds brand image
Vehicle for society stability	Vehicle for lifestyle changes

Figure 1.
Priorities for Sport-Centered and Marketing-Centered Paradigms.

tions. First, given ongoing changes in the marketing environment, sport organizations should focus more on cooperative strategy . Second, cost-effectiveness is a critical factor in influencing sponsors' decision-making processes. If sport organizations wish to become more involved in sponsorship, they must solve the problem of interest distortion (i.e., the problem of one side taking advantage of the other). Ultimately, corporations must develop a workable strategy that enhances both cooperation and cost-effectiveness.

3. Sport organizations are more likely to focus on Olympic performance through a sponsorship arrangement. Corporations, on the other hand, are more willing than are sport organizations to choose the most popular sporting event to build relationships that target grass-roots consumers. These two different strategic approaches—Olympic achievement and public appreciation (what the people want)—illustrate the divergence between sport organizations and commercial corporations when it comes to mission statements, expected objectives, organizational structures, resource management, implementation plans, and leader-

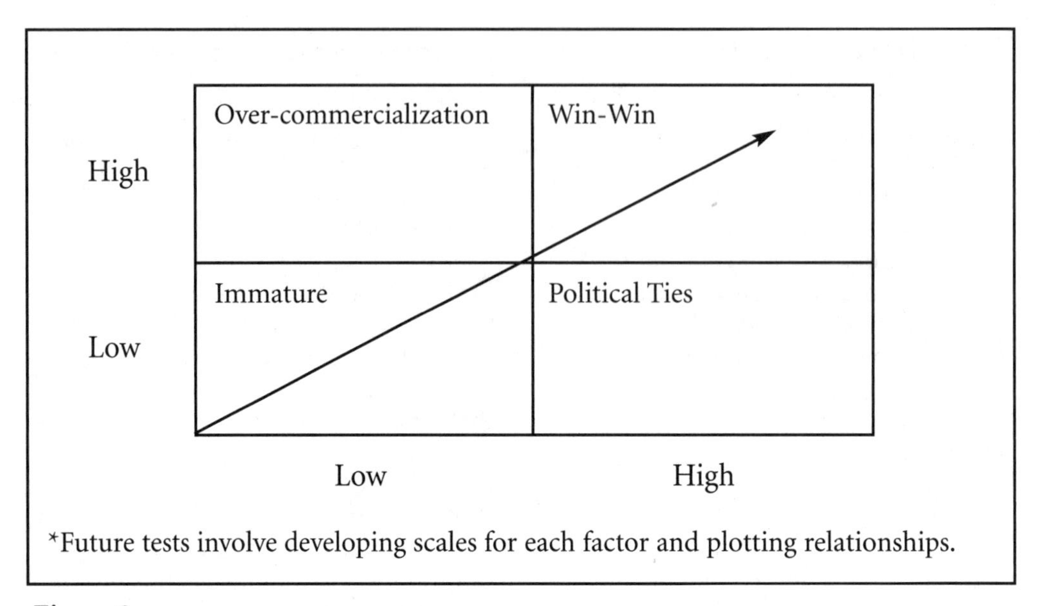

Figure 2.
The Sport Sponsorship Matrix: A Hypothetical Relationship Theory of Cost-Effectiveness vs. Cooperation*

ship styles. Unless a cooperative strategy, involving joint interests and a workable methodology, is created to benefit both government and private parties, problems will arise in sport sponsorship applications. The development of such a strategy would dramatically change the way sport sponsorship programs are conducted in China.

Discussion

It is understandable that the sport-centered ideas practiced in China for many years may be unfamiliar to practitioners in the West. Winning Olympic events, combined with serving China with glory, has long been the outstanding value defining Chinese sport culture. When Western corporations become involved in sponsoring Chinese athletic events or properties, their capitalistic attitudes (i.e., economic profit motives) conflict with China's distinct socialism (i.e., social profit motives). Sport organizations view sponsorship as an external resource to add to the value of Olympic success. Western corporations traditionally have seen sponsorship as a marketing vehicle to differentiate brands or organizations. Through sport, corporations wish to access the largest possible group of participants and audiences, thereby creating opportunities for product promotions and sales. Sport organizations wish to raise funds to enhance the power of the Chinese sport system. The clash between the sport-centered perspective and the market-driven one not only creates a conflict in values, but also gives rise to interest distortion problems.

The findings of this study provide clear evidence of the differences between sport organization groups and corporate groups with regard to sport sponsorship applications in China. The differences arise not only from divergent attitudes concerning the objectives of sport sponsorship, but also from implementation actions in conducting sponsorship programs. These differences create problems, which generate conflict in sport sponsorship applications. Attempts to explain the diversity that exists in Chinese sport marketing provide insight into the conflict between the sport-centered mindset and the marketing-centered mindset. The core value of the sport-centered perspective is emphasized through concepts of country, organization, groups, teams, and society. Judgmentally, the core value of the marketing-centered perspective, created through product and service, is more focused on mass society, service to the community, and quality of life, which is in line with the capitalistic orientation toward organizational profitability and attainment of individual wealth. Figure 1 delineates the strong differences that exist between the two viewpoints. In China, sport organizations' and commercial corporations' views regarding sport and sport sponsorship are so distinct that there are many reasons for the two working entities to excuse themselves from a marketing application of sport sponsorship. This may be because the act of marketing in China may be thought of by some as being overtly Western or capitalistic.

To complicate the situation, both the sport organizations and the commercial corporations believe their mindsets to be correct, because each group's mindset serves its own objectives purely. Problems arise when these opposing mindsets collide in the attempt to work together for a sponsorship arrangement. Sponsorship problems develop because of the strong influence these mindset barriers have on attitudes toward sponsorship value, business interest, and practical strategy (see Tables 2–5). The differing viewpoints create interest conflicts, which lead to stalemates in negotiation and application between sport organizations and commercial corporations.

In addition to the mindset barrier, our study identifies cost-ineffective implementation strategies as being another critical problem that can ruin the cooperation between sport organizations and commercial entities. When China began a nationwide economic reform, sport sponsorship created an appropriate way for the business community to explore new areas of marketing and for sport properties to explore new sources of revenue. While sport sponsorship can benefit both sport properties and commercial corporations, not everyone in both groups understands the nuances of sponsorship or the totality of China's economic reform and the evolving business model. The socialist approach to business, which has been practiced in various forms, can cause a distortion of intentions between two partners working together for the first time.

The findings in this study seem to indicate that, for various reasons, some sport sponsorship arrangements probably are not compatible at the present time. In addition to the common issues of overcommercialization, ambush marketing, endorsement scandals, cost-ineffectiveness, inappropriate communications, misuse of sports, unpredictability, lack of public support, and marketing clutter, the development of sport marketing in China also is threatened by the typical Chinese economic, political, and cultural factors. Resolving such conflicts becomes very complicated when external political, economic, and cultural practices attempt to coexist with internal marketing values. Positive influences such as economic reform and WTO acceptance (Burton, 2001; Wiseman, 2001) have made sport marketing and sponsorship both possible and workable in China. However, negative influences such as political control and Olympic-driven patriotism have positioned Chinese sport on two different tracks—leading to two different destinations. One track leads toward social-development objectives (i.e., national glory), and

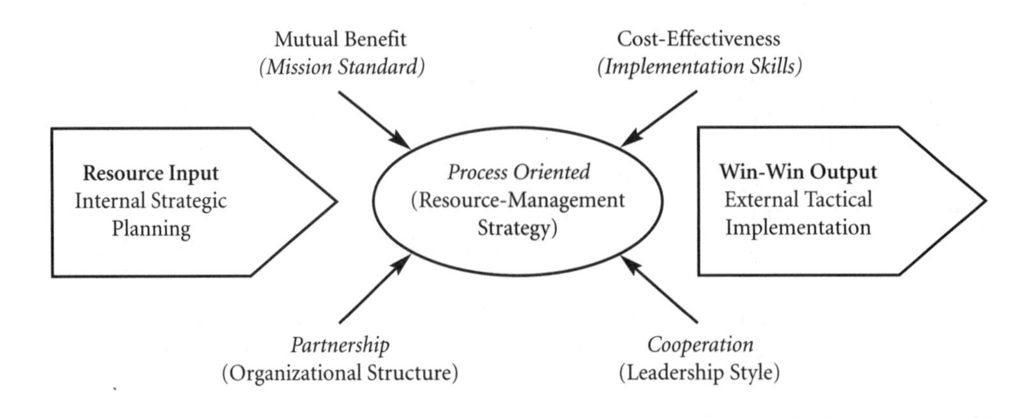

Extended Explanations: The Five Key Principles

Mutual benefit
- Mission statement
- Opportunities and threats
- Social, political, regulatory and citizenship considerations

Partnership
- Organizational structure
- Team management
- Organizational strengths and weaknesses

Process Oriented
- Resource management
- Performance in detail

Cost-effectiveness
- Implementation management
- Competitve capacities
- Business philosophies

Cooperation
- Relationship management
- Leadership style
- Shared value and cultures
- Ethical beliefs

Figure 3.
A Step-by-Step, Relational Sponsorship Management Strategy: The Five Key Principles for Successful Sport Sponsorship Programs

the other leads toward economic-development objectives. Confusion arises as to which destination should take priority.

A sport sponsorship matrix, displayed in Figure 2, shows a straight line indicating the possible relationship by which sport organizations and commercial corporations might work together in a win-win situation, with sport sponsorship cooperation. This hypothetical relationship theory demonstrates how the union between the two groups moves from a low degree of cooperation and cost-effectiveness to a high degree of cooperation and cost-effectiveness. In order to reach this ideal teamwork situation, both groups must make an equal effort. Cost-effectiveness and cooperation have equal weight in sport sponsorship applications, and neither of the two factors should be ignored. If one of the groups concentrates too much on cost-effectiveness and ignores the cooperation factor, the risk of overcommercialization emerges. If the working team pays too much attention to cooperation and forgets about the critical issue of cost-effectiveness, the sport sponsorship will lead to a social-serving objective rather than to a mutually beneficial and appropriately profitable business objective. This study reveals that each group is missing one or both of these key factors; it also indicates that the working relationships between sport organizations and commercial corporations run the risk of appearing overcommercialized or overly politicized. Unfortunately, some sport sponsorship agreements are even worse, because neither of the two critical factors is in operation. Rather, cost-ineffectiveness and a low level of cooperation result in a predictable chain of events: The cost-ineffective output triggers a low level of cooperation; a low level of cooperation leads to an interest distortion; and the interest distortion ultimately results in a break-up of the two working teams.

This study provides a warning signal: Chinese sport marketing is facing the serious threat of increased sponsorship withdrawal. The sponsorship demands of sport organizations greatly exceed commercial corporations' desires and abilities to supply those sponsorships. This unbalanced supply-and-demand situation, showing an inflation of Chinese sport marketing, indicates a potential risk for sport organizations. If this lack of balance continues, sport organizations will fail to attract corporate sponsors.

Chinese sport marketing has an emerging potential for both sport organizations and commercial corporations, but it has a long way to go. Even though sport organizations and commercial corporations desire to work together, they have yet to establish workable marketing policies and procedures. For a long time, the industry-controlled environment, with a politically influenced climate, placed sport organizations in nonprofit positions requiring no marketing skills. Sport organizations enjoyed not only financial support from the government, but also the opportunity to raise capital from social resources. In the course of China's economic reform, however, sport organizations have been redesigned to penetrate sport marketing and to play the roles of both nonprofit organizations and business entities. Sport organizations are growing hungry for more capital. The problem is that commercial corporations are unwilling to contribute in such a crowded market, because it is too difficult for them to differentiate themselves from others.

The findings of this study emphasize that if sport marketing is to succeed in China, it must be seriously improved—not only from the standpoint of marketing-environment and implementation strategies, but also with regard to the integration of two opposing mindsets. Changes from short-term sponsorship to long-term partnerships, shifts from business deals to mutual-benefit relationships, and concentration on a commitment input and a cost-effectiveness output are required for success. Additional research might further explore the growing sophistication of both sponsorship sellers and sponsorship buyers as China moves from a controlled, planning economy to a free market—all the while attempting to unify social and economic objectives.

Sport marketing in China currently is such a specialized area that it requires a complete-solution package to address these special problems. The popular, anecdotal belief is that sport marketing in China is striding toward a marketing-centered destination. Clearly, a successful sponsorship strategy for a long-term and cost-effective relationship between sport organizations and commercial corporations—along with a step-by-step, relational sponsorship management strategy—will lead Chinese sport and sport sponsorship toward a brighter future. Figure 3 provides a step-by-step, relational sponsorship management strategy based on information from this study. The strategy involves five principles, which offer a working strategy for sport sponsorship with the following management considerations:

1. *Purpose and Objectives.* The principle of mutual benefit indicates the core meaning in a cooperative mission statement. With social, political, regulatory, and citizenship considerations, a sponsorship program certainly will develop several objectives, both long-range and short-range, in a sport sponsorship strategy. The mission development, however, must cover overall needs and expectations—both from sport organizations and from commercial corporations. Sport organizations should find ways to satisfy the business needs of marketing promotions and product sales. Corporations should find ways to fulfill the social-development needs of sport groups.
2. *Organizational Structure.* The principle of partnership is the defining organizational structure for a sponsorship program. Sport sponsorship is a partnership, not a philanthropic donation. Both sport organizations and commercial corporations should invest their resources in a partnership structure that can accommodate the truthful interests of both parties; then, they should make that partnership work. Such a partnership structure is a risk-sharing system that ties sport organizations to commercial corporations while at the same time fostering a win-win outcome that allows for acceptable profit-taking and social gain.
3. *Implementation Plan.* The principle of cost-effectiveness must be a natural outcome of sponsorship. Even for popular sporting events with strong competitive capabilities, cost-effectiveness is requisite. Without a cost-effectiveness process, even attractive sponsorship programs will most certainly fail. In an implementation plan, practical skills in dealing with time, money, and people must be cost-effective while still meeting the desired outcomes of each party. Only with this scenario will a long-term relationship result.
4. *Leadership Style.* The principle of cooperation is a communication and leadership style that results in the marriage of a sport organization and a business corporation. It is a so-called husband-wife relationship, with shared values and a common culture. Both sides should have equal rights. The business philosophies and ethical beliefs of sport officials and business executives must be compatible.
5. *Resource Management.* The principle of process orientation is an integrative strategy for resource management. All other principles revolve around it. Both sport organizations and commercial corporations must understand their strengths, weaknesses, and competitive capabilities; and they must be able to successfully manage internal, strategic planning. In order to combat external influences, details must be controlled every step of the way, and both parties must be highly committed to their strategy.

This step-by-step, relational sponsorship management approach offers a possible solution to sport sponsorship problems in China. Implementation and practice of the strategy will involve not only technical designs, but system reforms as well. Making sport marketing work is a long-term project. It will happen, however, when sport marketing in China involves persistent efforts from both sport organizations and commercial corporations.

Conclusions

This study reveals serious conflicts between sport organizations and commercial corporations in China regarding their attitudes and behaviors toward the values, interests, and operational preferences for sport sponsorship. With a gap analysis to address these significant problems in sport sponsorship applications, this study explored the large philosophical gap that separates the sport-centered and marketing-centered mindsets of the parties involved—a gap that indicates the slow transition of Chinese sport from an Olympic-driven model to a marketing-driven model. Encouraging both sport organizations and commercial corporations to make considerable improvements in their sport sponsorship applications, this study presents a step-by-step, relational sponsorship management strategy, with five principles, to respond to critical sponsorship problems. The study also provides strategic considerations for a long-term, cost-effective relationship that will change future business involving sport sponsorship programs in China.

Recommendations for Future Research

The results of this study partially reveal barriers that hinder sport sponsorship in China, including selling strategies and buying motivations. Further research on the step-by-step management strategy, with more comprehensive investigation techniques, is recommended. A continued study of the hypothetical sport sponsorship theory, involving the development of scales for each indicator and the plotting of relationships, is suggested as well. If questionnaires are used in China for such data collection, it is recommended that multiple-choice questions be used, rather than a Likert Scale. Subjects are more responsive to such a format.

References

Andrus, R. (1996). *Sports marketing.* Provo, UT: Brigham Young University.

Andrus, R. (2000). *Marketing research.* Provo, UT: Brigham Young University.

Agnew, J. (1982, November 20). Corporate sports events can be a way to reach customers. *Marketing News,* p. 1.

Boone, L., & Kurtz, D. (1999). *Contemporary marketing* (9th ed.). Fort Worth: Harcourt Brace.

Burton, R. (2001a, July 8). China makes good business sense. *New York Times,* p. 29.

Burton, R. (2001b). *Sports administration in the new millennium—promotion and marketing.* Invited lecture presented to the Asian Basketball Confederation Sports Administration Seminar, Kuala Lumpur, Malaysia.

Echikson, W., Webb, A., & Fonte, D. (2001, July 9). Guess who wants Beijing to get the Games. *Business Week,* p. 48.

George, W. S., & William, G. C. (1989). *Statistical methods* (8th ed). Ames, IA: Iowa State University Press.

IEG Reports. (2001, December 18). IEG forecast: Sponsorship spending growth will slow in 2001. *IEG Reports, 19*(4), pp. 1, 4.

Johnson, D. (2001, October 12). Update 2002: China celebrates. *ESPN Soccernet* Retrieved from http://www.soccernet.com/columns/2001/update2002

Li, D. (1999). *Sports industry and the development of economics.* Beijing, China: National Sports Committee of China.

Lizhong, G. (1996). Sports marketing strategy: A consumer case analysis in China. *Multinational Business Review, 4*(1), 36–38.

McDonald, M., & Milne, G. (1999). *Cases in sports marketing.* Sudbury, MA: Jones and Bartlett.

Mullin, B., Hardy, S., & Sutton, W. (1993). *Sport marketing.* Champaign, IL: Human Kinetics.

Saxton, E. (1993, December). Motor sports sponsorship. *Marketing News,* p. 1.

Schlossberg, H. (1996). *Sports marketing.* Cambridge, MA: Blackwell Business.

Swanson, R., & Spears, B. (1995). *History of sport and physical education in the United States.* Madison, WI: Brown & Benchmark.

United States-China Business Council. (2001). *China's economic indicators, 1995–2000* Retrieved from http://www.uschina.org/press/econmarch99.html

Wilson, N. (1988). *The sports business.* London: Piatkus.

Wiseman, P. (2001, October 18). Deep financial problems threaten to bury China. *USA Today,* p. B1-2.

Wu, S. (1999). *The Chinese history of sports.* Beijing, China: People's Publisher of Sports.

21

Effect of Perceived Sport Event and Sponsor Image Fit on Consumers' Cognition, Affect, and Behavioral Intentions

Win Koo and Jerome Quarterman

Introduction

The value of commercial sponsorship of sports reached $26.2 billion in 2003, an increase of 7.4% from $24.4 billion in 2002 (Sport Business Associates, 2004). It dominated all other areas of sponsorship-linked marketing activities such as entertainment tours, festivals, and public causes. In 2003, corporations spent approximately $436 million on college football sponsorships (*Sport Business Daily*, 2003) and the projected growth rate of the value of "the sponsorship dollar" is expected to increase annually. Sport sponsorship has been one of the fastest growing areas of promotion. Marketers interested in building brand awareness and positive brand attitudes include sport sponsorship as part of their marketing communication mix (Cunningham & Taylor, 1995; Shanklin & Kuzma, 1992). Jonathan, Ashok, and Hong (1998) indicated that 93% of the companies' primary goal was to increase product awareness through sport sponsorship activities. In addition, research has also shown that sponsorship activities can improve consumer attitudes about corporations and increase product sales (Pope, 1998).

Much of the accessible research on sport sponsorship has been focused, however, on issues pertaining to the firms. Examples would be in the setting of sponsorship objectives or that of measuring sponsorship results. Consequently, they have been devoid of serious theoretical insight regarding how it functions from a marketing communication effects perspective (Cunningham & Taylor, 1995; Gwinner, 1997; McDaniel, 1999; McDaniel & Kinney, 1996). It has been argued that studies in this area should add more to our theoretical understanding of sponsorship's influence on consumer attitudes, beliefs, and behavioral intentions (Cunningham & Taylor, 1995; McDaniel, 1999; Kinney & McDaniel, 1996). The purpose of this study was two-fold: to examine the effects of perceived brand/sport event image fit on consumers' cognitive (corporate image, brand recognition) and affective (brand attitude) responses to sponsorship activities and to examine the effects of consumers' cognitive and affective responses on their purchasing intentions.

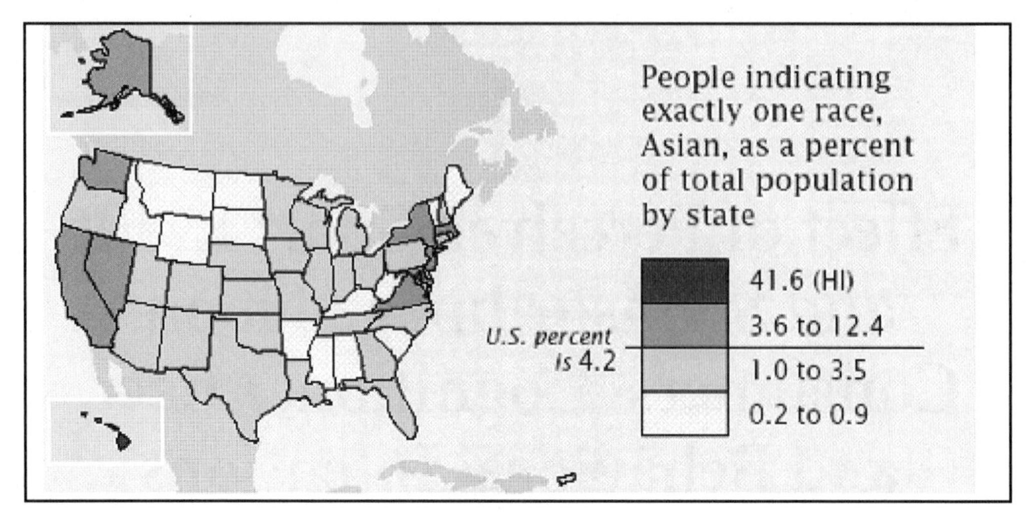

Figure 1.
Asian American Population by State

This study was intended to serve as a foundation that relates to the issue of sport sponsorship effectiveness as a strategic marketing tool, and to provide evidence of the efficacy of consumers' perceptions of brand/sport event image fit in shaping consumer-based brand equity. It is critical that sport sponsorship strategy becomes a function of the overall brand strategy and that it is used at the corporate level in order to contribute to a brand's overall equity and direct/indirect sales.

Theoretical Understanding of Sponsorship

Fiske (1982) defined a schema as "an active organization of past experiences, which must always be supposed to be operating in any well-adapted organic response" (p. 60). The primary motivation for the development of schema theory was to offer an alternative explanation for human information processing. Fiske's theory of schema-triggered affect was extended to explain consumers' processing of sport sponsorships because it could be used to investigate: 1) how consumers process the image fit of a brand and a sport event brought together through sponsorship, and 2) how the image fit leads to favorable cognitions and affects toward the sponsoring brand.

Schema theory has been used comprehensively in celebrity endorsement and spokesperson advertising research. A concept related closely to schema theory is the match-up hypothesis. Misra and Beatty (1990) defined a successful match-up as one in which "...the highly relevant characteristics of the spokesperson are consistent with the highly relevant attributes of the brand" (p. 161). For example, Seri Pak, a Ladies Professional Golf Association (LPGA) golf player, may be considered congruent with sporting goods or products that may have an image consistent with her wholesome image. On the other hand, Seri Pak may not be considered congruent with technical products, such as computers, or products with an image inconsistent with her wholesome image, such as tobacco or alcoholic beverages. Consumer responses to a celebrity endorsement, such as brand attitude and recall of brand information, are expected to be more positive if the endorser is a good fit with the brand (Misra & Beatty, 1990).

Evaluating consumer responses to sport sponsorships using schema theory is equivalent to celebrity endorsement and product spokesperson research in two ways. The first equivalence is that one objective of sponsorship is to transfer feelings about a peripheral cue, such as a sponsored sport event, to a brand. This corresponds to the transfer of feelings about celebrities, in endorsement advertising, to the brands endorsed (Gwinner, 1997). McDaniel (1999) argued that consumers possess schemas about sporting events, just as they possess schemas about celebrities. A second equivalence is that the effects of image fit on consumers' responses to corporate event sponsorship are expected to be similar to the match-up effects of a brand with a celebrity. The greater the image fit between sponsor and sport event, the more likely the schemas held in the consumer's memory will be stimulated, thereby allowing incorporation of ideas about the sponsorship activity with the existing schemas.

On the other hand, some studies (e.g., Hastie, 1980; Meyers-Levy & Tybout, 1989; Srull, 1981) have pointed out that moderate schema incongruity was related to increased cognitive evaluation. For instance, Meyers-Levy and Tybout's (1989) study was constructed in the context of describing a new soft drink and providing information that was completely congruent, moderately incongruent, or severely incongruent with the product category. The results of the study indicated that evaluations of moderately incongruent stimuli might be better predictors of behavior. Also Srull (1981) reported the results of an experimental study, based on research performed by Hastie (1980), in which people tended to recall a greater proportion of incongruent than congruent information. Despite the research results of those who support schema incongruity as the more effective means of stimulating affect, more research has supported the alternative position that schema congruency results in stronger affect on consumer behaviors (e.g., Cohen, 1982; Fiske, 1982; Fiske & Pavelchak, 1986; Misra & Beatty, 1990).

In this study, Fiske's theory of schema-triggered affect was used to interpret the existing phenomena that the linkage of a brand with an event, presented to consumers through sport sponsorship, could lead consumers to process the information about the linkage and compare it with existing information stored in their memory about the brand and the event. Therefore, utilizing schema theory to explain consumers' cognitive and affective responses to brand/sport event linkages provides reliable evidence that the sponsoring events exhibiting a good image fit with the brand can strengthen the development of consumers' cognitive and affective responses through exposure to a brand's sport sponsorship activity.

Effects of Image Fit on Consumers' Cognitive and Affective Responses

In consumer research, schema theory has been used to examine whether congruent information results in more favorable affective consumer behavior outcomes. Misra and Beatty (1990) found support for the contention that schema congruence is more influential in consumer evaluation than schema incongruity, by examining the effects of endorser/brand match-up on brand recall and affect toward the brand. Endorser/brand congruence resulted in higher brand recall than incongruence between endorsers and brands. Also, the transfer of affect from celebrity endorser to the brand, which is the primary reason celebrities are hired to endorse products, occurred only when the celebrity endorser and the brand were perceived as congruent. Those results were consistent with

Kahle and Homer (1985), and Kamins (1990), who found that a fit between a celebrity and an advertised product enhances product and advertisement evaluations.

Recognizing the results of these studies of course is essential for sponsorship activities. Consequently, outcomes of sport sponsorship effectiveness can be classified into corporate-based and consumer-based. More recent studies have determined that the primary goal for many companies engaging in sport sponsorship is their return on investment, which is corporate based outcome. However, a variety of sponsorship literature specified that the primary objectives of many sponsors were to increase brand awareness and enhance brand and/or corporate image (Gilbert, 1988; Quester, 1997; Shanklin & Kuzma, 1992). These objectives are consumer-based outcomes that a sponsor can evaluate to determine a sponsorship's effectiveness in communicating with the target audiences and ultimately consumer-based outcomes impact corporate-based outcomes. Examination of a brand's overall equity from the consumer's perspective focuses on the consumer behaviors in response to the marketing efforts of a brand. The framework of brand's overall equity used in this study is known as customer-based brand equity, which may be defined as the differential effect of brand knowledge on consumer cognitions and affect to the marketing of that brand (Keller, 1993, 1998). Keller (1993) suggested that brand awareness and brand image are the two dimensions of brand knowledge that can be used to measure the sources of brand equity. Also, the hierarchy-of-effects model (Lavidge & Steiner, 1961) used to explain a consumer's response to communications indicated that a consumer's initial response to marketing communications such as sport sponsorship tended to be cognitive and affective in nature.

Therefore, the implications for brand/sport event image fit on cognitive and affective responses to brand/sport event linkages generally point toward the benefits of image fit between brand and sport event. In the current study, a consumer's perceived brand/sport event image fit is expected to influence two cognitive responses (brand recognition and corporate image of the sponsoring firm), and an affective response (brand attitude toward the sponsoring firm). The following research hypotheses (RH) were proposed in relation to the foregoing discussion.

RH_1: Students classified as having high-perceived brand/sport event image fit have a more positive corporate image of the sponsoring brand than students with low perceived brand/sport event image fit.

RH_2: Students classified as having high-perceived brand/sport event image fit have a more positive brand attitude toward the sponsoring brand than students with low perceived brand/sport event image fit.

RH_3: Students classified as having high-perceived brand/sport event image fit have higher likelihood of correctly recognizing a brand as an event sponsor than students with low perceived brand/sport event image fit.

Effects of Consumers' Cognitive and Affective Responses on Purchase Intentions

Consumers' cognitive and affective reactions to sponsorship activities have important implications in terms of gauging the effectiveness of sport sponsorship. A unique association between the sport event and the sponsor's product is created through sport sponsorship activities (Abratte, Clayton, & Pitt, 1987). McDonald (1991) specified the importance of product relevance to the sponsored event, based on direct and indirect approaches. The direct process occurs when the sponsoring firm's products are used in the event. Indirectly, relevance can be achieved if some aspect of the sponsor's image corresponds with the event. In addition, Gwinner (1997) utilized the terms "functional based" and "image based similarity" to explain the potential association between sport events and sponsors.

Brand awareness, corporate image, and brand attitude make the brand a candidate for purchase. Keller (1993) identified three benefits resulting from high levels of brand awareness and positive brand image: 1) to increase the probability of brand choice, as well as to produce greater consumer loyalty, 2) to have specific implications for the pricing, distribution, and promotion activities related to the brand, and 3) to increase the effectiveness of marketing communication. In addition, the importance of image has been increasingly recognized in consumer behavior studies (e.g., Ferrand & Pages, 1999; Gwinner, 1997; Hart & Rosenberger, 2004; Poiesz, 1989; Shanklin & Kuzma, 1992; Sirgy, 1985) because consumers use heuristic decision processes, such as reliance on corporate image, for evaluative purposes. In many situations, consumer information processing is limited, and decisions and judgments are based on simplified product cues and symbolic association, such as corporate image (Poiesz, 1989). If the company successfully associates with a sporting event through sponsorship activity, we would expect attitudes toward the company to become more positive.

Many marketers have recognized that images have the power to influence the behavior of all those involved with a sporting event (Ferrand & Pages, 1999). According to a study conducted by Gardner and Schuman (1987), 53% of the respondents made a purchase as a result of a sponsorship. Sheth, Newman, and Gross (1991) also suggest five different values relating to the decision to purchase or not purchase a particular brand: functional value, social value, emotional value, epistemic value, and conditional value. The awareness and corporate image of sponsors have impacts on all or some of these five values in different ways (Pope, 1998).

Sport sponsorship activity may increase brand awareness and may enhance brand attitude and/or corporate image. These objectives will be successful in forming and strengthening a consumer's brand-knowledge structures. They would also be expected to increase the purchasing intention of the relative sponsoring brand products. Therefore, it can be argued that most consumers will assume that the positive image of a sporting event results in the positive image of its sponsors. This extends the notion of the schematic information process found in the relationship between the consumers' cognitive and affective responses and the purchase intentions context. This discussion leads to the following research hypotheses (RH):

RH_4: Students' corporate image of a sponsoring brand will have an effect on their purchase intentions.

RH_5: Students' attitude toward a sponsoring brand will have an effect on their purchase intentions.

RH_6: Students' correct recognition of a brand, as a sporting event sponsor, will have an effect on their purchase intentions.

Method

Design

The study employed a cross-sectional quantitative survey design. Data were collected from a sample to describe their perceptions of the image fit between the Bowl Championship Series (BCS) and the sponsors at one point in time. Data were obtained during two stages including a pre-test and main test stage. The pre-test stage facilitated a set of personality-oriented adjectives describing participants' image dimensions of the BCS and a set of appropriate sponsoring brands of the BCS. The main test stage was used to examine the effects of perceived brand/sport event image fit on consumers' cognitive and affective responses and the effects of consumers' cognitive and affective responses on their purchase intentions.

Participants

In the pre-test stage, participants were 162 undergraduate students enrolled in sport management and business courses at a major public university in the southeastern region of the United States, and who watched one of the final four college Bowl Championship Series (BCS) games. It was a necessary condition that participants had exposure to the sport event since this study evaluated students' cognitive information process. Of this amount more than half were males (88 or 54.3%) and the remaining were females (74 or 45.9%).

In the main test stage, a convenience sample of 452 undergraduate students enrolled in sport management and business courses were selected from two major universities in the southeastern region of the United States. Twenty-five (5.5%) did not complete the questionnaire and were not included in the final analysis. Of the 427 participants in this study, more than half (237 or 55.5%) were males and the remaining amount were females (190 or 44.5%). The majority (93.4%) of students' ages ranged from 18 to 25 and the largest ethnicity group was white Americans (76.7%).

Table 1.
Level of Image and Functional Based Similarity among the Sponsoring Brand

	Image based similarity		Functional based similarity	
Sponsors	*M*	*SD*	*M*	*SD*
Nokia	3.78	.07	4.10	1.12
Tostitos*	4.10	1.07	4.00	1.33
FedEx	3.24	.98	3.37	1.29
Sony PlayStation 2*	3.81	1.02	3.63	1.46
Coca Cola*	3.55	.89	3.92	1.11
Cingular	3.56	1.22	3.79	1.17
Pontiac*	3.24	.94	3.10	1.06

Note. * indicates selected sponsors subsequently used in the main survey.

Table 2.
Image Dimension of the 2003 Bowl Championship Series

	N	*M*	*SD*
Competitive	162	6.57	.79
Exciting	162	6.22	1.17
Energetic	162	6.10	1.24
Tough	162	6.02	1.13
Pressure	162	5.93	1.35
Aggressive	162	5.88	1.54
Emotional	162	5.83	1.30
Active	162	5.80	1.50
Masculine	162	5.78	1.64

Data collection procedures

Human subject's approval was obtained from the Institutional Review Board. The purpose of the research was explained to each student. Informed consent was provided by each student. In order to avoid multiple observations on the same respondent, each student was randomly assigned to respond to questions regarding one of the four sponsoring brands. The student sample was one of convenience from two major universities in the southeastern region of the United States.

Measures

Pre-test. To develop the test instrument, the pre-test consisted of two components. The first part of the pre-test sought to select appropriate sponsoring brands of the BCS to examine the effects of perceived brand/sport event image fit on consumers' cognitive and affective responses. Students have been exposed to various sponsoring brands of the BCS derived from the potential association between the BCS and its sponsors. That exposure in turn developed schema of each sponsor to the students. Regarding the potential association, Gwinner and Eaton's (1999) study demonstrated that when an event and a brand are associated with the basis of either image or function, the transfer process is enhanced. Therefore, in order to choose a variety of sponsors to reflect the different level of students' previous associations between the BCS and its sponsors, Gwinner and Eaton's (1999) 6-item scale for measuring the image and functional based similarity was applied to the sponsors relating to the BCS. In addition, the level of association was measured by 7-point Likert type scales anchored by strongly disagree (1) and strongly agree (7).

As illustrated in Table 1, the BCS was paired with seven different sponsoring brands. In general, there were seven original sponsors relating to the BCS in the pre-test, of which three were title sponsors of the BCS (Nokia, FedEx, and Tostitos), three were NCAA corporate sponsors, (Coca-Cola, Pontiac, and Cingular) and the last one a presenting sponsor of the BCS, (Sony PlayStation 2).

Unfortunately, the results of the pre-test demonstrated that students' perceptions of functional and image-based similarity of the BCS sponsors were parallel. Thus, due to the lack of distinction among sponsors in students' cognitive structure, four sponsoring brands out of seven associated with the BCS were selected for use in the main survey using a pattern of 2 (image/functional) by 2 (high/low) possibilities. For example, Tostitos had the highest image and the second-highest functional-based similarity with the BCS, while Pontiac had the lowest image and functional-based similarity with the BCS. The last two sponsors were a combination of high and low for each similarity; Coca-Cola had a high functioned-based similarity with a low image-based similarity, while Sony PlayStation 2 had a high image-based similarity with a low functional-based similarity.

The remaining pre-test was conducted to produce a set of personality-oriented adjectives that could be used to describe image dimensions of the BCS. A questionnaire for the pre-test was developed, containing 40 adjectives that had been selected from previous studies (Ferrand & Pages, 1996, 1999; Gwinner & Eaton, 1999; Koo & Cho, 1999) on people's perceptions of image dimensions of various sports. The pre-test was administered to students to rate the adjectives on a 7-point scale as they applied to the BCS.

As seen in Table 2, through this procedure, among 40 adjectives ranged 1.84 for "calm" to 6.57 for "competitive", nine adjectives were ranked the highest by student respondents. In addition, the finding from an exploratory factor analysis demonstrated that all nine adjectives loaded on one factor with appropriate factor loadings ranged from .57 to .75. Those nine adjectives were considered the most useful in describing the event, and were then chosen for use in the image fit effect test.

Main test. The study's hypotheses were tested in this phase of the study. Sirgy et al. (1997) suggested that a method directly measuring congruency is more appropriate for examining image congruence between a brand and one's own image. The traditional method of measuring self-image congruence is based on computing a discrepancy of the subject's perception of his or her self-image in relation to the product-user image. In this manner, self-image congruence may be used to measure the image fit between the BCS and sponsor since the notion of self-image congruence was to explain and predict aspects of consumer behaviors such as brand attitude, brand adoption, and purchase intentions.

Gwinner and Eaton (1999) also used the discrepancy index between the corresponding adjectives in the event and the band ratings because the event's image is expected to be more important in the spectator's mind since his/her primary focus is typically on the activities of the sporting event, rather than on the sponsors. For this reason, the test for image fit was conducted based on the degree of image differences between the event and its sponsors, and, therefore, the nine images (adjectives) selected from the pre-test used for rating the BCS were also used in rating the sponsors. For example, assume that a student rates "energetic," one of the main adjectives reflecting the BCS, as a six for the BCS. If a student regards Pontiac as having a very "energetic" image, it will probably mark 6th or 7th in a 7-point Likert scale and the absolute difference scores for those corresponding adjectives should be "1 or 2." A zero difference indicates the greatest image fit. We summed the nine absolute difference scores for the BCS/sponsor pair to generate an image fit indicator. The following mathematical rule indicates the sum of the absolute image difference scores, which were used as the image fit in this study (Claiborne & Sirgy, 1990; Sirgy, 1985).

$$\sum_{i=1}^{n} |Si - Ei|$$

Si= rating of sponsor image along image dimension i and
Ei=rating of BCS along image dimension i

A 4-item test comprised of 7-point Likert type scales used by Roy (2000) was slightly modified and applied to this study for measuring Corporate Image (- has good products and services, - is well managed, - responds to consumer needs, and - has a commitment to quality and excellence) because Roy (2000) found that two items from Johnson and Zinkhan's (1990) original 6-item scales had low-squared multiple correlations decreasing the reliability of the measure. Brand Attitude was examined by using three 7-point semantic differential scales anchored by favorable/unfavorable, bad/good, and negative/positive (McDaniel & Kinney, 1996). Brand Recognition tested a student's ability to recognize a brand as one of the BCS sponsors by a dichotomous response. Finally, the measures of Purchase Intentions were measured by a 2-item scale derived from the 3-item scale in Kinney and McDaniel (1996), comprised of 7-point semantic differential scales anchored by improbable/probable and unlikely/likely. Scale reliabilities met or exceeded the performance of the scales in previous research due to the deletion of one item that had a low item to total correlation. Initial reliabilities of each category for the main test ranged from .85 for the corporate image to .96 for the purchase intentions. Thus, scale reliabilities exceeded the .70 threshold were considered to have an acceptable level of reliability (Nunnally, 1978).

Data Analysis

The analysis of data from the survey was performed using the SPSS 11.5 and Lisrel 8.52 programs. Prior to testing the research hypotheses, the dimensionality and validity for the measures were tested by a confirmatory factor analysis (CFA). In order to test the hypotheses of the study the following statistical techniques were utilized; multiple analysis of variance (MANOVA), Chi-square (χ^2), and multiple regression analysis. MANOVA was used to examine the first and second research hypotheses. Perceived brand/sport event image fit was classified as the categorical independent variable of two levels and Corporate Image and Brand Attitude as the dependent variables. Chi-Square statistics were used to examine research hypothesis 3, with which to determine whether correct sponsor recognition differed between the two perceived brand/sport event image fit groups. Finally, multiple regression analysis was used to examine research hypothesis 4 through 6. Consumers' cognitive and affective responses were considered as the independent variables and Purchase Intentions as the dependent variable.

Results

Psychometric evaluation of the measures

The purpose of assessing convergent and discriminant validity was to determine whether the measures were indeed measures of the constructs they aimed to assess and whether the measures were isolated to the construct which they were said to gauge and not other constructs as well (Hair, Anderson, Tatham, & Black, 1995). Items of all scaled constructs were put into a measurement model as indicators of exogenous latent variables. The scale of each latent variable was fixed by assuming that the variance of each latent variable was equal to one.

Evidence of convergent validity was sought by examining each construct's average variance extracted (Hair, Anderson, Tatham, & Black, 1995) and a construct was considered to exhibit convergent validity if the average variance extracted was 0.50 or greater (Fornell &

Table 3.
Convergent and Discriminant Validity for the Measures

Measures	Average variance extracted	ϕ^2
Match-up Effect	.55	.00 - .01
Brand Attitude	.79	.00 - .40
Corporate Image	.59	.01 - .39
Purchasing Intention	.84	.00 - .40

Larcker, 1981). Shown in Table 3, since the average variance extracted estimates ranged from .55 to .84 for all latent constructs, the measure possessed convergent validity.

The discriminant validity for each construct was determined by comparing the average variance extracted with the square of the correlation (ϕ^2) between the factor and each of the other constructs (Lichtenstein, Netemeyer, & Burton, 1990). In this measurement model, the average variance extracted for each construct was greater than the squared correlations between it and each of the other constructs (See Table 3). In addition, the fit indices were larger than the common target of .90 that indicate a reasonable fit (e.g., NFI, CFI, NNFI > .90), χ^2 (129, N=427) = 459.91, p = .00, Root Mean Square Error of Approximation (RMSEA) = .07, Normed Fit Index (NFI) = .92, Non-Normed Fit Index (NNFI) = .93, and Comparative Fit Index (CFI) = .94 (Kelloway, 1998; Tate, 1998). In summary, the results of CFA indicated that the latent constructs examined in this study have an acceptable level in terms of convergent and discriminant validity.

Effects of image fit on consumers' cognitive and affective responses

Students classified as having high perceived brand/sport event image fit were expected to have more positive cognitive and affective responses, such as Corporate Image (CI), Brand Attitude (BA), and Brand Recognition (BR) than students with low perceived brand/sport event image fit. Accordingly, to examine research hypothesis 1, 2, and 3, the classification of high and low groups were achieved by using a median split of perceived brand/sport event image fit. Student group sizes were 215 for the high image fit group and 212 for the low image fit group.

The test of the assumption of homogeneity of covariance matrices in the two groups results in a reject decision: Box's M = 22.61, F(3, 32716833) = 7.50, p < .001, indicating a likely violation of the assumption. However, a follow-up analysis with Levene's test of the assumption of homogeneity of variance for each of the dependent variables resulted in failure to reject decisions for all variables, a result consistent with the assumption that the variances were equal over the groups: F(1, 425) = 1.68, p = .20 ; F(1, 425) = 3.67, p = .06.

Results of the MANOVA supported the first two hypotheses. First, the multivariate null hypothesis of equality of the means over the high image fit group and low image fit group for two variables, CI and BA, were rejected at the .05 level: Wilk's Λ = .98, F (2, 424) = 3.33, p = .03. As seen in Table 4, univariate F-tests provide additional support for research hypothesis 1 and 2. Support for research hypothesis 1 was found by the differences in CI of the sponsoring brands being statistically significant between students in the high image

Table 4.
Effects of Perceived Image Fit on Corporate Image and Brand Attitude

	N	*M*	*SD*	*F*	*p*
Corporate Image	High (215)	4.60	.07	5.86*	.01
	Low (212)	4.38	.08		
Brand Attitude	High (215)	1.04	.09	4.32*	.03
	Low (212)	.73	.11		

Notes. Multivariate test is significant (Wilk's Lambda= .98, F [2, 424]=3.33, p=.03*); *p<.05, **p<.01, ***p<.001

Table 5.
Effects of Perceived Image Fit on Brand Recognition

Number of Students	Identi-fication	Frequency	Percent	χ^2	*df*	*p*
High (215)	Correct	99	46.0	22.65***	1	< .001
	Incorrect	116	54.0			
Low (212)	Correct	51	24.1			
	Incorrect	161	75.9			

* p<.05; **p<.01; ***p<.001

fit group and students in the low image fit group: $F(1, 425) = 5.86$, $p = .01$. Thus, students having high perceived brand/sport event image fit had more positive CI of event sponsors than students having low perceived brand/sport event image fit. Second, a statistically significant difference in BA was found between students in the high and low image fit groups. The findings supported the hypothesis that students in the high image fit group had more favorable BA than students in the low image fit group: $F(1, 425) = 4.32$, $p = .03$.

Finally, a chi-square statistic was computed to determine whether correct sponsor recognition differed between the two image fit groups of students (see Table 5).

The result indicated that high perceived brand/sport event image fit increased the likelihood of a student correctly identifying a brand as an event sponsor: $\chi^2(1, 427) = 22.65$, $p < .001$. Students in the high image fit group correctly recognized event sponsors 46.0% of the time, compared with 24.1% correct recognition rate for students in the low image fit group. However, the majority of students in both image fit groups did not recognize the sponsors since the sponsors used for the study did not have higher students' perceptions of previous potential association with the BCS, which were found in the pre-test.

Effects of consumers' cognitive and affective responses on purchase intentions

Visual inspection of a plot of the model residuals versus the predicted outcomes did not suggest any violations of the regression assumptions of correct fit, constant variance, or normality. Also, a larger than .20 tolerance and a smaller than 3.0 Variance Inflation Factor indicated there was no significant multicollinearity among the independent variables (Fox, 1991; Hair, Anderson, Tatham, & Black, 1995).

The model R^2 of .51, reflecting the overall strength of relationship between Purchasing Intention (PI) and the independent variables, was statistically significant at the .05 level: $F(3, 423) = 144.30, p < .001$. The adjusted R^2 that compensates for the positive bias in R^2 was .50, indicating that about 50% of the variability of PI was explained by the model. The standard error of estimate was 1.34. Results of the multiple regression supporting the hypotheses that students' corporate image (CI), brand attitude (BA), and brand recognition (BR) of a sponsoring brand will have an effect on their purchase intentions are summarized in Table 6.

First, the positive effect of CI on PI, significant at the .05 level ($t = 5.90$, $p < .001$), reflects an estimated change of .421 PI units for every unit change in CI, controlling for the other variables. Second, BA's effect on PI was significant at the .05 level ($t = 12.32$, $p < .001$). The result indicated that an estimated change of .637 PI units associated with one unit change in BA, controlling for the other variables. Finally, the effect of BR on PI was also statistically significant at the .05 level ($t = 2.90$, $p < .001$), indicating that the predicted PI for the group recognizing the sponsoring brand is .481 units higher than that for the group not recognizing it, controlling for other IVs. Finally, the unique contributions of CI, BA, and BR of the model R^2 (R^2 in Table 4) were respectively .004, .018, and .014, which suggested that three independent variables were important in explaining PI.

Discussion and Conclusions

The primary purpose of our study was to gain a better understanding of the image fit effects on consumers' cognitive and affective responses that are considered elements of customer-based outcomes for the sport sponsorship and of the effects of consumers' cognitive and affective responses on purchase intentions. The findings were consistent with the match-up hypothesis and schema theory. Students with high perceived brand/sport event image fit may have transferred the favorable associations arising from the

Table 6.
Effects of Consumers' Cognitive and Affective Responses on Purchase Intentions

Variables	Effect Estimate	Standardized Error	Standardized Coefficient	*p*
Corporate Image	.421	.090	.242	.004***
Brand Attitude	.637	.080	.276	.018***
Brand Recognition	.481	.175	.271	.014***

Notes. The overall strength of relationship is significant ($F[3, 423] = 144.30, p < .001$***); * $p<.05$, ** $p<.01$, *** $p<.001$
* $p<.05$; ** $p<.01$; *** $p<.001$

brand/sport event image fit to their evaluation of the sponsor's corporate image (Roy, 2000). They also seemed to have a more favorable brand attitude toward the sponsoring brand. Fiske's theory of schema-triggered affect (1982) indicated that an elaboration of match-up stimuli results in the development of a more positive affect. A consumer who perceived the sport sponsorship activity as fit with his or her schema would assimilate that information into existing schemas for the brand, thus strengthening the schema. Subsequently, a positive relationship between sport event and brand will contribute to the consumers' favorability toward the sponsor (Speed & Thompson, 2000).

Another finding, that correct sponsor recognition is a function of relatedness between sponsor brand and event, was also consistent with predictions derived from the schematic information-processing model. This suggests that when an individual receives new information about a brand, any information that is irrelevant to existing schema may be filtered out, while information that is relevant will be more readily encoded. This leads to subsequent recall or recognition superiority for the relevant information (Taylor & Crocker, 1981).

Sport sponsorship activity increases brand awareness and enhances brand attitude and/or corporate image. Many sponsors achieve consumer-based outcomes that can be evaluated to determine sport sponsorship effectiveness in communicating with target audiences. Achievement of these objectives would imply that a sport sponsorship activity was successful in forming and strengthening a consumer's brand-knowledge structures (Keller, 1998). Specifically, the results of this study indicated that corporate image, brand attitude, and brand recognition are important dimensions in explaining purchase intentions.

For that reason, sponsors would be advised to take a proactive role in judging their target consumers and in measuring their target consumers' image perceptions of a specific event. In this manner, they will be able to use sport sponsorship activity to achieve the firm's brand positioning goals. Sport sponsorship activities can position the brand by using the elements of the marketing mix to make positive, unique associations with the brand. They can also increase their popularity by displaying an association through sport sponsorship. On the other hand, sponsees should demonstrate to potential sponsors that linking with their event would create added value for their brands (Roy & Cornwell, 2003). The awareness of the event image would help sponsees (sport associations, schools, and teams) to obtain financial supports from outside organizations.

Therefore, an understanding of consumers' brand/sport event image fit through a sponsorship activity is important for both sport marketers and event organizers. This is because consumers who perceive the brand/event image fit via sponsorship as being fit are likely to have more positive cognitive and affective responses toward the sponsors than consumers who perceive the brand/event image fit as being less congruent or incongruent. Perceptions of consumers' brand/sport event image fit through a sponsorship activity may be formed using either or both of these dimensions as evaluative criteria; image fit of sponsor with event using functional criteria and image fit of sponsor and event form a strategic target marketing viewpoint.

In the context of sport sponsorship activity, a consumer may assess the balance or congruence of a brand with a sport event in two different ways. First, some consumers might perceive a fit between a non-alcoholic beverage sponsor and a college football event because beverages are served at the event. Other consumers might perceive that a beverage sponsor would have no association with a college football event. Second, the audience of the event being sponsored is congruent with the sponsoring brand's target market. For example, the target market of some wireless phone brand (e.g., Nokia) might be perceived as being congruent with the audience of a college football event, while another phone brand (e.g., Samsung) might be perceived as not matching the event's audience.

Consequently, whenever this schematic information process is occurring, sport marketing programs that are considering sponsorship arrangements should not only consider exposure issues, but should also take into account the congruence between a sporting event's image and the image/positioning goals for their brands.

Limitation and Future Study

This investigation has limitations that suggest important directions for future research in sport marketing. First, the results of this investigation cannot be generalized beyond the present sample and the perceptions of sport event/sponsors image fit effect category. The sample was confined to a convenience sample of undergraduate students enrolled in sport management and business management courses of a major public university in the southeastern region of the United States. Therefore, the findings cannot be generalized to other consumer groups or geographical areas. Future studies should draw samples from larger groups of individuals in more diverse settings. Additionally, future research should be gathered from a longitudinal time frame to capture differences that may occur during different years. Second, the present investigation maybe limited since the students' responses may have been influenced by previous exposure to brand advertising, use of the products, or word-of-mouth communications with others who are familiar with the brand. Also, an effective sponsorship will depend on additional factors besides brand/sport event image fit. A sponsor's leveraging of the sport sponsorship through advertising and sales promotion might be important factors to sponsorship success.

Therefore, a similar research design could be implemented using fictitious brands and events instead of real brands and events. This approach would allow presentation of brand/sport event stimuli that are not affected by students' knowledge of brands and events from past experience and exposure. Finally, a conceptual study will be needed to examine the variables effecting schematic information processing activities and their influence upon on consumer behaviors.

References

Abratt, R., Clayton, B. C., & Pitt, L. F. (1987). Corporate objectives in sports sponsorship. *International Journal of Advertising, 6*, 299-311.

Claiborne, C. B., & Sirgy, M. J. (1990). Self-congruent as a model of attitude formation and change: Conceptual review and guide for future research. *Developments in Marketing Science, 13*, 1-7.

Cohen, J. B. (1982). The role of affect in categorization: Toward a reconsideration of the concept of attitude. In Mitchell, A. (Ed.), *Advances in Consumer Research* (pp. 94-100). Ann Arbor, MI: Association for Consumer Research.

Cunningham, M. H., & Taylor, S. F. (1995). Event marketing: State of the industry and research agenda. *Festival Management & Event Tourism, 2*, 123-137.

Ferrand, A., & Pages, M. (1996). Image sponsoring: Methodology to match event and sponsor. *Journal of Sport Management, 10*(3), 278-291.

Ferrand, A., & Pages, M. (1999). Image management in sport organizations: The creation of value. *European Journal of Marketing, 33*(4), 387-401.

Fiske, S. T. (1982). Schema-triggered affect: Applications to social perception. In Clark, M. S., & Fiske, S. T. (Eds.), *Affect and Cognition: The Seventeenth Annual Carnegie Symposium on Cognition* (pp. 55-78). Hllsdale, NJ: Lawrence Erlbaum Associates.

Fiske, S. T., & Pavelchak, M. A. (1986). Category-based versus piecemeal-based affective responses: Developments in schema-triggered affect. In Sorrentino, R. M., & Higgins, E. T. (Eds.), *Handbook of Motivation and Cognition* (pp. 167-203). New York: The Guilford Press.

Fornell, C., & Larcker, D. (1981). Evaluating structural equation models with unobservable variables and measurement error. *Journal of Marketing Research, 18,* 30-50.

Fox, J. (1991). *Regression diagnostics.* Thousand Oaks, CA: Sage Publications.

Gardner, M. P., & Schuman, P. J. (1987). Sponsorship: An important component of the promotion mix. *Journal of Advertising, 16*(1), 11-17.

Gilbert, D. (1988). Sponsorship strategy is adrift. *The Quarterly Review of Marketing, 14*(1), 6-9.

Gwinner, K. P. (1997). A model of image creation and image transfer in event sponsorship. *International Marketing Review, 14*(3), 145-158.

Gwinner, K. P., & Eaton, J. (1999). Building brand image through event sponsorship: The role of image transfer. *Journal of Advertising, 28*(4), 47-57.

Hair, J. H., Anderson, R. E., Tatham, R. L., & Black, W. C. (1995). *Multivariate data analysis,* (4th ed.) Upper Saddle River, NJ: Prentice Hall.

Hart, A. E., & Rosenberger, P. J. (2004). The effect of corporate image in the formation of customer loyalty: An Australian replication. *Australasian Marketing Journal, 12*(3), 88-97.

Hastie, R. (1980). Memory for information which confirms or contradicts a general impression. In Hasite, R. (Ed.), *Person memory: The cognitive basis of social perception,* Hillsdale, NJ: Lawrence Erlbaum Associates.

Johnson, M., & Zinkhan, G. M. (1990), Defining and measuring company image. *Proceedings of the thirteenth annual conference of the academy of marketing science* (pp. 346-350). New Orleans, LA.

Jonathan, L., Ashok, S., & Hong, S. W. (1998). Transference of skills between sports and business. *Journal of European Industrial Training, 22*(3), 93-112.

Kahle, L. R., & Homer, P. H. (1985). Physical attractiveness of the celebrity endorser: A social adaptation perspective. *Journal of Consumer Research, 11,* 954-961.

Kamins, M. A. (1990). Investigation into the match-up hypothesis in celebrity advertising: When beauty may be only skin deep. *Journal of Advertising, 19(1),* 4-13.

Keller, K. L. (1993). Conceptualizing, measuring, and managing customer-based brand equity. *Journal of Marketing, 59,* 1-22.

Keller, K. L. (1998). *Strategic brand management.* Upper Saddle River, NJ: Prentice Hall.

Kelloway, E. K. (1998). *Using LISREL for structural equation modeling.* SAGE publications. London, U.K.

Kinney, L., & McDaniel, S. R. (1996). Strategic implications of attitude-toward-the-ad in leveraging event sponsorships. *Journal of Sport Management, 10,* 250-261.

Koo, G. Y., & Cho, K. M. (1999). The comparative analysis of the Korean professional sports image. *Korean Journal of Sport Management, 4*(1), 185-205.

Lavidge, R. C., & Steiner, G. A. (1961). A model for predictive measurements of advertising effectiveness. *Journal of Marketing, 25,* 59-62.

Lichtenstein, D. R., Netemeyer, R. G., & Burton, S. (1990). Distinguishing coupon proneness from value conscious: An acquisition-transaction utility theory perspective. *Journal of Marketing, 54,* 54-67.

McDaniel, S. R., & Kinney, L. (1996). Ambush marketing revisited: An experimental study of perceived sponsorship effects on brand awareness, attitude toward the brand and purchase intention. *Journal of Promotion Management, 3,* 141-67.

McDaniel, S. R. (1999). An investigation of match-up effect in sport sponsorship advertising: The implications of consumer advertisings schemas. *Psychology & Marketing, 16*(2), 163-185.

McDonald, C. (1991). Sponsorship and the image of the sponsor. *European Journal of Marketing, 25*(11), 31-39.

Meyers-Levy, J., & Tybout, A. M. (1989). Schema congruity as a basis for product evaluation. *Journal of Consumer Research, 16,* 39-54.

Misra, S., & Beatty, S. E. (1990). Celebrity spokesperson and brand congruence: An assessment of recall and affect. *Journal of Business Research, 21*(2), 159-173.

Nunnally, J. C. (1978). *Psychometric theory* (2nd ed.). New York: McGraw-Hill.

Poiesz, T. B. C. (1989). The image concept: Its place in consumer psychology. *Journal of Economic Psychology, 10,* 457-472.

Pope, N. (1998). Consumption values, sponsorship, awareness, brand and product use. *Journal of Product & Brand Management, 7*(2), 124-136.

Quester, P. G. (1997). Awareness as a measure of sponsorship effectiveness: The Adelaide Formula One Grand Prix and evidence of incidental ambush effects. *Journal of Marketing Communications, 3,* 1-20.

Roy, D. P. (2000). *An examination of the influence of perceived brand-event congruence on consumer responses to event sponsorships.* Unpublished doctoral dissertation, University of Memphis.

Roy, D. P., & Cornwell, T. B. (2003). Brand equity's influence on responses to event sponsorships. *Journal of Product & Brand Management, 12*(6), 377-393.

Shanklin, W. L., & Kuzma, J. R. (1992). Buying that sporting image. *Marketing Management,* 59-67.

Sheth, J. N., Newman, B. I., & Gross, B. L. (1991). Why we buy what we buy: A theory of consumption values. *Journal of Business Research, 22,* 159-170.

Sirgy, M. J. (1985). Using self-congruence and ideal congruence to predict purchase motivation. *Journal of Business Research, 13,* 195-206.

Sirgy, M. J., Grewal, D., Mangleburg, T. F., Park, J., Chon, K., Claiborne, C. B., Johar, J. S., & Berkamn, H. (1997). Assessing the predictive validity of two methods of measuring self-image congruence. *Journal of the Academy of Marketing Science, 25*(3), 299-241.

Sport business daily (2003, March). College marketing notes. Retrieved from http://www.sportsbusinessdaily.com.

Speed, R., & Thompson, P. (2000). Determinants of sports sponsorship response. *Journal of the Academy of Marketing Science, 28,* 226-238.

Sport business associates (2004, October 1). The commercial value of sport sponsorship. Retrieved from http://www.sportbusinessassociates.com.

Srull, T. K. (1981). Person memory: Some tests of associative storage and retrieval models. *Journal of Experimental Psychology: Human Learning and Memory, 7,* 440-463.

Tate, R. (1998). *An introduction to modeling outcomes in the behavioral and social sciences,* (2nd ed.). Tallahassee, FL: Burgess Publishing.

Taylor, S. E., & Crocker, J. (1981). Schematic bases of social information processing in social cognition. *The Ontario Symposium on Personality and Social Psychology, 1,* 89-134.

SECTION VII.

Celebrity Athlete Endorsements

22

Celebrity Athletic Endorsement: An Overview of the Key Theoretical Issues

Christine M. Brooks and Kellee K. Harris

Introduction

In 1947 the *New York Times* devoted two pages commemorating the life, accomplishments, and personality of Babe Ruth. According to Susman (1984), Ruth was more than a baseball player. He was a cultural icon through whom a mechanized society reflected a rebellion against efforts to rationalize all aspects of man's activities. The middle class could delight in a personality who defied rationality. Ruth appealed to the intangible desires of those whom Henry Ford called "the common man" for whom Ford mass-produced cheap, mechanically efficient automobiles by cheap and mechanically efficient production methods in factories where statistics were proof of this mechanical efficiency. What Ford eventually discovered was that his common man wanted more than record-book cheapness and mechanical efficiency. People also wanted style (Susman, 1984), and Ruth resonated "style." He carried within his persona a web of meanings that filled the unfilled needs of certain segments of American society at that time.

Susman (1984) commented that Ruth was the ideal hero for this new era of American consumption:

> Ruth enjoyed spending money as well as earning it. An incorrigible gambler, and love for large sums, he never seemed concerned about winning or losing. He loved expensive and fancy clothes. His interest in sex seemed limitless. . . His gluttony became legendary. . . (p. 146)

Americans enjoyed Ruth's excess. Bill McGreehan, a sportswriter in the 1920s, referred to Ruth as "our national exaggeration" (quoted in Susman, p. 146).

Ruth was not the first sports hero, but he may have been the first to make sports celebrity status pay so well. Under the guidance of his agent, Christy Walsh, and with the added benefit of the insatiable appetite of the new breed of sportswriters for "good copy," Ruth converted his remarkable exploits as a baseball player, his persona or aura, and the images he represented in the minds of the American consumer, into one extremely successful marketable package. He endorsed products, appeared in movies, and organized live appearances so fans in dozens of small towns could see him in the flesh (Susman, 1984). The image, character, and style of Ruth, in conjunction with the ballyhoo of exaggerated promotion, is the archetype of the sports celebrity of today. These athletes represent more to society than their statistics. They contain a symbolic quality, an image or style, an aura of importance when being average is the norm. As was true in the Babe Ruth era, but perhaps even more so today, advertisers and the media perceive an economic value in these symbolic qualities. More frequently than ever, advertisers choose to use these larger-than-life sports heroes as spokespeople for their products or brands. Indeed, athletes have become a rather "hot" component of what is known as "celebrity endorsement" or "celebrity advertising."

It has also become a "hot" topic within the academic field of sports marketing. The first author of this paper has recently been asked to review three manuscripts encompassing celebrity endorsement as the general theme. As well, the projects and research papers handed in by her students during the past academic year have included at least one third that were, in some way, related to the newfound fame of athletes and their endorsement of products. This is up from only one or two during the previous year.

The common fault with all these efforts is that athlete endorsement is often discussed without any apparent theoretical understanding of the phenomenon. The papers frequently fall victim to a significant element of hype and contain little, if any, critical analysis of what the endorsement process is all about. Without doubt, it is interesting to know which athlete is the most popular, or who is the most recognized, or most trusted (Table 1). It is also quite an eye-opener to see the millions offered by companies to athletes for product endorsement purposes. Beyond interest value, there is very little elaboration about why this information is useful in an academic or practical sense. In this paper we will try to provide a conceptual framework in which we can place the athlete endorsement process. Throughout we will discuss the point of view of the practitioner and the associated critical research questions.

The Conceptual Framework

McCracken (1989) defines a celebrity endorser as "any individual who enjoys public recognition and who uses this recognition on behalf of a consumer good by appearing with it in an advertisement" (p. 310). Friedman and Friedman (1979) state that "a celebrity endorser is an individual who is known to the public (actor, sports figure, entertainer, etc.) for his or her achievements in areas other than that of the product class endorsed" (p. 63). Both these encompass the general definition of the celebrity athlete endorser for the purpose of this paper. That is, the celebrity athlete is well-known, and uses his or her fame to help a company sell or enhance the image of company, products, or brands.

A celebrity athlete can assume one or a combination of four product endorsement styles. McCracken (1989) has labeled these as (a) the explicit mode (I endorse this product), (b) the implicit mode (I use this product), (c) the imperative mode (you should use this product), and (d) the co-present mode (the athlete merely appears in some setting with the product). Within each mode the athlete may be positioned as a product expert and may or may not be presented as someone who has a strong, long-term association with the company. There are at least four key questions that concern us. First, under what condition is a celebrity athlete the most persuasive? Second, what type of celebrity athlete

Table 1.
The Top 10 Athlete Endorser Rankings

Most Appealing[1]	Most Recognized	Most Influential/ Trusted[2]	Most Controversial[2]	Highest Total Endorsements[3] ($)
Tiger Woods	O.J. Simpson	Michael Jordan	Dennis Rodman	Michael Jordan ($40 million)
Michael Jordan	Magic Johnson	Shaquille O'Neal	Michael Irvin	Tiger Woods ($25 million)
Grant Hill	Michael Jordan	Joe Montana	John Daly	Shaquille O'Neal ($23 million)
Dennis Rodman	Muhammed Ali	Tiger Woods	Darryl Strawberry	Arnold Palmer ($19.2 million)
Ken Griffey, Jr.	Mike Tyson	Cal Ripken, Jr.	Mike Tyson	Andre Agassi ($17 million)
Troy Aikman	Joe Montana	Troy Aikman	Jennifer Capriati	Jack Nicholaus ($16 million)
Scottie Pippen	Nancy Kerrigan	Steve Young	Albert Belle	Grant Hill ($7 million)[4]
George Foreman	Tonya Harding	Ken Griffey, Jr.	Pete Rose	Joe Montana ($12 million)
Bonnie Blair	Joe Namath	Dan Marino	Derrick Coleman	Ken Griffey, Jr. ($6 million)
Joe Montana	Hank Aaron	Wayne Gretzky	O.J. Simpson	Deon Sanders ($6 million)

1. Burns Sports Celebrity Services, April 1997
2. Sports Media Index, American Sports Data, February 1997
3. The ten most wanted spokesperson survey, Sports Marketing Newsletter, August 1997
4. According to Sports Marketing Newsletter, Grant Hill signed a new endorsement contract with Fila in October, 1997, worth at least $80 million over the next 7 years. This new deal would now place Hill significantly higher on the SMN survey list.

is the most persuasive? Third, how does a successful celebrity athlete endorsement work? Fourth, do celebrity athletes sell products?

These are not easy questions to answer. Some researchers theorize that celebrities, and by association, celebrity athletes, are useful because of the symbolic representations they have for certain consumer groups. Thus the celebrity endorsement advertising effect has been explained in terms of transferring cultural meaning (McCracken, 1989) from the celebrity to the product, a transfer that has its theoretical foundation in Oliver Wendell Holmes' (1863) notion of separating "form" from "structure." Others suggest that celebrity endorsers may be influential because they are viewed as highly dynamic and they have attractive and likable qualities (Atkin & Block, 1983), and besides that, their fame attracts attention to the product. Advertisers also often choose celebrity athletes based on "physical attractiveness" believing that they can add value to their products due to a potent mixture of physical attractiveness and status of the athlete (cf. Friedman & Friedman, 1979).

Within the sports industry, practitioners recognize that there are features of athletes that make some more effective endorsers than others. Brian Murphy, publisher of *The 10*

Most Wanted Spokespersons Survey, for example, asserts that besides athletic skill, athletes who want to endorse products must also have charisma and selling ability (personal communications). Similar statements were made about the qualities required of successful athlete endorsers back in the era of Babe Ruth. The difference between the 1920s and the 1990s, however, is that there are now efforts to quantify charisma and potential selling ability of a celebrity athlete.

Table 1, for example, presents a ranking of celebrity athletes that combines the data from several different sources that are attempting to provide some measure of selling ability. It is often quite confusing as to how to interpret these types of data. As Harvy Lauer, president of American Sports Data, has detected from ASD surveys, there often appears only a weak relationship between an athlete's name recognition and his credibility as an endorser (personal communications, Nov. 28th, 1997). Lauer used the example of retired '49ers quarterback Joe Montana, who was ranked sixth in ASD's Sports Media Index Study on athlete name recognition, but third among all athletes, retired or active, in ability to influence consumers. Montana was only surpassed by Michael Jordan and Shaquille O'Neal in this latter category. Although it might be debatable that there are any real statistical differences between the position Montana retains in each category of the ASD Media Index list, Lauer's point is reflective of the confusion that exists regarding how one should go about interpreting the data contained in these lists.

Part of the confusion can be attributed to lack of a theoretical understanding as to how the categories of athlete characteristics relate to product or brand marketing strategy. To fully understand the theoretical perspective of the celebrity endorsement process one must be cognizant of three interrelated content areas of knowledge. These are (a) an understanding of how and why society consumes images, (b) the concept of brand equity, and (c) the central theoretical characteristics of the endorsement process. The literature in the first two content areas is quite vast, and all we will try to do in this paper is to broadly capture the theoretical thinking of a selection of authors. The third content area has not earned quite the same attention and, according to McCracken (1989), has not inspired "especially illuminating theoretical accounts" (p. 310). He claims that present knowledge about celebrity endorsement is "modest and imperfect" and that many of the available models fail to capture the process in its entirety.

Consuming Images

It is not possible to fully comprehend the complex nature of athlete endorsement without some knowledge about the role "style" and images play in society. Style comes in many different forms and although it is hard for most consumers to define it, for most style is relatively easy to recognize. For some style means being elegant, or hip. For others it is a means of self-expression through which the individual tries to establish his or her own special niche in society. Ewen (1988) reports of a young man growing up in the South Bronx who spent much of his youth playing basketball and who illustrates this sense of self-expressive style:

> "I played the game from sun-up til sundown. It's never enough to just score the ball in the basket, or to simply block someone's shot. There's got to be style added to it. . . finesse, control, aggression. When a basketball is dunked in the basket, especially while an opponent is present, it says a statement and sense of style. "Get off of me, and take this!" is the clear message. To block an opponent's shot and send the

ball into another area of the park or gym is very threatening and shows style... When I grew up I wore basketball sneakers and Lee jeans. I wore my hair sometimes in braids or in waves, and I walked with a bop. It's a cultural statement that my friends and I identified with while growing up... It's the 'thing' to wear basketball sneakers in the ghetto." (p. 21)

According to Ewen (1988) this young man's sense of style was shaped by the choreography and competition of basketball. The act of playing basketball was then mediated by marketplace commodities to help him establish and express a cultural meaning. Advertisers understand that this sense of self-expressive style has a very dramatic influence on different consumer segments. For example, practitioners in the sports industry believe that the baby boomer and teen segments of the market have different perceptions of the type of athlete they admire. Baby boomers want athletes who follow the rules, show respect, and have "class." Corporate managers making endorsement decisions for this demographic group find the that older, more mature athletes with a proven record of performance are generally more acceptable to baby boomers (Roush, 1994).

When marketing to teens, on the other hand, many companies look for outrageous, in-your-face showmen who trash talk and head butt their way through the game. Their consumers are frequently attracted to the flamboyance of a Dennis Rodman, who has blatant disregard for traditional standards and mores—a hot button with the younger crowd. Sports industry "bad boys" such as Rodman may enrage older consumers, but they appeal to a teen crowd for defying the status quo (Stern, 1995).

The sense of what is style or class in sports for one group is perceived as being quite different from what these terms mean to the other. In each market segment, the perception of style is intertwined not only with the aspirations and yearnings of consumers in that segment, but also with their apprehensions and anxieties. It is perhaps the most complex consumption phenomenon to understand because it deals in a consumer's consumption and interpretations of illusions and images. The marketing activities designed to capture and sell these illusions and images, and their associated lacework of consumer interpretations, require successfully transporting them from one context (the athlete) and placing them onto another (the product) so that the consumer can then actively attach the desired image onto his or her own self. In 1932 Sheldon and Arens termed the process *consumer engineering.*

According to Ewen (1988), this "value added" notion of embellishing objects with intricate, powerful, and mysterious webs of interpretation has been practiced within cultures around the world for millennia. However, only the very wealthy could afford to consume these objects and their symbolic representation. Around the mid-1800s American marketers learned how to inexpensively reproduce images and style by what Oliver Wendell Holmes (1863) referred to as separating form from substance. According to Ewen (1988), architecture was perhaps the first to be effected by this separation. Prior to the 1830s, the form of the walls of a building were truly part of the structure of the building. Engineering for structure and style (or ornamentation) were combined into one work of art. After the 1830s, however, the linking of style and structure was severed when modern construction allowed an inner structural frame to be built that then permitted a "skin" or outer shell to be attached. It now became a relatively inexpensive process to mimic the style of almost any architecture around the world and transplant it any place within the world. Buildings could take on any style at a fraction of the cost of

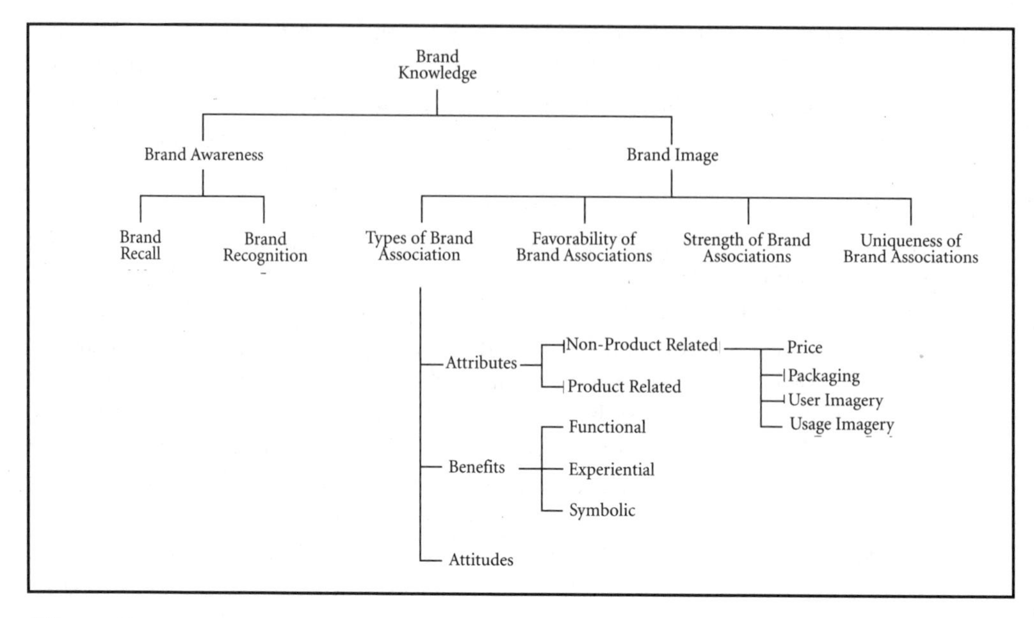

Figure 1.
Dimensions of Brand Knowledge

the handcrafted original: It could "look like the real thing" without "being the real thing."

This notion of separating form from structure so that the image of the original could be made widely available to the masses was embraced by American society and quickly became a seductive means of self-expression. By 1907 business was beginning to realize the powerful selling mechanism inherent in the form (style or image) once it was detached from the substance (Ewen, 1984). Psychoanalysts of the time—Freud, Jung, and Pavlov—provided business with the psychological understanding of how to reattach these detached images to their products so they would appeal to the unconscious urges and repressed senses of the masses. American marketers became so successful at doing this that by the 1930s Friedell (1954) commented there were no realities anymore. Consuming was all about living a life of images and illusions . He dubbed this form of consumerism *Americanism* (p. 301).

It is within this context of style and images—the world of the unreal where surfaces are stripped from their structure and converted into salable commodities—that we now turn our attention to the notion of brand equity.

Brand Equity

Brand equity is an inherent value a consumer attributes to a specific brand of product or service. It occurs when the consumer who is quite familiar with the brand "holds favorable, strong, and unique brand association in memory" (Keller, 1993, p. 2). Brand equity is generated from knowledge about the brand that has been created in consumers' minds as a result of previous marketing activities. Thus, understanding the dimensions of brand knowledge is important because these dimensions influence not only what comes to mind when a consumer thinks about a brand, but also the role the celebrity athlete can play in enhancing brand knowledge and thus brand equity.

Table 2.
Summary of Brand Knowledge Constructs[1]

Construct	Type of measurement(s)	Purpose of measurement	Brief Summary
Brand Awareness: Related to strength of memory trace that indicates ability to identify brand.			
1. Recall	Able to identify a specific brand within a product class when given some type of cue	Determine "top-of-mind" accessibility of brand in memory	Believed to relate to making decisions when choosing among brands. Raises likelihood that brand will be in the consideration set that will be considered for purchase. Also believed to influence strength of brand association
2. Recognition	Confirm exposure to the brand	Determine potential to recall brand from memory	
Brand Image: Perceptions about the brand as reflected by brand associations held in memory.			
(a) Characteristic of brand association			
1. Type	Free association, projective techniques, in depth interviews	Provide insight into nature of brand associations	See Figure 1. Requires an understanding of consumer knowledge about brand attributes, and benefits, and their attitudes towards the brand
2. Favorability	Ratings of evaluations of associations	Assess most important dimension giving the brand the competitive advantage	Believed to reflect the success of the marketing program.
3. Strength	Ratings of beliefs of associations	Assess most important dimension giving the brand the competitive advantage	Believed to depend upon how information is encoded in consumer memory and how it is stored. Also an important determinant of brand awareness
b) Relationship among brand associations:			
1. Uniqueness	• Compare characteristics of associations with those of competitors (indirect measure) • Ask consumers to state what is unique aspect of brand (direct measure)	Provide insight into how brand associations are unique to one brand	Believed to be affected by price, packaging, user imagery and usage imagery.
2. Congruence	• Compare patterns of associations across consumers (indirect measure) • Ask consumers conditional expectations about associations (direct measure)	Provide insight into the extent to which brand associations are shared, affecting their favorability, strength or uniqueness	Believed to affect ease of which existing associations can be recalled and how easily new associations can become linked to the brand in memory.
3. Leverage	• Compare characteristics of secondary associations with those for a primary brand association (indirect measure) • Ask consumers directly what inferences they would make about the brand based on the primary brand association (direct measure)	Provide insight into the extent to which brand associations to a particular person, place, event, company, product class, etc. are linked to other occasions	Secondary associations are believed to be created by linking product with another association (e.g., celebrity athlete).

1. Adapted from Keller, 1993, p. 14

Figure 1 presents Keller's (1993) dimensions of knowledge about the brand. There are two broad dimensions: brand awareness and brand image. *Brand awareness* is assessed by the ability of the consumer to recall the brand name and to recognize that he or she has some exposure to the brand at some point in time. *Brand image* refers to the associations the consumer has about the brand and the way these associations are stored in memory. Table 2 summarizes the types of measurements typically made, the purpose of each measurement, and a brief explanation as to why each measure is important to marketing a product or brand. There has been considerable research in each of these areas, and the reader is referred to Keller (1993) for an overview. What we will do here is try to explain how the celebrity endorser fits within the notion of enhancing brand equity process and to provide an overview of the research that is available in this area.

Dimensions of Brand Knowledge

The combination of awareness and image about a product or brand leads to knowledge about the brand that is stored in consumer memory. Brand recall and recognition are believed to indicate the level of brand awareness. The types of associations (attitudes, benefits, and product attributes), degree of favorability towards the brand, strength with which the brand is entrenched in consumer memory, and the unique qualities of the brand compared with competitive products are all believed to impact the image a consumer will have about a brand. A celebrity athlete can be used to influence one of, or a combination of all, these dimensions of brand knowledge.[1] Advertisers believe that messages delivered by well-known personalities draw attention to the advertisement and therefore such messages enhance recall for some consumers (Ohanian, 1990). However, the athlete may draw attention to the advertisement, but this may not result in consumer purchase. There are three models that attempt to explain the conditions under which the consumer might be persuaded to purchase the product. The first model is known as *the cultural meaning model* (McCracken, 1986, 1989), the second as *the source attractiveness model* (McGuire, 1985), and the third as *the source credibility model* (Hovland & Weiss, 1951). In its own way, each model contributes a unique understanding as to how an athlete potentially enhances brand awareness and brand image and thus brand equity.

The Cultural Meaning Model

To fully understand the cultural meaning model, we need to go back to the previous discussion of images. Benjamin (1985) observed that there were two effects that resulted from mass-producing original objects for the purpose of selling off their images. One effect is that objects lose their aura whereas the other is that objects gain an aura. When a work of art, a Picasso, for instance, is reproduced for mass consumption, it loses significant value. The original Picasso has a unique presence in time and space. There is an authenticity about what the art represents. It contains a notion of culture. Benjamin calls the special value inherent in the original its aura and by making the work available to the mass market this aura is liquidated or vaporized. The mass-produced copy is never as valuable as the original and never can be. It is possible that this has implications for sport sponsoring, where companies are attempting to transfer a sport's image onto their own company and products.

The celebrity, though, gains an aura through mass reproduction. Mass production in this case means exposure on television, in the media, and so on, whereby the image of the celebrity is made widely available. The difference, according to Benjamin (1985), relates to the symbolism involved. By mass-producing a work of art so it can be consumed by those who cannot afford the original, the mass-production process allows the artwork to be downwardly mobile. The celebrity, on the other hand, is often symbolic of the upwardly mobile. The symbolism of fame and fortune connects with consumers. Even if they never "make it" as athletes, consumers have access to the fantasy, the dream, or the identity with someone similar to them who has risen above common people. The press, agents, and image managers play a role in the mass-production process, but the phenomenon of the celebrity athlete is one of the ongoing message that anyone can achieve status in society through sports — particularly professional sports. Ewen (1988) claims that within celebrities "people not only find a piece of themselves, but also a piece of what they strive for." (p. 96). Hollywood was once the only significant accessible avenue, now sports opens up another path to the riches of American society. Stories of hard work, devotion to the game, and lucky breaks feed into consumer belief that the playground basketball player, and other aspiring professional athletes in high schools, colleges and club programs around the country can also "make it."

Besides the fantasy component, McCracken's (1989) research suggests that the athlete plays another role. His argument suggests that celebrity athletes can transfer meanings to consumer goods. However, celebrity athletes are only useful in so far as they consist of certain meanings that the consumer finds compelling and useful. The endorsement of a product by an athlete succeeds only when there is a successful transfer of meaning. The theoretical perspective of the process suggests that meanings begin as something resident in the culturally constituted world (McCracken, 1986) where the original symbolic meaning resides. This is the world as the consumer experiences and interprets it. Culture acts as the lens by which a consumer views the world, and culture determines how symbolic properties of an athlete will be captured and assimilated by consumers. Culture also acts as a blueprint that guides behavior. It provides consumers with a cultural category (e.g., age, sex, status, class) and provides them with cultural principles (methods by which to organize and evaluate cultural phenomena). In other words, culture constitutes the world by giving it meaning for the consumer.

In order for a meaning to move from the culturally constituted world to a consumer good, there must be a separation of the meaning from the original location so it can be transferred to the consumer good. According to McCracken (1986), this is accomplished by (a) advertising and (b) product design. Advertising serves two general purposes. First, it brings the consumer good and a representation of the culturally constituted world together. Second, it keeps the consumer informed about the present state and stock of cultural meanings that exist in consumer goods. In essence, advertising serves as an instrument of meaning transfer, and one role a celebrity athlete is believed to play here is to bring attention to the advertisement so this transfer can take place.

Product design transfers meaning in a more complex manner because the process has more sources of meaning, and agents of transfer (McCracken, 1986). In one respect, product design transfers meanings in a similar method as advertising by simply associating the product with meanings established in the culturally constituted world. Product design can also invent new styles by using opinion leaders who help shape and refine existing cultural meaning and encourage reform of cultural categories. The fashion system is an excellent example of this. Opinion leaders in the fashion industry are sources of meaning for consumers by prompting imitation. In another capacity, the fashion system can radically reform cultural meanings. Celebrity athletes may play a role as opinion leaders and thus prompt imitation of behavior, style, dress, etc., although to our knowledge, no research has been done in this area.

Once meaning has been moved to the consumer good, it then must move to the consumer. The movement of meanings from consumer goods to the individual consumer requires the specific efforts of the consumer. Consumers must take possession of these meanings and construct a new self (McCracken, 1989). Dressing like the athlete, wearing the same brand of shoes, using the same products, and mimicking the athlete's behavior are all examples of how consumers could take possession of the meaning of an athlete.

It is precisely because of the complexities described above that we see conflicting explanations as to why some companies find certain athletes a nightmare whereas others find them a dream. Sprite, for example, found Philadelphia 76er Alan Iverson's arrest on a gun charge to be an embarrassment, but he continues to be a marquee athlete for Reebok International. According to Dave Fogelson, PR Director for Reebok, "We have a big problem with what happened this summer to Alan, and we don't want people to think we condone his actions. However, when you're in the sports business everyday like we are, you must learn to ride these things out" (quoted in Benerza, 1997, p. 5). According to Bob Williams of Burns Sports, if athletes are dropped it is generally because a company does not want to appear as supporting someone with such negative publicity (Benerza). Out of fear of generating their own negative publicity by appearing not to stick by the athletes, some companies will appear to support the athletes by helping them overcome whatever problems befall them. Williams also comments that some corporations enjoy the attention the negative publicity may bring (Benerza). In essence, any awareness is good awareness.

The embracing of NBA "Bad Boy" image of Dennis Rodman can be particularly perplexing to some. Rodman, an endorser for Converse, has appeared on the cover of *Sports Illustrated* decked out in sequins and nine shades of eye makeup and has appeared with actor Jean Claude van Damm tearing up the movie screen. Despite his on- and off-court antics and ever-changing hair color, Rodman continues to draw a following for Converse's target audience: 12- to 18-year-olds. Converse has found Rodman a strong voice outside the United States. In fact, according to Jim Solomon, Executive Vice President of Marketing for Converse, Rodman was part of their international sales strategy in the Far East and Europe (Stern, 1995). According to Solomon, Rodman is huge in these markets: "Dennis does what kids admire: he speaks his mind, stays true to himself, doesn't care what others think, isn't artificial, and doesn't suck up. We adults may classify him as a rebel, but I don't think out of 1,000 kids, you'd ever hear one of them call him that" (quoted in Stern, 1995, p. 74). An interesting sidenote: Although controversial male athletes can attract a following, female athletes with a similar track record fare badly on all counts.

Despite the apparent embrace of the bad boy image by some companies, there is a preference for the nice guy. Tiger Woods and Michael Jordan are two examples. The Burns Sports Celebrity Survey (1997) indicates that Woods has firmly established himself as one of the top sports celebrity endorsers today. It is unclear as to what will happen if Woods has a mediocre career. The media may lose interest and exposure in the media is a crucial element to the perceived endorsement value of athletes. This phenomenon has been noticed before when Mark Spitz, winner of seven Olympic Gold medals in 1976, virtually disappeared from public consciousness almost immediately after the closing ceremony. Schick had hired Spitz to endorse their razors and were forced to abandon the campaign (Kaikati, 1987). Woods appears to have more cultural meaning than Spitz, that may result in Woods having more multidimensional endorsement capacity. As well, there may be other factors, such as credibility and likability, that impact the endorsement value of some athletes. We move now to a discussion of the phenomenon of credibility and attractiveness.

The Source Attractiveness Model and the Source Credibility Model

The source attractiveness model has its theoretical foundations in social psychology and asserts that the source of the information must be familiar, likable, and/or similar to the consumer for it to be effective (McGuire, 1985). Exposure of the athlete through the media provides the familiarity component, likability depends upon physical attractiveness and behavior, and similarity requires that the consumer identify with the athlete in some manner. Thus, if we were to select an athlete to endorse a product, we would choose one who had wide exposure, one who was similar to the target market, and one whom the target market found attractive. According to McGuire's model, this athlete would be a persuasive endorser for the product or brands.

On the other hand, a marketing and advertising practitioner may choose to use a celebrity athlete spokesperson on the assumption that if consumers believe the athlete has some expert knowledge about the product, and if consumers believe they can trust this athlete to not lead them astray, then they will be influenced to purchase the product. This thinking is referred to as the source credibility model, that has its foundations in the work of Hovland and Weiss (1951) within the field of social psychology. There are numerous attempts in the literature to examine how a credible spokesperson enhances the persuasiveness of a message.

There have also been efforts to determine the perceptual structure of source credibility and attractiveness. Several different scales have been developed (see Ohanian, 1990, for a summary of these attempts). According to Ohanian, trustworthiness appears to be one important dimension of credibility. Expertise is a second dimension that has empirical support. In attempting to develop reliable scales for these two dimensions of credibility, Ohanian developed a tri-component measure of credibility that included trustworthiness, expertise, and attractiveness.

The notion of the persuasive powers of an expert source, that is, a highly skilled athlete, has been one important reason for hiring athletes to endorse products in the sporting goods industry. When Wilson Sporting Goods pays top tennis players to use their brand of tennis racket, this company is buying into the notion that being the best implies being very knowledgeable about equipment. It also implies that consumers believe professional athletes of this caliber would not use the equipment unless it was of top quality. Unfortunately for Wilson, consumers are often skeptical about the fact that the athlete is being paid to use the product. One way around this problem has been to develop a long-term relationship with the athlete to show the consumer the endorsement is more about good quality equipment than about money.

Both the source attractiveness and source credibility models have been validated to some degree in the literature, and each provides an intuitively appealing reason why an athlete should be an effective endorser. There are also ample examples in the literature, however, where neither model adequately explains why some celebrity endorsements fail to sell products. McCracken (1989) claims that the source credibility and source attractiveness models place too much weight on the qualities of the celebrity and not enough on qualities of the product and cultural context. Others simply refer to these failures as a lack of match or congruence between product and celebrity (Friedman & Friedman, 1979; Kahle & Homer, 1985). Neither the source attractiveness nor the source credibility model takes the cultural context, or the apparent requirement of a congruence between source, product, and consumer into account. In essence, these authors suggest that a physically attractive celebrity football player who also played tennis would be an irrelevant endorser of tennis rackets if the consumer did not see the link between this athlete and tennis rackets. In this case the celebrity athlete's physical attractiveness would have nothing to do with tennis rackets. Thus, effectiveness of the endorsement would probably be minimal.

Kahle and Homer (1985) contend that the significance of "match-up" can be understood in terms of social adaptation theory. An attractive athlete may serve as an effective source of information for a product that is attractiveness related (e.g., razors, facial cream, shampoo). The consumer may believe that the product will enhance his or her physical attractiveness just as it did for the athlete. However, in the case of the football player endorsing tennis rackets, consumers must perceive that playing tennis will make them physically attractive before the message could be a useful tool for facilitating adaptation. It would be much better in this case to use a tennis player who is perhaps a credible source.

The significance of the match-up effect has also been explained from the perspective of attribution theory (Folkes, 1988). Attribution theory attempts to explain the process through which consumers infer the causes of behavior from observation of, in our case, the athlete's behavior. Miller and Basehart's (1969) research on the role attractiveness plays here has some interesting implications for athlete endorsement. According to Miller and Basehart (1969) attractive people are perceived to control their own fate and thus behave in ways that are out of their own choice. Unattractive individuals, on the other hand, were more likely to be seen as coerced, influenced by others, and more likely to be buffeted about by conditions in the environment. This research makes one wonder whether the highly developed physical skill of a professional athlete acts similarly to attractiveness in that consumers may believe that such athletes are complete masters of their own fate. Thus, a consumer may believe that endorsed sports products contribute to the celebrity athlete's level of skill because these athletes would not choose equipment that would cause them to lose. In all this, however, one cannot forget McCracken's (1986) culturally constituted world and the role played by attaching images to a commercial product.

Back to Brand Equity

After this admittedly cursory review of the key components of the literature relating to how celebrity athlete endorsement may work, let us return now to brand equity. As we are exposed to athletes who are endorsing products we are now able to discern what the company is trying to accomplish. For example, basketball player Grant Hill has his own Web site (www.granthill.com). Recently a Shoot the Net Sweepstakes contest originated from Hill's page requiring participants to search Web sites such as Wilson and Fila for answers to weekly questions. During the course of the Shoot the Net Sweepstakes, daily traffic at Hill's site increased from approximately 8,000 hits per day in late October to a peak of 42,000 per day in December and January. This represents a novel strategy by companies who have paid Hill to be spokesperson for their products to expose their products to consumers. The celebrity status of Hill is being used as a hook to draw his fans to the company's advertisements on the Internet. Table 2 shows brand awareness as one of the key dimensions to building brand equity. It is believed to be related to making decisions when choosing among brands. It also raises the likelihood that the brand will be among those considered when the consumer is faced with a purchase decision. Awareness is also believed to effect the strength of the brand association in memory. To fully understand the reason why strength of association is important to awareness, and thus to brand equity, one must know a little bit about memory structure.

One of the most widely recited conceptualizations of memory structure is the associative network memory model (see Wyer & Srull, 1989, for a complete description). Under this theory of memory structure, knowledge is viewed as a series of nodes of stored information that are linked together by paths. The formation of brand image requires that a brand node of knowledge about the brand be established in memory. The more links there are to this node the stronger the brand image is said to be. These links to this brand image node may, however, vary in potency. Weak links do not activate other nodes very easily, and thus it may not be possible for the consumer to retrieve information about the brand. The way in which this brand node has been stored and the way in which this node is linked to other nodes of information affect the ease by which the consumer recalls information about that brand. By using Hill's Internet site as a physical link to the advertisement, the assumption is that consumers will link Hill, and all his accompanying symbols, to the product. Upon seeing Hill's image in the store or on a package, the content of information stored in the brand node of the consumer's memory will be stirred, and the consumer will be drawn to the company's brand.

The "superbranding" concept of Michael Jordan is being used for similar reasons. By definition, a superbrand athlete limits his endorsement deals to a handful of companies and tries to synergize all parties to work together on mutually beneficial programs (Chandler, 1997). The concept was first tested during Jordan's 1996 movie, *Space Jam.* Every Jordan sponsor received a mention in the movie. The apparent theoretical notion here is that by tying Jordan and the products of three or four products together, there will be more ways in which a consumer will be stimulated to recall a specific brand of product. Does it work? We do not know because the data, if there are any, have not been published.

Other uses of athletes in endorsement situations can generally be understood in terms of belief of the advertiser in the source attractiveness model or the source credibility model. Other, perhaps more sophisticated, endorsement situations encompass setting the complex notion of a cultural meaning transfer into motion.

Important Research Questions

Researchers and practitioners clearly have much work to do to bring a sense of order to the understanding of celebrity athlete endorsement. Every aspect of Table 2 requires research attention. There is only a scattering of scholarly research specifically investigating the athlete as endorsers (e.g., Martin, 1996) or on the impact athletes and athletic excellence have on children and adolescents (e.g., Watkins & Montgomery, 1989). We require much more than mere demographic descriptive studies. We require insightful, in-depth, critical analyses of the *way* athletes effect consumers, *how* athletes affect consumers and *under what condition* this impact is positive and under what condition this impact is negative. Exactly how does the athlete endorser impact brand equity?

According to Kaikati (1987), the effectiveness of celebrities in advertising during the 1980s was less positive than before this era. Post-1980s consumers did not find celebrities very believable or trustworthy, and there was a high degree of skepticism about their motivations for endorsing the product. The sports industry is apparently finding similar problems with athlete endorsers today. The newly derived cultural category of Generation Xers has a disdain for anyone pitching products. These consumers see 'talking heads" as a commercial sell-out and reject any form of obvious commercialism. For this market of consumers, the best advertising is no advertising (Smith, 1995). What is their perception of athletes who endorse products?

From the practitioner's perspective, it seems that it would be essential to understand when and how certain uses of athletes can set self-destroying processes into action so that the entire value of the athlete endorser to a company collapses. Indeed, this should also be of concern to the researcher as well. Self-destroying processes, once set in motion, could adversely effect the entire structure of sport, not just the income potential of the celebrity athlete.

The final significant research area that requires exploration relates to the distinction between celebrity and hero. In reviewing the literature in this area Chalip (1997) argues that there is a difference and that the two conditions of athlete status are frequently interchanged. Celebrity athletes gain their status because they are well-known. Athletes become heroes, on the other hand, when they move beyond celebrity status and represent gallant quests that connect in some meaningful way with segments of consumers. Does a hero have more cultural meaning than a celebrity? If so, is the endorsement process more effective when the advertising agency uses heroes instead of celebrities?

Clearly, we need a great deal of research on all these issues.

References

Atkin, C., & Block, M. (1983, February/March). Effectiveness of celebrity endorsers. *Journal of Advertising Research, 23*, 57–61.

Benerza, K. (1997, December 9). Visa nets hockey deal; Sprite axes Iverson. *Brandweek, 38*, 5.

Benjamin, W. (1985). *Illuminations*, . New York: Schocken Books

Burns, Celebrity Sports Index (1997). *Most appealing sports endorser survey.* Retrieved from http://www.burns sports.com.

Chalip, L. (1997). Celebrity or hero? Toward a conceptual framework for athlete promotion. In D. Shilbury & L. Chalip (Eds.), *Advancing the management of Australian and New Zealand sport* (pp. 42–56). Melbourne: Sport Management Association of Australia and New Zealand.

Chandler, S. (1997, April 7). Michael Jordan's full corporate press. *Business Week, 3433*, 44.

Ewen, S. (1988). *All consuming images: the politics of style in contemporary culture.* United States: Basic Books.

Folkes, V. (1988, March). Recent attribution research in consumer behavior: A review and new dimensions. *Journal of Consumer Research, 14*, 548–565.

Friedell, E. (1954). *A cultural history of the modern age: The crisis of the European soul from the black death to the world war.* 3: 300–301. New York: Starmount Press

Friedman, H., & Friedman, L. (1979). Endorser effectiveness by product type. *Journal of Advertising Research, 19*(5), 63–71.

Holmes, O.W. (1863). Doings of the sunbeam. In B. Newhall (Ed.), *Photography: Essays and images* (pp. 25–50). New York: Museum of Modern Art

Hovland, C., & Weiss, W. (1951, Winter). The influence of source credibility on communication effectiveness. *Public Opinion Quarterly, 15*, 635–650.

Kahle, L., & Homer, P. (1985, March). Physical attractiveness of the celebrity endorser: A social adaptation perspective. *Journal of Consumer Research, 11*, 954–961.

Kaikati, J. (1987). Celebrity advertising: Review and synthesis. *International Journal of Advertising, 6*, 93–105.

Keller, K. (1993, January). Conceptualizing, measuring, and managing customer-based brand equity. *Journal of Marketing, 57*, 1–22.

Martin, J. (1996). Is the athlete's sport important when picking an athlete to endorse a nonsport product. *Journal of Consumer Marketing, 13*(6), 28–43.

McCracken, G. (1986, June). Culture and consumption: A theoretical account of the structure and movement of the cultural meaning of consumer goods. *Journal of Consumer Research, 13*, 71–84.

McCracken, G. (1989, December). Who is the celebrity endorser? Cultural foundations of the endorsement process. *Journal of Consumer Research, 19*, 310–321.

McGuire, J. (1985). Attitudes and attitude change. In G. Lindsey & E. Aronson (Eds.), *Handbook of Social Psychology* (pp. 233–346). New York: Random House.

Miller, G., & Basehart, J. (1969, March). Source trustworthiness, opinionated statements, and response to persuasive communication. *Speech Monographs, 36*, 1–7.

Murphy, B. (1997). *The ten most wanted spokesperson survey.* Westport, CT: Author

Ohanian, R. (1990). Construction of a scale to measure celebrity endorsers' perceived expertise, trustworthiness, and attractiveness. *Journal of Advertising, 19*(3), 39–52.

Roush, C. (1994, November 21). Big George and the over the hill gang. *Business Week, 3415*, 70.

Sheldon, R., & Arens, E. (1932). *Consumer engineering: A new technique for prosperity.* New York: Arno Press (reprinted in 1976).

Smith, G. (1995, March 13). Sneakers that jump into the past. *Business Week, 3415*, 71.

Stern, W. (1995). Rebel with a cache. *Business Week, 3433*, 74.

Susman, W. (1984). *Culture as history.* New York: Pantheon Books.

Watkins, B., & Montgomery, A. (1989). Conceptions of athletic excellence among children and adolescents. *Child Development, 60*(6), 1362–72.

Wyer, R., & Srull, T. (1989). Person memory and judgment. *Psychological Review, 96*(1), 58–83.

23

Athletes as Product Endorsers:
The Effect of Gender and Product Relatedness

Thomas C. Boyd and Matthew D. Shank

Introduction

Celebrity endorsers have long been used as the source of marketing messages to promote a wide variety of products and services. Celebrity images are featured in print, radio, and approximately 20% of all television commercials (Lane and Spiegel, 1996). The celebrities used as promotional tools come from a variety of areas including television, movies, music, corporate America, politics, and of course, athletics. Companies are spending huge sums of money to have athletes such as Michael Jordan ($30 million/year), Tiger Woods ($70 million/year) and Lance Armstrong ($16.5 million/year) endorse both sports and nonsports products (Isidore, 2003). Popular wisdom says that these athletes in particular can command huge sums to endorse products because of their universal popularity and clean images. The fame and popularity of these athletes make them popular as endorsers but little has been done to help us understand whether they are truly effective, or the circumstances under which effectiveness is increased.

U.S. companies paid $897 million to athletes, coaches, and sports personalities in 2001 (Sports Business Journal, 2002) to endorse their goods and services. In addition to the fees for signing these athletes, companies spend another $10 billion to promote their association with them. One study found that sports figures were used as endorsers in 98 of the 872 (11.9%) television commercials analyzed (Turner, Bounds, Hauser, Motsinger, Ozmore & Smith, 1995). Interestingly, only 3% of the advertisements used female athletes as endorsers. Although only a small percentage of the television commercials analyzed used female athletes, this number should continue to grow as women's sports become increasingly popular around the globe (Miller, 1997).

Based on the above studies, it seems that athletes remain a popular choice for advertisers of both sports and nonsports products. Dyson and Turco (1997) discuss a number of reasons for using celebrities as endorsers. First, research has shown that customers will have more positive brand attitudes toward products that are endorsed by celebrities (Petty, Cacioppo & Schuman, 1983) and are more likely to choose those products

(Agrawal & Kamakura, 1995). Second, celebrities gain and hold consumers' attention (Atkin & Block, 1983). Third, celebrities can provide expert testimonials for products that helped contribute to their success. This is especially true for sports celebrities who endorse products used in their competition. Wayne Gretzky endorsing hockey equipment or Rebecca Lobo endorsing basketball equipment are excellent examples of the powerful "match-up" that can be created between athlete endorsers and sports products. However, it has also been shown that in the presence of negative information about the celebrity, the endorser may have negative effects on attitudes toward the brand (Till & Shimp, 1998).

Although billions of dollars are spent using athletes as pitchmen for a host of products, little is known about choosing athletes as endorsers. Relatively few studies have explored the factors that influence the effectiveness of *athlete* endorsers. Moreover, even less is known about the use of female athletes as endorsers. The studies that have been conducted on the effectiveness of celebrity endorsers are grounded in understanding the characteristics of the source (DeSarbo & Harshman, 1985; Haley, 1996; Ohanian, 1990) and the match-up between source and product (Kahle & Homer, 1985; Kamins, 1990).

The purpose of the present study is to explore how the gender of the athlete endorser and type of product that they are endorsing (sport-related versus nonsport related) is related to respondents' perceptions of source expertise, trustworthiness and attractiveness.

Background

A number of theoretical approaches have been used to study the questions of how celebrity endorsers work. They include *attribution theory* (Mowen & Brown, 1981), the *elaboration likelihood model* (Petty, Cacioppo & Schuman, 1983), *adaptation theory* (Kahle & Homer, 1985), *transfer of cultural meaning* (McCraken, 1989), *source characteristics and credibility* (Ohanion, 1990), and *associative learning* (Till, 2001; Till & Busler, 2000; Till & Shimp, 1998). In this research, we are interested in the ways in which matches between source and consumer characteristics influence perceptions of the source as a model, making research on source characteristics and credibility the most appropriate to apply here.

Source Characteristics

Most research on celebrity endorsers has explored the characteristics of the source that affect the effectiveness of the message. Most notably, the *credibility of the source* has been linked with the persuasiveness of the message. In other words, the more credible the source, the greater the persuasiveness of the message on the target audience. As Haley (1996) points out, "[M]uch support has been found for the main effect of source credibility. That is, different perceptions of source credibility differentially affect message evaluation, attitude change, behavioral intentions and behavioral compliance."

While source credibility has been described as a multidimensional construct, there is no consensus on what factors compose source credibility. Ohanian (1990) provides an excellent review of source credibility scales and the dimensions measured. *Source expertise* and *trustworthiness* have been identified as the two most critical dimensions of credibility by a number of researchers (DeSarbo & Harshman, 1985; Appelbaum & Anarol, 1972; Hovland, Janis & Kelley, 1953). Additional dimensions such as *charisma* (attractiveness and enthusiasm), *objectivity*, and *dynamism* have also been used to describe source credibility.

Ohanian (1990) has conceptualized source credibility as having three distinct dimensions: *expertise*, *trustworthiness*, and *attractiveness*. It is important to note that (and as stated by Ohanian) research suggests that the three dimensions of source credibility can make independent contributions to the effectiveness of the source (Weiner & Mowen, 1985). For example, Dennis Rodman may be seen as an expert source of information about basketball shoes, but not very trustworthy. And his attractiveness is most certainly in the eye of the beholder.

Source expertise refers to the "extent to which a communicator is perceived to be a source of valid assertions" (Hovland, Janis & Kelley, 1953). Research has shown that a source's perceived expertise has a positive impact on attitude change and that topic specific expertise is important (i.e., athletes endorsing sport-related products). Moreover, expertise of the source is the one dimension of credibility that has been linked with intention to purchase products (Ohanian, 1991). For example, it is easy for a consumer to perceive Tiger Woods' expertise about Nike golf balls, but his expertise about automobiles may be doubted.

Source trustworthiness refers to the consumer's confidence in the source for providing information in an objective and honest manner (Ohanian, 1991). In her review of the literature, Ohanian (1990) stated that "trustworthiness of the celebrity is an important construct in persuasion and attitude-change research." However, she found in a later study (Ohanian, 1991) that trustworthiness did not have a significant impact on purchase intentions across four celebrities endorsing four products (one of which was John McEnroe endorsing tennis racquets).

Source attractiveness is a more difficult characteristic to conceptualize. Most researchers describe attractiveness in terms of physical appearance and facial attractiveness (Patzer, 1983). Other researchers believe that attractiveness is a more multidimensional construct. For instance, attractiveness may be described in terms of the perceived similarity of the source to the receiver of the message, familiarity, and whether the source is likeable or admired (Triandis, 1971). Regardless of how attractiveness is defined, studies have shown that attractive sources are able to enhance the target audience's perception of the ad (Baker & Churchill, 1977) and increase purchase intentions (Petroshius & Crocker, 1989) and purchase behavior (Caballero & Pride, 1984).

In addition to the dimensions of credibility, another source characteristic of importance to advertisers is the gender of the endorser. Gender has not received much attention in advertising research (especially in the context of athlete endorsers), although a few studies have examined gender of the endorser as it relates to attitude towards the ad (e.g., Baker & Churchill, 1977; Debevec & Iyer, 1986; Kahle & Homer, 1985; Kamins, 1990) and product images (e.g., Allison, Golden, Mullet & Coogan, 1980; Alreck, Settle & Belch, 1982). Baker & Churchill (1977) found that respondents judging the affective dimensions of ads, rated ads with endorsers of the opposite gender higher than advertisements using endorsers of the same gender. Langmeyer (1991) also found that respondents tend to rate models of the opposite sex more favorably on a number of items (e.g., sexier, nicer) than they rate endorsers of the same sex. In another study, Ohanian (1991) found a respondent's gender had no significant influence on purchase intentions or on ratings of celebritys' attractiveness, trustworthiness, or expertise.

Match-up Hypothesis

Related to all three dimensions of credibility is the notion that a good fit between endorser characteristics and the type of product being endorsed is beneficial (Kahle & Homer, 1985; Kamins, 1990). Kamins (1990) suggests that in an effective advertisement, the message conveyed by the image or characteristics of the celebrity and the image or characteristics of the product converge, thereby achieving a balance between celebrity and product. This suggests that the message is more effective when there is a match-up or congruence between the qualities of the endorser and the product being endorsed. In fact, the match-up hypothesis states the greater congruence between the image of the endorser and the image of the product being promoted, the more effective the message. This may also depend upon how we measure effectiveness (e.g., increased sales, improved attitude toward the ad or toward the brand).

Support for the match-up hypothesis is mixed. In two studies using a fictitious athlete endorser Till & Shimp (1998) found positive main effects for endorser attractiveness but no match-up interaction between endorser attractiveness and products that enhance attractiveness. Kamins (1990) only found support of the match-up hypothesis on two of seven measures of effectiveness, and not for the critical measures of brand attitude and purchase intentions.

Research suggests that expertise may be more important than attractiveness in influencing brand attitudes under match-up conditions. In a second study, Till & Busler (1990) found that there is an interaction effect between the endorser and product for perceived expertise. Specifically, they found that for an athlete endorsing an energy bar (match-up condition) brand attitudes were higher and the endorser was rated higher on expertise than in conditions of an actor endorsing an energy bar or on either person endorsing a candy bar.

Naturally, athletes are perceived to have high levels of expertise when endorsing sports-related products. In addition, athletes may be perceived to be attractive endorsers, if the definition of attractiveness is based on physical appearance and body shape. As such, any body enhancing or beauty-related products may represent good 'matches' for athletes. Unfortunately, the trustworthiness of many professional athletes is perceived to be questionable (e.g., Kobe Bryant), therefore a congruent match may be more difficult on this dimension.

Beyond the match-up between endorser and product is another equally important linkage between the target audience and the endorser. Mowen, Brown, and Schulman (1979) use balance theory (Heider, 1958) to describe the relationships that exist among target audience (i.e., the consumer) and endorser, product and endorser, and consumer and product. As Mowen, Brown, and Schulman (1979) state, "an endorser will be maximally effective when both a strong sentiment (affective) relationship exists between the consumer and the endorser, and a strong unit relationship exists between the endorser and the product." Because of this relationship between each of the elements in the triad, advertisers must carefully consider an endorser who 'fits' both the product and the target audience.

Research Questions

We now examine how the fit between the athlete endorser, the product, and the consumer influence consumers' perceptions of the important source characteristics. The source characteristics being measured have previously been shown to improve ad effectiveness. Thus, understanding how to enhance consumers' perceptions of source characteristics should lead to improved ad effectiveness. Based on the previously discussed literature on source characteristics (including expertise, trustworthiness, attractiveness and gender) and the match-up hypothesis, the following research questions have been formulated.

It is important to note the questions are meant to reflect issues of particular interest to practitioners who must make difficult decisions about selection of athletes as endorsers of products. From a practitioner perspective, the broad research question is as follows: "Given a particular product, target audience and advertising objective, how can I choose the most effective athlete endorser?" More specific research questions include

RQ1: Will athletes be seen as more attractive, more trustworthy and as having more expertise when endorsing a sports product versus nonsports product?

RQ2: Will respondents' gender have any impact on the evaluation of the athlete's attractiveness, trustworthiness, and expertise?

RQ3: Will the gender of the athlete endorser influence the target audience's evaluation of the endorser's perceived attractiveness, trustworthiness, and expertise?

RQ4: Will the gender of the consumer influence evaluations of the endorser's perceived attractiveness, trustworthiness, and expertise differently for sport versus nonsport products?

RQ5: Will the effects of gender matching between the consumer and athlete endorser impact consumers' evaluations of the athlete endorser's perceived attractiveness, trustworthiness, and expertise?

RQ6: Will the effect of gender matching between consumers and athlete endorsers show different patterns in the rating of perceived endorser attractiveness, trustworthiness, and expertise for sport versus nonsport products?

Method

Subjects

Participants were undergraduate marketing majors at a midwestern university. Gender was evenly split. Participation was voluntary and students received no credit for taking part. A total of 309 usable responses were received. Of particular interest to sport marketers is the question of whether or not the use of celebrity endorsers should be limited to sport enthusiasts or fans. We measured sport interests in order to determine whether or not responses differed by interest level. Subjects reported the following sport-related behaviors and interests: 90.8% described themselves as sport fans; their interest was equally divided between local and national teams; 66.2% said they would be willing to plan a day around a sporting event; 62% reported reading a newspaper sports section more than once a week for an average of 1.6 hours per week; and respondents spend an average of 5.3 hours per week watching sports on television.

Procedure

Data collection took place in classrooms where participants were arranged in rows. They were told that they were participating in a study that was looking at what people thought of different ads that were being considered for inclusion in an advertising campaign.

Participants were randomly assigned to evaluate one ad that was inside a folder. Subjects were told that they would first answer questions about their sports viewing habits because the ads were possibly to be run in sports magazines. On the cover of the folder was a questionnaire asking about sports involvement, sport-related media viewing habits, and sex. The sports involvement scale was taken from Shank and Beasley (1998). After completing the first written questionnaire, subjects opened the folder and viewed the ad. They then completed a written battery of fifteen items about their perceptions of the spokesperson in the ad. Perceptions of the athlete endorser's attractiveness, trustworthiness, and expertise were measured with a 7-point Likert scale using semantic differential anchors. Scale items were taken from Ohanian (1990) and included five items each for the three scales of credibility. After completing all questions, subjects placed the completed surveys inside the folders and returned them to the researcher.

Stimuli

A 2x2x2 full factorial between-subjects experimental design was used with gender of subject, gender of athlete endorser, and type of product advertised (milk or running shoes) as the three factors. Stimuli consisted of four magazine ads. There were two ads for milk using the familiar milk moustache appearing on an athlete. One milk ad showed Amy Van Dyken, a female Olympic gold-medal swimmer, and the other showed Oscar de la Hoya, an Olympic gold-medal boxer. The shoe ads were both for the Saucony Ultimate Cross Trainer running shoe. The female spokesmodel was Paula Newby-Fraser and the male was Dave Scott—both elite level triathletes. Both shoe ads showed pictures of both the spokesmodel and the product. Although the milk and shoe ads were made as similar as possible, they are not identical and therefore any effects of ad design will be confounded with the effects of product in our analysis. Thirty-six percent of respondents reported being familiar with the endorser in the ad they saw. Far more subjects were familiar with the milk endorsers (69% familiar with Amy Van Dyken, 56% familiar with Oscar de la Hoya) than with the shoe endorsers (6.5% familiar with Paula Newby-Fraser and 9.3% familiar with Dave Scott).

Analysis and Results

Care was taken to ensure random assignment to experimental conditions, but the use of a student sample means that caution should be used in generalizing results to other populations. To address the research questions, separate analysis of variance (ANOVAs) were run using attractiveness (ATTRACT), trustworthiness (TRUST) and expertise (EXPERT) as dependent measures. Additionally, ANOVAs were run with credibility (sum scale of trustworthiness and expertise) and with source liking (sum scale of all three subscales) as dependent variables. Although the models for credibility and source liking were significant (p=.013 and p=.045, respectively) the present study does not address these broader constructs. First, we believe that the models run on the individual subscales provide more information about the effects of our experimental factors. Second, the low item correlations between the subscales (.24, .34, and .56) and a low Cronbach alpha (.649) (Cronbach, 1951) indicate that these subscales represent distinctly different dimensions that should be interpreted separately. Further evidence is provided by the very different patterns of results we find for the experimental factors on each of the subscales. Table 1 reports p values from the ANOVAs and illustrates the

Table 1.
ANOVA Results for All Subjects

	Dependent variable (Pr>F)				
Independent variable	**Source liking**	**Attract**	**Trust**	**Expert**	**Credible**
Product	.0035	.001	.952	.016	.143
Respondent gender	.9067	.057	.584	.2323	.298
Celeb gender	.0172	.0001	.853	.1237	.286
Product * resgen	.0831	1.0	.0278	.1796	.044
Product * celeb gen	.7734	1.0	.396	.678	.659
Resgen * celeb gen	.3197	.271	.0106	.4256	.068
Product * resgen * celeb gen	1.000	.070	.1907	.1569	.1086
Model	.013	.0001	.05	.049	.045
R^2	.057	.299	.045	.044	.046

extent of differences in results between the three subscales, as well as the summed scales.

Table 1 shows the full ANOVA results for each of the five models run. All models were significant at the $p < .05$ level. Only the model for ATTRACT showed high explanatory power with the experimental factors accounting for 29.9% of the variation in rated attractiveness. For the other models, variation in the dependent variable explained by the experimental factors ranged from 4.4% (EXPERT) to 5.7% (LIKING). We now present a more detailed discussion of the results in the context of our research questions.

RQ1: Will athletes be seen as more attractive, trustworthy and as having more expertise when endorsing a sports product versus non-sports product?

The results provide mixed evidence that athlete endorsers are more effective when endorsing sport-related products. Looking at the main effect of product in our models we see that it is significant for both ATTRACT (F=107.97, p=.0001) and EXPERT (F=5.85, p=.0161). An examination of cell means, however, shows that the effects are in opposite directions. Subjects found milk endorsers to be more attractive than shoe endorsers (22.57 vs. 16.79)[1] while they found shoe endorsers to be more expert (29.49 vs. 27.92). The finding on perceived expertise is consistent with expectations based on previous literature (Ohanian, 1991) and supports the match-up hypotheses. Regarding the finding on attractiveness, it is possible that the endorsers in the milk ads were simply bet-

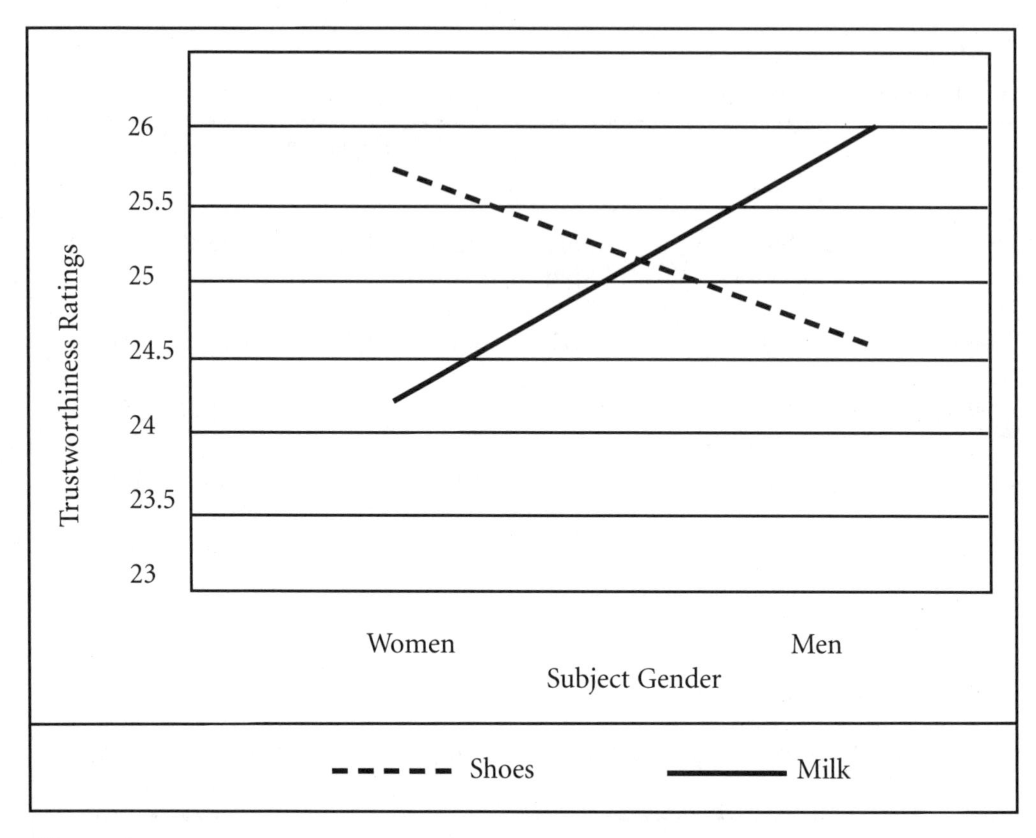

Figure 1.
Trustworthiness Ratings by Product and Subject Gender

ter looking or that the quality of photography was more flattering to the models. It is also possible that the milk models, by virtue of their Olympic accomplishments and greater familiarity, were more attractive in a nonphysical sense (i.e., familiar, likeable). To fully understand this effect, future research should place the same models in both ads (sport and nonsport products) so that the model and product effects are not confounded with the ad.

RQ2: Will respondents' gender have any impact on the evaluation of the athlete's attractiveness, trustworthiness, and expertise?

We examined the main effects of respondent gender (Resgen) to determine whether the gender of the target audience might affect endorser effectiveness. We found a significant main effect of Resgen on ATTRACT only (F=3.64, p=.0572). There were no significant respondent gender effects for expertise (F=1.43, p=.232) or trustworthiness (F=.30, p=.584). Comparing cell means, we see that female respondents rated endorsers as less attractive than did male respondents (19.26 vs. 20.33)[1] with marginal significance (F=3.64, p=.057). During respondent debriefing it was suggested that one possible reason for this result is that women have been socialized to have less appreciation for athletes' physiques. This possibility provides an opportunity for future study, perhaps exploring how social roles influence the effect of athlete endorsers.

RQ3: Will the gender of the athlete endorser influence the target audience's evaluation of the endorser's perceived attractiveness, trustworthiness, and expertise?

Testing for main effects of celebrity gender (Celebgen) tells us whether the gender of the athlete endorser will influence her or his effectiveness when results for both products are combined. As with Resgen we find that Celebgen is only significant in the model for ATTRACT (F=14.83, p=.0001). Cell means reveal that while male athletes were rated higher than female athletes on all dimensions, those differences were only significant for attractiveness (20.83 vs. 18.67). Future research might test the hypothesis that Americans have been socialized to appreciate the physical attributes of male athletes more than those of female athletes.

Thus far we have examined only main effects from our models. Although informative, most issues of real interest to practitioners and researchers involve the interaction effects of our experimental design. The two- and three-way interaction effects discussed below reveal information about the value and importance of matching the endorser to the product and the target market.

RQ4: Will the gender of the consumer influence evaluations of the endorser's perceived attractiveness, trustworthiness and expertise differently for sport versus non-sport products?

An examination of the Product by Resgen interaction shows a significant effect on TRUST only (F=4.89, p=.0278). Cell means show (see Figure 1) that men rated milk endorsers as more trustworthy than did women (25.5 vs. 24.2) while women rated shoe endorsers higher on TRUST than did men (25.7 vs. 24.6). This suggests that male target

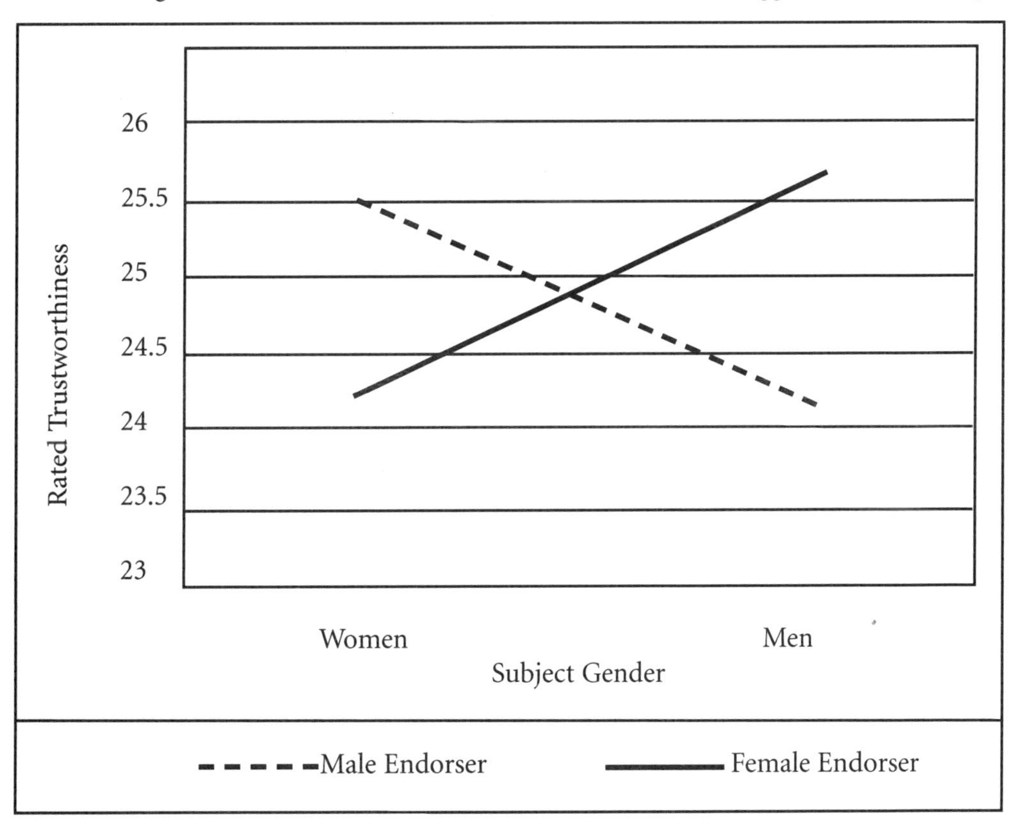

Figure 2.
Trustworthiness Ratings by Subject-Endorser Gender Match

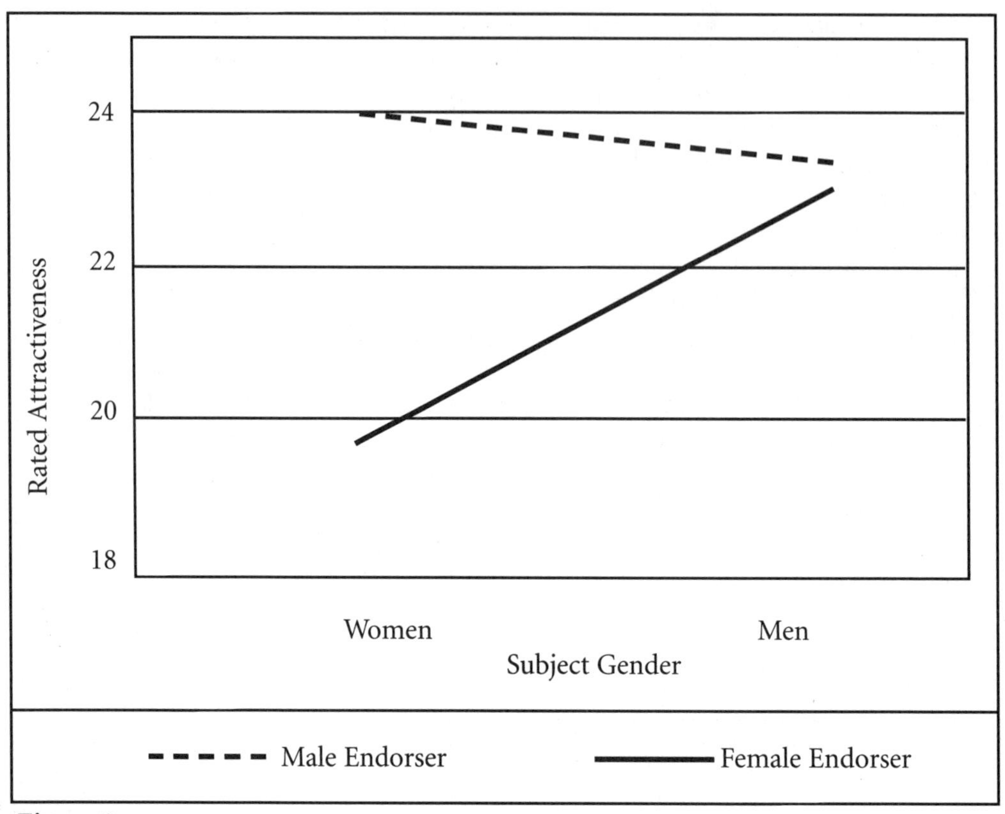

Figure 3a
Milk Endorser Attractiveness by Subject-Endorser Gender Match

markets (in this case college age males) may be more likely to trust athlete endorsers of nonsport products than women, thus, given a nonsport product, ads targeting men may be making better use of athlete endorsers than ads targeting women; this conclusion depends on the generalizeability of this research from a student sample.

RQ5: Will the effects of gender matching between the consumer and athlete endorser impact consumers' evaluations of the athlete endorser's perceived attractiveness, trustworthiness and expertise?

Although we see no significant effects on ATTRACT or EXPERT, we see a strong effect of the Resgen by Celebrity Gender interaction on TRUST (F=6.61, p=.0106). As expected, women rated female endorsers as more trustworthy than male endorsers (25.8 vs. 24.6) and men rated male endorsers as more trustworthy than female endorsers (25.6 vs. 24.1). Figure 2 shows this crossed effect independent of product. This is a strong finding in support of the notion that gender matching between the endorser and the consumer is important in creating trust. Interestingly, subjects did not follow this pattern of same-gender preference in evaluating attractiveness or expertise.

RQ6: Will the effect of gender matching between consumers and athlete endorsers show different patterns in the rating of perceived endorser attractiveness, trustworthiness and expertise for sport versus non-sport products?

Finally, we examine the three-way interaction of our experimental factors. Although we see p values that approach significance for TRUST (p=.19) and EXPERT (p=.16), we only

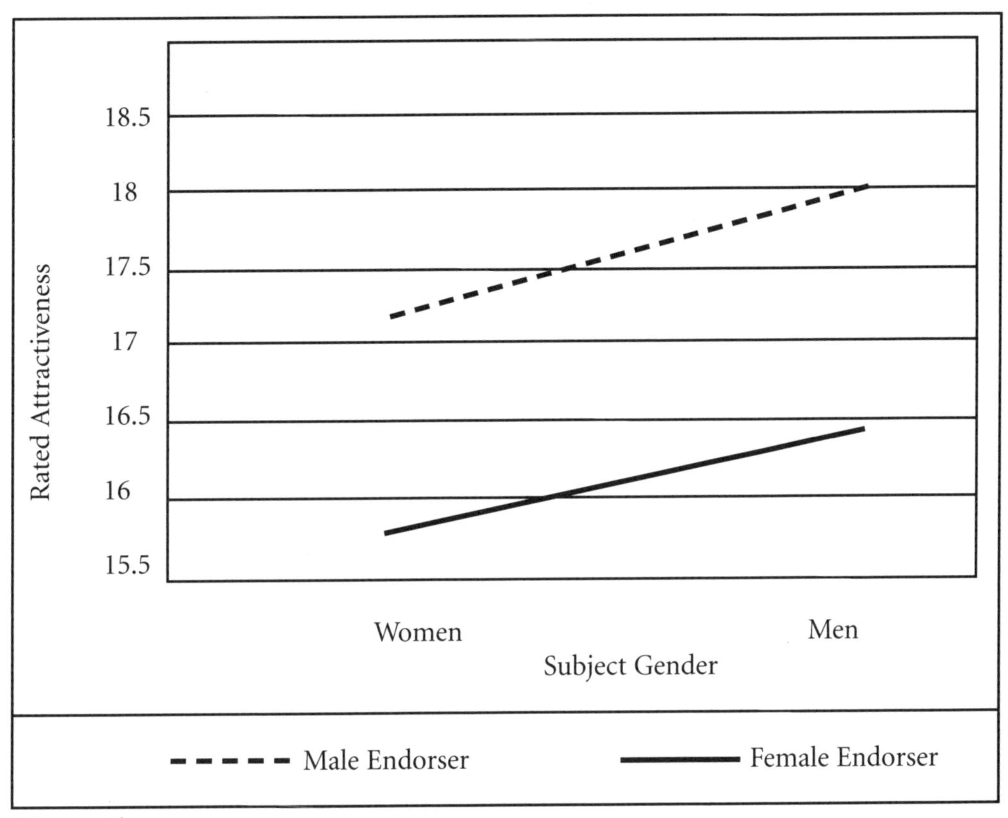

Figure 3b
Shoe Endorser Attractiveness by Subject-Endorser Gender Match

see significant three-way effects on ATTRACT (F= 3.31, p=.0700). Cell means show that for shoes, male endorsers were rated more attractive than female endorsers by both men (17.97 vs. 16.4) and by women (17.16 vs. 15.65). However, for milk, women rated the male endorser as much more attractive than the female (24.0 vs. 19.82) while men rated the male and female endorsers similarly (23.63 vs. 22.72). This three-way interaction is illustrated by Figures 3a and 3b where the pattern of effects differs between male and female subjects for the two products.

In addition to the effects related to our research questions, we see no significant effects of the Product by celebrity gender interaction in any model, suggesting that the gender of the athlete endorser does not matter more for a nonsport product than for a sport product.

The Role of Involvement

Obviously, there are consumer characteristics other than gender likely to influence athlete endorser effectiveness. Of particular interest to sport marketers is the question of whether or not the use of celebrity endorsers should be limited to sport enthusiasts or fans. We explore this issue by considering subjects' self-reported involvement with sport. Using an eight-item involvement scale developed by Shank and Beasley (1998) we divided subjects into split halves reflecting relatively low and high levels of felt involvement for sport. Subjects falling below the median for the involvement scale were treated as

Table 2.
ANOVA Results for Low Involvement Subjects

	Dependent variable (Pr>F)				
Independent variable	**Source liking**	**Attract**	**Trust**	**Expert**	**Credible**
Product	.1133	.0001	.7782	.0070	.0600
Respondent gender	.6422	.09812	.7930	.7546	.9700
Celeb gender	.1733	.0002	.5001	.7517	.9101
Product * resgen	.0613	1.000	.0428	.0614	.0245
Product * celeb gen	.2001	1.000	.5326	.0825	.1821
Resgen * celeb gen	.4481	.1768	.0026	.6735	.0754
Product * resgen * celeb gen	.2108	.9109	.2117	.0831	.0929
Model	.1098	.0001	.0290	.0185	.0248
R^2	.0749	.347	.0978	.1032	.1004

having low involvement and subjects falling above the median were treated as having high involvement with sport.

Because an ANCOVA using involvement as a covariate resulted in biased estimators and was uninterpretable, we instead compared ANOVAs on all dependent measures for subjects with high versus low involvement. Tables 2-3 show the results of ANOVAs on each of the five dependent measures comparing the high and low involvement subjects.

Results from the high and low involvement subjects indicate that most found effects for our experimental factors occur for low involvement subjects but not high involvement subjects. For high involvement subjects, only the model for ATTRACT is significant (F=11.48, p=.0001). In contrast, models for all three source characteristics are significant for low involvement subjects (see Table 2). In general, the pattern of significant effects for low involvement subjects mirrors the effects found for all subjects. This result indicates that it may be futile to attempt to predict the effects of gender or product matching to the target market when the target market is highly involved in sport, but it may make sense to do so when the target market has low felt involvement for sport.

Conclusions

Main Effects of Factors

Our findings from the main effects of the experimental factors suggest that athlete endorsers are most effective when the target market is male, the athlete is male, and the product is sport-related. First, from the effects of product on perceived expertise we conclude that athlete endorser credibility is enhanced by perceived expertise when the product is sport-related. We cannot, however, generalize about a product the athlete-endorser does not use. All else being equal, this suggests that athletes will be most effective when endorsing sport-related products. Second, there is mixed evidence to suggest that male consumers are more receptive to athlete endorsers. Independent of endorser gender, men tend to see athletes as more attractive; however, women rated the athletes as more expert and trustworthy although those differences were not statistically significant. Third, across all subjects we saw male athlete endorsers rated higher, although only attractiveness is significant. This finding suggests that male athlete endorsers may be more effective than their female counterparts, to the extent attractiveness influences credibility, regardless of audience gender.

Table 3.
ANOVA Results for High Involvement Subjects

	Dependent variable (Pr>F)				
Independent variable	**Source liking**	**Attract**	**Trust**	**Expert**	**Credible**
Product	.0124	.0001	.7081	.5079	.8475
Respondent gender	.4859	.2826	.5278	.0346	.1168
Celeb gender	.0391	.1049	.3515	.0533	.1060
Product * resgen	.8276	.5855	.2649	.8735	.5760
Product * celeb gen	.9768	.1081	.4264	.0806	.5267
Resgen * Celeb Gen	.9178	.9133	.6350	.4214	.4745
Product * Resgen * Celeb Gen	.6462	.0572	1.000	1.000	1.000
Model	.1274	.0001	.8410	.1204	.5456
R^2	.0735	.2614	.023	.0746	.0395

Interaction Effects of Factors

Men rated nonsport product endorsers as more trustworthy while women rated the sport product endorsers as more trustworthy. This raises the question of how consumer characteristics influence how generalizeable the match-up hypothesis is. It appears that women are more sensitive to the match between endorser and product. Alternatively, it may be that men see a closer match between athletes and milk consumption than do women.

We see strong evidence that the match-up between the consumer and the athlete may contribute to endorser/ad effectiveness. Simply put, men trust men and women trust women, regardless of the product-endorser match. This finding strongly suggests advertisers should consider target audience gender when choosing athlete endorsers.

Finally, we find that consumers with low sport involvement are more likely to be influenced by our experimental factors. Although low involvement and high involvement subjects showed no significant differences in their numerical ratings of endorser attractiveness, trustworthiness, or credibility, the amount of variance explained by subject gender, athlete gender, and product was much higher for the low involvement group. This indicates that low involvement consumers may be more predictable in their responses to athlete endorsers. Assuming that consumers who read sport magazines are more likely to be high sport-involvement consumers, our findings may apply more readily to advertising placed in magazines more likely to be read by low sport-involvement consumers.

The results here raise questions of how consumers' perceptions of their own expertise regarding a product influence their reliance on an endorser. It is possible that women are socialized to believe they should know about milk (nutrition/diet) and, therefore, see an endorser as less relevant, while the same might be true for men with athletic equipment. If true, this has implications for when it is effective to use an endorser. We suggest that future research should examine the relationship between consumer expertise, gender, product category, and consumer reliance on an endorser, and how that translates into perceptions of endorser credibility.

Managerial Implications

The current study suggests that when using product endorsers, marketers should consider the gender of the target market and the endorser. Our findings indicate that a match-up on gender will improve endorser credibility through greater trustworthiness. Further, marketers are likely to see improved effectiveness when there is a match between the product and the endorser. For athlete endorsers this means that they will be perceived as more credible when endorsing athletic equipment they use. We cannot generalize to athletic equipment they do not use, as we did not test that situation.

Future Research

The ultimate goal of the present study was to understand what makes athlete endorsers effective and how athlete endorsers differ from other types of celebrities. Some of our findings are consistent with previous studies while others are contradictory. For example, we found that respondents rated athlete endorsers of the opposite sex as significantly more attractive than athletes of the same sex. This finding is similar to other research (Baker & Churchill, 1997; Langmeyer, 1991). However, Ohanian (1991) reported no effect of respondents' gender on perceptions of attractiveness (or expertise and trustworthiness) regardless of the gender of the celebrity. One possible explanation for these differences among researchers is that the findings are highly dependent on the ads, the endorsers, and the sample.

While we attempted to find ads that were similar, it is likely that the ads themselves and the endorsers used varied enough to 'create' effects. Replication of this research is necessary before strong generalizations can be made. Ideally, ads using the same endorsers in the same poses could be used for both sport and nonsport products to minimize the effects of the ad. Also, future research could help reduce the effects of familiarity by using a larger number of endorsers and introducing familiarity as a covariate.

Although we have gained insight into athlete endorser effectiveness, it would be helpful to have a more direct contrast between athlete endorsers and nonathletes. Comparison of endorser credibility where athletes and nonathletes appear in the same ad would provide additional insights into the ways in which athlete endorsers are more or less effective than other endorsers. Considering the amount of money spent on celebrity endorsers, we know surprisingly little about what makes them effective and how to best match the endorser with our products and target markets to maximize effectiveness.

References

Agrawal, J., & Kamakura, W. A. (1995). The economic worth of celebrity endorsers: An event study analysis. *Journal of Marketing, 59*(3), 56-63.

Allison, N., Golden, L., Mullet, G. & Coogan, D. (1980). Sex-typed product images: The effects of sex, sex role self-concept and measurement implications. In J. Olsen (Ed.). *Advances in consumer research 7* (p. 604-609). Ann Arbor, MI: Association for Consumer Research.

Alreck, P., Settle, R. B., & Belch, M. (1982). Who responds to 'gendered' ads, and how? *Journal of Advertising Research, 22*, 25-31.

Appelbaum, R. F., & Anarol, W. E. (1972). The factor structure of source credibility as a function of speaking situation. *Speech Monographs, 39*, 216-222.

Atkin, C., & Block, M. (1983). Effectiveness of celebrity endorsers. *Journal of Advertising Research, 23*, 57-61.

Baker, M. J., & Churchill, G. A. (1977). The impact of physically attractive models on advertising evaluations. *Journal of Marketing Research, 14*, 538-555.

Caballero, M. J., & Pride, W. M. (1984). Selected effects of salesperson sex and attractiveness in direct mail advertisements. *Journal of Marketing, 48*, 94-100.

Cronbach, L. J. (1951). Coefficient alpha and the internal structure of tests. *Psychometrika, 16*, 297-334.

Debevec, K., & Iyer, E. (1986). The influence of spokespersons in altering a product's gender image: Implications for advertising effectiveness. *Journal of Advertising, 15*(4), 12-20.

DeSarbo, W. S., & Harshman, R. A. (1985). Celebrity-brand congruence analysis. In J. Leigh and C. Martin (Eds.). *Current issues and research in advertising* (pp. 17-52). Ann Arbor, MI: The Graduate School of Business Administration.

Dyson, A., & Turco, D. (1997). The state of celebrity endorsement in sport. *The Cyber-Journal of Sport Marketing.* Retrieved from http://www/cad.gu.edu.au/cjsm/dyson.htm.

Haley, E. (1996). Exploring the construct of organization as source: Consumers' understandings of organizational sponsorship of advocacy advertising. *Journal of Advertising, 25*(2), 19-36.

Heider, F. (1958). *The psychology of interpersonal relations.* New York: John Wiley and Sons.

Hovland, C. I., Janis, I. K., & Kelley, H. H. (1953). *Communication and persuasion.* New Haven, CT: Yale University Press.

Isidore, C. (2003). Advertisers worry: Who's next? Retrieved from CNNMoney.com.

Kahle, L., & Homer, P. M. (1985). Physical attractiveness of the celebrity endorser: A social adaptation perspective. *Journal of Consumer Research, 11*, 954-961.

Kamins, M. A. (1990). An investigation of the match-up hypothesis in celebrity advertising: When beauty may be only skin deep. *Journal of Advertising, 19*(1), 4-13.

Lane, R. (1996, December). Nice guys finish first. *Forbes, 158*(14), 237-242.

Lane, R., & Spiegel, P. (1996, December). The Year of the Michaels. *Forbes, 158*(14), 244-252.

Langmeyer, L. (1991, June). Exploring gender influences of meaning in celebrity endorsers. Gender and Consumer Behavior Conference, Salt Lake City, UT.

McCracken, G. (1989). Who is the celebrity endorser? Cultural foundations of the endorsement process. *Journal of Consumer Research, 16*(3), 310-321.

Miller, C. (1997). Marketers look to score with women's sports. *Marketing News, 31*(16), 1, 16.

Mowen, J. C., & Brown, S. W. (1981). On explaining the effectiveness of celebrity endorsers. In K. B. Monroe (Ed.). *Advances in consumer research* (pp. 437-441). Ann Arbor, MI: Association for Consumer Research.

Mowen, J. C., Brown, S., & Schulman, M. (1979, month). Theoretical and empirical extensions of endorser effectiveness. In Neil Beckwith et al. (Eds.). Marketing Educators' Conference Proceedings. Chicago: American Marketing Association.

Ohanian, R. (1990). Construction and validation of a scale to measure celebrity endorsers' perceived expertise, trustworthiness, and attractiveness. *Journal of Advertising, 19*(3), 39-52.

Ohanian, R. (1991). The impact of celebrity spokespersons' perceived image on consumers' intention to purchase. *Journal of Advertising Research*, 46-53.

Patzer, G. L. (1983). Source credibility as a function of communicator physical attractiveness. *Journal of Business Research, 11*(2), 229-241.

Petty, R. E., Cacioppo, J. T., & Schumann, D. (1983). Central and peripheral routes to advertising effectiveness: The moderating role of involvement. *Journal of Consumer Research, 10*(2), 135-146.

Petroshius, S. M. & Crocker, K. E. (1989). An empirical analysis of spokesperson characteristics on advertisement and product evaluations. *Journal of the Academy of Marketing Science, 17*, 217-225.

Shank, M. D., and Beasley, F. (1998). Fan or fanatic: Towards a measure of sport involvement. *Journal of Sport Behavior, 21*, 435-443.

How $194.64 billion is spent in sports. *Street and Smith's Sports Business Journal*, special issue "By the numbers 2003," *5*(36), 150-151. Charlotte, NC.

Till, B. D. (2001). Managing athlete endorser image: the effect of endorsed product. *Sport Marketing Quarterly, 10*, 35-42.

Till, B. D., & Busler, M. (2000). The match-up hypothesis: Physical attractiveness, expertise, and the role of fit on brand attitude, purchase intent and brand beliefs. *Journal of Advertising*, 29(3), 1-13.

Till, B. D., & Shimp, T. A. (1998). Endorsers in advertising: The case of negative celebrity informaiton. *Journal of Advertising*, 27(1), 67-82.

Triandis, H. C. (1971). *Attitudes and Attitude Change.* New York: John Wiley and Sons.

Turner, E. T., Bounds, J., Hauser, D., Motsinger, S., Ozmore, D., & Smith, J. (1995). Television consumer advertising and the sports figure. *Sport Marketing Quarterly, 4*(1), 27-33.

Weiner, J. & Mowen, J. (1985). The impact of product recalls on consumer perceptions. *MOBIUS: The Journal of the Society of Consumer Affairs Professionals in Business, 14*(1), 18-21.

24

To Catch a Tiger or Let Him Go? The Match-up Effect and Athlete Endorsers for Sport and Non-Sport Brands

Stephen K. Koernig and Thomas C. Boyd

Introduction

Advertising has infiltrated every part of our day-to-day lives. Each day, consumers are exposed to over 1,500 advertising messages from a variety of sources: television, billboards, radio, flyers enclosed with credit card and utility bills, mobile phones, the grocery store floor, and even public restrooms (Grede, 2002). This onslaught of ad clutter across a myriad of media is also intensifying within each medium. For example, the amount of commercial time in an hour-long television program has steadily increased to 21 minutes (Downey, 2002; Grede, 2002). Not surprisingly, the vast (and increasing) amount of ad clutter has been identified as one of *the* leading problems for advertisers (Downey, 2002).

One commonly used strategy to slice through this ad clutter is to include celebrity endorsers in advertisements (Erogan, Baker, & Tagg, 2001; Lin, 1993; Solomon, 2007). In fact, ads with celebrities account for approximately 20% to 25% of all advertisements (Agrawal & Kamakura, 1995; Stephens & Rice, 1998). Among the most popular celebrity endorsers are athletes, coaches, and other sports personalities (Bush, Martin, & Bush, 2004). Celebrity athletes are demanding increasingly large sums of money to lend their name and image to products, and earned over $897 million for endorsements in 2001 (Agrawal & Kamakura, 1995; *SportsBusiness Journal*, 2002). In many cases, athletes earn much more for endorsements than they do in their sport career. For example, LeBron James signed endorsement contracts for over $90 million with Nike and Upper Deck trading cards *before he was even drafted* by a professional basketball team (CBS News, 2003). Perhaps the most mentioned example is Tiger Woods, who in 2000 signed a five-year contract extension with Nike valued at over $105 million, and in 2002 extended his contract with Buick five years for an additional $40 million (DiCarlo, 2005).

Despite the significant expense associated with celebrity spokespersons, firms continue to pay them large sums of money to endorse their brands. Some research evidence supports this expense; using celebrities as endorsers can be an effective strategy to gain and hold consumer attention (Atkin & Block, 1983), enhance message recall (Friedman & Friedman, 1979), increase believability of the ads (Kamins, Brand, Hoeke, & Moe, 1989), and create positive word of mouth communications (Bush et al., 2004). Celebrities also can help improve brand attitude (Friedman & Friedman, 1979; Kamins, Brand et al., 1989; Petty, Cacioppo, & Shumann, 1983), increase purchase likelihood (Friedman & Friedman, 1979; Kamins, 1989), and increase brand loyalty (Bush et al., 2004). Other research evidence indicates that ads with celebrities are rated as more interesting, strong, and effective; that products in the ads are rated as more pleasant and enjoyable; and that the celebrities themselves are rated as more trustworthy, attractive, and competent (Atkin & Block, 1983). Additionally, investors react positively to the announcement of celebrity endorsement deals, indicating that they perceive the value of the celebrity to exceed the cost (Agrawal & Kamakura, 1995).

Research evidence also indicates, however, that celebrities might not be effective for all brands in all situations, and companies have started to question whether paying celebrities to endorse their brands is the most effective use of company resources (Duncan, 2004; Marketing Week, 2003). In fact, only one out of five commercials containing celebrity endorsers meets companies' strategic expectations (Miciak & Shanklin, 1994). Aside from their high cost, the value of celebrity endorsers may be diminished if they endorse multiple products, or if they endorse (or use) rival products (Agrawal & Kamakura, 1995; Tripp, Jensen, & Carlson, 1994). Celebrities also may prove ineffective when negative press about the celebrity occurs that tarnishes their image and subsequently damages the image of the associated brand (Louie & Obermiller, 2002; Till & Shimp, 1998). Additionally, the effectiveness of the specific celebrity may depend on the *type of product* being endorsed (Kamins, 1990; Solomon, 2007). For example, Tiger Woods has been effective as an endorser for Nike; however, contrary to expectations, Buick's use of Tiger Woods in car ads has not stemmed the sales decline for their automobiles; nor has it resulted in a decrease of the average age of their buyers. In fact, the average age increased by two years to 65 years old (Popely & Mateja, 2007). Given the high cost and prevalence of using celebrity endorsers in our culture, coupled with the potential downsides of using celebrity endorsers, it is critical for a firm to understand when a specific celebrity (or type of celebrity) should be used for a particular brand. This is particularly true in the case of athletes, whose fame and achievements stem from their sport, but whose private behaviors are increasingly scrutinized by the media. Although frequently used to endorse non-sport brands, the circumstances under which an athlete is effective as an endorser have not been fully explored.

Research on the "match-up hypothesis" has empirically addressed the issue of how endorser effectiveness varies based on the type of product being endorsed. More specifically, the match-up hypothesis explains how the congruence between the image of a spokesperson and the image of a brand results in more positive evaluations of the endorser, the brand, and the advertisement. This match could relate to the congruency of the brand with endorser attractiveness, expertise, or other relevant characteristics (Hsu & McDonald, 2002; Kahle & Homer, 1985; Till & Busler, 2000). While empirical research exists investigating the effects of the match-up effect in the context of attractiveness, the match-up hypothesis has received limited empirical attention for other match-up conditions, especially in the area of sport marketing and the impact of celebrity athlete endorsers. Athlete endorsers are of particular interest because they are used not only to endorse sports brands but also to endorse non-sport brands. Although the match-up hypothesis suggests that using athletes to endorse non-sport brands may be ill advised, the heavy use of athletes to endorse non-sport products and brands continues; this mismatch between theory and practice warrants empirical exploration, and the study of the match-up effect in the context of athlete endorsers is an important omission given the frequency and high cost of using celebrity athletes as endorsers. Further, athletes present a special case as endorsers because our attitudes and knowledge about them derive not only from seeing them in contrived situations (e.g., movies or events) but also how they behave and perform in spontaneous situations on the field of play. This authenticity may create a different kind of relationship with fans and could result in the high levels of brand adoption by sports fans of brands used by athletes (O'Keefe, 2005).

This research seeks to fill this gap in the literature by using the match-up hypothesis as a guide to predict and empirically test the effectiveness of athlete endorsers in two experimental studies. In the first experiment, the importance of matching up the image of the brand with the image of the endorser is examined. Specifically, a well-known celebrity athlete is paired with both a sport-related brand and a non-sport-related brand to determine if the match-up between brand image and sport celebrity image affects consumer attitudes and intended behavior. In the second experiment, the match-up effect is tested using an anonymous model identified as either a famous athlete or not, for either a sport-related brand or a non-sport brand. In both experiments, schema theory is tested as the mechanism driving these effects. The implications for the use of celebrities in advertising are discussed and recommendations are provided based on the results.

Literature Review

McCracken (1989, p. 310) defined a celebrity endorser as "any individual who enjoys public recognition and who uses this recognition on behalf of a consumer good by appearing with it in an advertisement." Celebrity endorsers can include actors, athletes, business people, entertainers, military leaders, models, politicians, and singers (Freiden, 1984; Friedman & Friedman, 1979; Hsu & McDonald, 2002; McCracken, 1989). Even animated spokes-characters can serve as celebrity endorsers (Callcott & Lee, 1994).

In general, the multidimensional image of the celebrity (or the cultural meaning embodied by the celebrity) is transferred to the product, and then to the consumer, via advertisements (McCracken, 1989). For example, Walker, Langmeyer, and Langmeyer (1992) measured consumer images of three different products (jeans, bath towels, and VCRs) when they were associated with two celebrities with extremely different images (Madonna and Christie Brinkley). They found that the unique images of the celebrity endorsers were transferred to the various products when they were paired with that celebrity. Celebrity images can also be transferred to organizations. Perceptions of an organization become more positive after being linked with a celebrity who consumers like; similarly, perceptions of the organization become more negative when the celebrity is disliked (Langmeyer & Shank, 1993).

Certain specific characteristics of the celebrity endorser affect their influence on consumer attitudes and behavior. One widely studied characteristic in the literature on endorser effectiveness is the credibility of the endorser. Several studies have identified source expertise and trustworthiness as key dimensions of credibility (Appelbaum & Anatol, 1972; DeSarbo & Harshman, 1985; Dholakia & Sternthal, 1977; Hovland, Janis,

& Kelley, 1953; Ohanion 1990). These components of credibility can work in conjunction or independently to contribute to the effectiveness of an endorser (Wiener & Mowen, 1985). Endorser credibility is important because when endorser credibility is high, consumers are more likely to accept arguments presented in the advertisement, but tend to reject arguments in ads with a source low in credibility (Grewal, Gotlieb, & Marmorstein, 1994). Source credibility may also be impacted by the fit between the brand and the celebrity endorser.

The Match-Up Hypothesis

The match-up hypothesis provides a theoretical framework that helps link the relationship between the endorser-brand fit and endorser credibility and explains how the image of a spokesperson, in conjunction with the image of a brand, affects consumers' brand and advertisement evaluations. The match-up hypothesis has its roots in the work of Mowen, Brown, and Schulman (1979), who used balance theory (Heider, 1958) to describe the relationships between the endorser, the brand, and the target audience and asserted that an endorser would be most effective when there is a close relationship between all three elements. According to the match-up hypothesis, an endorser will not have a beneficial effect on consumer attitudes and behavior unless the image of the endorser "matches up" with the image of the brand (Kahle & Homer, 1985; Kamins, 1990; Parekh & Kanekar, 1994). For example, an attractive spokesperson would be more effective than an unattractive model in a cosmetics advertisement because cosmetics are related to beauty and an attractive endorser is consistent with this image. However, the attractive model would not be more effective than the unattractive model in an ad for computers because computers are not related to beauty. The attractive celebrity is effective because the match-up between the beautiful celebrity and the beauty enhancing brand results in high credibility—but only for brands related to beauty.

Much of the early match-up research focused on physical characteristics of the spokesperson and especially on physical attractiveness. For example, Kahle and Homer (1985) examined the impact of attractive versus unattractive celebrities in razor print ads. They found that attractive celebrities elicited higher purchase intent and more positive attitudes toward the brands than unattractive celebrities. They argued, but did not verify, that razors are associated with attractiveness, and that the congruency of the brand image (as one that increases attractiveness) with the attractive endorser led to the more positive evaluations. Expanding on Kahle and Homer's (1985) study, Kamins (1990) experimentally manipulated the degree to which the brand was related to attractiveness and found a significant relationship between celebrity attractiveness and product type, whereby the ad with the attractive celebrity and the attractiveness-related brand elicited higher evaluations of perceived endorser credibility and more favorable attitudes of the advertisement. The attractiveness of the celebrities did not have any impact in the ads with the brands not related to attractiveness.

In contrast, Till and Busler (2000) found evidence of an attractiveness effect but not a match-up effect. In their study, an attractive endorser had a positive effect on brand attitude and purchase intent, but the effect was not significantly greater for an attractiveness-related product. Till and Busler (2000) speculated that this finding might have been an artifact of the product chosen because the link between the product (cologne) and attractiveness may not have been apparent to subjects. Alternatively, they suggested that their manipulation of attractiveness was overly strong, creating effects for attractiveness that led to increased credibility (c.f. Ohanian, 1991).

Athletes and the Match-Up Effect

Athletes provide an excellent opportunity to examine match-up effects. From a practical standpoint, athletes are widely used as brand endorsers and are an obvious match with brands that are related to athletic activity or that are related to fitness. Athletes presumably have high expertise in athletics, providing them with credibility, and thus they may be more effective as endorsers for sport-related brands. For example, in a study examining the credibility of famous endorsers (Joe Montana and Paula Abdul) of L.A. Gear shoes, Nataraajan and Chawla (1997) found that Joe Montana was rated as more credible than Paula Abdul. If consumers perceived Montana's image to match up with that of the shoes, then these results would support the match-up hypothesis. Nataraajan and Chawla (1997) did not find any difference between the credibility ratings of Paula Abdul and a non-famous male model, suggesting that her celebrity status alone did not make up for the absence of an obvious fit between Abdul and the brand. However, the goal of this study was not related to the study of the match-up effect, and as such they did not measure whether subjects thought of the shoes as related to sports (or to Montana). Additionally, only a single measure of credibility was used; ad attitudes, brand attitudes, and intended behavior were not measured.

Research evidence also exists suggesting that a perceived match-up between a less well-known (or even unknown) athlete and the brand is sufficient to elicit the more positive response. For example, although not tested in the context of the match-up hypothesis, Yoon and Choi (2005) found that subjects preferred, and reported higher purchase intentions for, ads for sports brands that contained both the product and an athlete, even though the athletes were not famous. Similarly, Boyd and Shank (2004) found higher credibility for less famous tri-athletes endorsing a sport-related product (cross-trainer shoes) than for more famous Olympic stars endorsing a non-sport product (milk). Although Boyd and Shank (2004) found that the match-up between the endorser and the product resulted in higher perceived expertise, they used different athletes (tri-athletes versus Olympic stars) for their different product categories (cross-trainer shoes versus milk) and thus confounded the results. They also did not examine the impact of this match-up on evaluations of the ad or the product.

Even an anonymous model purported to be an athlete might elicit match-up effects. In a study using fictional candy bars and energy bars, Till and Busler (2000) used an anonymous model and presented him as either an actor or an athlete for both products. They found a match-up effect of a more positive brand attitude for the athlete compared to the actor for the energy bar. They suggest that these results were caused by increased ratings of expertise of the athlete over the actor. Similarly, Lynch and Schuler (1994) matched an anonymous model in various stages of muscularity with numerous products related to or unrelated to muscularity in print ads. They found that the more muscular the spokesperson was, the more knowledgeable he was perceived to be, but only in ads for products that were related to muscularity. The muscularity of the spokesperson had no impact on attitudes for those products without a relationship to muscularity. It is significant that the endorser had a positive impact, even though he was not known as an expert or celebrity in the fitness industry (nor depicted as one).

Taken together, the attractiveness match-up research coupled with the limited sport-related research suggests that a celebrity athlete should be most effective when endorsing a sport-related brand. In particular, the match-up between the image of the celebrity and the image of the brand should contribute to more positive perceptions of the endorser, attitudes toward the brand and ad, and increased purchase behavior. Additionally, even an unknown athlete or a person depicted as an athlete should elicit more positive responses when endorsing a sport versus a non-sport brand. This leads to the following hypotheses:

H1: When the endorser *is a famous athlete*, attitudes toward the endorser, the advertisement and the brand, and purchase intent will be more positive for a sport-related brand than for a non-sport related brand.

H2a: For a sport-related brand, attitudes toward the endorser, the advertisement and the brand, and purchase intent will be more positive if the endorser *is identified as an athlete* compared to if the endorser *is not identified as an athlete.*

H2b: For a non-sport related brand, there will not be any difference in attitudes toward the endorser, the advertisement and the brand, or purchase intent if the endorser *is identified as an athlete* compared to if the endorser *is not identified as an athlete.*

A Theoretical Perspective – Schema Theory

Schema theory can be used to explain the anticipated attitudes and behavior that will result when a celebrity athlete matches up (or doesn't match up) with the brand. According to Fiske's (1982) two-category model, judgments about the endorser and brand are influenced by the endorser-brand match. According to this model (see also Fiske & Pavelchak, 1986; Sujan, 1985) a two-stage process, including categorization and evaluation, affects judgments about the brands. When the image of the endorser in the advertisement matches with the brand category, the affect associated with the endorser is immediately applied to the brand category. When a mismatch occurs between the endorser and the brand and is thus inconsistent with the stimulus individual, increased thinking about the inconsistency results (Sujan, 1985). Thus, an advertisement with an endorser whose image is consistent with consumer expectations of the brand will induce immediate affect; however, if the endorser's image is inconsistent with expectations, increased elaboration will result over the inconsistency.

In the context of celebrity endorsers and sport marketing, when an athlete endorses a sport-related brand (versus a non-sport brand) the advertisement should generate fewer ad-related thoughts than when the same model is not identified as an athlete (or is not an athlete) because the brand and endorser images are consistent with one another; this consistency induces immediate affect. However, when there is an inconsistency between the athlete and the brand, consumers will think more about this mismatch. This leads to the following hypotheses:

H3: When the endorser *is a famous athlete*, there will be fewer thoughts generated for a sport-related brand than for a non-sport related brand.

H4a: For a sport-related brand, there will be fewer thoughts generated if the endorser *is identified as an athlete* compared to if the endorser *is not identified as (and not known as) an athlete.*

H4b: For a non-sport related brand, there will more thoughts generated if the endorser *is identified as an athlete* compared to if the endorser *is not identified as (and not known as) an athlete.*

Method – Experiment 1

Overview

In order to explore the role of the match-up effect in the context of celebrity athletes as product endorsers, Experiment 1 consisted of a between subjects design with two experimental conditions. In the first condition, subjects viewed an advertisement with a well-known athlete endorsing a sport-related brand, and in the second condition subjects saw him endorsing a non-sport related brand. Subjects were randomly assigned to one of these conditions and after viewing the ad, they responded to items measuring the dependent variables and demographic characteristics in a self-administered questionnaire. The total sample size was 55 subjects recruited from undergraduate business courses consisting of 43.6% females (56.4% males) with a mean age of 22.9 years (ranging from 20 to 38 years of age). The subjects were familiar with the product categories and the brands included in this study and thus were considered satisfactory for the purposes of this study.

Pre-test

A pre-test was conducted to select a sport-related brand and a non-sport related brand for inclusion in the ads. Forty-two subjects from the same population as those individuals that participated in the main study (but who were not included in the main study) rated a number of different clothing brands on two seven-point semantic differential scales. One was anchored with *non-sport brand* and *sport brand*, and the other was anchored with *non-fashion brand* and *fashion brand*. The brand's relation to fashion was important because the impact of consumer involvement with the product category was tested in the main experiment. Clothing brands were selected as the product category because they would be familiar to the subject population and are purchased by the population. Based on the results of the pre-test, the non-sport related brand selected for this study was The Gap and the sport related brand was Champion, rated as low (M=2.05) and high (M=6.10) as a sport brand, respectively (t=10.499, p <.001). Regarding the brands' relation to fashion, The Gap was rated high (M=6.25) and Champion was rated low (M=2.72); this difference was also significant (t=8.635, p <.001).

Procedure

Full-page print advertisements for the non-sport and sport brands were created by a professional graphic designer and included an actual National Football League player, Tom Brady, as the endorser for the brands. In both conditions, Brady was shown prominently from the waist up wearing a tee shirt and looking into the camera; he was identified by name and as "Quarterback for the New England Patriots and Two Time Superbowl MVP." The two ads were identical except for the brand name; the Champion logo was included at the bottom of the ad in the sport condition, while in the non-sport condition The Gap logo was used.

Subjects were provided with a three-page self-administered questionnaire and were advised that that they would view an advertisement for an upcoming tee shirt ad campaign and would be asked for their overall impressions about the endorser, the ad, and the brand. A projected image of the ad for the condition to which they were assigned was then shown to all subjects at the same time. While viewing the full-screen advertisement, subjects completed the questionnaire containing items measuring the dependent variables.

Dependent Variables

The dependent variables used in this experiment included widely used items measuring attitudes toward the endorser, attitudes toward the advertisement, attitudes toward the brand, and purchase intent. Attitudes toward the endorser included *Liking, Perceived Trust,* and *Perceived Expertise. Liking* of the celebrity was measured with a one-item scale (e.g., Kahle & Homer, 1985; Kamins, 1990). *Perceived Trust* and *Perceived Expertise* were measured using five-item scales developed and tested by Ohanian (1990). *Attitude Toward the Brand* and *Attitude Toward the Ad* were both four-item scales from Mitchell and Olsen (1981). A three-item scale from Till and Busler (2000) was used to measure *Purchase Intent.* For all of the items in the above measures, subjects indicated their responses on seven-point semantic differential scales. Additionally, subjects were asked to report their involvement with both sports and fashion using an eight-item scale adapted from Shank and Beasley (1998). The subjects were also asked to write down all of the thoughts they experienced while participating in this experiment. They were instructed to include all thoughts, no matter how simple, complex, relevant, or irrelevant they might seem. Lastly, the subjects were asked to respond to questions about their demographic characteristics.

Results – Experiment 1

Multi-item scales for the dependent variables were constructed by averaging the item responses for each variable. Cronbach's alpha scores for these multi-item factors were: *Perceived Trust* (.83), *Perceived Expertise* (.88), *Attitude Toward the Brand* (.85), *Attitude Toward the Ad* (.78), *Purchase Intent* (.96), *Sport Involvement* (.86), and *Fashion Involvement* (.96) and were deemed sufficiently high based on the standard of .70 established by Nunnally (1978).

Subjects' written responses to the thoughts-generated section of the survey were separated into individual ad-related thoughts and were subsequently independently classified by two judges as positive, negative, or neutral (c.f., Koernig & Page, 2002; Sujan, 1985). The agreement between the two judges was 88.9%, and in the cases where they disagreed, discussion between the judges resolved the disagreement so that all thoughts were coded into one of the three groups. The total number of thoughts was calculated for each subject by adding the number of positive, negative, and neutral thoughts.

Hypothesis Testing

Hypothesis 1 would be supported if the celebrity athlete elicited more positive responses endorsing the sport-related brand compared to the non-sport brand. A multivariate test was conducted across the two brands to test this hypothesis. The results of the MANOVA indicate that the main effects of endorser type were significant: Wilkes' Lambda=.779, $F(1, 53)=2.270$, $p<.052$. Univariate tests were conducted to further explore the impact of an athlete endorser for a sport-related brand versus a non-sport related brand. The results of these analyses and the mean values of the dependent variables for each of the

Table 1.
Comparison of Attitudes and Behaviors for Sport and Non-Sport Brand Endorsed by a Celebrity Athlete

Dependent Variable	Brand Type	N	M	SD	*F*	*p*
Liking	Non-Sport	27	4.52	1.91	7.985	.007**
	Sport	28	5.71	1.15		
Perceived trust	Non-Sport	27	4.16	1.21	4.337	.042*
	Sport	28	4.86	1.26		
Perceived expertise	Non-Sport	27	4.88	1.16	1.288	.262
	Sport	28	5.29	1.50		
Attitude toward brand	Non-Sport	27	4.69	1.27	.008	.931
	Sport	28	4.71	1.19		
Attitude toward ad	Non-Sport	27	4.35	1.45	.417	.521
	Sport	28	4.12	1.25		
Purchase intent	Non-Sport	27	3.61	1.93	.128	.722
	Sport	28	3.43	1.71		

* $p < .05$ ** $p < .01$ *** $p < .001$

Table 2.
Comparison of Thoughts Generated for Sport and Non-Sport Brands Endorsed by a Celebrity Athlete

Dependent Variable	Brand Type	N	M	SD	*F*	*p*
Ad related thoughts	Non-Sport	27	4.67	1.84	8.666	.005**
	Sport	28	3.43	1.23		
Positive thoughts	Non-Sport	27	.52	.75	11.632	.001***
	Sport	28	1.64	1.54		
Negative thoughts	Non-Sport	27	1.59	1.34	9.937	.003**
	Sport	28	.61	.96		
Neutral thoughts	Non-Sport	27	2.56	1.22	21.325	.001***
	Sport	28	1.18	.98		

* $p < .05$ ** $p < .01$ *** $p < .001$

Table 3.
Comparison of Attitudes and Behaviors for Sport and Non-Sport Brand Endorsed by an Athlete (A) vs. a Non-Athlete (NA)

Dependent Variable	Brand & Endorser Type	N	M	SD	*F*	*p*
Liking	Non-Sport (A)	43	4.72	1.61	1.723	.191
	Non-Sport (NA)	44	5.05	1.83		
	Sport (A)	46	5.33	1.30		
	Sport (NA)	52	5.04	1.56		
Perceived trust	Non-Sport (A)	43	4.50	1.01	4.498	.035*
	Non-Sport (NA)	44	4.66	.91		
	Sport (A)	46	4.76	.87		
	Sport (NA)	52	4.34	.69		
Perceived expertise	Non-Sport (A)	43	5.15	1.06	8.727	.004**
	Non-Sport (NA)	44	5.11	.85		
	Sport (A)	46	5.49	.95		
	Sport (NA)	52	4.62	.92		
Attitude toward brand	Non-Sport (A)	43	4.58	1.18	4.373	.038*
	Non-Sport (NA)	44	4.88	.73		
	Sport (A)	46	5.22	.96		
	Sport (NA)	52	4.89	1.15		
Attitude toward ad	Non-Sport (A)	43	4.42	1.38	4.293	.040*
	Non-Sport (NA)	44	4.74	1.08		
	Sport (A)	46	4.84	1.33		
	Sport (NA)	52	4.41	1.11		
Purchase intent	Non-Sport (A)	43	3.80	1.56	6.177	.014*
	Non-Sport (NA)	44	4.11	1.09		
	Sport (A)	46	4.23	1.61		
	Sport (NA)	52	3.40	1.80		

$^{*}p < .05$ $^{**}p < .01$ $^{***}p < .001$

experimental conditions are shown in Table 1. For all of the dependent variables except *Attitude Toward the Ad* and *Purchase Intent*, the mean score was higher in the sport-related brand condition. However, ANOVA tests indicated that there was only a significant main effect of the type of brand for *Liking* $F(1, 53)=7.985$, $p=.007$ and *Perceived Trust* $F(1, 53)=4.337$, $p=.042$. These results provide only partial support for hypothesis 1. The failure to find significant results across some of the dependent variables could have resulted from the use of a real sport celebrity in the advertisements. Subjects may have

Table 4.
Comparison of Thoughts Generated for Sport and Non-Sport Brand Endorsed by an Athlete (A) vs. a Non-Athlete (NA)

Dependent Variable	Brand & Endorser Type	N	M	SD	*F*	*p*
Ad related thoughts	Non-Sport (A)	39	4.38	2.14	15.144	.000***
	Non-Sport (NA)	42	3.07	1.89		
	Sport (A)	46	3.04	1.74		
	Sport (NA)	47	3.94	1.71		
Positive thoughts	Non-Sport (A)	39	.82	1.17	4.595	.033*
	Non-Sport (NA)	42	1.21	1.35		
	Sport (A)	46	.89	1.29		
	Sport (NA)	47	.53	.75		
Negative thoughts	Non-Sport (A)	39	1.18	1.27	32.978	.000***
	Non-Sport (NA)	42	.14	.35		
	Sport (A)	46	.33	.63		
	Sport (NA)	47	.89	1.13		
Neutral thoughts	Non-Sport (A)	39	2.38	1.70	8.519	.004**
	Non-Sport (NA)	42	1.71	1.58		
	Sport (A)	46	1.83	1.35		
	Sport (NA)	47	2.51	1.49		

* $p < .05$ ** $p < .01$ *** $p < .001$

had preexisting affect for Brady, and this could have influenced their responses to some of the dependent measures.

Hypothesis 3 would be supported if there were main effects of brand type on the number of thoughts generated. A multivariate test was conducted across the two brands to test this hypothesis. The results of the MANOVA indicate that there was a significant main effect of brand type: Wilkes' Lambda=.543, $F(1, 53)=10.527$, $p <.001$. Univariate tests were conducted to further explore the nature of this relationship. The mean values of the dependent variables for each of the experimental conditions are shown in Table 2. Subjects did notice an incongruity with the inclusion of a sport celebrity in an ad for a non-sport brand, as evidenced by the number of advertisement-related thoughts generated by the ad. The number of thoughts was further analyzed based on whether they were positive, negative, or neutral. In addition to generating significantly more ad-related thoughts (M=4.67 vs. M=3.43), the non-sport ad with the sport celebrity generated significantly more negative thoughts (M=1.59 vs. M=.61), more neutral thoughts (M=2.56 vs. M=1.18), and fewer positive thoughts (M=.52 vs. M=1.64) than the ad for the sport brand endorsed by the same sport celebrity. The mismatch between the endorser's image and the image of the brand was inconsistent with expectations and this inconsistency elicited increased elaboration. Examples of thoughts in this mismatch condition include "Tom Brady???," "Sports fans don't like GAP!," What does he have to do with GAP?," and "You use a sports character to advertise for a casual clothing store? Not a good idea." These results provide strong support for hypothesis 3.

Lastly, even though the hypotheses did not predict any interactive effects of the subjects' involvement with sport or fashion, univariate tests were done to determine if any differences might exist between subjects high and low in sport and fashion involvement. The scores from the eight *Sport Involvement* items were summed for each subject, and a median split of the overall scores was done, dividing the subjects into high involvement and low involvement groups. This process was repeated for the *Fashion Involvement* scores. ANOVA tests did not reveal any significant interaction between *Sport Involvement* and brand type, or between *Fashion Involvement* and brand type, for any of the dependent variables.

Method – Experiment 2

Overview

Experiment 2 further explored the match-up effect using an anonymous model as a product endorser in a 2 X 2 between subjects design. The same two brands (sport brand and non-sport brand tee shirts) and the same dependent variables that were used in Experiment 1 were used in Experiment 2. The difficulty with using a famous endorser to test for match-up effects is that pre-existing knowledge about and affect for the famous person may influence perceptions of the celebrity and the brand. The goal of Experiment 2 was to determine the impact of a fictional "celebrity," which was accomplished by using an anonymous model and presenting the endorser as either an accomplished athlete or with no personal information supplied, as is commonly done with models. Thus, a major departure from Experiment 1 was the inclusion of an unknown male model in the ad instead of a real celebrity. In one condition, the anonymous model was given a fictional name, "Gregg Sanders," and was falsely identified as a "Wide Receiver for the Two Time NFL Champion New England Patriots." In the second condition, the model was not identified, consistent with ads that use unknown models. The ads were created by a professional graphic designer for the four different experimental conditions and were presented in the same way to subjects as in Experiment 1. The total sample size was 185, consisting of 37.6% females (62.4% males), who were recruited from the same population as in Experiment 1. The mean age was 24.4 years (the minimum age was 19 and the maximum age was 40).

Results – Experiment 2

Multi-item scales for the dependent variables were constructed by averaging the item responses for each variable. Cronbach's alpha scores for these multi-item factors were: *Perceived Trust* (.76), *Perceived Expertise* (.87), *Attitude Toward the Brand* (.85), *Attitude Toward the Ad* (.84), *Purchase Intent* (.95), *Sport Involvement* (.92), and *Fashion Involvement* (.93) and were deemed sufficiently high based on the standard of .70 established by Nunnally (1978). The same procedure from Experiment 1 was used to classify the thoughts generated by the ads. The agreement between the two judges was 83.4%, and in the cases where they disagreed, discussion between the judges resolved the disagreement so that all thoughts were coded into one of the three groups.

Hypothesis Testing

Hypothesis 2a would be supported if the model elicited more positive responses when identified as an athlete compared to a non-athlete when endorsing the sport-related brand. Hypothesis 2b would be supported if there were no differences in the responses elicited by the model when depicted as a non-athlete and athlete in the non-sport brand ad. A multivariate test was conducted across the two types of endorser and the two brands to test these hypotheses. The results of the MANOVA indicate that there was a significant interaction between the brand and type of endorser: Wilkes' Lambda=.947, $F(3, 181)=2.483$, $p=.045$. Univariate tests were conducted to further explore the nature of these relationships and the results of these analyses are presented in Table 3. These tests revealed a significant interaction between the type of brand (sport or non-sport) and the type of endorser (athlete or non-athlete) for most of the dependent measures. Specifically, interactive effects were found for *Perceived Trust* $F(1, 183)=4.498$, $p=.035$; *Perceived Expertise* $F(1, 183)=8.727$, $p=.004$; *Attitude Toward the Brand* $F(1, 183)=4.373$, $p=.038$; *Attitude Toward the Ad* $F(1, 183)=4.293$, $p=.040$; and *Purchase Intent* $F(1, 183)=6.177$, $p=.014$.

Post hoc tests were conducted to determine the nature of these interactions. Regarding the sport-related brand, the ads with the athlete elicited significantly more favorable responses than the ads with the non-athlete for *Perceived Trust* ($M=4.76$ vs. $M=4.34$), *Perceived Expertise* ($M=5.49$ vs. $M=4.62$), and *Purchase Intent* ($M=4.23$ vs. $M=3.40$). These results support hypothesis 2a. Regarding the non-sport brand, a comparison of the ads depicting the athlete with the ads depicting the non-athlete did not reveal any significant differences for any of the dependent variables, thus providing strong support for hypothesis 2b.

Hypothesis 4a would be supported if the ad for the sport brand generated fewer total thoughts when the endorser was identified as an athlete compared to when the endorser was not identified as an athlete. Hypothesis 4b would be supported if the ad for the non-sport brand elicited more thoughts when the endorser was identified as an athlete compared to when the endorser was not identified as an athlete. A multivariate test was conducted across the two types of endorser and the two brands to test these hypotheses. The results of the MANOVA indicate that there was a significant interaction between brand and type of endorser: Wilkes' Lambda = .784, $F(3, 181)=15.451$, $p<.001$. Univariate tests were conducted to further explore the nature of the interaction effect between endorser type and brand and the results of these analyses are presented in Table 4. The results revealed a significant interaction between the type of brand and type of endorser for the total number of thoughts generated $F(1, 183)=15.144$, $p<.001$. The number of thoughts was further analyzed based on whether they were positive, negative, or neutral. This analysis revealed a significant interaction between the type of brand and type of endorser for the total number of positive $F(1, 183)=4.595$, $p=.033$; negative $F(1, 183)=32.978$, $p<.001$; and neutral thoughts $F(1, 183)=8.519$, $p=.004$.

Post hoc tests were conducted to determine the nature of these interactions. In the advertisement for the sport-related brand, the endorser labeled as an athlete generated significantly fewer total thoughts ($M=3.04$ vs. $M=3.94$), fewer negative thoughts ($M=.33$ vs. $M=.89$), and fewer neutral thoughts ($M=1.83$ vs. $M=2.51$) compared to the ad with the non-athlete. Similarly, the ad for the non-sport brand with the non-athlete generated significantly fewer total thoughts ($M=3.07$ vs. $M=4.38$), fewer negative thoughts ($M=.14$

vs. M=1.18), and fewer neutral thoughts (M=1.71 vs. M=2.38) compared to the ad with the athlete. Examples of thoughts induced by the mismatch condition with the non-sport brand endorsed by the athlete included "this guy should be in a sporty ad," "athletes should endorse sport clothing, tennis shoes, etc.," "I don't associate athletes with Gap," and "I thought it was weird that Gap would use a football player as an endorser." Similarly, the mismatch condition with the non-athlete endorsing the sport brand included "He should be in Cosmo" and "This ad doesn't work for the product being advertised." These results strongly support hypotheses 4a and 4b.

Lastly, univariate tests were done to determine if any differences existed between subjects high and low in both sport and fashion involvement. The same method used in Experiment 1 was used to form high involvement and low involvement groups. ANOVA tests did not reveal any significant interaction between *Sport Involvement*, brand type, and endorser for any of the dependent variables; nor were significant results found for an interaction between *Fashion Involvement*, brand type, and endorser.

Discussion

A critical issue for marketers paying famous celebrities to be endorsers for their brands revolves around which celebrity, or type of celebrity, would maximize advertising effectiveness for their particular brand. The match-up hypothesis suggests that an athlete would be ideally suited as an endorser for a brand related to athletics, but not for a non-sport brand. However, the results of the first experiment only partially support the predicted match-up effects and indicate that using a famous athlete endorser may be no more effective for sport-related brands than for non-sport brands. Significantly, matching the athlete with a sport-related or unrelated brand did not make any difference on evaluations of the brand and ad, and did not impact purchase behavior. The only benefit of matching an athlete with a sport brand was limited to increased liking and trust of the endorser. From a managerial standpoint, this raises the issue of whether a highly accomplished athlete endorser benefits more than the brand they endorse (e.g., Did Tom Brady overshadow the brands in the advertisements?). Advertising agency executives rank the risk of celebrities overshadowing the brands as a significant one (Erogan et al., 2001), and because of this potential problem, companies including Pepsi and Chrysler have recently moved away from linking their brands with high profile celebrities. Instead, they are refocusing consumer attention on the brand through ads without celebrities (Duncan, 2004).

Strong support for the match-up hypothesis was found when an unknown model was used (instead of the well-known celebrity) in ads for sport and non-sport brands. Specifically, the findings from the second experiment suggest that a spokesperson depicted as an athlete is more effective than as a non-athlete when endorsing a sport-related brand. No difference existed between athletes and non-athletes when endorsing a non-sport brand. Thus, this study and its sport marketing perspective more fully integrate research on the match-up hypothesis with celebrity endorsers. These results are consistent with much of the previous research done on the match-up hypothesis (e.g., Kahle & Homer, 1985; Kamins, 1990; Lynch & Schuler, 1994) and underscore the importance of fit of the endorser with the brand to help maximize ad and brand attitudes, as well as to increase purchase behavior. These results suggest that the current industry practice of linking athletes who have no obvious match with the product category (e.g., Tiger

Woods endorsing Buick) may not be the most efficient use of company resources. In fact, these results mirror what is happening in practice.

Furthermore, while a direct comparison between an anonymous athlete and a famous athlete cannot be made, the fact that the model *depicted* as a star athlete elicited more positive responses for a sport brand than a non-sport brand suggests that on a cost-benefit basis, a company may want to consider using either a model depicted as an athlete (or a lesser known athlete) instead of spending a much larger sum for a more famous athlete. Similarly, La Ferle and Choi (2005) found only a relatively small advantage of using an extremely well-known and liked celebrity over a non-celebrity, and based on these results, they suggested that a non-celebrity might be a better use of company resources. These results are in contrast to earlier studies, which have shown an advantage of using celebrities over non-celebrity spokespersons (e.g., Atkin & Block, 1983; Frieden, 1984; Kamins, 1989). The results of the present study provide a framework to help companies select a specific type of non-celebrity endorser. Specifically, telling consumers that someone is famous, or highlighting a lesser known athlete's achievements, will elicit more positive responses for the brand, the ad, and the endorser when they are endorsing a sports-related brand.

This research also contributes to the literature by identifying the underlying mechanism driving the match-up effects. The lack of a match between the image of the brand and the image of the endorser induced increased elaboration and resulted in more negative thoughts compared to a match-up of the images. These results can be explained in the context of schema theory. Schema theory explains that when a match is present, consumers are more likely to engage in fewer thoughts about the ad because the ad already fits an existing schema; therefore, consumers are more likely to accept the ad and its message. When there is no match present, consumers will engage in more elaboration about the ad in an attempt to resolve perceived inconsistencies with existing schemas. These thoughts will include negative reactions to the observed inconsistency, resulting in more negative attitudes about the ad and the endorser (Fiske, 1982; Fiske & Pavelchak, 1986; Sujan, 1985).

Perhaps the most significant contribution of this research is its separation of the two dimensions of an athlete endorser's image. Athletes are popular as endorsers because they are both famous and they are respected for their achievements on the field of play. Prior research had not separated these two dimensions of an athlete's image and thus they have always been confounded with other factors in the study. Thus, in prior research it could never be said whether it is the fame of the athlete, similar to other celebrities, or their achievements that make them effective endorsers. In this research, two separate studies were performed using identical brands, allowing an examination of the differences between a famous athlete and an unknown, albeit accomplished athlete. In the first, fame and achievement were confounded as in prior research and the results were mixed as to the benefits of using a famous athlete. However, in the second study, there is no existing fame for the athlete. He is a fictional character, and while subjects could make assumptions about his achievements by virtue of his portrayal as a professional football player, there is no additional knowledge due to his fame. In study two, strong support was found for the use of the athlete endorser for the sports brand with results similar to but stronger than for the famous athlete. These findings suggest that it is the fit of the athlete with the brand that is driving positive attitudes rather than the fame of the athlete.

Some limitations of this study must be noted. First the use of student subjects limits the generalizeability of the findings to other populations, and thus replication with non-student subjects would be appropriate. Second, the results reported here in Experiment 1 are limited to one celebrity athlete, and as such it is impossible to predict whether the same results would occur if a different famous athlete were used. Therefore, future research should replicate this study using a variety of real celebrity endorsers. Third, only two brands from a single product category were included in the research design. Future researchers should use additional product categories and brands. Future research could also replicate these findings using fictional brand names to eliminate any pre-existing bias resulting from the use of actual brands. Fourth, only a male endorser was included in the ads. Another opportunity for future research includes the use of male and female endorsers (both together and alone in ads) to examine the effects of the gender of the endorser. Finally, all of the ads had people in them. Given the recent strategies of Pepsi and Chrysler of eliminating high profile celebrities (and all people) from their ads to refocus attention on the brand, future researchers should compare the impact of ads that include celebrity endorsers to those that do not include people in them.

References

Agrawal, J., & Kamakura, W. A. (1995). The economic worth of celebrity endorsers: An event study analysis. *Journal of Marketing, 59*(3), 56-63.

Appelbaum, R. F., & Anatol, K. W. E. (1972). The factor structure of source credibility as a function of speaking situation. *Speech Monographs, 39*(3), 216-222.

Atkin, C., & Block, M. (1983). Effectiveness of celebrity endorsers. *Journal of Advertising_Research, 23*(1), 57-61.

Boyd, T. C., & Shank, M. D. (2004). Athletes as product endorsers: The effect of gender and product relatedness. *Sport Marketing Quarterly, 13*(2), 82-93.

Bush, A. J., Martin, C. A., & Bush, V. D. (2004, March). Sports celebrity influence on the behavioral intentions of generation Y. *Journal of Advertising Research*, 108-118.

Callcott, M. F., & Lee, W. (1994). A content analysis of animation and animated spokes-characters in television commercials. *Journal of Advertising, 23*(4), 1-12.

CBS News (2003). *LeBron James hits $90M jackpot.* Retrieved from http://www.cbsnews. com/stories/2003/05/22/national/ main555131.shtml

DeSarbo, W. S., & Harshman, R. A. (1985). Celebrity-brand congruence analysis. In J. H. Leigh & C. R. Martin (Eds.), *Current issues and research in advertising* (pp. 17-52). Ann Arbor, MI: The Graduate School of Business Administration.

Dholakia, R. R., & Sternthal, B. (1977). Highly credible sources: Persuasive facilitators or persuasive liabilities? *Journal of Consumer Research, 3*(March), 223-232.

DiCarlo, L. (2005). *With Tiger Woods, it's Nike, Nike everywhere.* Retrieved from http://www. msnbc.msn. com/id/4554944/

Downey, K. (2002). *TV ad clutter worsens, and buyers grouse.* Retrieved from http://www. medialifemagazine. com/news2002/feb02/feb11/5_fri/news2friday.html

Duncan, A. (2004). *Companies ditch celebrity endorsers.* Retrieved from http://advertising. about.com/cs/advertising/a/endorsements.htm

Erogan, B. Z., Baker, M. J., & Tagg, S. (2001). Selecting celebrity endorsers: The practitioner's perspective. *Journal of Advertising Research, 41*, 39-48.

Fiske, S. T. (1982). Schema-triggered affect: Applications to social perception. In M. S. Clark & S. T. Fiske (Eds.), *Affect and cognition: The 17th annual Carnegie Symposium on cognition* (pp. 55-68). Hillsdale, NJ: Lawrence Erlbaum.

Fiske, S. T., & Pavelchak, M. A. (1986). Category-based versus piecemeal-based affective responses: Developments in schema triggered affect. In R. M. Sorrentiono & E. T. Higgins (Eds.), *The handbook of motivation and cognition: Foundation of social behavior* (pp. 167-203). New York: Guilford Press.

Freiden, J. B. (1984). Advertising spokesperson effects: An examination of endorser type and gender on two audience. *Journal of Advertising Research, 24*(5), 33-41.

Friedman, H. H., & Friedman, L. (1979). Endorser effectiveness by product type. *Journal of Advertising Research, 19*(5), 63-71.

Grede, R. (2002, March 29). Rising above the advertising clutter. *Small Business Times,* Retrieved from http://www.thegredecompany.com/docs/Rising%20Above%20Advertising%20Clutter.pdf

Grewal, D., Gotlieb, J., & Marmorstein, H. (1994). The moderating effects of message framing and source credibility on the price-perceived risk relationship. *Journal of Consumer Research, 21*(1), 145-153.

Heider, F. (1958). *The psychology of interpersonal relations.* New York: John Wiley and Sons.

Hovland, C. I., Janis, I. L., & Kelley, H. H. (1953). *Communication and persuasion.* New Haven, CT: Yale University Press.

Hsu, C., & McDonald, D. (2002). An examination on multiple celebrity endorsers in advertising. *Journal of Product and Brand Management, 11*(1), 19-29.

Kahle, L. R., & Homer, P. M. (1985). Physical attractiveness of the celebrity endorser: A social adaptation perspective. *Journal of Consumer Research, 11,* 954-961.

Kamins, M. A. (1989). Celebrity and noncelebrity advertising in a two-sided context. *Journal of Advertising Research, 29*(3), 34-42.

Kamins, M. A. (1990). An investigation of the match-up hypothesis in celebrity advertising: When beauty may be only skin deep. *Journal of Advertising, 19*(1), 4-13.

Kamins, M. A., Brand, M. J., Hoeke, S. A., & Moe, J. C. (1989). Two-sided versus one-sided celebrity endorsements: The impact on advertising effectiveness and credibility. *Journal of Advertising, 18*(2), 4-10.

Koernig, S. K., & Page, A. L. (2002). What if your dentist looked like Tom Cruise? Applying the match-up hypothesis to a service encounter. *Psychology & Marketing, 19,* 91-110.

La Ferle, C., & Choi, S. M. (2005). The importance of perceived endorser credibility in South Korean advertising. *Journal of Current Issues and Research in Advertising, 27*(2), 67-81.

Langmeyer, L., & Shank, M. D. (1993). Celebrity endorsers and public service agencies: A balancing act. In E. Thorson (Ed.), *Proceedings of the 1993 Conference of the Academy of Advertising* (pp. 197-207). Columbia, MO: American Academy of Advertising.

Lin, C. A. (1993). Cultural differences in message strategies: A comparison between American and Japanese commercials. *Journal of Advertising Research, 33,* 40-48.

Louie, T. A., & Obermiller, C. (2002). Consumer response to a firm's endorser (dis)association decisions. *Journal of Advertising, 31*(4), 41-52.

Lynch, J., & Schuler, D. (1994). The matchup effect of spokesperson and product congruency: A schema theory interpretation. *Psychology & Marketing, 11*(5), 417-445.

Marketing Week (2003, October 16). Marketing society claims celebrity ads 'become a thing of the past'. *Marketing Week,* p. 6.

McCracken, G. (1989). Who is the celebrity endorser? Cultural foundations of the endorsement process. *Journal of Consumer Research, 16*(3), 310-321.

Miciak, A. R., & Shanklin, W. I. (1994). Choosing celebrity endorsers. *Marketing Management, 3*(3), 51-58.

Mitchell, A. A., & Olson, J. C. (1981). Are product attribute beliefs the only mediator of advertising effects on brand attitude? *Journal of Marketing Research, 18*(3), 318-332.

Mowen, J. C., Brown, S. W., & Schulman, M. (1979). Theoretical and empirical extensions of endorser effectiveness. In N. Beckwith et al. (Eds.), *Marketing educators' conference proceedings* (pp. 258-263). Chicago: American Marketing Association.

Nataraajan, R., & Chawla, S. K. (1997). 'Fitness' marketing: Celebrity or non-celebrity endorsement? *Journal of Professional Services Marketing, 15*(2), 119-129.

Nunnally, J. C. (1978). *Psychometric theory.* New York: McGraw Hill.

Ohanian, R. (1990). Construction and validation of a scale to measure celebrity endorsers' perceived expertise, trustworthiness, and attractiveness. *Journal of Advertising, 19*(3), 39-52.

Ohanian, R. (1991). The impact of celebrity spokespersons' perceived image on consumers' intention to purchase. *Journal of Advertising Research, 31,* 46-54.

O'Keefe, B. (2005, September 5). America's fastest growing sport. *Fortune,* 48-64.

Parekh, H., & Kanekar, S. (1994). The physical attractiveness stereotype in a consumer-related situation. *The Journal of Social Psychology, 134*(3), 297-300.

Petty, R. E., Cacioppo, J. T., & Schumann, D. (1983). Central and peripheral routes to advertising effectiveness: The moderating role of involvement. *Journal of Consumer Research, 10*(2), 135-146.

Popely, R., & Mateja, J. (2007, May 26). Age-old battle for Buick. *Chicago Tribune,* Section 2, pp. 1-2.

Shank, M. D., & Beasley, F. M. (1998). Fan or fanatic: Towards a measure of sport involvement. *Journal of Sport Behavior, 21*(4), 435-443.

Solomon, M. R. (2007). *Consumer behavior: Buying, having, and being.* Upper Saddle River, NJ: Prentice Hall.

Sports Business Journal (2002). How $194.64 billion is spent in sports. *SportsBusiness Journal, 5*(36), 150-151.

Stephens, A., & Rice, A. (1998). Spicing up the message. *Finance Week, 76*(26), 46-47.

Sujan, M. (1985). Consumer knowledge: Effects on evaluation strategies mediating consumer judgments. *Journal of Consumer Research, 12,* 31-45.

Till, B. D., & Busler, M. (2000). The match-up hypothesis: Physical attractiveness, expertise, and the role of fit on brand attitude, purchase intent and brand beliefs. *Journal of Advertising, 29*(3), 1-13.

Till, B. D., & Shimp, T. A. (1998). Endorsers in advertising: The case of negative celebrity information. *Journal of Advertising, 27*(1), 67-82.

Tripp, C., Jensen, T. D., & Carlson, L. (1994). The effects of multiple product endorsements by celebrities on consumers' attitudes and intentions. *Journal of Consumer Research, 20,* 535-547.

Walker, M., Langmeyer, L., & Langmeyer, D. (1992). Celebrity endorsers: Do you get what you pay for? *Journal of Services Marketing, 6*(4), 35-42.

Wiener, J., & Mowen, J. C. (1985). The impact of product recalls on consumer perceptions. *MOBIUS: The Journal of the Society of Consumer Affairs Professionals in Business, 14*(1), 18-21.

Yoon, S., & Choi, Y. (2005). Determinants of successful sports advertisements: The effects of advertisement type, product type and sports model. *Journal of Brand Management, 12*(3), 191-205.

SECTION VIII.

Ethical Issues

25

Good Morning, Vietnam:
An Ethical Analysis of Nike Activities in Southeast Asia

Lynn R. Kahle, David M. Boush, and Mark Phelps

Introduction

In recent years Nike has received a great deal of criticism regarding its manufacturing policies in less developed countries, such as Vietnam. Although Nike is a United States (U.S.) company, virtually all of its manufacturing is done overseas in countries with low wages. Nike has been accused of manufacturing shoes and apparel in "sweatshop" conditions. The allegations center on the notion that young workers are paid low wages to work long hours in unpleasant and unhealthy conditions. Reports have circulated of physical abuse and of exposure to toxic substances, such as the chemical solvents toluene and acetone, which can lead to serious health impairment, including birth defects (Herbert, 1997; O'Rourke, 1997). Because the modal worker in Asian footwear factories is a young woman in prime fertility years, this concern is especially serious and poignant.

Nike has from the beginning endeavored to build high-quality products at affordable costs for North American and, more recently, worldwide consumers. Part of the core marketing strategy has always been to sell products with good value for the money (Katz, 1994). This result has been achieved in part by using low-cost Asian labor, moving from Japan to Korea and Taiwan to South China, Indonesia, and Thailand to North China and Vietnam. Asian sourcing has allowed low manufacturing costs relative to the quality of the products. Thus, Asian sourcing has always been nearly as central to Nike strategy as using famous athletes to attest to the virtues of Nike equipment in athletic performances.

We recently had the opportunity to visit a factory (Changshin) in Vietnam that produces only Nike shoes and another factory owned by an apparel company (Huy Hoang) that manufactures for both Nike and Adidas (but for neither at the location we visited). We also visited the headquarters of NikeVietnam in Ho Chi Minh City. None of us has ever worked in or owned stock directly in the shoe or apparel industries, including Nike. We did not begin working on this project with preconceived convictions regarding the outcome of our investigation. The purpose of this paper is to report on and examine our experiences in hopes of continuing the dialogue about the ethical issues associated with marketing strategy.

Vietnam

Vietnam is a country of contrasts. Its population is 78 million in spite of the heavy toll of war and disease. For a country that has been ravaged by war with France and then the United States during the second half of the 20th century, it has enormous natural, tropical beauty. Gorgeous beaches, spectacular mountains, and the lush Mekong Delta are all part of this country of abject poverty.

The dominant city in northern Vietnam is Hanoi, the political capital. The dominant city in southern Vietnam is Ho Chi Minh City, formerly Saigon, the unofficial economic capital and the most populous city. Most shoe and apparel manufacturing is located in the general vicinity of Ho Chi Minh City. Although Ho Chi Minh City does not yet have the traffic nightmare of other Southeast Asian cities such as Bangkok, public transportation is poor. Recent economic progress has upgraded the modal source of transportation from the bicycle to the motor scooter.

Today Vietnam has a mixed economy. After the war with the United States ended in 1975, the political leaders tied Vietnam's economic future to the Soviet Union, which itself has tumbled economically during the following two decades. Vietnam's economic plight worsened because of that relationship (Harvie & Hoa, 1997), and the most recent economic crisis in Asia has not been beneficial to Vietnam. Official government rhetoric still often carries Marxist overtones, but in recent practice, signs of capitalism abound beneath the Marxist rhetoric. The Vietnamese apparently sense little contradiction in tolerance of capitalist-type economic opportunity while espousing their historic Marxist ideals. Relaxation in the collectivist philosophy of rice production has transformed Vietnam from a net importer of rice to one of the world's leading rice exporters, for example. Although the literacy rate is 94%, per capita income is only $320 per year (World Bank Group, 1999).

The minimum wage in Vietnam varies by factory ownership and district. State-owned factories have a minimum wage of $13 per month, but private, foreign companies generally must honor minimum wages in the $35 to $45 per month range, depending on their location. Foreign companies must pay a minimum wage that is specified in U.S. dollars, although employees are of course paid in Vietnamese dong. The exchange rate used to compute wages is adjusted periodically by the collective bargaining units. Most blue-collar workers belong to labor unions.

Because of the relaxing of political intolerance, the high literacy rate, the abundant natural resources, and the availability of eager and inexpensive labor, some people believe Vietnam is poised for tremendous growth in the next decade (Harvie & Hoa, 1997; Murray, 1997). Although Asian "tigers" have experienced economic trouble recently, the two-decade-old profile of the newly prosperous Asian economies resembles the profile of Vietnam today. A fairly educated and ambitious workforce is rapidly industrializing. Some scholars believe that Vietnam is on the brink of a new day economically and that the morning greeting is coming from such factories as Changshin.

Changshin

The Changshin factory is located in the rural exurbs of Ho Chi Minh City, approximately a one-hour drive (40 km) from the central business district. We selected the factory we wanted to visit based on its location relative to our travel schedule, and after several prompts our request to visit Changshin was granted. Nike did not dictate which factory we visited, but Nike certainly could have prevented us from visiting any particular factory. We were told by sources both within and outside Nike that Changshin is neither the best nor the worst Nike-associated facility in Vietnam. We were also told by several sources that current variability among Nike-associated factories is relatively small. Changshin is 100% owned by a Korean company with historic ties to Nike. The factory was built with a vision toward subcontracting with Nike, and that has been the exclusive use of the plant since it was completed in July 1995. Building such a factory costs between $16 million and $20 million. The profit margin for the factory owners is reportedly from 5% to 8%.

We wanted to inspect the physical environment of the factory. It was clean, well lighted, and had no foul smell of chemical bonding agents. Seemingly endless rows of sewing machines provided work stations for employees on the shoe assembly line in the approximately 100,000 square meter facility. More than 32 lines were devoted to cutting and stitching. The factory campus had a large, pleasant lunchroom, an office complex for management, attractive lawn and landscaped areas, and some covered parking for bicycles and motor scooters. Both air and water filtration systems were in place, prompting one of the Korean managers to say, "The conditions here are cleaner than at my home." The physical working conditions of the plant seemed quite in line with North American environmental expectations for a factory of this type. We base this on subjective impressions, however, not biochemical analysis.

The factory subcontracts with Nike to manufacture men's footwear. The maximum shoe production capacity is 350,000 pairs per month with the current single shift. More than 50% of the shoes manufactured at Changshin are exported to Europe because Vietnam does not, at this writing, enjoy Most Favored Nation trade status with the United States.

This factory and its sister plant have about 5,000 employees, including 365 staff members, 39 of whom are experts from Korea and the Philippines. It has 4 directors, 4 assistant directors, 22 supervisors, 4 Vietnamese top managers, and 4 Vietnamese assistant managers. The Nike Vietnam Headquarters in the business district of Ho Chi Minh City employs about 100 experts in efficiency, quality control, technology, safety, and work standards, who visit and advise this factory and the other Nike subcontractors in Vietnam (4 other footwear factories, 9 apparel factories) daily. These people, about 75% of whom are Vietnamese, seem well aware of the criticisms Nike has received for manufacturing policies, of the consequences of those criticisms, and of how to avoid further problems.

The shoe or apparel manufacturing process we observed is labor intensive and relatively menial, although some level of skill is necessary to operate the machines. The wide variety of styles, sizes, materials, and choices in high-end shoes dictates a manufacturing process that is unwieldy. The ideal employee in such a factory does not require advanced technical or professional skills at the time of hiring.

The modal employee at Changshin is a young, rural woman. Employees are selected by a hiring service provided by the government. All workers that we saw wore blue shirts and dark pants, making them both literally and figuratively blue-collar workers. We were told by sources unassociated with Nike that in Vietnamese culture, sewing is viewed as "woman's work," as it is in much of the rest of the world, which explains why 85% of the workers are women. As sex-role norms change throughout the world, this role may change, too. Although child labor laws would allow Changshin to employ workers beginning at age 16, Nike imposes a minimum age of 18 at footwear factories. We saw no evidence that Changshin is violating this policy. Although formal education is mandatory

Table 1.
The NIKE Code of Conduct

Nike, Inc., was founded on a handshake.

Implicit in that act was the determination that we would build our business with all of our partners based on trust, teamwork, honesty and mutual respect. We expect all of our business partners to operate on the same principles.

At the core of the NIKE corporate ethic is the belief that we are a company comprised of many different kinds of people, appreciating individual diversity, and dedicated to equal opportunity for each individual.

NIKE designs, manufactures and markets products for sports and fitness consumers. At every step in that process, we are driven to do not only what is required, but what is expected of a leader. We expect our business partners to do the same. Specifically, NIKE seeks partners that share our commitment to the promotion of best practices and continuous improvement in:

1. Occupational health and safety, compensation, hours of work and benefits.
2. Minimizing our impact on the environment.
3. Management practices that recognize the dignity of the individual, the rights of free association and collective bargaining, and the right to a workplace free of harassment, abuse or corporal punishment.
4. The principle that decisions on hiring, salary, benefits, advancement, termination or retirement are based solely on the ability of an individual to do the job.

Wherever NIKE operates around the globe, we are guided by this Code of Conduct. We bind our business partners to these principles. While these principles establish the spirit of our partnerships, we also bind these partners to specific standards of conduct. These are set forth below:

1. Forced Labor. (Contractor) certifies that it does not use any forced labor—prison, indentured, bonded or otherwise.
2. Child Labor. (Contractor) certifies it does not employ any person under the age of 15 (or 14 where the law of the country of manufacturing allows), or the age at which compulsory schooling has ended, whichever is greater.
3. Compensation. (Contractor) certifies that it pays at least the minimum wage, or the prevailing industry wage, whichever is higher.
4. Benefits. (Contractor) certifies that it complies with all provisions for legally mandated benefits, including but not limited to housing; meals; transportation and other allowances; health care; child care; sick leave; emergency leave; pregnancy and menstrual leave; vacation, religious, bereavement and holiday leave; and contributions for social security, life, health, worker's compensation and other insurance.
5. Hours of Work/Overtime. (Contractor) certifies that it complies with legally mandated work hours; uses overtime only when employees are fully compensated according to local law; informs the employee at the time of hiring if mandatory overtime is a condition of employment; and, on a regularly scheduled basis, provides one day off in seven, and requires no more than 60 hours of work per week, or complies with local limits if they are lower.
6. Health and Safety. (Contractor) certifies that it has written health and safety guidelines, including those applying to employee residential facilities, where applicable; and that it has agreed in writing to comply with NIKE's factory/vendor health and safety standards.
7. Environment. (Contractor) certifies that it complies with applicable country environmental regulations; and that it has agreed in writing to comply with NIKE's specific vendor/factory environmental policies and procedures, which are based on the concept of continuous improvement in processes and programs to reduce the impact on the environment.
8. Documentation and Inspection. (Contractor) agrees to maintain on file such documentation as may be needed to demonstrate compliance with this Code of Conduct, and further agrees to make these documents available for NIKE or its designated auditor's inspection upon request.

Adapted from Nike, Inc., website at www.Nikebiz.com.

and provided until age 18 in Vietnam, many of the workers are high-school dropouts. The turnover rate is less than 5% per year, and most attrition is due to change in the employee's stage of family life cycle (marriage or childbirth).

We noticed several informational signs. Outside the plant a sign displayed in perhaps 10-foot-tall English letters Nike's "Just do it" slogan and a Nike swoosh. We saw a much smaller sign in English promoting the "ABC Campaign" (Aggressive mind, Best quality, Clean) and several prominent signs detailing the Nike Code of Conduct in both English and Vietnamese. The code of conduct spells out fairly stringent and explicit standards of employer-employee relations (Nike, 1999), as can be seen in Table 1.

About 87% of the workforce belong to the union, whose leaders meet with management at least monthly to discuss working conditions. Topics of discussion at these meetings include safety, management style, training, education, motivation, environmental conditions, and labor practices. We saw no evidence of physical or psychological abuse of workers.

By U.S. standards, wages are low in Vietnamese footwear factories. Minimum legal wage at Changshin is $35 per month. Nike reports that the average wage for direct labor at Nike-associated factories in Vietnam is about $52 per month. We asked several workers at Changshin how much they earned at the factory, and the modal response converted to about $45 per month. Our sample was too small for inferential purposes, but we have no reason to doubt Nike's estimate that pay exceeds minimum wage by some modest amount. Worker benefits include social security, free health care, and one free or subsidized meal per day. At Changshin that meal costs employees about 10 cents (1,290 dong) per day. Most employees presumably live near the factory, and it appeared that workers mostly ride bicycles to work. At the more urban Huy Hoang factory, employee transportation to work is subsidized. Labor costs account for approximately 20% of the retail cost of footwear, according to Nike executives.

Changshin employees who have not completed high school have free access to night classes on the factory campus to complete their high school equivalency. They are promised a 5% pay raise upon completion of their high school education. The company also provides 10 scholarships and some computers to Van Lang University in Ho Chi Minh City, and it encourages managers to pursue higher education.

Overall, we did not see anything that struck us as out of the ordinary for a manufacturing facility. We also did not notice fundamental differences between the Huy Hoang factory working conditions and the Changshin factory. Our general conclusion agrees with that of Andrew Young, former U.S. Ambassador to the United Nations (Nike, 1998). At the request of Nike founder Phil Knight, Young visited four factories in China, four factories in Vietnam, and four factories in Indonesia. He reported that those 12 factories were "clean, well-organized, adequately ventilated, and well-lit" and that he found "no evidence or pattern of widespread or systematic abuse or mistreatment of workers" (Nike, 1999; see Table 2 for a complete listing of findings and recommendations). Recent reports in *Time* magazine also came to the same general conclusion (Saporito, 1998). The dispute over conditions in factories subcontracting from Nike is far from over, however, and the Young Report has been severely criticized (Herbert, 1997; O'Rourke, 1997).

Business Ethics

In a sense, ethics are subjective, but some principles of ethics have relatively widespread following. The United Nations has produced a book on human rights that most nations

Table 2.
Findings and Recommendations of the GoodWorks International Report

Findings

1. Factories we visited that produce NIKE goods were clean, organized, adequately ventilated and well lit. They certainly did not appear to be what most Americans would call "sweatshops."
2. I found no evidence or pattern of widespread or systematic abuse or mistreatment of workers in these twelve factories.
3. Generally speaking, these twelve factories are controlled by absentee owners, managed by expatriates who, in Vietnam in particular, do not speak the local language fluently and are overseen by a relatively small number of NIKE technical supervisors focused largely on quality control.
4. The concept of "workers' rights" is not a well-developed or well-understood principle in the three Asian countries where NIKE and its major competitors produce shoes and apparel.
5. Some system of third-party monitoring is necessary because of the ownership structure of these Asian factories.
6. In some factories, workers are offered housing as an additional benefit but it is entirely voluntary. By Western standards, the rooms are small and the furnishings sparse. The workers I talked with said that it was "better than their home."
7. There needs to be a better system to enable individual factory workers to file a complaint or grievance and know that it will be seriously considered and/or investigated without fear of retribution.
8. The NIKE Code of Conduct should be the basis of the relationship between NIKE, the plant ownership and management and the workers. The Code is not visible on the factory floors and not well understood by the workers.

Recommendations

1. NIKE should continue its efforts to support and implement the provisions of the Apparel Industry Partnership, which resulted in the first major agreement—across industry lines—to set voluntary, global standards and goals for international labor practices.
2. NIKE should take more aggressive steps to explain and enforce the Code of Conduct.
3. NIKE should promote the development of "workers' representatives" in the factories to effectively represent the workers' individual and cumulative interests.
4. NIKE should insist that the factories that manufacture its products create and enforce a better grievance system within the factory.
5. NIKE should expand its dialogue and relationship with the human rights community and the labor groups within the countries where they produce goods and with their international counterparts.
6. NIKE should consider some type of "external monitoring" on an ongoing basis to ensure effective application of the Code of Conduct. It is important that NIKE's professional audits conducted by Ernst & Young and Price Waterhouse be continued. It should consider establishing an "ombudsman" in each major country with manufacturing facilities. NIKE also might assemble a small panel of distinguished international citizens to monitor factories.

Adapted from Nike, Inc., website at www.Nikebiz.com.

have adopted, for example. In the area of business ethics, the major accounting firm of Arthur Anderson has produced educational materials regarding ethics that are widely used throughout North America (Cooke, 1990). Their premise is that ethical behavior is good business because at its core human interaction requires some trust in a civil reciprocity. No matter how explicit a contract, for example, at some point the potential exists to find uncovered circumstances. Partners need to trust that the spirit of the contract will prevail when those circumstances arise.

The Arthur Anderson materials suggest that most business ethics philosophies center on one of three principles: the Golden Rule, Enlightened Self-Interest, and Utilitarianism. The Golden Rule, "Do unto others as you would have them do unto you," is widely disseminated in one form or another among the world religions, and it has also received serious philosophical attention. Enlightened Self-Interest maintains that you should not do things to hurt others because they otherwise will be motivated to practice retribution. Utilitarianism in its core form asserts that one should do the greatest good for the greatest number of people. All three, then, emphasize social interactions among participants in business transactions.

Several primary participants dominate the social aspects of business transactions. The most important elements in business social exchanges are usually the stockholders, the managers, the employees, and the consumers. Political units (countries) also experience consequences from business.

Nike and the Ethical Principles

How does Nike relate to these ethical principles? To the extent that Asian sourcing succeeds at producing quality, cost-competitive products, both consumers and stockholders benefit. Managers, therefore, benefit as well. The market has a saleable product, and consumers have a reasonably priced product they want. The success of both Nike's stock and marketing efforts attests to the essentially ethical outcome for these two important participants according to all three ethical principles.

The case for nonmanagement employees is far more complicated. The first question is who is responsible for inappropriate behavior when it occurs in Nike-associated factories? Some instances of abuse have occurred in Nike's far-flung worldwide operations, but they have always occurred at the hands of Nike subcontractors, not Nike itself. Nike insists that subcontractors meet certain standards and obey local laws. Nike tries to enforce those standards, but it has regrettably had less than perfect success.

Although no one can defend certain abuses, the abuses are currently far from the norm and certainly not the goal of Nike. Both Nike and its subcontractors appropriately accept blame for past injustices and apparently seek to minimize them today. From an Enlightened Self-Interest perspective, it might make sense for Nike to try to pass the blame onto the subcontractors, but Nike is not doing that. From a Golden Rule and Utilitarian perspective, that is an admirable outcome.

Nike subcontractors today do not apparently practice systematic physical, environmental, or psychological abuse against Vietnamese workers. Neither the Young Report nor our own observations showed evidence of a policy of abuse, as would be expected based on current Nike pronouncements. Of course, one can never truly prove the null hypothesis. In some places or times that we did not visit, abuses could occur. We saw no evidence that abusiveness exists as a policy, however.

Nike and its subcontractors have had hundreds of thousands of employees worldwide, and one can expect a certain amount of tension simply because that sometimes occurs when people interact with other people. The epidemiology of mental illness cases, for example, implies that occasionally people with serious mental health problems will become employees or even supervisors of footwear manufacturing facilities. The problem is exacerbated by cultural differences. When a Korean company is supervising a Vietnamese factory for a U.S. company, opportunities abound for cultural miscommunication and misunderstanding. Something that is normal or acceptable in one culture may not be acceptable in another. All three cultures need to learn how to meld. Cultural understanding and patience toward others would seem to be a virtue in all three ethical systems, and Nike has recently improved on this moral dimension.

Nike supervisors did not deny that in the past some abuses have occurred, although in some instances the supervisors believed that the media sensationalized abuses. By all indications we could detect, the commitment to improved working conditions seemed genuine. A single instance of abuse identified by media representatives may not represent a widespread policy of abuse.

Wages are always a complicated topic. Nike and its subcontractors are apparently not violating any laws regarding wages. That fact probably meets the Enlightened Self-Interest standard. Consumers and stockholders benefit when wages are low. Workers in general prefer higher wages. At least Golden Rule and Utilitarian ethics would probably imply higher wages, but how much higher?

One reason that wages are low in developing counties is that poor infrastructure suppresses productivity. In Vietnam the infrastructure is fundamentally different from that in the United States. We also visited Amata, a "modern industrial park" near Ho Chi Minh City, whose positioning statement promises "non-stop power supply." In North America or the European Union, a nonstop power supply would be considered a given. To make the Changshin plant functional, it was necessary to buy four electrical generators, drill water wells, establish a water filtration system, and upgrade telecommunication infrastructure, among other things. The roads to Changshin are marginally passable but certainly not superhighways. The vicinity of Changshin has an upgraded, modernized infrastructure because of the footwear factory, which in turn enhances its attractiveness to other types of manufacturing. If workers at Changshin earned the same wages as workers in the United States, Nike would have no marketing motive to manufacture overseas.

Although wages at Changshin clearly fall below U.S. levels, the local norms also enter into determining fair wages. The low turnover rate implies that workers consider the wages acceptable relative to alternatives. One danger in overshooting the local wage norms too dramatically is that it could invite corruption. As we look at wages through North American lenses, the wages do seem low. However, as economic conditions in a developing country improve, the wage discrepancy usually decreases (Donaldson, 1996).

A second factor to consider in wage levels is automation and its effect on employment. One of us recently visited two automobile factories, one for Nissan in Tokyo and one for a Beijing Autoworks/Jeep joint venture in Beijing. The high labor costs in Japan today motivated a highly automated, low employment factory, whereas the low Chinese labor costs motivated a labor-intensive manufacturing process. Undoubtedly some point exists at which it would be cost-effective from a manufacturing perspective to eliminate many low-end jobs from the footwear manufacturing process and replace them with machines.

Probably most employees of Changshin prefer employment to automation from an Enlightened Self-Interest perspective.

The ethics on the country level are also interesting. From the Vietnam government perspective, the fact that Nike subcontractors supply employment in Vietnam is acting in an ethical manner according to all three theories of ethics. Countries with very low levels of development that move up the ladder of economic development need pioneer companies, such as Nike, that are willing to enter the risky contexts of weak infrastructure and political uncertainty to create the environment that will foster further economic growth. Japan a generation ago and Korea or Taiwan half a generation ago are examples of places where pioneers such as Nike helped to create an environment and infrastructure for economic progress. In 1950 Japan was a source of cheap labor, and "Made in Japan" implied low cost but shoddy goods. Today Japan has the world's second largest economy, and "Made in Japan" implies quality. Japan's journey to economic development would not have occurred without foreign pioneers launching development activities.

Why the Controversy?

If Nike has behaved ethically, why then is it embroiled in such controversy? The answer is to be found in three areas. First, Nike must contend with a variety of stakeholder groups, each of which has an identifiably different set of interests, many of which conflict. Second, in business it is not sufficient to behave within the bounds of law and ethical principle; public perceptions are crucial. Third, management practices can be mistaken without being unethical (Markus, 1996; Miller & Cross, 1998).

Stakeholder Conflict

A stakeholder is "any group or individual who can affect or is affected by the achievement of the organization's objectives" (Freeman, 1984, p. 46). Nike's principal stakeholders are consumers, stockholders, Asian workers, American workers, nongovernment organizations (NGOs), competitors, and the media.

Nike consumers. Consumers are best served by low-priced, high-quality products that fit their individual needs. Secondarily, some consumers may have a preference for products that cause less harm to others or that are manufactured in their own home countries. The latter characteristics may be called "ethical" factors. Within their capacity to take in all the relevant information, consumers can get the best combination of price, quality, and "ethical factors" by maximizing choice and information. In general, Nike consumers benefit from low Asian wages.

Nike stockholders. Stockholders are concerned with maximizing return on their investment. This goal is facilitated in the long run by satisfying consumers. Although stockholders may be the first to be seen as "greedy," it is problematic to argue that their wealth is derived from exploiting Asian workers. Nike's profitability hinges on its ability to outsell its competitors, all of which employ Asian workers. The implication for labor practices at Nike subcontractors is that competition constrains how much or how fast Nike can lead wages and benefits upward.

Asian labor. Workers at Nike's Asian subcontractors are interested in maximizing wages, benefits, and job security and in optimizing working conditions. Nike probably would prefer to hire subcontractors that use U.S. labor if it were not for the large wage differential. Therefore, job security and maximum wages are competing objectives for

Asian workers, and Asian workers compete with workers in the United States and around the world. With a restricted range of skills and alternatives, they are vulnerable to exploitative practices. Their demographic and cultural profile makes them less vocal than other groups but also more sympathetic as victims.

U.S. labor. Objections also come from North American organized labor. Providing jobs in Southeast Asia probably reduces jobs and perhaps wages in the United States to some extent, although those jobs could also go to other less developed countries, such as Mexico. Wages are low in countries with low development because their infrastructure for modern interaction lags behind other places.

One issue is whether American workers deserve jobs more than do workers in other countries who are willing to work for less. China, for example, is trying to enter the world economy after a generation of Marxist-style human rights and previous economic policies have left widespread suffering as their legacy. One could argue that China, Vietnam, and similar countries with long-standing economic problems need the jobs more than the United States does. Workers in the United States have access to more lucrative jobs, which is another reason that wages are higher in the United States.

U.S. workers have the same interests as Asian workers but are in a completely different competitive position. With wage rates many times those of Asian workers, U.S. workers require commensurate productivity advantages in order to be competitive. Lacking such productivity advantages in shoe manufacture, they may benefit from a strategy of making "ethical factors" salient in consumers' minds. Their primary interest in improving safety, wages, and benefits for Asian workers (decrying sweatshops) is to drive up the cost of foreign labor.

One generic, systemic issue presented by the critics of Nike and other similarly situated multinational corporations is how, in a global economy, employment opportunities should be allocated among citizens of different nations and on what terms. For the companies the issue of whether they are obligated to their parent nations to maximize domestic employment has proven to be much less perplexing than those issues regarding to what extent they should take advantage of lower cost foreign labor markets in economically developing nations.

Nongovernmental organizations (NGOs). NGOs advocating labor rights in economically developing nations, particularly for employees working for multinational corporations, have been prominent and powerful critics. They often have ties to one another and to counterparts in international and domestic labor organizations. Their missions typically are labor rights, human rights, or religion. They often have an extensive organizational history of activism, professional staff and supporters, and financial and political clout at the grassroots level. Their tactics against Nike have included media attacks, political pressure, public protests including recent acts of violence, consumer boycotts, shareholder resolutions, and lawsuits for unfair trade practices.

Some NGO representatives have admitted that Nike has been targeted not so much due to its practices being appreciably different from those of others, but instead due to its market share leadership, profitability, visibility, and vulnerability to moral public challenges, given the potential receptiveness of its core target market to the criticisms and its other past public moral issues. Apparently the strategy is that by causing the market leader to improve workers' compensation and conditions, smaller competitors will follow, because they will not be at a relative cost disadvantage and will not want to allow Nike a first-mover competitive advantage.

These NGOs are political advocates for their stakeholders' interests similar to consumer and environmental advocacy organizations. The moral standards by which they judge multinationals are derived from the normative ethical reasoning traditions of human rights, justice, and duties, which tend to reject egoism and even utilitarian approaches to deciding moral issues. Their arguments, however, now often include utilitarian and egoistic justifications, too. The resulting labor standards are asserted as universal with some marginal adjustments for differences in nations' stages of economic development, comparative economic advantages, and culture. Consequently, although NGOs may welcome improvements in labor conditions, they will accept nothing less than their standards as morally adequate. Their standards are akin to natural law rights, and such standards lead to rigid dialogue.

Nike competitors. Nike competitors, such as Adidas and Reebok, are interested in taking market share away from Nike. They have mixed motives, however, regarding human rights issues in Asia because their labor practices are subject to the same types of criticisms that have plagued Nike. If they are seen as leading the public criticism, the spotlight could be turned on them. To some extent they are shielded by not being the market leader, a position that any of them would probably trade places to acquire. In the short run, they benefit from criticism of Nike because such criticism affects both their costs and their sales less than it does Nike. In the long run, if they become linked with extremist ideologues who object to Nike and all other capitalist elements of the world economy, Nike competitors will only be hurting themselves.

The media. The international media have an interest in filling airtime with content that attracts an audience and in selling papers. Large companies with high-profile products, spokespersons, and advertising campaigns place themselves in the middle of a high-stakes media game. The media find that criticizing large companies can attract an audience. The celebrity element of the athletic apparel industry also attracts media attention. Michael Jordan sells shoes and also makes Nike a bigger story. Very public figures make for interesting public discussions, which leads us to the issue of public perceptions. Celebrity endorsement also can heighten a sense of wage unfairness, a sense that Nike treats factory workers badly "even as it lavishes millions of dollars on star athletes to endorse its products" (Greenhouse, 1997, p. 1).

Public Perceptions

One lesson to be learned from Nike's experience is that behaving legally is sometimes insufficient from a public relations perspective. Historically, firms could use subcontractors as a legal "firewall" to shield them from responsibility. For high-profile market leaders, such a strategy does not work well in some instances. The argument that a firm does not control its manufacturing subcontractors may be particularly problematic for strong brand names. If the public is expected to buy shoes because they are Nikes, it will not believe that someone else is responsible for making them.

For high-profile firms, the standard seems to be social-responsibility leadership. That is, it seems insufficient merely to adhere to ethical standards, to *not* be unethical. Market leaders are expected to be out in front on issues of worker safety, wages, and benefits improvement.

Although the Young Report did not find evidence of worker mistreatment, it did report problems with communication and with cultural conflict. For example, it noted that "factories are controlled by absentee owners, managed by expatriates, who in

Vietnam in particular, do not speak the local language fluently." In such a situation, the opportunity for cultural conflicts and miscommunication seems very high. The expectation is that market leaders work to alleviate these kinds of problems as well.

Nike's Alternatives

Nike and other multinationals have three basic alternatives regarding labor practices in Asia. First, they may take full advantage of the lower labor standards presented to them in some nations by the global economy and governmental policies. Second, they can attempt to meet the demands of their critics. Third, they can seek to improve incrementally compensation and conditions of foreign workers.

Certainly any labor compensation, conditions, or practices that are illegal under a particular nation's laws cannot be morally justified in that nation. Such practices normally would be prohibited by an independent contractor's agreement with its customer. Beyond the minimum legal standards, labor practices or conditions that demonstrably threaten workers with serious physical or emotional harm violate basic tenets of human rights. Further, tolerating such practices because they are allowed economically and legally in some host nations, when they have long been condemned legally or morally in parent nations, is unjust discrimination and should be expected to bring criticisms of exploitation. Such practices would also violate Kant's categorical and practical imperative principles, as well as the Golden Rule. Most multinationals would not willingly disclose publicly their association with these types of labor practices. Thus, the first option will often be morally deficient without careful analysis of potential host nation's laws and actual labor conditions, especially in today's environment of global oversight.

The second alternative is difficult to reject because it sets universal, largely nondiscriminatory standards and satisfies commonly asserted labor rights. It is, however, subject to valid ethical and practical constraints if implemented immediately. The host nations may view this alternative as cultural imperialism or an impediment to their economic development. Their cultural and governmental sovereignty can be threatened by multinational companies imposing Western standards on their economies. Because this activity would likely also increase their relative labor costs, these nations may also believe their competitive advantage in the global economy would be reduced or eliminated, especially because they normally suffer from other comparative disadvantages. For companies this alternative would create significant risks of their becoming less competitive on costs unless all competitors acted together or there were substantial first-mover advantages.

The third alternative seems to be the present choice of Nike and others. It is a conservative response to the critics, which they predictably have rejected. Other stakeholders who could be negatively affected by the second alternative, though, are exposed to less risk, while having the satisfaction that progress is being made.

Nike's Strategic Responses

Historically, many corporations have responded to public moral challenges in a reactive manner followed by an attempted defense that often is ineffective in quelling the critics. Forced to reflect on the criticisms and the increasing damage to their reputations, these companies move toward accommodation with the critics' issues. Commentators assert that this reactive strategy is inadequate and instead urge a proactive approach that predicts and prepares for social responsibility challenges.

Nike originally responded to critics by explaining that its manufacturers were foreign companies with which it merely contracted for the production of finished products (Katz, 1994). This type of relationship is legally known as an independent contractor one, in which generally the hiring party has no legal right to control the means by which the contractor meets its contract obligations and no legal responsibility for the contractor's behavior. Nike also compared its practices to the similar practices of its competitors. This response, of course, is technically correct, but not relevant or material to the critics. These issues are not ones of legal responsibility, but of social and moral responsibility. The law does not require Nike or its competitors to leave its product manufacturers free to set their own labor practices, and these companies possess sufficient buyers' power to demand certain labor standards be met by their contract manufacturers.

Nike thereafter embarked upon plans to cause the contract manufacturers to improve the compensation, health, safety, and other working conditions of their production employees.

It installed employees to monitor compliance by the contractors with Nike's Code of Conduct. It employed international CPA firms to audit contractors for code compliance and commissioned Andrew Young's consulting firm to inspect them. Nike also joined the White House-initiated Apparel Industry Partnership dedicated to establishing industry standards regarding the use of foreign labor. More recently, in the face of the economic crisis in Asia, Nike has caused compensation and food supplements for the contractors' employees to be increased. To the critics all these actions were too little, too late. The CPA audits have been severely challenged based upon their lack of public disclosure, potential bias, inadequate methodology, and alleged underreporting of legal and code violations. The report by Young has been criticized as based on inadequate investigation and bias, in spite of the fact that it both documented numerous problems and recommended that further actions be taken, many of which were acted upon quickly.

The difficulties Nike has encountered have been experienced by many other companies that were caught in a reactive-defense posture to public moral challenges. Recapturing the moral high ground in the public perception becomes a difficult long-term process. A proactive stakeholder analysis prior to making decisions to identify the likely social responsibility issues embedded in the decision, the power of the stakeholder proponents, and the ethics of their position would reduce the risks of making decisions subject to strong moral challenges. It would also help companies be prepared to explain the moral bases for their decisions when challenged without appearing defensively guilty. This approach seems particularly advisable for those companies that are market leaders or otherwise very visible publicly.

Conclusion

Nike has made mistakes, but one could argue that Nike has paved the way for economic development in some of the countries that most desperately need it. International welfare often perpetuates social problems in countries, but bringing countries into the world economic order often starts countries down the path to a better standard of living. Nike subcontractors in Asia operate 150 factories employing more than 450,000 workers (Greenhouse, 1997). As the old proverb says, "If you give people fish, they can eat for a day. If you teach people to fish, they can eat for a lifetime." Nike has metaphorically been teaching people to fish, or at least make shoes. One estimate is that 5% of the Vietnamese gross domestic product is related to Nike, which has only operated there since 1995.

Thus, Nike's activities have provided a jump-start to a nearly dead economy. Especially from a utilitarian perspective, this activity can be seen as laudable.

We have no reason to believe that Nike's practices are fundamentally worse or better than those of other shoe and apparel manufacturers, and indeed we believe Nike has been the target of attention because it is the market leader, not because it is extreme in its practices. If anything, we saw some evidence that Nike is trying harder to correct problems because of the negative publicity it has received. For example, Nike has pioneered the use of less toxic water-based solvents and bonding agents.

Does the fact that Nike is better than, or at least no worse than, its competitors mean that its critics should stop putting pressure on Nike to improve its practices? Perhaps not. The point of advocacy activities is to push companies past simple compliance with the law. Therefore, "fairness" toward a particular company is not an overarching objective of Nike critics. Putting pressure on the market leader has had the demonstrable effect of improving working conditions at the factories that Nike has the power to influence, if not the legal responsibility to control.

Should consumers who are interested in increasing ethical treatment of Asian workers boycott Nike products? Almost certainly not. Although the threat of a boycott arguably puts pressure on Nike to lead its industry toward better pay and conditions for workers, consumers who reward Nike's competitors for equivalent ethical behavior do nothing to improve the lot of Asian workers. Boycotting all footwear from Southeast Asia, if successful, would end many jobs.

Nike did not invent the world economy, but merely figured out how to operate successfully in it. No one is forcing Southeast Asian countries to make Nike footwear or apparel. The host countries actively court Nike factories. Providing employment to developing countries has many positive effects. Although wages are indeed low in Vietnamese footwear factories, the ethics of manufacturing in Vietnam are more complicated than sometimes implied in popular media.

References

Cooke, R. A. (1990). *Ethics in business: A perspective.* Boston: Arthur Andersen & Co.

Donaldson, T., (1996, Sept.–Oct.). Values in tension: Ethics away from home. *Harvard Business Review, 74*(5)4–12.

Freeman, R. E. (1984). *Strategic management: A stakeholder approach.* Boston: Pitman.

Greenhouse, S. (1997, Nov. 8). Nike shoe plant in Vietnam is called unsafe for workers. *New York Times,* p. 1.

Harvie, C., & Hoa. T. V. (1997). *Vietnam's reforms and economic growth.* New York: St. Martin's Press.

Herbert, B. (1997, March 28). Brutality in Vietnam. *New York Times,* p. 8.

Katz, D. (1994). *Just do it: The Nike spirit in the corporate world.* New York: Random House.

Marcus, A. A. (1996). *Business & society: Strategy, ethics, and the global economy* (2nd ed.). Homewood, Illinois: Irwin.

Miller, R. L., & Cross, F. B. (1998). *The legal environment today,* Cincinnati: ITP-West.

Nike. (1999). Retrieved from http://www.Nikebiz.com/labor/code.shtm/

O Rourke, D. (1997). Smoke from a hired gun: A critique of Nike's labor and environmental auditing in Vietnam as performed by Ernst &Young. *Transnational Resource and Action Center,* San Francisco, CA.

Saporito, B. (1998). Taking a look inside Nike's factories. *Time, 151*(12), 52.

Young, Andrew. (1998). "The NIKE Code of Conduct" by Goodworks International, LLC: A report on conditions in international manufacturing facilities for NIKE, Inc. Atlanta: Goodworks.

World Bank Group. (1999). Retrieved from www.worldbank.org

26

Marketing Implications of Title IX for Collegiate Athletic Departments

Carol A. Barr, William A. Sutton, and Erin M. McDermott

Introduction

Title IX has become one of the most prevalent managerial and financial issues affecting collegiate athletic departments in the '90s. Title IX is federal legislation that states that "No person in the United States shall, on the basis of sex, be excluded from participation in, be denied the benefits of, or be subjected to discrimination under any education program or activity receiving federal financial assistance" (Education Amendments of 1972, 1990).

Since the passage of Title IX in 1972, a myriad of events have taken place that have affected the impact and application of Title IX to scholastic and collegiate athletic departments. In looking at the law's history, the application of Title IX to athletic departments was virtually nonexistent from 1972 to 1979. With the passage of Title IX in 1972, there was much confusion as to how Title IX should be interpreted and implemented and whether Title IX applied to athletics at all. In 1975, the Department of Health, Education & Welfare (HEW), the governing organization responsible for the implementation of Title IX, released a set of regulations designed to implement Title IX (U.S. General Accounting Office, 1996). Although athletic administrators were now aware that Title IX included athletics, there was still disorder surrounding what these regulations actually covered and how they should be implemented. In 1979, the Office for Civil Rights (OCR) succeeded HEW and released policy interpretations that helped to alleviate some of the confusion surrounding Title IX. Title IX's impact was beginning to be felt as the percentage of female participants in intercollegiate athletics rose from 15% in 1972 to 30.8% in 1984 (Berry & Wong, 1986).

In 1984, though, Title IX's impact on collegiate athletic departments was virtually extinguished through the *Grove City College v. Bell* Supreme Court ruling. In this ruling, the Supreme Court stated that only departments or programs that received direct federal funding needed to comply with Title IX (*Grove City College v. Bell*, 1984). After the *Grove City College* decision, the OCR dropped 23 Title IX cases because it could not establish that the collegiate athletic department involved was receiving direct federal financial assistance (Wong & Ensor, 1985/86).

In March of 1988, Congress passed the Civil Rights Restoration Act of 1987 (1988), which stated that entire institutions and agencies are covered by Title IX, and other federal antidiscrimination laws, if any program or activity within the organization receives federal aid. Since the enforcement of Title IX was restored with the passage of the Civil Rights Restoration Act, collegiate athletic departments have found themselves in the position of having to once again understand and comply with the requirements of Title IX. The 1996/97 NCAA statistics found that the percentage of women participants in intercollegiate athletics had risen to 38.9% as collegiate athletic departments were taking action to comply with Title IX (Basinger, 1998).

Title IX's Impact on Collegiate Athletic Departments

As Title IX regained its enforcement power as far as collegiate athletic departments were concerned, and as more athletes, coaches, and parents have become aware of what the law entails, an increase in Title IX litigation and settlement agreements has occurred. Some of these court cases and settlements include *Favia v. Indiana University of Pennsylvania* (1993), *Roberts v. Colorado State Board of Agriculture* (1993), *Cohen v. Brown University* (1995), and *Pederson v. Louisiana State University* (1996). These court cases all involved female plaintiff student-athletes bringing a Title IX complaint alleging that they were being discriminated against by not being provided with the opportunity to participate in intercollegiate athletics. It is interesting to note that in each of these court cases, the courts have ruled that the institution was discriminating against the female student-athletes. This carries a strong message to collegiate athletic department and university administrators that the majority of collegiate athletic departments are out of compliance with Title IX. This statement is supported by the results of a recent study performed by *USA Today* using the Equity in Athletics Disclosure Act, which requires colleges and universities to make athletic participation and financial data public (Brady, 1997). This study found that at only 28, or 9%, of Division I institutions the percentage of female student-athletes was within five percentage points of women undergraduates enrolled at the institution.

Although participation ratios of female student-athletes to female undergraduate students have primarily received the most attention in Title IX court cases, Title IX legislation covers other component areas as well. These additional component areas include financial assistance, which analyzes the percentage of athletic scholarship aid provided by sex to the percentage of athletic participants by sex; and other benefits and opportunities, an area that analyzes the treatment of student-athletes by sex in a multitude of categories, including equipment and supplies; scheduling of games and practice times; travel and per diem allowances; tutors; coaches; locker rooms, practice, and competitive facilities; medical and training facilities and services; housing and dining facilities and services; publicity; support services; and recruitment (*Title IX Athletics Investigator's Manual*, 1990). The allocation of scholarship funding as well as benefits and opportunities provided to male and female student-athletes is starting to receive increased attention in the courts and in settlement agreements between the plaintiff female student-athletes and the institution's athletic department. In 1997, the National Women's Law Center brought sex discrimination complaints against 25 institutions dealing solely with allocation of female athletic scholarship funding (Arace, 1997). Therefore, it is important for collegiate athletic administrators to collect information and understand these other Title IX component areas in terms of the male and female student-athletes and to make appropriate changes to ensure compliance with Title IX in these areas as well.

Since 1988 and the restoration of the application of Title IX to collegiate athletic departments, much has happened in terms of participation opportunities for female collegiate athletes. In 1996/97, women collegiate athletic participants reached a record high of more than 128,200 or 38.9% of all collegiate athletic participants (Basinger, 1998). This record number of participants carries with it increased pressures in funding as far as scholarship aid, recruiting dollars, and operational funds are concerned in addition to pressures placed on facility usage and an increase in personnel support needed.

Collegiate athletic administrators state that gender equity plays a big part in all their decision making (Jensen, 1994), but collegiate athletic administrators also must be cognizant of the financial pressures found within athletic departments today. This presents a very difficult task for collegiate athletic administrators: how to juggle achieving Title IX compliance while working within very restrictive budgetary constraints. For example, Colorado State, citing budgetary problems, dropped its baseball and women's softball programs in June of 1992. The women softball players filed a Title IX lawsuit claiming that Colorado State was not in compliance with the law. The lower court, affirmed by the Circuit Court of Appeals, ruled that Colorado State had to reinstate its women's softball team because the school was in fact out of compliance with Title IX by not providing enough opportunities for female student-athletes to participate (*Roberts v. Colorado State Board of Agriculture*, 1993).

Title IX's Impact on Collegiate Athletic Marketing

Collegiate athletic marketing has experienced tremendous growth as institutions and athletic administrators are relying on marketing to help with the financial difficulties they are experiencing. In a study of the status of athletic marketing in National Collegiate Athletic Association (NCAA) Division I-A universities, 84% of the presidents and 96% of the athletic directors who responded stated that expanding marketing efforts will be very important in increasing athletic revenue (Lehnus, 1996). It is interesting to note that in this study, 51% of the presidents and 75% of the athletic directors responded that gender equity was the most important problem facing athletics in the next decade (Lehnus, 1996). As Title IX and its requirements for increased funding for women's athletics have taken place during a time of funding cuts at many schools, numerous institutions have turned to placing a larger emphasis on athletic fund-raising, promotions, and marketing efforts in order to keep their programs alive (Stevens, Louden, & McConkey, 1995).

In 1980, it was unusual to find a collegiate athletic program that had any staff member whose job title contained the word "marketing" (Stevens et al., 1995). Yet, in a 1995 study of Division I and II athletic directors regarding the nature and extent of sport marketing, Stevens et al. (1995) found that 66% of Division I and II institutions responding reported having someone responsible for sport marketing activities. In addition, 63% of the people in charge of sport marketing were employed full-time whereas 37% were employed part-time (Stevens et al., 1995). A second study involving athletic marketing administrators found that 60.3% of the respondents (members of the National

Association of Collegiate Marketing Administrators [NACMA] representing Division I, II, and III institutions) reported that they would probably be working in intercollegiate sport marketing in the next 5 years. However, 46% indicated they had applied for a different job in the past year. Reasons found in this study for the retention (or lack thereof) of collegiate marketing administrators included salary dissatisfaction and the desire to "move up" within the athletic department (Sutton, McDonald, & Covell, 1995).

The growth of collegiate athletic marketing has also seen the emergence of NACMA, which was founded in 1990 and serves those working in collegiate marketing, promotion, and related fields at NCAA, NAIA, and NJCAA member institutions. This association operates in an advisory and supportive capacity, enabling members to exchange ideas, formulate concepts and practices, provide continuing education, and establish operating and ethical standards (Lipsey, 1996).

Title IX contains compliance guidelines regarding the marketing and promotional activities of collegiate athletic departments. Although the terms *marketing* and *promotions* are not explicitly stated within the Title IX Policy Interpretations, the marketing and promotional activities of a collegiate athletic department are reviewed for Title IX purposes under the publicity component area (*Title IX Athletics Investigator's Manual*, 1990). This component area of Title IX addresses the availability and quality of personnel, the access to other publicity resources for men's and women's programs, and the quantity and quality of publications and other promotional devices featuring men's and women's programs (*Title IX Athletics Investigator's Manual*, 1990). Marketing can be used as a tool to promote sporting activities and generate funds, but collegiate athletic administrators need to take appropriate steps as well to ensure that both the men's and women's sport programs are receiving the attention and benefits of the marketing activities.

With the increase in participation, the focus of gender equity will now start to change from simply wanting a female team to wanting a team that is equitably funded or provided with similar benefits and opportunities according to the other component areas of Title IX. In some cases, the courts have addressed various funding and benefit areas and have provided some foresight into how these issues will be handled. One funding and benefit area receiving recognition by the courts is the sport promotions and sport marketing area. As part of the Consent Decree in *Haffer v. Temple University* (1981), Temple University agreed to hire a full-time employee to promote Temple's women's athletic programs. Temple also agreed to provide resources for the promotion of the women's athletic programs in order to attract increased spectator interest and, where feasible, raise revenues. The court in *Favia v. Indiana University of Pennsylvania* (1993) found that at each home football game and men's basketball game, a scholarship for tuition for one semester was raffled off. This special incentive helped to heighten interest and increase student attendance at these games, whereas a similar practice was not conducted at any women's games. Indiana University of Pennsylvania was found to be in violation of Title IX. In the *Cohen v. Brown University* Settlement Agreement involving Title IX component areas other than the proportionality argument, C.A. No. 92-0197-P (D.R.I. 1994), Brown University agreed that the number of promotional events for home competitions must be substantially equivalent for the men's and women's teams. In addition, Brown University agreed to supply the men's and women's sport programs with comparable media and/or recruiting guides, printed competitive schedules, and staff support from the sport information department. Some institutions have voluntarily implemented changes to help with compliance in these Title IX component areas; Penn State decided to increase funding in sport promotions and marketing in addition to other changes being implemented, whereas the University of Virginia decided to enhance their sport information and sport promotions areas to assist with Title IX compliance issues (Grant & Curtis, 1996).

Collegiate athletic marketing is a component area of Title IX that will receive increased attention as the focus of Title IX compliance changes from athletic participation ratios to athletic scholarship funding and to benefits and opportunities provided to male and female student-athletes. As such, the activities, funding, and personnel involved in the marketing of male and female sport programs should be of concern to collegiate athletic administrators. In addition, as collegiate athletic departments experience the effects of financial cutbacks at the university and federal levels, the pressure to achieve compliance with Title IX is even greater and necessitates innovative thinking on the part of collegiate athletic administrators. Marketing is one area that can serve as an important tool in assisting with the financial pressures being experienced by collegiate athletic departments in achieving Title IX compliance.

Method

Questionnaire

Based on a review of the literature regarding Title IX and athletic marketing studies, a survey was designed to collect data on the demographic profiles of the respondents and the marketing support and attention given to men's and women's sport programs in their athletic departments. Further refinement of the original questions was based on feedback from a pretest of the survey instrument. This feedback was provided from an expert panel consisting of seven administrators (4 males, 3 females) holding various positions within athletic departments at institutions among the various NCAA divisional levels.

The final questionnaire for this study consisted of 26 questions divided into two parts: (a) demographic information and (b) support of and activities surrounding men's and women's sport programs in athletic departments. The first part of the questionnaire asked the subjects to provide information on their gender, ethnicity/race, degree, job title, and division of their institution. The second part consisted of a variety of items measuring the types of activities and marketing support given to women's sport programs compared to men's sport programs in athletic departments.

Respondents

The survey questionnaires were mailed to NACMA members, $N = 245$, representing the different NCAA Division I, II, and III institutions. The survey respondents consisted of 88 NACMA members (males = 70 or 80%, females = 18 or 20%), resulting in a response rate of 36%. Information on the survey respondents can be found in Table 1.

The data are presented both descriptively and statistically. *T*-tests, chi-square, and analysis of variance tests were performed on some of the key questions to show the relationships between information provided and the gender of the respondent, in addition to the institution's NCAA membership classification.

Table 1.
Survey Respondent Profiles

Division of Respondent's Institution	Division I-A	Division I-AA	Division I (no football)	Division II	Division III
N = 85	42 (49.4%)	16 (18.8%)	12 (14.1%)	10 (11.8%)	5 (5.9%)
Position Held by Respondent	Athletic Director	Associate Athletic Director	Assistant Athletic Director	Director of Marketing/ Promotion	Other
N = 87	8 (9.2%)	11 (12.6%)	23 (26.4%)	36 (41.4%)	9 (10.4%)
Educational Degree of Respondent	Bachelor's Degree	Master's Degree or Candidate	Ph.D. Degree or Candidate	Other	
N = 88	25 (28.4%)	57 (64.8%)	5 (5.7%)	1 (1.1%)	

Results

Athletic Department and Athletic Marketing Budgets

Respondents were asked to give specific figures for total annual athletic department budget, percentage of this budget allocated directly to men's and women's sport program budgets (including scholarships, travel expenses, operating expenses, salaries, recruiting expenses), the total annual athletic marketing budget, and the percentage of this budget allocated to men's and women's sport programs. Overall results found the average athletic budget to be $9,200,000 and the average marketing budget, $120,000. Of the $9,200,000 mean athletic department budget, 61.8% was allocated to men's sports, and 38.2% was allocated to women's sports. Of the mean $120,000 athletic marketing budget, 62.8% was allocated to men's sports, and 37.2% was allocated to women's sports.

The annual budget and marketing budget data were then analyzed by division and were compared between men's and women's sport programs. Tables 2 and 3 show the results of these analyses. Due to small sample sizes and similar marketing practices, Divisions II and III were grouped together. The division listed as Division I represents institutions that are Division I but have no football program, whereas the Division I institutions that sponsor football are classified according to their I-A and I-AA NCAA membership status.

Number of Sport Programs Offered

Respondents were asked to specify the number of varsity sport programs offered to men and women respectively in their athletic department. The mean number of sport teams supported for men was 9.1 and for women, 9.2. The equality of these two figures suggests that Title IX has had an impact on the number of sport programs being offered. In 1977 the average number of teams offered for women in an athletic department was 5.61, in 1992 it was 7.09, and in 1994 it was 7.22 (Acosta & Carpenter, 1994). Table 4 presents

Table 2.
Annual Athletic Department Budget by Division and Sport Program

Division	# of Responses	Mean	Men's Sports	Women's Sports
Division I-A	40	$15,600,000	65.8%	34.2%
Division I-AA	15	6,290,000	61.9%	38.1%
Division I (no football)	11	3,300,000	57.7%	42.3%
Divisions II & III	15	1,320,000	57.2%	42.8%

Table 3.
Athletic Marketing Budget by Division and Sport Program

Division	# of Responses	Mean	Men's Sports	Women's Sports
Division I-A	37	$204,000	66.1%	33.9%
Division I-AA	16	76,000	53.1%	46.9%
Division I (no football)	11	57,000	67.5%	32.5%
Divisions II & III	13	22,000	60.0%	40.0%

Table 4.
Number of Sport Teams Offered by Gender and Division

Division	# of Responses	Men's Teams*	Women's Teams**
Division I-A	39	10.0	10.2
Division I-AA	15	9.1	8.7
Division I (no football)	12	8.7	8.8
Divisions II & III	15	7.3	7.7

* F. Prob. for men's teams by division = 0.01
** F. Prob. for women's teams by division = 0.01

data on the number of male and female sport teams by division. A statistical difference was found between divisions in the number of men's and women's sport teams offered.

Sport Programs Benefiting from Marketing and Promotional Campaigns

Respondents were asked to provide information regarding the number of varsity men's and women's sport teams that benefited from marketing and promotional campaigns geared toward increasing event spectatorship. The mean number of men's programs benefiting from such campaigns was 4.6, and for women's programs, 4.5. This suggests that almost an equal number of men's and women's sport programs benefit from marketing and promotional campaigns geared toward increasing event spectatorship. These

Table 5.
Number of Sport Teams Benefiting from Marketing and Promotional Campaigns by Gender and Division

Division	# of Responses	Men's Teams*	Women's Teams**
Division I-A	41	5.4	5.4
Division I-AA	15	4.4	4.2
Division I (no football)	12	3.3	2.9
Divisions II & III	15	3.5	3.4

* F. Prob. for men's teams by division = 0.02
** F. Prob. for women's teams by division = 0.02

data were also analyzed by division and are shown in Table 5. The results show statistically significant differences between divisions in the number of men's teams and women's teams benefiting from marketing and promotional campaigns.

Criteria Used to Determine Marketing Attention Provided to Sport Programs

The next section of questions was aimed at determining the reasons institutions use for providing marketing attention to a particular sport program. Respondents were given 10 criteria to rank from 1 (*most important*) to 10 (*least important*) when deciding the reasons behind giving sport programs marketing attention in athletic departments. The criteria given are listed in Table 6. Table 6 shows the overall rank of these criteria according to the average of the mean ranking by each division. An analysis by division is also in Table 6, comparing the rankings by respective division. Revenue potential was the only criterion that showed a significant difference (F Prob.=0.05) between divisions. All other criteria had no significant differences between divisions.

Perceptions Regarding Marketing and Promotional Efforts

The next section of questions was included to assess the respondents' attitude toward marketing efforts taking place. Respondents were asked to rate their level of agreement to a set of nine statements on a 6-point Likert scale ranging from 1 (*strongly disagree*) to 6 (*strongly agree*). All statements were geared toward measuring Title IX's impact on marketing and promotional efforts given to women's sport programs in athletic departments. An analysis of these statements and their mean level of agreement by division and gender of respondent is shown in Table 7. No statistically significant differences were found by division or gender for any of the items.

The results from Table 7 indicate that the respondents were leaning toward the agreement end of the Likert scale as far as Title IX's having a positive impact on the marketing efforts directed at women's sports, attendance at women's sports increasing over the past 3 years, and attributing this growth in attendance to the marketing efforts for women's programs. Another key result found respondents in all divisions, as well as both the male and female respondents, disagreeing with the statement that women are more effective than men in marketing and promoting women's sports. Another unique finding from

Table 6.
Criteria Used by Athletic Departments in Determining Why Sport Programs Receive Marketing Attention

Ranking Scale— 1 = most important <------------> 10 = least important

Rank		Criteria	I-A			I-AA			I (no football)			II & III			F.
R	M		*n*	M	R	*n*	M	R	*n*	M	R	*n*	M	R	Prob.
1	2.5	Revenue potential *	41	3.1	(2)	16	2.3	(2)	12	1.3	(1)	11	2.0	(1)	0.05
2	2.7	Attendance	41	2.0	(1)	16	2.1	(1)	11	2.5	(2)	11	3.1	(3)	0.55
3	4.2	Tier level**	15	4.5	(4)	7	4.9	(3)	5	3.8	(3)	6	3.0	(2)	0.67
4	4.5	Athletic director decision	41	4.3	(3)	16	4.9	(3)	12	4.5	(4)	11	4.6	(4)	0.85
5	5.2	Past performance	41	5.2	(5)	16	5.2	(5)	12	5.3	(5)	10	4.8	(6)	0.70
6	5.3	Funding received	40	5.4	(6)	16	5.3	(6)	11	5.7	(6)	11	4.6	(4)	0.70
7	5.8	Marketing director decision	41	5.5	(7)	16	5.9	(7)	12	6.4	(7)	9	6.0	(7)	0.69
8	6.6	Consistency with conference	40	6.6	(9)	16	6.8	(10)	11	6.9	(8)	10	6.2	(8)	0.93
9	6.6	Coach influence	40	6.2	(8)	16	6.7	(9)	11	7.4	(9)	9	7.8	(10)	0.10
10	7.4	President/ Chancellor/ CEO influence	39	7.5	(10)	16	6.4	(8)	11	8.0	(10)	10	7.5	(9)	0.36

n = number of responses, M = mean, R = rank within that division classification
* F prob. ≤ .05
** = if the athletic department used a tiering system of sport programs that also played a part in determining marketing attention received

these questions was that the respondents felt that marketing dollars spent on men's sports generally provide a higher return on investment compared to dollars spent on women's sports. This could be seen as a dilemma when budgetary decisions are made. To spend more money on marketing men's sports may provide a larger return on the investment, but this practice may deprive the women's programs from budgetary support needed for marketing efforts to help increase attendance that would be seen as showing a return on investment. It is important to keep in mind that the surveys were mailed to members of NACMA and that a possible limitation of any survey questionnaire involves the possibility

Table 7.
Level of Agreement With Statements on Marketing and Promotional Efforts According to Division and Gender of Respondent

Likert scale: 1 = strongly disagree <-- 2 --- 3 --- 4 --- 5 --> 6 = strongly agree

Statement	I-A		I-AA		I (no football)		II/III		Division F Prob.	Male		Female		Gender T-test
	n	M	*n*	M	*n*	M	*n*	M		*n*	M	*n*	M	
Marketing dollars and resources should be allocated only to revenue sports.	40	2.9	16	3.3	12	3.4	12	2.8	0.62	67	3.1	18	2.7	0.41
We promote women's sports via special events (clinics, tournaments, booster club activities).	40	4.2	16	4.5	11	3.9	11	4.2	0.85	66	4.3	17	4.2	0.86
Women are more effective in marketing and promoting women's sports than men.	40	2.2	16	2.5	12	2.0	13	2.3	0.68	66	2.2	17	2.4	0.68
Title IX has positively impacted marketing efforts directed at women's sports.	41	4.4	16	4.4	12	4.2	14	3.6	0.23	67	4.2	18	4.4	0.63
Attendance at women's sports has increased during the past 3 years.	41	4.4	16	4.1	12	3.9	14	4.4	0.70	67	4.2	18	4.7	0.17
Marketing efforts for women's programs have influenced their game attendance levels.	41	4.3	16	3.9	12	4.1	15	4.3	0.73	68	4.1	18	4.6	0.18
We allocate equal amounts of time and effort for marketing women's sports as we do for men's sports.	41	3.8	16	3.7	12	3.1	14	3.9	0.59	67	3.7	18	3.6	0.82
Title IX has resulted in additional dollars being allocated to market and promote women's sports.	41	4.0	16	4.0	12	3.8	13	2.9	0.13	66	3.8	18	3.8	0.99
Marketing dollars spent on men's sports generally provide a higher return on investment compared to dollars spent on women's sports.	41	4.7	16	4.8	12	4.7	13	4.5	0.94	67	4.7	17	4.5	0.56

n = number of responses, M = mean value on the 6-point Likert scale

of responses' being influenced by the personal motives or concerns of the individual respondent, not necessarily the practices occurring at the institution.

Marketing Activities Surrounding Women's Sports

A series of yes/no questions was asked to determine the marketing activities surrounding women's sport programs. Respondents were asked whether they charged admission for women's sport programs, whether they produced separate media guides for men's and women's sport programs, whether they actively solicited sponsors for women's sports, and whether they had a staff member devoted to marketing women's sports. These data were analyzed by division and are shown in Table 8. There were statistically significant differences between divisions in the areas of producing separate media guides (prob.=0.02) and having a staff member devoted to marketing women's sports (prob.=0.00).

Table 8.
Marketing Activities Surrounding Women's Sports

Activity	Div. I-A		Div. I-AA		Div. I (no football)		Div. II & III		Chi Square
	n	%	*n*	%	*n*	%	*n*	%	
Charging admission	41	100	15	93.8	10	83.3	14	93.3	0.11
Separate media guides *	40	100	16	100	12	100	12	85.7	0.02
Actively solicit sponsors	40	97.6	14	87.5	10	83.3	14	93.3	0.30
Staff member devoted to marketing women's sports **	23	56.1	3	18.8	1	8.3	1	6.7	0.00

* Statistical difference was found between Divisions II & III response and all other division categories.

Table 9.
Practices Used for Men's and Women's Sport Programs

Description of Practice Used	# of Responses	Men's Teams—Yes Responses	Women's Teams—Yes Responses	*T*-Value	Significance Value
A strategic marketing plan (2–3 years) *	84	37	29	2.62	0.01
An annual marketing plan *	85	78	73	2.29	0.02
Staff training and development in marketing/promotions	84	44	42	1.42	0.16
Merchandising programs *	84	51	44	2.53	0.01
Sport-specific logos and merchandise	84	45	45	0.00	1.00
Sponsor appreciation activities *	85	72	67	2.29	0.02
Golf tournaments or other fund-raisers	84	66	55	3.54	0.00

* Statistical differences were found in these categories between what was being done for the men's sport programs versus the women's sport programs.

Practices Used for Men's and Women's Sport Programs

The respondents were asked whether they utilized certain practices for both the men's and women's sport programs. A comparison was then made utilizing the overall results to determine if statistically significant differences occurred in utilizing these practices with both the men's and women's sport programs. The results are presented in Table 9.

In each of the categories except sport-specific logos and merchandise, the respondents stated that the practice provided less for the women's sport programs than for the men's sport programs. In addition, the results revealed that in the majority of categories, dif-

Table 10.
Number of Sport Programs With Corporate Sponsorship Affiliation

Sport Program	Division I-A		Division I-AA		Division I (no football)		Divisions II & III		F Prob.
	n	Mean	*n*	Mean	*n*	Mean	*n*	Mean	
Men's Teams *	34	6.35	16	4.63	10	3.10	11	3.55	.01
Women's Teams *	34	6.15	16	3.94	10	2.60	10	3.70	.03

* For both the men's teams and women's teams sport programs, the statistical difference was found between Division I-A results and Division I (no football) results.

Table 11.
Characterization of Promotional Efforts for Women's Sports

Characterization	Division I-A		Division I-AA		Division I (no football)		Divisions II & III	
	n	%	*n*	%	*n*	%	*n*	%
Media-directed	15	62.5	8	66.7	3	33.3	6	60.0
Grassroots-directed	9	37.5	4	33.3	6	66.7	4	40.00

ferences were found in the practices provided for men's sport programs in comparison to the practices provided for women's sport programs.

Corporate Sponsors

In order to further assess the marketing support given to women's sport programs, respondents were asked how many men's and women's varsity teams respectively are affiliated with corporate sponsors. These data were then analyzed by division, and statistically significant differences were found between divisions for both men's and women's teams. No statistical difference was found within division between men's and women's teams affiliated with corporate sponsors. Table 10 lists the mean values calculated for the number of men's and women's teams that are affiliated with corporate sponsors. The significant difference between men's teams by division is 0.01, and the significant difference between women's teams by division is 0.03. The top four women's sport programs given by the respondents as being affiliated with corporate sponsors are basketball (30.7%), volleyball (26.1%), soccer (10.2%), and softball (9.7%).

Characterization of Promotional Efforts for Women's Sports

In order to evaluate the promotion activities designed for women's sport programs, respondents were asked to characterize the promotional efforts and activities for women's sports as either primarily media-directed (advertising, poster, flyers, etc.), or grassroots-directed (distributing tickets/hosting clinics, etc.). The data were analyzed by division, and no statistically significant differences were found. Table 11 lists this data analysis by division.

Table 12.
Summary of Key Results and Title IX Implications

Key Results	Potential Title IX Implications
1. Revenue and attendance were the top two criteria overall used to determine marketing support for sport programs.	• If this practice involves primarily men's teams receiving marketing support, a potential Title IX violation may be occurring. • Sport marketers should look at potential revenue and higher attendance women's sports, such as basketball, volleyball, softball, and soccer, to name a few. • Television contracts are emerging in some women's sports, such as basketball, volleyball, and softball. This contains a potential for additional revenue for these sport programs.
2. Staff support devoted to marketing women's sport programs is low.	• Although data for men's sport programs are not available to make a comparison, sport marketers can look within their own athletic department, keeping in mind that Title IX requirements investigate availability and quality of personnel involved.
3. Both male and female respondents disagreed with the statement that women are more effective in marketing and promoting women's sports than men are.	• Quality of the personnel employed is important under Title IX requirements.
4. Respondents were in agreement that marketing dollars spent on men's sports generally provide a higher return on investment compared to dollars spent on women's sports.	• Sport marketers should be cautious not to become too concerned with higher returns from men's sport programs which will in turn create more funding and support for these men's sport programs. • Some women's sport programs created high returns as well, that is, women's basketball, volleyball, and softball, to name a few.
5. Statistically significant differences were found concerning certain practices used for both men's and women's sport programs (i.e., merchandising programs, sponsor-appreciation activities, golf tournaments and other fund-raisers).	• A potential Title IX violation may be occurring if one gender is being discriminated against by not receiving adequate attention and support.

It was also found that most institutions from all divisions are using primarily a media-directed approach in promoting women's sport programs. The only exception was Division I (no football), which described their promotional efforts as grassroots-directed. Although the respondents were not asked reasoning behind their promotional approach, one explanation regarding the grassroots method used by Division I (no football) institutions may involve the media appeal of the sport of football in comparison to other sport programs.

Discussion

The annual athletic department budgets and athletic marketing budgets at the institutions of the respondents showed the men's sport programs received a higher percentage of funding than that of the women's sport programs. A comparison between the two budgets showed the percentage of funding received for athletic marketing by the women's sport programs to be fairly close to the overall percentage of the athletic department budget in Division I-A and Divisions II and III. This comparison also found the Division I-AA institutions represented in the study provided more athletic marketing budgetary support for the women's programs, by almost 9%, whereas the Division I (no football) institutions exhibited less athletic marketing support, by almost 10%, for the women's sport programs in comparison to percentage of athletic budgetary support. In comparing the athletic marketing funding percentages with female student-athlete participation data in each of these divisions—Division I-A: 34%, Division I-AA: 35%, Division I (no football): 45%, Division II: 35%, Division III: 38% (1997 NCAA Gender Equity Study)—there was not much discrepancy except in Division I-AA, 11.9% difference, and Division I (no football), 12.5% difference. The discrepancy in Division I-A, though, was in favor of the women's sport programs receiving athletic marketing funding, whereas in Division I (no football), the discrepancy existed in the lack of athletic marketing funding being provided to the women's sport programs.

When deciding which sport programs receive marketing attention in athletic departments, the overall results found revenue potential and attendance as the top two criteria (see Table 6). Revenue potential and attendance were ranked either number one or two in all divisions, except in Division III, which ranked revenue potential number one, but instead of attendance, tier level was ranked number two. Attendance closely followed, with only a 0.1 differential between the mean values. In Divisions I-A and I-AA, attendance was ranked number one with revenue potential ranked second. Although revenue is important to these institutions, this result makes sense, especially at the Division I-A level, because attendance is crucial to Division I-A football membership criteria.

It can be inferred from the overall ranking of revenue potential and attendance as the top two criteria used in determining marketing attention, that there exists a self-fulfilling prophecy on the part of marketing departments. The level of marketing support given to a program is mainly decided based on revenue potential and attendance, and as a result, the programs with high attendance and high revenue potential will receive the most marketing support. They will thrive and continue to receive more marketing support, which will lead to consistently higher revenue potential and higher attendance levels. Those with lower revenue potential and attendance will lack the initial marketing attention and support, potentially preventing them from achieving the necessary levels of either of these criteria to receive marketing support. Yet, in asking the respondents about their attitudes toward marketing efforts (see Table 7), the results of this study found the respondents to be neutral or leaning slightly toward disagreement that marketing dollars and resources should be allocated only to revenue sports. Philosophically, sport marketers may not agree that marketing support be allocated only to revenue sports, and yet budgetary decisions and even lack of personnel support may dictate that this practice be followed. Sport marketers and athletic administrators must exhibit caution, though, as the courts in Title IX cases have found that budgetary reasons are not a valid excuse for Title IX violations. If the revenue sports receiving marketing attention and support are primarily men's sport programs, a potential Title IX violation may be occurring.

There was also speculation as to whether any significant differences between divisions and between gender of respondents would be found in terms of perceptions of marketing and promotional efforts (see Table 7). Some of the questions referred to revenue sports, game attendance levels, and allocation of dollars that might have had an impact on how the respondents in the various divisions or by gender would agree or disagree with the statement. There were no statistically significant differences found based on division level or gender of respondent. Some key results found the respondents in all divisions disagreed with the statement when asked whether they felt women are more effective in marketing and promoting women's sports than men are. Another interesting finding saw the respondents in all divisions agreeing with the statement that marketing dollars spent on men's sports generally provide a higher return on investment compared to dollars spent on women's sports. The results seem to indicate that marketing decisions are made similarly by marketing administrators regardless of division or gender of the marketing administrator. It is also apparent that the perception of Title IX's impact on marketing activities and the progress of women's sport events in relation to this support are not dependent on division level of the institution or gender of the marketing administrator.

Results from this study also found that admission is being charged, separate media guides are being produced, and a high number of athletic departments are actively soliciting corporate sponsorship for some women's sport events at most institutions at all division levels (see Table 8). A key finding associated with the marketing activities surrounding women's sports was the lack of a full-time staff member devoted to marketing women's sports. At Div. I-A institutions, 56.1% responded that they had a staff member devoted to marketing activities surrounding women's sports. The percentage of institutions employing such a person in the other divisions was lower: 18.8% in Div. I-AA, 8.3% in Div. I (no football), and 6.7% in Div. II and III institutions. Although a limitation of this study was that comparison data regarding staff members devoted to marketing men's sport programs were not obtained, these results can still provide helpful information. Results from Table 7 indicate the respondents across divisions were fairly neutral when asked whether they allocate equal amounts of time and effort for marketing women's sports and for men's sports. Perhaps a bigger commitment to the marketing of women's sport programs through the employment of a full-time staff member committed to the task could assist in this area. Once again, sport marketers and athletic administrators must keep in mind that Title IX policy interpretations under this component area investigate the availability and quality of personnel being provided to both the men's and women's sport programs.

Respondents who indicated they had a staff member devoted to women's sports were asked which programs received the attention of this person. The top four programs from the 49 sport programs given were basketball (32.7%), volleyball (18.4%), all sports (16.3%), and softball (8.2%). Relating this to the important criteria found for sport programs to receive marketing attention, mainly attendance and revenue potential, it makes sense that basketball and volleyball are being focused on by many staff members devoted to women's sport programs. The growth in women's basketball and volleyball has led to increased attendance and greater revenue potential. It is common for these events to charge admission for spectators. Television contracts emerging in women's basketball, volleyball, and softball have also provided these sports with more potential for additional revenues that have contributed to greater marketing attention.

The survey also asked respondents to indicate what types of marketing practices were utilized for both men's and women's sport programs (see Table 9). Numerous statistically significant differences were found when comparing results overall between men's and women's sport programs. For instance, merchandising programs, sponsor-appreciation activities, golf tournaments, or other fund-raisers were performed more often for the men's sport programs than women's sport programs. Again, sport marketers and athletic administrators must keep in mind the requirements of Title IX in providing benefits and opportunities to the men's and women's sport programs.

Summary and Implications

As the focus of Title IX litigation has extended beyond the participation opportunities area to other component areas such as marketing and promotional activities, sport marketers and athletic administrators must be aware of the Title IX requirements in this area as well. The athletic marketing funding and support being provided to the men's and women's sport programs need to be monitored in order to assure compliance with Title IX. Table 12 contains a summary of the key results as well as potential Title IX implications surrounding these findings.

Conclusion

Institutions and marketing departments at all levels seem to have good intentions in supporting women's programs, but athletic departments are not adding the personnel necessary to effectively promote and market women's sports. There is no question that an increase in support personnel and funding in areas such as marketing should accompany the growth that has taken place in the number and operation of the women's sport programs. The Title IX component area that addresses marketing and promotional activities surrounding the men's and women's sport programs specifically investigates the policies, procedures, and criteria used in determining who gets what, as well as compares the number and quality of personnel assigned to cover the men's and women's teams. Thus, in terms of Title IX compliance, it is imperative that institutions not only provide sufficient marketing support to the women's teams in relation to the men's teams, but also provide appropriate personnel and budgetary resources to carry out these marketing goals and activities.

Athletic administrators and marketers should monitor the courts and the Title IX decisions that are being handed down. If the courts start to look more intensely into the benefits and opportunities component area of Title IX compliance, the marketing and promotional activities under the Title IX publicity component area, personnel, and operational budgets surrounding the men's and women's sport programs will be closely scrutinized, and could, in fact, lead to another round of Title IX litigation.

References

Acosta, R.V., & Carpenter, L.J. (1994). *Women in intercollegiate sport. A longitudinal study—seventeen year update.* Unpublished manuscript, Department of Physical Education, Brooklyn College, Brooklyn, NY.

Arace, J. (1997, June 3). Title IX complaint about scholarships. *USA Today*, p. 8C.

Basinger, J. (1998, May 22). NCAA sets new record for student participation. *The Chronicle of Higher Education*, p. A47.

Berry, R.C., & Wong, G.M. (1986). *Law and business of the sports industries, common issues in amateur and professional sports, II*, Dover, MA: Auburn House Publishing Company.

Brady, E. (1997, March 3). Colleges score low on gender-equity test. *USA Today*, p. 1C.

Civil Rights Restoration Act, Pub. L. No. 100-259, 102 Stat 28 (1988).

Cohen v. Brown University, 8879 F.Supp. 185 (D.R.I. 1995).

Cohen v. Brown University Settlement Agreement, C.A. No. 92-0197-P (D.R.I. 1994).

Education Amendments of 1972, Pub. L. No. 92-318, 20 U.S.C.A. § 1681(a) (1990).

Favia v. Indiana University of Pennsylvania, 812 F.Supp. 578 (W.D. Pa. 1993).

Grant, C.H.B., & Curtis, M.C. (1996). *Gender equity: Judicial actions and related information.* Iowa City, IA: University of Iowa.

Grove City College v. Bell, 465 U.S. 555 (1984).

Haffer v. Temple University, 524 F.Supp. 531 (E.D. Pa. 1981).

Jensen, M. (1994, October 28). The lines remain drawn between the sexes in sports. *Philadelphia Inquirer*, p. A1.

Lehnus, D.L. (1996). The status of athletic marketing in Division IA universities. *Sport Marketing Quarterly, 5*(3), 31–40.

Lipsey, R.A. (Ed.). (1996). *Sports market place.* Princeton, NJ: Sportsguide, Inc.

Pederson v. Louisiana State University, 912 F.Supp. 892 (M.D.La. 1996).

Roberts v. Colorado State Board of Agriculture, 998 F.2d 824 (10th Cir. 1993).

Stevens, R.E., Loudon, D.L., & McConkey, C.W. (1995). Sport marketing among colleges and universities. *Sport Marketing Quarterly, 4*(1), 41–47.

Sutton, W.A., McDonald, M.A., & Covell, D. (1995, October). Collegiate marketing directors survey. *Athletics Administration*, 38–42.

Title IX athletics investigator's manual. (1990). Washington, DC: Office for Civil Rights, Department of Education.

United States General Accounting Office (1996, October). Intercollegiate athletics: Status of efforts to promote gender equity. Report to the Honorable Cardiss Collins, House of Representatives.

Wong, G.M., & Ensor, R.L. (1985/86). Sex discrimination in athletics: A review of two decades of accomplishments and defeats. *Gonzaga Law Review, 21*, 345.

27

More Than Just a Game? Corporate Social Responsibility and Super Bowl XL

Kathy Babiak and Richard Wolfe

More Than Just a Game? Corporate Social Responsibility in Super Bowl XL

The Super Bowl attracts more viewers and creates more revenue than any other single sport event. The Super Bowl, however, is more than just a game to the National Football League (NFL) and the communities that host it. Increasingly, organizing (host) committees, nonprofit organizations, and local governments in cities that are awarded the game use the event as a catalyst to address pressing social issues (Kott, 2005). The opportunities that a mega-event such as the Super Bowl affords a community for hosting the game in terms of economic, social, and political benefits are considerable. Kwame Kilpatrick, the mayor of Detroit, reflected on this opportunity:

> In truth the game is not nearly as important as the events that go on around the game. Those events will give us a platform to start changing the image of the City of Detroit around this nation and around the world. Only 12 cities have hosted the Super Bowl. This is our shot. (Kleinefelter, 2006a, Audio source)

In a reciprocal fashion, the NFL is becoming progressively more invested in corporate social responsibility (CSR) initiatives in an effort to establish itself as a socially conscious organization, one based on the twin pillars of football and the community (Tagliabue, 2006). As the proverbial jewel in the NFL's crown, the Super Bowl is an institution composed of many inter-linked parts: the league, competing teams, corporate entities, governments, and nonprofit organizations. Increasingly, the NFL is investing its efforts around the Super Bowl on social issues and concerns in cities that host the event.

This paper addresses community outreach initiatives delivered in conjunction with Super Bowl XL (SBXL) hosted by the City of Detroit in February 2006. We position the paper within the CSR construct developed by Carroll (1979, 1999), focusing on the ethical and discretionary aspects of social responsibility. Further, we discuss the strategic relevance of these efforts in enhancing the image of the NFL as a socially responsible organization. We provide an overview of the main tenets of CSR next.

CSR: A brief overview

CSR has been addressed in the organizational/management and economic literatures from a number of different perspectives (Carroll, 1979, 1999, 2000; Margolis & Walsh, 2003; van Marrewijk, 2003; Wood, 1991). Friedman (1962, 2002) offered the view that the only responsibility of business is to make a profit, within the limits of the law. An opposing stance, however, is that the corporation has responsibilities to others, in addition to shareholders. Increasingly, organizations have faced pressures to address societal concerns (Lewis, 2003; Margolis & Walsh, 2003; Matten, Crane, & Chapple, 2003; Moir, 2001). As a result, organizations have been sensitized to the importance of making a positive contribution to society, and many act accordingly. CSR involves a broad range of issues related to the role, position, and function of business in contemporary society (Jonker, 2005). Van Marrewijk (2003) stated that CSR "...refers to company activities – voluntary by definition – demonstrating the inclusion of social and environmental concerns in business operations and in interactions with stakeholders" (p. 236).

The seminal theme of CSR, thus, is that organizations have responsibilities beyond profit maximization (Carroll, 1979, 1999; Moir, 2001). The challenge faced by companies in the current environment is to "use their capabilities and capacities to contribute in a traditional business sense while accepting a social role" (Jonker, 2005, p. 20). Adopting this dual perspective, many leading U.S. corporations have been shifting from a traditional charity perspective to strategic CSR which attempts to integrate corporate donations and community service activities with business operations and interests (Dean, 2003). Similarly, cause-related marketing, whereby firms link the promotion of their

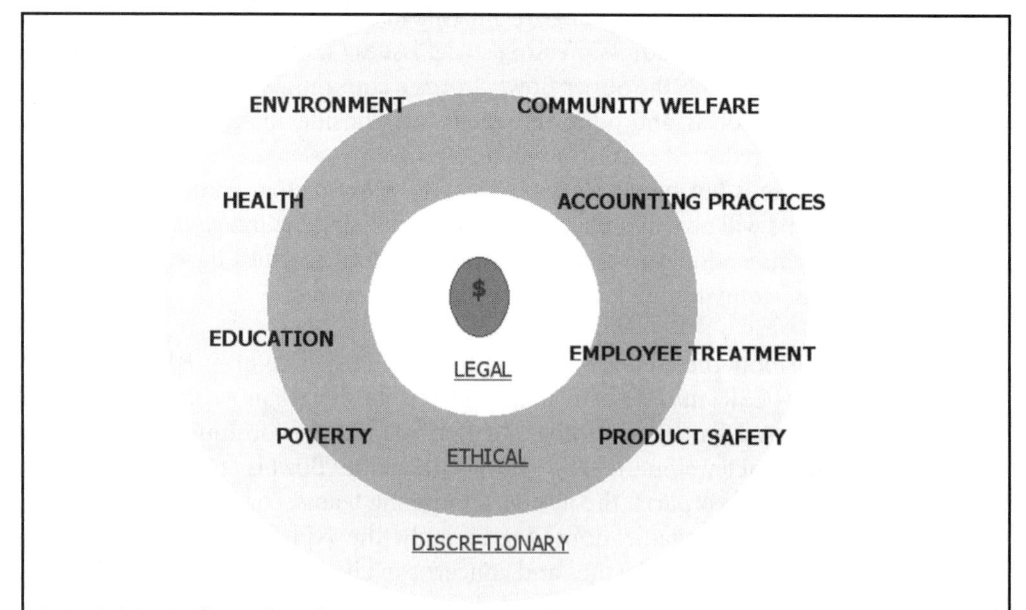

* Activities indicated such as environment, education, or health for example, may cut across all four dimensions of CSR.

Figure 1.
Carroll's (1979, 1999) framework of corporate social responsibility

product to a social cause and contribute a share of the revenues to the cause, is an increasingly common manifestation of business-society linkages (File & Prince, 1998; Gupta & Pirsch, 2005; Higgins, 2003; Irwin, Lachowetz, & Clark, 2003; Irwin, Lachowetz, Cornwell, & Clark, 2003; Meyer, 1999).

Engaging in CSR activities can help a company in various ways (Alperson, 1995; Foley, 1998; Graham, 1994; Mullen, 1997; Stark, 1999). Increasingly, companies and brands associate themselves with a cause as a means to: differentiate from competition; build an emotional bond with their customer; engender employee satisfaction/loyalty; create a cushion for greater customer acceptance of price increases; generate favorable publicity/counter negative publicity; help win over skeptical public officials (who might determine expansion/growth); and build corporate reputation and brand loyalty.

In order to structure our investigation of the CSR activities surrounding the Super Bowl in Detroit, we have adopted Carroll's (1979, 1999) framing of CSR. Carroll argued that CSR is composed of four components: economic (the basic responsibility to make a profit and, thus, be viable), legal (the duty to obey the law), ethical (responsibility to act in a manner consistent with societal expectations), and discretionary (activities that go beyond societal expectations). This paper focuses on the ethical and discretionary components of CSR—that is, activities consistent with societal expectations as well as activities which go beyond societal expectations. We chose to focus on these two areas of CSR as we were interested in voluntary, as opposed to obligatory conformity with economic and legal dimensions of CSR (Godfrey, 2005). A number of CSR areas have been identified which cross each of Carroll's CSR dimensions; examples include: employee treatment, product safety, community welfare, and the environment (McAdam & Leonard, 2003). See Figure 1 for an overview of Carroll's CSR framework and CSR areas.

CSR and Sport.

The concept of CSR is gaining considerable currency in the sport industry. As recently as 10 years ago, CSR issues did not play a significant role in sport (Kott, 2005; Robinson, 2005). Professional sport organizations, however, are entering into socially responsible initiatives at a rapid pace. Currently, most if not all, professional sport organizations have a community affairs or community outreach department, and many are creating foundations to support social causes in their communities (Robinson, 2005). Strong relations with the local community are essential for a sport organization's success (i.e., it is believed to affect an organization's ability to attract fans, secure corporate sponsors, and to have effective dealings with local and state governments). The growing focus on community outreach activities by these organizations, therefore, is understandable.

A number of levels of socially responsible behavior are evident in the sport industry. First, professional sport leagues such as the NFL, NBA, NHL and MLB have initiated league wide programs to address social concerns (e.g., the NBA's Read to Achieve program). Second, teams / franchises have their own programs which address social concerns (e.g., Atlanta Braves' "Grand Slam" and "Straight A" programs). Third, athletes are increasingly engaging in socially responsible initiatives, frequently through their own foundations (e.g., Peyton Manning's PeyBack Foundation). Finally, major events such as the Olympics and the Super Bowl implement socially responsible projects (Kott, 2005). These events have the potential to create a legacy in host cities via a number of related factors: improved infrastructure, increased private and public investment, enhanced tax base, new jobs, and improved image (Ahmed, 1991).

CSR initiatives of sport organizations have advantages that organizations in other industries do not. Among these are the cachet of celebrity athletes, and the media exposure of the events, leagues, teams, and athletes themselves. These advantages result in sport organizations having greater effects than other businesses in providing inspiration in areas such as education and health care for children; health and exercise; concern for the environment; and social/cultural enrichment (Headlee, 2006). Partnering with sport organizations in CSR initiatives, therefore, is very attractive to corporate and nonprofit organizations wanting to increase their CSR impact and be perceived as good corporate citizens by stakeholders.

Mega-events such as the Olympics and the Super Bowl face pressures to be socially responsible in addition to those addressed above. These often result from stakeholder concerns related to potential negative social and environmental impacts of the events. Concerns have been expressed related to impacts on transportation, efforts to relocate homeless people, and how public money spent on these events can best contribute to social well-being (Jennings, 2000; Lenskyj, 2000). Notably, the International Olympic Committee (IOC) has included socially related concerns in its mandate. For example:

> More than ever, sport is a universal language and plays the role of catalyst in today's society as a means of improving quality of life and well-being. The Olympic Movement is about more than sport. ... the Olympic Movement is continuously involved in humanitarian aid efforts, environmental efforts as well as the world-wide goal of elevating the status of women in sport. (http://www.olympic.org, Development Through Sport Section, para. 2)

Thus, at an increasing rate, mega-events are being designed to include CSR related programs. These efforts can be motivated by altruistic values of top management, to develop and to project a positive corporate image, and/or to alleviate negative perceptions stakeholders might have of an event.

Super Bowls and CSR

For the past several years, the NFL has made efforts to take the social responsibility associated with the Super Bowl very seriously. Its website states that "As part of each Super Bowl's community investment, the NFL works with local organizations to develop programs focusing on youth outreach, health and wellness, the arts, education, business advancement for racial and gender minorities, and community rebuilding" (National Football League, 2006, In the Community, para. 1).

NFL commissioner, Paul Tagliabue, has been instrumental in guiding the league and the Super Bowl towards greater social responsibility. He has stated that:

> The Super Bowl may last just four hours, but its legacy lasts forever in the host city. The NFL and the host city give equal attention to the game and the community each year. Throughout the week preceding the game, the NFL stages multiple events and activities to enliven, enrich, and assist the Super Bowl host community. Community outreach is an important element of the Super Bowl experience. Our goal is to take a leadership role and encourage others to join us in public service. (http://www.jointheteam.com, Super Bowl Outreach, para. 1)

Consistent with this, recent Super Bowls in Houston (2004) and Jacksonville (2005) implemented many community outreach initiatives including programs to encourage children to read; projects devoted to build new, or refurbish existing, homes for the underprivileged; and initiatives to address health related issues such as physical inactivity in children and youth.

In what follows, we examine some of the community outreach efforts implemented in concert with SBXL hosted by the City of Detroit in February 2006. First, however, we describe the social context of Detroit, outline the approach we used to gather the data for this preliminary study on CSR and the Super Bowl, and present an overview of the key CSR initiatives delivered in conjunction with SBXL.

SBXL Site – Background

Many accounts detail the social ills facing Detroit. Among the most pressing issues are poverty (over one third of the population lives below the poverty line [Census Bureau, 2006]), crime, and poor education (Murray, 2006). The city faces serious financial hardship, being on the verge of bankruptcy. This has resulted in recent reductions in police officers and firefighters and the closing of eight local community centers. Detroit is a largely minority city surrounded by affluent white suburbs; it has seen decades of population decline (50% of population has gone to suburbs since the 1960s; Karush, 2006). Given the many social problems facing Detroit, there were many opportunities for SBXL CSR initiatives to positively impact the city.

The SBXL Host Committee spent $18.5 million to attract and stage the game (Rovell, 2006). With such large amounts being spent on hosting such events, sport organizations and host cities are increasingly focusing on the impact on a community of hosting an event. Although the final number is still being debated, some have estimated that SBXL had an economic impact of approximately $250 million on the deflated Detroit economy (Walsh, 2006).

Data Collection

Data was collected primarily from secondary sources including media clippings (print and audio) and webpage analysis. Several local newspapers and business sources were systematically scanned daily for six months prior to the game and for six months subsequent to the game. These sources included the Detroit News, Detroit Free Press, Crain's Detroit Business, and other community based media outlets (such as National Public Radio). All sections of these newspapers were reviewed, as many articles related to the community impact of SBXL appeared in non-sport sections. In total, over 90 articles related to community outreach and SBXL were reviewed and analyzed from these sources. Further, an ongoing analysis of four key web pages allowed the researchers to collect a broad range of information regarding specific Super Bowl community outreach efforts. The four web pages were those of the Detroit Lions (www.detroitlions.com), SBXL (www.sbxl.org/community), the Super Bowl (www.superbowl.com/features/community), and the NFL (www.jointheteam.com).

Research Findings and Discussion

In this section we present the socially responsible programs enacted by the NFL and the Host Committee for SBXL. We categorize the programs based on Carroll's (1979, 1999)

Table 1.
Ethical Corporate Social Responsibility and Super Bowl XL

Name of Program	Partners	Purpose
Emerging Business	Corporate: 1 *Nonprofit: 1 (750 companies registered, contracts offered to 250)	To provide women and minority owned businesses Program with opportunities for participation in Super Bowl business process
Super Makeover	Corporate: 1 **Government: 4	Initiative to enhance City of Detroit: picking up trash, painting over graffiti, and killing and removing weeds in high traffic pedestrian areas
Project "Green"	Corporate: 1 Nonprofit: 2 Government: 4	2,500 trees and plants planted to offset carbon emissions

* Nonprofit partners include charities, nonprofit organizations, schools, and foundations
** Government partners include local/municipal governments and organizations, state or federal governments

framework, focusing on ethical and discretionary CSR-related activities. We provide an overview of some of the major programs and then offer our thoughts on how the NFL may build its corporate image by engaging in CSR-related programs. Under the NFL's "Community Impact" umbrella, more than 50 CSR-related events in 12 communities were held during SBXL (Smith, 2006). Tables 1 and 2 present the major ethical and discretionary outreach efforts examined for this paper.

Ethical CSR

Carroll (1999) described the ethical portion of his framework as "...the kinds of behaviors and ethical norms that society expects business to follow. These extend to behaviors and practices that are beyond what is required by the law" (p. 283). The impact of mega sport events on a community has tended to draw criticism from various stakeholders. Critics point to the negative social and environmental impact a major sport event can have on a local community. A primary concern is that money spent by governments on a mega-event could be better used to improve education, infrastructure, health care, and/or the environment. Further, as tickets for an event often cost considerably more than the average citizen can afford, the latter thus has limited chances of attending the event.

In order to prevent being perceived in a poor light, and/or to do the "right" thing, the NFL and Host Committee may engage in CSR-related efforts to proactively address the concerns of critics, and thus comply with societal expectations. As a result, a number of

Table 2.
Discretionary Corporate Social Responsibility and Super Bowl XL

Name of Program	Partners	Purpose
Education related CSR		
Super Reading Program	Corporate: 11 Nonprofit: 3	Encourage children in Detroit schools to read and use local public libraries
Youth Education Town	Corporate: 8 Nonprofit: 5 Government: 2 Individuals: 3	The creation of educational and recreational centers for youth in at-risk neighborhoods in Super Bowl Host cities including tutoring, mentoring, career training, computer education, and athletics. YETs are physical legacies of the Super Bowl.
Cultural CSR		
One World, One Detroit	Corporate: 1 Nonprofit: 10 Government: 1	Tolerance and diversity conference
Rock my Soul		A celebration of art, dance, and music of African Americans throughout history
Infrastructure		
SuperBuild	Corporate: 16 Nonprofit: 6	In partnership with Habitat for Humanity, 40 homes were built for families displaced by Hurricane Katrina
Rebuilding Together		A one-day blitz of much needed home improvements to families, the elderly, or disabled homeowners
Charity Events		
Super Bowl NFL Charities Bowling Classic	Corporate: 1 Nonprofit: 1	Proceeds to benefit Detroit Youth Education Town
NFL Experience	Corporate: 34 Government: 1	An event which provides an opportunity for families to have a 'Super Bowl experience' by experiencing interactive exhibits, clinics, and autograph signings. Proceeds from this charitable event go to the Detroit Youth Education Town
Taste of the NFL	Corporate: 8 Nonprofit: 3	To raise money and awareness for the hungry

'ethically' related outreach activities were planned around SBXL. Table 1 outlines a sample of these ethical practices which include addressing environmental concerns, and ensuring fair business practices and opportunities for underrepresented groups. Below, we describe these initiatives in greater detail.

Addressing Environmental Concerns: A concern for environmentalists is the long-term consequences of major sport events on local communities. This issue was triggered by concerns related to the impact of un-recycled waste at Super Bowl events (Kleinefelter, 2006a). For over a decade, the NFL has addressed this matter by implementing programs to reuse left over food, recycling trash from the game, and coordinating a tree planting effort to offset carbon emissions generated by the increased vehicle traffic. In Detroit, 1,500 trees were planted as part of this program, and 50,000 pounds of food were donated to needy recipients. Local environmental groups believed that although planting 1,500 trees would not have much impact on offsetting carbon emissions during the event, the visibility of the effort and being associated with the NFL and Super Bowl was of greater value than anything they could communicate to the public themselves (Kleinefelter, 2006a). For the NFL, being perceived as an organization that cares about the environment helped to create an image of an organization that is socially responsible (Anderson, 2006).

Combating Unfair Business Practices: Another aspect of ethical CSR related to the Super Bowl has to do with how the NFL conducts its business leading up to the event. In order to address local business concerns, the NFL created a program to ensure that minority owned businesses benefit from a Super Bowl hosted in their community. The Emerging Business Program, launched by the NFL in 1994, is a program that was open to firms certified to be at least 51% owned, operated, and controlled by minorities and/or women. Detroit's version of the program was judged as being particularly successful, having 750 firms on its resource guide, more than any previous Super Bowl. During SBXL, approximately 250 firms received contracts worth an estimated $5.8 million for products and services (http://www.sbxl.com). Not only does this program help the NFL's image as an organization that cares about minorities and women (two large fan bases), they believe that it makes for good business "reaching out to minority and women-owned businesses is part of the NFL's commitment to community service. More than that, the program makes good business sense for all involved" (http://www.superbowl.com, In the Community, Emerging Business Program para. 2).

Addressing Concerns Related to the Homeless – A Different Perspective: As mentioned above, there exist concerns associated with potential negative effects of the Super Bowl on the homeless (Martin, 2006). While the NFL does implement a variety of socially related programs around the Super Bowl, the homeless may have been overlooked. For instance, according to advocates for the homeless, efforts were made at Jacksonville's Super Bowl in 2005 to keep the homeless off the streets and out of sight. In fact, a shelter which was opened for the Jacksonville Super Bowl was closed the day after the game (Bianchi, 2005).

Similar issues occurred in Detroit. It is estimated that as many as 13,000 people in Detroit are homeless, though many of those find shelter with friends or family. As many as 3,000, however, are on the city's streets at any given time (Albom, 2006; Kleinefelter, 2006b). It was left to nonprofit organizations in Detroit to organize a SBXL 'party' to get the city's homeless into shelters. When police encountered a homeless person during

Super Bowl week, they were to contact service providers who would be dispatched to persuade the person into going to a shelter. "They just want to get us (homeless) off the street, keep us from panhandling. When the game is over and we wake up the next morning, I still got nothing in my pockets" said a Detroit homeless man (Martin, 2006, para. 20). It was expected that the Super Bowl would cost homeless service providers as much as $100,000; however, the NFL did not help pay for those costs (Martin, 2006).

Discretionary CSR

Carroll (1999) describes discretionary responsibilities as:

> Voluntary roles that business assumes but for which society does not provide as clear-cut an expectation as it does in the ethical responsibility. These are left to individual managers' and corporations' judgment and choice. ... Examples include making philanthropic contributions, or conducting programs for drug abusers... (p. 284)

A number of discretionary CSR activities were implemented by the NFL and the Host Committee to coincide with SBXL. Many of these efforts are beyond the core competencies of the NFL's business. We have grouped these in the following categories: education, culture, infrastructure related activities, and charitable events and contributions.

Supporting Education: In concert with the NFL, Detroit's SBXL Host Committee implemented the Super Reading Program Book Drive, a program which partnered with Charter One Bank, the Detroit Lions, and the Comcast Foundation (Detroit Lions, 2005). Through this program, over 14,000 books were collected at bank branches and Detroit Lions' games and 3,000 new books were purchased for the Detroit Public School system. As stated by Susan Scherer, Executive Director of SBXL:

> Super Bowl is not just about the game. It is also about the community. Detroit Public Schools had an established program that could use the Super Bowl as a chance to reach their goals and encourage reading. We are proud to be able to support such an important initiative. (http://www.sbxl.com, Community Outreach, Super Reading, para. 10)

In addition to the book drive, the Super Reading Program had three focus areas: the Host Committee's adoption of 40 third-grade classes at Detroit Public Schools; support of an accelerated reader program implemented by Detroit Public Schools to encourage reading; and a library card challenge to encourage children to use the Detroit public library system.

One of the most visible and important (physical) legacies of SBXL will be a Youth Education Town (YET), a $6 million project which will provide broad educational support for local youth. The center will be an after-school educational and recreational facility designed to enhance academics, physical fitness, and job-related skills for disadvantaged youth. For more than a decade, the NFL, in partnership with Boys & Girls Clubs of America and other leading community organizations, has constructed YETs in Super Bowl host cities. The YET initiative is aimed at positively impacting at-risk youth, and would not have been built had Detroit not hosted the Super Bowl (Michigan Economic Development Corporation, 2006). The NFL will support this program indefinitely.

Cultural CSR: In an effort to promote diversity and to create an environment of tolerance, a number of cultural and diversity related CSR events were held in conjunction with SBXL. One of the events held was One World, One Detroit, where 240 ethnically diverse teens participated in a day-long conference addressing issues of tolerance and diversity. Another event held as part of the community outreach efforts of SBXL was Rock my Soul, a celebration of African American art, dance, and music.

Building Infrastructure. In partnership with Habitat for Humanity, the NFL and the Host Committee participated in SuperBuild XL, a project in which 40 homes were built and shipped to Forth Worth, Houston, and College Station, Texas, to help families that were displaced by Hurricane Katrina. Rebuilding Together is a renovation project conducted each year in underserved neighborhoods of Super Bowl host cities. The first project of Rebuilding Together involved revamping the Cass Avenue Activity Center which works with nearly 70 adults who have mental and physical disabilities (Khatri, 2006a).

Some suggest that SBXL has had a dramatic effect on Detroit, doing more to change the city's physical appearance than have corporate relocations, new casinos, two new stadiums, and the last three mayors (Howes, 2006). Infrastructure improvements include upgrades on two main highways and a new streetscape on Lower Woodward, a main street in the city. Former Detroit Mayor Dennis Archer believes Detroit has capitalized on the Super Bowl where other cities have not. "In cities such as Miami, which has hosted eight Super Bowls, there is little redevelopment in preparation for a game. But downtown redevelopment ... has been so successful, Detroit will be in the running for another Super Bowl in five to eight years" (Howes, 2006, para. 8).

Charitable Efforts: The NFL and the SBXL Host Committee established the Sanctioned Event Program to provide local residents who would not otherwise have the opportunity to enjoy Super Bowl-related programming to do so, and at the same time, raise funds for local charities (McDonald, 2005). The NFL provided Super Bowl tickets to organizations to be raffled or auctioned off; this initiative raised $625,000. Another event held was a bowling weekend with proceeds going to charity (Carter, 2005). Usually NFL charities host a golf tournament the day before the game. However, since golf in January in Detroit was not an option, bowling became an alternative. The bowling weekend raised $200,000 and included 75 celebrities, mostly former and current NFL players.

The Taste of the NFL, a high-end food and wine-tasting fund-raiser for area food banks, is estimated to have raised $1 million during SBXL (Smith, 2006). Taste of the NFL is a sanctioned NFL event where funds and awareness are raised for hunger relief organizations. The event provides food and grocery products to those at risk of hunger. Funds raised are distributed to food bank members of America's Second Harvest in each NFL city, as well as other hunger-relief agencies.

In total, the NFL estimates that Super Bowl-related charity events in Detroit raised $8 million (Smith, 2006), but this number is very difficult to confirm. Over 200 of the state's nonprofit organizations expect to benefit from this money (Khatri, 2006b) which will help compensate for the decrease in donations seen in the state of Michigan over the past few years.

Concluding Thoughts: The Super Bowl and CSR

CSR has been viewed as an effective tool for corporations to enhance their reputation and build brand image and customer loyalty, as well as to positively influence society (Lewis, 2003). For the NFL, particularly with an event of the magnitude of the Super Bowl, engaging in CSR-related activities may help to soften some of the criticism surrounding the event (i.e., cost constraints on who is able to attend; issues of who really benefits from such mega–events; effects on the underprivileged, particularly the homeless). Doing the "right thing," in an environment where corporations are increasingly criticized for unethical activity, may ward off backlash and contribute to the NFL's reputation as an entity that cares, and thus may enhance its image.

We suggest that sport organizations have no choice when it comes to CSR—they cannot ignore it, whether they are motivated by altruistic principles of helping others, and/or by pragmatic concerns related to the bottom line. As we have seen above, the Super Bowl is an event which is surrounded by considerable CSR activity. While we cannot definitively say what the NFL's motivation for this is, it is likely a combination of altruism and pragmatism. On the one hand, the NFL is enacting its core value of being a socially conscious organization—on the other, it is a means to pragmatic outcomes such as generating favorable publicity and building its reputation, and establishing an emotional bond with its customers. As argued by Mintzberg (1984), organizational leaders believe that "doing good is the right thing to do" and/or "doing good is good business."

We believe that the growing area of mega-events and social responsibility provides opportunities for researchers to investigate a number of relevant questions. As little work has explored CSR in sport, areas worthy of exploration may include: devising criteria by which to measure the extent and/or impact of CSR-related activities, efforts at uncovering the degree to which CSR-related activities are motivated by pragmatics or principles, tracking the development and evolution of CSR initiatives, identifying customer perceptions of CSR-related efforts and whether they have any impact on brand image, and the extent to which multi-sectoral partnerships are being included in an organization's CSR efforts.

Further, we believe that this paper may provide food for thought for practitioners in the NFL and other parts of the sport industry. Overall, it appeared that the NFL is relatively consistent with its values/beliefs regarding its social responsibility purpose. With the exception of the issue of the homeless during the lead up to the Super Bowl, this may serve to further enhance the strong brand image the NFL is building as an organization who cares about both football and the community. One issue practitioners may want to consider and one which we intend to explore in further research is the extent to which many of these CSR-related programs are 'boiler plate' programs (that is implemented in the same manner in each Super Bowl host city). One drawback from a purely socially responsible perspective is that by being so focused on existing programs, it may prevent the opportunity from addressing real issues/social causes and having long term impact in areas in which their business operates (i.e., poverty, crime, homelessness in Detroit.)

Author Note

Special thanks to Matthew Tapping and James Harasin, who contributed greatly to this paper.

References

Ahmed, Z. U. (1991). Marketing your community: Correcting a negative image. *Cornell Hotel and Restaurant Administration Quarterly, 31*(4), 24.

Albom, M. (2006, February 2). *Party on, but keep on giving.* Retrieved from http://www.freep. com/apps/pbcs.d11/article?AID=/20060202/sports1101/602020556/1082

Alperson, M. (1995). *Corporate giving strategies that add business value* (1126). New York: The Conference Board.

Anderson, S. E. (2006). *Greening the gridiron: Environmental responsibility at the Super Bowl and beyond.* Retrieved from http://www.greenbiz.com/news/news_third.cfm?NewsID=302828CFID=11385223&CFTOKEN=67754566

Bianchi, M. (2005, February 5). *Super Bowl brings shelter for homeless.* Retrieved from http://www.ezilon.com/information/article_1126.shtml

Carroll, A. B. (1979). A three-dimensional conceptual model of corporate social performance. *Academy of Management Review, 4*, 497-505.

Carroll, A. B. (1999). Corporate social responsibility: Evolution of a definitional construct. *Business and Society, 38*(3), 268-295.

Carroll, A. B. (2000). Ethical challenges for business in the new millennium: Corporate social responsibility and models of management morality. *Business Ethics Quarterly, 10*(1), 33-42.

Carter, K. L. (2005). *Super Bowl will bowl for charity.* Retrieved http://www.freep.com

Census Bureau. (2006). *Quick Facts from the US Census Bureau.* Census Bureau. Retrieved from http://quick-facts.census.gov/qfd/states/26/2622000.html

Dean, D. H. (2003). Associating the cooperation with a charitable event through sponsorship: Measuring the effects on corporate-community relations. *Journal of Advertising, 31*(4), 77-88.

Detroit Lions. (2005). *Super Reading book drive scores a TD for Detroit's youth.* Retrieved from http://www.detroitlions.com/document-display.cfm?document-id=437063

File, K. M., & Prince, R. A. (1998). Cause related marketing and corporate philanthropy in the privately held enterprise. *Journal of Business Ethics, 17*(14), 1529-1540.

Foley, J. (1998). Picking a philanthropic partner. *Marketing Magazine, 103*(33), 16-20.

Friedman, M. (1962). *Capitalism and Freedom.* Chicago: University of Chicago Press.

Friedman, M. (2002). *Capitalism and Freedom* (40th Anniversary ed.). Chicago: University of Chicago Press.

Godfrey, P. C. (2005). The relationship between corporate philanthropy and shareholder wealth: A risk management perspective. *Academy of Management Review, 30*(4), 777-792.

Graham, J. (1994). Corporate charity. *Incentive, 168*(7), 51-53.

Gupta, S., & Pirsch, J. (2005). *The company-cause-customer 'fit' in cause-related marketing: A social identity perspective.* Paper presented at the American Marketing Association Conference, Chicago.

Headlee, C. (2006). *Environmental impact of Super Bowls on host cities. Day to day.* National Public Radio. Retrieved from http://www.npr.org/templates/story/story.php?storyId=5180609

Higgins, K. T. (2003). Marketing with a conscience. *Marketing Management, 11*(4), 12-16.

Howes, D. (2006). *Super Bowl XL has game-changing impact on Detroit.* Retrieved http://www.detnews.com

Irwin, R., Lachowetz, T., & Clark, J. (2003). Cause-related sport marketing: How should it work? *International Journal of Sport Management, 4*(3), 173-178.

Irwin, R., Lachowetz, T., Cornwell, T. B., & Clark, J. (2003). Cause-related sport sponsorship: An assessment of spectator beliefs, attitudes, and behavioral intentions. *Sport Marketing Quarterly, 12*(3), 131-139.

Jennings, A. (2000). *The Great Olympic Swindle.* London: Simon & Schuster Ltd.

Jonker, J. (2005). CSR wonderland: Navigating between movement, community and organization. *Journal of Corporate Citizenship, 20*, 19-22.

Karush, S. (2006). *Super Bowl host is U.S.'s poorest city.* ABC News. Retrieved from http://www.abcnews.go.com/US/wirestory?10=15577103&page=1

Khatri, S. S. (2006a). *Big game may be huge for charities.* Retrieved from http:///www.freep.com

Khatri, S. S. (2006b). *Center scores renovations through big game.* Retrieved from http://www. freep.com

Kleinefelter, Q. (2006a). *Detroit freshens up for the Super Bowl.* National Public Radio. Retrieved from http://www.npr.org/templates/story/story.php? storyId=5189921

Kleinefelter, Q. (2006b, February 1). *Detroit throwing Super Bowl 'party' for homeless.* News and Notes. Retrieved from http://www.npr.org/templates/story/story.php?storyID=5182373

Kott, A. (2005). The philanthropic power of sport. *Foundation News and Commentary.* January/February, 20-25.

Lenskyj, H. (2000). *Inside the Olympic industry: Power, politics, and activism.* Albany: SUNY Press.

Lewis, S. (2003). Reputation and corporate responsibility. *Journal of Communication Management, 7*(4), 356-365.

Margolis, J. D., & Walsh, J. P. (2003). Misery loves companies: Rethinking social initiatives by business. *Administrative Science Quarterly, 48*(2), 268-289.

Martin, A. H. (2006). *Homeless people to get Super Bowl party.* Retrieved January 8, 2006, from http://www.freep.com

Matten, D., Crane, A., & Chapple, W. (2003). Behind the mask: Revealing the true face of corporate citizenship. *Journal of Business Ethics, 45*(1), 109-127.

McAdam, R., & Leonard, D. (2003). Corporate social responsibility in a total quality management context: Opportunities for sustainable growth. *Corporate Governance, 3*(4), 36-49.

McDonald, K. (2005). *Metro Detroit Taubman Malls win host committee's first ok to sponsor an officially-sanctioned Super Bowl XL event.* Retrieved from http://www.taubman.com

Meyer, H. (1999). When the cause is just. *Journal of Business Strategy, 20*(6), 27-32.

Michigan Economic Development Corporation. (2006). *Super Bowl XL: Reaching out to the community* (4). Lansing.

Mintzberg, H. (1984). Who should control the corporation? *California Management Review, 27*(1), 90-116.

Moir, L. (2001). What do we mean by corporate social responsibility? *Corporate Governance, 1*(2), 16-22.

Mullen, J. (1997). Performance-based corporate philanthropy: How 'giving smart' can further corporate goals. *Public Relations Quarterly, 42*(2), 42-49.

Murray, S. (November 6, 2005). Turnaround dreams take root in Detroit. *USA Today.*

National Football League. (2006). *Super Bowl Community Outreach.* Retrieved from http://www.superbowl.com/features/community

Robinson, R. (2005). *Sports philanthropy: An analysis of the charitable foundations of major league teams.* Unpublished Master's thesis, University of San Francisco.

Rovell, D. (2006, February 2). *What is a Super Bowl worth? Good question.* Retrieved from http://www.sports.espn.go.com/nfl/playoffs05/news/story?id=2315303

Smith, J. (2006). *Crowded calendar for charities.* Retrieved from http://www.crainsdetroit.com

Stark, M. (1999). Brand aid: Cause effective. *Brandweek, 40*(8), 20-22.

Tagliabue, P. (2006). *Join the team. Message from the Commissioner.* Retrieved from http://www.jointheteam.com/about/commissioner.asp

van Marrewijk, M. (2003). Concepts and definitions of CSR and corporate sustainability: Between agency and communion. *Journal of Business Ethics, 44*(2/3), 235-247.

Walsh, T. (2006, March 16). *Super boost for Detroit.* Detroit Free Press. Retrieved from http://www.highbeam.com/doc/1G1:143285148/Detorit+Free+Press+Tom+Walsh+column%7eC%7e+Super+Bowl+boost+for+Detroit

Wood, D. J. (1991). Corporate social performance revisited. *Academy of Management Review, 16,* 691-718.

28

Communicating Socially Responsible Initiatives:
An Analysis of U.S. Professional Teams

Matthew Walker, Aubrey Kent, and John Vincent

Communicating Socially Responsible Initiatives: An Analysis of U.S. Professional Teams

As sport has evolved from its participant-oriented past into the global phenomenon we know today, a business-oriented model has taken over the day-to-day operations by embracing several strategic initiatives. In line with the 21st century business model, public pressure has increased on North American companies to become more community oriented, resulting in a growing interest in pro-social business practices. As a result, more and more organizations (including those in professional sport) have either adopted socially responsible programs or have at least been more open about what they do in this area. From Nike to NASCAR, examples abound of activities undertaken to bring messages and resources to members of society who would not otherwise interact with these organizations.

Numerous social programs of professional teams exist, including the Philadelphia Eagles' "Go Green" and "Youth Partnership" initiatives, the Toronto Maple Leafs' "Be our guest" and "Leafs at School" programs, and the Minnesota Timberwolves' "Fast-Break Foundation." At the league level, more broadly functioning programs can be seen such as the NHL's "Hockey Fights Cancer" and "Green Partnership," the NBA's "Read to Achieve" and "Basketball Without Borders," the PGA TOUR's "Giving Back" initiative, NASCAR's "Drive for Diversity," and the NFL's "Play 60" campaign. Immediately observable is that these activities take on many forms and are driven by a diverse array of motives, possibly creating varying consumer responses.

Broadly conceptualized, the foregoing examples have led to the emergence of several theories used to describe the *business-society-relationship* (Carroll & Buchholtz, 2008; Wood, 2000) and fall under the broad umbrella of corporate social responsibility (CSR). CSR is understood to mean that businesses and society are interwoven rather than distinct entities responsible for their wider impact on society (Waddock, 2004). Drawing on the model for corporate-community integration (Marquis, Glynn, & Davis, 2007), organizations concerned with CSR seek to "do good" (Sen & Bhattacharya, 2001, p. 228) and attempt to project the image of a good community citizen. Empirical data has shown that CSR is an effective marketing tool when used to enhance or proactively defend a corporate reputation (Pollach, 2003). However, communicating CSR programs as a means of linking external stakeholders to the organization has been relatively under-explored (Morsing, 2006). The little work that has been done anecdotally indicates that many consumers appreciate discretion and reject bragging about CSR (Morsing & Beckman, 2006). The widespread presence of CSR coupled with the societal importance of the concept (Meijer & Schuyt, 2005) makes understanding how social initiatives are communicated particularly noteworthy.

Stemming from the lack of research on the communication side of the CSR information exchange process, this study assessed the extent to which sport teams are using e-newsletters to disseminate CSR information. The main thesis was that CSR communication (i.e., designed and distributed by the organization about its socially responsible efforts) could influence various relational (e.g., reputation) and transactional (e.g., patronage) business outcomes. Thus, the need existed to identify and categorize CSR activities and (based on the results) suggest some industry-specific best-practice strategies.

Stakeholder Communication and CSR

It has generally been acknowledged that organizations should effectively manage their relationships with stakeholders; the ways in which they choose to do so, however, vary considerably. Messages about CSR are likely to evoke strong and positive stakeholder reactions (Morsing & Schultz, 2006). Moreover, as a reflection of ethics that can create additional (i.e., secondary) value for the organization (van de Ven, 2008; Walker & Kent, 2009) the marketing of CSR initiatives have increased in popularity (Pomering & Dolnicar, 2009). Yet, there is an observable disconnection between consumer attitudes and actual behaviors regarding CSR. This apparent disconnect (some feel) stems from a general lack of awareness of companies' CSR achievements (Bhattacharya & Sen, 2004).

Consumers are important stakeholders with respect to CSR information and organizations must realize the strategic implications their awareness of CSR can have (Mohr, Webb, & Harriss, 2001). In fact, Dawkins (2004) maintained that the awareness issue stems directly from CSR communication, asserting that effectively communicating CSR initiatives are "... rare achievements" (p. 4). Echoing the findings in the marketing literature (Mohr et al., 2001; Sen, Bhattacharya, & Korshun, 2006; Ross, Stutts, & Patterson, 1990-91; Webb & Mohr, 1998), two recent studies of CSR in the sport industry (Walker & Kent, 2009a, 2009b) found both golf and professional football fans to be largely unaware of the CSR activities of the PGA TOUR and two National Football League (NFL) teams. Building on this work, the present study was partially motivated by "in practice" CSR initiatives particularly regarding the lack of (1) empirical work on the awareness levels of salient stakeholders, and (2) research on how sport firms are communicating CSR to their stakeholders.

Supporting Theory

Within the realm of normative stakeholder theory (Carroll, 1989; Kuhn & Shriver, 1991; Marcus, 1993), it is assumed that support of organizational affiliates (i.e., positive identification), is a precondition for an organization's ability to manage stakeholder relations

(Morsing, 2006). Further, communication and consumer behavior theories suggest that when consumers have a preference for a brand, they are more willing to receive information and also to search for information about that brand (Mersavio & Raulas, 2004).

This idea parallels van de Ven's (2009) idea of a communicated organizational identity. The author stated that "... the communicated identity [of an organization] is most clearly revealed through 'controllable' corporate communication" (p. 343). This typically encompasses advertising, sponsorship, and public relations and is derived also from "non-controllable" communication (e.g., word-of-mouth and media exposure). Correspondingly, Berger and Mitchell (1989) argued that repeated exposure to a brand enhances brand attitudes by allowing the customer to process more salient information. The preceding suggests that when a consumer receives information about, spends time with, and processes information about a brand, positive affective responses can be evoked (Mersavio & Raulas, 2004).

Organizations in the sport industry have recognized the benefits of actively communicating with their stakeholders to induce affiliative connections (Brown, 2003; End, 2001; Sutton et al., 1997). Primarily using *social identity theory* (Tajfel & Turner, 1979), research has revealed that identification levels based on team communication can lead to fan loyalty (Dutton, Dukerich, & Harqual, 1994), affective reactions (Branscombe & Wann, 1991; Wann & Branscombe, 1995), and purchasing behaviors (Kwon & Armstrong, 2006).

Recognizing the existence of an imbedded relationship between an organization and the extent to which consumers identify with the organization, Ahearne and colleagues (2005) noted that among consumers, "... efforts toward preserving, supporting, and improving the organization proceed naturally from identification" (p. 577). This sentiment implies that managers should to determine the organization's ideal identity (van de Ven, 2008) and thereafter be willing to define a revised conception to salient consumer groups. Therefore, the conceptual understanding of the business environment and formulation of an ideal identity should reflect how the firm wishes to deal with the social aspects of its operations.

E-Newsletter Communication

Several marketing techniques can be used to facilitate this process, that is, promote "good" causes in effective ways (van de Ven, 2008). However, communicating CSR through traditional advertising channels is perceived by many as over-accentuating the good deeds of the company, which can lead to skepticism about the message and cynicism regarding firm motives (Pomering & Dolnicar, 2009). In a recent study that addressed this challenge, Morsing and Schultz (2006) found that consumers preferred CSR initiatives to be communicated through "minimal release" channels (e.g., annual reports and websites). This finding aligns closely with the sport marketing literature, suggesting that web-based content is the most effective way of reaching interested consumers (Brown, 2003). While many electronic communication methods exist, among the most frequently used are newsletters (sent via email) which correspond to the idea of a "minimal release" channel described by Morsing and Schultz (2006).

According to Nielsen Media, 276.9 million individuals (up 21% from a year prior) in the US, several European countries, Australia, and Brazil, used email to communicate in August of 2009 (Vascellaro, 2009). With email representing one of the most popular communication methods among internet users (Godin, 1999) it is not difficult to see why e-newsletters have become a popular trend in marketing communications (Brondmo, 2000; Roberts, Feit, & Bly, 2001). Costs are minimal, targeting specific consumers is easy, product and service information can be conveniently distributed, and they offer concise information that may be used over extended periods.

Newsletters are excellent vehicles for engaging in dialogue with customers because personalized information, entertainment, and promortions can be easily distributed (Brondmo, 2000). Research on e-newsletters has primarily focused on their effectiveness as promotional tools (Gilbert, Powel-Perry, & Widijoso, 1999; Graham & Harvey, 1996) with surprisingly little work documenting their utility in disseminating pro-social content. Heath (1997, p. 290) stressed the importance of developing strong "... mutually beneficial" relationships with stakeholders focusing on "... an appropriate sense of corporate responsibility" through various communication outlets. Similar research (notably by Grunig & Grunig, 1992; Grunig & Hunt, 1984; Grunig & White, 1992) on two-way (i.e., symmetrical) communication proposed that organizations should be actively engaged in developing mutually beneficial communication relationships with stakeholders. Although communication will not likely be the only way for an organization to engage with its stakeholders, it can play an important role in how the organization satisfies various stakeholder demands.

Based on the preceding, we explored the extent to which professional sport teams communicated their CSR agendas to their stakeholders. We sought to discern if team communication strategies are designed to simply disseminate information, or inform the public in an objective manner. To address this query, several professional teams' e-newsletters were content analyzed to explore the magnitude and focus of CSR reporting. The results are presented thematically, and the discussion provides implications for social responsibility among sport managers and researchers interested in communicated CSR efforts.

Method

In order to identify and classify team CSR activities, we adopted a qualitative content analysis approach (Hsieh & Shannon, 2005), which is a systematic and replicable technique for examining communication methods (Berger, 2000). Qualitative content analysis was appropriate since existing research literature on CSR communication in sport is quite limited (Hsieh & Shannon, 2005). Hence, from this initial inquiry it should be possible to draw inferences (i.e., analytical not statistical generalizability; see Yin, 2003) about how sport teams communicate CSR to their stakeholders.

Evidenced by previous research (e.g., Esrock & Leichy, 1998; Maignan & Ralston, 2002; Pollach, 2005), content analyses dealing with CSR communication have focused mainly on the types of messages directed to various publics. However, there is a lack of scholarship examining the content of CSR communication by firms outside of *Fortune's 500, Fortune's Most Admired Companies,* and *Forbes' Top 100* lists (Walker & Parent, 2010). In light of the interest in CSR among sport firms, along with the rise of social reporting in the sport industry, this research advances the CSR communication literature in sport.

Data Collection

An essential stage in any content analysis is deciding which documents to analyze (Krippendorff, 1980). The proliferation of online content dedicated to sport (both domestically and internationally) makes it possible to closely follow an organization's social reporting on many levels. As mentioned, e-newsletters are conveniently available, free to the subscriber, and provide the most up-to-date information on the organization, in addition to serving active information-seeking audiences rather than more passive publics who are reached via traditional mass media (Esrock & Leichty, 1998).

The selection of teams for this study was a key methodological decision to combine the representativeness and characteristics of the four major sport leagues (i.e., NFL, NBA, MLB, NHL) with the manageability of data gathering and analysis. The inclusion of nearly 30 organizations is comparable with studies in the management literature (Chapple & Moon, 2005). The data collection procedure followed a series of steps. First, an exhaustive list of all teams residing in all four major sport leagues in the United States was compiled. From this list, 30 teams were randomly selected (i.e., ¼ of the professional teams housed in the four sport leagues) for use in the analysis. Next, we subscribed to every team's e-newsletter and as they were disseminated, all of the newsletters were archived in an email folder over a three-month period, yielding a total of 818 team newsletters.

The e-newsletter from each of the selected teams was examined for the existence of CSR activities. In this initial examination, a rigid definition of CSR was not imposed; instead we allowed the data to inform the emergent CSR profiles among the teams. Thus, all of the initiatives, codes, policies, and programs that involved stakeholder interaction (or impact) were regarded as CSR activities. Using the grounded theory approach (Glaser & Strauss, 1967), we provided emergent profiles of CSR activities among the teams. Where CSR activities were found, these specific e-newsletters were subjected to further analysis.

Coding the Variables

The unit of analysis was the 29 selected sport organizations' e-newsletters. While 30 teams were selected for coding, we encountered an issue accessing one of the team's e-newsletters, and then encountered additional problems with links to the team's website. Therefore, this one team was removed from the analysis. From the remaining sample, coders determined whether the articles in the e-newsletters communicated the organizations' CSR activities as well as documenting the type of CSR disseminated.

To reduce researcher bias, two independent coders used Holsti's (1969) formula to determine the reliability of the coding using 10% of the overall sample. One member of the research team trained two graduate students during two separate two-hour training sessions to acquaint them with the coding task. Consequently, extensive coding practice opportunities were provided for the coders. Any coding ambiguities were thoroughly discussed and resolved, with the primary author being the final arbiter for reliability. Inter-coder reliability improved to 100% in determining whether the articles communicated CSR, and 97% for categorizing the type of CSR before coding for this study began. Reliability checks were performed at regular intervals throughout the coding process. Agreement between coders was well above 90% and Scott's (1955) *Pi. Percentage* of agreement corrected for chance agreement between coders (all were above .944). The results are presented using basic descriptive statistics.

Preliminary Analysis

The sample of 818 newsletters from 29 different professional teams (MLB=9, NFL=7, NHL=7, NBA=6) yielded a total of 240 (29%) articles that reported past or future CSR activities. The majority of the e-newsletters were distributed weekly (n=152, 65.8%), fol-

Table 1.
Examples of Documented CSR Initiatives

Classifications	Examples
Philanthropic Event	Donations to a partnering organization and general donations to the local community.
Charitable or Volunteer Event	Illnesses or diseases, camps or clinics free for disadvantaged youth, shopping days for youth, back-to-school drives, toy drives, food drives, blood drives, clothing drives, any event where the proceeds benefitted the teams' or other foundation.
Community Appreciation Event	Ethnic heritage days, youth or senior's days, autograph signings that were free and open to the public or for terminally ill children, free parties, movie nights, or event where the stakeholder paid but the proceeds went to charity.
Educational Event	Children and/or adults taught something and the proceeds went to a charitable organization.
Community Involvement	Opening a Boys and Girls Club, rebuilding homes, providing opportunities for kids to showcase their skills, recognizing players and coaches in the community that give back and excel in sports and/or the classroom.
Promotional Giveaway	Camps and/or clinics (that charged a fee) and community events where money was raised. Events where the proceeds did not go to a charity or philanthropic event were not included as examples of CSR

lowed by bi-weekly (n=72, 31.2%), and monthly (n=7, 3.0%). Many of these e-newsletters contained multiple CSR articles, reports, and promotions. Therefore, 273 different articles, features, and reports that communicated CSR were identified.

Results

Coding Categories

After careful analysis of the articles, the two coders entered the information gleaned from the 273 articles onto a more detailed final coding sheet. The final coding sheet was designed to provide more information about each team's CSR activities. After re-analyzing the articles, the total number was reduced to 231 due to the inability to code specific initiatives that were not deemed to be CSR-related. Based on the re-evaluation, six classifications were developed that accurately encompass all CSR events found in the e-newsletters (see Table 1).

Descriptive Results

For the type of CSR communicated, monetary charitable events (e.g., auctions, raffles, and golf tournaments) returned the highest number of occurrences (*n*=93, 40.3%). Non-monetary charitable events (e.g., food, clothing, toy, and back-to-school drives) were next (*n*=33, 14.3%). Volunteerism and community outreach (*n*=29, 12.6%) were the third most popular (e.g., free sports camp, visiting schools/hospitals, and community service). Fourth were articles related to social awareness and promotions (*n*=26, 11.3%; e.g., wear pink for breast cancer, heritage days, foster children awareness, battered women and children, health and fitness screenings, environmental awareness, and illness awareness). Next were community appreciation initiatives (*n*=25, 10.8%) followed by events designed to honor "meritable" work (*n*=21, 9.1%; e.g., community coach/player of the week, scholar athlete, and public service appreciation). Additional analysis of the data revealed that athletes or coaches were involved 59.7% of the time, 81.4% of the e-newsletters reported three or fewer CSR initiatives, and 78.3% featured 10 or fewer non-CSR related articles.

Discussion and Implications

The focus of this study was to examine e-newsletter communications of professional sport teams operating in a community-based sector of economic activity. The secondary focus was to illustrate the diversity of messages most prevalent in this context. The results highlight the ways professional teams disseminate information about their CSR practices (i.e., via their e-newsletters). For the most part, general statements about organization-specific initiatives set the tone for this one-way communication method. These broad involvement messages were (seemingly) designed to inform team stakeholders of the teams' commitment to their respective communities. Our analysis led to

Table 2.
Classifications of CSR Initiatives

Classifications	Operational Definitions
Monetary Charitable Event	Any event that monetary donation was the primary outcome, regardless of how it was acquired.
Non-Monetary Charitable Event	Any event that non-monetary donations were the primary outcome.
Volunteerism / Community Outreach	Organizational member(s) donated time (and/or services) to the community or persons in need.
Event to Honor "Meritable" Work	Events to recognize outstanding achievement or sacrifice by members of the organization or others.
Community Appreciation	Events to honor community support with the proceeds going to charity.
Social Awareness Promotion	Any event that raised awareness about a social, environmental, or health-related causes.

the identification of strategies which appear to encapsulate sport organizations' communicated CSR activities. These findings contribute to the CSR communication literature and also add to the discussion of how professional sport teams communicate CSR information to their stakeholders.

In addition to the above commentary, our findings address some recent calls for research on CSR awareness among organizational stakeholder groups (Du, Bhattacharya, & Sen, 2007). Research has revealed that CSR perceptions affect the image of the firm and the propensity of consumers to patronize the firm (Du et al., 2007; Luo & Bhattacharya, 2006; Sen et al., 2006). However, when gauging awareness, some have noted that stakeholders are not aware of the breadth of CSR activities in which most firms are engaged (see Ellen, Webb, & Mohr, 2006), making the distribution of this information of critical value.

The awareness issue (with regard to CSR information) raises the question of whether teams should determine first whether or not fans care to hear these messages. We argue that this logic is backwards. Teams invest millions in CSR programs with the primary purpose being to initiate positive community outcomes (e.g., environmental, youth health/education, etc.) and performing these activities in a vacuum defeats the aim of having broad social impact. Therefore, dissemination of information is critical, and not just because there may also be reciprocal "secondary" benefits for the team.

The point of caring about reciprocation is to sustain these activities when times are tough, and altruistic motivation may not be as dependable (under these circumstances) as we might hope. Thus, while it may be true that CSR is of little importance to the majority of fans, the point of communicating these activities is to make fans aware of these issues since the team is considered a valued source of information. Due to a strong preexisting relationship (i.e., team identification, loyalty, etc.), we argue that the team has a duty to use its pulpit for the greater good, and not just to sell tickets.

Therefore, while one-way CSR information is necessary to bolster stakeholder awareness, it may not be enough to yield intended social outcomes. New information detailing how two-way CSR communication can bolster both relational and transactional rewards should be noted. This process means that the transfer of information from the organization to the stakeholder (i.e., objectively, not necessarily with a persuasive intent) is interactive and ongoing. Described by Morsing and Schultz (2006), this two-way exchange was articulated as "sensegiving" and "sensemaking" (p. 352). As the name entails, sensegiving relates to the availability of information to salient stakeholders, which seems to accurately depict the communication processes seen in the current study. Conversely, a two-way sensemaking communication approach combines stakeholder involvement with organizational priorities, affording the stakeholder the ability to respond to CSR information (i.e., a pulling effect). This process would allow the organization to better craft their messages to align with stakeholder interests.

Based on the *stakeholder information strategy*, communication is typically a one-way (i.e., pushing), from the organization to its stakeholders (i.e., "telling, not listening"; Grunig & Hunt 1984, p. 23), as was the case here. Thus, a response strategy using both sensegiving and sensemaking (i.e., pushing and pulling) should result in an impactful CSR dialogue with the most active information seeking audiences for the sport firm.

In line with this idea, social networking sites (SNS) have gained popularity and as a result, marketers are drawn to this new communication mode because costs are minimal and their ability to reach new audiences and active (information-seeking) publics is prolific. While many of the technological features are consistent, the social and communication exchanges that emerge around SNSs are varied (e.g., fan groups that subscribe to team newsletters and spend time in team chat rooms). The surge in SNS usage makes the discussion of sensemaking even more salient. Armed with this new technology, sport marketers now have the ability to "pull" information from team stakeholders on a wide array of CSR-related initiatives. By integrating a sensegiving and sensemaking approach to CSR dialogue (i.e., pushing and pulling), marketers can begin to understand what matters most to their fans and select community partnerships and social initiatives that serve mutual interests, as well as promote social change.

Stakeholder communication aside, one of the more telling results was the lack of partnerships between the teams and outside organizations. Previous cause-related marketing (CRM) research has shown that well-conceived promotional initiatives lead (in theory) to more positive consumer attitudes (e.g., Lachowetz & Gladden, 2002; Roy & Graeff, 2003). Team promotions emphasizing a partnership affiliation (for which a consumer may have a high degree of affinity) are likely to have a more positive effect on consumer judgments than similar initiatives that either deemphasize or emphasize affiliations for which the consumer may have little affinity (Strahilevitz & Myers, 1998). This seemingly simple exchange could increase the firm's return on CSR, especially if the social program helps the community, resulting in the "win-win-win strategy" (Polansky & Wood, 2001, p. 8). However, such a strategic partnership dynamic was not the case with the teams analyzed. Among the 231 coded CSR activities, 121 (52.4%) had no affiliation with an outside organization, while 110 (47.6%) explicitly stated a partnership dynamic. This dichotomy leaves some room for conjecture as the strategic partnership process has not been fully explored by the teams included in our sample.

Finally, while our empirical observations serve to partially illustrate the magnitude of social reporting by teams, the complexities faced by managers as they engage in CSR communication can be a slippery slope. Brown and Dacin (1997, p. 81) maintained that "... if a company focuses too intently on communicating CSR, is it possible that consumers may believe that the company is trying to hide something." Correspondingly, strategic goals inherent to a firm's survival are among the most widely accepted motives for engaging in CSR (Ellen et al., 2006). Yet, these activities may actually run the risk of a "consumer backlash" if individuals question the appropriateness of a firm's actions (Drumwright, 1996; Osterhus, 1997). Thus, pursuing a proactive (i.e., actively engaged) CSR strategy may be the most logical mode of social engagement. In this vein, proactive CSR communication represents efforts to disseminate information to create a social image before any negative information is released (Wagner, Lutz, & Weitz, 2009). In sum, we believe that this analysis contributes to a more recent academic focus on the dissemination of information without an overtly persuasive intent.

Limitations

Although the aim of this paper was to assess the level of CSR communication by sport teams, additional research should investigate how these findings apply to the larger sport industry. We acknowledge that our reported findings bracketed for the purposes of this investigation, rendering our findings as partial. Nonetheless, a focus on basic message dissemination (in isolation) still provides a view of the processes by which sport teams seek to inform their more "information seeking" audiences.

In light of our reported findings, we recognize several limitations (both analytical and practical); we offer three in particular. First and most obvious to the coders was that many of the sport organizations' newsletters provided limited information about their CSR activities. We found this to be quite alarming given that space restrictions do not apply to online content. Many articles referred the reader to a website link where additional information was presented. However, the researchers experienced several problems when attempting to open the links provided in the e-newsletters. To partially explain this issue, there was approximately a three-month time lag between collecting the majority of the original 273 CSR articles, preliminarily analyzing them, and coding them into the final detailed coding sheet. Unfortunately, during those months some of the links had become obsolete. This explains the reduction in articles from 273 to 240. The remainder of the reduction can be explained by links not being available or insufficient information being provided, or ambiguities that meant that upon further examination (e.g., reliability checks) the article did not fit the operational definition of CSR.

Second, we should note that we based our analysis on self-reporting of activities by organizations (i.e., auto-communication) and recognize the potential biasing of this information. For this query, we were interested only in establishing a framework for the type of CSR communicated via the e-newsletter. In subsequent analyses, we will endeavor to compare what a team *says* it does versus what it *actually* does. One related caveat was a complete absence of reporting the outcomes of the CSR events—for example, how much money was raised or how many in-kind gifts were donated (i.e., the social impact of the CSR practice was largely ignored).

Third, many of the reported CSR activities may not necessarily be reflective of their social responsibility practices. Reporting CSR may exaggerate the practices and performance of the initiatives (e.g., impact). As a result, the prominence given to these activities may serve as a strategic tool used to transmit marketing and reputational branding messages. Given the visibility of many teams to external stakeholder scrutiny, there may even be an added incentive for social reporting in this manner (Chappel & Moon, 2005). Thus, future research should examine the actual impacts of sport organizations' social responsibility activities.

Final Thoughts

For our study, CSR implies that the rights that sport organizations demand in society come with the voluntary agreement to behave responsibly and avoid problems that would otherwise emerge. Previous CSR communication literature has underscored the importance of minimal releases such as annual reports and e-newsletters as a preferred means of CSR communication to stakeholders (Morsing & Schultz, 2006). However, in order for this information to be well-received it needs to be included in communication strategies and dispersed to a greater degree. Therefore, we suggest that sport firms continue to attend to minimal releases but expand to other mediums with their messages as well (e.g., SNSs like Facebook and Twitter). And to improve the impact of this strategy, teams would benefit from involving stakeholders in construction of CSR communication (Morsing & Schultz, 2006). Simply, organizations should actively "give sense" to salient stakeholders as well as "make sense" of stakeholders' responses.

References

Ahearne, M., Bhattacharya, C. B., & Gruen, T. (2005). Antecedents and consequences of customer–company identification: Expanding the role of relationship marketing. *Journal of Applied Psychology, 90*(3), 574-585.

Argenti, P. A., & Druckenmiller, B. (2004). Reputation and the corporate brand. *Corporate Reputation Review, 7*(4), 368-374.

Bergami, M., & Bagozzi, R. P. (2000). Self categorization, affective commitment, and group self-esteem as distinct aspects of social identity in the organization. *British Journal of Social Psychology, 39*(4), 555-577.

Berger, A. A. (2000). Semiotic analysis. In A. A. Berger (Ed.), *Media and communication research methods* (pp. 35-51). Thousand Oaks, CA: Sage.

Berger, I. E., & Mitchell, A. A. (1989). The effect of advertising on attitude accessibility, attitude confidence, and the attitude-behavior relationship. *Journal of Consumer Research, 16*(3), 269-279.

Branscombe, N. R., &Wann, D. L. (1991). The positive social and self concept consequences of sports team identification. *Journal of Sport and Social Issues, 15*(2), 115-127.

Brondmo, H. P. (2000). *The eng@ged customer: The new rules of internet direct marketing.* New York: Harper Collins Publishers.

Brown, M. (2003). An analysis of online marketing in the sport industry: User activity, communication objectives, and perceived benefits. *Sport Marketing Quarterly, 12*(1), 48-55.

Brown, T. J., & Dacin, P. A. (1997). The company and the product: Corporate associations and consumer product responses. *Journal of Marketing, 61*(January), 68-84.

Carroll, A. B. (1989). *Business and society: Ethics and stakeholder management.* Cincinnati, OH: South-Western.

Carroll, A. B., & Buchholtz, A. K. (2008). *Business and society: Ethics and stakeholder management* (7th ed.) Mason, OH: South-Western Cengage Learning.

Chapple, W., & Moon, J. (2005). Corporate social responsibility in Asia: A seven country study of CSR website reporting. *Business & Society, 44,* 415-441.

Drumwright, M. E. (1996). Company advertising with a social dimension: The role of noneconomic criteria. *Journal of Marketing, 60*(4), 71-87.

Du, S., Bhattacharya, C. B., & Sen, S. (2007). Reaping relational rewards from corporate social responsibility: The role of competitive positioning. *International Journal of Research in Marketing, 24*(3) 224–241.

Dutton, J. E., Dukerich, J. M., & Harqual, C. V. (1994). Organizational images and member identification. *Administrative Science Quarterly, 39*(2), 239-263.

Ellen, P. S., Webb, D. J., & Mohr, L. A. (2006). Building corporate associations: Consumer attributions of corporate social responsibility programs? *Journal of the Academy of Marketing Science, 34*(2), 147-157.

End, C. (2001). An experiment of NFL fans' computer mediated BIRGing. *Journal of Sport Behavior, 24,* 162-181.

Escrock, S. L., & Leichty, G. B. (1998). Social responsibility and the corporate web pages: Self presentation or agenda-setting? *Public Relations Review, 24*(3), 305-319.

Gilbert, D., Powell Perry, J., & Widijoso, S. (1999). Approaches by hotels to use the internet as a relationship marketing tool. *Journal of Marketing Practice: Applied Marketing Science, 5*(1), 21-38.

Glaser, B., & Strauss, A. (1967). *The discovery of grounded theory.* Chicago: Aldine.

Godin, S. (1999). *Permission marketing: Turning strangers into friends, and friends into customers.* New York: Simon & Schuster.

Graham, J. R., & Harvey, C. R. (1996). Market timing ability and volatility implied in investment newsletters' asset allocation recommendations. *Journal of Financial Economics, 42*(3), 397-422.

Griffin, J. J., & Mahon, J. F. (1997). The corporate social performance and corporate financial performance debate. *Business and Society, 36*(1), 5-31.

Grunig, J. E., & Hunt, T. (1984). *Managing public relations.* Fort Worth, TX: Holt, Rinehart and Winston.

Holsti, O. R. (1969). *Content analysis for the social sciences and humanities.* Reading, MA: Addison-Wesley.

Hsieh, H. F., & Shannon, S. E. (2005). Three approaches to qualitative content analysis. *Qualitative Health Research, 15*(9), 1277-1288.

Joinson, A. N., & Harris, P. R. (1995). *Self-enhancement and self protection on the Internet: A study of football fans on the WWW.* Paper presented at the BPS London Conference, Institute of Education, London.

Krippendorff, K. (1980). *Content analysis: An introduction to its methodology. The Sage Commtext Series.* London: Sage Publications Ltd.

Kuhn, J. W., & Shriver, D. W., Jr. (1991). *Beyond success: Corporations and their critics in the 1990s.* New York: Oxford University Press.

Kwon, H., & Armstrong, K. (2006). Impulse purchase of sport team licensed merchandise: What matters? *Journal of Sport Management, 20,* 101-117.

Lachowetz, T., & Gladden, J. (2002). A framework for understanding cause-related sport marketing programs. *International Journal of Sports Marketing and Sponsorship, 4*(4), 205-225.

Mael, F., & Ashworth, B. E. (1992). Alumni and their alma mater: A partial test of the reformulated model of organizational identification. *Journal of Organizational Behavior, 13*(2), 103-123.

Maignan, I., Ferrell, O. C., & Hult, G. T. M. (1999). Corporate citizenship: Cultural antecedents and business benefits. *Journal of the Academy of Marketing Science, 27*(4), 455-469.

Maignan, I., & Ralston, D. A. (2002). Corporate social responsibility in Europe and the U.S.: Insights from businesses' self-presentations? *Journal of International Business Studies, 33*(3), 497-514.

Marcus, A. A. (1993). *Business and society: Ethics, government and the world economy.* Homewood, IL: Irwin.

Marquis, C., Glynn, M. A., & Davis, G. (2007). Community isomorphism and corporate social action. *Academy of Management Review, 32*, 925-945.

Meijer, M. M., & Schuyt, T. (2005). Corporate social performance as a bottom line for consumers. *Business & Society, 44*(4), 442-461

Mersavio, M., & Raulas, M. (2004). The impact of e-mail marketing on brand loyalty. *Journal of Product and Brand Management, 13*(7), 498-505.

Mohr, L. A., Webb, D. J., & Harris, K. E. (2001). Do consumers expect companies to be socially responsible? The impact of corporate social responsibility on buying behavior. *The Journal of Consumer Affairs, 35*(1), 45-72.

Morsing, M. (2003). Behind the mask: Revealing the true face of corporate citizenship. *Journal of Business Ethics, 45*, 109-120.

Morsing, M. (2006). Corporate social responsibility as strategic auto-communication: On the role of external stakeholders for member identification. *Business Ethics: A European Review, 15*(2), 171-182.

Morsing, M., & Beckman, S. C. (Eds.). (2006). *Strategic CSR communication.* Copenhagen: DJØF Publications.

Morsing, M., & Schultz, M. (2006). Corporate social responsibility communication: Stakeholder information, response and involvement strategies. *Business Ethics: a European Review, 15*(4), 323-338.

Osterhus, T. L. (1997). Pro-social consumer influence strategies: When and how do they work? *The Journal of Marketing, 61*(4), 16-29.

Polansky, M. J., & Wood, G. (2001). Can over commericilization of cause related marketing harm society? *Journal of Macro Marketing, 21*(1), 8-22.

Pollach, I. (2003). Communicating corporate ethics on the world wide web. *Business & Society, 42*(2), 277-287.

Pollach, I. (2005). Corporate self-presenation of the WWW. Strategies for enhancing usuability credibility and utility. *Corporate Communications: An International Journal, 10*(4), 285-301.

Roberts, S., Feit, M., & Bly, R. W. (2001). *Internet direct mail: The complete guide to successful E-mail marketing campaigns.* Chicago: NTC Business Books.

Ross, J. K., Stutts, M. A., & Patterson, L. T. (1990-1991). Tactical considerations for the effectiveness of cause related marketing. *The Journal of Applied Business Research, 7*(2), 58-65.

Roy, D. P., & Graeff, T. R. (2003). Consumer attitudes toward cause-related marketing activities in professional sports. *Sport Marketing Quarterly, 12*(3), 163-172.

Scott, W. A. (1955). Reliability of content analysis. *Public Opinion Quarterly, 19*, 321-325.

Sen, S., & Bhattacharya, C. B. (2001). Does doing good always lead to doing better? Consumer reactions to corporate social responsibility. *Journal of Marketing Research, 38*, 225-243.

Sen, S., & Bhattacharya, C. B., & Korschun, D. (2006). The role of corporate social responsibility in strengthening multiple stakeholder relationships. *Journal of the Academy of Marketing Science, 34*(2), 158-166.

Strahilevitz, M., & Myers, J. G. (1998). Donations to charity as purchase incentives: How well they work may depend on what you are trying to sell. *The Journal of Consumer Research, 24*(4), 434-446.

Sutton, W. A., McDonald, M. A., Milne, G. R., & Cimperman, J. (1997). Creating and fostering fan identification in professional sports. *Sport Marketing Quarterly, 6*(1), 15-22.

Tajfel, H., & Turner, J. C. (1979). An integrative theory of intergroup conflict. In W. G. Austin, & S. Worchel (Eds.), *The social psychology of intergroup relations* (pp. 33-47). Monterey, CA: Brooks/Cole.

Vascellaro, J. E. (2009, October). Why email no longer rules. *Wall Street Journal.* Retrieved from http://online.wsj.com/article_email.html

Waddock, S. (2004). Parallel universes: Companies, academics, and the progress of corporate citizenship. *Business and Society Review, 109*, 5-42.

Wagner, T., Lutz, R. J., & Weitz, B. A. (2009). Corporate hypocrisy: Overcoming the threat of inconsistent corporate social responsibility perceptions. *Journal of Marketing, 73*(6), 77-91.

Walker, M., & Kent, A. (2009a). Do fans care? Assessing the influence of corporate social responsibility on consumer attitudes in the sport industry. *Journal of Sport Management, 23*(6), 743-769.

Walker, M., & Kent, A. (2009b). CSR on tour: Attitudes towards corporate social responsibility among golf fans. *International Journal of Sport Management, 11*(1), 1-28.

Walker, M., & Parent, M. M. (2010). Toward an integrated framework of corporate social responsibility, responsiveness, and citizenship activities in sport. *Sport Management Review, 13*(3), 198-213.

Wann, D. L., & Branscombe, N. R. (1995). Influence of level of identification with a group and physiological arousal on perceived intergroup complexity. *British Journal of Social Psychology, 34*(3), 223-235.

Webb, J. D., & Mohr, L. A. (1998). A typology of customers' responses to cause related marketing: From skeptics to socially concerned. *Journal of Public Policy and Marketing, 17*(2), 226-239.

Wood, D. J. (2000). Theory and integrity in business and society. *Business & Society, 39*(4), 359-378.

Yin, R. K. (2003). *Case study research: Design and methods* (3rd ed.). Thousand Oaks, CA: Sage Publications.

Conclusion

What the Future Holds for Sport Marketing Researchers and Scholars

My esteemed co-editor, Nancy Lough, began her introduction of this handbook by quoting from my favorite Shakespeare play, "Hamlet." To continue that theme, I offer you Banquo's thoughts regarding the future from "Macbeth."

"If you can look into the seeds of time and say which grain will grow and which will not, speak then to me." — William Shakespeare

My interpretation and application of Banquo is to state that in this conclusion I will do my best to identify what I would consider to be promising and fertile areas for scholarly exploration. But just as it is difficult to see which seeds will grow and which seeds will not grow, the same can be said for scholarly lines of research inquiry. In some cases it is the breadth of the topic that gives it life, in others it may be the timeliness of the issue at hand. In some other cases, like the farmer and the condition of the soil, it may lay with the ability and investigative skills of the first author, who in an exploratory role identifies and examines a problem. By that I mean the quality and depth of that examination—how deep did it go, how broad did it stretch, and was the author able to pique the academic curiosity of a student to follow up with a dissertation or a colleague to take the initial inquiry to the next level? Like Banquo, I am dependent upon powers and talents far greater than mine to attempt to see into the future, but, nevertheless, I will do my best to identify the areas of inquiry that I feel are most likely to emerge in the coming years in sport marketing.

But before looking ahead, it is important to reflect back and trace the evolution of sport marketing research, and particularly the scholarly works contained in this collection of sport marketing research, which Lough did an excellent job of accomplishing in the introduction to this handbook. My reflection is based upon my experience and perspectives as an author whose work is included in this volume; a founding member of the *Sport Marketing Quarterly* (*SMQ*)—feeling there was a need for a scholarly outlet for academics specializing in sport marketing (and at the time practitioners); an editor of *SMQ* who served two terms; a faculty member who advised doctoral students in the area of sport marketing (a number of whom whose works are also included in this volume); and finally as a practitioner who has worked in the industry in various full- and part-time capacities over the past 25 years—and can attest to how the views of the practitioner, particularly with regard to the value of research and analysis, has changed significantly along with the level of respect and acceptance for faculty and students who can provide this research and analysis.

The articles contained in this handbook span the 20-year history of *SMQ* and the topics that scholars and researchers felt represented the best lines of inquiry during that time period. Much of the research has focused on what we will refer to as consumer-related marketing issues. These issues include

- consumer interests and habits;
- motivational impact on behavior;
- the basis for consumer preferences—including demographic and psychographic factors;
- the effect of promotional activities on consumer participation and purchasing;
- consumer reaction, recall, and activity related to sponsorship;
- the effectiveness of marketing communication efforts in reaching consumers and influencing subsequent behavior; and
- the impact of ethical and social responsibility on marketing initiatives and activities.

There are two areas of inquiry that I feel were under-represented, namely sales and sales-related issues, and global examinations of marketing development and activities (I am not referring to examinations and analyses of activities within one country, but activities and approaches that are multi-country in nature; for example, NBA marketing and sponsorship activities in the two most populous areas of the world—China and India). While both of these topics have been addressed via special issues in *SMQ* focusing solely on each of these areas, there has not been a consistent area of inquiry by a number and variety of scholars over a period of time.

In 1999, as Steve Hardy and I were ending our second term as co-editors of *SMQ*, we co-authored an article titled "The SMQ and the Sport Marketplace: Where We've Been and Where We're Going." In that article, we offered our thoughts on topics that we thought might be productive areas for scholars to examine going forward. These areas included the Internet, the experiential elements of the sport experience, the role of technology and entertainment, branding, facility design and development, expanding sponsorship opportunities, and multi-cultural influences on sport offerings, presentations, and development (Hardy & Sutton, 1999). Many of these areas were the subject of a number of scholars and were not only published in *SMQ*, but in a variety of refereed business journals, textbooks, mainstream press books, trade journals, and most recently web pages devoted to special topics and blogs and other cyber forms of opinion and expression.

As we look toward the future once again, I thought I would take the same approach and offer a list and short exploration of topics that I feel would make excellent lines of productive inquiry for scholars while at the same time offering insight and perspective to our industry brethren.

It is also worth noting that at this point, industry professionals employ business analysts and utilize statistics and modeling in a much more scientific approach than at any point in the past. These tools assist them as they try to become more accurate in projecting revenues, more adept at utilizing the consumer data they are collecting to devise different products and services, and better at targeting their sales efforts to a variety of consumer targets. This bodes well for closer relationships between industry and academe that we have also strived for but never quite realized.

The topical areas listed and described below are those that, based on my experience and consulting activities in the sport industry, I would recommend inquiry into, not only for established scholars and researchers, but also doctoral candidates looking for a dissertation topic or young scholars seeking to establish their fields of focus and their research lines.

The Secondary Ticket Market: We Are All in the Ticket Sales Business

StubHub and a variety of secondary market web sites have established a viable business without a product of their own and without many of the production costs associated with producing a product and offering that product for sale and in this case re-sale. These types of companies enjoy an economic model where the profits are fee based, thus the prices at which tickets are re-sold is not a point of concern for the secondary seller. With that in mind, if ticket prices in the secondary market are lower than the price the team is selling them for, the team is unable to sell additional tickets at the expected higher prices, and the season ticket buyers who are trying to sell their tickets for games that they cannot attend or are not interested in attending are unable to realize ticket prices near what they paid and become dissatisfied. Thus the problem to be studied is the impact of the secondary ticket sales market on team revenue, sales efforts, customer renewal and customer retention, and ultimately the packaging of tickets and how they are sold, which leads to the more global issue, namely the long-term profitability and sustainability of the professional sports model as it relates to live attendance and ticketed admission.

Drayer and Martin (2010) launched an area of inquiry regarding the perception of these secondary market sellers and raised the issue of legitimacy and authenticity. At one time this was a significant issue and the authors made several very valid points regarding issues and concerns facing the teams and the leagues and the types of questions they should be considering before determining how to proceed. That decision has been made as leagues and teams have accepted sponsorship contracts and dollars from these same secondary market sellers. In the process and according to the terms of these contracts, the secondary sellers are now viewed as authentic and legitimate purchasing options as they are advertising on the team web sites, during team broadcasts, and also in the venues where the games are played. Helyar wrote, “Leagues have made peace—and, more importantly, deals—with firms that provide an online market for buyers and sellers of tickets. That’s a big shift in a short time. Owners long believed in their divine right to control the distribution of, and collect all the revenue from, their teams’ tickets” (2007, para. 4).

By providing this legitimacy and authenticity, the teams and leagues have created a competitor who is viewed as a much more affordable and desirable purchasing option than the team itself. The opportunity for further studies exploring the economic model of such competition, the long-term effects of legitimizing the competition, and how that competition and the availability of being able to buy an incremental number of tickets (not just the ticket plans offered by the team or league) at a price lower than the team is selling them for should provide scholars with a variety of topics and satisfy an industry craving the results of those inquiries and analyses.

The Role of Social Media: We Are All Reporters Capable of Delivering News Instantaneously to a Variety of Audiences

Twitter, Facebook, MySpace, and so forth offer many platforms for communication, interaction, influencing opinion and behavior, and other forms of expression. Ted Leonsis, Vice Chairman emeritus of AOL and owner of Monumental Sports (Washington Capitals, Wizards, and Mystics) articulates this well when discussing the impact of his blog.

> I am my own media company. I announce things on my blog and depending upon the topic I have 40,000 to 90,000 coming to my blog. I have a direct, unfiltered way to reach our audience now, and I think that harnessing that is what you have to do as an ownership, because we are media brands. We're in the subscription business. We call them season ticket holders. We're in the sponsorship business. We are in the same business as the Washington Post. (Leonsis, 2011)

The issues relating to these mediums are plentiful and should be a popular source of examination and scholarly inquiry as they are complex and multi-faceted. A list of issues could include:

1. Ethical considerations and obligations related to the truth and accuracy of cyber communication. Is there an effective management approach that can be utilized to control content in terms of its accuracy and veracity so as to protect the subjects of these postings from damage to their persona, image, and reputation?
2. Measuring ROI and trying to assess the true value of marketing and promotional efforts conducted through social media. Do all of the "likes" and "followers" provide a revenue stream?
3. Related to No. 2, is it important that these activities generate a revenue stream, and would commercialization of these mediums by third parties wishing to interact with these audiences cause these communications sources to be abandoned in favor of newer mediums that have not been commercially compromised?

The Widespread Availability and Affordability of Technology and the Availability of On-Demand Programming (Including Global Sports) and Its Potential Effect on Live Attendance at Sporting Events

One of my favorite research pieces regarding the impact of technology on sport was written in 1953 by John Rickards Betts, who focused on the impact of what he referred to as the technological revolution that occurred between 1850 and 1900 and the role that "revolution" played in the growth, popularity, and dissemination of the American sport product. Betts (1953) discussed the effect of the light-bulb (growth of indoor sports, night-time competition, and after working hours participation and spectatorship), as well as the railroad (ability for teams to travel further distances and the opportunity for their fans to follow them) and the telegraph (ways to disseminate scores, results, and stories about sports teams and their exploits in a more timely fashion.

Portability, mobility, on-demand, high definition, and 3D television are the telegraph, telephone, radio, and television of the day. All of these technologies are contributing to providing an enhanced and all-access window to the sports world. In addition, all of these factors are contributing to the reality that the consumer doesn't have to be there to see it first hand. In many cases consumers can view the sport product much better at a location away from where it is actually being played, namely in the comfort of their own homes. Crutchfield Communications identifies the impact 3D will have on sports: "While high-definition TV improved sports watching with its clarity and detail, 3D goes further—it's like surround sound in the way it draws you in and makes you feel like a part of the action. It's closer to actually sitting in the stands. That third dimension makes the players' athleticism and skill seem even more superhuman."

Compare the technology advances with the expense of attending sporting events, the argument of convenience and comfort versus being at the venue, and the attitude of the host and the venue toward the fans while they are in attendance, and you may have the opportunity to explore and identify the issues affecting live attendance at sporting events not only in the US but throughout the world. Will the opportunity to watch any team or any sport in any country in high-definition 3D television affect the motivation to attend live sporting events?

Ethical Considerations, Responsibilities, and Obligations Related to Tracking Consumer Internet Behavior

Big Brother is alive and well, studying our cyber habits and behaviors and using that knowledge to refine its marketing communications, approaches, tactics, and offers. Clarke (1998) authored a very perceptive article on Internet privacy concerns. Thirteen years ago, Clarke had identified that cyberspace was invading private space. According to Clarke, "controversies about spam, cookies and the clickstream are merely the tip of the iceberg. Behind them loom real-time person-location technologies including intelligent transfer systems, geo-location, biometric identification, 'hard' authentication techniques and miniaturized processors embedded in plastic cards, anklets, watches, rings, products, product packaging, livestock, pets and people" (para. 1).

It should be common knowledge that sport franchises, based on the success and practices of mainstream businesses, have the ability to monitor the online behavior of their followers, visitors, and customers. It has become common practice in the sport industry to send out regular communications in a variety of forms, including offers and special targeted commercial messages and to track the acceptance of those messages and the subsequent behavior and actions of the consumer after opening the message (were they opened, if so how long did the reader engage with them, were they forwarded, etc.).

The issues here are abundant. In addition to privacy issues there are marketing effectiveness issues and ethical issues relating not only to how the information is obtained, but also to how it is utilized, monetized, and inevitably how the information is controlled and shared.

The Importance of Personalization, Customization, and Exclusivity as It Relates to Consumer Expenditures and Lifetime Value

In recent years, many brands have embraced a customization concept that enables consumers to take part in designing their own unique items. NIKEiD allows consumers to design their own pair of shoes. The successful premise behind Build-A-Bear Workshop is that children design and build their own stuffed animals. LEGO adopted a similar approach with its Designed by Me program that enables the unique creation and design of LEGO sets. Jones Soda allows users to customize bottle labels, and even allows those bottles to be sold in stores. Auto makers and apparel companies have used similar approaches to consumer customization.

These examples are but a small sample of the customization concepts that corporations have developed, taking advantage of web portals that enable consumers to have the ability to customize products. The potential is there for this customization concept to explode. And once it does, consumers will begin to demand the ability to customize products. No longer will companies be able to live by the mantra made popular by auto maker Henry Ford when he stated, "You can have it in any color you want as long as it's black" (Daye & VanAuken, 2008).

Technology, combined with a wealth of consumer information and the affordability of that technology and data, provides the opportunity for any sport organization to offer a high level of personalization and customization to their customers if they so choose. It is only logical that if the product offerings (goods, services, and experiences) are customized to a degree that they are a better fit for the consumer than the mass-marketed product offerings usually provided. The consumers now become purchasers who are much more satisfied with what they have purchased and in all probability are better equipped to make maximum utilization of the product that they have purchased. For example, if ticket packages, golf club memberships, fitness center memberships, and so forth that are sold and priced on the assumption that the consumer will utilize and consume the majority of that product were broken down into frequency consumption packages truly based upon the past usage patterns of the buyer, would the lifetime value of that consumer (the amount spent over the lifetime associated with that product) provide enough of a financial return to make the customization package the normal and accepted product?

The Effect of Athlete and Coaching Behavior on the Level of Interest and Support of Collegiate Athletic Programs

In researching this section, I was sadly not surprised that there were web sites devoted to the Top 10 Scandals in College Sports as well as the Top 10 Coaching Scandals in College Sports History. In 2010 and 2011, three institutions—Auburn University, The Ohio State University and The University of Southern California—were all tainted and painted as institutions whose obsession with college athletics and winning football programs caused them to disregard NCAA rules and regulations. Auburn has not been penalized (although in the court of public opinion many feel it is guilty of such transgressions), The University of Southern California has forfeited victories and returned cash payments for using an ineligible player, and that ineligible player made history by surrendering his Heisman Trophy. Finally, The Ohio State University saw its coach resign and its most talented player leave school and as of this writing is still waiting for the NCAA to determine the exact type of punishment to be meted out.

Does an athletic department scandal affect the ability of that particular athletic department to successfully generate the revenue through ticket sales, television contracts, corporate partnerships, licensed merchandise sales, and donations to sustain itself and its support of all of its athletic programs until such time that the sanctions or penalties are lifted? Further, does the same athletic department issue affect perceptions and finances outside of the athletic department but within the university itself in terms of new student applications, gifts to the university, alumni support, and even legislative funding and support of state institutions? This is a very interesting research question and I am sure that some scholars who are well versed in the issues related to fan identification and fandom in general might find this a very stimulating line of inquiry to pursue.

Traditional Team Sport (Baseball, Basketball, Football, and Hockey) Attendance in the United States and the Effect of Demographic Changes in Age and Ethnicity on that Attendance

Will soccer crack the Big Four? Does the growth and economic power of the Hispanic market change interest and viewing patterns as they relate to the popularity and broadcast frequency of those Big Four sports? In examining the current state of soccer in the US, a number of issues are quite apparent:

1. The most powerful and influential media partnership in the United States, ESPN/ABC, has made a significant movement to not only schedule more soccer programming (not only the MLS but games from the English Premier League and international competitions), but to create programming and opportunities to market and promote this additional coverage, which was demonstrated by their successful programming package of the 2010 World Cup in South Africa. According to *New York Times* columnist Ken Belson, "Even though the American team had long left the tournament, more than 24 million fans watched the World Cup Final match between Spain and the Netherlands—a figure more than the average viewership for last year's World Series games between the New York Yankees and the Philadelphia Phillies" (2010, para. 2).
2. DirecTV and other satellite and cable providers are making international soccer programming available on a subscription basis.
3. The world view of the American sport consumer is evolving, and consumers are beginning to follow athletes that are dominant or the best at what they do regardless of their geographic origin and those athletes' achievements in international as well as American-based competitions.
4. The spending and viewing habits of the Hispanic market in the United States continue to grow. According to the Greater Austin Hispanic Chamber of Commerce,

> Hispanics account for more than 13% of the U.S. labor force and are expected to increase to nearly 20% by 2030. In addition, higher-paying management and professional occupations are the fastest-growing job categories for Hispanics, propelled by growing educational attainment. All of this comes as Hispanic employment has grown more than 16% since 2000, while overall U.S. employment has barely grown 2%. (2009, para. 6)

The Effect of Personality in American Individual Sports, Particularly Tennis and Golf

It would be interesting to examine the power of personalities such as Tiger Woods and their effect in terms of generating interest and how that interest converts into attendance, viewership, and equipment purchasing through participation. Subsequently, the effect of the decline of such personalities and their impact upon the sport and its corporate partners that was so heavily invested in them and tied to their performance, both as an athlete and as an endorser, should be examined.

The TV ratings for the 2011 PGA Tour U.S. Open (which was won by Rory McIlroy and did not include Tiger Woods) were down 26% when compared to the 2010 U.S. Open with Woods as a competitor (Kirk, 2011). This begs the question, is an American media audience (all forms of media) influenced positively or negatively by the presence or lack thereof of a bonafide American competitor?

Further lines of inquiry might address whether or not this factor also affects interest and participation in those particular sports, funding opportunities at the collegiate level for those sport programs, allocated media coverage and programming promotion, and so forth.

Conclusion

The past 20 years have witnessed the growth and popularity of sport marketing as an accepted academic discipline in terms of coursework and scholarly inquiry. Sport management programs with an emphasis on sport marketing have become abundant, with two of the most prominent examples being the University of Oregon's Warsaw Sport Marketing Center and the University of Massachusetts' Mark H. McCormack Department of Sport Management. The Warsaw Center has become involved with companies and universities in the Pacific Rim, which should lead to more types of global marketing perspectives involving the US, China, and Japan that I detailed previously in this chapter. The University of Massachusetts' department serves as the archival home of the writings, photographs, and client-related memorabilia of McCormack, who was the founder and chief executive of the world's largest sport management firm, IMG International. The collection has the potential to generate a cornucopia of research opportunities related to sport marketing agencies, made-for-television events, the evolution of endorsement, and promotional opportunities dating from Arnold Palmer through Tiger Woods, as well as global expansion and event development.

To paraphrase the Shakespeare quote that my co-editor used in the introduction of this handbook, while we may not know where we are going, sport marketing scholars have a wealth of options to determine their journeys and destinations as well as some very qualified academicians to act as Sherpas—helping them prepare for their own research journeys and offering suggestions along the way.

References

Belson, K. (2010, July 24). Soccer's growth in the US seems steady. *The New York Times.* Retrieved from http://www.nytimes.com/2010/07/24/sports/soccer/24soccer.html

Betts, J. R. (1953). The technological revolution and the rise of sport 1850-1900. *The Mississippi Valley Historical Review, 40*(2) 231–256.

Clarke, R. (1998). Internet privacy concerns confirm the case for intervention. *Proceedings of the Association for Computing Machinery.* Retrieved from http://www.rogerclarke.com/DV/CACM99.html

Crutchfield. (n.d.). Retrieved from http://www.crutchfield.com

Daye, D., & VanAuken, B. (2008, September 28). Branding strategy insider: The branding blog. Retrieved from http://www.brandingstrategyinsider.com/2008/09/customization-b.html

DeLoach, C. (1998). *Quotable Shakespeare* (Macbeth, 1.3.58, p. 165). Jefferson, NC: McFarland and Co.

Drayer, J., & Martin, N. T. (2010). Establishing legitimacy in the secondary ticket market: A case study of an NFL Market. *Sport Management Review, 13*(1) 39–49.

Greater Austin Hispanic Chamber of Commerce. (2009). *Hispanic market & its buying power.* Retrieved from http://www.gahcc.org/Hispanic-Buying-Power.861.0.html

Hardy, S., & Sutton, W. A. (1999). The SMQ and the sport marketplace: Where we' been and where we're going. *Sport Marketing Quarterly, 8*(4), 9–14.

Helyar, J. (2007). *In change of heart, leagues embrace secondary ticket sellers.* ESPN.com. Retrieved from http://sports.espn.go.com/espn/news/story?id=3165059

Kirk, J. (2011, June 20). 2011 U.S. Open ratings lower than 2010's, but last year was huge. *SB Nation.* Retrieved from http://www.sbnation.com/golf/2011/6/20/2233818/us-open-tv-ratings-2011-golf-rory-mcilroy

Leonsis, T. (2011). Ted Leonis on social media's impact on sports. *Sportology.* Retrieved from http://sportology.us/2011/01/ted-leonsis-on-social-medias-impact-on-sports/

Index

N

O

P

R

S

T

V

W

Y

About the Editors

Nancy L. Lough, EdD, is a professor at the University of Nevada, Las Vegas. She teaches in the Higher Education Leadership program in the College of Education. She provides leadership for the sport administration concentration and directs both master's and doctoral degree programs. She teaches sport marketing, leadership development, governance, and sport in higher education. Previously, she taught courses in consumer behavior, sport business, and women in sport.

Her areas of expertise include marketing women's sport, corporate sponsorship of sport, leadership in college athletics, gender equity, Title IX, and work life balance in sport. Lough's recent research examines antecedents for professional advancement in athletic administration, exploration of work-life balance policies affecting institutional climate, sponsorship valuation and enhancement for women's sporting events, marketing and media influence on the success of women's sport properties, and the use of social marketing to promote social change through sport.

Lough has extensive experience in college sport inclusive of both NCAA Division I and II programs in California, Texas, and Colorado. She has served as a consultant for professional sport organizations such as the LPGA, and for amateur sport organizations such as the Native American Sports Council, the New Mexico Sports Commission, and the Nevada Interscholastic Athletics Association. As a consultant, Lough assists with evaluation and strategic planning to achieve gender equity and Title IX compliance.

Lough was a founding board member of the Sport Marketing Association and continues to serve SMA as an executive board member. Similarly, she has held leadership positions in multiple sport management organizations including the North American Society for Sport Management, National Association for Girls & Women in Sport, National Association for Collegiate Women Athletic Administrators, and the Sport Management Program Review Council, predecessor to the Commission on Sport Management Accreditation. Twice, she received the President's award from the National Association for Girls and Women in Sport and was recognized by the YWCA as a "Woman on the Move."

She currently serves as the editor of *Sport Marketing Quarterly* (*SMQ*) and was recently a featured author in the top 20 articles over the first 20 years of *SMQ*. She previously served as editor of the *Journal of Contemporary Athletics*, and continues to serve on multiple editorial review boards. Lough has presented work at national and international conferences and authored book chapters on sponsorship and sales, financial management in sport, and women in sport business. She has published articles in a variety of academic journals including the *International Journal of Sports Management, Journal of Applied Marketing Theory, Excellence and Equity in Education, Women's Sport and Physical Activity Journal*, and the *Journal for the Study of Sports and Athletes in Education*. She has been quoted as an expert on sport sponsorship in publications such as the *Los*

Angeles Times and Canada's *Globe and Mail.* Similarly, she has published opinion pieces in sport industry publications such as Street & Smith's *SportsBusiness Journal, Women's Sport & Fitness,* and *Athletic Management.*

Prior to assuming her position at UNLV, Lough assisted in the revitalization of the sport administration program at the University of New Mexico. She also served as a member of the sport management faculty at Iowa State University and initiated her academic career at Kent State University.

Lough is a native of Colorado and received her doctorate from the University of Northern Colorado. She and her partner currently reside in Henderson, Nevada.

William A. Sutton, EdD, is s professor and associate department head on the faculty of the DeVos Sport Business Management Graduate Program at the University of Central Florida. He teaches sport marketing and sales and promotional management in sport and serves as the internship coordinator for the program.

Sutton is also the founder and principal of Bill Sutton & Associates, a consulting firm specializing in strategic marketing and revenue enhancement. Sutton's consultation work has spanned the industry, working with professional leagues, teams, organizations, brands, universities, agencies, and facilities. His consulting clients include the NBA, WNBA, NHL, Orlando Magic, Phoenix Suns, MSG Sports, Pittsburgh Pirates, and Cleveland Cavaliers.

He is the co-creator and architect of the innovative and groundbreaking Sports Sales Combine. CNBC.com hailed the Sports Sales Combine, a careers concept inspired by the NFL Draft Combine, as potentially "the next great idea in sports marketing."

Sutton employs a hybrid approach, influenced heavily by his wide-ranging work experiences; including tenures at sports marketing agencies, professional leagues, and nationally acclaimed sport management programs. Prior to assuming his current positions, Sutton served as Vice President, Team Marketing and Business Operations for the National Basketball Association. In this capacity, Sutton assisted NBA teams with marketing related functions such as sales, promotional activities, market research, advertising, customer service, strategic planning, and staffing. In addition to working at the NBA, Sutton's professional experiences also included service as a special events coordinator for the City of Pittsburgh, a YMCA director, vice president of information services for an international sport marketing firm, and commissioner of the Mid-Ohio Conference. He has held academic appointments at Robert Morris University, The Ohio State University, and the University of Massachusetts at Amherst.

Sutton is a co-author of *Sport Marketing* (3rd ed., 2007) and *Sport Promotion and Sales Management* (2nd ed., 2008), published by Human Kinetics. He has also authored more than 200 articles (refereed and non-refereed), and has made more than 250 national and international presentations. Sutton, a past president of the North American Society for Sport Management, is a founding member and past president of the Sport Marketing Association. He also previously served as the co-editor of the *Sport Marketing Quarterly.*

Sutton is a featured author for Street and Smith's *SportsBusiness Journal*, where his Sutton Impact column is a monthly feature. Sutton is also a contributor for the basketball strategy and business magazines *Basketball Gigante* and *FIBA Assist*, published in Italy. Sutton is frequently called upon by members of the media for his insight and commentary on the sports business industry, including *USA Today*, *The New York Times*, *CNBC.com*, *The Washington Times*, *Fox Business*, *The Orlando Sentinel*, *South Florida Sun-Sentinel*, *Advertising Age*, and *Brandweek*.

A native of Pittsburgh, Sutton was inducted into the College of Education Hall of Fame at Oklahoma State University, his alma mater, in 2003. He is also an inaugural member of the Robert Morris University Sport Management Hall of Fame (2006). Sutton serves on the Board of Directors for the Folds of Honor Foundation and also on the Central Florida Sports Commission. He and his wife Sharon reside in Orlando, Florida.

About the Authors

Artemisia Apostolopoulou is an associate professor of sport management in the School of Business at Robert Morris University. Her research interests include branding and brand extension strategies, sport sponsorship, and the fusion of sport and entertainment.

Ketra L. Armstrong is a professor of sport management in the School of Kinesiology at the University of Michigan. Her research focuses on the social psychology of sport consumption with a special emphasis on elements of race and ethnicity.

Kathy Babiak is an associate professor of sport management in the School of Kinesiology at the University of Michigan. Her research interests include organizational theory, interorganizational relationships, strategic alliances, corporate social responsibility, and philanthropy in sport.

Carol A. Barr is an associate professor in the Mark H. McCormack Department of Sport Management and the associate dean for Undergraduate Programs and Campus Relations in the Isenberg School of Management at the University of Massachusetts Amherst. Her research interests include gender equity in sport and management issues within collegiate athletics.

Anthony A. Beaton is a post doctoral research fellow in the Department of Tourism, Leisure, Hotel, and Sport Management at Griffith University. His research interests include understanding the psychological connection of individuals to sport and exercise activities.

Gregg Bennett is an associate professor and Director of the Center for Sport Management Research and Education at Texas A&M University. His research interests include the action sports segment and effective event marketing.

David M. Boush is the Gerald B. Bashaw Professor and the associate dean of administration in the Lundquist College of Business at the University of Oregon. His research interests center on the relationship between consumer behavior and marketing management decisions.

Thomas C. Boyd is dean of the School of Business and Management at Kaplan University. His research interests include sport marketing, celebrity endorsers, and sport promotions.

Dallas D. Branch is a professor of sport management in the College of Physical Activity and Sport Sciences at West Virginia University. His research interests focus on sport marketing, brand building, and sport property valuation.

Christine M. Brooks is CEO of Learnitez.com and is the online science coordinator for the USA Track and Field Coaching Education certification program. Her online courses are used by Griffith University (Australia), Ball State University, and the University of Florida.

Rick Burton is the David B. Falk Distinguished Professor of Sport Management in the David B. Falk College of Sport and Human Dynamics at Syracuse University. His research interests include sport marketing, sport sponsorship and endorsements, women in sports, and the history of the Olympics.

John Cimperman is the managing partner of Cenergy Communications.

Connie Blakemore Cook is a professor emeritus at Brigham Young University in the College of Health and Human Performance. Her research developments include mastery learning, body-mind connection, cohort teacher development, and international culture exploration.

Lawrence W. Fielding is a professor in the Department of Kinesiology at Indiana University. His research interests include the history of the sporting goods industry and the development of commercial sport.

Kevin Filo is a lecturer in the Business School at Griffith University in Australia. His research interests include the synergy of sport and charity, as well as internet marketing communication in sport.

Sam Fullerton is a professor of marketing in the College of Business at Eastern Michigan University. His research interests include business and consumer ethics, sport marketing, and cross-cultural comparisons of consumer attitudes.

Daniel C. Funk is a professor and Washburn Senior Research Fellow for the School of Tourism and Hospitality at Temple University and also holds an appointment as a professor of sport marketing in the Griffith Business School, Australia. His research examines individual and external determinants that shape consumer involvement with sport and recreation experiences.

Lizhong Geng is the China director in ICON Health and Fitness Inc. His working experiences include serving for the Chinese Olympic Committee and Nike Company.

James ("Jay") M. Gladden is dean of the IU School of Physical Education & Tourism Management at Indiana University-Purdue University Indianapolis. His research interests include sport branding, sport sponsorship, and athletic fundraising.

Frederick G. Grieve is a professor in the Department of Psychology, coordinator of the clinical psychology master's program, and director for the clinical/applied research group at Western Kentucky University. In addition to sport fan behavior, his research interests lie in the area of eating disorders and male body image.

Kellee K. Harris is the business development manager at Package Containers, Inc. She previously was the owner and president of MarketSpark, a marketing consulting company, and has more than 20 years experience in consumer product marketing and communications, primarily in the sporting goods industry.

Dennis Howard is the Philip H. Knight Professor of Business in the Lundquist College of Business at the University of Oregon. His research interests include sport finance, sport marketing, and sport and leisure management.

Richard L. Irwin is a professor in the Department of Health and Sport Sciences and associate dean of University College at the University of Memphis. His research interests include sport marketing, promotion, and sales.

Jeffrey D. James is a professor and chair of the Department of Sport Management at Florida State University. His research interests include sponsorship, sport consumer behavior, and consumers' psychological connection to sport products.

Lynn R. Kahle is the Ehrman Guistina Professor of Marketing and the chair of the Department of Marketing at the University of Oregon. His research interests include marketing communication, international marketing, consumer psychology, applied social psychology, and sustainability.

Steven M. Kates is an associate professor in the faculty of Business Administration at Simon Fraser University in Canada. His research interests focus brand management and consumer socialization.

Aubrey Kent is an associate professor in the School of Tourism and Hospitality Management at Temple University. His research interests include consumer and employee attitudes in sport.

Stephen K. Koernig is an associate professor in the Department of Marketing at DePaul University. His research interests include sport marketing, celebrity endorsers, and services marketing.

Win Koo is a teaching assistant in the recreation and sport management program at the University of Arkansas. His research interests include the different aspects of marketing, consumer behavior, and economics in sport and recreation.

Tony Lachowetz is a lecturer in the Mark H. McCormack Department of Sport Management at the University of Massachusetts Amherst. His research interests include cause-related sport marketing and corporate selling activities and sponsor retention.

Robert Madrigal is an associate professor of marketing in the Lundquist College of Business at the University of Oregon. His research interests center on the application of pertinent theories of social psychology and consumer behavior to issues related to sport and tourism.

Daniel F. Mahony is a professor of sport management and the dean of the College and Graduate School of Education, Health, and Human Services at Kent State University. His research interests include sport consumer behavior and intercollegiate athletics.

Erin M. McDermott is the executive associate athletic director at Princeton University.

Mark A. McDonald is an associate professor in the Mark H. McCormack Department of Sport Management at the University of Massachusetts Amherst. His research interests include management education and leadership in sport.

G. Russell Merz is a professor of marketing in the College of Business at Eastern Michigan University. His research interests focus on measurement and modeling of marketing issues related to customer satisfaction, sport marketing, media engagement, advertising creativity, and brand management.

Lori K. Miller is a professor emeritus with the Department of Sport Management at Wichita State University. Her research interests include legal issues in sport.

George R. Milne is a professor in the Department of Marketing at the University of Massachusetts Amherst. His research interests include online consumer and marketer behavior, privacy and public policy, sport marketing, and consumer consumption.

Matthew Nicholson is an associate professor in the Centre for Sport and Social Impact at Latrobe University in Australia. His research interests focus on policy development and practice, the relationship between sport and the media, the contribution of sport and volunteering to social capital, and the cultural and commercial development of the football codes.

Dale G. Pease is an emeritus professor in the Department of Health and Human Performance at the University of Houston. His research interests are in the areas of sport fandom, leadership, and performance enhancement.

Mark Phelps is the Donald A. Tykeson Senior Instructor of Business in the Lundquist College of Business at the University of Oregon. His research interests include sport marketing, law as it relates to international business, and entrepreneurial organizations.

Mark Pritchard is an associate professor of marketing in the Department of Management at Central Washington University. His research focuses on issues in services marketing and the factors that influence repeat patronage in the sport and tourism industries.

Jerome Quarterman is an associate professor in Health, Human Performance and Leisure Studies and coordinator of Sport Management Studies at Howard University. His research interests include assessments of the managerial roles and skills of practicing managers in sport organizations, barriers and choices confronting student athletes, and research of research methods applied to sport management studies.

Lynn Ridinger is an associate professor in the Department of Human Movement Sciences at Old Dominion University. Her research interests include gender equity, consumer behavior, and college athletics.

Stephen D. Ross is an associate professor of sport management at the University of Minnesota. His research interests include sport brand management, sport consumer psychology, and sport marketing as it relates to the youth segment.

Matthew D. Shank is the president of Marymount University. His research interests include sport marketing, services marketing, and marketing education.

Aaron C. T. Smith is a professor and deputy pro-vice chancellor at Royal Melbourne Institute of Technology (RMIT University), Australia. His research interests include sport and health, and the management of psychological, organizational, and policy change in business.

Bob Stewart is an associate professor in the School of Sport and Exercise Sciences at Victoria University in Australia. His research interests include drug use cultures in elite and community sport, player regulation in professional team sports, and the commercial and managerial progress of Australian Rules football.

David K. Stotlar is a professor in the sport management program at the University of Northern Colorado. His research focuses on sport marketing and sport sponsorship.

Terese M. Stratta is the director of special academic initiatives in the Office of the Provost at Winston-Salem State University.

John Vincent is an associate professor in the Department of Kinesiology at the University of Alabama. His research interests include sport media and the intersection of gender, race, and national identity.

Matthew Walker is an assistant professor in the Department of Tourism, Recreation, and Sport Management at the University of Florida. His research focuses on business strategy with particular emphasis on business ethics and corporate social responsibility.

Daniel L. Wann is a professor of psychology at Murray State University. His research interests include team identification and the social well-being of sport fans.

Richard Wolfe is a professor of business strategy in the Peter B. Gustavson School of Business at the University of Victoria in Canada. His research interests include business strategy and sport management.

Ryan K. Zapalac is an assistant professor in the Department of Health and Kinesiology at Sam Houston State University. His research interests include sport consumer behavior, sport spectator and fan psychology, and psychological burnout.